GENERAL METALS
SIXTH EDITION

John L. Feirer

McGraw-Hill Book Company

New York   Atlanta   Dallas   St. Louis   San Francisco
Auckland   Bogotá   Guatemala   Hamburg   Lisbon
London   Madrid   Mexico   Montreal   New Delhi   Panama   Paris
San Juan   São Paulo   Singapore   Sydney   Tokyo   Toronto

Sponsoring Editor: Don Hepler

Editing Supervisor: Larry Goldberg

Design and Art Supervisor: Karen Tureck

Production Supervisor: Laurence Charnow

Cover Designer: Renée Kilbride Edelman

Cover Photographer: Ken Karp

Library of Congress Cataloging in Publication Data

Feirer, John Louis
    General metals.

    (McGraw-Hill publications in industrial education)
    Includes index.
    Summary: An industrial education textbook in basic
metalworking.
    1. Metal-work—Juvenile   literature.   [1. Metal-
work]
I. Title.   II. Series.
TS205.F37   1985   671   85-184
ISBN 0-07-020398-9

    3 4 5 6 7 8 9 0 DOCDOC 8 9 2 1 0 9 8

ISBN 0-07-020398-9

EDITOR'S FOREWORD

The McGraw-Hill Publications in Industrial Education constitute a functional and practical series of textbooks designed to cover the broad areas of industrial education. The publisher and the consulting editor aim to provide the finest publications possible. All the authors are experts and have demonstrated their abilities as master teachers, teacher educators, skilled workers, or consultants. The several books contain carefully selected and well-organized subject matter. They are written and prepared in an interesting style at the proper readability level. These textbooks carefully explain technical terms when they first appear. Line drawings and photographs are used extensively to illustrate and clarify many meaningful statements and phrases. This edition makes use of the second color to accent illustrations and to emphasize significant points and topical headings. Not only does *General Metals* contain many illustrations, but it uses them as a most powerful and effective teaching tool.

The sixth edition of *General Metals* is based upon a very careful analysis of introductory metalworking courses in many schools. New techniques in the vast metalworking industry, refinements of the basic technology, a fuller knowledge of industrial technology, and greater interest in the career opportunities in the field have necessitated changes.

The author, editor, and publisher hope that this publication will supply the student with many contemporary metalworking activities. They trust that it will assist the student to realize and appreciate more fully the impact and significance of metals in the industrial technological society of today.

Chris H. Groneman

McGraw-Hill Publications in Industrial Education
Chris H. Groneman, Consulting Editor

Books in Series

GENERAL INDUSTRIAL EDUCATION AND TECHNOLOGY Groneman and Feirer
GENERAL METALS Feirer
GENERAL POWER MECHANICS Crouse, Worthington, Margules, and Anglin
GENERAL WOODWORKING Groneman
GETTING STARTED IN DRAWING AND PLANNING Groneman and Feirer
GETTING STARTED IN ELECTRICITY AND ELECTRONICS Groneman and Feirer
GETTING STARTED IN METALWORKING Groneman and Feirer
GETTING STARTED IN WOODWORKING Groneman and Feirer
TECHNICAL ELECTRICITY AND ELECTRONICS Buban and Schmitt
TECHNICAL WOODWORKING Groneman and Glazener
UNDERSTANDING ELECTRICITY AND ELECTRONICS Buban and Schmitt

CONTENTS

v

ABOUT THE AUTHOR

John L. Feirer is a distinguished faculty scholar at Western Michigan University in Kalamazoo. He received his B.S. degree from the University of Wisconsin-Stout, where he majored in metalworking. He also holds an M.S. degree from the University of Minnesota and a doctorate from the University of Oklahoma. His many years of teaching experience include positions in a number of junior and senior high schools in the Midwest.

Dr. Feirer is active in industrial arts organizations and has written widely in the field. He is past executive editor of *Industrial Education* magazine, co-author (with C. H. Groneman) of *General Industrial Education and Technology* (McGraw-Hill, 1986) and the *Getting Started* series (McGraw-Hill, 1979), and author of *Machine Tool Metalworking* (McGraw-Hill, 1973).

PREFACE

General Metals has been widely accepted as a basic metalworking textbook for almost three decades. Revisions since the publication of the first edition have been founded upon two primary bases: (1) the results of questionnaires sent to teachers using the book and (2) extensive review of literature in metals technology. With this approach, the author has made every attempt to keep abreast of both educational and technical advances.

This, the sixth edition of *General Metals,* represents another revision. However, the major features of the original edition are retained. The basic structure is essentially the same. The book is divided into main sections and units, each unit treating the basic tools, materials, processes, and related information for a specific step in metalworking. The book stresses the illustrative approach to instruction, and each illustration has been carefully selected for the purpose.

While this functional pattern has been maintained, numerous changes have been made to reflect contemporary directions in the field, including the following:
1. Technical information in text and illustrations has been updated throughout.
2. Major technical terms are printed in boldface type and defined on first use; other technical terms are italicized and defined. All boldfaced terms are included in a new glossary.
3. Information on the metric system of measurement has been expanded throughout. Metric equivalents follow customary measurements in the text. Metrics have been added to most tables and many illustrations.
4. A new unit on leaded stained glass and new materials on safety, careers, welding, and gating systems have been added.
5. Important new units on computers in metalworking industries, industrial robots, and manufacturing systems help the student learn about current metal technology.
6. Several new project suggestions are included.

General Metals is planned for the general-metal shop and the general-metal area of general shop in a range of career-education programs. While beginning classes may do creative work only in the areas of bench, sheet, and art metal, students have an opportunity to read about all areas of metalwork. As time and experience permit, students may make representative projects and study occupations and techniques in other areas. This new edition meets today's need for an introductory, yet comprehensive, metalworking text.

John L. Feirer

METALWORKING

Unit 1
Introduction to General Metals

Are we living in the metal age, the electronic age, the atomic age, the jet age, or the aerospace age? Actually, we are living in all of these ages at once. However, the products of today's technology are dependent on parts made of metal (Fig. 1–1). Look up! The loud blast you hear could be a jet, a rocket, or a missile. These machines are made of metal. The attractive new buildings in your city

Fig. 1–1 This modern helicopter is an all-metal vehicle built mostly of light materials such as aluminum and titanium. (United Technologies Corp.)

contain many metal parts. Did you ever stop to consider how these things came to be made? The answer is that they are the products of the skill and cooperation of thousands of engineers, technicians, and skilled workers who make use of metals and other materials.

The United States is a huge workshop for metalworking. The metalworking industry employs a great number of workers. The value of its finished products exceeds that of most other industries. Metal is the raw material of this industry. Electricity is its source of power. Since so many products are made of metal, the field of metalworking is very large. Think of it—the chances are more than one in ten that you will be working in the metalworking industry someday.

What is general metals?

General metals is the study of all aspects of metalworking. These include bench, sheet, and art metal; jewelry; metal finishing; forging; casting; machining; heat treating; materials testing; welding and other fastening methods; and metal manufacturing. You will do work similar to that done by the millions of engineers, technicians, and skilled and semiskilled workers in the metalworking industry (Fig. 1–2).

Why take a course in general metals?

There is much more to general metals than making a few small metal objects that

Fig. 1-2 This skilled aircraft worker must know how to use hand tools. The job of aircraft worker is one of the many careers in the metals industry. (Lockheed Aircraft Company)

you can take home. Here is what you will accomplish in your course in general metals:

1. You will gain an understanding of American industry (Fig. 1-3).

2. You will acquire hand and machine skills.

3. You will develop safe working habits.

4. You will learn what good design is and how to plan, design, and construct projects (Fig. 1-4).

Fig. 1-3 These students are learning how industry produces metal products. (United Technologies Corp.)

5. You will have the opportunity to apply what you have learned in mathematics and science.

6. You may develop a hobby.

7. You will learn how to construct metal products and how to select appropriate materials.

8. You will explore careers that exist in the field of metalworking.

9. You will build interesting projects with the skills you acquire and feel pride in a job well done.

10. You will learn to live and work with others.

Skills basic to metalworking

Before you can begin to make a project in metalwork, you should learn how to work safely in the shop, how to select and design projects, how to read drawings, how to plan a project, how to choose metals, and how to measure and make layouts. When you have

Fig. 1-4 This unique hotel is built mostly of metal and plastics. A great amount of lead is used for sound barriers between rooms. (Lead Industries Association)

learned these things, you are ready for the interesting experience of making something worthwhile of metal. Though you may not have the time or skill to make projects in every area, you will have a chance to learn about them all.

? QUESTIONS

1. Name the areas of metalworking covered by the term *general metals.*
2. List 10 reasons why you should take a course in general metals.

✓ EXTRA CREDIT

1. Find out all you can about one of the following people. Report on that person's activities in the metalworking field: Paul Revere, Eli Whitney, Thomas Edison, Henry Ford, Walter Chrysler, William Knudsen, Henry Bessemer, Jan Matzeliger, and Elijah McCoy.
2. Talk to a friend or neighbor who works in the metalworking industry. Ask the person about the job and about training for it. Report on this in class.

Unit 2
Safety in the Metal Shop

You will get more out of shop activities and your future career if you avoid accidents. It is smart to be careful, for an accident can change your life.

Safety is important in all industrial education activities. When you get a job in industry or business, you will be required to observe the safety standards that were established by the U.S. Congress in 1970 with the passage of the Occupational Safety and Health Act (OSHA). These strict regulations provide protection for both the employee and the employer in all aspects of work. Many states have passed laws similar to the federal law. More and more, these regulations apply to both industries and schools.

Safety standards established by law are very comprehensive. These standards include not only the obvious, such as safety

Fig. 2-1 This woman is a mechanic in a steel mill. She is wearing safety glasses and a hard hat. For work around noisy machines, the ear protectors on the hard hat must be lowered to cover the ears. (Inland Steel Company)

glasses or goggles, but also standards for guards, noise and air pollution, electrical hazards, and every other aspect of working conditions (Fig. 2-1). Each employer must

3

Fig. 2-2 Safety regulations must be posted, and every person must observe them. (Snap-on Tools Corporation)

establish and maintain conditions of work that are safe and healthy. All employees must follow all safety regulations (Fig. 2–2). No employee may willfully remove, displace, damage, destroy, or carry off any safety device or safety item (Fig. 2–3).

It is important in your school activity to develop proper attitudes toward health and safety. By the time you take a job in industry, you will have developed safe working procedures. The basic purpose of a comprehensive safety program is to provide you and your fellow students with a safe and healthy working environment. It is mandatory that you follow the safety regulations outlined in this unit and in each of the sections where safety regulations apply.

It is important for you to learn how to be both a good and a safe worker. The best way is to do each part of a job carefully and correctly as described in this book or as demonstrated by your instructor. Accidents usually happen when you do the wrong thing "just this once" or when you fail to follow proper methods. The *right* way is the *safe* way.

The metal shop is planned to be a safe place in which to work. All machines are guarded and in good working order. You must help maintain the tools and machines so that the shop will remain a safe place in

which to work. Let your teacher know if you find any unsafe tools or machines in the shop.

To have an accident-free shop, remember the ABC of safety: *Always be careful.* Here are some important safeguards:

1. Remember that the shop is a place for work, not horseplay.

a. Any tricks or pranks are dangerous to you and your friends.

b. Do not be responsible for sending a fellow student to the hospital by playing a practical joke. For one moment of laughter, you will pay with a lifetime of regret.

2. Whenever possible, use the buddy system when working at a difficult task.

3. Dress safely.

a. Roll up your sleeves, tuck in or remove your tie, and wear a shop coat or an apron.

b. Remove all jewelry, including rings and watches. A watchband, for example, can catch in moving machinery (Figs. 2–4, 2–5).

c. Keep your hair cut short or out of the way. Long hair around moving parts is dangerous and must be covered with a net or cap.

Fig. 2-3 Safety education is required in most industries. (National Steel Corporation)

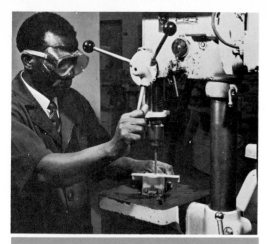

RIGHT

Fig. 2–4 This is the right way to operate a drill press.

Fig. 2–5 The drill press can be dangerous. Find the following unsafe practices: quill extended too far; sharp edges on metal; workpiece being held by hand; chuck key, drill, and other tools lying on table; loose sleeves on operator; operator not wearing apron or goggles; and operator wearing watch and ring.

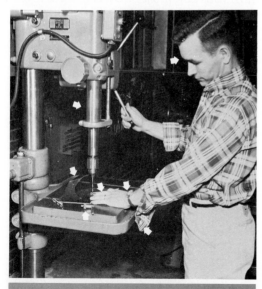

WRONG

Fig. 2–6 When using welding equipment, be sure that you wear a shield with proper filter glass, gloves, and proper clothing.

d. Always wear special protective clothing when working in the welding, forging, and foundry areas (Fig. 2–6).

4. Protect your eyes.

a. Wear goggles or a shield whenever there are sparks. You have only two eyes. Protect them.

b. Wear safety glasses when grinding or buffing or whenever there is danger of flying chips (Fig. 2–7).

Fig. 2–7 Grinding can be a dangerous operation. Make sure your eyes are well protected. Never take chances. (Mercury Marine Company)

5

Fig. 2-8 The cold chisel at the top is sharp and in good condition. The one at the bottom is dull and has a "mushroom" head. Take care of your tools.

c. Wear special goggles or a shield for gas and arc welding.

d. Wear goggles and protective clothing when pouring hot metal in the foundry or when working with acids.

5. Take proper care of hand tools.

a. Most accidents are caused by incorrect use of hand tools or poor tool maintenance. Leaving scraps of metal lying around is always a hazard.

b. Dull tools are dangerous. Always keep tools sharp.

c. Make sure that hammer heads and screwdriver blades are fastened tightly to their handles.

d. Always put a handle on a file before using it.

e. Grind "mushroom" heads and all burrs off cold chisels, center punches, and other small hand tools (Fig. 2-8).

f. Always keep pliers, screwdrivers, and metal shears in good working condition.

6. Use tools correctly.

a. Choose the right tool or equipment for the job. The work can, then, be done faster and more safely (Fig. 2-9).

b. There is always a right and a wrong way to use a tool. Learn to use a tool the right way.

c. Never carry sharp tools in your pockets.

d. You can pinch your fingers with pliers or snips. You can get burned with hot metals or hot tools. Always be careful.

7. Use portable electric hand tools correctly. These tools operate on 110 volts. This voltage can kill or cause a serious shock or burn under certain conditions.

a. Always check the electric hand tool before using it. Make sure the cord is in good condition and that it does not have a broken plug or switch.

b. Always keep the cord away from oil or hot surfaces.

c. Never use electric tools around inflammable vapors and gases. This could cause an explosion.

d. Always be sure that your hands are dry when using an electric hand tool.

8. Observe safety rules when running machines.

a. Always follow the safety rules given in each unit on each machine.

b. Stop the machine before it is oiled, lubricated, or adjusted.

Fig. 2-9 This employee is using an electric chain hoist to move heavy metal parts.

6

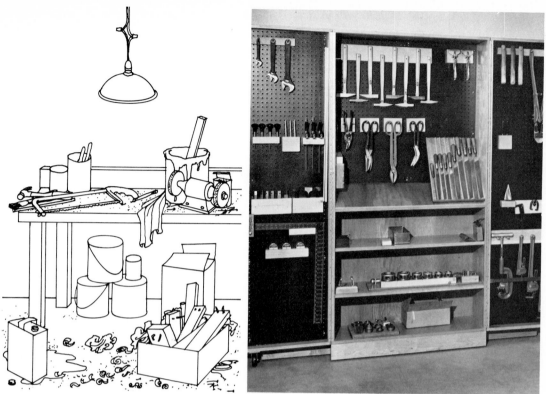

Fig. 2-10 Which kind of housekeeper are you?

c. Never feel the surface of metal while it is being machined.

d. Clean chips off with a brush—never with a rag or your hand.

e. Never allow anyone to stand near the machine you are using.

f. Never use measuring tools on metal while it is being machined.

g. Keep the guards in place. They were put there for your protection.

h. Operate a tool or machine only after you have had thorough instructions on using it.

i. Remember, you must know what you are doing before you start the machine.

j. Never try to hold a piece of metal in your hand while it is being machined. It takes only one accident to change your life. Do not let that accident happen.

9. Be a good housekeeper (Fig. 2-10).

a. Do your part in keeping the shop clean and in order.

b. Clean the tool or machine after using it.

c. Put away all tools and accessories.

d. Wipe up any oil or grease on the floor.

e. Get rid of the waste materials.

f. Put your work away at the end of the period.

g. A clean shop is likely to be a safe shop. Do not wait for someone else to clean up.

10. Ask for first aid every time you need it.

a. Do not laugh off a small injury or burn. Get first aid no matter how slight the

7

injury. Infection may start many days after you scratch your hand.

b. Report every accident to your instructor. If necessary, he or she will send you to the school nurse or to a doctor.

c. A small burn, a metal sliver in your finger, or a cut can easily cause blood poisoning. A piece of metal in the eye can cause blindness. Do not say it never happens, for each year there are over 153,000 eye injuries to students. Do not add to this number.

Remind yourself of these basic rules of safety, and practice them:

1. Dress properly.
2. Know your job.
3. Do it correctly.

 QUESTIONS

1. What is the ABC of safety?
2. What is the proper way to dress in the shop?
3. In what ways can the eyes be protected?
4. What is the right way to use a file?
5. Why should the right tool be used for a job?
6. What should you do in case of an accident in the shop?
7. What are the three basic rules of safety?

 EXTRA CREDIT

Write to an insurance company or to the National Safety Council for information about school shop and industrial safety practices. Give a report.

Unit 3
Metalwork Design

Every product made starts with a design. In the beginning, the design is only an idea in the designer's mind. Then, it is a sketch on a piece of paper and perhaps an experimental model. Next, it is a finished product (Fig. 3–1). Products may be well designed or poorly designed. A well-designed product is one that is built correctly, is useful, and makes you want to buy it.

Good design in metals is achieved by planning and making projects that not only suit your needs but also are attractive. Deciding on the right design is not easy, but here are a few suggestions that may help:

1. Look at well-designed metal products in magazines.
2. Stop in at hardware and furniture stores to see what kinds of metal products are available.
3. Visit shops featuring good design.
4. Visit antique dealers and art galleries.

You will begin to get a feel for what is good and will be able to discard a design that is bad.

Elements of design

There are five basic *elements of design* that are present in every kind of product. They include lines, shapes, solids, color, and texture. These elements are arranged by designers to create the form of a product.

1. *Lines.* All things have lines in their form, for there are many kinds of lines. These kinds include lines that are straight, curved, zigzag, and circular (Fig. 3–2).

2. *Shapes.* Lines are combined to give an object its shape, or form. These shapes

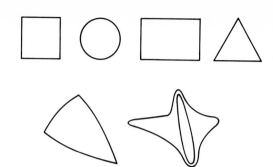

Fig. 3-3 Lines were used to make these shapes.

Fig. 3-1 A truck of the early 1900s compared with today's service vehicle. (Western Electric Company)

Fig. 3-4 Shapes are combined to form these common solids.

Fig. 3-2 Lines are an important design element.

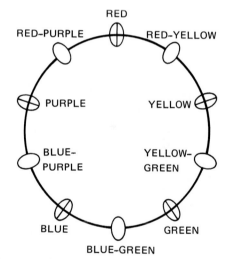

Fig. 3-5 The color wheel.

are, in fact, two-dimensional objects, such as squares, circles, rectangles, triangles, and free-form shapes (Fig. 3–3).

3. *Solids.* Plane shapes are, in turn, joined to make a solid object. The pieces of metal you work with are solid shapes, such as cylinders, rectangular solids, cubes, rods, bars, and spheres (Fig. 3–4). When you put these pieces together, they form a large solid object whose precise shape is determined by width, height, and length.

4. *Color.* There is color everywhere. All metals have a color of their own. For example, brass is gold, and aluminum is silvery

white. Colors can also be added with paint, lacquer, or other finishes. Colors can appear to be pleasant or unpleasant, depending on the way they are used. Some colors, such as red, yellow, or orange, seem warm. Other colors, such as green, blue, and purple, seem cool (Fig. 3–5).

5. *Texture.* **Texture** refers to the character of the surface (Fig. 3–6). Texture can be added to metal by pressing, cutting, rolling, shaping, expanding (making larger), and perforating (making holes through).

Principles of design

It is difficult to say why one project is attractive and another is not. There are many rules that can be followed. However, rules alone will not make a good design. For example, some pieces of contemporary metal furniture do not follow all the rules but are still quite attractive. The *principles of design,* however, guide designers as they assemble the elements of design to create a pleasing, useful object. Generally, a good design has the characteristics of balance, proportion, rhythm or repetition, harmony, and emphasis.

1. Balance is a state in which the parts of an object are equal in weight or appearance. An article is said to have balance when it resembles a balanced scale. It then appears to have equal weight or equal areas on both sides of the center. Most things in nature—people, trees, and animals—are in balance.

Things lacking balance look as if they might tip over. Balance does not mean that the two sides must be equal. Balance can be obtained by using different materials or colors or by placing the parts at different distances from the eye. *Formal balance* is present when both sides are exactly equal (Fig. 3–7). *Informal balance* is shown by an object in which opposite sides *seem* equal, or at rest, when actually they are not (Figs. 3–8, 3–9).

2. Proportion is the relationship between the sizes of the various parts or the relationship of areas. Generally, the rectangle

Fig. 3–7 This contemporary candleholder is an example of formal balance. (Georg Jensen Silversmiths, Ltd.)

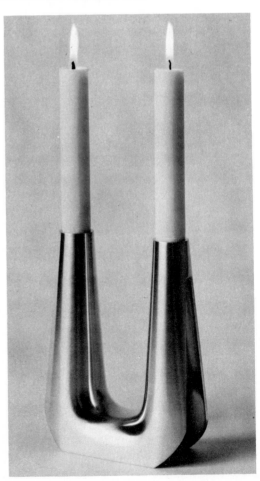

Fig. 3–6 Note the contrasting textures and materials used in this desk. It is a superb blending of metal, leather, and wood. (Dunbar Industries)

10

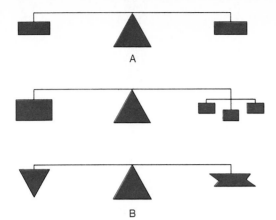

A

B

Fig. 3–8 The chart shows formal (A) and informal (B) balance.

Fig. 3–9 This teapot is balanced informally. The handle provides the balance for the spout. The two parts seem to have the same weight. (Sterling Silversmiths Guild of America)

Fig. 3–10 The rectangular shapes have a proportion of about 5 to 8—the golden section in design. (McDonald Products)

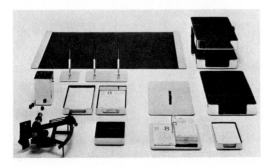

has better proportion than the square. The height and width of the rectangle are easily seen by the eye. The **golden section,** a rectangle with a proportion of about 5 to 8, is very pleasing (Fig. 3–10). Metal projects such as serving trays, picture frames, and chairs look best when they show this proportion. Proportion is also important when planning parts of an object. For example, if you place a large shade on a small lamp, the entire lamp is out of proportion. The same shade on a larger base might show good proportion. Proportion and balance are closely related.

3. Rhythm or **repetition** is the effect achieved by repeating a line or shape at regular intervals (Fig. 3–11). It gives an article a pleasing appearance and a feeling of movement.

4. Harmony is a condition in which the different parts of an object fit and look well together. For example, you would not build a table with heavy welded metal legs attached to a thin, expanded metal top. Color harmony is also important.

Fig. 3–11 The metal supports and lamps for the storage units provide a pleasing repetition of shapes. (Herman Miller, Inc.)

Fig. 3–12 This beautiful table, made of stainless steel and glass, shows good proportion. The center structure is a point of emphasis.

Fig. 3–13 This telephone is an example of a very functional product. (Western Electric Company)

5. Emphasis is a way of pointing out the focus, or center of interest (Fig. 3–12). A certain part of the article may be emphasized through the shape of the object, the use of color, or the way the object is decorated.

Trends in metal design

For many years, there has been a strong trend toward simplicity, especially in the design of metal products. When you compare older articles with those designed today, you can easily see this change. Metal products of many years ago made much use of hammered surfaces, bent edges, scroll work, and heavy design. Today, metal products are generally simpler. There are many reasons for this. Products that are simply made and lightly decorated are easier to manufacture, more efficient in use, and easier to maintain. You should remember this in designing your first project. Many beginning metalworkers want to overdecorate their projects or make them fancy. To decide whether a metal project is well designed, ask yourself the following questions:

1. Does it do the job well? In other words, does it fulfill its **function?** If you design a project to do its job, the object will be useful and functional (Fig. 3–13).

2. Is it good-looking? You can make a metal table by attaching four straight legs to a top, but the result probably will not be in-

Fig. 3–14 These simple pieces of tableware are examples of style in metalwork. (Fraser's Stainless)

teresting or look good. The project should have **style** (Fig. 3–14).

3. Is it well made? The project you make in the metal shop should be well put together. Close attention to construction will improve the final appearance of your project.

4. Have the best materials been used? Metals are beautiful in themselves. Copper, brass, stainless steel, and aluminum all have a naturally beautiful finish. Make sure that you know something about the metals you are using. Be sure you know how they act in forming, bending, shaping, and soldering. Will the metal suit the article you want to make? A copper dish, for example, cannot be used with acidic foods unless it is plated or tinned.

Kinds of design

There are many projects you can make in the metal shop. Here are some groups to think about:

1. *Craft projects.* These are small metal objects that are clever and popular but may not show good design. For example, you may make a wall plaque featuring your high school mascot. Maybe it is a mule or a tiger. You will probably keep it for a few years and then say, "That was fun to make, but I'm tired of it now." The craft objects you make in the metal shop should be attractive, useful pieces, not novelty items.

2. *Utility projects.* Many things built in the school metal shop are utility items such as tools or parts of machines. Just because an article is practical and useful, it does not have to be ugly. A hammer, for example, can be a thing of beauty.

3. *Home furnishing projects.* Many metal projects, such as chairs, tables, lamps, and stands, can be used in your home (Fig. 3–15). These should follow a certain style. The most common styles are modern or contemporary, early American or colonial, and traditional. The kind of metal you use, the way it is finished, and the shape of the parts make the difference in style.

Selecting a good design

In choosing a design, remember these points:

1. Make sure the design meets a practical need.

2. See that the design expresses the spirit or idea of our time and fits in with the way we live.

3. Make use of new tools and materials and methods of fastening.

4. Use the materials best suited for the project. Apply the correct techniques in handling these materials.

5. Make sure that metal products look

Fig. 3–15 This unusual metal table stand can be made in the school shop.

like metal. Do not try to imitate wood, plastic, or other materials.

6. Modern design should be simple. The structure of the parts in themselves is interesting. Do not try to hide anything.

 QUESTIONS

1. What steps can you take to develop your taste for good design?
2. Name five basic elements of design.
3. List the five principles of design.
4. What is the trend today in the design of metal products?
5. List four questions that you can ask to decide if a metal product is well designed.
6. Name three kinds of projects that can be made in metals shop.

 EXTRA CREDIT

1. Make a chart or display illustrating the elements or principles of design. Use illustrations from magazines, catalogs, and other sources.
2. Review an article from the magazines *Industrial Design* or *Interiors*.

Unit 4
Designing a Product

You will probably have the opportunity to design projects or parts of projects in your metalworking class. Whether you design a project or not, it is a good idea to begin to understand the general procedure that a designer follows in solving a design problem (Figs. 4–1, 4–2).

Steps in designing

First, select a project. Second, clarify the design problem. If, for example, the project selected is a bookrack or a set of bookends, you must decide how and where it will be used. A small bookrack used on your study desk to hold notebooks and classroom papers

Fig. 4–2 The top of this solar stove opens on all fours sides to make an enclosed cooking system that traps the heat from the sun and holds it, allowing for even, continuous heat. (Zinc Institute, Inc.)

Fig. 4–1 While there are many solar cookers on the market, this student designer researched existing similar solar products and then developed a very efficient unit of unique design. See Fig. 4–2. (Zinc Institute, Inc.)

will have to be of a particular design in order to provide proper support. A set of bookends used to support a number of volumes of an encyclopedia will require an entirely different design. The bookends may also have to be of a specific style, such as early American or contemporary, in order to fit into a particular surrounding.

You will also have to be concerned with size. What are the sizes of the books to be stored, and about how many books are there? This knowledge will give you some idea as to how big and how strong you must make the bookrack or bookends.

A third question deals with the kinds of materials to be used. If, for example, you plan to use the bookrack or bookends on a walnut record cabinet, you may decide to add a wood-grained vinyl covering to the metal selected.

After the above questions have been answered, you should proceed to make some sketches of the object. Several sketches are shown in Fig. 4–3. These are all possible solutions to the design problem, but each must be refined before it can be used.

After completing your sketches, you may wish to make a model or mockup of the product before going ahead and preparing the final drawing. It is often helpful to experiment with a design first in order to find out whether or not your idea will work.

The next step is to prepare a detailed working drawing of the product. A working drawing shows the size and shape and kind of materials to be used and how the product is to be made. The foregoing are not only steps in designing but also factors related to good design. In addition, you should consider the following points:

1. Function is a very important aspect of design. The project that you make must

Fig. 4-4 These wall telephones were designed with a place to "park" the receiver to make them more functional. (Western Electric Company)

Fig. 4-3 Sketches of possible bookrack ideas.

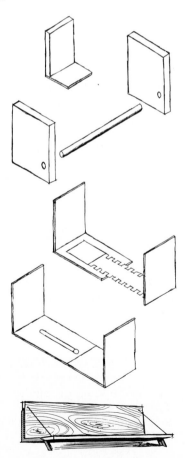

Fig. 4-5 This table combines metal and glass in its construction. (Baker Company)

work properly. If a product does not function as it is supposed to, it is poorly designed. Study the telephones shown in Fig. 4-4. Are these designs functional?

2. It is very important to try out new ideas in design. Look at the table illustrated in Fig. 4-5. Note the attention to shape and combination of materials. Very often, an ordinary product can be made much more serviceable and beautiful by a little extra experimental effort.

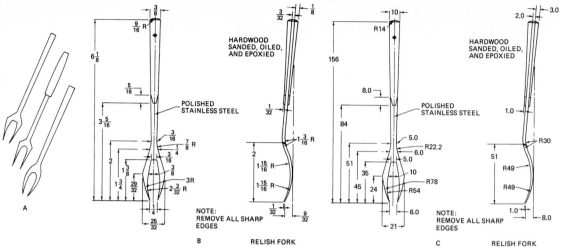

Fig. 4–6 In designing a small relish fork, prepare (A) several simple sketches. Refine these sketches. Prepare a working drawing in (B) customary or (C) metric units.

Fig. 4–7 Redesigning a bracket. (A) Note how many parts and operations were needed to make the original bracket. (B) This redesigned unit is easier to make and less expensive.

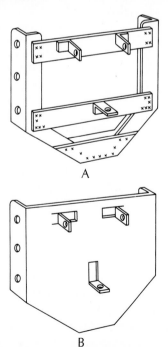

3. Work out a system for designing. Note the procedure used for designing the kitchen utensil shown in Fig. 4–6.

Redesigning

Do not overlook the possibility of redesigning a project or product that was made in the past (Fig. 4–7). A redesigned product is often superior to the original one. Participating in this type of design activity will help you to better understand the way products are designed.

 QUESTIONS

1. What must you do before sketching a design?
2. What kinds of design drawings should be made?

 QUESTIONS

1. Prepare some colored sketches of a project you wish to make.
2. Develop a design for a project sugested by your teacher.

Unit 5
Measurement

Measurement is one of the most common, yet most important, activities in our lives. We thrill at a football player running 98 yards (90 m) for a touchdown. A baseball hit 400 feet (122 m) is a home run in anybody's ball park. And every household has a ruler and a tape measure for measuring changes in height or the size of a rug.

Most everyday measurements are satisfactory if they are no more than a fraction of an inch or a millimeter off. However, in mass production industries, where things are made by the millions, measurements have to be more accurate. Rulers may be alright for measuring some things. However, many dimensions have to be accurate within thousandths of an inch (or hundredths of a millimeter). Why? Because mass production is based on **interchangeability,** which demands that everything fit together just right. The only bridge between the engineers who design things and the skilled workers who make them is the blueprint that contains the **dimensions,** or measurements. Factory assembly lines can run smoothly only when directions are followed exactly.

What is measurement?

When we measure something, we compare it to a **standard unit.** Each of the measures we spoke of earlier—the changes in height, the size of the rug, the length of the touchdown runs, the distance the baseball was hit—is an example of this comparison. We use standard units such as inches or millimeters, pounds or kilograms, gallons or liters, and hours to measure things. To measure, we must find the number of units there are in the object we are measuring.

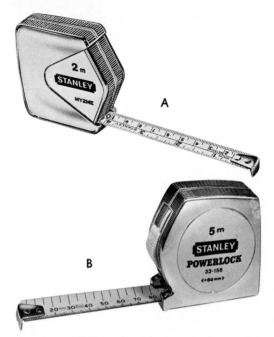

Fig. 5-1 (A) This steel tape rule is graduated in customary and metric units. Note that 1 inch equals about 2.5 centimeters, and 2 inches are about the same as 5 centimeters. This type is not as useful as one with the metric scale graduated in millimeters. (B) This is the best kind of graduation to use in metalwork. (Stanley Tools)

Two kinds of measurement are in common use today in the United States: the **customary system** and the **metric system.** The customary system is sometimes called the *English system* in the United States and the *Imperial system* in Great Britain, Canada, and Australia (Fig. 5-1). The United States and Canada are moving toward the metric system, along with the rest of the world. This applies particularly to manufacturing, especially making such items as automobiles, farm machinery, tools, equipment, and other items exported throughtout the world. In the years ahead, everyone will need to know how to use the metric system. Therefore, it is a good idea to learn to measure in metrics and to build a project to metric

17

measurements following the suggestions included in this unit.

The SI metric system

The history of the metric system began in France in 1790. During the French Revolution, a group of French people recommended a new unit of length based on a natural measurement. This was to replace the variety of measures then used in Europe. They suggested *one* system for all countries. The basis of measurement selected was the distance from the North Pole to the equator through Paris, France. This distance is so great that one ten-millionth of it was chosen as the new basic unit of length. This unit was called the *meter* (or *metre*). It became the basis of the *metric system*. The metric system was tried and modified, and finally in 1840, it became the law in France. After that, the system began to spread throughout the world.

The older metric system has been in use in many countries for a long time. In recent years, it has been replaced by the updated *SI metric system*, or *Système International d'Unités*. This system consists of seven **base units** (Table 5–1) plus two **supplementary units** and many derived units. A **derived unit** is one that is computed from one or more base, supplementary, and other derived units. For example, the liter, used for liquid capacity, is a derived unit. It comes from a base unit, the meter. It is the same as one cubic decimeter. The newton (N) is the unit used to measure force. It comes from a formula, $N = kg \times m/s^2$, which is mass in kilograms (kg) times acceleration in meters per second per second (m/s^2).

The metric system, like the monetary system of the United States, is based on multiples of 10. For example, a meter is divided into 10 decimeters, 100 centimeters, and 1000 millimeters. A meter multiplied by 1000 equals a kilometer. *Kilo-* means *thou-*

Table 5–1
Base Units
of the SI Metric System

Unit	Symbol
meter (length)	m
kilogram (mass)	kg
second (time)	s
kelvin (temperature)	K
ampere (electric current)	A
candela (luminous intensity)	cd
mole (amount of substance)	mol

sand. Therefore, a kilometer is 1000 meters, a kilogram is 1000 grams, and a kilowatt is 1000 watts (Table 5–2). As you can see, the same prefixes are used for all units.

Only five metric units are used in everyday life: the meter, the kilogram, the cubic meter, the liter, and the degree Celsius. They are discussed below.

Length. The **meter** (m), the metric unit of length, is equal to about 39.37 inches. Thus, it is slightly longer than a yard, which is equal to 36 inches, or 3 feet. The meter is divided into 100 equal parts called **centimeters** (cm) and 1000 equal parts called **millimeters** (mm).

The meterstick is a little longer than the yardstick. A 300-millimeter **rule** (another word for *ruler*) is slightly shorter than a 12-inch rule (Fig. 5–2). The millimeter is the smallest division on many metric rules. Measurements in the customary system are

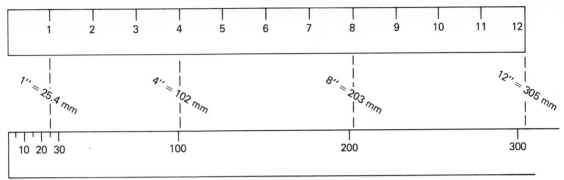

Fig. 5-2 Note that a 300-millimeter rule is a little shorter than a 12-inch rule.

often made to the nearest 1/16 inch. Working in the metric system and measuring to the nearest millimeter would therefore be somewhat more accurate. For even greater accuracy, measurements may be rounded off to a half millimeter (0.5 mm). A half millimeter is about 1/50 inch in size, or about halfway between 1/32 inch and 1/64 inch, the smallest division on precision machinist's rules.

Metric tools are usually available in 150-millimeter and 300-millimeter lengths in addition to the meterstick. Use a rule that is graduated in millimeters, with every tenth line marked 10, 20, 30, and so on (Fig. 5-3). This kind is easier to read than one with the numbered lines graduated in centimeters.

Weight or mass. The metric unit of mass is the **kilogram** (kg), equal to 1000 grams. For everyday purposes, mass is the same as

Table 5–2
SI Unit Prefixes

Multiple or submultiple	Prefix	Symbol	Pronunciation*	Means
$1\ 000\ 000\ 000 = 10^9$ $1\ 000\ 000 = 10^6$ $1\ 000 = 10^3$ $100 = 10^2$ $10 = 10^1$	giga mega kilo hecto deka	G M k h da	*jig′ a* (a as in *about*) as in *megaphone* as in *kilowatt* *heck′toe* *deck′a* (a as in *about*)	one billion times one million times one thousand times one hundred times ten times
base unit $1 = 10^0$				
$0.1 = 10^{-1}$ $0.01 = 10^{-2}$ $0.001 = 10^{-3}$ $0.000\ 001 = 10^{-6}$ $0.000\ 000\ 001 = 10^{-9}$	deci centi milli micro nano	d c m μ n	as in *decimal* as in *centipede* as in *military* as in *microphone* *nan′oh* (an as in *ant*)	one tenth of one hundredth of one thousandth of one millionth of one billionth of

* The first syllable of every prefix is accented.

Fig. 5–3 This 150-millimeter rule replaces the 6-inch rule.

weight. The kilogram is about the same as 2.2 pounds, or slightly more than twice the pound in weight. The weight or mass of materials such as sand, metal, and other bulk items is given in kilograms.

Volume. The metric volume measure is the **cubic meter** (m^3), which is a rather large cube. It is about 30 percent more than a cubic yard. A cube that measures 1 decimeter on each side is called a **cubic decimeter** (dm^3).

Liquid capacity. The cubic decimeter, when used as a unit of liquid capacity, is called the **liter** (L or l). A cubic decimeter, or liter, of water has a mass of 1 kilogram. The liter is slightly larger than the quart (about 6 percent more). It is the metric unit used for the liquid capacity of such finishing materials as paints and oils. Since most of these materials are normally packaged in quart and pint (half-quart) sizes, the metric equivalents are the liter and half liter (500 milliliters). Since the liter and half liter are a little larger than the quart and pint, the contents of the metric containers will cover a little more area.

Temperature. Metric temperature is shown in **degrees Celsius** (°C). On this scale, water freezes at 0°C and boils at 100°C, and normal body temperature is 37°C.

To convert Fahrenheit temperature to Celsius, use this procedure: First, subtract 32 from the Fahrenheit temperature. Next, multiply the result by 5/9.

$$°C = (°F - 32)5/9$$

Technical (derived) units

The more common derived units are called **technical units** (Table 5–3). In the metric system, there is only one unit for any physical quantity. For example, all power is expressed in watts and kilowatts, not horsepower. The more common technical units you will use in metalwork are discussed below:

1. *Speed.* Speed in the SI metric system is given in **meters per second** (m/s). However, highway speed limits will be shown in kilometers per hour (km/h). Machine speeds will be in meters per second (m/s) or in meters per minute (m/min).

2. *Force.* Force in metrics is given in **newtons** (N). The force of gravity on a 1-kilogram mass would be 9.8 newtons at sea level and 1.6 newtons on the moon. The force of gravity on a person with a mass of 80 kilograms (176 lbs.) would be 784 newtons on earth and 128 newtons on the moon.

3. *Pressure.* The unit of pressure is the **pascal** (Pa). This is a small unit. For example, a medium-sized apple (100 grams) squashed evenly on a 1-square-meter table would exert a pressure of about 1 pascal. Therefore, pressures are often given in **kilopascals** (kPa), or 1000 pascals. One pound per square inch (psi) is equal to about 7 kilopascals. Tire pressure of 25 pounds per square inch is about 172 kilopascals in metrics.

4. *Energy.* The unit of energy or work is the **joule** (J). This is a very small unit, so the kilojoule (kJ) is often used. A kilojoule is

Table 5-3
SI Metric Derived Units with Special Names

Measurement	Name	Symbol	Formula
frequency	hertz	Hz	l/s
force or weight	newton	N	$kg \cdot m/s^2$
pressure or stress	pascal	Pa	N/m^2
energy	joule	J	$N \cdot m$
power	watt	W	J/s
electric charge	coulomb	C	$A \cdot s$
electric potential	volt	V	W/A
capacitance	farad	F	C/V
electric resistance	ohm	Ω	V/A
conductance	siemens	S	A/V
magnetic flux	weber	Wb	$V \cdot s$
magnetic flux density	tesla	T	Wb/m^2
inductance	henry	H	Wb/A
luminous flux	lumen	lm	$cd \cdot sr$
illuminance	lux	lx	lm/m^2

about the same as a British thermal unit (Btu).

5. *Power.* The unit for *all* power—*not* just electricity—is the **watt (W)** or **kilowatt (kW)**. A popular size of electric lamp consumes 100 watts. One horsepower equals about 3/4 kilowatt. Therefore, a 100-horsepower engine would be a 75-kilowatt engine.

Metric standards

In industry, changing to the metric system involves a great deal more than converting units of measure. Changing inches to millimeters, pounds to kilograms, and quarts to liters is called a "soft" conversion. In other words, the *actual size* of the object does not change. If the thickness of metal is listed as one inch, it can also be listed as 25.4 millimeters. A quart can be shown as 0.946 liters.

SI metric is a measurement system only. It is totally separate and different from the problem of developing metric standards for all materials used. Establishing metric standards is the responsibility of the worldwide organization called the ISO (International Organization for Standardization). The United States is represented in the ISO by the American National Standards Institute (ANSI). These organizations are establishing metric standards for the actual sizes of materials. As these standards are developed, the actual size of a material may change. This is called "hard" conversion. You will find information on these metric standards throughout this book. The ISO paper sizes used in machine drafting and the ISO thread standards used in metalworking are but two examples.

About 150 to 200 metric standards are now available. It has been estimated that, in the years ahead, we will need about 1100 metric standards in order to have true interchangeability of parts.

Tools and machines

The usual gage found on metalworking machines has customary measurement in inches and fractions of an inch. This gage lets the worker measure and adjust the depth or width of cut. These machines can be converted to metric measurement by placing a

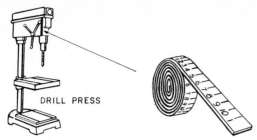

DRILL PRESS

Fig. 5-4 Metric tape can be added to machines for cutting to metric sizes.

metric tape alongside the customary gage or over it (Fig. 5-4). On machine tools such as lathes, shapers, and grinders, dual reading dials must be added that have both thousandths of an inch and hundredths of a millimeter. On the lathe, a separate set of gears is needed to cut metric threads. All measuring tools, such as rules and micrometers, must be available in metric units. Other tools, such as metric drills, taps and dies, and wrenches, are needed to work in the metric system.

 **QUESTIONS**

1. Why must measurements in industry be very accurate?
2. What five metric units are you likely to use in daily life?
3. What are five metric technical measuring units used in metalwork?
4. What is the difference between a "soft" conversion and a "hard" conversion to the metric system?
5. How can the gage on a metalworking machine be converted to metric measurement? How can the dial on a machine tool be converted?

 EXTRA CREDIT

1. Make a poster-sized conversion chart for common customary and metric units.
2. Write a research report on the history of the metric system.

Unit 6
Reading a Print and Making a Sketch

In general metals, you will need a drawing or sketch for just about anything you make. You must be able to read the drawing or **print,** which is a reproduction of a drawing. It is sometimes called a *blueprint.* You must also be able to transfer measurements from the drawing to the metal. Often, you will want to make a sketch of some project you have designed. If you have had a course in drawing or drafting, this should be easy. If you have not, read this unit thoroughly, and then have your teacher suggest a good drawing book. Drawing is a language a skilled worker must understand if she or he is to be successful.

Kinds of drawings

1. Many books and magazines contain drawings that look something like a photograph. These are called **pictorial drawings** (Fig. 6-1). There are three kinds:

a. The **perspective drawing** shows the object as it would appear to the eye. There are two kinds of perspective drawings, parallel and angular. *Parallel perspective* is not

Fig. 6-1 Pictorial drawings of several metal products.

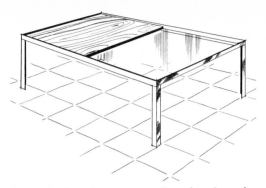

Fig. 6-2 Angular-perspective drawing of a coffee table.

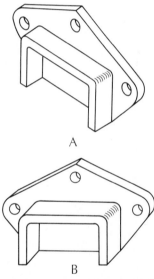

Fig. 6-3 (A) Isometric drawing of a metal part. (B) Oblique drawing of this same part.

used very often. It has only one **vanishing point.** That is the point at which various lines of the drawing meet when they are extended. *Angular perspective,* which has two vanishing points, is the more common. Many of the metal products, such as cars and appliances, that you see in magazine advertisements are drawn in angular perspective (Fig. 6–2).

    b. An **isometric drawing** is a pictorial drawing in which the sides of the object are shown 120 degrees apart. It is used mostly for drawing objects in the shape of rectangular solids (Fig. 6–3A).

    c. An **oblique,** or **cabinet, drawing** is shown in Fig. 6–3B. Note that one side appears close to the viewer and the other sides are inclined, or slanted.

    2. **Multiview,** or **orthographic,** drawings are used for building projects. The drawing used for construction is often called a **working drawing.** The multiview drawing usually shows two or three views of the object. A standard three-view drawing of this

type is made with the front view in the lower left-hand corner of the page. The top view is above, and the right-side, or end, view is to the right (Fig. 6–4). Sometimes, only two views are needed (Fig. 6–5).

    Working drawings are made as assembly drawings and as detail drawings (Fig. 6–6). An **assembly drawing** shows how the parts fit together to make the complete product. A **detail drawing** shows a single part of the product and contains all the information

23

necessary to make the part. For some simple projects, both the assembly and detail drawings are shown on the same sketch or print.

Larger projects require an assembly drawing and other drawings for each individual part or detail.

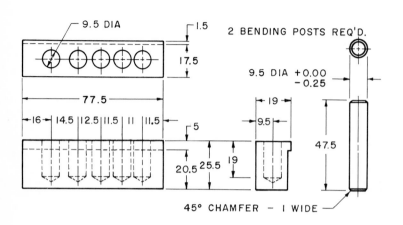

Fig. 6-4 Multiview drawing of a bending tool, showing front, top, and side views.

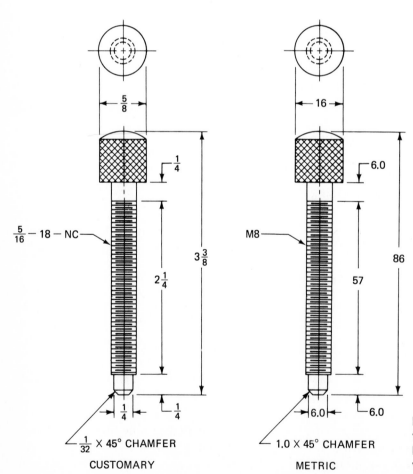

CUSTOMARY

METRIC

Fig. 6-5 Only two views of this screw are needed, because the front and side views are identical.

24

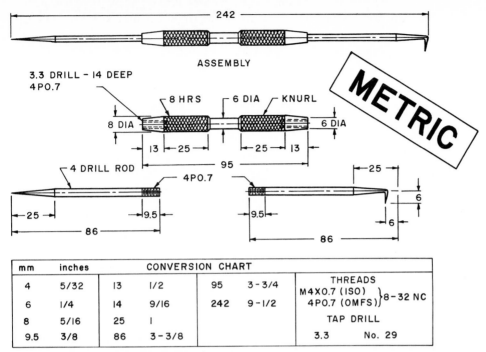

Fig. 6-6 A detail drawing of each part of a scriber and an assembly drawing showing how the parts go together.

mm	inches					CONVERSION CHART		
4	5/32	13	1/2	95	3-3/4	THREADS		
6	1/4	14	9/16	242	9-1/2	M4X0.7 (ISO) 4P0.7 (OMFS)	8-32 NC	
8	5/16	25	1			TAP DRILL		
9.5	3/8	86	3-3/8			3.3	No. 29	

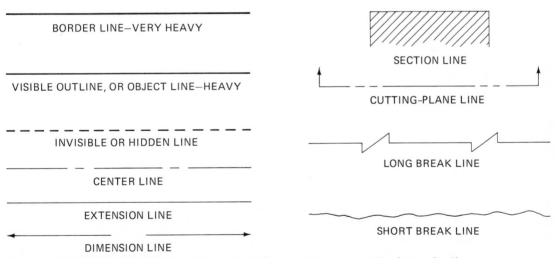

Fig. 6-7 Here is the alphabet of lines. Each line must be correctly shown for the drawing to be read properly.

Meaning of lines

A variety of lines are used to convey information in a drawing. It is important in reading a drawing and making sketches that you understand the meaning of each line (Fig. 6-7).

1. Object lines show all the edges or surfaces that can be seen.

2. Hidden lines show edges and details that cannot be seen.

3. Center lines locate the center of arcs and circles and divide an object into symmetrical, or equal, parts.

4. Extension lines are continuations of the lines of the drawing. The dimensions can be shown between them.

5. Dimension lines show the dimensions, or distances, between lines. They have arrowheads at one or both ends and are broken in the center.

Dimensions

Dimensions tell the size of each of the various parts of an object or job to be produced. A drawing that is correctly made contains all the dimensions necessary to make the part. Sometimes, a metalworker finds it necessary to calculate or add a dimension or two to make a job easier.

There are four common ways to make a drawing so that the product can be built to customary and/or metric standards:

1. *Customary drawing.* There are two common methods of dimensioning in the customary system. The method used depends on how accurate the part to be made needs to be.

a. It is common practice to dimension drawings in inches and common fractions of inches when the part to be made does not need to have a fine degree of accuracy. This is often the case in working with sheet metal. This method of dimensioning is used in most of the projects in this book. You have to have good judgment to fit parts together when only fractional dimensions are shown.

b. For parts that require precision measurements, dimensions are always given in inches and decimal parts of an inch, such as 1.5 inches or 3.254 inches. Most machine drawings are dimensioned in decimals. This method is used in order to obtain greater accuracy in making the part, to help eliminate errors, and to make it easier to show the tolerances and allowances for each part and between the mating parts. This method also lets a machinist or toolmaker know that dimensions must be measured with precision measuring tools, such as a micrometer or vernier instruments. These measuring tools measure directly in decimals. Dimensions that require the use of precision measuring tools are given in thousandths (0.001) or ten-thousandths (0.0001) of an inch.

2. *Dual dimensioning.* With this method, both the metric (in millimeters) and the customary (in inches) dimensions are shown directly on the drawing. For example, if the design or primary dimension is 2 inches, this would be shown as $\dfrac{2}{[51]}$ or, more accurately, as $\dfrac{2}{[50.8]}$ (Fig. 6–8). A symbol or note on the drawing such as $\dfrac{in}{[mm]}$ indicates that the top dimension is in inches and the dimension in brackets is in millimeters. Note also that the exact conversion of 2 inches is 50.8 millimeters, which would be used for precision work, such as in a machine shop. The metric dimension can be rounded to 51 millimeters for less precise work, such as with sheet metal. If the design or primary dimension is in metrics, this dimension is shown above and the inch dimension is shown in brackets, such as $\dfrac{12}{[0.472]}$ for an accurate conversion or $\dfrac{12}{[0.5]}$ for a rounded conversion. With dual dimensions, the product can be made using either system of measurement.

3. *Metric drawing with readout chart.* Most manufacturers are designing new products

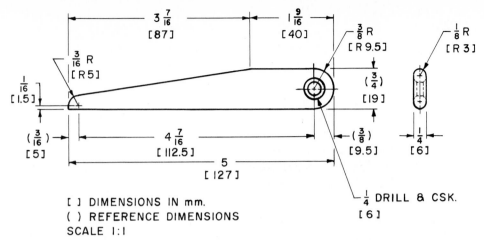

Fig. 6–8 A dual-dimensioned drawing. A note on the drawing shows that the dimensions in brackets are in millimeters.

in metric, using only millimeter dimensions on the drawing itself. A small conversion chart is then added to the drawing, usually as a paste-on. This conversion chart shows the dimensions on the drawing itself in millimeters and their equivalents in inches.

Therefore, anyone can make the product in either the metric or the customary system (Fig. 6–9).

4. *All-metric drawing.* On an all-metric drawing, only metric measurements are shown (Fig. 6–10).

Fig. 6–9 A metric drawing with a readout chart showing the equivalents of the metric dimensions in inches.

mm	in.
1	1/32
5	3/16
10	13/32
13	1/2
16	5/8
17.5	11/16
20.5	13/16
25	1
41	1 5/8
104	4 1/8

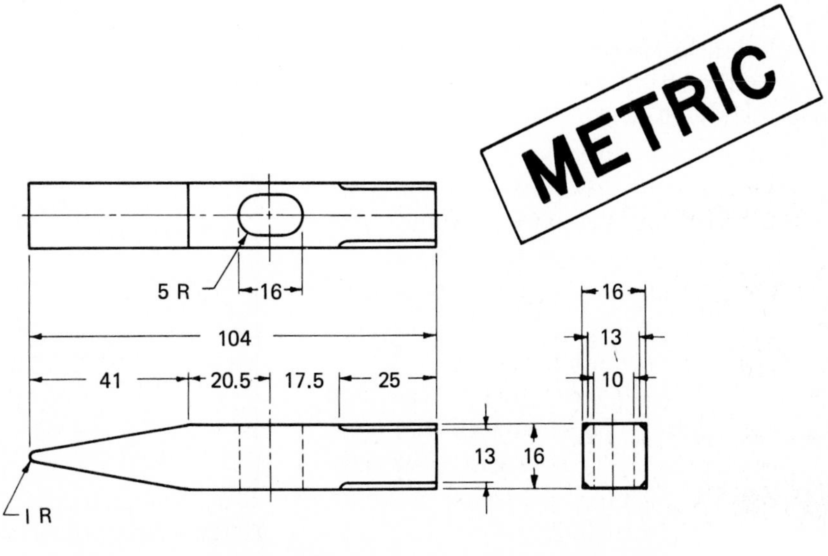

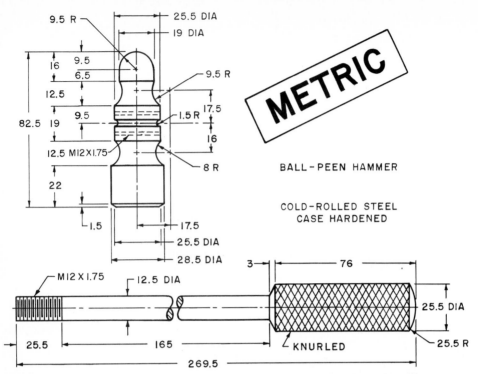

Fig. 6–10 An all-metric drawing. To identify a metric drawing clearly, either use a different-color paper (yellow) or stamp the drawing with some identification.

Scales

There are two kinds of **scales** used in drawing. One kind of scale is used to show the relationship between sizes as drawn and the true dimensions of the object. When the object is not drawn full size, drawings are made to either reduced or enlarged scales. This kind of scale is usually found on maps. A comparison of the common metric and customary scales is shown in Table 6–1.

The second kind of scale is a measuring device. When working with metal, you call it a *rule*. The three common drafting scales are the architect's scale, the engineer's scale, and the metric scale. The architect's and engineer's scales are used for making customary drawings. The metric scales are used for making metric drawings.

Table 6–1
Metric and Customary Scales

Metric scale	Customary equivalent
1:1 (full size)	1″ = 1″ or 12″ = 12″ (full size)
1:2 (half size)	1/2″ = 1″ or 6″ = 12″ (half size)
1:3 (third size)	3/8″ = 1″ or (three-eighth size)
1:5 (fifth size)	1/4″ = 1″ or 3″ = 12″ (quarter size)
1:10 (tenth size)	1/8″ = 1″ or (eighth size)

☐ approximate equivalent

28

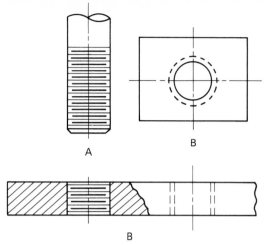

A   B

B

Fig. 6–11 Thread symbols: (A) external, (B) internal.

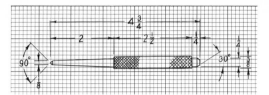

Fig. 6–12 A one-view sketch of a center punch with fractional dimensions.

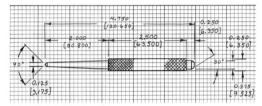

Fig. 6–13 A sketch of the center punch showing dual decimal-metric dimensions.

Pattern development

Sheet-metal objects, such as boxes or cylinders, which are formed from flat sheets, must first be drawn on a flat surface. This is called *pattern development* or *making a stretchout*. Additional information on pattern development can be found in Unit 25.

Symbols

Symbols are simplified drawings of certain things. They are used in order to save drawing time. The common symbols for threads are shown in Fig. 6–11.

Making a customary shop sketch

You should make a shop sketch, or simple working drawing, before trying to build a project. You make shop sketches on cross-sectional, or squared, paper. All you need is a soft pencil, an eraser, and a 12-inch rule or straightedge. You will find that it is easier to make shop sketches on cross-sectional paper than to draw them freehand.

1. Decide on the views you will need to build the project. Only one view may be necessary for a simple project.

2. Decide on the scale. If the paper has eight squares to the inch, each square can represent 1/8 inch, 1/4 inch, 1/2 inch, or any other suitable fraction.

3. Draw the project. Figure 6–12 shows a one-view shop sketch of a center punch with fractional dimensions. Figure 6–13 is the same object dimensioned with the dual decimal-metric dimensions. The dimensions in brackets are in millimeters.

Metric shop drawings

Metric cross-sectional paper has small squares measuring 1 millimeter by 1 millimeter (1 mm × 1 mm) with slightly heavier lines for the squares measuring 10 millimeters by 10 millimeters. A design based on the metric system should be in units of 10, 5, or 1 millimeters. To make the metric drawing full size, each small square would equal 1 square millimeter (1 mm^2). If the drawing is to be half size, each small square would equal 2 mm^2.

? QUESTIONS ▮▮▮▮▮▮▮▮

1. What is a pictorial drawing?
2. Name the different kinds of pictorial drawings.
3. What kind of drawing should be used for building projects?
4. Name five different kinds of lines used to convey information in a drawing.
5. What is dual dimensioning?
6. What are the two kinds of scales?
7. What kind of paper do you use for a shop sketch?

✔ EXTRA CREDIT ▮▮▮▮▮▮▮

Get a print of a simple metal part from a manufacturer of metal products. Show the print to the class, and explain how to read it.

Unit 7
Metals

Metals are desirable materials for product manufacturing because of their many outstanding properties. For example, they are excellent conductors of heat and electricity; they are opaque and are easily shined; they are strong, tough, and ductile; and they are easily machined.

Metallurgy is the science and technology of metals and their behavior. A scientist who specializes in metals and their use is called a **metallurgist.** In this unit, you will become acquainted with some basic information on metals and metallurgy.

Metals and alloys

Metals are among nature's most common elements. Iron, copper, and aluminum are examples. An **alloy** is a mixture of two or more metals. Usually, it consists of a **base metal** and a smaller amount of other metals. Brass, for instance, is an alloy of copper, the base metal, and zinc. In the metal shop, metals and alloys are both called metals. Metals are divided into two groups: the **ferrous metals,** which have a large percentage of iron, and the **nonferrous metals,** which have little or no iron.

Mechanical properties of metal

1. Strength is the ability of a metal to resist applied forces. Bridge girders, elevator cables, and building beams all must have this property.

2. Hardness is the ability of a metal to resist penetration, or piercing. The harder the metal, the less likely it is to change in shape. Hardness can be increased by work hardening or heat treating (explained in later units).

3. Brittleness is the tendency of a metal to break easily. Certain kinds of cast iron are brittle and break if dropped. Hardness and brittleness are closely related, since hard metals are more brittle than soft metals.

4. Malleability is the ability of a metal to be hammered or rolled out without breaking or cracking.

5. Ductility is the ability of a metal to be drawn out thin without breaking. Copper is very ductile and can be easily made into wire. Deep-formed automobile bodies and fenders, washing machines, and other stamped and formed products are made possible by this property.

6. Elasticity is the ability of a metal to return to its original shape after bending. The steel used to make springs is very elastic.

7. Fusibility is the ability of a metal to become liquid easily and join with other metals. Metals that readily weld usually have this property.

8. Machinability involves several properties. Some of these are the rate at which the material can be removed in machining, the kind of chip produced, the amount of tool wear, and the kind of surface finish that can be obtained.

The ferrous metals— iron and steel

Iron as a pure metallic element is not suitable for use in industry. However, a small amount of the nonmetallic element **carbon** can be added to iron to produce cast iron, wrought iron, and steel. **Steel,** which is very tough and useful, is an alloy mainly of iron and carbon. Other alloying elements, such as manganese and chromium, give steel other properties, such as corrosion resistance and strength. Steel is the most important metal known to people. Most of the metal used in the world today is steel (Fig. 7–1).

Following is a short description (from Joseph T. Ryerson and Son, Inc.) of how iron and steel are made:

The first step in the production of iron is the mining of iron ore. Most of the iron ore in the United States comes from the Lake Superior states of Minnesota, Wisconsin, and Michigan. A low-grade iron ore called **taconite** is increasingly being used. The **recycling,** or reuse, of iron and steel is also growing (Fig. 7–2).

Iron ore is smelted in blast furnaces. The other raw materials needed to produce iron are coke, limestone, and air. **Coke,** the fuel

Fig. 7–1 Steel is the most important metal known to people. Here you see the completed steel structure of the world's longest main-arc span, the New River Gorge Bridge in West Virginia. (United States Steel Corporation)

Fig. 7–2 Pollution control equipment on this basic oxygen furnace collects and recycles more than 99.9 percent of the dust generated during the steelmaking operation. (American Iron and Steel Institute)

Fig. 7-3 The final product of the ironmaking process is many kinds and shapes of steel. (Specialty Metals Corporation)

in ironmaking, is made from coal. Limestone acts as a **flux,** or cleaner, to remove impurities from the iron ore. It takes about 2 short tons (1.8 metric tons, or t) of iron ore, 1 ton (0.9 t) of coke, 1/2 ton (0.45 t) of limestone, and 4 tons (3.6 t) of air to produce 1 ton (0.9 t) of iron (Fig. 7-3).

The **blast furnace,** which produces iron, is a large steel shell nearly 100 feet (30 m) high, lined with heat-resistant brick. It is **charged,** or loaded, through the top with alternate layers of coke, ore, and limestone. Each blast furnace has three or more stoves to heat air for the hot blast. Air is forced through the hot flues, or pipes, of these stoves and delivered to the bottom of the blast furnace at temperatures ranging from 1200 to 1600°F (650 to 870°C). The coke burns in the blast of heated air to produce a temperature of about 3500°F (1925°C).

When the oxygen in the hot air comes in contact with the highly heated coke, large quantities of carbon dioxide gas are produced. This gas breaks down into carbon monoxide gas, an active **reducing agent.** That means that carbon monoxide has the power of combining with oxygen and also has the power of taking oxygen away from other compounds, such as iron ore. The car-

bon of the coke also reacts with the oxygen of the ore. Eventually, by means of these reactions, the iron is separated as a spongy, porous mass. This mass of iron moves downward into the higher temperature zone and begins to melt. Before it reaches the bottom of the furnace, it becomes entirely molten.

The limestone that has been added with the other raw materials has the power of combining at high temperatures with the earthy impurities of the ore to form a **slag.** Since this slag is lighter than the molten iron, it floats to the top. The slag is drawn off through the **cinder notch,** leaving the clean iron to be drawn off through a lower **iron notch,** or tapping hole. A flowchart of this process is shown in Fig. 7-4, pages 33 and 34.

During these operations, the iron has picked up 3.5 to 4 percent carbon from the coke.

A blast furnace operates without stopping. The raw materials are supplied at the top as rapidly as needed to provide enough hot metal for tapping at set intervals, usually 4 to 6 hours apart. At each tapping, 100 to 125 tons (90 to 115 t) of liquid iron are taken from the furnace. The liquid iron flows through troughs into huge ladles mounted on cars. This product of the blast furnace is called **hot metal.** When cast into molds, it is called **pig iron.**

Steel is produced from either hot metal or pig iron. The steelmaking process consists of refining blast-furnace iron to remove excess carbon and impurities. At the same time, the steelmaker controls the quantity of the alloying elements other than iron that are an essential part of steel.

Steelmaking methods

Steel is made by the open-hearth, electric-furnace, and basic oxygen processes.

In the **open-hearth process,** scrap iron and limestone are placed in a furnace on an open hearth, which looks like a huge rectan-

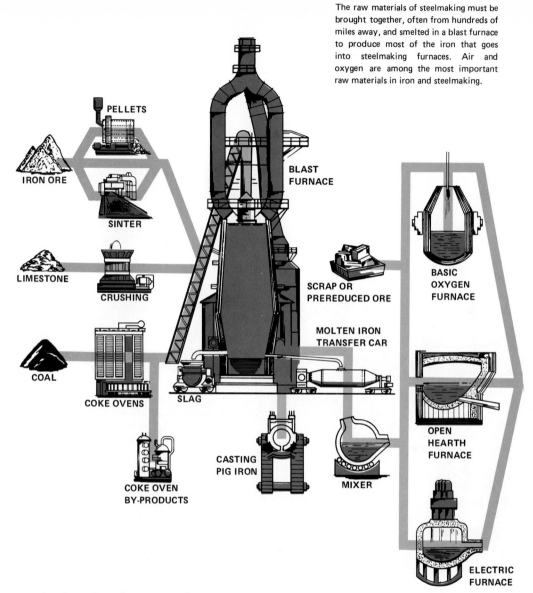

The raw materials of steelmaking must be brought together, often from hundreds of miles away, and smelted in a blast furnace to produce most of the iron that goes into steelmaking furnaces. Air and oxygen are among the most important raw materials in iron and steelmaking.

PELLETS

IRON ORE

SINTER

LIMESTONE

CRUSHING

COAL

COKE OVENS

COKE OVEN BY-PRODUCTS

SLAG

CASTING PIG IRON

MIXER

BLAST FURNACE

SCRAP OR PREREDUCED ORE

MOLTEN IRON TRANSFER CAR

BASIC OXYGEN FURNACE

OPEN HEARTH FURNACE

ELECTRIC FURNACE

Fig. 7-4 The flowchart for steelmaking.

gular dish. Fuel, gas, and air are then pumped into the furnace and ignited. The flame is directed over the iron, which melts. Carbon is produced in the form of a gas, and it combines with the air in the furnace. Other nonmetallic elements combine with

the limestone to form a slag. This slag floats on top of the molten metal and keeps it from direct contact with the flame. When the scrap iron is all melted, hot pig iron from a blast furnace is added, and refining continues.

Molten steel must solidify before it can be made into finished products by the industry's rolling mills and forging presses. The metal is usually formed first at high temperature, after which it may be cold-formed into additional products.

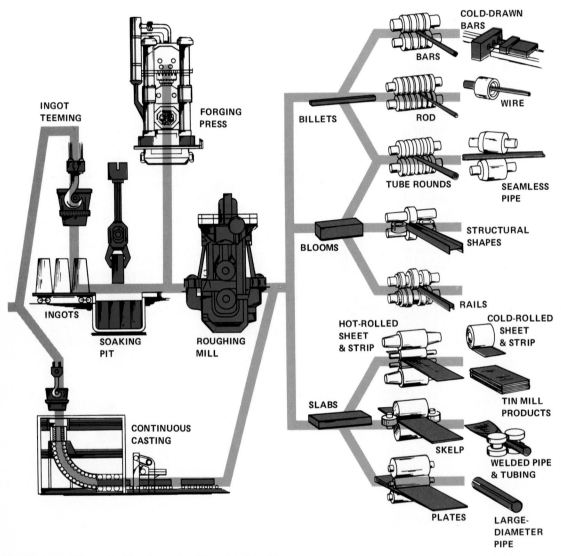

Fig. 7-4 (*continued*) The flowchart for steelmaking.

The **electric-furnace process** closely resembles the open-hearth process, except that the heat is provided by electricity, and the amount of metal processed is much smaller. The electric furnace can regulate heat very precisely. It is, therefore, used particularly for careful alloying and for producing steel to exact specifications, or specialty steel.

In the **basic oxygen process,** a pear-shaped furnace is used. Pig iron is placed in the bottom. Then, through the top, an oxygen lance is lowered until its tip is about 6 feet (2 m) above the metal. This lance pumps in huge amounts of oxygen. The oxygen combines with carbon and starts a high-temperature churning action. This very rapidly burns impurities from the iron and turns it into steel.

The finished product

Steels produced by the above methods are cast into **ingots,** or steel castings. The steel is poured from the large ladles that receive it at the furnaces into molds and allowed to cool long enough to form the ingots.

The succeeding steps in the manufacture of steel vary, depending on the product that is desired. Usually, ingots are reheated and then rolled into blooms, slabs, or billets. These three shapes of steel can also be made by a new process called continuous casting (Fig. 7–5).

Fig. 7–5 The continuous-casting process.

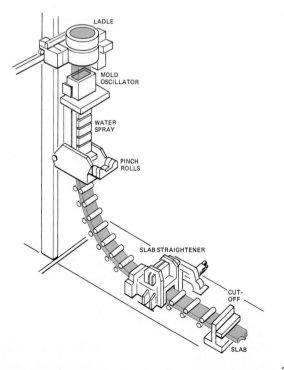

LADLE

MOLD OSCILLATOR

WATER SPRAY

PINCH ROLLS

SLAB STRAIGHTENER

CUT-OFF

SLAB

Kinds of iron and steel

Most of the projects you will make will be of carbon, alloy, or tool-and-die steel. In addition, you will probably use some of these other common ferrous metals: wrought iron, galvanized steel, tin plate, and perforated and expanded metal.

1. Cast iron is used for the heavy parts of many machines. It is the most common material for making castings. It contains 2 to 4 percent carbon. The basic kinds of cast iron are white, gray, and malleable iron. *White iron* and *gray iron* are low in cost and wear well. They are very brittle, however, and cannot be hammered or formed. *Malleable iron* is cast iron that has been made more malleable by annealing (discussed in later units). Malleable-iron castings are not so brittle or hard. They can take a great deal of hammering. Many plumbing fixtures are made of malleable iron. Cast irons are difficult to weld.

2. Wrought iron is almost pure iron. It contains only minor amounts of carbon. It is often used for ornamental ironwork. However, wrought iron is seldom used in the school shop because of its high cost. Wrought iron forges well, can easily be bent hot or cold, and can be welded.

3. Carbon steels are classified by the amount of carbon they contain. This amount is given in *points* (100 points equals 1 percent) or by *percentage*.

a. Low-carbon steel, often called *mild* or *soft steel,* contains 0.1 to 0.3 percent carbon (10 to 30 points). It does not contain enough carbon to be hardened. This type of steel is available as black-iron sheet, band iron, bars, and rods. Because it is easily welded, machined, and formed, low-carbon steel is suitable for products and projects in which an easily worked metal is needed. It is used for most bench-metal and ornamental ironwork.

b. *Medium-carbon steel* has 0.3 to 0.6 percent carbon (30 to 60 points). It is used for many standard machine parts. In the school shop, it is used for projects like hammer heads and clamp parts.

c. *High-carbon steel* contains 0.6 to 1.7 percent carbon (60 to 170 points). The best kind for school shops contains 75 to 95 points. It is used for making small tools or for any item that must be hardened and tempered.

4. **Alloy steels** have special properties determined by the mixture and the amount of other elements, particularly metals, added. Each alloy steel has a "personality" of its own. Some of the common alloying elements are described below:

a. *Nickel* is added to increase strength and toughness. It also helps steel resist corrosion.

b. *Chromium* adds hardness, toughness, and resistance to wear. Gears and axles, for example, are often made of chromium-nickel steel because of its strength.

c. *Manganese* is used in steel to produce a clean metal. It also adds strength to the steel and helps in heat treating.

d. *Silicon* is often used to increase the resiliency of steel for making springs.

e. *Tungsten* is used with chromium, vanadium, molybdenum, or manganese to produce high-speed steel, used in cutting tools. Tungsten is said to be *red-hard,* or hard enough to cut even after it becomes red-hot.

f. *Molybdenum* adds toughness and strength to steel. It is used in making high-speed steels.

g. *Vanadium* improves the grain of steel. It is used with chromium to make chrome-vanadium steel, from which transmission parts and gears are manufactured. This type of steel is very strong and has excellent shock resistance.

5. **Tool-and-die steels** are a large group of steels used when careful heat treating must be done. You will use these steels to make tools that must have a cutting edge.

6. **Rolled steel,** which includes bar, rod, and structural steels, is produced by rolling the steel into shape. *Hot-rolled steels* are formed into shape while the metal is red-hot. The metal passes through a series of rollers, each one a little closer to the next. As the steel passes through the last rollers, hot water is sprayed over it, forming a bluish **scale.** The steel produced by this method is fairly uniform in quality and is used for many kinds of parts. Hot-rolled bars of the best quality are used to produce cold-finished steels. *Cold-finished steels* are used when great accuracy, better surface finish, and certain mechanical properties are needed. There are several ways of producing cold-finished bars. The most common results in what is called *cold-worked steel.* First, the scale is removed from the hot-rolled bars. Then, the bars are either *cold-drawn,* drawn through dies a little smaller than the original bar, or *cold-rolled,* rolled cold to the exact size.

7. **Galvanized,** or **galvannealed, steel** is mild sheet steel coated with the metal zinc to keep it from rusting.

8. **Tin plate** is mild steel coated with tin.

9. Metals are available in many different patterns. **Perforated metal** has a design stamped through it (Fig. 7–6). **Expanded metal** is made by cutting slits in the metal and pulling it open to expand it. **Embossed metal** has the design pressed into its surface.

Identifying steels

All steels look very much alike. Thus, it is difficult to identify the type of steel merely by looking at it. There are three methods of identification:

1. *Number system.* A number system, or series, to identify carbon and alloy steel has been developed by the American Iron and

Table 7-1
Identifying Steels

Principal element	AISI or SAE number	How used

carbon
  low 0.1 to 0.3%
  medium 0.3 to 0.6%
  high 0.6 to 1.7%
	1	nails, screws, body parts, ships, axles, rails, wheels, springs, tools, cutters, drills

nickel	2	casting, boiler plate, structural steel
nickel-chromium	3	stainless steel, kitchen utensils, gears, shafts
molybdenum	4	machinery, automobile parts, ball and roller bearings, springs
chromium	5	hammers, bearings, axles, gears
chrome-vanadium	6	tools, springs, gears
nickel, chromium, and molybdenum	8	machining tools
manganese-silicon	9	coil and leaf springs
manganese, nickel, chromium, and molybdenum	9	parts for dies and molds

Fig. 7-6 The sides of this magazine rack are made of perforated metal.

Steel Institute (AISI) and the Society of Automotive Engineers (SAE) (Table 7-1). You will find complete information about these numerical systems in *The New American Ma-chinist's Handbook*[1] or *Machinery's Handbook*.[2] The systems are based on the use of numbers composed of four digits:

a. The first number tells the kind of steel: 1 shows carbon steel, 2 is nickel steel, 3 is nickel-chromium steel, 4 is molybdenum steel, and so forth.

b. The second number in alloy steel shows the approximate percent of alloy elements. For example, 2320 shows a nickel steel with about 3 percent nickel.

c. The last two (and sometimes three) numbers show the carbon content in points (100 points equals 1 percent). For example, AISI C1095 or SAE 1095 is a carbon steel with 95 points of carbon.

Another letter-and-number system is used to identify tool-and-die steels.

[1] Rupert LeGrand (ed.), McGraw-Hill Book Company, New York, 1955.
[2] Holbrook Horton (ed.), 20th ed., The Industrial Press, New York, 1975.

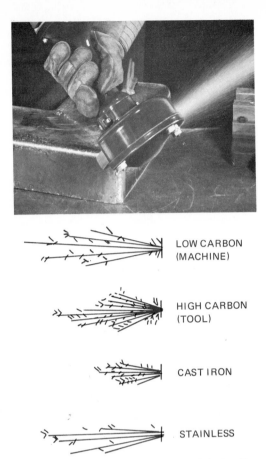

paint only the ends. Others paint all along the bar. This is done to avoid confusing the steel bars when they are stored on racks. If a certain steel is painted red, it may mean that it is high-carbon steel. Each company has a different color code.

3. *Spark test.* This method of identification is rather inaccurate. The test is made by watching the sparks given off when the metal is ground. The kind, frequency, position, and color of the sparks are all considered in making the identification. Figure 7-7 shows the sparks given off by various metals. Spark tests are often used in choosing a particular type of steel from among a group of unidentified steels. Always wear eye protection when doing this test.

Standard shapes and sizes

Metals can be purchased in many shapes and sizes (Fig. 7-8). Standard lengths range from 10 to 24 feet (3 to 8 m). Not all shapes, sizes, and kinds of metal are available in

Fig. 7-8 Some common shapes of metal standard stock are loaded on this toy train. (Westinghouse Corporation)

LOW CARBON (MACHINE)

HIGH CARBON (TOOL)

CAST IRON

STAINLESS

Fig. 7-7 Identifying ferrous metals by the spark test. What kind of metal is being ground?

The American Iron and Steel Institute has also developed a system for identifying the kind of furnace in which the steel was made:

B = acid Bessemer carbon steel
C = basic open-hearth or basic
       electric-furnace carbon steel

The letter is placed before the number of the steel. For example, AISI C1018 is a low-carbon, general-purpose steel suited to project work in wrought metal.

2. *Color code.* Most manufacturers paint each different kind of high-carbon alloy and tool-and-die steel a different color. Some

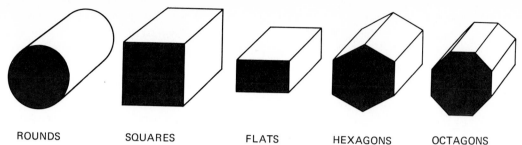

| ROUNDS | SQUARES | FLATS | HEXAGONS | OCTAGONS |

Fig. 7-9 Common shapes of bar stock.

every length. The best way to purchase metals is to use a stock list or reference book available from the supplier. You will find that most suppliers have the following common shapes and sizes or their metric equivalents in stock (Fig. 7-9):

1. Rounds, or shafting, in diameters from 3/16 to 9 inches (Table 7-2).

2. Squares from 1/4 by 1/4 inch to 4 1/2 by 4 1/2 inches (Table 7-2).

3. Flats, or rectangular shapes, from 1/8 by 5/8 inch to 3 by 4 inches (Table 7-3).

4. Hexagons, or six-sided shapes, from 1/4 to 4 inches measured across opposite flat sides (Table 7-2).

5. Octagons, or eight-sided shapes,

from 1/2 to 1 3/4 inches measured across opposite flat sides.

Nonferrous metals

There are many kinds of nonferrous metals. They are grouped as follows:

1. *Base metals:* copper, lead, tin, nickel, zinc, and aluminum.

Table 7-2
Round, Square, and Hexagon Bar Sizes

inch	mm *
1/8	3
1/4	6
3/8	10
1/2	12
5/8	16
3/4	20
1	25
1-1/4	30
1-1/2	40
1-3/4	45
2	50

*Metric replacement sizes are based on ANSI B32.4-1974.

Table 7-3
Flat, or Rectangular, Bar Shapes

Thickness		Width	
inch	mm *	inch	mm *
1/16	1.6	3/8	10
1/8	3	1/2	12
3/16	5	5/8	16
1/4	6	3/4	20
5/16	8	1	25
3/8	10	1-1/4	30
7/16	11	1-1/2	40
1/2	12	1-3/4	45
9/16	14	2	50
5/8	16		
11/16	18		
3/4	20		
7/8	22		
1	25		
1-1/8	28		
1-1/4	30		
1-5/16	32		
1-3/8	35		
1-1/2	40		
1-3/4	45		
2	50		

*Metric replacement sizes are based on ANSI B32.3-1974.

2. *Alloys:* brass, bronze, nickel silver or German silver, pewter or Britannia metal, and gar-alloy.

3. *Precious metals:* sterling silver, gold, and platinum.

Many of the nonferrous metals listed above are not used very often in the school shop. Some are too expensive. Others do not have good working qualities.

Some common nonferrous metals and their characteristics and applications are described below:

1. Copper is a warm reddish brown metal used for much art-metal work (Fig. 7–10). It is easy to work and is an excellent conductor of electricity. Copper becomes hard when it is worked. However, it can easily be softened by heating it to a cherry-red color and then cooling it. Copper can be joined with rivets or by silver soldering, bronze

brazing, or soft soldering. It will take an excellent polish and finish and is used for many decorative pieces, such as bowls, trays, and containers. It is easy to form by stretching, but it does not machine easily. For example, it is more difficult to cut threads on copper rod than on mild steel. Copper becomes covered with a green tarnish, which is easily removed by brushing and polishing or by chemical means.

2. Brass is one of the more important of the copper alloys. Brass is very ductile and can be made into wire. It is also a good base for plating. There are many kinds of brass, each with different working qualities. The principal alloying element in most brass is the metal zinc. *Gilding brass,* a rich bronze in color, is 5 percent zinc. It is used for jewelry, coins, and plaques. *Commercial bronze,* actually a brass, contains about 10 percent zinc. The *red,* or *colonial,* brass that contains 15 percent zinc is somewhat softer and is used for jewelry. It has a gold color that is very similar to real gold. *Cartridge brass,* which is 30 percent zinc, is used to make artillery and ammunition. *Yellow brass,* 35 percent zinc, is characterized by its bright yellow color. *Leaded brass* and *forging brass* each have a little lead added to the copper and zinc.

3. Bronze, another copper alloy, has a reddish gold color. Bronze may or may not contain some zinc. Common alloying elements used in bronze include:

a. Tin to increase strength and resistance to corrosion.

b. Aluminum to increase resistance to corrosion.

c. Nickel to make the bronze whiter. Nickel bronze is a beautiful metal for castings, plaques, and similar articles.

4. Nickel silver, sometimes called **German silver,** is usually made of about 64 percent copper, 18 percent nickel, and 18 percent zinc. The more nickel it contains, the whiter it is. Nickel silver can be soldered,

Fig. 7–10 Copper is used in the piping systems of an active solar energy house. (Georgia-Pacific Corporation)

formed, and annealed, much like brass. Its color varies from a light pink to a silver white. Nickel silver is a good imitation of sterling silver. However, it is quite brittle, cannot be hammered into shape, and discolors easily. Nevertheless, it is easy to solder, bends quite well, and is very good for etching. Nickel silver is used for bracelets, rings, and other jewelry. It is used as a base for all good silver-plated tableware.

5. Zinc is most often seen in the form of a protective coating on sheet metal. Zinc is also used as an alloying element in making brass and some bronze. Sheets of pure zinc can be used for protecting other materials.

6. Lead is one of the heaviest metals. The surface of lead is quite gray, but a scratch in the surface looks white. Lead is very soft. Thus, a lead block is a good thing to use as a backing when punching holes with a hollow punch or when bumping or hammering sheet metal. Lead is most often used as an alloy with some other metal. When lead is alloyed with tin, it becomes soft solder.

7. Tin is seldom used except as an alloying metal. It is used with copper to produce bronze and with lead to make soft solder. Tin is nonpoisonous. A coating of tin is put on mild-steel sheets used for making food containers.

8. Aluminum has become one of the leading metals of industry and everyday life. Embossed sheet aluminum is used in building construction, furniture, and appliances (Fig. 7–11). It is being used more and more because it is lightweight, is easy to work, and has a pleasing appearance. Aluminum resists corrosion and is a good conductor of electricity. Pure aluminum is soft. Making it into alloys adds strength and provides other desirable characteristics. Elements added to aluminum include:

a. Copper to add strength and hardness and to make it easier to machine.

Fig. 7–11 Aluminum is widely used in aircraft because it is light in weight and easy to shape. (Cessna Corporation)

b. Magnesium to improve ductility and resistance to impact.

c. Manganese to increase strength and hardness.

d. Silicon to lower the melting point and improve castability.

e. Zinc to improve strength and hardness.

There are well over 100 different alloys of aluminum. Some of the more common ones you might use include:

a. Wrought alloys, which are used for rolling, pressing, and hammering. These are indicated by an S. Wrought alloy 1100 is pure aluminum.

b. Alloy 3003, which has some manganese in it. This can be purchased as 3S–O, which is dead-soft or annealed, or in the forms 3S–1/2H, 3S–3/4H, or 3S–H, which vary in degree of hardness.

c. Alloy 5052, which has a little magnesium in it.

d. Casting aluminums used in sand molds include 43, which contains a little silicon, and 113, which contains some copper and silicon.

41

9. Sterling silver is used in jewelry and tableware. It has a warm silver luster. Pure silver is soft. Sterling silver, although not so ductile as copper, can be formed and shaped well. It is suited to chasing, etching, spinning, and all other surface decorations. It hard-solders well. To be marked *sterling,* an article must contain at least 0.925 parts of silver, with 0.075 parts or less of copper and other alloying elements to give it hardness.

10. Pewter, or **Britannia metal,** has a pleasing gray color. It is 92 percent tin, 6 percent antimony, and 2 percent copper. Because of its high tin content, it is quite expensive and often hard to obtain. It was used a great deal during colonial days. Some of the early pewter contained lead, which made it poisonous in combination with acid foods. Pewter is very soft and easy to work cold. It is difficult to solder, however, because of its low melting point.

11. Gar-alloy is bluish gray. It is a zinc-base alloy, with copper and silver added to give it strength. It has good cold-working qualities for drawing, spinning, and hammering. It resists corrosion well and buffs to a high polish.

Space-age metals

When people began to approach the threshold of space, they needed new metals that could withstand great heat and cold, were light and tough, and were easy to fabricate. Three new metals are particularly important in the aerospace industry and in other areas of new technology:

1. Titanium is a very desirable metal because it is light and strong and resists corrosion. Though titanium is heavier than aluminum, titanium alloys are much stronger than aluminum alloys. Titanium alloys are much lighter than steel alloys but are comparable to them in strength. Titanium is very expensive because it is difficult to produce and fabricate. It melts at a very high

Fig. 7-12 Molybdenum is used in electronic devices such as this microwave oven. (Amana Corporation)

temperature and must be worked in an atmosphere of inert gases.

2. Beryllium, which is lighter than aluminum, is as strong in proportion to its weight as high-strength steel. Beryllium conducts heat well and is slow to heat up. Thus, it can be used where other metals would melt. Beryllium is frequently used as an alloy with copper, nickel, or aluminum.

3. Molybdenum has a high melting point and a high strength-to-weight ratio. It is a good conductor of heat and electricity (Fig. 7–12).

 QUESTIONS

1. What is the difference between a metal and an alloy?
2. What is the difference between ferrous and nonferrous metals?
3. Name the mechanical properties of metals.
4. What are the four raw materials for making iron?
5. What are three ways of making steel?
6. How do cast iron and wrought iron differ in composition?
7. What is mild steel?

8. Name seven elements used in making alloy steels.
9. What are the three methods of identifying steel?
10. What is the base metal in brass and bronze? What are the chief alloying elements?
11. What elements are alloyed with aluminum?
12. What three metals are very important in the aerospace industry?

EXTRA CREDIT

Find out all you can about one of the following metals: tungsten, molybdenum, nickel, chromium, cadmium, titanium, magnesium, beryllium.

Unit 8
Planning a Product

When the drawing for the project is complete, a great deal of planning must be done before construction can begin. In industry, these plans are submitted to a section called *production planning* or *production control.* Here **specifications,** or descriptions, are written for the product, and the routing, or shop, orders made. Planning the work before building the project is the best way to avoid making needless mistakes. The extra time spent in planning is well worth it.

It is good practice to use a plan sheet when planning your project. A plan sheet has three major parts: the bill of materials; the equipment and tools to be used; and the procedure, or steps, for making the project.

Making a bill of materials

It is important to list the materials needed to build the project. Each item should be written accurately and clearly so that the list could be sent to a metal-supply house and the proper items obtained in return. The bill of materials includes the number of pieces, the size of each piece, its description, the cost per unit, and the total cost. Table 8–1 includes a list of the common materials and a description of how to order them in the customary system. As materials become available in metric sizes, these can be used instead. A stock list or handbook of materials can be obtained from most companies that manufacture and sell metal supplies.

Equipment and tools

All the equipment and tools you need should be listed. It will save time and energy later if all tools are obtained before work is started on the project. Tools should be kept in a convenient place when not in use. In that way, they will be close at hand when you need them.

Table 8–1
Common Materials Used in Metalwork

Material	Common sizes (suggested sizes for average projects)	How sold (in general)	Characteristics
A. Sheet stock			
galvanized steel (iron)	United States Standard gage numbers 28 to 26 for light projects; United States Standard gage numbers 22 to 20 for heavier projects	24 × 96″ by sheet or bundles	mild steel with zinc coating
galvannealed steel	same as above	same as above	mild steel with zinc coating that is part of the sheet
tin plate	United States Standard gage number 30 or 28 (IC or IX) for light items	20 × 28″ by sheet or by package of 56 or 112 sheets	mild steel with tin coating cold-rolled to thickness
black annealed sheet (iron)	United States Standard gage numbers 26 to 22 for lighter projects; United States Standard gage numbers 20 to 18 for heavier projects	24 × 96″ by sheet or bundle	mild steel with oxide coating hot-rolled or cold-rolled
aluminum (1100S or 3003S; soft temper)	Brown & Sharpe gage number 18 or 0.040 for light projects; Brown & Sharpe gage number 14 or 0.064 for heavier projects	24 × 72″ by sheet or by lineal foot on rolls	commercially pure metal
copper (soft)	16-oz for light work; 24-oz for medium work; 32-oz for heavy work	24 × 96″ by sheet	pure metal
brass (soft)	Brown & Sharpe gage 18 for average work	24 × 76″ by sheet or by lineal foot on rolls	copper and zinc; standard or red brass for easier hammering and finishing
nickel silver (German silver)	Brown & Sharpe gage numbers 20 and 16	6 or 12″ by lineal foot	65% copper, 17% zinc, and 18% nickel

Table 8–1 *(Continued)*

Material	Common sizes (suggested sizes for average projects)	How sold (in general)	Characteristics
B. Mild steel and nonferrous metals			
band (hot-rolled strips)	1/8 × 1/2″, 1/8 × 3/4″, 1/8 × 1″ for bench-metal or wrought-metal projects	16′ lengths per lb or ft or 100 ft	AISI C1018 rolled mild steel with oxide coating
rounds (shafting)	1/2″, 3/4″, 1″ for machine or small tool parts not requiring hardening	12′ or 16′ lengths per lb or ft	AISI C1018 hot-rolled with oxide coating or cold-finished or aluminum
squares (bar)	1/2 × 1/2″, 3/4 × 3/4″, 1 × 1″, 1-1/2 × 1-1/2″ for small tools that are to be case-hardened or for wrought-metal projects	12′ or 16′ lengths per lb or ft	same as above
flats	1/2 × 1-1/4″, 1/2 × 2″ for small tools	12′ lengths	AISI C1018 cold-finished
angle	1-1/2 × 1-1/2 × 1/8″, 2 × 2 × 3/16″ for bench legs and frames	12′ or 14′ lengths per lb or ft or 100 ft	AISI C1015 hot-rolled or aluminum
C. High-carbon and tool steel			
flats	1/8 × 1-1/2″ for knives	12′ or 14′ lengths by lb	AISI C1095 or tool steel (water hardening)
rounds	1/2″, 9/16″, or 5/8″ for punches	12′ or 14′ lengths by lb	same as above
hexagon	1/2″ or 3/4″ for chisels or punches	12′ or 14′ lengths by lb	same as above
octagon	3/8″, 1/2″, or 5/8″ for chisels or punches	12′ or 14′ lengths by lb	same as above

Table 8-1 (*Continued*)

Material	Common sizes (suggested sizes for average projects)	How sold (in general)	Characteristics
C. High-carbon and tool steel (*continued*)			
drill rod	various diameters 1/8″, 3/16″, 1/4″, 3/8″ for small tools	3′ lengths	polished round; good tool steel; diameter is extremely accurate; smooth finish
D. Other items			
pipe	1/8″ mild steel, brass, and copper for electric lamps	12′ lengths by lb or ft	AISI C1018 mild steel and copper or brass; may be continuous-threaded
rivets	1/8 × 1″, 3/16 × 1″ roundhead and flathead, black (soft) iron for bench metal or wrought metal	by lb or per 1000 pieces	
	1/8 × 1″ aluminum, copper, and brass roundhead	by lb	
	1 and 2-1/2 lb black-iron and tinned tinner's rivets	by box (1000 pieces)	
machine screws and nuts	6-32-1″-1-1/2″, 8-32-1″-1-1/2″ steel, roundhead or flathead, and brass roundhead for small machine assembly	by gross (144 pieces)	
wire	United States Standard gage numbers 10, 12, 14, 18 black soft annealed wire or coppered. Bessemer wire or soft galvanized wire for sheet-metal work. Brown & Sharpe gage numbers 18 and 20 aluminum	by weight of coil	
foundry metal	aluminum casting alloy number 43 or 113	by lb	
	Die-cast metal	by lb	

___Candle Sconce_____ ___October 5_____ ___October 19_____
(Name of project)   (Date started)   (Date completed)

Bill of Materials:

No.	Size T	Size W	Size L	Name of part	Material	Unit cost	Total cost
1	18 Ga. (1.2mm)	2" (50mm)	14" (355mm)	hanger	black iron sheet		
1		3/4" (19mm) ID	1" (25mm)	candle cup	pipe, mild steel		

Tools and Machines: Combination square, layout fluid, scriber, dividers, round and flat files, grinder, drill and drill press, center punch, hammer, sheet-metal brake, hacksaw, brazing equipment, steel wool, C clamp, flat black paint, paint thinner, and a brush

Outline of Procedure or Steps:
1. Cut hanger to size shown in bill of materials.
2. Apply layout fluid to hanger.
3. Layout patterns for each end; layout bend lines and center-punch holes.
4. Cut hanger to shape with hacksaw, grinder, and files. Remove all burrs.
5. Bend hanger to shape.
6. Cut pipe to length; remove all burrs.
7. Clamp pipe in position on hanger.
8. Braze pipe to hanger.
9. Clean sconce with paint thinner and steel wool; wipe dry.
10. Apply two coats of flat black paint.

Fig. 8-1 The planning sheet used to make a candle sconce.

Procedure, or steps

An outline of procedure is simply a list of steps to follow in building something. First, list all the parts of the project. Next, think through what you must do to make each part, and write this down. And finally, list the steps to follow in assembling and finishing the project. Study all these steps to make sure they are correct. Figure 8-1 shows the plan sheet used to make a candle sconce, or wall-mounted candleholder. Customary and metric drawings are shown in Fig. 8-2 and a photograph of this project in Fig. 8-3.

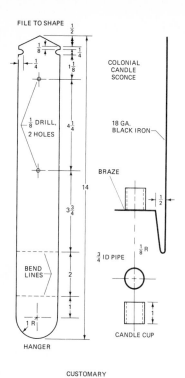

FILE TO SHAPE

COLONIAL
CANDLE
SCONCE

18 GA.
BLACK IRON

⅛ DRILL,
2 HOLES

BRAZE

¾ ID PIPE

⅛ R

BEND
LINES

1 R

CANDLE CUP

HANGER

CUSTOMARY

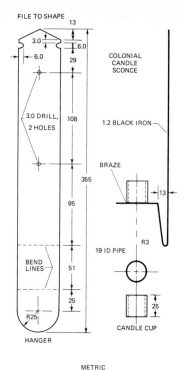

FILE TO SHAPE

COLONIAL
CANDLE
SCONCE

1.2 BLACK IRON

3.0 DRILL,
2 HOLES

BRAZE

19 ID PIPE

R3

BEND
LINES

R25

CANDLE CUP

HANGER

METRIC

Fig. 8–2 Customary and metric drawings of the candle sconce.

Fig. 8–3 The completed candle sconce.

 QUESTIONS

1. Why must you plan a project before starting to build it?
2. What is a bill of materials?
3. What is an outline of procedure?

✔ **EXTRA CREDIT**

Obtain a stock list and reference book from some metal company, Find out all you can about a certain kind or shape of metal. For example, what are the kinds and sizes of tubing available in copper, aluminum, or steel?

48

Unit 9
Measuring and Marking Out

Measuring and marking out stock are important steps in making any project. It is important to learn to use the common layout tools correctly so that you will not make any mistakes. Layout tools are precision instruments. Use them carefully and properly (Fig. 9–1).

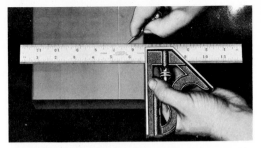

Fig. 9–1 Learn to use layout tools properly for accurate work.

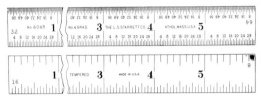

Fig. 9–2 Front and back views of a 6-inch steel rule.

Customary rules and scales

1. The 6- or 12-inch *steel rule* is the most common rule for taking and laying out measurements (Fig. 9–2). Most steel rules are marked on all four edges. The first edge is divided into eight parts to the inch, with each small division representing 1/8 inch. Every second division represents 1/4 inch, and every fourth division represents 1/2 inch. The second edge is divided into sixteenths of an inch, the third into thirty-seconds of an inch, and the fourth into sixty-fourths of an inch. Each 1/64 inch represents a little less than sixteen-thousandths (actually 0.015625) of an inch. In measuring, the experienced machinist can judge half or one-fourth of this amount. He or she can therefore read the rule as close to the exact size as 0.003 to 0.005 (three to five thousandths) of an inch.

Fractions of an inch and their decimal and millimeter equivalents are shown in Table 9–1. Fractional and decimal parts of an inch are in common usage in the United States.

In measuring or marking out distances, the rule must be held on edge to be accurate. If the end is worn, start measuring from the 1-inch mark.

Be sure that you can read a rule. It is surprising how many people have difficulty finding the 7/16 or 13/32 division on a rule. Many errors are made through incorrect measuring and layout. Study Fig. 9–3 if you have trouble reading the rule.

2. The *hook rule*, which has a hook on the end for keeping the rule in place, measures inside and outside diameters and through holes (Fig. 9–4). The hook serves as the starting point of the measurement.

3. A 36-inch steel *circumference rule* is very useful for sheet-metal layout (Fig. 9–5). As its name implies, it is used to measure the circumference, or rim, of a circle. Along one edge of the circumference rule, there is a regular rule, divided into sixteenths, for measuring diameters. Along the other edge, there is a scale that shows the circumferences for those diameters. For example, if you want to lay out a piece of sheet metal that is to be rolled into a 4-inch-diameter cylinder, first locate the 4-inch mark on the rule. Then look across to the mark on the scale, which indicates about 12 9/16 inches.

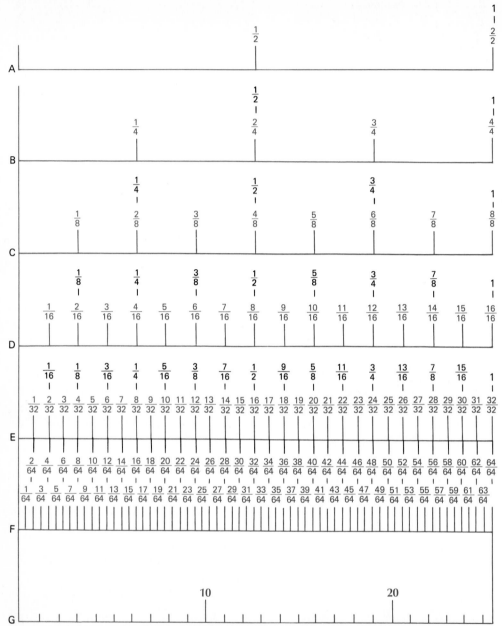

Fig. 9-3 This chart will help you to learn to read a rule. Notice that 8/64 inch at line *F* is the same as 4/32 inch at line *E*. It is the same as 2/16 inch at line *D*, which is 1/8 inch at line *C*. A millimeter comparison scale is shown at line *G*. Note that an inch equals about 25 millimeters.

Fig. 9–4 A hook rule, front and back.

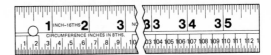

Fig. 9–5 A circumference rule is useful in sheet-metal work. It will give the circumference needed when the diameter is known.

Table 9–1
Fractions of an Inch and Their Decimal and Millimeter Equivalents

Inches		in.	mm	Inches		in.	mm
	1/64	0.01563	0.397		33/64	0.51563	13.097
1/32		0.03125	0.794	17/32		0.53125	13.494
	3/64	0.04688	1.191		35/64	0.54688	13.890
1/16		0.06250	1.587	9/16		0.56250	14.287
	5/64	0.07813	1.984		37/64	0.57813	14.684
3/32		0.09375	2.381	19/32		0.59375	15.081
	7/64	0.10938	2.778		39/64	0.60938	15.478
1/8		0.12500	3.175	5/8		0.62500	15.875
	9/64	0.14063	3.572		41/64	0.64063	16.272
5/32		0.15625	3.969	21/32		0.65625	16.669
	11/64	0.17188	4.366		43/64	0.67188	17.065
3/16		0.18750	4.762	11/16		0.68750	17.462
	13/64	0.20313	5.159		45/64	0.70313	17.859
7/32		0.21875	5.556	23/32		0.71875	18.256
	15/64	0.23438	5.953		47/64	0.73438	18.653
1/4		0.25000	6.350	3/4		0.75000	19.050
	17/64	0.26563	6.747		49/64	0.76563	19.447
9/32		0.28125	7.144	25/32		0.78125	19.844
	19/64	0.29688	7.541		51/64	0.79688	20.240
5/16		0.31250	7.937	13/16		0.81250	20.637
	21/64	0.32813	8.334		53/64	0.82813	21.034
11/32		0.34375	8.731	27/32		0.84375	21.431
	23/64	0.35938	9.128		55/64	0.85938	21.828
3/8		0.37500	9.525	7/8		0.87500	22.225
	25/64	0.39063	9.922		57/64	0.89063	22.622
13/32		0.40625	10.319	29/32		0.90625	23.019
	27/64	0.42188	10.716		59/64	0.92188	23.415
7/16		0.43750	11.113	15/16		0.93750	23.812
	29/64	0.45313	11.509		61/64	0.95313	24.209
15/32		0.46875	11.906	31/32		0.96875	24.606
	31/64	0.48438	12.303		63/64	0.98438	25.003
1/2		0.50000	12.700	1		1.00000	25.400

Fig. 9-6 A steel tape is especially useful for measuring around curved sections. (Lotkin Tools)

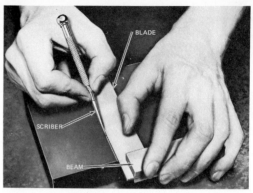

Fig. 9-8 Using a toolmaker's try square to mark a line across a workpiece.

Fig. 9-7 A 150-millimeter rule with one edge graduated in millimeters (1 mm) and the other edge in 1/2 millimeters (0.5 mm).

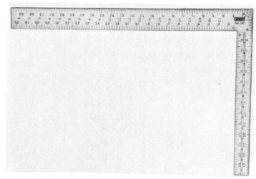

Fig. 9-9 A large steel square.

4. The *steel tape* can be bent around curved or circular objects. You can use it to measure on the inside or outside of openings. The tape has a little hook on the end that holds it in place for making long measurements (Fig. 9-6).

Metric rules

Metric rules are commonly available in 150-mm and 300-mm lengths (Fig. 9-7). The rules are divided into full millimeters (1 mm) for most work and into half millimeters (0.5 mm) for more precise work. Steel tapes are available with dual or only metric graduations.

Squares and protractors

1. A *toolmaker's try square* is very accurate. It has both a steel beam and blade. It is used to check whether two adjoining surfaces are at right angles to each other, to make a square, and to square off a line in measuring stock to length (Fig. 9-8).

2. A large *steel square* is very useful in sheet-metal work (Fig. 9-9).

3. The *combination set* is one of the most useful measuring tools (Fig. 9-10). It has four parts:

   a. A *steel rule,* made in lengths from 9 to 18 inches with a slot or groove running lengthwise along one side. Any one of the three heads (described below) can slide along the groove on the rule and be locked in place with a knurled nut.

   b. The *combination square head,* which makes a 90-degree angle on one side and a

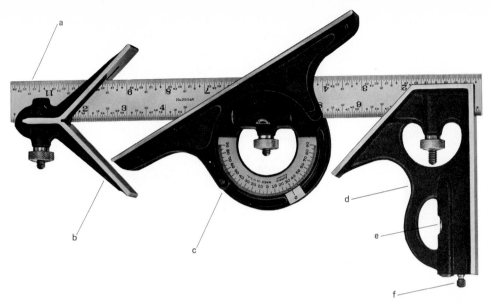

Fig. 9-10 Parts of a combination set: (a) steel rule, (b) center head, (c) protractor head, (d) square head, (e) spirit level, (f) scriber.

Fig. 9-11 A combination square with a blade that is graduated in 1/2 millimeters (0.5 mm) on one edge and 1/32 inch on the other.

45-degree angle on the other (Fig. 9–11). There is a *spirit level* in the head for leveling up a machine or workpiece. This head can be used for laying out lines at 45- or 90-degree angles, for checking the squareness of

stock, for measuring depths, and for other operations shown in Fig. 9–12.

c. The *center head*, sometimes called the *center square*, used for locating the center of the end of a cylinder.

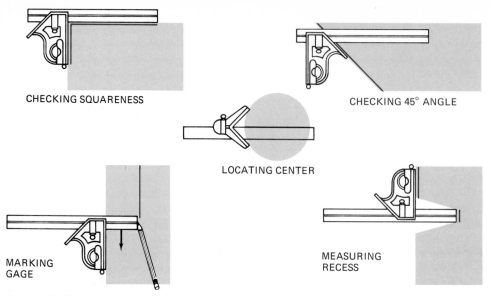

CHECKING SQUARENESS

CHECKING 45° ANGLE

LOCATING CENTER

MARKING GAGE

MEASURING RECESS

Fig. 9–12 Common uses for the square and center heads.

d. The *protractor head,* used to lay out and check any angle from 0 to 180 degrees (Fig. 9–13).

Sheet-metal gages

Sheet-metal gages are round disks of metal with slots cut around the outside. They are used to measure the thickness of sheet metal and wire in the customary system. (No gages are used in the metric system. A metric micrometer is used to measure the thickness or diameter in millimeters.) Each slot of a gage is numbered. The numbers represent a certain thickness or diameter in decimals of an inch. The gage of the sheet metal or wire is the number of the slot in which it fits.

There are two common customary gage systems used for metal (Table 9–2). The *United States Standard* (USS) gage is used for black and galvanized mild-steel sheets, steel plates, and steel wire. The *Brown & Sharpe,* or *American,* gage is used for measuring nonfer-

Fig. 9–13 Using the protractor head.

rous metals such as copper, brass, and aluminum. To measure a piece of galvanized sheet, select a gage that is stamped United States Standard. Then try the metal in the various slots until you find the one in which

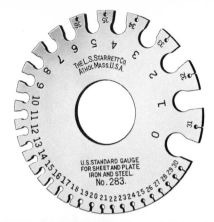

it just slips (Fig. 9-14). If the metal is 16 gage, it will be 0.0598 inch thick. To measure brass, use the Brown & Sharpe, or American, gage. If it is 16 gage, it will be 0.050 inch thick.

Scribers and other marking tools

A **scriber** is a slender steel rod about 8 to 12 inches (200 to 300 mm) long with a sharp point on one or both ends. Sometimes, one end is bent at a right angle. The scriber is used to **scribe,** or scratch, lines on most metal surfaces (Figs. 9-15, 9-16). For marking on metal plate, a *soapstone crayon* is good because it shows up well. For marking bend lines on sheet metal, a *pencil* is used.

Measuring and marking out heavy stock

To measure the thickness of a piece of metal, *hold the rule on edge* with one edge of the metal on the 1-inch or 10-mm mark. The mark above the other edge will show the thickness. Measure the width the same way.

Fig. 9-14 The disk gage is used to measure the thickness of sheet metal. Use the right gage for each kind of material.

Table 9-2
Sheet-Metal Gages and Thicknesses

Gage	Ferrous		Nonferrous	
	inch	mm *	inch	mm *
16	0.0598	1.60	0.050	1.20
18	0.0478	1.20	0.040[a]	1.00
20	0.0359	0.90	0.032[b]	0.80
22	0.0299	0.80	0.025[c]	0.65
24	0.0239	0.65	0.020[d]	0.50
26	0.0179	0.45	0.015	0.40
28	0.0149	0.40	0.012	0.30
30	0.0120	0.35	0.010	0.25
32	0.0097	0.22	0.007	0.18

[a]32-ounce   [b]24-ounce   [c]20-ounce   [d]16-ounce
*Metric replacement sizes are based on ANSI B32.3-1974.

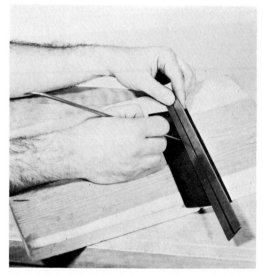

Fig. 9-15 A scriber.

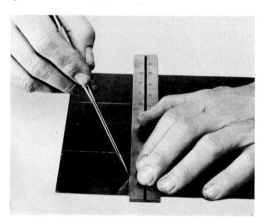

Fig. 9-16 Hold the scriber as you would a pencil. Tilt the point in toward the corner formed between the rule and the metal.

Fig. 9-17 Measuring the length of stock. The rule is held on edge with the inch mark over the end of the stock. A scriber is used to mark the length accurately.

There are no strict rules for measuring and marking out in all instances. However, here are a few suggestions:

1. Make sure the end of the workpiece from which the marking is done is square.

2. Hold the rule on edge in contact with the surface of the workpiece (Figs. 9-17,

9-18). If the end of the rule is worn, hold the 1-inch or 10-mm mark over the edge of the workpiece.

Fig. 9-18 Measuring with a metric rule.

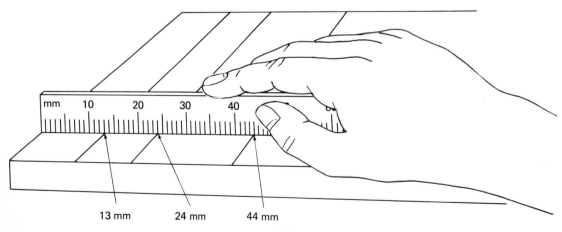

Fig. 9-19 Using a scriber and the square head of a combination set to mark a line across the stock.

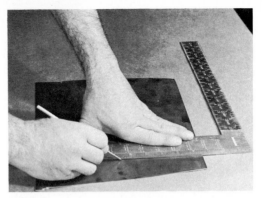

Fig. 9-20 When laying out on a flat sheet, mark several points to indicate length or width of the stock. Then hold the straight edge or square over these points and scribe a line.

3. Make sure the rule is kept parallel along the workpiece so that the exact length can be obtained.

4. Mark the exact length shown on the rule with a scriber.

5. Hold a square firmly against the side of the workpiece. Mark a line across the workpiece (Fig. 9-19). Turn the scriber at a slight angle so that the point will draw along the lower edge of the rule.

Marking stock to be cut from sheet

1. Make sure that an edge and an end are at right angles to each other.

2. Hold a rule over the end of the workpiece, and mark out a point that shows the length of stock to be cut.

3. Move the rule over, and mark out another point for the length.

4. Join these two points with a scribed line.

5. Mark several points to indicate the width.

6. Lay a straightedge along these points, and scribe a line (Fig. 9-20).

 QUESTIONS

1. What are the common divisions of an inch on a steel rule?
2. What is measured with a hook rule?
3. What is the circumference of a 35-inch circle? Find the answer by reading the scale in Fig. 9-5.
4. What is a steel tape used for?
5. What are the common divisions on a metric rule?
6. What are the four parts of a combination set?
7. What does a sheet-metal gage measure?

✓ EXTRA CREDIT

Obtain the following tools, and explain to the class how they are used: rule, caliper, square, universal bevel protractor.

Unit 10
Making a
Simple Layout

A **layout** is a flat pattern made directly on the metal. It shows the shape and size of an object, the location of all holes or openings, and the areas to be machined. A layout is similar to a working drawing (Fig. 10–1). In making a layout, accuracy is very important. If you make an error in a layout, your job can be ruined before you even start it. To make a good layout, you must be able to (1) read and understand drawings and prints, (2) use layout tools, and (3) transfer measurements carefully and exactly from a drawing to the material itself.

Layout tools

1. The **bench,** or **machinist's, vise,** usually has a swivel base. It is the kind most often used in the shop. It has two hardened jaws with faces that are lightly grooved to hold workpieces securely. One jaw, the solid jaw, is fixed, and the other, the adjustable jaw, moves in and out when you turn the handle. Vise-jaw caps, or false jaws, of copper, brass, or aluminum are put over the hardened jaws in clamping finished workpieces (Fig. 10–2).

Fig. 10–1 A drawing of a sheet-metal box is on the left. On the right is the layout.

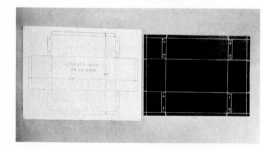

2. A **hammer** is used for striking, driving, and pounding. The most common hammers are the ball peen, straight peen, and cross peen (Fig. 10–3). The *ball peen hammer* is used most often. The flat face of the hammer is used for general work and the rounded end for riveting and hammer-tracking, or decorating, art-metal projects. The *straight peen hammer* and *cross peen hammer* are used for hammering in tight corners and making sharp bends in metal.

The size of a hammer is determined by the weight of the head, which varies from 4 to 48 ounces. A 9-ounce hammer, sometimes called a **mallet,** has a head of lead, brass, rawhide, plastic, rubber, or wood. These hammers are used when a steel hammer might mar the metal surface (Fig. 10–4).

3. There are two kinds of **punches,** the prick punch and the center punch. A *prick punch* is a hardened steel rod with a knurled handle and a point ground to a sharp angle

Fig. 10–2 A common bench vise used by metalworkers. The vise-jaw caps protect the finished surface of a workpiece.

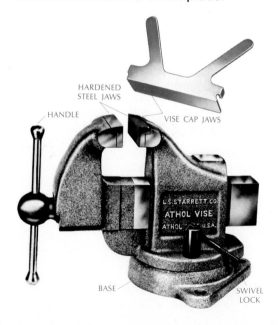

HARDENED
STEEL JAWS

HANDLE

VISE CAP JAWS

L.S.STARRETT CO.
ATHOL VISE
ATHOL U.S.A.

BASE

SWIVEL
LOCK

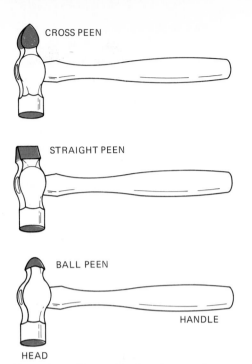

CROSS PEEN

STRAIGHT PEEN

BALL PEEN

HANDLE

HEAD

Fig. 10-3 Three kinds of peen hammers.

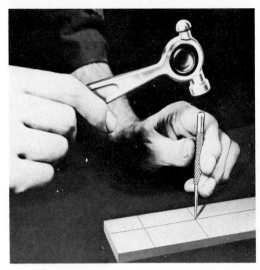

Fig. 10-5 Using the prick punch. (The L. S. Starrett Company)

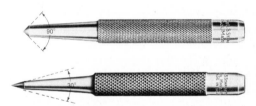

Fig. 10-6 A center punch is ground at an angle of 90 degrees. The prick punch is ground at 30 degrees. (The L. S. Starrett Company)

Fig. 10-4 (A) Soft-faced hammer with plastic head, and (B) wooden mallet.

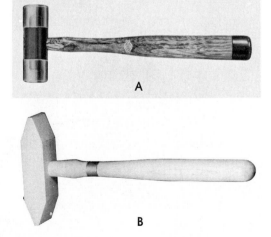

A

B

of about 30 degrees (Fig. 10–5). It is used to make the first marks locating holes and other points needing machining. In transferring patterns from paper layouts to sheet metal, the prick punch is used to make small dents to locate lines and corners. It is important to keep the point sharp.

A *center punch* is similar to a prick punch, except that the point is usually 90 degrees (Fig. 10–6). It is used to enlarge prick-punch marks so that the drill will start easily and correctly.

4. Dividers are used to lay out arcs and mark the size and location of holes to be

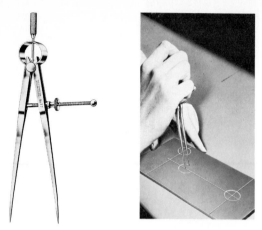

Fig. 10–7 Typical dividers used to draw a circle.

drilled. Divider legs must be sharp and of equal length. To set dividers, place one point on a rule line and adjust the other for the desired radius (Fig. 10–7). To use dividers, place the point of one leg into the prick-punch mark, tip the dividers, and turn them clockwise.

Fig. 10–8 Hermaphrodite caliper and typical use in layout. (Brown & Sharpe Manufacturing Company)

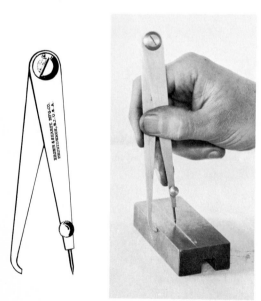

5. A **hermaphrodite caliper** has one outside-caliper leg and one divider leg (Fig. 10–8). It is used to locate the center of an irregularly shaped workpiece or to lay out a line parallel to an edge.

6. An **angle plate** has two finished surfaces at right angles to each other. It is a bracket used to hold workpieces in making a layout (Fig. 10–9).

7. A **toolmaker's,** or **parallel, clamp,** is used to hold parts together in making a layout. It is also used for holding workpieces during machining operations such as drilling (Fig. 10–10).

Fig. 10–9 (A) Angle plate. (B) Angle plate in use.

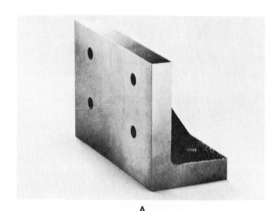

A

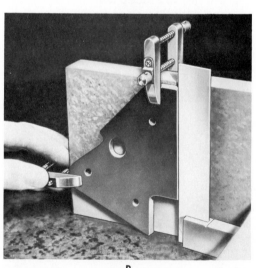

B

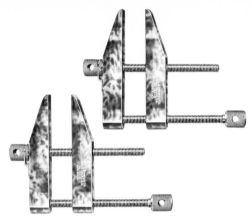

Fig. 10-10 A pair of toolmaker's clamps.

Fig. 10-11 V-blocks.

Fig. 10-12 Applying layout die to the metal before making the layout. (The L. S. Starrett Company)

8. The **V-block** is a rectangular steel block in which deep V-shaped grooves have been cut (Fig. 10–11). It is used to hold round workpieces in making a layout or drilling.

Layout surface preparation

Layout fluids and other materials are used to coat the surface of metal to make the layout show up better. Some common ones are the following:

1. *Chalk,* such as that used on chalkboards, for simple layouts, such as those locating the center for drilling center holes.

2. *Layout dye* or *ink,* a commercial preparation that can be spread on with a brush or with a spray can. It leaves an even, blue-colored surface on which scribed lines show up sharp and clear (Fig. 10–12).

3. *Blue vitriol,* made by mixing 4 to 5 ounces or 115 to 140 grams of copper sulfate in a quart or liter of water and adding 4 or 5 drops of sulfuric acid. When applied to metal, it turns a copper color.

4. *Showcard white* or *poster paint.*

5. A mixture of alcohol, shellac, and aniline dye for aluminum or other nonferrous materials.

Enlarging a pattern

Sometimes, you have to enlarge a pattern to full size before you can do a layout. For example, the typically irregular designs found on art-metal projects often have to be enlarged. This is quite easy to do:

1. Most patterns are already on squared paper. If yours is not, lay out squares on the original drawing. The size of the squares will depend on the scale of the drawing. For example, if the drawing is one-fourth full size, and you are working in the customary system, lay out 1/4-inch squares on the original drawing. Then you

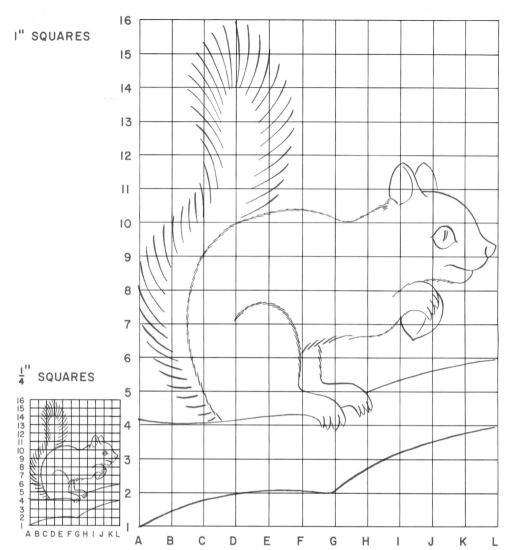

Fig. 10–13 Enlarging a pattern. The small figure on the left is the original. By making 1-inch squares on the larger sheet of paper and transferring several reference points, the full-size pattern can be drawn.

can use inch squares for the full-size pattern, and the drawing will be enlarged correctly. If you are working in the metric system, lay out millimeter squares on the drawing. Then you can use metric squared paper for the full-size pattern, taking 1-millimeter squares for full size, 2-millimeter squares for double size, and so on.

2. For a customary full-size pattern, lay out inch squares on a large piece of wrapping paper. For a metric full-size pattern, mark off the squares you need on metric squared paper, as explained above.

3. Letter across the bottom and number up the left side on both the original drawing and the pattern (Fig. 10–13).

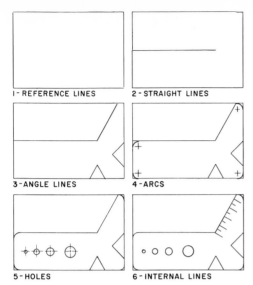

Fig. 10-14 Steps in making a layout for a drill gage.

Fig. 10-15 The layout for this project was done by attaching the design to the metal with tape.

4. Locate a point on the original drawing, and transfer it to the same point on the enlarged pattern. Do this until you have marked enough points to draw the pattern layout full size.

5. Connect these points with a pencil, using a straightedge for the straight lines and a French curve or bent wire for the curved lines. If the design is symmetrical, the same on both sides, you need to enlarge only half the pattern.

Making a layout directly on metal

Since the layout will vary for each different project, only general suggestions can be made for making a layout directly on metal (Fig. 10-14). Before starting, be sure that you have the right size and kind of metal.

1. Cut or file one edge and end at right angles to each other. Use this edge and end as reference lines, and make all measurements from them.

2. Apply some kind of layout fluid.

3. Lay out all straight lines to show the widths and lengths of the various parts.

4. Lay out all angles and irregular lines.

5. Lay out all arcs.

6. Mark all holes to be drilled.

7. Lay out all internal lines.

Transferring a design

There are several ways of transferring an irregular or complicated design:

1. Draw the design on thin paper and glue the paper to the metal surface with household cement or tape (Fig. 10-15).

2. Apply a coat of showcard white, and then transfer the design to the metal with carbon paper. First, place a piece of carbon paper and then the design over the metal, and clip the two in place. Next, outline the design with a pencil or stylus, a sharp instrument used for marking (Fig. 10-16).

3. If you are making many parts that have the same shape, you can cut a **template,** or pattern, of plywood or sheet metal. Hold the template on the metal, and trace the pattern with a scriber (Fig. 10-17).

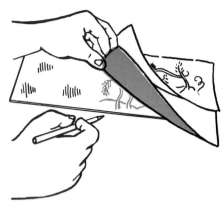

Fig. 10-16 Transferring the design to the metal by placing a piece of carbon paper between the design and the metal.

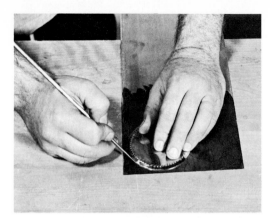

Fig. 10-17 Using a template is the simplest way to transfer a design. This is an especially good method when many parts of the same kind must be laid out.

QUESTIONS

1. What is a layout?
2. Name four kinds of hammers.
3. Name some materials that can be applied to metal to make layout markings show up better.
4. What kinds of designs often have to be enlarged?
5. Is it possible to make a layout directly on metal?
6. What are three ways of transferring a design?

EXTRA CREDIT

Get a surface gage to show to the class, and explain how it is used.

Unit 11
Careers in Metalworking

The metalworking industry contributes to the production of goods in many ways. It produces metal raw materials, tools, machines, and structures for other industries. It delivers a wide variety of goods and services directly to consumers. The metalworking industry is subdivided into three basic types: manufacturing, construction, and service

(Table 11-1). Each group includes many different occupations in which metalworking skills are essential (Fig. 11-1). The purpose of this unit is to help you learn more about these careers and occupations.

The field of metalworking offers many exciting careers and occupations. Engineers and technicians are needed to plan and supervise the work. Skilled workers are needed to perform the difficult operations. Semi-skilled workers are required to operate production machines. Routine jobs are done by unskilled workers. Detailed information on occupations in the metalworking field is

Table 11-1
Metalworking Industries

Manufacturing	Construction	Service

mining
transportation
  equipment
communication
  equipment
consumer
  products
machinery
power
  equipment
	homes
	bridges
	structures
	commercial
	  buildings
	factories
	schools
		appliance
		  repair
		automotive
		  repair
		communication
		  repair
		education

available in *Occupational Outlook Handbook,* published by the U.S. Government Printing Office, Washington, D.C.

General job categories and a number of specific jobs are discussed below. The skilled workers, technicians, engineers, and scientists serve on technical teams in the metalworking industry. Each job has certain educational and training requirements.

Skilled metalworkers

The metalworkers of modern industry are trained to do skilled work and to use precision tools and machines to build, operate, and maintain many different products. These workers include the toolmakers, diemakers, wood and metal patternmakers, millwrights, electricians, welders, plumbers, sheet-metal workers, and many others (Fig. 11–2).

Fig. 11–1 People with many kinds of skills work in the metal industries. (Republic Steel Corporation)

Fig. 11–2 Skilled workers are highly trained to use precision tools and machines. (L. S. Starrett Company)

Fig. 11-3 The all-around machinist must be able to use many different kinds of machines. (Sheldon Corporation)

A brief description of some of the skilled occupations and a list of typical jobs done in each follow. These are not all the skilled trades. Several of the skills of one trade may be common to a number of other trades. Nonetheless, the occupations described below represent the types of skill generally found in the metalworking industry.

All-around machinist. The all-around machinist is a skilled worker who uses machine tools to make metal parts. Machinists can set up and operate most machine tools. A wide knowledge of shop practice and the working properties of metals, plus an understanding of what the various machine tools can do, enable the machinist to turn a block of metal into an intricate part meeting precise specifications (Fig. 11-3).

Variety is the main characteristic of the job of the all-around machinist. This worker plans and carries through all operations needed in turning out machined products, sometimes switching from one kind of product to another. A machinist selects the tools and material needed for each job and plans

the cutting and finishing operations in order to make the product according to blueprint or written specifications. A machinist makes standard shop computations relating to dimensions of work, tooling, feeds, and speeds of machining. A machinist often uses precision measuring instruments, such as micrometers and gages. After completing machining operations, a machinist may finish the work by hand, using files and scrapers, and then assemble the finished parts with wrenches and screwdrivers. The all-around machinist may also heat-treat cutting tools and parts to improve their machinability.

Diemaker. The diemaker is a skilled machinist who specializes in making the molds and dies used for die casting, stamping, and pressing out metal parts. This worker also repairs damaged or worn dies and sometimes makes tools and gages. This trade requires a very high degree of manual skill as well as a good knowledge of shop mathematics, blueprint reading, and the properties of many kinds of metal. Imagination and ingenuity are also important, for the diemaker must be able to visualize the completed die or part before starting to work.

Toolmaker. The work of the toolmaker is closely related to that of the diemaker, since both must be skilled machinists. The toolmaker also constructs precision gages and measuring instruments for checking the accuracy of parts.

Patternmaker. The patternmaker constructs the wood or metal patterns and core boxes that are used to make molds in casting parts from metal or plastic. This worker must have a high degree of manual skill because of the many hand operations involved in pattern building. Accuracy is crucial in patternmaking because any imperfection in the pattern will show up in casting. The patternmaker must also have the artistic ability to visualize the parts the patterns will be used to make. A knowledge of metal shrinkage and foundry practices is essential in both wood and metal patternmaking.

The wood patternmaker, working from blueprints, first lays out each section of the pattern to be made. Next, this worker uses woodworking machines and hand tools to shape the pieces. The patternmaker then fits the pieces together to form the final pattern or core box.

Metal patternmakers use metalworking machines and equipment to make patterns. This skill is similar to that of the toolmaker and diemaker. Unlike the wood patternmaker, the metal patternmaker makes patterns that are normally used many hundreds of times.

Machine maintenance worker. The machine maintenance worker makes certain that the machinery of the plant is kept in good condition. Such workers must be able to repair breakdowns as quickly as possible (Fig. 11-4). A complete knowledge of the structure and operation of every machine used in the shop is needed. It is necessary to know all types of bearings and the lubricating requirements of the machines serviced. Doing routine maintenance work and making replacement parts and doing repairs for presses, lathes, mills, and other machines are also parts of the job.

Sheet-metal worker. The sheet-metal worker must be able to read blueprints to lay out complicated metal shapes and surfaces. The job requires the skillful use of hand and power tools for cutting, forming, and fabricating sheet metal. The job may also involve constructing aircraft parts, hoppers, air-conditioning ducts, paint-spraying booths, furnace piping, or safety shields for the shop machines (Fig. 11-5). In the automobile industry, the sheet-metal worker makes and assembles the parts for the handmade metal bodies of experimental and preproduction automobiles.

Millwright. Millwrights install, dismantle, move, and set up the machinery and industrial equipment used in factories. They often prepare the platforms and concrete foundations on which the machines are mounted. They also frequently help plan the location of new equipment.

Fig. 11-4 A machine maintenance worker must know how to repair and rebuild equipment. (Caterpillar Tractor Company)

Fig. 11-5 Sheet-metal workers in the aircraft industry. (Lockheed Aircraft Company)

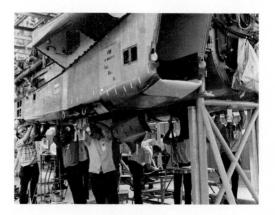

Fig. 11-6 Many welders are employed in the manufacturing industry. (Firestone Company)

The millwright must have a thorough knowledge of the structure of the buildings and the operation of the machines. A good knowledge of blueprint reading is also needed. The millwright must also be skillful in welding and many other trades in order to install and service overhead tracks and cranes, conveyors, bins, chutes, and structural members.

Welder and oxygen cutter. Welders join metal parts together by applying gas flames or electricity to cause melting, then either letting the parts fuse by themselves or pressing them together. Welders must know how to weld different metals. They must also know how to select and operate welding equipment. The ability to read blueprints is important. Welders are employed in making and repairing thousands of metal products (Fig. 11-6). Some welders specialize in setting up welding work for others. Other welders work with engineers on designing new welding equipment.

An oxygen cutter's job is like gas-flame welding, except that instead of joining the metal parts together, the cutter cuts them apart.

Learning to become a skilled metalworker

There are several ways you can learn the skills of a metalworker. A craft or trade can be learned in a vocational or trade school or in an industrial apprenticeship program. Many vocational courses, such as machine shop, welding, foundry, and drafting, can be taken in high schools. These are useful if you enter a trade apprenticeship program. The length of the program varies with the trade. Tool-and-die work, machine operation, and patternmaking frequently take 4 years. Some maintenance trades can be completed in 3 years. In every case, you must satisfactorily complete a certain number of work hours set down in the training schedule for each skill and operation in your chosen trade.

While on the job, you will be under the guidance of the supervisor of the department in which you work. Complete records will be kept on all phases of your training. Your shop supervisors and instructors will review your progress from time to time. They will comment on your learning ability, skill, initiative, and attitude toward the job.

In addition to your work in the shop as an apprentice, you may also be required to attend classes in shop mathematics, blueprint reading, mechanics, and other subjects related to your trade. Here your practical courses and shop training in school will be a great help. The more you have learned in school, the less extra study you will have to do to complete your apprenticeship.

Vocational programs in high schools, trade schools, and community or junior colleges often can prepare you for jobs in small local industries. You can then receive extra training on the job in the special skills needed in your particular craft.

Technicians

There are many different scientific and technical careers available to technicians. In industry, technicians apply the science and mathematics learned in a technical institute or a community or junior college. They use specialized and highly accurate measuring devices. They build special machinery to test new devices. They collect data and compile reports (Fig. 11–7). In short, they work with engineers and scientists, helping them change ideas into reality.

Many technicians work in the metalworking industry. Some of these are drafters, designers, and mechanical, metallurgical, building-construction, and instrumentation technicians.

Drafters and designers. Drafting and design technicians are the graphic communicators on the technical team (Fig. 11–8). They translate scientific and engineering sketches and notes into accurate drawings. Prototypes or other kinds of experimental equipment are then made from these drawings. These technicians have a background in technical drawing, mathematics, and processes. This knowledge enables them to produce graphical and tabular data that the skilled worker uses. Technical sketching, rendering, and writing are parts of this job.

Mechanical technician. Mechanical technology is an important part of industrial activities that involves machines, mechanisms, and industrial processes. The work done by the mechanical technician is a part of, or is related to, research and engineering activities. The job requires a broad understanding of engineering design and production.

The work of the mechanical technician involves two general areas: design and production. The design area includes such jobs as design drafter, tool designer, research as-

Fig. 11–7 Technicians work as members of specialized teams. These oil-industry technicians are checking pump equipment. (Phillips Petroleum Company)

Fig. 11–8 The design technician must learn the art of graphic reproduction. (Eastman Kodak Company)

sistant, or engineering assistant. The production area relates to mechanical manufacturing functions. It includes activities such as quality control, production planning, methods analyzing, and job estimating (Fig. 11–9).

Fig. 11-9 The technician is using a precision measuring device that makes use of a laser beam. (Hewlett-Packard Company)

Metallurgical technician. The metallurgical technician is an important member of a technical team engaged in product or process research and development or in production. The work requires special knowledge of the principles of chemistry, physics, and mathematics as applied in the metallurgical industry. The work also requires a broad knowledge of laboratory procedures, metallurgical processes, and laboratory analyses. This background enables the technician to work closely with scientists and engineers. As a member of the metallurgical research team, the technician obtains test data on processes for developing new products or improving production methods (Fig. 11-10).

Building-construction technician. The construction technician works closely with the civil engineers. The job involves detailed design work, materials testing, surveying, estimating, construction, supervision, report writing, and other engineering work. Many tasks previously done by a civil engineer are now performed by the building-construction technician. However, the technician will not be chiefly responsible for the design or construction of engineering projects but will remain accountable to the professional engineer. Nevertheless, the building-construc-

tion technician may head a surveying crew or supervise the materials-testing laboratory as well as hold other responsible positions.

Instrumentation technician. Scientific instruments extend human senses and control in space exploration, weather prediction, communications, environmental control, industrial research, automated processing and production, and many other areas of applied science.

Instrumentation technicians must be able to work closely with instrumentation engineers and scientists. They must also be able to supervise and coordinate the efforts of skilled workers and instrument maintenance workers. Technicians are members of the scientific team that plans, assembles, installs, calibrates, evaluates, and operates instruments in metalworking processes or systems (Fig. 11-11).

Because instrumentation technicians are employed in so many different and specialized situations, they must have a broad range of scientific knowledge and technical skills.

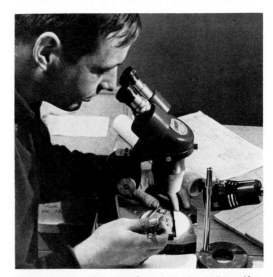

Fig. 11-10 This technician is using the electron microscope to inspect a piece of material. (Gulf Oil Corporation)

70

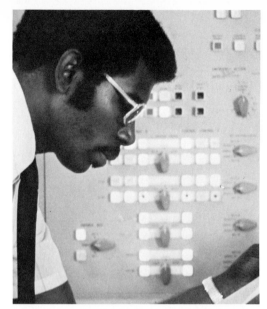

Fig. 11-11 One of the jobs of an instrumentation technician is to punch data into a numerical-control machine tape to be used on an automatic production line. (General Electric Company)

Engineers

Engineers who work in the metalworking industry are trained in mathematics and the physical sciences. They apply their knowledge, experience, and judgment to develop economical ways of controlling and using the materials and forces of nature. They transform raw materials into useful devices and harness energy to help people do work. They are builders or inventors who apply scientific knowledge to solve the practical problems of life, to build better systems, and to create new products. *Engineering could be called the art of making science useful.*

Although there are many types of engineers, only those closely related to the metalworking industry will be described here. These are civil, mechanical, metallurgical, mining, aerospace, and industrial engineers (Fig. 11-12).

Civil engineer. Civil engineers are chiefly interested in the relationships between people and the physical environment. They design and construct structures and systems that add to comfort, convenience, and safety. They are trained in soil mechanics, building materials and structural analysis, hydrodynamics, fluid mechanics, and environmental health. Civil engineers help develop commercial buildings, expressways, pipelines, waterways, sanitary systems, urban renewal projects, and bridges of all types.

Mechanical engineer. Mechanical engineers develop the hardware for the generation, transmission, and application of heat and mechanical energy. Mechanical engineers design power sources, such as reactors, gas turbines, internal-combustion engines, and heat exchangers and transmissions. They also design the machines and tools used in manufacturing operations. Their training in applied mechanics, strength of materials, thermodynamics, and fluid mechanics gives them broad knowledge that can be applied in many industries.

Metallurgical and mining engineers. These engineers employ new techniques to design systems for locating and extracting increas-

Fig. 11-12 There are many opportunities for mining engineers to work for energy-producing companies. (Sun Oil Company)

71

ingly scarce minerals from the ground and for converting them into useful raw materials or consumer products. Mining engineers use their knowledge of geology, chemistry, surveying, materials handling, and mining operations in working with solid minerals such as iron ore, coal, and limestone. Metallurgical engineers help extract impurities to refine the ores and help produce useful metals and alloys.

Aerospace engineer. Aerospace engineering deals with the application of many areas of engineering to all types of flight vehicles from aircraft to missiles. Aerospace engineers study aerodynamics, hydraulics, electronics, structural design, materials strength, and flight mechanics. They develop and test guidance and propulsion systems for airplanes and spacecraft. This field demands a broad base of scientific and engineering knowledge and rapid adjustment to changes and discoveries.

Industrial engineer. Industrial engineers help make manufacturing and assembly processes more efficient by combining people, materials, machines, and methods in new and better ways. Industrial engineers need a broad knowledge of engineering and manufacturing and an understanding of plant operations, cost analysis, personnel relations, and applied statistics. They must be familiar with human as well as technical concerns when designing and managing systems for the production of quality products at a reasonable cost.

Becoming an engineer

If you are interested in engineering, your objective in high school should be to lay a firm foundation for further training in college. To qualify for most engineering schools, you must take several basic subjects. These subjects provide the groundwork for any field of engineering and are the basic tools of the engineer—mathematics, science, and communication. If you do not enter an engineering school directly after high school, you may attend a 2-year technical institute or a community or junior college and then transfer to a university to complete your engineering degree. All engineering programs are at least 4 years long. After graduating from such a program and, perhaps, working for a while, you may wish to study for an advanced degree.

Scientists

The scientist on the technical team is the discoverer, the person who seeks new knowledge. The scientist is an *inquirer*—someone trained in the basic laws of nature who investigates the physical world and its secrets to learn more about why and how things behave as they do. Although the various branches of science demand different skills and training, scientists in every field possess several similar characteristics. Perhaps the most important trait is *curiosity*—a driving need to know. It is a desire for knowledge that compels the scientist to search until a reasonable explanation has been found for something not understood before. This curiosity forces the scientist to question even accepted facts and theories established earlier (Fig. 11–13).

Though there are many specialized fields in science, almost all scientific careers are based on some studies in the basic sciences—chemistry, physics, biology, and mathematics. After gaining a fundamental knowledge of these subjects, most prospective scientists advance to higher levels of study and select a field in which to concentrate.

Careers in science cover a wide range of activities that are difficult to define in specific terms. In various industries, the same type of scientific work may be known by several different names. There are, however, a

72

Fig. 11-13 The scientist on the technical team serves as the discoverer of new knowledge. (Exxon Company)

few basic descriptions that cover the work of most scientists.

Basic research. Scientists engaged in basic research are trying to gain a better understanding of the natural and physical world and are seldom concerned with the immediate use of their discoveries.

Applied research. Scientists in applied research usually seek new knowledge with a well-defined goal and a specific application in mind. Applied scientists often work closely with engineers in developing new products or techniques.

Teaching. Scientists who are teachers help fill the need for future qualified scientists. In addition, college and university instructors often do individual research on projects supported by their school or by business or government. Like most scientists, science educators usually hold at least a master's degree.

Learning to become a scientist

If you are interested in science, courses such as English, mathematics, science, and social studies will help you fulfill the basic requirements for most college programs in science.

Getting started in a career in metalworking

There is no certain way of telling whether you will make a good metalworker or engineer until you actually try. However, aptitude tests may help you find out what skills you already have. As in any occupation, success depends a good deal on your attitude, temperament, and willingness to work and learn.

There are, however, a few qualifications you must have in order to be on the technical team. You must have acquired mechanical ability. You must like working with materials, machines, and ideas. If you have ever built a birdhouse, put an alarm clock back together, or fixed a bicycle, you probably have some idea of these aptitudes. Your school metals class will give you an excellent opportunity to find out whether you will enjoy this type of work as a career.

A knowledge of blueprint reading and drafting is essential in nearly all technical jobs. Your school courses in these subjects will be a big help to you. Take as many science courses as you can, particularly physics. Your shop classes will give you a good foundation in shop practice and theory. They will also give you a chance to use many of the hand and machine tools skilled workers use (Fig. 11-14).

English, speech, history, and civics will round out your education and aid you in expressing your opinions. The information and skills gained from them may be helpful in future promotions to supervisory positions.

But most of all, you will have to answer this question: Do I think I have the ability and the desire for a career in metalworking?

Fig. 11-14 Education is the single most important part of a career in metalworking. Stay in school—get as much education as you possibly can. (The Boeing Company)

 QUESTIONS

1. What are the three main kinds of metalworking industries?
2. Which four types of workers serve on technical teams in the metalworking industry?
3. List the eight types of skilled metalworkers.
4. What six kinds of technicians are employed in the metalworking industry?
5. What six kinds of engineers work in the metals industry?
6. What are three kinds of careers open to scientists?

 EXTRA CREDIT

1. Interview a friend or relative who works in the metalworking industry. Write a short description of the job.
2. Discuss a career in metals with your teacher and counselor.

SECTION 2

BENCH METAL

Unit 12

Introduction to Bench Metal

One of your first experiences in the metal shop will probably be in the area of bench metal. This is because bench-metal work is basic to all other metalwork. Working in bench metal is sometimes called elementary machine shop, benchwork, cold-metal work, metal fitting, or hand tools. Whatever the name, the purpose is to introduce you to common metal tools. You will soon learn how to use and to care for them (Fig. 12–1).

Tools

You will learn to use hand tools for cutting, forming, fastening, and finishing. These tools include hammers, drills, wrenches, hacksaws, vises, and benders. Using them can be more difficult than operating some machines. All metalworkers and mechanics must know how to handle bench-metal tools. Even people in the professions of medicine and dentistry must have a knowledge of precision, or very accurate, tools.

No matter how you plan to earn a living, learning to use these hand tools and machines is a rewarding accomplishment. You can make many interesting projects. You can

also do many small maintenance jobs in the shop and home. These might include repairing a bicycle or automobile or putting a new lock in a door.

Materials

In bench-metal operations, the metal is usually worked cold. It is therefore important to use soft metals. One common material is mild steel in the form of flats, rounds, angles, and heavy sheets. Aluminum and copper are also used, especially for ornamental metalwork.

Processes

The basic bench-metal processes are shown in Table 12–1. You will need to master them in order to make your projects.

Fig. 12–1 Learning to use and care for hand tools correctly is a main purpose of a bench-metal course.

75

Table 12–1
Bench-Metal Processes

Type	Equipment used
Cutting	
sawing	hand and power hacksaws, bandsaw
shearing	cold chisel, bench shears, bolt cutter
drilling	hand and electric drills, drill press, reamers, taps (related dies)
abrading	grinders and polishers
filing	files
Forming	
bending	vises, forks, bending machines
Fastening	
riveting	rivets and sets
threading	threaded fasteners, wrenches, and screwdrivers
Finishing	
polishing and buffing	polishing and buffing wheels and compounds
texturing	hammers

Fig. 12–2 This fireplace set is an example of good design in bench-metal work.

Your bench-metal experience may help you to a career in metalworking. Bench-metal work may also become a satisfying hobby. There are many things that can be made of wrought metal—floor lamps, foot scrapers, house-number plaques, porch furniture, dune buggies, sports equipment (Fig. 12–2).

Both hand and machine processes are used in bench metal.

An interesting part of bench metal is **ornamental metalwork,** sometimes called **wrought-metal work.** It involves some cutting operations plus a few others such as bending curves and scrolls and twisting metal. As you master your bench-metal skills, keep in mind the things you have learned about safety. Know how you are to do something before you do it. Keep your tools in good condition. Avoid unsafe working habits.

 QUESTIONS

1. List some bench-metal operations.
2. What kinds of workers must know how to handle bench-metal tools?
3. Why are soft metals used in bench-metal work?
4. What is wrought-metal work?

 EXTRA CREDIT

Trace the history of one of the common hand tools from its beginning. Prepare a written or oral report for presentation to your class.

Unit 13
Cutting Heavy Metal

There are several ways of cutting heavy metals. Sawing is done with hand saws and power saws. Shearing is done with cold chisels, bench shears, and bolt cutters.

Safety

1. When using a hacksaw, make sure the blade is properly tightened.

2. Always wear safety goggles when striking with tools such as hammers and chisels.

3. Remember that the **burr,** or rough area along a cut edge, is sharp and can cause a serious injury.

4. Never use a dull chisel or one with a "mushroom," or flattened, head.

Cutting with a hand hacksaw

A **hacksaw** has a fine-toothed blade held under tension in a frame. Hacksawing is probably the most common method of metal cutting (Fig. 13–1). The hand hacksaw has a U-shaped frame with handle and replaceable blades. The frame itself may be either solid, to take one length of blade, or adjustable for different lengths (Fig. 13–2). The posts that hold the blade can be adjusted to four different positions. For ordinary cutting, the blade is placed in line with the frame.

Blades

Here are some facts you should learn about hand hacksaw blades:

1. *Size.* Available in lengths of 8, 10, and 12 inches (203, 254, and 305 mm), a width of 1/2 inch (13 mm), and a thickness of 0.025 inch (0.6 mm).

2. *Kind of material.* Carbon steel, tungsten alloy steel, molybdenum steel, molyb-

Fig. 13–1 Hacksawing is a simple and common method of cutting heavy metal.

denum high-speed steel, and tungsten high-speed steel.

3. *Types of blades. All-hard, semiflex,* and *flexible backs.* The flexible back has a hard edge that makes it good for general sawing.

4. *Number of teeth* (per inch or 25 mm):

a. 14 teeth: for cutting soft steel, brass, and cast iron.

b. 18 teeth: for cutting drill rod, mild steel, light angle iron, and tool steel; for general work.

c. 24 teeth: for cutting brass tubing, iron pipe, and metal conduits.

d. 32 teeth: for cutting thin tubing, thin sheet metal, and channels (Fig. 13–3).

5. *Tooth set.* **Set** refers to the way the teeth are bent to one side or the other and the amount of bend. The set makes the **kerf,** or width of the cut made by the saw, wider than the blade itself. Thus, the blade will not bind or stick. In an *alternate,* or *raker, set,* the teeth are bent alternately to right and left, with a straight tooth between. In a *wave set,* several teeth are bent in one direction, and then several are bent the other way. Blades with 14 and 18 teeth are made in the alternate set. Those with 24 and 32 teeth are made in the wave set.

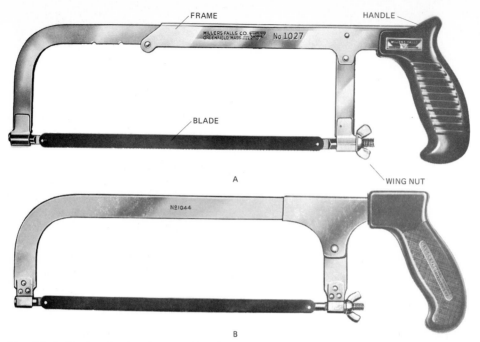

Fig. 13-2 Parts of a hacksaw: (A) adjustable hacksaw frame that can be used with blades of different lengths; (B) solid frame. (Millers Falls Company; Crescent Tool Company)

MINIMUM THICKNESS FOR SAFE CROSSCUT

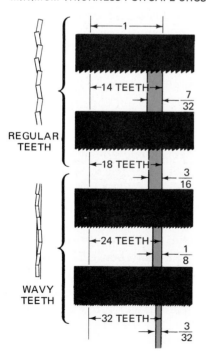

REGULAR TEETH

14 TEETH — $\frac{7}{32}$

18 TEETH — $\frac{3}{16}$

WAVY TEETH

24 TEETH — $\frac{1}{8}$

32 TEETH — $\frac{3}{32}$

Fig. 13-3 To cut thin tubing, use a wave-set blade with 32 teeth per inch (25 mm). Notice the simple method of holding the tubing. A hole is drilled in a piece of wood about the size of the tubing, and then the piece is cut in two. The chart will aid in blade selection.

78

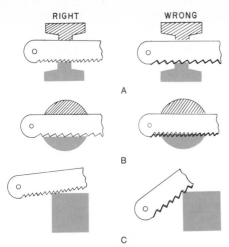

Fig. 13-4 (A) Right: Three blade teeth in contact with the material. Wrong: Blade too coarse. (B) Right: Coarse teeth, ample chip clearance. Wrong: Teeth too fine. (C) Right: Start cut at slight angle. This is easier and safer. Wrong: Angle of cut is too steep.

Fig. 13-6 Clamping the workpiece tightly in the vise with the layout line close to the vise jaws. Notice that the jaws have been covered with soft jaw caps (arrows).

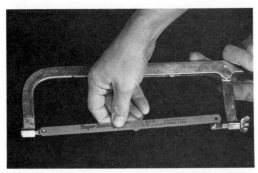

Fig. 13-5 Put the blade in the frame with the teeth pointing away from the handle. Make sure that the blade is taut.

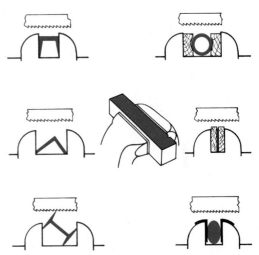

Fig. 13-7 Common methods of holding metal for cutting.

Sawing

1. Select the correct blade, making sure that the blade will have at least *three teeth* in contact with the metal at all times (Fig. 13-4). Place it in the frame with the teeth pointing *away* from the handle (Fig. 13-5).

2. Tighten the wing nut on the handle until the blade is tight. After a few cuts, retighten it with a turn or two.

3. Cover the jaws of the vise with jaw caps (Fig. 13-6). Fasten the workpiece with the layout line as close to the end of the jaws as possible. Figure 13-7 shows the right ways to fasten different metal shapes.

4. If thin sheet stock is to be cut, sandwich it between two pieces of scrap wood (Fig. 13–8).

5. Start the cut by guiding the blade with the thumb of the left hand and taking one or two light strokes with the hacksaw (Fig. 13–9). Then, grasping the end of the frame firmly with the left hand, take full-length strokes (Fig. 13–10). Move both hands in a straight line. If you do not, the blade will twist, making the cut uneven.

6. Apply pressure on the forward stroke. Release the pressure on the return stroke. Do not allow the teeth to drag over the metal. Use a uniform motion, with about 40 to 60 strokes per minute.

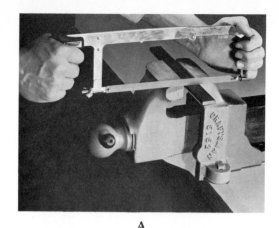

A

Fig. 13–8 Sheet metal can be sandwiched between two pieces of wood for cutting.

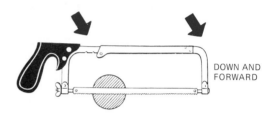

DOWN AND FORWARD

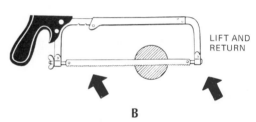

LIFT AND RETURN

B

Fig. 13–10 (A) The correct way to hold the hacksaw. (B) Apply pressure on the forward stroke and release the pressure on the return stroke.

Fig. 13–9 Guide the saw blade with your thumb as you start the cut.

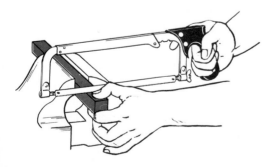

7. When the cut is about completed, hold the end to be removed with your left hand (Fig. 13–11). Make the last few cuts by holding the saw with the right hand only.

8. For making deep cuts, turn the blade at right angles to the frame after you have cut as deep as you can with the blade in the regular position (Fig. 13–12).

9. Check your work. Did you twist the blade? Is the cut crooked? Does it follow the layout line?

Fig. 13-11 Hold the workpiece with your left hand as you make the last few cuts.

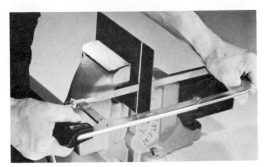

Fig. 13-12 Turn the blade at right angles to the frame for deep cuts.

Chisels

A **chisel** is a wedge-shaped cutting tool used to cut, shear, and chip metal. One end is hardened and sharpened to make a good cutting edge. There are four kinds of chisels used in the machine shop (Fig. 13–13):

1. The *flat cold chisel* is a plain flat chisel used for cutting or chipping metal and for splitting nuts or rivets. The common widths are 1/8 to 3/4 inch (3 to 19 mm).

2. The *diamond-point chisel* has a square end and a cutting edge at one corner. It is used for cleaning out sharp corners or for cutting a sharp bottom groove.

3. The *cape chisel* has a narrow blade for cutting keyways and grooves.

4. The *roundnose chisel* is used for cutting grooves or for moving a drilled hole that was started wrong.

Sharpening a flat cold chisel

1. The cutting edge of a cold chisel is ground at an angle of 60 to 70 degrees, with the edge at a slight arc (Fig. 13–14).

2. Use a medium wheel for grinding.

3. Hold one side of the cutting edge lightly against the face of the wheel, and move it back and forth in a slight arc.

4. Cool the chisel often. Never allow the cutting edge to become overheated or the edge will lose its hardness.

5. Grind first one side and then the other to form a sharp edge.

6. The body of the chisel is softer than the cutting edge. The head will therefore

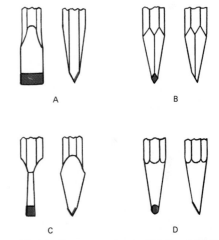

Fig. 13-13 Four common kinds of chisels: (A) flat cold chisel, (B) diamond-point chisel, (C) cape chisel, (D) roundnose chisel.

Fig. 13-14 The correct way to grind the cutting edge of a cold chisel.

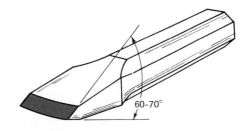

mushroom after it has been used for a while. This mushroom is dangerous. It could cut your hand, or a piece of it could break off and hit your eye. Always grind off the mushroom when it forms.

Cutting with a flat chisel on a plate

1. Lay out the area to be cut with a chisel. Put on safety glasses.
2. Place the workpiece over a soft metal plate. *Never use a surface plate, or an anvil, or the finished surface of a machinist's vise.*
3. Hold the chisel firmly in your left hand with the thumb and fingers around the body.
4. Place the cutting edge on the layout line, and strike the tool with a hammer. Keep your eye on the cutting edge, not on the tool.
5. Go over the layout line lightly (Fig. 13–15). Then start back, and strike the tool with a firmer blow to cut through the metal. If necessary, turn the stock over, and cut from the opposite side.

Shearing in a vise

1. Clamp the work in the vise with the layout line just above the edge of the jaw.
2. Hold the chisel at an angle of about 30 degrees with the side of one cutting edge parallel to the layout line. If the chisel is held too high, it will dig into the vise jaw. If it is held too low, it will tear the metal.
3. Strike the chisel firmly to shear off the metal (Fig. 13–16).
4. The chisel is also used to shear off a rivet or bolt (Fig. 13–17).

Cutting an internal opening

1. Drill a series of small holes close together just inside the waste material.
2. Cut out the opening with a chisel (Fig. 13–18).
3. File to the layout line.

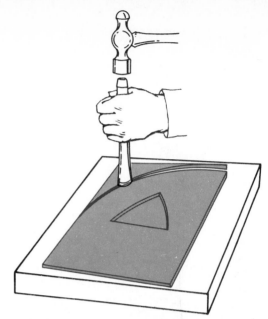

Fig. 13–15 Hold the chisel firmly. Make light indentations along the layout line first. Then strike with heavier blows to cut through the metal.

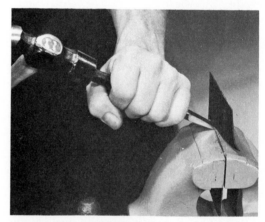

Fig. 13–16 Hold the chisel at an angle of about 30 degrees to the vise when shearing metal in a vise.

Bench shears

There are two kinds of **bench shears.** The *bench lever*, or *slitting, shears* have straight blades. They are used for cutting band or

Fig. 13-17 For some kinds of work, it is a good idea to hold the chisel with a special chisel punch holder. This will give you a firm grip while keeping your hands out of the way of the hammer. (Snap-on Tool Corporation)

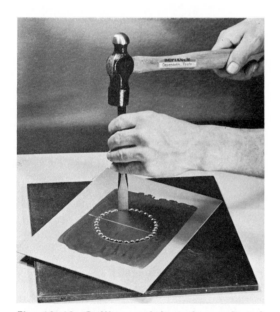

Fig. 13-18 Cutting an internal opening. A series of holes is drilled just inside the waste stock. This makes it easy to cut out the opening with a chisel. Finish the inside edge by filing.

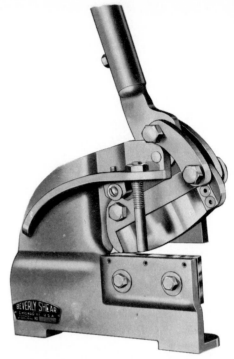

Fig. 13-19 Bench lever, or slitting, shears. (Beverly Shear Company)

with the layout line directly over the shearing edge. Then carefully lower the handle to cut the metal (Fig. 13-19). The *throatless bench shears* have curved blades. They are used to make curved or irregular cuts as well as straight cuts on sheet stock. When cutting an irregular shape, constantly move the stock as you cut, following the layout line (Fig. 13-20).

Bolt cutters

The **bolt cutter** is a special type of shears used to cut or part rods, wire, or bolts. To cut, merely insert the rod into the right hole, and press the handles together. Use this only for mild steel or nonferrous metals (Fig. 13-21A). *End-cutting nippers* are used for similar cutting on lighter metals (Fig. 13-21B).

strap iron and black-iron sheet. *Never cut nails, rivets, or bolts with these shears.* To operate, open the blades, and insert the metal

Fig. 13-20 Using throatless bench shears. Make sure that the metal is inserted as far into the shears as possible. Keep your fingers away from the sharp cutting blade (arrow).

Fig. 13-21 This bolt and rod cutter (A) has a capacity of 3/8-inch (9.5-mm) mild steel. The end-cutting nipper (B) is used for lighter work. (Stanley Tools)

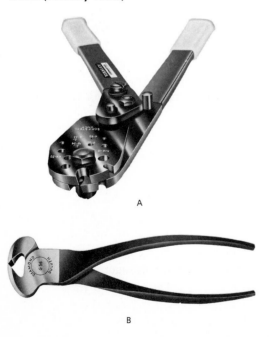

A

B

Power sawing

Metal can be rough-cut to length with either a **power hacksaw** or a continuous-blade **horizontal band saw** (Figs. 13–22, 13–23). The power hacksaw operates much like a hand hacksaw. A blade of the correct length, 12 or 14 inches (305 or 356 mm), for the saw, with 6 to 10 teeth per inch (per 25 mm), should be used. Blades for the horizontal band saw are made to fit a particular size of machine. They have 6 to 24 teeth per inch (per 25 mm). They vary in width from 1/16 to 1 inch (1.5 to 25 mm). To operate either saw, do the following:

1. Make sure the vise is at right angles to the blade.

2. Open the jaws until the long bar or rod slips through under slight pressure.

3. Lower the frame until the blade just clears the top of the metal. Now move the metal back and forth until the cutoff line is under the saw blade.

4. Tighten the vise.

5. Turn on the power, and lower the blade slowly to the cutting position. The actual cutting is automatic. The saw will turn off when the cut is complete. Most models have a stop rod that can be set when cutting several pieces to the same length. Use an oil coolant if needed.

Vertical band saws

Large, specially equipped **vertical band saws,** sometimes called *contour saws* (Fig. 13–24), are used to cut stock to size and to cut out shapes, particularly for tool-and-die work. These machines have a blade welder, table, fence, and crosscut gage. Many also have a coolant system. The work done on these machines is called **band machining.** In job shops, the vertical band saw is just as important as the lathe, milling machine, or grinder.

Fig. 13-22 A power hacksaw. (The L. S. Starrett Company)

Fig. 13-23 A horizontal band saw. (Kalamazoo Saw Company)

Fig. 13-24 A vertical band saw. (DoAll Company)

Fig. 13-25 Using a saber saw to cut aluminum. (Disston Tool Company)

Portable power saws

There are several kinds of portable power saws. One is the **saber saw,** or **portable jigsaw.** It can saw through thin metal, such as aluminum or steel 3/32 inch (2.5 mm) or more thick, with a very clean, even cut (Fig. 13-25). Thinner sheet metal should be sandwiched between scraps of plywood or other thin wood to prevent the sawed edges from bending or crinkling. Make sure that the saw blade is for cutting metal. Such blades are normally of high-speed steel.

The **reciprocating saw** can be used to saw metal pipe and other shapes, provided that a blade for metal sawing is used (Fig. 13-26).

The **portable band saw** works like a horizontal band saw. It can be used near the stock rack to cut materials to length (Fig. 13-27).

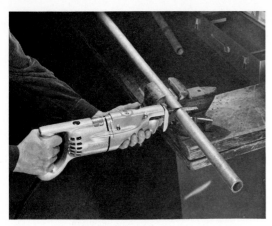

Fig. 13-26 Cutting pipe with a reciprocating saw. (Black & Decker Company)

Fig. 13-27 A portable band saw. (Milwaukee Electric Company)

In general, for best cutting results:

1. Keep the blade off the work until the motor has been started.

2. Start cutting on a surface where the greatest number of teeth will be in contact with the work at one time.

3. Place the steady rest against the work, and lower the saw blade into the cut.

4. Do not bear down while cutting. The weight of the tool will supply enough pressure.

5. When completing a cut, hold the tool firmly so that it will not fall against the work.

 QUESTIONS

1. Name the tools used for cutting heavy stock.
2. When a blade is put into a hacksaw frame, which way should the teeth point?
3. What should you do when a mushroom forms on the head of a chisel?
4. What do you cut with bench lever shears? With throatless bench shears?
5. What tool is used to cut rods?
6. When cutting with a portable power saw, should you bear down with the blade?

✓ EXTRA CREDIT

Write a report on other methods of cutting metal.

Unit 14
Drilling and Reaming

Drilling is cutting round holes in a material (Fig. 14-1). Drilling machines, including the drill press, are used for this purpose. They are used also for countersinking, reaming, boring, and tapping.

Drill-press safety

1. Wear safety glasses.

2. Make sure the drill is tight and straight in the **chuck,** or special clamp.

3. Remove the chuck key before starting the drill.

4. Never force the drill.

5. Do not try to hold work pieces by hand when drilling. Make sure your work is firmly clamped to the table or is held tightly in a drill-press vise.

Fig. 14-1 Drilling is cutting round holes in a material. (Clausing Corporation)

6. Never leave the drill press when it is moving.

7. Never try to stop the drill with your hand.

Drilling machines

Drill presses include bench models and floor models (Fig. 14–2). The major parts are the *base, column, table,* and *head.* The head contains all the operating parts. There is usually a four-step pulley on the spindle drive and the motor for setting different speeds. Some machines have a convenient speed-dialing mechanism instead of the step pulley (Fig. 14–3). The *spindle* moves the cut-

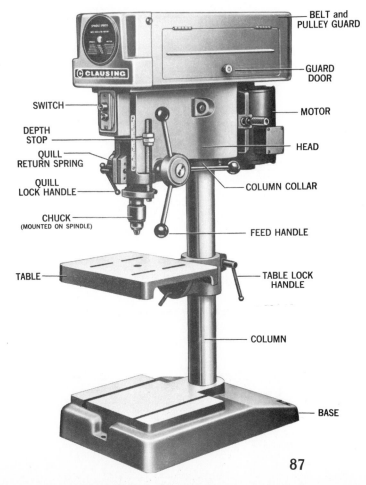

SWITCH

DEPTH STOP

QUILL RETURN SPRING

QUILL LOCK HANDLE

CHUCK
(MOUNTED ON SPINDLE)

TABLE

COLUMN

BELT and PULLEY GUARD

GUARD DOOR

MOTOR

HEAD

COLUMN COLLAR

FEED HANDLE

TABLE LOCK HANDLE

BASE

Fig. 14-2 Parts of a bench-model drill press. (Clausing Corporation)

Fig. 14-3 This floor-model drill press has a variable speed control on the head. (Clausing Corporation)

ting tool up and down. The size of a bench or floor drill press is equal to twice the distance between the drill and the column. Thus, if the distance between drill and column is 7 inches (178 mm), the machine is called a 14-inch (356 mm) drill press.

A *portable electric drill* can be used for many jobs (Fig. 14–4). The size is indicated by the largest drill it will handle. Common sizes are 1/4, 3/8, 1/2, 3/4, and 1 inch (6.35, 9.53, 12.7, 19.05, and 25.4 mm).

The *hand drill* and the *breast drill* are hand tools that can be used for drilling smaller holes (see Fig. 14–29).

Twist drill

Twist drills with two flutes, or grooves, running around the body are most often used for drilling. They are made with either *straight* or *taper shanks* (Fig. 14–5). The straight shank is most common, especially on drills 1/2 inch (12.7 mm) or smaller.

Drills are made of either high-speed steel or carbon steel. High-speed-steel drills are stamped HS or HSS on or near the shank. Though a little more expensive than car-

bon-steel drills, high-speed-steel drills are much better. They wear much longer and do not break so easily. The main parts of a twist drill are shown in Fig. 14–6.

Drills larger than 1/2 inch (12.7 mm) are available in fractional or metric sizes only. Three sets of customary drills 1/2 inch or smaller are in common use:

1. Wire-gage sizes from 80, the smallest, to 1, the largest.

2. Letter sizes from A, the smallest, to Z, the largest. Lettered drill sizes begin where numbered drill sizes end.

3. Fractional-size drills from 1/64 to 1/2 inch, increasing by 1/64 inch (Fig. 14–7).

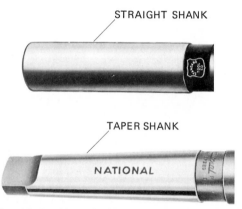

Fig. 14–5 **Straight-shank and taper-shank twist drills.**

Fig. 14–6 **Parts of a taper-shank drill.**

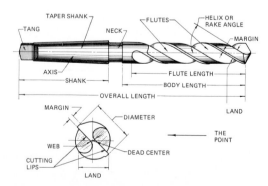

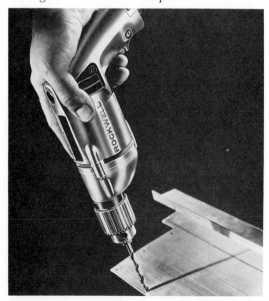

Fig. 14–4 **A portable electric drill. (Rockwell International)**

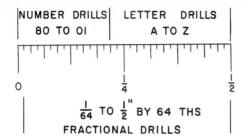

| NUMBER DRILLS | LETTER DRILLS |
| 80 TO 01 | A TO Z |

$\frac{1}{64}$ TO $\frac{1}{2}$" BY 64 THS
FRACTIONAL DRILLS

Fig. 14-7 There are three sets of customary drills with diameters smaller than 1/2 inch.

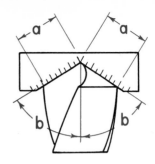

Fig. 14-9 The lips of the drill are ground to the same length (a) and at the same angle (b).

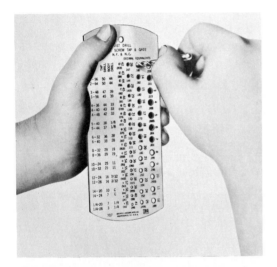

Fig. 14-8 Use a drill gage to find the size of a customary drill. Insert the drill into the holes until you find one it just fits. There is a separate gage for each set of drills—number, letter, and fractional. Use a micrometer to check the size of metric drills. (The L. S. Starrett Company)

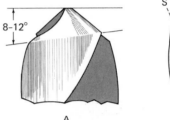

Fig. 14-10 (A) The relief, or clearance, angle of the cutting edge is between 8 and 12 degrees. (B) S indicates the cutting edges. The distance between line a and line b is the actual clearance.

Metric drills are used in all equivalent sizes. A conversion chart for drills can be found in the appendix to this book.

Note that all three sets are made so that each drill differs by only a few thousandths of an inch from the next size. No two drills are exactly the same size, except the 1/4-inch and the E drill, which are both 0.2500 inch (6.35 mm). The size of the drill is stamped on the shank. If the mark is worn off, you can check the size with a *drill gage.* There is a drill gage made for each different set of drills (Fig. 14–8). The drill size can also be checked with a *micrometer* (see Unit 61).

To cut properly, the drill point must meet these requirements:

1. The included angle must be correct. For most work, this angle is 118 degrees, or 59 degrees on either side of the axis (Fig. 14-9).

2. The lips of the drill must be the same length.

3. There must always be proper relief, or clearance, behind the cutting edge. This lip relief must be 8 to 12 degrees for ordinary drilling (Fig. 14-10).

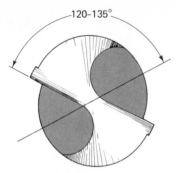

Fig. 14-11 The line across the dead center, or chisel edge, of the drill should be at an angle of 120 to 135 degrees to the cutting edge.

4. The chisel edge must be ground at the proper angle (Fig. 14–11). See Unit 20 for information on sharpening twist drills.

Holding devices

1. A *drill-press vise* is best for holding rectangular or heavy flat pieces for drilling (Fig. 14–12).

2. A *V-block* holds round pieces (Fig. 14–13). On some V-blocks, a *U-shaped clamp* holds the workpiece in place.

3. *C-clamps* can be used to fasten the work to the table. Put a piece of scrap wood underneath the work, or center it directly over the table hole.

4. Special *hold-down clamps* can be used to hold irregularly shaped workpieces (Fig. 14–14).

5. A *monkey wrench* or a *pair of pliers* can sometimes be used as a holding device (Figs. 14–15, 14–16). This must be done with extreme care.

Fig. 14–12 Most workpieces can be held safely in a drill-press vise for drilling.

Fig. 14–13 Drill round stock with the workpiece held in a V-block.

Fig. 14-14 Holding a workpiece to the table using a special cam clamp. Many other clamping devices are available.

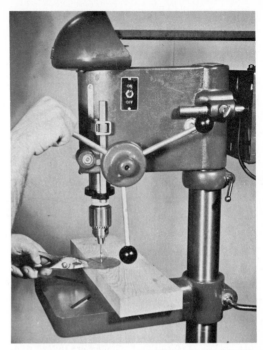

Fig. 14-16 You can sometimes use a pair of pliers to hold thin, small sheet stock while drilling. Never hold workpieces with your fingers.

Fig. 14-15 A monkey wrench can sometimes be used to hold workpieces of irregular shape while drilling.

Speeds, feeds, and lubricants

Drill speed is the distance the drill would travel in 1 minute if it were rolled on its side. Generally, the larger the drill, the slower the speed. The softer the material, the higher the speed. Using a coolant or cutting fluid allows higher drill speeds.

The drill press with belt and pulley has only four to eight speeds. Set the belt on the pulley below highest speed for a 1/4-inch (6.35 mm) drill (Fig. 14-17). Increase the speed for smaller sizes, and decrease it for larger ones (Table 14-1). To adjust the speed on a variable-control machine, dial the desired speed while the machine is running. The dial mechanism generally has a range of 450 to 5000 revolutions per minute (rpm) (Fig. 14-18).

Feed is the distance the drill moves into the stock with each complete turn. Apply just enough pressure to make the drill cut the metal. Too much pressure will cause the drill to burn or break. Too little will produce a scraping or dulling action. You can easily learn how much pressure to use by looking at the chips.

Table 14-1
Drill Speeds in Revolutions per Minute *

Diameter		Aluminum, brass, bronze	Cast iron, hard steel	Mild steel
in.	mm			
1/8	3.18	9170	2139	3057
1/4	6.35	4585	1070	1528
3/8	9.53	3056	713	1019
1/2	12.7	2287	535	764
1	25.4	1143	267	282

* Rpm should be reduced one-half for carbon-steel drills.

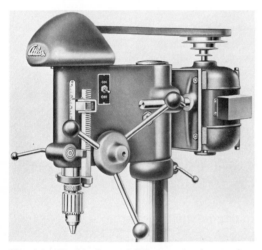

Fig. 14-17 Various drilling speeds can be obtained by changing the position of the belt on the pulley.

Fig. 14-18 A drill press with variable-speed pulleys. (Clausing Corporation)

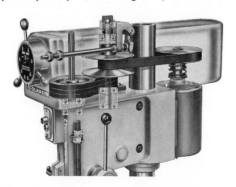

Table 14-2
Cutting Fluids

Material	Drilling	Reaming
aluminum	kerosene kerosene and lard oil soluble oil	kerosene soluble oil mineral oil
brass *	soluble oil kerosene and lard oil	soluble oil
cast iron *	air jet soluble oil	soluble oil mineral lard oil
copper *	soluble oil mineral lard oil kerosene	soluble oil lard oil
malleable iron *	soda water	soda water
mild steel	soluble oil mineral lard oil sulfurized oil lard oil	soluble oil mineral lard oil
tool steel	soluble oil mineral lard oil sulfurized oil	soluble oil lard oil sulfurized oil

* Also drilled and reamed dry, without the use of cutting fluids.

Cutting fluid is used in drilling as a lubricant to reduce friction and to keep the drill cool (Table 14-2).

Drilling on the drill press

1. To locate a hole for drilling, scribe two lines at right angles to show the center of the hole. Mark this center with a prick punch.

2. Enlarge the mark with a center punch, so the drill will start easily.

3. Select the correct size of drill. Your drawing or sketch shows this. Insert the drill in the chuck, and tighten it with a key (Fig. 14-19). Always remove the key immediately.

4. If a taper-shank drill is used, insert it directly in the spindle or first into a drill sleeve and then into the spindle (Figs. 14-20, 14-21). The drill is removed with a *drill drift* (Fig. 14-22).

5. Turn on the power, and check to see that the drill is running straight. If it wobbles, it may be bent, or it may be in the chuck the wrong way. The shank may also be worn. Turn off the power.

A   B

Fig. 14-20 (A) A drill sleeve is sometimes needed if the taper hole in the spindle is larger than the taper shank on the drill. (B) A drill socket is used when the taper shank on the drill is larger than the taper hole in the spindle. (The Cleveland Twist Drill Company)

Fig. 14-21 Some drill presses are equipped with a taper-hole spindle that takes a taper-shank drill. Insert carefully. Make sure the sleeve is seated properly.

Fig. 14-19 Inserting a drill into a drill chuck. This chuck takes a drill up to 1/2 inch (12.7 mm) in diameter. Be sure to remove the chuck key when the drill is tight.

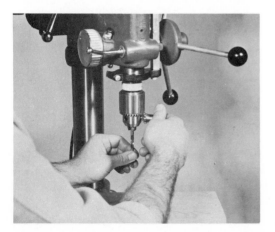

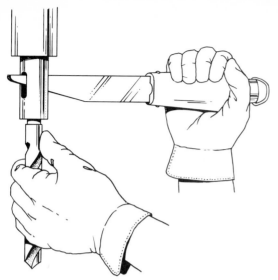

Fig. 14–22 Removing a taper-shank drill with a drill drift. A board should be placed on the table to keep the point of the drill from striking the metal of the table if the drill drops.

Fig. 14–23 Shavings from steel can easily cut your hand. Remove these with a brush or stick of wood, never with your fingers.

6. Adjust for the correct speed.

7. Fasten the workpiece securely in a vise or to the table.

8. Move the drill down with the hand feed to see if the point is exactly over the punch mark. If necessary, move the workpiece or the table slightly. Also check to see that the drill can go all the way through the work. Raise the table if necessary. Make sure that there is a piece of scrap wood or a clearance space between the workpiece and the table.

9. Turn on the power, and bring the point of the drill down to the workpiece. Feed the drill in to enlarge the punch mark. Now release the drill slightly, and apply a little cutting fluid, if needed.

10. Begin the drilling. Apply even pressure, and let the drill do the cutting. When it is cutting correctly on steel, thin ribbons of metal rise from the flutes in the hole. Brush away the shavings as they pile up. Use a stick or brush for this (Fig. 14–23). Watch carefully as the drill begins to go through the other side of the workpiece. Release the pressure slightly. Do not bear down on the feed handle. This is when the drill tends to catch, breaking the workpiece or twisting it.

11. After the drilling is finished, release the pressure on the feed handle, and turn off the power.

Drilling larger holes

To drill a hole larger than 3/8 inch (10 mm), it is a good idea to drill a **pilot,** or **lead, hole** first. The chisel edge, or dead center, of a twist drill does no cutting. If a smaller center hole is drilled first, the larger drill will go through with less friction. The pilot hole should be equal to, or slightly larger than, the web of the larger drill (Fig. 14–24). *Hole saws* can be used to cut large holes in cast iron, mild steel, and nonferrous metals (Fig. 14–25). They range in size from 5/8 to 6 inches (16 to 152 mm) in diameter. The increments, or fractional steps, are 1/8 inch (3 mm). To use the saw, fasten the workpiece firmly, and locate the

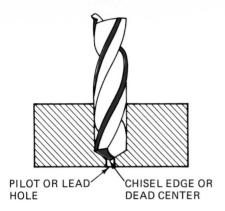

PILOT OR LEAD
HOLE

CHISEL EDGE OR
DEAD CENTER

Fig. 14-24 Drill a pilot hole before drilling a large hole in metal.

Fig. 14-25 A hole saw is used for cutting holes in metal sheet stock.

hole to be drilled. Use a slow speed, as indicated on the chart for the hole-saw kit. Feed slowly until the saw teeth engage the workpiece. Increase the feed, and proceed with the cutting. The workpiece may chatter if you drill too fast or if it is loose. Add cutting oil as needed, and lessen the feed as the cut is finished.

Drilling blind holes

A **blind hole** is one that is cut only part way through the workpiece. Move the workpiece aside, then lower the drill until the right depth is reached. Then set the depth gage to stop the drill. Place the workpiece under the drill, and drill as above.

If the hole is to be deep, release the drill several times, and apply a cutting fluid. This helps clean out the hole and keeps the drill cool.

Drilling round stock and irregular shapes

1. To drill a hole in a rod, pipe, shaft, or other round piece, hold the workpiece in a V-block. Make sure that the bottom of the V is centered under the point of the drill (see Fig. 14-13).

2. A drill jig can be used to drill a large number of holes in parts that are alike.

3. To drill a hole in a scroll, first clamp a small wooden rod to the table. Swing the table out of the way, with the extended rod under the drill. Support the scroll on the rod while drilling (Fig. 14-26).

4. A workpiece can also be held for drilling with a monkey wrench or pliers (see Figs. 14-15, 14-16).

5. Use special clamps or a drill jig for special drilling jobs (Fig. 14-27).

Using a portable electric drill

1. Clamp the work in a vise or to the bench so that the drilling can be done either vertically or horizontally.

2. With the power off, place the point of the drill in the center-punch hole. Rotate the drill chuck by hand, applying a little pressure (Fig. 14-28).

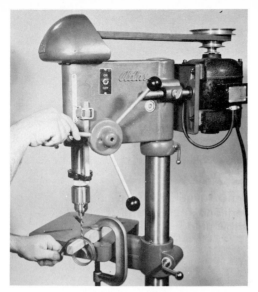

Fig. 14-26 The correct way of drilling a scroll. The table is swung out of the way, and a round wooden stick is clamped to the table with a C-clamp to support the workpiece.

Fig. 14-27 End-drilling with a special vise.

3. Turn on the power, and apply forward pressure with your right hand. Hold the drill back, and steady it with your left hand. Remember: It is easy to break a drill. The slightest jerk will catch it and break it off. Use cutting oil as needed.

Using a hand drill

1. To insert a drill, hold the shell of the chuck in your left hand. Pull back on the handle with your right hand in a counter-clockwise direction until the jaws are open wide enough to allow the shank to enter. Then turn the handle forward to tighten the drill.

2. If the workpiece is thin and tends to bend, place a piece of scrap wood behind it. If possible, clamp the workpiece in a vise so that the drilling can be done horizontally.

3. Place the point of the drill in the center-punch mark. Check to see that the hand drill is square with the metal surface.

4. Drill the hole as described above (Fig. 14-29).

Fig. 14-28 Here is the correct way to start a hole with a portable electric drill. Rotate the chuck a little before you turn on the power.

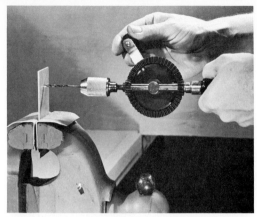

Fig. 14-29 Clamp the workpiece in a vise and drill with a hand drill at right angles to the work surface. If the metal is thin, put a piece of wood behind it to give it extra support.

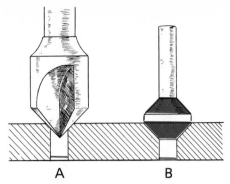

Fig. 14-30 (A) A countersink. (B) The countersink hole should match the size of the flathead fastener.

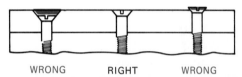

WRONG   RIGHT   WRONG

Fig. 14-31 The correct and incorrect ways of countersinking a hole. The hole is correct when the opening at the top is the same as the largest diameter of the head.

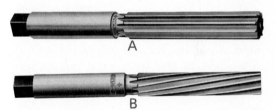

Fig. 14-32 Hand reamers with (A) straight flutes and (B) spiral flutes. (The Cleveland Twist Drill Company)

Countersinking

Countersinking is machining a cone-shaped recess at the outer end of a hole. This recess is needed when using countersunk rivets and flathead bolts or screws. An 82-degree countersink is used (Fig. 14–30).

1. Insert the countersink in the drill chuck.

2. Adjust for a slower speed—about half that for drilling.

3. Feed the countersink slowly until about the right amount of material is removed. Check the size of the hole by turning the rivet, screw, or bolt upside down over the hole (Fig. 14–31).

4. When countersinking several holes, set the stop on the depth gage.

Reaming

Reaming is smoothing the surface of a hole and finishing it to a standard size. This process is also called *sizing the hole*. When a very accurate, smooth hole is needed, the hole is first drilled a little undersize and then reamed to exact size. Hand reamers are identified by the square on the end. Machine reamers have either a straight or a taper shank (see Unit 64).

There are two common kinds of reamers:

1. *Hand reamers* are solid, straight reamers with either straight or spiral flutes (Fig. 14–32). They are made of carbon or high-speed steel. A tap wrench is used on the square of the shank to rotate the tool. Hand

Fig. 14-33 An adjustable hand reamer. A similar machine reamer is available. (The Cleveland Twist Drill Company)

reamers are available in sizes from 1/8 to 1 1/2 inches (3 to 38 mm). The cutting end is ground with a starting taper to make sure the reamer starts easily in the hole.

2. *Adjustable hand reamers* have blades inserted in tapered slots along their threaded bodies (Fig. 14-33). They are used to ream odd-sized holes, as in repair work. The size of these reamers can be adjusted from 1/32 to 5/16 inch (1 to 8 mm). About 20 reamers are needed for all hole sizes from 1/4 to 3 inches (6 to 76 mm).

Reaming is done as follows:

1. Drill the hole 1/64 inch (0.5 mm) undersize.

2. Clamp the workpiece in a vise, with the hole vertical. (If the workpiece is small, the reamer is sometimes clamped in the vise and the workpiece rotated.)

3. Fasten a double-end tap wrench to the square end of the reamer.

4. Hold the reamer at right angles to the surface of the workpiece, and apply

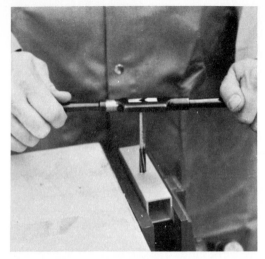

Fig. 14-34 Hand reaming.

slight pressure to it. Turn the reamer slowly and evenly, making sure it aligns itself with the hole.

5. Feed the reamer into the hole steadily. In one turn, it may go into the hole as much as one-fourth the length of its diameter (Fig. 14-34).

6. Use a cutting fluid if needed.

7. Continue turning the reamer clockwise until the hole is reamed. Continue rotating the reamer forward as you remove it from the hole. *Never turn a reamer backward.*

 QUESTIONS ▬▬▬▬▬

1. Name the major parts of a drilling machine.
2. What kind of shank is most common on drills 1/2 inch (12.7 mm) or smaller?
3. Why is a high-speed-steel drill better than a carbon-steel drill?
4. Where on a drill is the size marked?
5. What is used to hold rectangular or flat pieces for drilling?
6. What is drill speed?
7. Define *feed.*
8. How do you know when a drill press drill is cutting correctly on steel?
9. What is a pilot hole? A blind hole?
10. How are round pieces held for drilling?
11. How might you break off the drill on a portable electric drill?
12. What is a countersink?
13. Name the two common kinds of reamers.
14. How much undersize should you drill a hole that will be reamed?

 EXTRA CREDIT ▬▬▬▬▬

1. Find out how square holes can be cut or drilled in metal.
2. Select a twist drill that needs sharpening. Sharpen it, and have it checked by your instructor.

Unit 15
Filing

Filing is one of the most useful of bench-metal operations. It is used to take the burrs off a piece of hacksawed metal, for smoothing a ground workpiece, or for cutting intricate shapes. Filing is a form of metal milling. If you were to take a milling cutter and stretch it out, you would have a file (Fig. 15–1).

Files

A **file** is a hardened steel tool that forms, shapes, and finishes metal by removing small chips. A good metalworker has a variety of files and uses each for its own particular purpose.

The parts of a file are shown in Fig. 15–2.

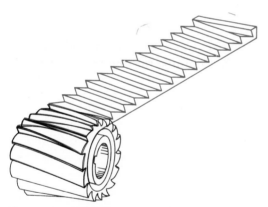

Fig. 15–1   Filing is a form of metal milling. This illustration shows how the file and the milling cutter are similar.

Note that the length is measured from the *point,* or *tip,* to the *heel,* or *shoulder.* The length does not include the *tang.*

Files differ in the following ways:

1. *Length.* File lengths vary from 4 to 18 inches (102 to 457 mm). In general, files increase by 1 inch (25 mm) from 4 to 8 inches (102 to 203 mm) and by 2 inches (51 mm) from 8 to 18 inches (203 to 457 mm). The most common lengths are 6, 8, 10, and 12 inches (152, 203, 254, and 305 mm).

2. *Shape.* Files are made in four common geometric shapes: square, triangular, round, and rectangular (Fig. 15–3).

3. *Cut.* A *single-cut file* has one row of teeth cut at an angle (from 65 to 85 degrees) across the face. A *double-cut file* has two rows of teeth cut to form individual diamond-shaped cutting points. The first row is called the *overcut.* The second row is finer and deeper and is called the *upcut.* The angle of the two cuts is not the same. The double-cut removes metal faster than the single-cut, but leaves a rougher surface.

The *rasp-cut file* has individually shaped teeth and is used only on softer metals. Some special files have *curved* teeth (Fig. 15–4). An *all-purpose file* has teeth that are divided into small cutting sections.

Fig. 15–3 Common shapes of files.

Fig. 15–2   Parts of a file: (a) point, (b) face, (c) edge, (d) heel, (e) tang, (f) length.

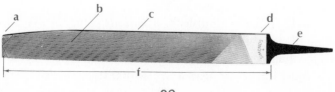

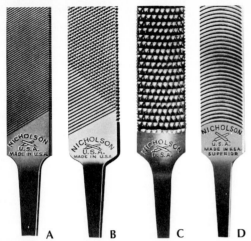

Fig. 15-4 Cuts of files: (A) single cut, (B) double cut, (C) rasp cut, (D) curved-tooth cut.

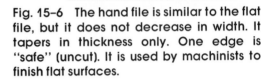

Fig. 15-5 The flat file is rectangular and slightly tapered toward the point in both width and thickness. It is cut on both edges and sides. It is a good general-purpose file for fast removal of metal.

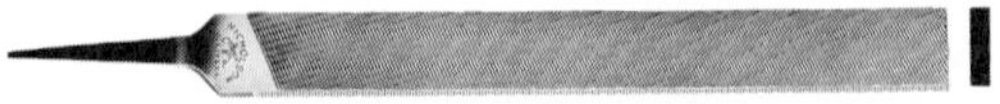

Fig. 15-6 The hand file is similar to the flat file, but it does not decrease in width. It tapers in thickness only. One edge is "safe" (uncut). It is used by machinists to finish flat surfaces.

Fig. 15-7 The half-round file has one rounded side (back) and one flat side. The flat side is always double-cut. The rounded side is double-cut, except in all-smooth and 4- and 6-inch (102- and 153-mm) second-cut files. The latter are single-cut. The half-round file is very useful for filing either flat or concave surfaces.

Fig. 15-8 The round file is made in a tapered shape and is generally used to file round and curved surfaces.

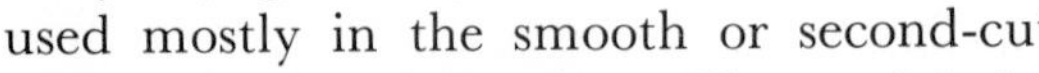

Fig. 15-9 The square file is used mostly for filing slots and for general surface filing.

4. *Coarseness.* The common grades of coarseness are as follows:

a. Bastard—quite coarsely spaced teeth. Bastard files are used for the heavy removal of stock.

b. Second cut—medium spacing of teeth for average cutting.

c. Smooth—closely spaced teeth for fine finishing.

With files of the same grade of coarseness, the teeth on a shorter file are closer together than the teeth on a longer file.

Classification of files

Files are divided into the following three groups:

1. *Machinist's files.* These are the files most commonly used in the metal shop. They remove metal fast and are used when a very smooth finish is not needed. These files come in nine standard shapes, as shown in Figs. 15-5 through 15-13. All are double-cut, except the very small round files and the back of the smooth-cut half-round files. In addition to these, the machinist often uses a

mill file (Fig. 15-14). This is a single-cut file used mostly in the smooth or second-cut grades. It is used for draw-filing and lathe filing. It produces a very fine finish.

Fig. 15–10   The pillar file has a rectangular cross section. It is somewhat like the hand file but is thicker and not as wide. It also has one "safe" (uncut) edge. It is used for filing slots or openings of which one side is not to be filed.

Fig. 15–11   The three-square file is double-cut with the edges left sharp and cut. It is used for internal filing and for cleaning up square corners.

Fig. 15–12   The warding file is rectangular, but it tapers to a point in width. It is used for filing notches in keys and locks.

Fig. 15–13   The knife file has a knife-blade shape and is used for filing sharp angles.

Fig. 15–14   The mill file has single-cut teeth. It is tapered with square edges. It is rectangular and has the same thickness throughout. This file is widely used for lathe work, draw-filing, and filing brass and bronze. It can also be used for finish hand filing. The 6-, 10-, and 12-inch (152-, 254-, and 305-mm) sizes are most common.

2. *Swiss-pattern* and *jeweler's files.* These are used mostly for fine precision filing. They are sold in sets (Fig. 15–15).

3. *Special-purpose files.* There are hundreds of files designed for special purposes. One commonly found in the metal shop is

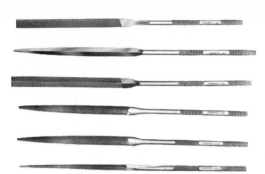

Fig. 15–15   Jeweler's files come in sets of different shapes for doing precision filing.

Fig. 15–16   The long-angle lathe file is especially good for filing on the lathe.

Fig. 15–17   This curved-tooth file works well on aluminum and on other soft metals such as brass. Because its teeth are curved, it readily clears itself of chips.

the *long-angle lathe file.* It has teeth cut at a much longer or shallower angle than those of a mill file. This file gives a good shearing action, cuts faster, and produces a very fine finish. It is used for both draw-filing and lathe filing (Fig. 15–16). The *curved-tooth file* is also common. It is designed for filing aluminum and other soft metals (Fig. 15–17).

File care and safety

1. *Attach a tight-fitting handle* (Fig. 15–18). It is very dangerous to use a file without a handle. The tang can pierce your hand. Choose a handle of the correct size. Slip the tang into the hole, and tap the handle on the bench until the file and handle are tight. A screw-on handle can also be used. *Never strike a file with a hammer to push it into the handle.*

Fig. 15–18 Always fit a handle on a file before using it.

Fig. 15–19 Keep the file clean by brushing it at regular intervals with a file card. Always follow the angle at which the teeth are cut (arrow).

2. *Keep the file clean.* Tap the handle on the bench after every few strokes to remove the loose chips. Brush the file in the direction of the teeth with a *file card* (Fig. 15–19). If a *pin*, or a small chip, remains in the teeth, pick it out with a metal *scorer*. This is a piece of wire or soft metal sharpened to a point. *Never clean the teeth by striking the file against a bench. The teeth are brittle and break easily.*

3. *Keep files separated.* Do not put files together in a drawer or on a bench. Bumping or rubbing files together can damage their teeth.

4. *Chalk the file teeth.* Rub ordinary chalk across the face of the file to help keep pins from wedging between the teeth. These pins scratch the workpiece. Chalking is especially important when filing nonferrous metals, such as copper, brass, and aluminum.

5. *Keep files dry so they will not rust.*

Cross-filing

Cross-filing, the usual method of filing, is done in the following way:

1. Cover the jaws of the vise with jaw caps (Fig. 15–20). Then lock the workpiece in place. The top of the workpiece should be about as high as your elbow when your arm is bent.

2. Stand with your feet about 2 feet (0.6 m) apart, your left foot ahead of your right foot. You should be able to swing your arms and shoulders freely.

3. Grasp the handle of the file in your right hand. Your thumb should be along the top and your fingers curled around the handle.

a. For heavy filing, place the palm of the hand over the tip of the file and the fingers underneath (Fig. 15–21).

b. For light filing, place the thumb over the file and the other fingers underneath (Fig. 15–22).

Fig. 15-20 Install vise-jaw caps before clamping the workpiece for filing. Make sure that the part to be filed is just above the vise jaws.

Fig. 15-22 Here is the way to hold the file for light-pressure filing.

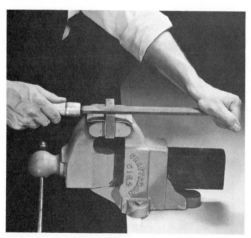

Fig. 15-21 The correct way to hold a file for heavy-pressure filing. Place the palm of the left hand on the file point with the fingers curved and pressed against the underside. Remember that the amount of pressure must vary with the hardness of the metal. Press just hard enough to make the file cut throughout the forward stroke.

4. Files cut only on the forward stroke. Apply pressure to the point at the start of the stroke, then with both hands, and finally with only the right hand. Move the file forward in a straight line. Do not rock it. Press only hard enough to make the file do the cutting.

5. Lift the file slightly on the return stroke. When filing soft metal, you might allow the file to drag slightly to help clean and position it for the next stroke. Beginners often make the mistake of moving the file back and forth in short, jerky strokes.

6. Work from one side of the workpiece to the other, filing evenly.

7. Every few strokes, tap the handle lightly on the bench to loosen the chips. Then clean the file with a file card. It is good practice to chalk the teeth before doing the final filing.

8. When grinding, drilling, or cutting, a small burr usually develops. Remove this by running the file across the corner.

Draw-filing

Draw-filing is done to get a very smooth, level surface. A mill file or a long-angle lathe file is generally used. If more metal must be

Fig. 15-23 Draw-filing. You should push the file sideways across the workpiece. Always use a new portion of the file after each stroke.

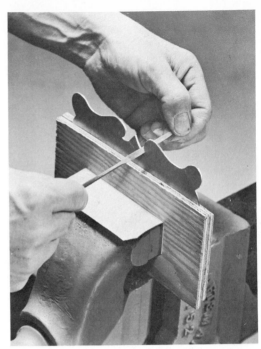

Fig. 15-24 Use jeweler's files for precision filing. They break very easily. If the metal is thin, sandwich it between two pieces of wood.

removed, a second-cut or bastard hand file or a flat file may be used.

1. Grasp the handle in your right hand, the file in your left hand (Fig. 15–23), with only enough space between for the workpiece. In this position, push the file. Turning the file around (with the handle in your left hand), file on the draw stroke. Curl your fingers around the far edge of the file, and put your thumb under the near edge.

2. Hold the file steady. Use the part of the face near the tang. Start the stroke at the end of the workpiece.

3. Apply moderate pressure, and push the file forward. Release the pressure on the return stroke.

4. After each stroke, move your hands to expose a new part of the file. This is important because any pin caught between the teeth would make a heavy scratch on the filed surface.

5. After the entire face has been used, clean the file.

6. Always remove the sharp wire edge by holding the file at an angle and making a light stroke across the edges of the workpiece.

Fine filing

Be especially careful when working with small files, for they break very easily.

1. Fasten the workpiece in a vise. If the metal is thin sheet, place it between two pieces of plywood.

2. Choose a file of the correct shape. No handle is needed because the tang is large and round.

3. To file a concave or round opening, twist the file slightly during the forward stroke (Fig. 15–24).

? QUESTIONS

1. Name the parts of a file.
2. By what four features can files be identified?

3. When would you use a machinist's file? A jeweler's file?
4. Why must the file be equipped with a handle?
5. What do you use to remove metal chips from file teeth?
6. In cross-filing, do you apply pressure on the forward or backward stroke?
7. In draw-filing, what must you do after each stroke?

✓ EXTRA CREDIT

Make a study of how files are made. Several manufacturers have booklets they will send you that describe the methods in detail.

Unit 16
Bending and Twisting Metal

Bending is a way of forming metal in one direction only. When you take a piece of wire in your hands and form a U shape with it, you are bending it. Metal can be bent to form round scrolls or angular V shapes (Fig. 16–1). Sheet metals, rods, bars, and wires are easily bent. In this unit, you will learn how to bend heavy metals.

Most metals 1/4 inch (6 mm) thick or less can be bent cold. The most common angular bends are made at *right angles,* or 90 degrees. However, it is sometimes necessary to bend other angles. An *obtuse angle* is greater than 90 degrees. An *acute angle* is less than 90 degrees.

Making angular bends

1. Make a full-size drawing of the part to be bent. Bend a piece of soft wire to the shape of the bend to find the length of material needed. In bending right angles, add an amount equal to one-half the thickness of the metal for each bend. For example, if you are using metal 1/4 inch (6 mm) thick and must make two right-angle bends, add 1/4

Fig. 16–1 A magazine rack of wrought iron that includes both angular bends and scrolls.

inch (6 mm) to the length of material needed.

2. If the piece has more than one bend, decide which is to be made first (Fig. 16–2).

3. Fasten the metal vertically in the vise, with the bend line at the top of the jaws. The extra material allowed for the bend must be above the vise jaws. Use a square to check the workpiece.

4. Bend the metal by striking it with the flat of a hammer near the bend line (Fig. 16–3). If the piece is long, apply pressure with one hand, and strike the metal at the same time. Do not strike it so hard that you thin out the metal near the bend.

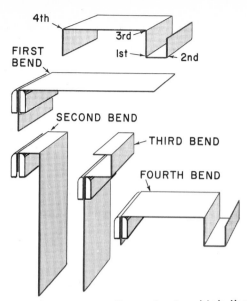

4th

FIRST BEND

3rd

1st — 2nd

SECOND BEND

THIRD BEND

FOURTH BEND

Fig. 16-2 Notice the order in which the bends are made.

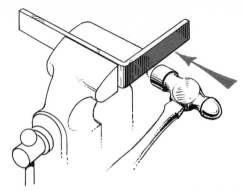

Fig. 16-4 Squaring off a bend. Notice that the workpiece is held in a vise with the edge parallel to the top of the vise jaw. This is the way to get an accurate right-angle bend.

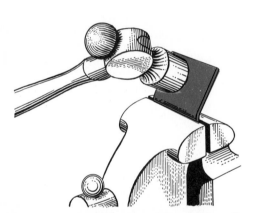

Fig. 16-3 Start the bend by striking the metal firmly with the flat of the hammer near the top of the vise jaw.

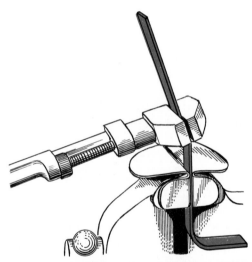

Fig. 16-5 Making a bend that is greater than 90 degrees, using a monkey wrench as a bending tool.

5. To square off the bend, place it in the vise as shown in Fig. 16-4. Strike directly over the bend. Make the other bends as needed.

6. To make an obtuse bend, use a monkey wrench, as shown in Fig. 16-5.

7. To make an acute bend, first make a right-angle bend. Then, place the bend between the vise jaws, and squeeze the two sides together (Fig. 16-6). Another method is to hold one side of the right-angle bend over the anvil and strike the other side with a hammer.

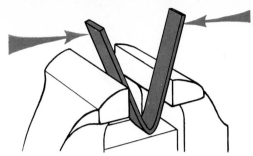

Fig. 16-6 Bend an acute angle by squeezing the metal in a vise.

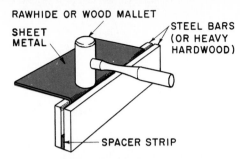

Fig. 16-7 Place the sheet metal between wood jaws or angle iron. Use a wooden or a rawhide mallet to make the bend.

Making an angular bend on sheet stock

1. Clamp the metal sheet between two pieces of hardwood or angle iron that are longer than the width of the metal (Fig. 16–7).

2. Apply pressure with both hands to start the bend.

3. Finish the bend with a wooden, rawhide, or rubber mallet.

Twisting metal

1. Cut off a piece of metal somewhat longer than the finished piece will be. Metal decreases in length when it is twisted. You can check the amount of "shrinkage" on a particular length of metal by making a single twist on a piece of scrap.

2. Mark a line at the beginning and end of the twisted section.

3. If the piece is short, place it vertically in the vise with the top of the jaws at one end of the twist. Place a monkey wrench at the other end.

4. Clamp long pieces horizontally in the vise. If you wish, you can slip a piece of pipe over the section to be twisted to keep it from bending out of line.

5. Hold your left hand over the jaws of the wrench to steady the metal. Then apply

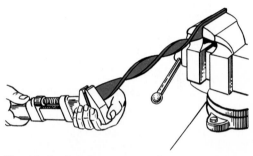

Fig. 16-8 Twisting metal. The twist may be either right-hand or left-hand, depending on the way you turn the wrench.

pressure to the handle, making a definite number of twists (Fig. 16–8).

Bending a scroll

A scroll is a strip of metal that forms a constantly expanding circle. It is similar in shape to an open clock spring. You bend a scroll in the following way:

1. Enlarge the drawing of the scroll to full size for a pattern (see Unit 10).

2. Measure the length of stock needed. This can be done by forming the scroll with a piece of soft wire and then straightening it out.

3. Cut the stock to the needed length.

4. Flare the end of the stock, if desired, by holding the end flat on a metal surface and striking it with glancing blows.

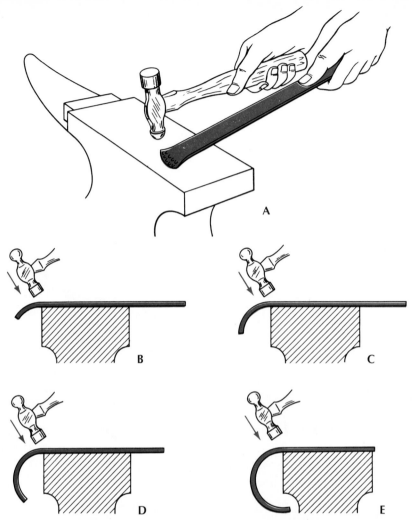

Fig. 16-9 Starting a scroll. (A) Place the metal flat on an anvil and flare the end. (B) Extend the end over the edge a little and strike with a glancing blow. (C, D, E) Strike and move it alternately, a little at a time, until the curve begins to form.

5. Start the scroll by placing the metal flat on an anvil or bench block, with one end extending slightly beyond the edge. Use the flat of a ball peen hammer to strike the metal with glancing blows to start the curve (Fig. 16-9). Continue extending the metal beyond the edge, a little at a time, as the beginning of the scroll is formed. Check often by holding the metal over the pattern. If the curve is too tight, open it slightly by holding the curved section over the anvil horn and striking the edge.

6. When the first part of the scroll is complete, the remainder can be formed better on a *bending jig* or *fork*. Figures 16-10 and 16-11 give examples of two common bending jigs. Most of these are adjustable to take different thicknesses of metal. If these are not available, a bending fork can be made by bending a rod into a U shape. The opening should be equal to the thickness of the metal being bent.

7. Lock the bending fork in a vise, and adjust it to the proper opening. Slip the partly bent scroll into the fork to the point at which the scroll is already bent. Now, grasp the straight end of the metal in your left hand. Apply pressure with the thumb and fingers of your right hand to continue forming the curve.

8. Bend the scroll a little at a time as you feed the stock into the jig.

9. Constantly check the scroll as it is formed by holding it over the pattern (Fig. 16–12). You will have to open the scroll a little if it is too tightly bent.

10. Two scrolls are often formed on the same piece, usually bent in opposite direc-

tions. There should be a continuous curve from one scroll to the other for the most pleasing appearance.

Bending curves

Here are three ways of bending curves of different sizes:

1. Select a short pipe or rod with an outside diameter equal to the inside diameter of the curve. Place one end of the workpiece and the pipe or rod in a vise. Pull the workpiece toward you to begin the curve (Fig. 16–13). Loosen the jaws, feed the workpiece in around the pipe or rod, and reclamp it as before. Continue forming the curve by drawing the workpiece toward you.

2. Lock a stake or pipe in a horizontal position in a vise. Hold one end of the work-

Fig. 16–10 A metal block with pins that can be set for different thicknesses of metal.

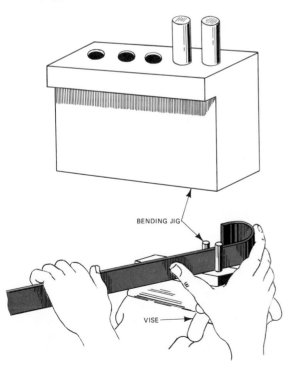
BENDING JIG
VISE

Fig. 16–11 A bending device with the top part attached off-center. This makes it possible to adjust it to different thicknesses of metal.

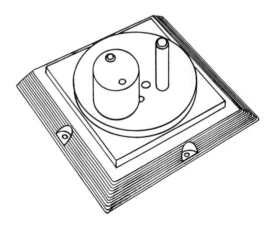

Fig. 16–12 Hold the partly bent scroll over the pattern to see if it is correct.

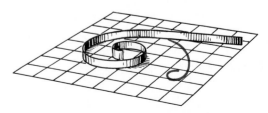

piece over it. Strike the metal with glancing blows just beyond the curve of the bending device. Continue feeding and striking the workpiece until the curve is bent (Fig. 16–14).

    3. Fasten the rod or pipe in a vertical position. Hold the workpiece in a horizontal position behind it. Grasp both ends with pli-ers or your hands. Pull with equal pressure (Fig. 16–15).

Bending an eye

    Find a rod or pipe with an outside diam-eter equal to the inside diameter of the eye to be formed. Figure 16–16 shows the four steps in bending an eye.

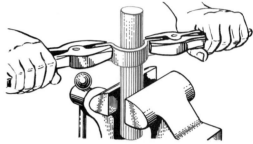

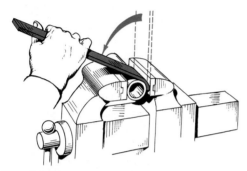

Fig. 16–13   Fasten both the pipe and the metal in the vise. Draw the metal around the pipe.

Fig. 16–15   This is a good way to bend a semicircle. Hold both ends with pliers and pull the metal around the rod.

Fig. 16–16   Steps in forming a metal eye. Use a rod or pipe with a diameter that equals the inside diameter of the eye.

Fig. 16–14   Bending metal over a stake. Alternately move and strike the metal a lit-tle at a time.

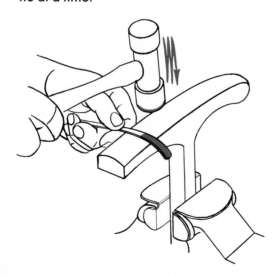

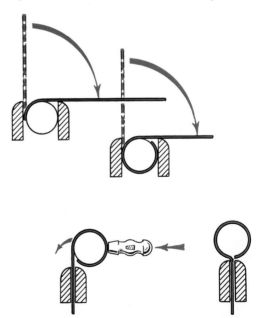

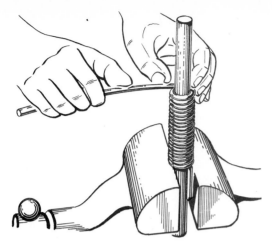

Fig. 16-17 Fasten the wire and rod in a vise. Draw the wire around the rod to form wire rings.

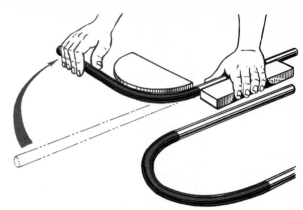

Fig. 16-18 Bending pipe or tubing, using a simple wooden form.

Making wire rings

Choose a rod or pipe with a diameter equal to the inside diameter of the ring. Fasten the rod and one end of the wire in a vise. Bend the wire around the rod to form a coil (Fig. 16-17). With a hacksaw, cut the coil along the length of the rod. You will now have several rings that can be closed and, if necessary, soldered or welded together.

Bending tube or pipe

Cut a wooden form to the shape of the bend and with a round groove in its edge. Fasten a metal clip to one end of the curve. Slip the tube or pipe under the clip, and slowly draw it around the form until the desired shape is obtained (Fig. 16-18). Be careful not to bend the curve too sharply. This kinks the metal, giving it a bad appearance. If a sharply rounded corner is needed, first fill the tube or pipe with wet sand or melted lead. Bend it around a form, and then empty it. This will prevent the tube from collapsing.

 QUESTIONS

1. What is bending?
2. What kinds and thicknesses of metal can be bent cold?
3. What allowance in length must be made for a right-angle bend?
4. With what tool do you strike metal to bend it?
5. What has been done incorrectly if the metal is thinned out at the bend line?
6. What tool can you use to complete a bend in sheet stock?
7. When metal is twisted, what happens to its length?
8. What is a scroll?
9. After you have hammered part of a scroll, what tool can you use on the remainder?
10. What can you bend a workpiece around to form a curve?
11. What will happen if you bend a tube or pipe too sharply?

EXTRA CREDIT

Find out the exact amount by which a particular length of metal shortens when it is twisted once, twice, and three times. Does the metal shorten by the same amount if it is heated before twisting?

Unit 17
Machine Bending

In Unit 16, you learned a number of different ways to bend metal by hand. This unit explains the methods used in machine bending. Machines are used to make bending easier and more accurate and to make duplicate parts. Several different kinds of bending machines are found in the school shop. Some of these are discussed in this unit.

Plate and bar bender

Plate and bar benders are mounted on the floor or on a bench. They can be used to bend heavy metal plates or flat bar stock, usually up to 1/4 inch (6 mm) thick. Some nonferrous soft metals of a slightly larger gage can also be bent on them. The capacity of the machine is usually stamped near the jaws. Do not exceed this capacity or you may damage the machine. To use the plate bender, carefully mark the bend line with chalk so that it can easily be seen. Place the workpiece between the jaws, and close them just enough to hold the workpiece. Then, grasp the bending lever with both hands, and pull hard to make the bend. Next, carefully open the jaws, and remove the workpiece (Fig. 17–1).

Vise-mounted or bench-mounted benders

Several companies manufacture small vise-mounted or bench-mounted benders that can bend materials up to 3/8 inch by 1 inch (10 by 25 mm) in cross section. These machines can bend flats, rounds, wire, and heavy sheet stock. Three of the most common are discussed below:

Fig. 17–1   A plate and bar bender. (Hall Enterprises)

1. The *Metl-Former* is a vise with rollers and jaws that can be used to form strips, tubes, and rods (Fig. 17–2). It is best for bending aluminum and steel rods of small diameter. To use this machine, follow these instructions carefully:

   a. Make a full-size drawing of the project on a piece of wrapping paper. Determine the length by using a piece of soft wire to make a pattern.

   b. To figure the length of material needed to make a bend of any radius, first find the radius of the arc from its center to the center line of the material (Fig. 17–3). Then use this simple formula: *The length of circular part equals radius times number of degrees in arc times 0.0175.* For example, if the radius is 2 inches (51 mm) and you wish to bend a 90-degree angle with a rounded corner, the material needed would be, in customary units: $2 \times 90 \times 0.0175 = 3.150$, or about 3 5/32 inches. In metric units, it would be as follows: $51 \times 90 \times 0.0175 = 80.325$ mm.

Fig. 17—2 Parts of a Metl-Former kit: (a) basic metal-forming tool, (b) three tubing and rod rollers, (c) three flat-metal rollers, (d) a sheet-metal bender, (e) a flat-metal bending wedge, (f) a roller handle. (Swayne, Robinson & Company)

c. To roll flat, round, or square metal, open the jaws wide enough to insert the metal between the drive roller, the one with the handle, and the two driven rollers.

d. Close the jaws until the rollers just touch the metal.

Fig. 17-3 Measure the radius to the center of the material and the angle of the arc before figuring the amount of material needed.

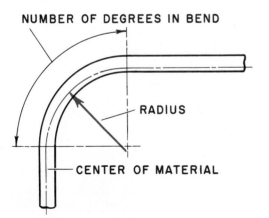

NUMBER OF DEGREES IN BEND

RADIUS

CENTER OF MATERIAL

e. Tighten the vise jaws about one-fourth turn, and crank through the correct distance until the right length of curve is formed.

f. Continue tightening the vise a little at a time, and crank the metal back and forth until the correct radius is obtained (Fig. 17–4). If the metal is formed too far, reverse it in the rolls, and proceed as above to straighten it out.

g. By using tubing and rod rollers, you will be able to form a tube or a rod in the same way (Fig. 17–5).

h. In using three-form rollers, the extreme ends of the rolled piece are not bent. In the piece shown in Fig. 17–5, the straight ends are about 1 3/8 inches (35 mm) long. To roll a full circle, find the amount of material needed and add 1 3/8 inches to each end. Then roll until the ends meet. Cut off 1 3/8 inches (35 mm) from each end, and roll through repeatedly until the circle is closed.

Fig. 17-4 Forming flat stock.

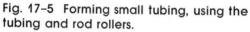
Fig. 17-5 Forming small tubing, using the tubing and rod rollers.

i. Figure 17–6 shows how to use the forming machine to make an angle bend.

j. Figure 17–7 shows how you can make a sheet-metal bend between the jaws of the forming machine. The height of the bend is limited to a maximum of 2 1/2 inches (63.5 mm).

2. The *Kan bend* is a hand bender that can be used on wire, flat metal, and tubing

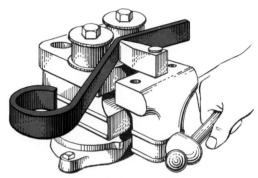

Fig. 17-6 Making a sharp-angle bend, using two flat-metal rollers and the flat-metal bending wedge. To bend flat stock, rods, and bar stock, mark off the bending lines. Then use the power of the vise screw to bend to the angle you want.

Fig. 17-7 Bending sheet metal between the sheet-metal jaws. Feed the metal between the jaws and use the power of the vise screw to gradually bend the metal.

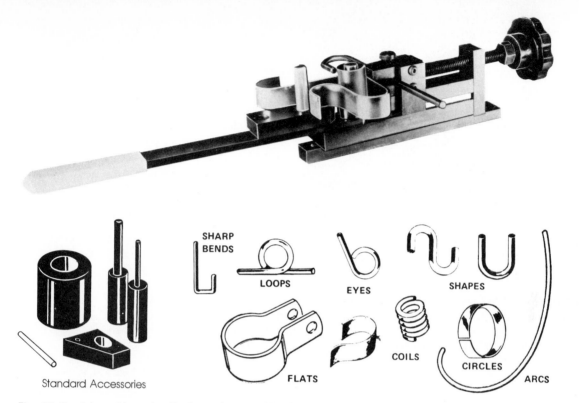

Fig. 17-8   A hand bender that can be used to do many kinds of bending. (Karl A. Neise, Inc.)

(Fig. 17–8). It can do repairs, make parts for small projects, and do designing and sculpturing. The unit is held in a vise or mounted on a bench top. It can bend wire or rounds up to 5/16 inch (8 mm) in diameter and flats up to 1/2 inch by 1 inch (13 mm by 25 mm) in cross section. The setups for bending are made quickly using various bending dies and blocks.

3. The *hand-operated scroll bender* is held in a vise (Fig. 17–9). It can produce five scroll sizes from 2 1/2 inches (63.5 mm) diameter single turn to 8 inches (203 mm) diameter one and one-half turn on stock up to 3/16 inch by 1 inch (5 mm by 25 mm) in cross section. Three sizes of scroll dies are available for this bender.

Di-Acro bender

The *Di-Acro bender* makes it possible to bend a variety of metals and shapes (Fig. 17–10). It consists of a form that has the

Fig. 17-9   A scroll bender. (Hossfeld Manufacturing Company)

115

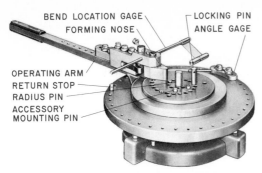

BEND LOCATION GAGE
FORMING NOSE
LOCKING PIN
ANGLE GAGE
OPERATING ARM
RETURN STOP
RADIUS PIN
ACCESSORY
MOUNTING PIN

Fig. 17–10   Parts of a Di-Acro bender. (Di-Acro/Division of Houdaille Industries)

same shape as the bend to be made and a forming roll that moves around the form to shape the metal. Since all metals are somewhat elastic, they spring back a little after they have been formed. Because of this, the bending form is usually made with a smaller radius than that needed for the bend.

Here is the correct way to use this bending machine:

1. Make a full-size drawing of the part to be bent on a piece of wrapping paper.

2. Use a piece of soft wire to find the length needed. Then cut a piece of metal to this length.

Fig. 17–11   (A) Adjust the forming nose so that the material will fit snugly between the nose and the point of the radius block. (B) Clamp the material close to the bending edge, using a locking pin or holding block as shown. (C) Move the operating arm until it strikes the gage. You will thus obtain the exact degree of bend you want. (D) The completed bend.

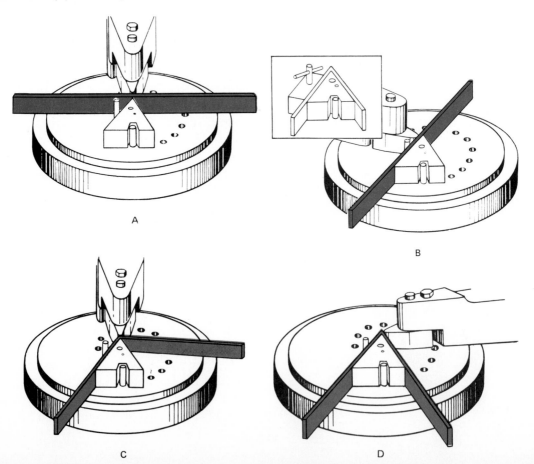

A

B

C

D

Fig. 17–12 Making a right-angle bend in a piece of angle iron. This type of bend is made when constructing the frame for a wrought-metal table.

3. Mark the start of the bend on the metal with a piece of chalk.

4. Place the metal in the bender with the mark against the form or against the radius collar. For example, in bending a sharp right angle with a 0-radius form, a form designed to bend sharp corners, the mark should be to one side, not at the center of the forming nose. Clamp the material close to the bending edge, as shown in Fig. 17–11.

5. Move the operating arm until it starts to bend the metal. After it has bent a short distance, take the metal out, and check it over the drawing. If the bend is not right, move the bend location mark, and put the metal back into the bender. It is better to have to move the mark toward the starting end.

6. Figure 17–12 shows how you can bend angle iron with a sharp right-angle corner. Notice how you must cut a 90-degree notch before forming.

Universal bender

The *universal bender* is so called because it can make any kind of bend. It is excellent for bending pipe, rounds, flats, squares, tubing, conduit, and angle iron. This bender can be put together without wrenches. It is a simple

job to choose and assemble the correct set of dies and bending blocks to do any kind of bending.

Figure 17–13 shows the parts of the bender. After you have used this bender for a few of the basic setups, you will be able to assemble it to do every kind of bending. Here are a few of the more common bending operations that you can do on the universal bender:

1. Bending angles, offsets, and other bends on heavy cold metal:

a. Connect the main frame and a swinging frame with the No. 20 center pin.

b. Place the No. 11 square bending block on a No. 22 support plug in the main frame, and hold in place with a No. 19 U-shaped pin.

c. Place a No. 11 square block or No. 9 flat surface roller in the swinging frame, and hold in place with a No. 18 eye pin.

d. Place the metal between the center pin and the bending block or roller. Pull the swinging frame clockwise to the degree of bend you want (Fig. 17–14).

2. Bending sharp square bends, U's, and various irregular shapes:

a. Place the No. 23 adjustable yoke in the oscillating block of the main frame. Adjust the yoke so that it lies flat against the center pin. The workpiece will be at right angles to the main frame at the start of the bend when bending pressure is applied.

b. Connect the main frame and a swinging frame with the No. 20 center pin.

c. When bending 1/4-inch (6.5 mm) round or flat metal, place the No. 18 eye pin at the first 5/8-inch (16-mm) hole in the swinging frame, as shown in Figs. 17–15 and 17–16.

3. Bending pipe and conduit. The setup is shown in Fig. 17–17.

4. Bending sharp square bends on wide flat stock. The setup is shown in Fig. 17–18.

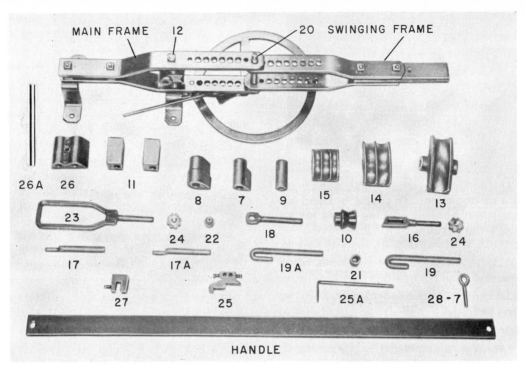

Fig. 17–13 Parts of the universal bender. The numbers are the part numbers used for identification in the manufacturer's catalogue:

7. Cam die, 1 1/2 inch.
8. Cam die, 1 3/4 and 2 inch.
9. Flat-surface bending roller.
10. V-grooved roller for numbers 13 to 15.
11. Bending blocks, square.
12. Oscillating block.
13. Grooved-pipe bending die, 1 1/4 inch.
14. Grooved-pipe bending die, 3/4 and 1/4 inch.
15. Grooved-pipe bending die, 1/4, 3/8, and 1/2 inch.
16. Eyebolt bending dog.
17. Flathead pin, regular.
17A. Flathead pin, offset for small eyes.
18. Eye pin.

19. U-shaped pin, regular.
19A. U-shaped pin, with lug for small eyes.
20. Center pin for 1/2-, 5/8-, and 3/4-inch eye.
21. U-pin roller.
22. Support plug.
23. Yoke for sharp square bending.
24. Thumb nut for numbers 16 and 23.
25. Sliding gage.
25A. Extension rod.
26. Sharp square bend block.
26A. Pin for number 26.
27. Circle gage.
28-7. Hand-level pin.

Fig. 17–14 Bending an angle on heavy cold bar stock.

Fig. 17–15 Bending a U-bolt.

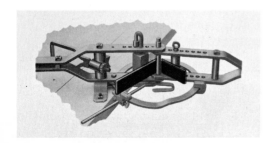

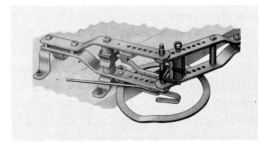

Fig. 17-16 Bending ornamental ironwork. This setup is similar to that in Fig. 17-15.

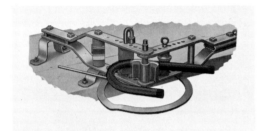

Fig. 17-17 Bending pipe.

Fig. 17-18 Making a sharp bend on wide flat stock.

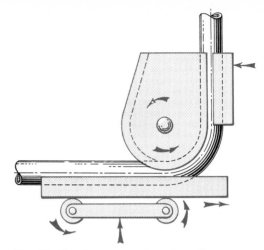

Fig. 17-19 Draw, or rotary, bending.

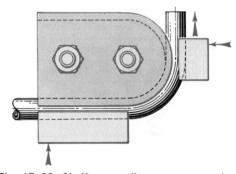

Fig. 17-20 Stationary-die, or compression, bending.

Industrial machine bending

There are four common bending techniques used in industry: draw or rotary, stationary-die or compression, roll, and stretch. Many others are used for special bending operations.

Draw, or *rotary, bending* is done on a machine having a rotating bending die and stationary wiper block or die clamp. The tube is clamped to the die and bent as the die rotates (Fig. 17-19).

Stationary-die, or *compression, bending* is done on a machine having a fixed bending die and a movable wiper block. The tube is wrapped around the die by the wiper block (Fig. 17-20).

Roll bending is used to produce circular bends. The equipment consists of three or four rolls, positioned one above the other (Fig. 17-21). This machine is used to bend rod, bar, or tubing into full or partial circles and to bend sheet or plate into cylinders.

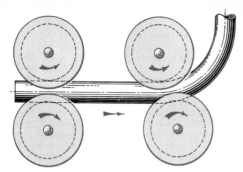

Fig. 17–21   Roll bending.

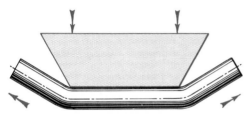

Fig. 17–22   Stretch forming or bending.

Wheel-shaped rolls are used to bend narrow sections.

When forming smoothly contoured parts by other methods is difficult, *stretch forming* or *bending* can be done. In this method, the material is stretched over a tool or stretch die (Fig. 17–22). The entire piece is stretched by tension. Unlike other types of bending, stretch forming uses no compression. This process can be used with strip, sheet, and plate metal. It is economical because only one die is required.

Sharp bends in tubing are difficult to make because a hollow tube collapses or flattens at the bend. Thus, the tube must be supported from inside.

In industry, two methods are commonly used to make short-radius bends in tubing. One way is to fill the tube with fillers, such as alloys that have low melting points. The alloys are melted, poured into the tube, and

allowed to solidify. The tube is then bent, and the filler is removed by heating the tube. The second method is to use a mandrel. A **mandrel** is a metal piece that serves as a core around which metal can be cast, molded, bent, or otherwise shaped. The mandrel, in this case, is a small, round rod or ball that is slightly smaller than the inside of the tube. It is inserted into the tube to the point where bending is to begin. The mandrel supports the tube at the point of bending. It is withdrawn as bending progresses so that it is not bent with the tube.

 QUESTIONS

1. What is the thickest metal plate or bar that most plate and bar benders can handle?
2. On what materials does a Metl-Former work best?
3. What is the formula for finding the length of material needed to make a bend of any radius?
4. Besides the Metl-Former, what are the two other vise-mounted or bench-mounted benders?
5. Why is the bending form on the Di-Acro bender made with a smaller radius than that required for the bend itself?
6. How did the universal bender get its name?
7. What are the four common bending techniques used in industry?
8. Low-melting-point alloys and mandrels are used to make what kind of bends?

✓ EXTRA CREDIT

1. Write a report on industrial metal bending.
2. Select a product photograph showing parts made by bending. Explain the bending procedures to the class.

Unit 18
Decorating the Surface and Ends of Metal

The appearance of many wrought-metal projects can be improved if the surface is finished by **texturing.** Texturing is done by peening or hammering. **Peening** is striking the metal with the peen of a hammer. The **peen** is the ball-shaped or wedge-shaped end of the hammer head. **Hammering** is striking the metal with the face, the other end of the head. Peening or hammering is done to prevent metal surfaces from looking scratched or dented.

Peening or hammering

Beginners often pound metal without any thought. The result is a piece of metal that is beaten out of shape, with an unattractive finish. The cut end may not be pleasing. It must be shaped and decorated in keeping with the design.

The appearance produced by peening or hammering depends on the shape of the tool used, its size, and the force with which the metal is struck. The ball peen hammer is most often used, but a cross peen or straight peen hammer will also give a good texture (Fig. 18–1). The proper technique for peening or hammering is given below:

1. Outline the area to be decorated. Decide whether one or both sides are to be finished.

2. Choose the right kind of hammer or peening tool, usually a 14-ounce (397-g) hammer or one slightly lighter or heavier.

3. Place the metal over a flat surface, either an anvil or a flat bench plate. Strike the metal with firm, even blows that slightly

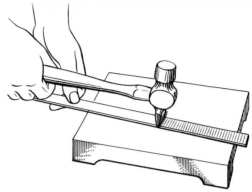
Fig. 18–1   A cross peen hammer gives a different texture to the surface of metal.

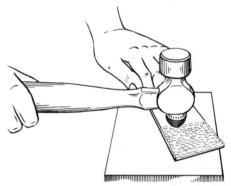
Fig. 18–2   Peening the surface with a ball peen hammer.

overlap one another (Fig. 18–2). Do not strike so hard that the metal stretches. If the surface is fairly wide, peen first from one side and then from the other to even out the stretching. At intervals, flatten out the metal with a wooden or rubber mallet. Keep the blows firm and evenly spaced.

4. If both surfaces of the metal must be peened, either of two methods can be followed:

a. Fasten a ball peen hammer with the peen upward in a vise. Hold the metal

121

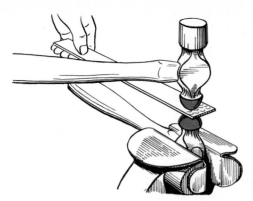

Fig. 18-3 Peening both surfaces at the same time. Be careful to strike the upper surface directly over the ball of the lower ball peen hammer.

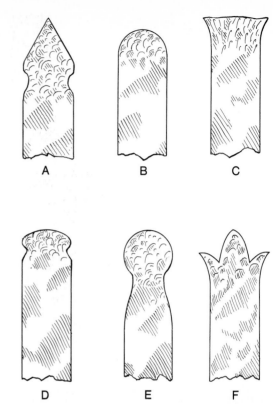

Fig. 18-4 Typical end designs for wrought-metal projects: (A) arrowhead, (B) rounded, (C) flared, (D) pinched, (E) ball, (F) split end.

over it, and strike the metal with another ball peen hammer (Fig. 18-3).

b. Peen one surface; then turn the metal over. Place a piece of soft annealed copper under the metal to protect the first peened surface. Peen the second surface.

Decorating the ends of metal

There are many ways to decorate the ends of metal. Figure 18-4 shows some of the possible decorations. These usually require grinding or cutting, filing to shape, and then peening. A typical example is the arrowhead design. To make it, first lay out the arrowhead shape on the end of the metal and grind to the outline. Then peen the end, striking more powerful blows toward the edge of the design and less powerful ones in the center. This will round off the end. The split-end effect is made by splitting with a hacksaw and filing to shape.

Decorating the edge of sheet stock

The edge of heavy sheet stock can be given either a bevel, or slant, or a rippled

Fig. 18-5 Rippling the edge of sheet stock by striking it with the peen end of a hammer.

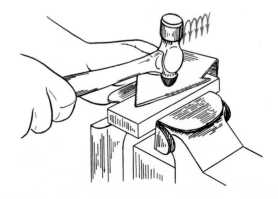

effect. Hold the edge of the metal directly over the edge of an anvil or bench plate. For beveling, strike the metal edge with glancing blows with the flat of a hammer. The rippled effect is a little harder to get because it is uniform. Place the metal as above. Strike with the peen of the hammer right on the edge two or three times in one spot. Then move the metal about 1/8 to 1/4 inch (3 to 6 mm) and repeat (Fig. 18–5). Practice on a piece of scrap metal. If you rub the surface lightly with abrasive paper after hammering, you will highlight it. This is a very pleasing effect.

 QUESTIONS

1. Why are metal surfaces textured?
2. On what three factors does the appearance produced by peening depend?
3. What kind of hammer is most often used in peening?
4. Over what kind of surface should the metal be held for peening?
5. What operations are usually involved in decorating the ends of metal?
6. What are two ways of decorating the edge of heavy sheet stock?

✔ **EXTRA CREDIT**

Make a sample display board showing several kinds of surface decoration.

Unit 19
Grinding Metals

Abrading is cutting or grinding away metal with abrasives. An **abrasive** is a material that will wear away something softer than itself. Abrasive grains are used to make abrasive paper, abrasive cloth, and grinding wheels. These can then be used on metal to remove small pieces and make it smooth. (Fig. 19–1).

Kinds of abrading

In metal finishing, there are three main kinds of abrading. **Grinding** is using abrasives to remove relatively large amounts of metal quickly. **Polishing,** which follows grinding, is used to smooth the surface and remove the scratches from grinding. **Buffing,** the final smoothing operation, gives a bright, mirrorlike finish or a softer, satinlike appearance. Abrading is done either by hand or by machine. This unit deals with

Fig. 19–1   Metal grinding is a form of abrading. (Norton Company)

grinding. (Unit 21 presents information on polishing metals. Buffing is treated in Unit 48.)

Kinds of abrasives

There are two main kinds of abrasive materials (Fig. 19–2). *Natural abrasives* are found in nature. *Artificial abrasives* were in-

Fig. 19-2 Abrasives come in many forms and shapes. (Carborundum Company)

emery and corundum, is also produced artificially from bauxite. This abrasive, like silicon carbide, is made in an electric furnace. The crystals are tougher than silicon carbide but not so hard. Aluminum oxide is used to grind such materials as steel.

Grain size

Abrasives come from a furnace or a mine in chunks. These chunks are then crushed into *grains,* or fine particles. The grains are sorted by being passed through screens of different sizes. For example, one screen may have 36 openings per inch (per 25 mm). The next smaller screen may have 40 openings per inch (per 25 mm). Grains that pass through the screen with the 36 openings but not through the next are numbered 36. This identifies the grain size, or coarseness. The higher the number, the smaller the grains. As you see in Table 19-1, the sizes range from coarse to fine. For sizes 280 and above, the grains are sorted in a different way and are called *flour sizes.*

Artificial abrasives can be graded very accurately. The uniform size, shape, and hardness of each grain make them better than the natural abrasives.

Grinding wheels

Wheels for grinding metal are available in many shapes, sizes, and **grits,** or grades. Thus, there is a wheel that is right for each grinding operation. Grinding wheels are made by pressing and bonding, or gluing,

vented by scientists and engineers. *Emery* and *corundum* are the two most common natural abrasives. Emery is about 60 percent aluminum oxide. Corundum is about 75 to 95 percent aluminum oxide.

Artificial abrasives were invented toward the end of the nineteenth century. *Silicon carbide,* the first artificial abrasive, is made from coke, sand, salt, and sawdust. This mixture is heated to a high temperature in an electric furnace until an iridescent, or rainbowlike, blue-black crystalline material is produced. Silicon carbide is used to grind materials such as cast iron and bronze. *Aluminum oxide,* although found naturally in

Table 19-1
Grain Sizes of Abrasives

Coarse ——————→ to ——————————→ Fine												Flour sizes		
10		20		46		80		150		220		280	400	600
	14		30		60		100							
	12	16	24	36	54	70	90	120	180	240		320	500	

the abrasive grains into the desired size and shape. The finer grains are bonded together with resin, rubber, or shellac. *Vitrified,* or ceramic-bond, wheels are also made for precision work. Soft metals are best ground with coarse grit wheels, such as numbers 36 and 46. For hard and brittle metals, use grit numbers 60 or 80.

Metal grinding

Every metal shop has one or more grinders for sharpening tools and for general grinding. This kind of grinding is called *offhand* because the workpiece is applied to the grinder freehand. The *bench grinder* is small and is mounted on a bench (Fig. 19–3). It has grinding wheels at both ends of a shaft that extends out from an electric motor. The *pedestal grinder* is similar except that it stands on the floor and is usually much larger (Fig. 19–4).

Grinder safety

1. Always wear goggles or an eye shield. Do this even when the grinder is equipped with safety eye shields (Fig. 19–5).

2. Make sure the toolrest just clears the grinding wheel by about 1/16 to 1/8 inch (1.5 to 3 mm). Most accidents happen when the workpiece becomes lodged between the

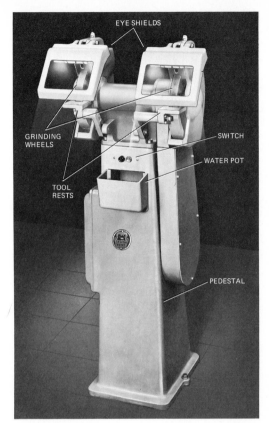

Fig. 19–4 Parts of the pedestal grinder. (South Bend Lathe Works)

revolving wheel and the toolrest. This can break the wheel and seriously injure the operator.

3. Always choose the right kind of grinding wheel for the material. The most common for general grinding is an aluminum oxide wheel. When you replace a grinding wheel, use one that has the same thickness, diameter, and size of arbor hole as the original wheel.

4. Use only the face of the wheel, never the sides.

5. Make sure the wheel is dressed, or sharpened, properly.

6. When a shop has two grinders, use one for general grinding and the other for sharpening tools.

Fig. 19–3 A bench grinder. (The Ridge Tool Company)

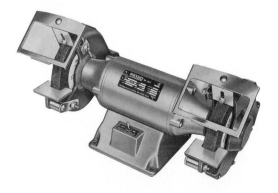

125

Fig. 19-5 Use all abrasives safely. Wear eye protection.

Fig. 19-6 A wheel dresser.

ABRASIVE STICK

Fig. 19-7 An abrasive-stick dresser.

Dressing and truing a wheel

As a grinding wheel is used, several things happen:

1. The wheel becomes clogged with small bits of metal. It is then called a **loaded wheel.**

2. The abrasive grains on the wheel face wear smooth, and the wheel loses its grinding action. It is then called a **glazed wheel.**

3. The wheel wears irregularly with grooves or high spots.

When any of these things happen, the wheel must be dressed and trued. **Dressing** is sharpening the edge of the wheel by exposing new abrasive grains. **Truing** is straight-

ening and balancing the wheel. Both can be done at the same time:

1. Use a *wheel dresser* that has a very hard, star-shaped steel wheel at one end of a holder (Fig. 19-6). Wear goggles.

2. Adjust the toolrest so that the dresser will make contact with the grinding wheel on the wheel's centerline.

3. Start the wheel turning. Then place the dresser on the toolrest with its handle tilted upward at an angle.

4. Slowly press the dresser against the face of the wheel until it "bites." Then move the dresser from side to side across the wheel to make the wheel surface straight.

⚡ **CAUTION**

Hold the dresser rigidly on the toolrest so that it does not vibrate.

Abrasive-stick and *diamond-tip dressers* are also used in the shop (Fig. 19-7). They are used in much the same way as mechanical dressers. You smooth a wheel by passing the dresser back and forth over the face of the wheel. Use very light pressure.

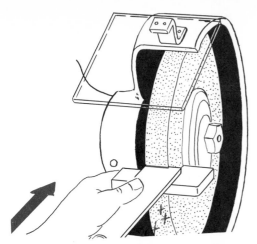

Fig. 19-8 Grinding a piece of metal. Hold the metal firmly on the toolrest and push it gently into the wheel. When grinding, use adequate lighting, keep the eye shield in place, and wear goggles.

Grinding metal

1. Check the safety rules.

2. Hold the workpiece firmly on the rest, and guide it back and forth to grind a straight edge (Fig. 19-8). Keep the metal cool by dipping it in water.

3. To grind a curve or a semicircle, swing the workpiece in the proper arc.

4. Whenever an edge is ground, a small burr forms on the lower side. Dress this off with a file or grinder.

 QUESTIONS ▬▬▬▬▬▬▬▬

1. Name the two main types of abrasive materials.
2. What artificial abrasive is used on cast iron and bronze? On steel?
3. What determines how abrasives are graded?
4. How are grinding wheels made?
5. For safety, how much clearance should there be between the wheel and the toolrest?
6. What part of the wheel should you always use for grinding?
7. Define *dressing* and *truing*.

✔ EXTRA CREDIT ▬▬▬▬▬▬▬▬

Report to the class on how grinding wheels are made.

Unit 20
Sharpening Hand Tools

All hand tools used for metal cutting must be carefully maintained. Dull tools can be both dangerous and frustrating. Be sure you have learned the procedures for sharpening them properly. Otherwise, you may ruin the tools.

General instructions

1. Make certain that you select the right wheel for sharpening. Use a fine wheel of 60 to 80 grit.

2. Check to see that the wheel and grinder are in good condition. The wheel should not be cracked or loose. The toolrest should be tight and the eye shield in place.

3. Be sure that the water pot is filled. Keep the tool cool by dipping it into water often. This will prevent overheating and softening of the tool.

Fig. 20-1 Sharpening a screwdriver. Grind each side so that it tapers a little, and then grind the tip square. Dip the tool in water often to keep it cool.

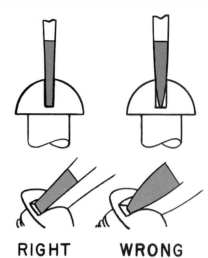

RIGHT   WRONG

Fig. 20-2 The right and the wrong tip on a screwdriver. Notice that the correctly ground tip tapers slightly to a blunt point.

4. Wear goggles. Be sure you have no loose clothing to get caught in the machine.

5. Wipe all grease or oil from your hands and the tools. Oily tools are difficult to hold while grinding and may slip.

Sharpening screwdrivers

1. *Screwdrivers* used for slotted-head screws should have a flat, blunt point with tapered sides. Grind or file either side of the point a little at a time. Then hold the screwdriver flat, and grind or file off the end (Fig. 20-1). Never sharpen a screwdriver to a sharp edge (Fig. 20-2). Do not overheat the tool as this will soften it.

2. *Phillips screwdrivers* should be dressed or sharpened lightly with a sharp file.

Sharpening cold chisels

1. The cutting edge of a *flat cold chisel* is ground to an angle of 60 to 70 degrees with the edge at a slight arc (Fig. 20-3).

Hold one side of the cutting edge lightly against the face of the wheel, and move it back and forth in a slight arc. Grind first one side and then the other to form a sharp edge.

Cool the chisel often. Never allow it to become overheated and lose hardness.

Fig. 20-3 Grinding a cold chisel. The point should be ground at an angle of about 60 to 70 degrees. Never let the chisel get so hot that you cannot hold it comfortably in your bare hand while grinding. Too much heat can remove the controlled temper in the metal.

The body of the chisel is softer than the cutting edge. The head will therefore mushroom, or flatten, after it has been used for a while. This mushroom is dangerous. It could cut your hand, or a piece of it could break off

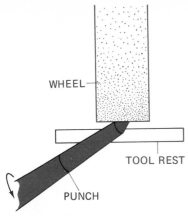

Fig. 20-4 **Grinding a center punch. Turn the tool slowly to form a nicely rounded shape, ending in a sharp point.**

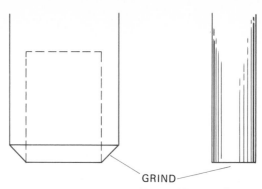

Fig. 20-5 **Grind only the cutting surfaces of solid and hollow punches.**

and hit your eye. Always grind off the mushroom when it forms.

2. *Cape, diamond-point,* and *roundnose chisels* should be ground in a similar way. Grind them carefully to retain their normal shapes. They can easily be ruined.

Sharpening punches

Because punches are round or cone-shaped, they should be turned slowly against the grinding wheel. This will keep their shape. Cool the punches often in water.

1. Grind a *center punch* to an included angle of 90 degrees (Fig. 20–4). *Prick punches* should be ground to angles of 30 degrees. Be careful not to burn the fragile points.

Adjust the toolrest so that the punch meets the wheel face at the desired angle. Turn the punch during grinding to make the point symmetrical, the same shape all around. Dip the punch in water often to avoid overheating it. Do not grind away more metal than is necessary.

2. *Hollow punches* should be ground on the outside only. Never attempt to grind the inside because this will change the size. The bevel should be ground slowly to an angle of about 45 degrees. *Solid punches* are ground only at the cutting tip. Do not change the diameter by grinding the sides (Fig. 20–5).

Sharpening twist drills

1. Check the condition of the *twist drill*. Usually, only a small amount of grinding is necessary to put the drill in good condition. Get a new, larger-size drill as a sample or guide. Make sure that the face of the grinding wheel is trued and dressed.

2. Grasp the drill near the point in your right hand, with your left hand holding the shank.

3. Hold the lip of the drill at an angle of 59 degrees to the grinding wheel. Grind the cutting edge slightly (Fig. 20–6). Then turn the drill in a clockwise direction, at the same time swinging the shank down in an arc of about 12 to 15 degrees (Fig. 20–7). Practice this before you grind the drill.

4. Grind a little off each cutting edge.

5. Check with a *drill-grinding gage* to make sure that the cutting edges are the same length and at the same angle with the axis—59 degrees. Check also to see that there is relief, or clearance, of 12 to 15 degrees from the cutting lips to the heel (Fig. 20–8). Do not overheat the drill. The point of carbon-steel drills may be cooled in water.

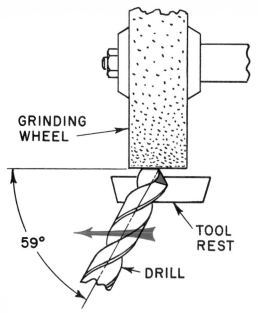

Fig. 20–6 Note that the drill is held at an angle of 59 degrees to the grinding wheel.

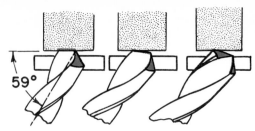

Fig. 20–7 Turn the drill while grinding.

Fig. 20–8 Checking the point with a drill-grinding gage. Make sure it is ground so that the lips are of the same length and at the same angle. (The L. S. Starrett Company)

Watch for the following:

1. Make sure there is enough, but not too much, lip relief.

2. Make sure both lips are the same length.

3. See that the lips are ground at the same angle.

 **QUESTIONS**

1. What grit, or grade, of wheel should you use for sharpening tools?

2. Why should tools be kept cool while being sharpened?
3. To what angle should the cutting edge of a cold chisel be ground?
4. Why should you turn punches slowly against the grinding wheel?
5. At what angle should you grind drills?

 **EXTRA CREDIT**

Prepare a wall chart showing the proper grinding angles for some selected cutting tools.

Unit 21
Using Abrasives
for Polishing

In Unit 19, you learned that polishing follows grinding in finishing metal. Polishing makes the metal smoother and removes grinding scratches. This is done by holding the surface of a workpiece against an abrasive-coated wheel or belt. Both hand and machine methods can be used.

 SAFETY RULE

Always wear safety goggles when machine-polishing metal.

Three main methods of machine-polishing metal are used in the school shop: (1) polishing compounds and cloth wheels; (2) abrasive-covered wheels; (3) abrasive-coated belts, disks, sheets, and drums.

Using abrasive cloth for hand polishing

Abrasive cloth has abrasive material attached to it with glue or some other adhesive. It comes in 9- by 11-inch (229- by 279-mm) sheets or in rolls 1/2 inch to 3 inches (13 mm to 76 mm) wide. Sheets are sold individually or by the quire (24 sheets) or ream (20 quires). Abrasive cloth used in the shop comes in the common grain sizes: 60 for medium-coarse work, 80 to 90 for medium-fine, and 120 to 180 for very fine.

Flexible abrasive sheets made of soft nylon web filled with abrasive grains and resins are also used. These sheets are made with either silicon carbide or aluminum oxide. They come in grades of very fine, fine, medium, and coarse (Fig. 21–1).

Crocus cloth is a very fine abrasive cloth made with red iron oxide coating. It is used to produce a very fine finish in final buffing

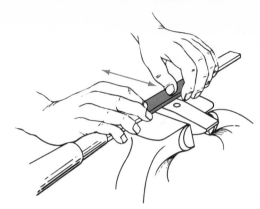

Fig. 21–2   Use abrasive cloth wrapped around a file to smooth the metal surface.

operations (see Unit 48). The procedure for hand polishing is as follows:

1. Cut a strip of abrasive cloth from a roll or sheet.

2. Wrap it around a flat stick or file (Fig. 21–2).

3. Apply a few drops of oil to the metal surface.

4. Rub the cloth back and forth as if you were sanding. Do not rock the tool; keep it flat.

5. After all scratches have been removed, the abrasive grains will float in oil on the surface.

6. Reverse the cloth, exposing the back. Rub back and forth to get a high polish.

Polishing with compounds and wheels

Attach a clean, soft cloth wheel to the head of the polishing machine (Fig. 21–3). Then select a stick of greaseless polishing compound. This is an abrasive mixed with glue in stick form. Turn on the machine, and hold the abrasive stick against the turning wheel until the face is coated. This coating will dry quickly. Then, holding the workpiece firmly in your hands, move it back and

Fig. 21–1   Because these abrasive sheets are flexible, they are ideal for applying a variety of attractive finishes to metal surfaces. (Norton Company)

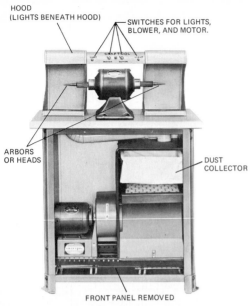

HOOD
(LIGHTS BENEATH HOOD)

SWITCHES FOR LIGHTS,
BLOWER, AND MOTOR.

ARBORS
OR HEADS

DUST
COLLECTOR

FRONT PANEL REMOVED

Fig. 21-3 This polishing machine is also used for buffing metal. The front panel has been removed to show the dust collector.

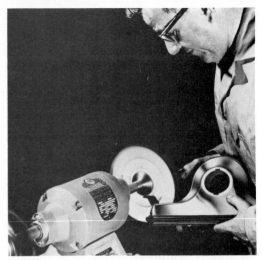

Fig. 21-4 Polishing mild steel. Hold the work below the centerline of the wheel for safe operation.

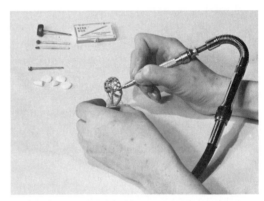

Fig. 21-5 Polishing a small part with a hand polisher and wheel.

forth across the wheel until the scratches have been removed. Keep the workpiece below the centerline of the wheel for safety (Fig. 21-4).

Polishing with abrasive-covered wheels

Polishing is often done with a wheel covered with an adhesive and abrasive grains. Wheels are commonly made from rope, felt, canvas, or leather. Hard wheels are sewn tightly or glued to make the face, or outer edge, of the wheel stiff but flexible. To do this with glue or water glass, an adhesive, pour some abrasive grains in a line on a piece of wrapping paper. Use grain of about No. 60 for medium polishing. Brush the glue or water glass on the face of the wheel. Then roll the wheel in the abrasive until it is covered. Allow the wheel to dry for several hours before using it. Small parts can be polished with a hand polisher and small, specially shaped wheels (Fig. 21-5).

Polishing with coated abrasives

Coated abrasives are available in belt, disk, sheet, and drum forms. Abrasive grains are adhered to cloth or fiber backings to provide a durable polishing surface. Flexible abrasive belts operate around two or three pulleys (Fig. 21-6). These belts are covered with an aluminum oxide abrasive for use on

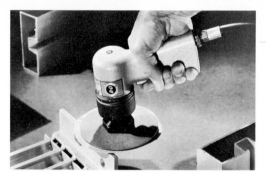

Fig. 21-7 A polishing disk is handy for rounding edges and corners. (Black & Decker Company)

Fig. 21-6 An abrasive belt can be used for polishing metal. (Baldor Company)

the belt in the areas between the pulleys. Apply even pressure as you work the piece back and forth. Polishing disks, sheets, and drums are also used (Fig. 21-7).

 QUESTIONS

1. What safety rule should always be followed when machine polishing?
2. How is abrasive material attached to abrasive cloth?
3. What is a polishing compound?
4. In what forms are coated abrasives available?

 EXTRA CREDIT

Make a report on the method of manufacturing one of the two artificial abrasives. The manufacturers will send you bulletins giving you this information.

steel or with silicon carbide for use on non-ferrous metals. To do the polishing, hold the work on the underside of the sheet or against

Unit 22
Cutting Threads

Threaded fasteners are used to join parts semipermanently. This joining system is used in many products. For example, the

axle on a bicycle is held to the fork with nuts. This feature makes it possible to remove the wheel to repair a tire.

A **thread** is a helical, or spirallike, cut on the inside of a hole or the outside of a rod or pipe (Fig. 22-1). Threads are used to assemble parts; transmit, and pass along, motion; and make adjustments.

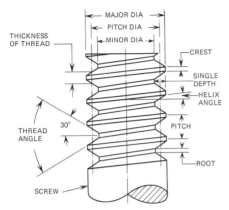

Fig. 22-1 Parts of a customary thread.

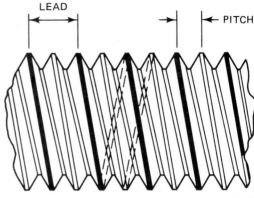

Fig. 22-2 The difference between pitch and lead for a double thread.

Screw-thread terms and definitions

1. An **internal thread** is a screw thread cut on the inside of a hole, as in a nut.

2. An **external thread** is a screw thread cut around the outside surface of a rod or pipe, such as a bolt.

3. The **major diameter,** sometimes called the *outside diameter,* is the largest diameter of a screw thread.

4. The **minor diameter,** sometimes called the *root diameter,* is the smallest diameter of a screw thread.

5. The **pitch diameter** is the diameter of an imaginary cylinder. This cylinder is of such size that its surface would pass through the screw-thread forms at the level where the width of the forms equals the width of the spaces between the forms. This definition holds true for straight threads.

The pitch diameter determines thread size in the customary system. For metric threads, size is found by gaging.

6. The **crest** is the top intersection of the two sides of a screw thread.

7. The **root** is the bottom intersection of the sides of two adjacent, or neighboring, screw-thread forms.

8. The **axis** of a thread is a line running lengthwise through the center of the material on which the thread is formed.

9. The **depth** of a thread is the distance between the crest and the root on a line that is at right angles to the axis of the thread.

10. The **thread angle** is the angle formed by the sides of two adjacent screw-thread forms.

11. The **pitch** is the distance from a point on one screw-thread form to the corresponding point on the next form. Pitch in inches is equal to 1 divided by the number of threads per inch. For example, a screw with 10 threads per inch has a pitch of 1/10 inch. Pitch for metric threads is given in millimeters.

12. Lead is the distance a screw will move into a nut in one complete turn (Fig. 22-2).

Forms of threads

The *American National thread system,* based on customary units, is the most common one in the United States (Fig. 22-3). In this system, the sides are at an angle of 60 degrees, and the crest and root are flat. The two common series are as follows:

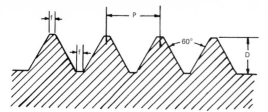

Fig. 22-3 American National thread form; *P* is the pitch, *f* is the width of the root and crest, and *D* is the single depth of thread. The ISO metric thread has the same thread form, but it is not interchangeable with customary threads.

1. *National Coarse* (NC), which has threads in sizes from 1 to 12 and from 1/4 to 4 inches, is for general-purpose work.

2. *National Fine* (NF), which has threads in sizes from 0 to 12 and 1/4 to 1 1/4

inches, is used for precision assemblies like automotive and aircraft engines.

Below 1/4 inch, taps and dies are marked by a gage number corresponding to the machine screw size (Table 22-1). For example, the next size smaller than 1/4-inch National Coarse is 12-24. This does not mean 12/24 inch. It means that the tap or die is for a machine screw made from stock with a No. 12 gage diameter and that there are 24 threads per inch.

Taps and dies are specified as follows:

1. 8-32 NC for a hole. This means that you need a tap made for a No. 8 machine screw that has 32 threads per inch, which is the National Coarse series.

2. 1/4-28 NF for a rod. This means that you must use a 1/4-inch die that will cut 28 threads per inch, which is the National Fine series.

Table 22-1
Thread Series

American National Fine (NF)			American National Coarse (NC)		
Size of tap	Threads per in.	Tap drill	Size of tap	Threads per in.	Tap drill
#4	48	43	#4	40	43
#5	44	37	#5	40	38
#6	40	33	#6	32	36
#8	36	29	#8	32	29
#10	32	21	#10	24	25
#12	28	14	#12	24	16
1/4	28	3	1/4	20	7
5/16	24	I	5/16	18	F
3/8	24	Q	3/8	16	5/16
7/16	20	25/64	7/16	14	U
1/2	20	29/64	1/2	13	27/64
9/16	18	33/64	9/16	12	31/64
5/8	18	37/64	5/8	11	17/32
3/4	16	11/16	3/4	10	21/32
7/8	14	13/16	7/8	9	49/64
1	14	15/16	1	8	7/8

Tap drill based on 75 percent full thread.

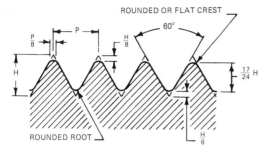

Fig. 22-4 Unified thread.

In 1948, Great Britain, Canada, and the United States agreed on a thread form that is very similar to the American National system. It is called the *Unified system.*

The two most common thread series are Unified Fine (UNF) and Unified Coarse (UNC) (Fig. 22–4). These series have a 60-degree angle thread. The crest of the external thread may be flat or rounded. The root of the external thread is rounded either on purpose or as a result of a worn tool. The internal thread has a flat crest and rounded root. This makes it possible to interchange these series with the American National series.

The *Acme screw thread* is a heavy-duty thread with a thread angle of 29 degrees. It is used for producing movement on machine tools and the like (Fig. 22–5).

American Standard pipe threads come in three series. The most common is the taper pipe thread (NPT), 3/4 inch per foot (Fig. 22–6). You will find that a 1/8-inch

pipe tap is about the same size as a 3/8-inch National Fine or National Coarse tap. This tap requires a letter R tap drill. Most electrical connections are made to fit this size.

Metric threads are designated much like the American National and Unified systems. They are similar in appearance, and similar gages are used to check them (Fig. 22–7). However, metric threads are not interchangeable with Unified threads, as their outside diameters and pitches are sized in millimeters. A typical designation for a metric thread is M5 $\times$ 0.8–C. In this example:

M = **the thread symbol for the International Organization for Standardization (ISO)**
5 = **the diameter in millimeters**
0.8 = **the thread pitch in millimeters**
C = **the class of fit, or tightness**

There are two classes of fit for metric threads: *general purpose* and *close fit.* The grade designation for general purpose is 6g for external threads and 6H for internal threads. These grades are comparable to Unified thread classes 2A and 2B, respectively. The external thread grade for close fit is 5g 6g. The internal thread grade is 6H, the same as for general purpose. If a thread symbol does

Fig. 22-6 Taper pipe thread.

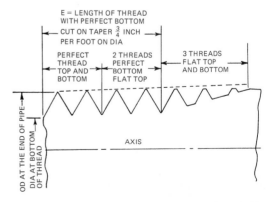

Fig. 22-5 Acme thread.

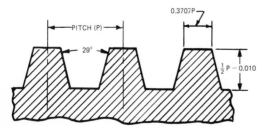

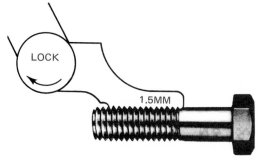

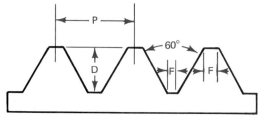

Fig. 22-7 Metric threads. A screw-pitch gage and ISO profiles are shown. (The L. S. Starrett Company)

not have any designation after the pitch, it is a general-purpose thread. For close fit, the capital letter C is used after the pitch, as shown in the example above. The complete ISO metric thread standards include three pitch series: *coarse, fine,* and *constant.* Metric countries around the world use 57 different combinations of pitches and diameters in the *fine* and *coarse* series. The United States, however, has decided to use only 25 diameter-pitch combinations. The diameters in these combinations range in size from 1.6 mm (about 1/16 inch) to 100 mm (about 4 inches). Spark plugs have always had ISO metric threads in the constant-pitch series.

Thread cutting is identical for both the customary and metric systems. Tap-drill sizes can be found on the ISO metric thread chart in Table 22-2.

Measuring the diameter and pitch of threads

The diameter of a thread is measured with a *hole gage* or a *micrometer.* There are two common ways of measuring pitch. For customary threads, place a customary rule along the threads. Count the number of

Table 22-2
ISO Metric Threads

Diameter	Pitch	Tap drill	Diameter	Pitch	Tap drill
M 1.6	0.35	1.25	M 20	2.5	17.50
M 2	0.40	1.60	M 24	3.0	21.00
M 2.5	0.45	2.05	M 30	3.5	26.50
M 3	0.50	2.50	M 36	4.0	32.00
M 3.5	0.60	2.90	M 42	4.5	37.50
M 4	0.70	3.30	M 48	5.0	43.00
M 5	0.80	4.20	M 56	5.5	50.50
M 6	1.00	5.00	M 64	6.0	58.00
M 8	1.25	6.75	M 72	6.0	66.00
M 10	1.50	8.50	M 80	6.0	74.00
M 12	1.75	10.25	M 90	6.0	84.00
M 14	2.00	12.00	M 100	6.0	94.00
M 16	2.00	14.00			

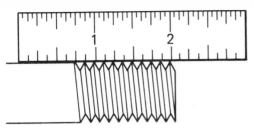

Fig. 22-8 A simple method for finding the number of threads per inch with a steel rule. Notice that there are eight threads per inch.

Fig. 22-9 A screw plate. This is a group of the more common sizes of taps and dies. (Morse Twist Drill & Machine Company)

Fig. 22-10 Three styles of taps: (A) taper, (B) plug, (C) bottoming.

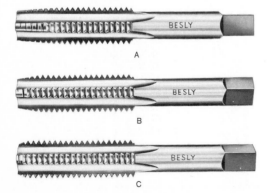

A

B

C

grooves in 1 inch (Fig. 22-8). This will be the pitch. For metric threads, place a metric rule along the threads, and check the pitch in millimeters. This method is difficult, however. A simpler way to find the pitch for metric threads is to use a *screw-pitch gage* of the proper type. This gage consists of a group of thin blades. Each blade has sawlike teeth that equal standard threads cut along one edge. These blades are stamped with the pitch in millimeters. Try several blades against the screw thread until one fits exactly. There are also customary screw-pitch gages stamped in threads per inch.

Cutting threads

Threads are cut at the bench with taps and dies. A **tap** is a hardened steel tool with a threaded portion. It is used for cutting internal threads. This is called **tapping.** A **die** is a tool used to cut external threads. This is called **die cutting.** A **screw plate** is a set of taps and dies of the most common sizes (Fig. 22-9).

Taps

A tap is a hard, brittle tool. It is turned with a special wrench that is placed on a square at the end of the shank. Hand taps come in three styles: *taper, plug,* and *bottoming* (Fig. 22-10). When cutting threads completely through a hole, only a taper tap is needed. When cutting threads to the bottom of a blind, or closed, hole, the taper tap is used first, then the plug tap, and finally the bottoming tap (Fig. 22-11). On a customary tap, the diameter and the number of threads per inch are stamped on the shank. For example, if it is stamped 1/2-13 NC, it means that the thread is 1/2 inch in diameter, there are 13 threads per inch, and it is an American National coarse thread. A metric tap shows diameter and pitch in millimeters, as in, for example, the legend M6×1. Small

138

OPEN   PARTLY OPEN   CLOSED

Fig. 22-11 Three holes that show the use of taps. For an open hole, use a taper tap. For a partly open hole, use both a taper tap and a plug tap.

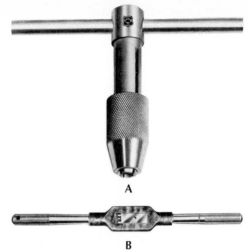

A

B

Fig. 22-12 (A) T-handle tap wrench, (B) bar tap wrench. (Standard Tool Company)

taps are held in a T-handle tap wrench. Larger sizes are held in a bar tap wrench (Fig. 22–12).

Dies

A die is held in a **diestock** (Fig. 22–13). Diestocks usually have a guide to help get the workpiece started square. There are three main kinds of dies (Fig. 22–14). The most common is the *adjustable split die*. Its pitch diameter can be adjusted by (1) three screws in the diestock, one entering the split to make it larger and two on either side to make it smaller; and (2) a setscrew in the die to change its size. The size is stamped on the front of the die.

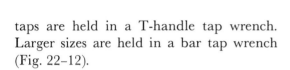

Fig. 22-13 Diestock.

The *adjustable two-piece die* has two parts that fit into a special diestock. A *solid rethreading die* is sometimes used.

Fig. 22-14 Three kinds of dies: (A) round adjustable split die, (B) adjustable two-piece die, (C) solid rethreading die.

A   B   C

Cutting internal threads

1. Determine the thread size and pitch needed. Select the correct tap drill. For customary-sized threads, look at a tap-drill chart (see Table 22-1). Suppose, for example, that you need a tap drill for an 8–32 NC tap. The table calls for a No. 29 drill. If number or letter drills are not available, use the closest fractional drill. In this case, it would be 9/64. Another way of finding what customary-sized tap drill you need is to subtract the pitch of one thread from the tap's diameter. For example, to find the tap-drill size for a 3/4–16 NF, subtract 1/16 from 3/4:

$$12/16 - 1/16 = 11/16 \text{ inch}$$

The tap drill cuts a hole slightly larger than the minor diameter of the thread. The tap-drill sizes given in Table 22-1 produce a thread 75 percent of full-thread depth. It is only 5 percent weaker than a 100 percent thread.

To find a tap drill for a metric thread, simply subtract the pitch from the diameter. For example, for a tap labeled M6×1, the right drill would be 6 minus 1, or a 5-mm drill (see Table 22-2).

2. Lay out the location for the hole, and drill it carefully.

3. Choose the correct tap, and fasten it in the tap wrench.

4. Clamp the workpiece firmly in a vise, with the hole in a vertical position, if possible.

5. Insert the tap in the hole. Grasp the tap wrench with one hand directly over the tap. Apply some pressure to it to turn it.

6. Check to see that the tap is at right angles to the workpiece. Once the tap is started, you need not apply pressure. It feeds itself into the hole.

7. Apply a little cutting oil to the tap, and turn it clockwise (Fig. 22-15). Every turn or so, reverse the direction a quarter

Fig. 22-15 Cutting internal threads with a hand tap.

turn or less to free the chips. Never force a tap. If it sticks, back it out a little. It can easily be broken.

8. Remove the tap by backing it out. Sometimes, it may stick. If it does, work it back and forth before removing it.

9. Check the threaded hole. Is it a good, clean-cut, sharp thread? Are the threads cut to the correct depth?

10. In cutting a thread in a blind hole, you must be especially careful as the tap nears the bottom. Remove the tap quite often to clean out the chips. If you fail to do this, the tap will not reach the bottom. After using a taper tap, follow with a plug tap and then a bottoming tap.

Cutting external threads

1. Grind a slight bevel on the end of the rod or pipe to get the die started more easily (Fig. 22-16).

2. Fasten the die in the diestock, with the side with the size to the top or away from the guide. The die has tapered teeth that should start the threading.

Fig. 22-16 Grind a bevel on the end of a rod or pipe before cutting an external thread with the hand die.

3. If necessary, put in a guide sleeve, or adjust the guide so that it just clears the workpiece.

4. Clamp the workpiece in a vise in either a vertical or a horizontal position.

5. Place the die over the end.

6. Cup your hand over the die, and turn to start it.

7. Apply some cutting oil when cutting steel.

8. Turn the die clockwise about two turns and then back about one turn (Fig. 22–17).

9. After the thread is cut to the right length, remove the die.

10. Try the threaded rod or pipe in the threaded hole or nut. If the thread binds, close the die slightly by turning the setscrew. Recut the thread.

Pipe threads

Pipe threads are used for joining pipes that carry liquids or gases. The thread most used is the American Standard Taper Pipe Thread (NPT). It has the same form as the American National thread, but it tapers by

Fig. 22–17 Cutting external threads on a rod. A die and a diestock are being used.

3/4 inch per foot. Pipe taps and dies are marked to correspond to pipe sizes. But since these sizes are larger than their fractional markings indicate (Table 22–3), so are the pipe taps and dies. For example, a 1/8-inch (3-mm) pipe tap is much larger than 1/8 inch (3-mm). It is roughly equal to a 3/8-inch (9.5-mm) UNC tap (Fig. 22–18). For most pipe work, only the external thread needs to be cut since the fittings are already threaded. Pipe is first cut to length with a hacksaw or pipe cutter. Then a tapered

Table 22–3
Pipe Threads

Pipe diameters		Actual outside	Threads per inch	Tap-drill size
Nominal size	Actual inside			
1/8	0.270	0.405	27	11/32
1/4	0.364	0.540	18	7/16
3/8	0.494	0.675	18	19/32
1/2	0.623	0.840	14	23/32
3/4	0.824	1.050	14	15/16
1	1.048	1.315	11-1/2	1-5/32
1-1/4	1.380	1.660	11-1/2	1-1/2
1-1/2	1.610	1.900	11-1/2	1-23/32
2	2.067	2.375	11-1/2	2-3/16
2-1/2	2.468	2.875	8	2-5/8

Fig. 22-18   A pipe tap.

Fig. 22-19   Using a pipe reamer. (The Ridge Tool Company)

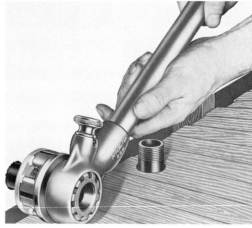

Fig. 22-20   An adjustable pipe die. (The Ridge Tool Company)

reamer is used to remove the burr on the inside of the pipe (Fig. 22-19).

Pipe dies are made so that one size can cut a range of pipe threads (Fig. 22-20). For example, one size can be used to cut threads from 1/2 inch (13 mm) through 3/4 inch (19 mm). On most die heads, the dies can be removed and reversed for cutting threads close to a wall.

Industrial threading and tapping

In industry, machines are used to produce screw threads on cylindrical surfaces. Threading is performed on external surfaces and tapping on internal.

Threading is done with machines by four general methods: cutting on a lathe, die chasing, grinding, and rolling. All can produce various external thread shapes.

Cutting on a lathe is done by using a single-point cutting tool shaped to match the thread to be produced (Fig. 22-21). Automatic controls feed the tool along the turning workpiece at the proper rate to make a uniform spiral cut. Several cuts along the same path are needed to finish the thread.

Die chasing is done with a hollow die having internal cutters, similar to that used for hand threading. A typical die head is shown in Fig. 22-22. The end of the workpiece is placed against the opening in the die head. Either the die or the workpiece is rotated as

Fig. 22-21   Cutting on a lathe.

Fig. 22-22 A die head.

the other remains stationary. The process is the same as screwing a nut onto a bolt except that the die cuts threads as it or the workpiece turns. The die has a series of cutting edges. Each edge "chases" the preceding edge along the same path so that the thread is cut deeper.

Die chasing can be done on a lathe by attaching the die to the spindle of the machine, clamping the workpiece in the chuck, and mounting the die on the tailstock. Special threading machines similar to lathes are also used.

The *grinding* of threads is done with a grinding wheel shaped to match the thread contour desired on the workpiece. Otherwise, it is like surface and cylindrical grinding. Thread grinding can be done by using table or wheel motion to produce a shaped path along the surface of the workpiece (Fig. 22-23).

Bolts and screws made by cold heading, and extrusion are usually threaded by *rolling*. The rolling of threads is entirely a forming process. No metal is cut from the piece.

Thread rolling is most often performed by rolling the workpiece between two flat dies (Fig. 22-24). The faces of the two dies are cut with the pattern of the thread to be formed. The space between them is less than the diameter of the unthreaded bolt or screw. One die does not move while the other one moves over it. As the fastener is rolled, metal is forced into the grooves of the dies to form the threads.

Threads are also rolled by using three rotating, cylindrical dies with threads cut in their surfaces (Fig. 22-25). They are mounted so that each almost touches the other two, a triangular arrangement similar to a three-roll bender. The fastener is inserted into the space between the three dies. The rotating dies form the threads.

Tapping is the most common method of machining internal threads. It is done with a

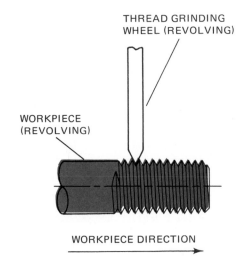

Fig. 22-23 Thread grinding.

Fig. 22-24 Thread rolling between flat dies.

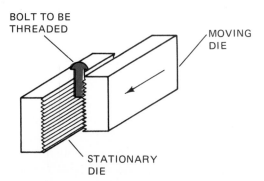

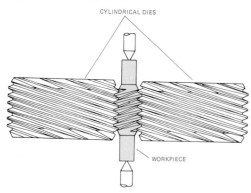

CYLINDRICAL DIES

WORKPIECE

Fig. 22-25 Thread rolling between cylindrical dies. Three dies are used; one has been removed to make this illustration clearer.

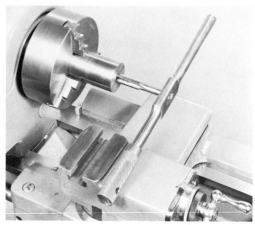

Fig. 22-26 Tapping internal threads on a lathe.

cylindrical tap that has cutting edges shaped like threads around its surface. Either the tap or the workpiece is rotated as the tap is fed into the hole or into the end of a tubular part. Machines used for tapping include drill presses, lathes, and special machines similar to drill presses (Fig. 22-26).

 QUESTIONS ▬▬▬▬▬

1. What is a thread?
2. Define the screw-thread terms *pitch* and *lead.*
3. What thread system is usually used in the United States?
4. What is the measuring unit for the diameters and pitches of metric threads?

5. What is a simple way to find the pitch of a metric thread?
6. What are the three kinds of hand taps?
7. What type of die is most common?
8. Should you apply pressure when starting a tap? After starting a tap?
9. To get a die started easily, what should you do to the end of a rod or pipe?
10. What is the most commonly used kind of pipe thread?
11. Name four methods of industrial threading.

 EXTRA CREDIT ▬▬▬▬▬

1. Write a report on the different uses for these threads: National Fine, Acme, NPT.
2. Write a report on industrial methods of threading.

Unit 23
Assembling with Metal Fasteners

There are many fasteners you can use to assemble metal projects. Rivets are used to put a project together permanently.

Threaded fasteners such as bolts or screws are used when the project may need to be taken apart or adjusted.

Rivets and riveting tools

A **rivet** is a permanent fastener with a head and a shank. Rivets for assembling mild-steel or wrought-metal projects are made of soft steel, sometimes called *soft iron.* They are available with flat, round, oval, or countersunk heads, in diameters from 1/16 to 3/8 inch (1.6 to 10 mm), and in lengths from 1/14 to 3 inches (6 to 76 mm) (Fig. 23–1, Table 23–1). The most common are the 1/8- and 3/16-inch (3- and 5-mm) round-head or flathead 1-inch (25-mm) rivets. If the project is made of copper, brass, or aluminum, choose nonferrous rivets of the same or contrasting metal. The most common size for small art-metal projects is the 1/8-inch (3-mm) roundhead rivet.

A *rivet set* or a *riveting plate* protects the roundhead rivet as it is set. Rivet sets come in various sizes with cone-shaped holes that fit the rivet heads tightly.

Assembling with rivets

1. Select the rivets. If the rivet is to be part of the design, a roundhead may be chosen. A flathead should be selected if the assembly is not meant to be noticed. If there are to be roundheads on both sides of the project, the rivets must be long enough to go through both pieces and extend beyond by one and one-half times the length of the diameter (Fig. 23–2). If the back is to be flush, the rivet must extend by only a small amount, just enough to fill the countersunk holes.

Table 23–1
Common Rivet Sizes
(Shank Diameters)

Customary (in.)	Nearest ISO metric equivalent (mm)
1/16	1.6
1/8	3
5/32	4
3/16	5
1/4	6
5/16	8
3/8	10

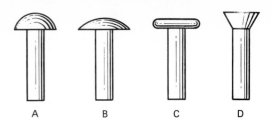

Fig. 23–1 Common rivet shapes: (A) roundhead, (B) ovalhead, (C) flathead, (D) countersunk.

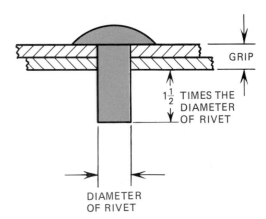

Fig. 23–2 A rivet that extends through both workpieces. About one and one-half times the diameter of the rivet is needed when forming a roundhead.

2. Lay out the location of the rivet, and drill the hole.

3. Countersink if necessary. On most projects, at least the back will be flush, but when countersunk rivets are used, both sides must be countersunk.

4. Check the rivet for length. Cut off any excess with a saw or with bolt clippers.

5. Insert the rivet in the hole. Be sure that the two pieces are pressed firmly together with no burr separating them. If the rivets are roundhead, protect the head by holding it in a rivet set or riveting plate (Fig. 23–3).

6. To round off the shank, strike it first with the flat of the hammer to fill up the

145

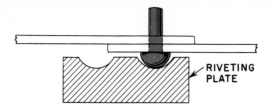

Fig. 23-3 A riveting plate or rivet set should be used to protect the head of the rivet.

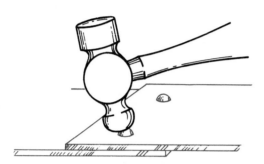

Fig. 23-4 Use the face of the hammer to flatten the shank and then round it off with the peen of the hammer.

hole. Then round it off with glancing blows (Fig. 23-4). If the back is to be flat, strike the rivet with the peen of the hammer to fill in the countersunk hole. Then finish by striking it with the flat of the hammer.

7. To rivet together curved parts or scrolls that cannot be held against a flat surface, proceed as follows:

a. Cut off a piece of scrap rod of a size that will slip into the curve under the rivet hole.

b. Drill a cone-shaped hole about the size of the rivet head toward the center of the rod.

c. Place the rivet head in the hole in the rod, and do the riveting as before (Fig. 23-5). It may be necessary to open the scroll slightly to complete the riveting.

8. Check the riveting job. Is the head damaged? Did you bend your project in riv-

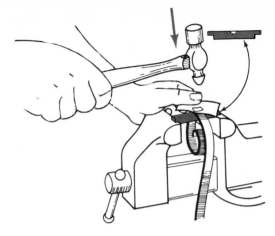

Fig. 23-5 Riveting a base to a scroll. A cone-shaped hole has been drilled in the small metal rod that supports the rivet.

eting it? Is the second head misshapen? If the back is flush, is the surface rough? Are the two parts too loosely fastened together?

Threaded fasteners

A **screw** is an externally threaded fastener. A **bolt** is a screw used with a nut. Both are measured by the diameter and length of the body. The head is not included in the length except in the case of flathead and ovalhead screws. Unfinished or semifinished screws are rolled, pressed, or punched out of steel. Finished screws are cut on special screw machines. Threaded fasteners are made of many different metals, such as steel, brass, and aluminum. They are finished in many ways, such as bluing, plating, or oxide coating. These finishes protect them from rusting. Some of the fasteners generally used in the metal shop are described below.

Machine screws are made in many different head shapes and are usually of steel or brass (Fig. 23-6). Customary-sized ones range from number 0 (.060 inch) to 3/8 inch in diameter and up to 3 inches in length. They come in both UNF and UNC thread

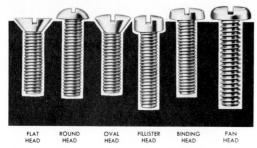

FLAT HEAD ROUND HEAD OVAL HEAD FILLISTER HEAD BINDING HEAD PAN HEAD

Fig. 23–6 Common machine-screw heads. These are also available with a Phillips head.

Fig. 23–7 A machine bolt and nut.

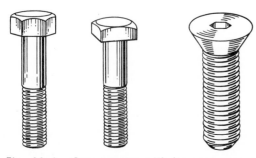

Fig. 23–8 Cap screws with hexagon and square heads. The flathead hexagon-socket type is also shown.

Fig. 23–9 Stove bolts: (A) flathead, (B) roundhead.

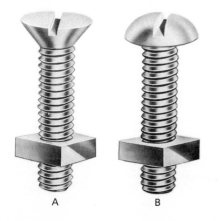

A   B

series. They are used for assembling with nuts or for joining two parts, one of which has a tapped, or threaded, hole.

Machine bolts have either hexagonal (six-sided) or square heads and are commonly used with nuts in heavy-duty assembly (Fig. 23–7). These bolts come in finished and unfinished styles and in UNF and UNC series. Common customary sizes have 1/4- to 1/2-inch diameters and 1- to 6-inch lengths.

Cap screws are available in a variety of head shapes, such as round, flat, and hexagonal, and are finished all over (Fig. 23–8). They come in both UNC and UNF series. These screws are generally used to join two parts where one part has a tapped hole. The common customary sizes range from 1/4 to 1 1/2 inches in diameter and 1/2 to 6 inches in length. They are usually made of steel.

Stove bolts are either flathead or round-head (Fig. 23–9). They have a coarse (UNC) thread. They are used with nuts to fasten metal parts. The common customary size ranges are from 1/8- to 5/16-inch diameters and 3/8- to 3-inch lengths.

Carriage bolts are used to fasten two pieces of wood or to join wood and metal (Fig. 23–10). These are commonly used in assembling farm equipment, trailers, and small buildings. They are useful because the square neck sinks into the wood, holding the bolt securely while the nut is tightened. The common customary sizes range from 1/4 to 1/2 inch in diameter. They are usually 1 to 6 inches long. These bolts are steel with a black finish.

Fig. 23–10 A carriage bolt.

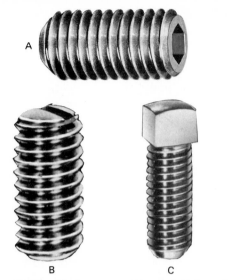

Fig. 23–11 Setscrews: (A) socket-head, (B) slotted-head, (C) square-head.

Fig. 23–12 Common washers and nuts: (A) plain or flat washer, (B) lock washer, (C) hexagon nut, (D) square nut, (E) cap nut, (F) wing nut.

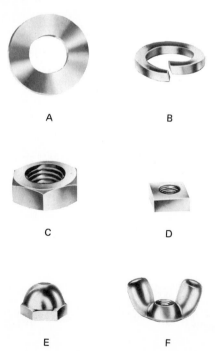

Setscrews are made in a range of head and point shapes and are used to fasten pulleys and collars to shafts (Fig. 23–11). They come in a variety of sizes according to need.

Many other threaded fasteners are available. *Nuts* and *washers* are often used with screws and bolts in fastening operations. *Cap nuts* enclose the thread for protection and appearance. *Square* and *hexagon nuts* are used for general holding jobs. *Wing nuts* are finger-tightened and are used where quick and easy assembly is needed. *Flat washers* prevent nuts from becoming loose. All these devices come in a wide range of kinds, materials, and sizes (Fig. 23–12).

Metric fasteners

Many kinds of machine screws, bolts, and nuts are available in metric sizes. Some sizes of metric machine bolts have a 12-spline head that plainly marks them as metric (Fig. 23–13). With hexagon bolts and nuts, however, it is difficult or impossible to tell the difference merely by looking. For example, the metric $M6 \times 1$ and the customary 1/4–28 UNF look almost identical.

The two are very close in diameter, but the metric fastener has about 25 threads per inch while the customary one has 28 threads per inch. Therefore, they are *not* interchangeable. The only way to tell the difference is to use a micrometer to check the diameter and a screw-pitch gage to check the pitch. Some of the larger bolts made in Europe are stamped with an M on the head to identify them as metric.

Fig. 23–13 A 12-spline head used **only** on metric fasteners.

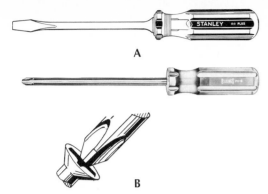

Fig. 23–14 (A) A screwdriver for slotted heads. (B) A screwdriver for recessed Phillips heads. (Stanley Tool Company; The Billings & Wilkins Tool Company)

Fig. 23–15 Pliers: (A) side-cutting, (B) groove-joint, (C) slip-joint, (D) flat-jaw, (E) long-nose, (F) diagonal.

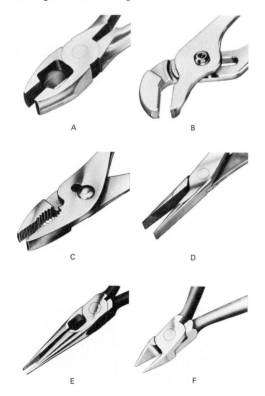

Tools for assembling with bolts, nuts, and screws

1. *Screwdrivers* are made in many diameters and lengths. The larger sizes have a square shank. This makes it possible to get extra leverage by using a wrench with the screwdriver. The blade is made for either slotted heads or for recessed (Phillips) heads (Fig. 23–14). In choosing a screwdriver, make sure that the blade fits the slot in the screw to be driven. The *offset screwdriver* is used to reach screws in out-of-the-way places.

2. *Pliers* are used to hold and grip small articles and to make adjustments (Fig. 23–15). They are not substitutes for wrenches, however, and should never be used as such. There are four common types:

    a. Slip-joint, for holding round bars and pipe and for doing general work.

    b. Side-cutting, for cutting and gripping wire to do electrical work.

    c. Long-nose, or *chain,* for getting into out-of-the-way places and for holding small parts.

    d. Diagonal, for cutting wire.

3. *Open-end* and *engineer's wrenches* are made with an opening in one or both ends (Fig. 23–16). Customary-sized ones are available with openings from 5/16 to 1 inch. The head and opening are set at an angle,

Fig. 23–16 (A) Open-end and (B) engineer's wrenches. (The Billings & Wilkins Tool Company)

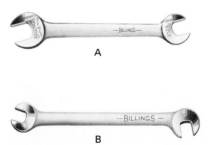

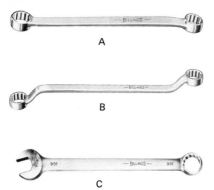

Fig. 23–17   Box wrenches: (A) 15-degree box wrench, (B) 45-degree box wrench, (C) box-and-open-end wrench. (The Billings & Wilkins Tool Company)

Fig. 23–18   An adjustable wrench.

Fig. 23–19   A monkey wrench. (The Billings & Wilkins Tool Company)

Fig. 23–20   A pipe wrench. (The Billings & Wilkins Tool Company).

Fig. 23–21   An L-socket wrench.

usually 15 or 22 1/2 degrees, to the body. This is so that the nut can be tightened in small areas. The smaller the openings, the shorter the lengths. *S-handle wrenches* have a handle bent in the shape of an S.

4. *Box wrenches* are very popular because they can fit into small places for tightening nuts. The modern box wrench is a 12-point wrench that has 12 notches around the circle for gripping the nut. The nut can be moved a short distance and then the wrench changed to another position. The box wrench is made with a straight end or with the end offset at an angle of 15 or 45 degrees to the handle. Some are made with a box wrench on one end and an open wrench on the other (Fig. 23–17). Customary-sized ones are made in sizes from 1/4 to 1 1/4 inches.

5. *Adjustable wrenches* are also very popular, since one or two sizes can take care of a wide range of bolts and nuts. One jaw is fixed. The other can be opened or closed (Fig. 23–18). An adjustable wrench should not be used in place of a box, open-end, or socket wrench.

6. *Monkey wrenches* are adjustable wrenches best used on squarehead nuts and bolts (Fig. 23–19). They also have many other uses in the shop, such as bending metal and making adjustments.

7. *Pipe wrenches* are designed for tightening pipe and rod parts. Their sharp teeth grip pipe or rod to prevent slippage when turning (Fig. 23–20).

8. *Socket wrenches* can be used to get at hard-to-reach places. One of the simplest is the L-socket wrench (Fig. 23–21). Most socket wrenches come in sets, with each socket having a 12-point grip (Fig. 23–22). The set includes an extension bar, a ratchet handle, and a swivel-joint connector. This set is ideal for the automobile mechanic.

9. *Spanner wrenches* are used to adjust or tighten nuts that have notches around the outside (Fig. 23–23).

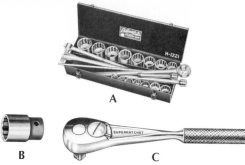

Fig. 23-22 (A) A socket set. (B) Note that each socket is notched with 12 points. (C) The ratchet wrench speeds up assembly.

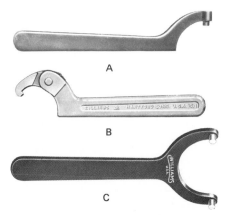

Fig. 23-23 Spanner wrenches: (A) pin, (B) adjustable-hook, (C) double-pin.

Fig. 23-24 A hexagon key set.

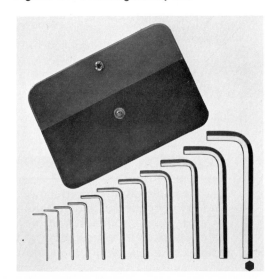

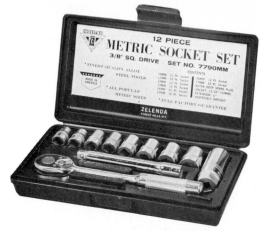

Fig. 23-25 A set of metric socket wrenches. (Zelenda Corporation)

10. *Hexagon key wrenches* are used with hexagon socket fasteners, including setscrews and cap screws (Fig. 23-24).

Metric wrenches

All styles of fixed-opening wrenches are available in metric sizes (Fig. 23-25). The size in millimeters is stamped on the wrench. It is the width of the bolthead across the flats, *not* the diameter of the bolt's threaded part. For example, an M16 bolt requires a 24-mm wrench (Table 24-2).

Table 23-2
Metric Bolts and Nuts and Matching Metric Wrench Sizes

Bolt and nut	Wrench size (mm)
M6	10
M8	13
M10	17
M12	19
M14	22
M16	24
M20	30
M22	32
M24	36

151

Hints for using assembly tools

1. Never use a screwdriver as a punch or chisel (Fig. 23–26).

2. Never use a pliers with a round-shank screwdriver. Some square-shank screwdrivers are designed for use with a wrench.

3. Always choose the wrench that fits the nut or bolt. A loose-fitting wrench will round off the corners of the head. It may cause serious injury if it slips.

4. Always pull on a wrench. Never push it, because then you cannot control it.

5. Never use a piece of pipe for added leverage. It is better to get a heavier wrench.

6. Never strike a wrench with a hammer. Sometimes, it may be absolutely necessary to tap it if a nut or bolt sticks. In those cases, be sure to use a soft-faced hammer.

Assembling with screws

1. Select the machine screw and a nut, if needed. The screw must be long enough to fasten the two pieces. If the clearance hole is drilled through, the screw should extend beyond the second piece so that a nut can be fastened to it. Usually, however, a clearance hole is drilled in the first piece, and the second hole is tapped.

2. Lay out the location of the hole, and drill the clearance hole in the first piece. This hole should be the same size as the outside diameter of the screw threads. If a flat-head screw is used, countersink the hole.

3. Drill and tap the hole in the second piece (see Unit 22). Sometimes, it is a good idea to clamp the pieces together and drill them with a tap drill. The first hole can then be enlarged to the clearance-hole size.

4. Choose the right size screwdriver so that you will not mar the screw head or the workpiece. Thread the screw into the tapped hole or nut.

Fig. 23–26 Remember, hand-tool safety depends mostly on the person who uses the tool. Knowing what a tool is designed to do and how to use it properly is the key. So think safety and avoid surprises. (Snap-on Tool Company)

 QUESTIONS

1. What different shapes can rivet heads have?
2. How are screws and bolts measured?
3. What is a machine screw used for? A setscrew?
4. How can you tell the difference between a metric hexagon bolt and a customary one?
5. What is a box wrench used for? A monkey wrench?
6. How can you tell the size of a metric wrench?
7. What will a loose-fitting wrench do to a bolt?

 EXTRA CREDIT

Make a sample display board showing some of the common metal fasteners. You can obtain samples from your school shop or from your hardware dealer.

SECTION 3

SHEET METAL

Unit 24
Introduction to Sheet Metal

There are about 65,000 skilled sheet-metal workers in the United States today. Many additional thousands work with sheet metal in factories producing a wide range of goods (Fig. 24–1). These factory workers are mainly assembly-line operatives, who perform only a few specific operations.

Skilled sheet-metal construction workers make and install a variety of sheet-metal products, including roofing, siding, storefronts, and ducts (Fig. 24–2). The ducts are

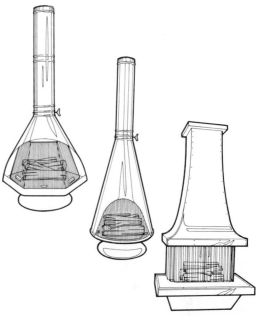

Fig. 24–2 These free-standing fireplaces are constructed of sheet metal.

Fig. 24–1 These employees in the aerospace industry are working with sheet aluminum. (Reynolds Metals)

used in ventilating, air-conditioning, and heating systems.

In duct work, the sheet-metal worker lays out and plans the job and determines the size and type of sheet metal to be used. Sheet-metal workers cut the metal with hand snips, power-driven shears, and other cutting tools. They shape the metal with a variety of machines, hammers, and anvils. They then weld, bolt, rivet, solder, or cement the seams and joints.

153

Table 24-1
Sheet-Metal Operations

Cutting operations	Purpose	Tools used
shearing	cut to size, separate metal	tin snips, hand and power shears, squaring shears, notcher, circle shears
punching	make holes	hollow punch, solid punch
Forming operations	**Purpose**	**Tools used**
bending	create angular, cylindrical, and conical shapes	forming stakes, hand seamer, bar folder, cornice brake, box-and-pan brake, press brake, forming rolls
turning	produce functional shapes on circular pieces	rotary machine with beading, crimping, wiring, burring, and turning rolls
Fastening operations	**Purpose**	**Tools used**
riveting	produce a permanent joint	rivet set, pop-rivet tool
threaded fasteners	produce a semipermanent joint	sheet-metal screws, self-tapping screws
seaming	produce a permanent mechanical joint, such as grooved, standing, folded, or double seams	hand groover, forming stakes, rotary machine
soft soldering	produce a permanent watertight joint	soldering copper, torch, gun, furnace, bunsen burner
gluing	produce a permanent watertight joint	contact cement, epoxy cement, clamps

Tools

To work with sheet metal, you must learn to use a number of hand tools and machines. You must also learn tool and machine safety. In this section, you will be learning to use hand tools such as hand snips and punches; layout tools; special equipment for bending, cutting, and seaming; and equipment for soldering and welding to make joints. The skills you learn will also help you at home. You can use them, for example, for the many small repair jobs to be done on home appliances, fixtures, and automobiles.

Materials

Sheet metal ranging from a few thousandths of an inch to one inch (25 mm) in thickness is made from both ferrous and nonferrous metals. In the school shop, most of the metals you use will be between 20 and 25 gage thick. The most common metals are in brass, aluminum, mild steel, and copper sheets. Some of these will be embossed or have etched patterns in them. Some sheet steels may have coatings of zinc (galvanized sheet) or black iron oxide.

Sheet-metal work calls for extra caution to prevent accidents. Each piece of sheet metal as it is being cut and handled is a potentially dangerous cutting tool. The razor-sharp burrs that appear on metal as it is cut can easily slice into your finger and produce a painful scratch or cut. Be very careful in working with sheet metal. Remove dangerous burrs or snags with a hand file.

Processes

Some of the more important sheet-metal processes you will be learning about in this unit are shown in Table 24–1. These operations must be mastered in order to produce satisfactory work. They are widely used in manufacturing. You can also use them to make a number of interesting projects, such as mailboxes, storage cabinets, toolboxes, bookends, and containers of many kinds.

? QUESTIONS

1. List some of the things sheet-metal construction workers make and install.
2. List three kinds of tools that sheet-metal workers use.
3. Name four metals commonly used in sheet metal.
4. Name three main groups of sheet-metal operations.

✓ EXTRA CREDIT

Find out all you can about the sheet-metal worker, and give a report to the class. Use the **Occupational Outlook Handbook** (U.S. Government Printing Office, Washington, D.C.) and other sources to get this information.

Unit 25
Developing Patterns

Before a sheet-metal project can be made, a pattern must be developed. A **pattern,** or **stretchout,** is a flat shape laid out on a piece of sheet metal prior to cutting. If patterning is done correctly, the metal can then be formed into a three-dimensional object (Fig. 25–1). A stretchout can be drawn directly on the metal. Most often, however, the pattern is first developed on paper, then transferred to the metal. This can be done by placing the paper pattern over the metal with a piece of carbon paper between them and tracing. However, in sheet metal, the usual practice is to place the pattern over the

metal and prick-punch around the outline. If many pieces of the same kind are to be made, a **template,** or heavy pattern, is made of metal. Then this can be held firmly in place, and you can trace around it.

Hems, edges, and seams

In making a pattern, you must also make allowances for hems, edges, and seams. A **hem** is a folded edge used to improve the appearance of the work and to strengthen it. A *single hem* may be any width. In general, the heavier the metal, the wider the hem. A *double hem* is used when additional strength is needed (Fig. 25–2). Hems are made in standard fractions such as 1/4 inch (6 mm), 3/8 inch (10 mm), 1/2 inch (13 mm), and so on.

A **wired edge** is a sheet-metal edge folded around a piece of wire (Fig. 25–3).

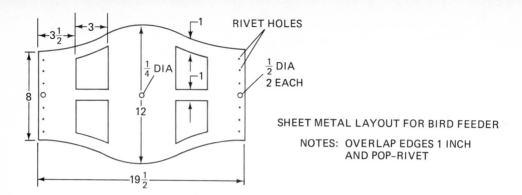

SHEET METAL LAYOUT FOR BIRD FEEDER

NOTES: OVERLAP EDGES 1 INCH
AND POP–RIVET

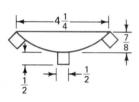

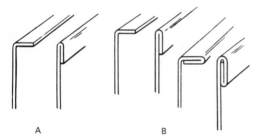

LAYOUT FOR END PIECES—2 EACH

NOTES: FOLD TABS BACK AND
SPOT WELD

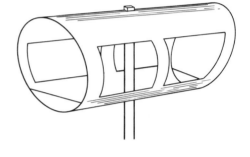

Fig. 25–1 Typical stretchout for a bird feeder. The parallel-line method for developing this is described in this unit.

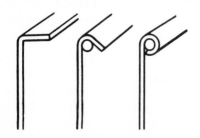

Fig. 25–2 (A) Single hem. (B) Double hem.

Fig. 25–3 A wired edge is used to strengthen the edge of metal and to improve its appearance.

The edges of such items as trays, funnels, and pails are often wired for added strength. The amount allowed for a wired edge is two and one-half times the diameter of the wire itself. For example, if the wire has a diameter of 1/8 inch (3 mm), then 5/16 inch (8 mm) is allowed for the edge.

Seams are mechanical joints between pieces of sheet metal. The common kinds of *lap seams* are plain, offset or countersunk, and inside or outside corner (see Unit 30). Lap seams are usually finished by riveting, soldering, or a combination of both. *Grooved seams* are used most often in joining two parts of a cylindrical object. There are three thicknesses of metal for the seam above the place where the two pieces join. For example, on a 1/4-inch (6 mm) seam, an allowance of 3/4 inch (19 mm) of extra metal must be made. On the layout, half this amount, or 3/8 inch (10 mm), is added to either side or end.

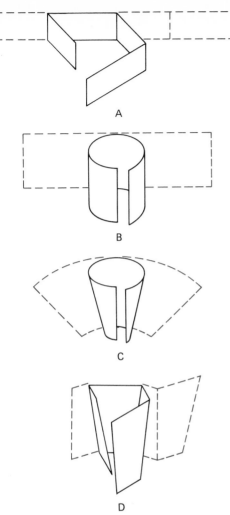

A

B

C

D

Fig. 25-4 Three kinds of pattern developments: (A) parallel-line development to make a box, (B) parallel-line development to make a cylinder, (C) radial-line development to make a cone, (D) triangulation to make a two-transition piece.

Kinds of patterns

Three kinds of pattern developments are used in sheet-metal work (Fig. 25-4):

1. *Parallel-line,* for making rectangular objects, such as boxes and trays, and cylindrical objects, such as funnels, tubes, pipes, scoops, and the like.

Fig. 25-5 The piping for this veneer dryer is a good example of triangulation and other kinds of pattern development. (Georgia-Pacific Corporation)

2. *Radial-line,* for making cone-shaped objects, such as funnels, buckets, or tapered lampshades.

3. *Triangulation,* for making transition pieces, such as the pipes that join square and round shapes (Fig. 25-5). These are commonly used in making fittings for air-conditioning and heating systems.

Making a simple layout for a box

1. Draw the square or rectangle equal to the size of the box bottom (Fig. 25-6).

2. Draw the side and ends so that they are of equal height.

3. Add material for the corner lap seam.

4. Add material for the hem.

The seams may be joined by soldering, spot welding, or riveting.

Laying out notches

Notches are laid out on a pattern to help in forming, assembling, and completing the

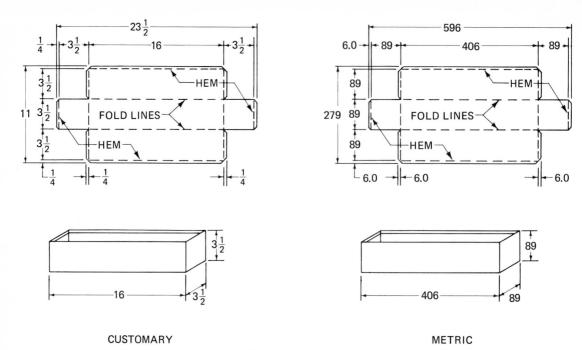

CUSTOMARY   METRIC

Fig. 25–6 A simple sheet-metal box with customary and metric dimensions is a good example of parallel-line development.

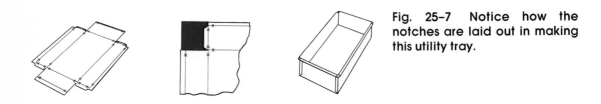

Fig. 25–7 Notice how the notches are laid out in making this utility tray.

sheet-metal object. The notches eliminate bulky excess material. A slant notch is cut at 45 degrees across the corner when you use a single hem. A V-notch is often used at the corner of the box (Fig. 25–7).

Parallel-line development of a cylinder

The stretchout of a simple can-shaped object is rectangular (Fig. 25–8). One dimension of the rectangle will equal the height of the cylinder, or can. The other dimension will be the circumference of the cylinder. The circumference rule can be used to find the circumference of any cylinder for which you know the diameter (see Fig. 9–5).

To make the pattern for the layout of a scoop or any other object that has one end shaped, follow these directions:

1. Make a top-view and a front-view drawing of the object (Fig. 25–9).

2. Divide the top into several equal parts. The more parts, the more accurate the stretchout.

3. Draw light vertical lines from the top view to the front view. Number the lines. For clarity, only even numbers are shown.

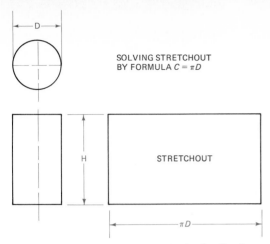

SOLVING STRETCHOUT
BY FORMULA $C = \pi D$

STRETCHOUT

πD

Fig. 25-8 Developing a cylinder by finding the circumference.

4. Make a stretchout to the right of the front view. Draw light, vertical, equally spaced lines. Number them in the same way as those on the top view.

5. Locate line 1 on the front view, and project it to line 1 on the stretchout. Do this for all the other lines.

6. Join the points with a French curve.

7. Add a certain amount on the ends for a grooved seam.

Radial-line development

To develop the pattern for a funnel, do the following (Fig. 25–10):

1. Get a piece of paper large enough to make the flat-pattern layout.

2. Draw a front view of the funnel to full size. Continue the lines that indicate the tapered sides of the body and the spout until they intersect, or cross, at points a and a'.

3. Draw semicircle bc at the large end of the body.

4. Divide this semicircle into an even

Fig. 25-9 The development for a scoop.

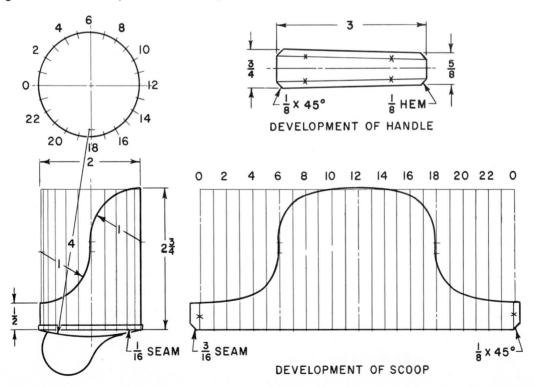

DEVELOPMENT OF HANDLE

DEVELOPMENT OF SCOOP

159

number of equal segments, or parts, perhaps 16.

5. Make a flat-pattern layout for the body of the funnel as follows:

    a. With the distance *ab* as a radius, draw an arc that will be the outside edge of the flat-pattern layout.

    b. With the distance *ad,* draw another arc using the same center.

    c. Space off twice the number of segments that are on the semicircle *bc* along the outer edge. Draw a line to the center at either end of the arc to form the flat pattern *fghj*. This will become the top cone of the funnel.

    d. Add an allowance two and one-half times the diameter of the wire along the outer edge for making the wired edge.

    e. Add an allowance on both sides of the pattern for making a grooved seam.

6. Follow the identical procedure for making a flat-pattern layout for the spout.

Sheet-metal project layout

When you have selected a sheet-metal project, you should make a layout of each part on paper. Then assemble all the paper layouts on a sheet of metal to determine how large a sheet you will need (Fig. 25–11). This will save you time, material, and money.

Fig. 25–10 Radial-line development of a funnel.

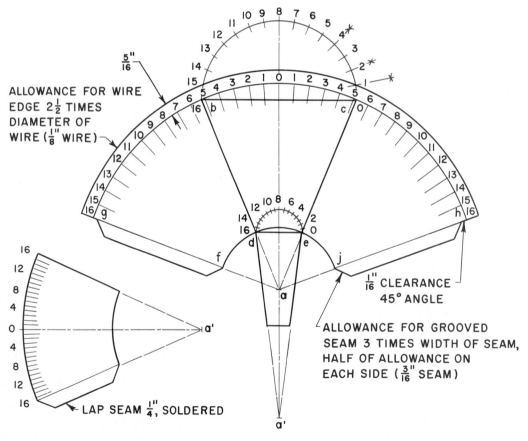

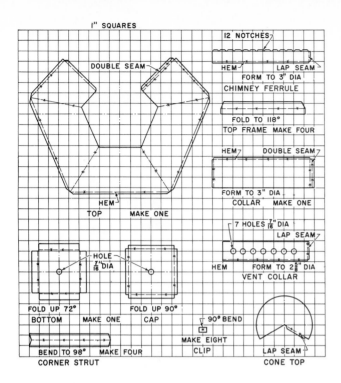

I" SQUARES

12 NOTCHES

DOUBLE SEAM

HEM — LAP SEAM
FORM TO 3" DIA
CHIMNEY FERRULE

FOLD TO 118°
TOP FRAME MAKE FOUR

HEM — DOUBLE SEAM

FORM TO 3" DIA
COLLAR   MAKE ONE

HEM

TOP   MAKE ONE

7 HOLES $\frac{7}{16}$" DIA
LAP SEAM

HOLE
$\frac{7}{16}$ DIA

HEM   FORM TO $2\frac{5}{8}$" DIA
VENT COLLAR

FOLD UP 72°   FOLD UP 90°
BOTTOM   MAKE ONE   CAP

90° BEND

MAKE EIGHT
CLIP

BEND TO 98°   MAKE FOUR
CORNER STRUT

LAP SEAM
CONE TOP

Fig. 25-11 Typical sheet-metal project layout and the finished product.

? QUESTIONS

1. How is a pattern on paper usually transferred to sheet metal?
2. What is a hem? A seam?
3. How much extra metal is needed for a wired edge?
4. What type of pattern development is used for a box? A scoop? A funnel?
5. What is triangulation used for?

✓ EXTRA CREDIT

Develop a pattern for a funnel that can be used for some special purpose, such as filling fruit jars, freezer containers, or the gas tank of a power mower.

Unit 26
Cutting Sheet Metal

The sheet metal you use in the school shop usually requires some kind of cutting. Cutting metal sheets is called **shearing.** *Squaring shears* are used to cut large sheets into pieces that can be more easily handled.

Hand snips and *shears* are used to cut the workpiece to the size and shape of the pattern. In the sheet-metal industry, large machines do this shearing (Fig. 26-1).

Another kind of sheet-metal cutting is called **punching.** This is making holes in the metal. These holes are usually round, but other shapes can be cut with special dies.

In this unit, you will learn how to cut sheet metal with shears and punches.

Fig. 26-1 Industrial shearing using a power shear. (Niagara Machine & Tool Works)

Hand snips and shears

There are five basic types of hand snips and shears used in sheet-metal work (Fig. 26–2):

1. *Straight snips* are used for cutting straight lines in sheet metal that is 22 gage or thinner. They are made in different sizes, with cutting jaws from 2 to 4 1/2 inches (51 to 114 mm) long. Straight snips are also used to make outside cuts on large-diameter circles.

2. *Hawk-billed snips* are used for inside cutting of intricate work. These snips have narrow curved blades that allow you to make sharp turns without bending the metal.

3. *Aviation snips* can be used for all kinds of cutting. They are made with left, right, or universal cutting blades.

4. *Bench shears* are designed to have one handle held in a vise or bench plate while the other handle is moved up and down. They can cut sheet metal 16 gage in thickness.

5. *Double-cutting shears* have three blades used to cut around cylindrical objects, such as cans and pipes. A single blade is pushed through the metal to start the cut.

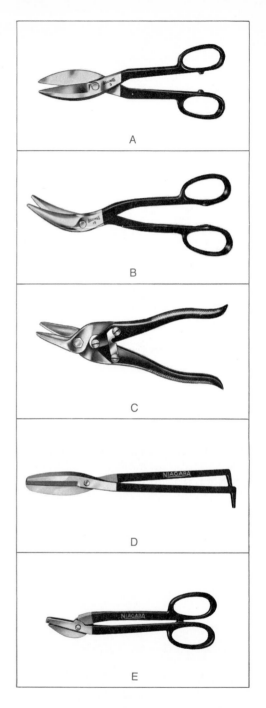

Fig. 26–2 Common hand snips and shears: (A) straight snips, (B) hawk-billed snips, (C) aviation snips, (D) bench shears, (E) double-cutting shears. (The Billings & Wilkins Company; Niagara Machine & Tool Works)

A double blade on the outside prevents the metal from twisting out of shape.

Making straight cuts

1. Select straight snips or aviation snips. Hold the sheet metal in your left hand and the snips in your right hand. Be careful of sharp edges.

2. Open the snips as far as possible, and insert the metal. Hold the straight side of the blade at right angles to the sheet.

3. Squeeze the handle firmly, and cut to about 1/4 to 1/2 inch (6 to 13 mm) from the point of the blade. Reopen the snips, and complete the cut. The edge should be even and clean. Avoid jagged, slivered cuts.

Whenever possible, cut to the right of the layout line (Fig. 26–3).

Cutting outside curves

1. Hold the metal in your left hand, and rough-cut to within about 1/8 to 1/4 inch (3 to 6 mm) of the layout line.

2. Carefully cut up to the layout line and around it, making a continuous cut. The scrap metal will tend to curl out of the way during the cutting (Fig. 26–4).

Notching

To cut notches or tabs in sheet metal, open the snips only part way, and use the portion near the point of the blade for cutting. This will prevent any cutting past the layout line (Fig. 26–5).

Punching large holes

Hollow punches are used to punch holes larger than those cut with a solid punch (Fig. 26–6). They can be used to cut holes 1/4 to 3 inches (6 to 76 mm) in diameter, in sizes varying by 1/8 inch (3 mm). You must punch or drill a hole before cutting an internal opening in sheet metal. To punch a hole:

1. Locate the hole on the sheet metal, and draw its exact size with dividers.

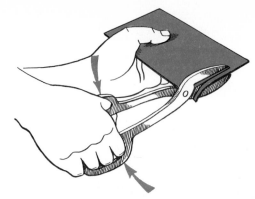

Fig. 26–3 Cutting with the straight snips. Cut at the right side of the material whenever possible. (Cut at the left side if you are left-handed.)

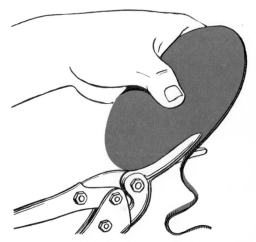

Fig. 26–4 Cutting an outside curve with aviation snips. Notice how the thin edge of metal curls away.

Fig. 26–5 When cutting notches, make certain that the blade just covers the cutting line.

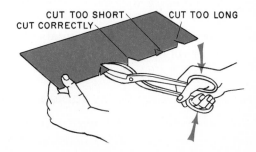

CUT TOO SHORT
CUT CORRECTLY
CUT TOO LONG

A

B

Fig. 26–6 The standard hollow punch (A) is used to cut larger holes in sheet metal. The size is stamped near the cutting edge (arrow). The spring-point hollow punch (B) is used to locate punched holes more accurately. (Niagara Machine & Tool Works)

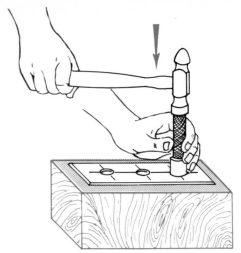

Fig. 26–7 Place the metal over end-grain hardwood or a lead block. Strike the punch firmly.

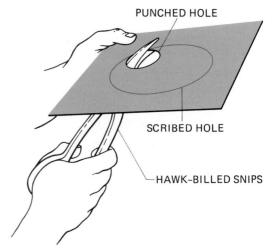

PUNCHED HOLE

SCRIBED HOLE

HAWK-BILLED SNIPS

Fig. 26–8 The punched hole permits you to start the cut.

2. Choose a punch of the correct size.

3. Place the metal over end-grain hardwood or a soft lead block (Fig. 26–7).

4. Hold the punch firmly over the layout, and strike it solidly with a heavy ball peen hammer. Try to punch the hole with one or two blows. Never tap lightly, as this makes ragged edges.

Cutting inside curves

1. Punch or drill a hole in the waste stock. You can also make this opening by cutting two slits at right angles with a cold chisel and a hammer. This hole should be large enough to allow hawk-billed snips to get started (Fig. 26–8).

2. Insert the snips from the underside. Rough out the inside opening to about 1/4 inch (6 mm) of the layout line.

3. Trim the hole to size.

Cutting with electric portable shears

Electric shears are used to cut corrugated metal sheets or sheet metal 18 gage or lighter

(Fig. 26–9). The machine will cut a minimum radius of about 1 inch (25 mm). To use it, place the metal between the cutters. Then turn on the switch, and guide the shears along the line to be cut.

Cutting with a hand ripping shear

Hand ripping shears are handy tools for ripping light-gage sheet metal (Fig. 26–10).

Fig. 26-9 Cutting metal with portable electric shears. Sheet metal up to 18 gage can be cut with this kind of shears.

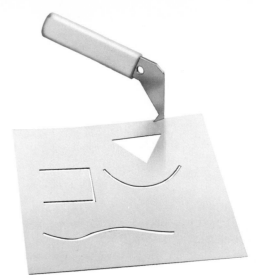

Fig. 26-10 The hand-ripping shear and typical internal cuts.

The shearing point can be inserted with a light hammer blow. Successive blows will drive the shear on a scribed line for almost any shape. A strip of metal about 3/32 inch (2.5 mm) wide is removed in this shearing operation.

Cutting with a multipurpose tool

Multipurpose tools will cut metals and many other materials (Fig. 26–11). This pistol-grip, spring-action tool comes with three tempered steel blades to do various kinds of cutting.

Cutting sheet metal by machine

Sheet metal can be cut with a number of simple machines:

Squaring shears, operated by foot, are used to square and trim large pieces of sheet metal (Fig. 26–12). The size of the machine is determined by the width of sheets it will cut. The common sizes are 30 or 36 inches (762 or 914 mm). A back gage controls the

Fig. 26-11 A multipurpose tool for cutting sheet metal, plastics, and many other materials. (Bernzomatic Corporation)

length of cut when the metal is inserted from the front. A front gage does the same for metal inserted from the back. The side gage is adjustable and is kept at right angles to the cutting blade. Sheet 18 gage or lighter can usually be cut on the squaring shears.

1. To cut long sheets, insert them from the back. To cut several pieces to the same

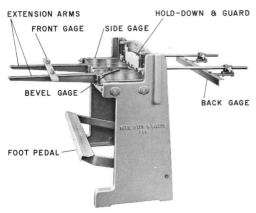

Fig. 26-12 Parts of the squaring shears. (Peck, Stow & Wilcox Corporation)

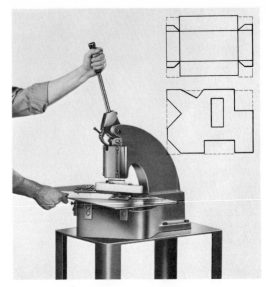

Fig. 26-13 Using a notcher for cutting tabbed corners. The insert shows the kinds of cuts that can be made on this machine.

length, set the front gage to this length. Use the graduated scale on the top of the bed for this purpose.

2. The left edge of the sheet should be firmly pressed against the left gage and the end of the sheet against the front gage.

3. Hold the sheet down on the bed with both hands. Then press the foot pedals with your foot.

 CAUTION

Keep your fingers away from the cutting blade at all times.

They will also cut tabs and notches for box corners (Figs. 26-13, 26-14). To use, just slide the workpiece up tightly against the guides, hold firmly, and pull the handle down.

Fig. 26-14 Using a power shearing and forming machine to make a series of notches in an airplane part. (Lockheed Aircraft Company)

Also, never let anyone near the front of the cutting blade when you are working there.

4. When cutting smaller pieces, feed the metal in from the front of the shears against the back gage. This gage can also be set easily to the right length. *Never attempt to cut band iron, wire, or any heavy metal on the squaring shears.* This will nick the blade, which will then make a notch in every edge you cut.

Tab notchers will handle small cutting jobs. They will cut a 6-inch by 6-inch (152-mm by 152-mm) corner notch in one stroke.

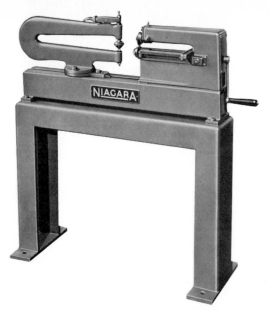

Fig. 26–15 A ring-and-circle shears. (Niagara Machine & Tool Works)

Ring-and-circle shears are used to cut rings or circles of sheet metal up to 20 gage in thickness (Fig. 26–15). Industrial models are used for heavier stock. Set the machine to the desired diameter of cut. Then place the workpiece between the holding jaws, and clamp tightly. Turn the handle slowly, and use your hand to ease the metal through the slitters, or cutting wheels. Be careful of sharp edges.

Hand punch presses are used for shearing holes in sheet metal (Fig. 26–16). On most machines, the dies can be changed for holes of different sizes and shapes. You use the machine as you would the tab notcher.

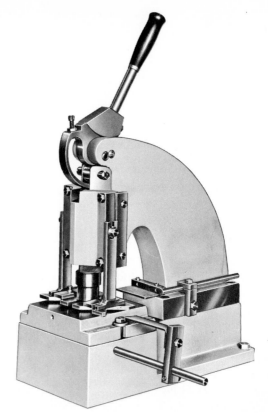

Fig. 26–16 The hand punch press can punch holes in sheet metal up to 20 gage. (Niagara Machine & Tool Works)

sheet-metal cutting?
4. What hand tool is used for cutting around cylindrical objects?
5. When punching, should you strike the punch solidly or lightly?
6. What machine is designed to cut large pieces of sheet metal?
7. What kinds of pieces should you never cut on the squaring shears?
8. What is the hand punch press used for?

 QUESTIONS

1. What is cutting metal sheets called?
2. Straight lines and outside curves are cut with what hand tool? Inside curves and intricate work?
3. Can aviation snips perform all kinds of

 EXTRA CREDIT

The hand snips and squaring shears both apply the principles of a lever and inclined plane in cutting sheet metal. Explain how these principles aid in cutting.

Unit 27
Bending Sheet Metal by Hand

Every sheet-metal project you make will have to be bent into some shape. Sheet metal can be formed or bent in many ways. Some of the common methods are described in this unit.

Bending equipment

A **stake** is a device for supporting or giving shape to metal that is being formed. *Metal stakes* are made in many sizes and shapes for bending all kinds of work (Figs. 27–1, 27–2). Some of the most common ones are listed below:

1. The *conductor stake,* for forming round sheet-metal objects.

2. The *hollow mandrel stake,* for forming, seaming, and riveting.

3. The *hatchet stake,* for making sharp-angle bends.

4. The *blowhorn stake,* for forming large cone-shaped objects.

5. The *double-seaming stake,* for making seams on large workpieces.

Stakes are held in a *stakeholder* or *bench plate* that is fastened to the bench. If stakes are not available, many other common metal pieces, such as round, square, and flat bar stock or pieces of railroad rail or of angle iron, can be used.

The hand, or handy, seamer can be used for bending an edge or folding a hem (Fig. 27–3).

A *wooden* or *rawhide mallet* with a smooth face is needed for bending, since a metal hammer would dent the metal workpiece. A

Fig. 27–1 Common kinds of stakes: (A) conductor, (B) hollow mandrel, (C) hatchet, (D) blowhorn, (E) double-seaming. The stakes are placed in the openings of the bench plate (F) when in use. (Peck, Stow & Wilcox Company)

Fig. 27–2 Universal stakeholder and stakes: (A) stakeholder and the rectangular end of a breakhorn stake; (B) breakhorn stake; (C) conductor stake, large end; (D) conductor stake, small end; (E) needle-case stake; (F) creasing stake with horn; (G) candle-mold stake; (H) blowhorn stake; (I) double-seaming stake. (Peck, Stow & Wilcox Company)

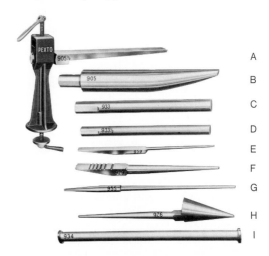

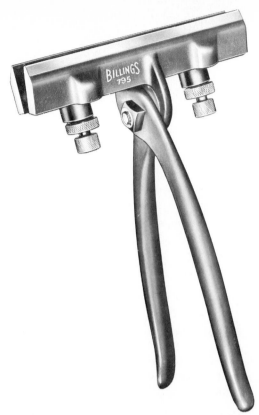

Fig. 27-3 A hand seamer. Note the two adjusting screws for setting the depth of the bend. (The Billings & Wilkins Company)

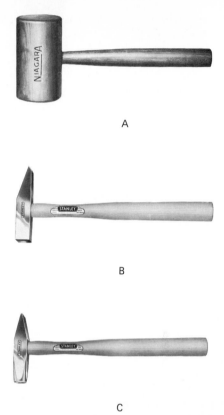

A

B

C

Fig. 27-4 Hammers for sheet-metal work. A wooden mallet (A) is used for most sheet-metal work. Rawhide and plastic mallets are also used, as well as setting-down hammers (B) and riveting hammers (C). (Niagara Machine & Tool Works; Stanley Tools)

setting-down hammer is used for setting down flanges and hems and for making certain kinds of seams. A *riveting hammer* is used for sheet-metal riveting (Fig. 27–4).

Making angular bends

1. To make a right-angle bend by hand, clamp two pieces of wood or angle iron in a vise, with the metal between them (Fig. 27–5). The layout line should be at the upper surface of the jig. Press the metal down with your left hand. Square off the bend with a mallet or with a block of wood and a hammer. To do a neat job, bend the metal slowly and gradually.

2. Another way of making a sharp

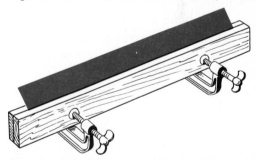

Fig. 27-5 Bending sheet metal by clamping the workpiece between two pieces of wood.

angle bend is to use a hatchet stake. Hold the work over the stake, with the bend line over the sharp edge. Now, press down with your hands on either side of the stake to start the

Fig. 27-6 Squaring off a sharp bend over a hatchet stake with a mallet.

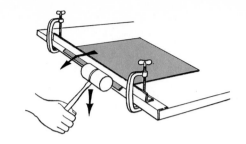

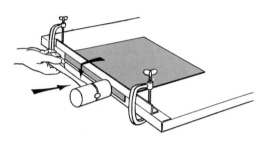

Fig. 27-7 Start the bend by striking the metal with the side of the mallet, forming the metal a little at a time. Square off the bend with the face of the mallet. If a hem must be bent, reverse the metal and flatten the edge.

bend. A wooden mallet is used to square off the bend (Fig. 27-6).

3. To bend a wide piece of metal by hand, place the metal on the bench with the bend line over the edge. Clamp a piece of angle iron over the bend line with one or two C-clamps. Press the metal down with your left hand, or strike it with the side of a mallet. Strike the metal with the face of the mallet to square off the bend (Fig. 27-7). Bend slowly. If you bend one part too much, a kink may form.

4. To bend a box by hand, bend two ends in a vise or over a stake. Then cut a block of wood of exactly the width of the box. Place this as shown in Fig. 27-8, and clamp in position. Now, bend up the sides of the box.

5. To make a hem by hand, first bend the hem at a right angle over the edge of a bench. Reverse the workpiece, and reclamp it on the bench. Close the hem by striking it with a wooden mallet.

6. If a hem must be bent on a small piece of metal, use a hand seamer (Fig. 27-9). Grasp the metal, with the edges of the jaws at the bend line, and turn the edge to the right angle. If you are making a hem,

bend it as far as it will go. Then open the seamer, and squeeze the metal to close the hem.

7. For irregular bends, cut two pieces of hardwood to shape. Squeeze the metal between them (Fig. 27-10).

Bending cylinders

1. Choose a stake, pipe, or rod with a diameter equal to, or smaller than, the diameter of the curve to be bent. Place the metal over the stake, with one edge extending slightly beyond the center of the bending device.

2. If the metal is thin, force the sheet around the stake with your right hand to form it. If the metal is heavy, use a wooden mallet to strike the sheet with glancing blows as you feed it across the stake (Fig. 27-11).

A

B

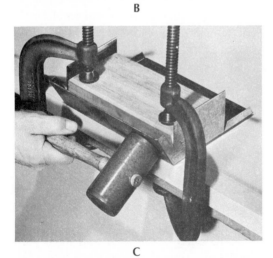

C

Fig. 27-8 (A) To make a box, bend two sides first. (B) Then, cut a block of wood the exact size of the bottom of the box and clamp in place. (C) Finally, bend the other sides.

Fig. 27-9 The hand seamer can be used to make sharp-angle bends or to form hems by hand.

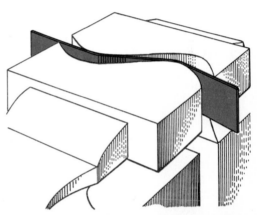

Fig. 27-10 Bending an irregularly shaped piece by squeezing it between two wooden forms.

Fig. 27-11 Using a mallet to form heavier metal into a cylindrical shape. Strike the metal as you push it over the form.

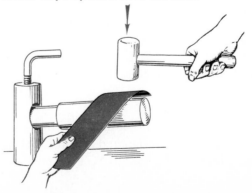

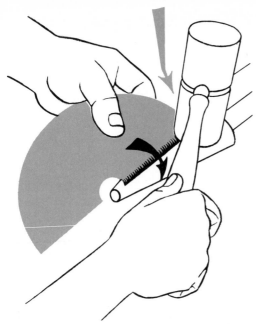

Fig. 27-12 Forming a cone-shaped object, such as a funnel, with a mallet.

Forming cone-shaped objects

When you must form cone-shaped objects, such as parts of a funnel or a spout for a watering can, it is best to have a stake with a tapered form. If you are forming a funnel top, for example, bend it over the apron of a blowhorn stake. Force the metal around it, using your hand or, if necessary, a wooden mallet to do the forming (Fig. 27-12).

 QUESTIONS ▬▬▬▬▬

1. List five kinds of sheet-metal stakes.
2. If metal stakes are not available, what are some substitutes you can use?
3. What device is used for bending an edge or folding a hem?
4. Why should you use a wooden or rawhide mallet for bending?
5. On what kind of stake would you bend a funnel?

 EXTRA CREDIT ▬▬▬▬▬

Suggest methods of bending sheet metal, using common objects found around the home. Sketch the items you could use.

Unit 28
Bending Metal on the Bar Folder or Brake

Metal sheets can be bent better and faster on a bar folder or brake than by hand. Bar folders and brakes are especially useful in industry for precision bending (Fig. 28-1).

The bar folder

The *bar folder*, or folding machine, comes in various sizes, designated by the maximum length of bend (Fig. 28-2). The most common size is 30 inches (762 mm). The bar folder will form open and closed locks in widths 1/8 to 1 inch (3 to 25 mm) on metal as heavy as 22 gage. It is used to fold edges and to prepare folds for various seams and wired edges. It is adjusted in two ways:

1. To regulate the depth of fold, turn the gage-adjusting screw knob in or out.

2. To regulate the sharpness of the fold, loosen the nuts or lever on the wing, and adjust the wing.

The wing is lowered when the bar folder is used to make a rounded fold for a wired edge. There are stops at the left end of the bar folder that will limit the fold to 45 or 90 degrees. An adjustable collar can be set for any angle. Figure 28-3 shows some common bends that can be made on a bar folder.

Fig. 28-1 Workers using a cornice brake to fold the lead sheet to be assembled on a roof by a roofing contractor. (Lead Industries Association)

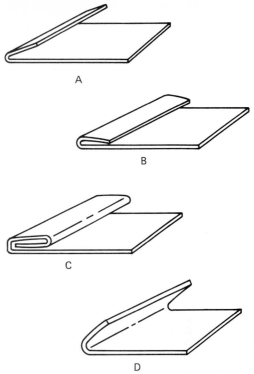

Fig. 28-3 Some common bends that can be made on a bar folder: (A) sharp bend for seam or hem, (B) single hem, (C) double hem, (D) open bend for wire-reinforced edge.

Fig. 28-2 Parts of a bar folder, or folding machine. (Peck, Stow & Wilcox Company)

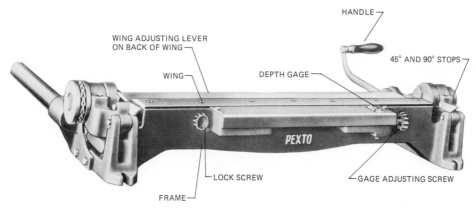

Making a fold or hem

A fold must be made before making a folded or grooved seam or a hem:

1. Adjust for the depth of fold by turning the gage-adjusting knob in or out until the depth is shown on the depth gage. Adjust

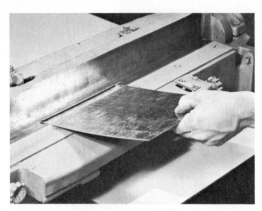

Fig. 28–4 Place the metal with the folded edge up on the bed. Then pull down on the handle with some force to flatten the hem.

the back wing for the correct sharpness of bend. If it is a 45- or 90-degree bend, set the stop. Make a trial fold on a piece of scrap sheet metal.

2. Insert the metal in the holder, and hold it firmly in place with your left hand.

3. Pull up on the handle with your right hand until the correct amount of fold is obtained.

4. If a hem is being made, remove the metal from the folder. Place it on the flat bed with the hem upward. Then flatten the hem (Fig. 28–4).

Making a rounded fold for a wired edge

1. Hold the wing vertically, and loosen the wedge lock nut. Then turn the wedge-adjusting screw until the distance between the wing and the edge of the blade is about equal to the wire diameter. Tighten the wedge lock nut.

2. Set the gage to a distance equal to one and one-half times the wire diameter. Insert the metal in the bar folder, and make the bend.

Try this on a piece of scrap metal before

attempting it on your project. With practice, you can make a variety of other bends on the bar folder.

Brakes

The *cornice brake* is used for making bends and folded edges on large pieces of stock (Fig. 28–5). The size is determined by the maximum length of bend it can make. The 5- and 7-foot (1.5- and 2.1-m) lengths are the most common. This machine is quite easy to operate:

1. Lift the clamping bar levers, and insert the metal in the brake. Tighten the bar levers, with the layout line directly under the front edge of the upper jaw. Check one edge of the metal and the front edge of the upper jaw with a square.

2. Now, lift up the bending wing until you have the angle of bend you want. Go a few degrees past this angle, because the metal tends to spring back.

The cornice brake works well for most jobs. It is not possible, however, to bend all four sides of a box on it. A *box-and-pan brake* is

Fig. 28–5 Parts of a cornice brake. (Peck, Stow & Wilcox Company)

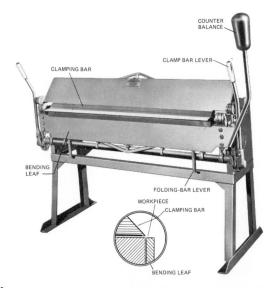

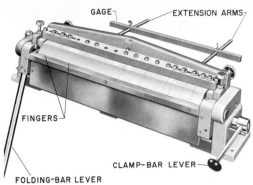

Fig. 28-6 Parts of a box-and-pan brake. Notice that the fingers are of different widths so that they can be put together to make any standard width. (Di-Acro/Division of Houdaille Industries)

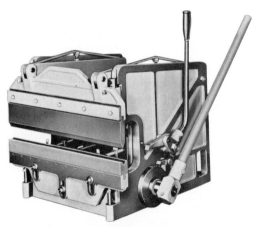

Fig. 28-8 A hand-operated press brake. (Di-Acro/Division of Houdaille Industries)

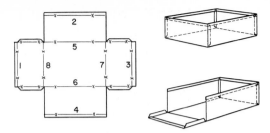

Fig. 28-7 Steps in completing a box on a box-and-pan brake:

1. Make the first hem.
2. Make the second hem.
3. Make the third hem.
4. Make the fourth hem.
5. Make a 90-degree bend on one side.
6. Make a 90-degree bend on the second side. These first six steps can be completed with all the fingers in the bar folder.
7. Fit just enough fingers together to equal the width of the box. Bend the first end.
8. Reverse the metal and bend the second end. When you complete steps 7 and 8, the sides may flatten a little as you bend the two ends.

used for this purpose (Fig. 28-6). The upper jaw is made up of various widths of removable fingers. You use only the numbers of fingers necessary for the length of bend you want. Figure 28-7 shows the steps in bending all four sides of a box.

The *hand-operated press brake* will perform not only simple angle and radius bends, but also flanging, hemming, seaming, flattening, punching, blanking, and drawing operations (Fig. 28-8). Six tons of power are avail-

able with many hand-operated brakes, making it possible to form a 16-gage (1.6-mm) mild steel over the full 24-inch (610-mm) bed. Industrial press brakes are made in many models, sizes, and capacities.

 QUESTIONS

1. On the bar folder, how do you regulate the depth of fold? The sharpness of fold?
2. Can a bar folder make any degree of bend?
3. What kind of brake is needed to bend all four sides of a box?
4. Name some special operations that can be performed on the hand-operated press brake.

 EXTRA CREDIT

Report on a trip you make through a sheet-metal shop.

Unit 29
Forming Cylindrical Parts on the Forming Rolls

The quickest and easiest way to form cylinders and cones is to use *forming rolls,* also called *slip-roll forming machines.* These machines are used in both school shops and industry (Fig. 29–1).

Forming rolls

The most common forming rolls have 2-inch (51-mm) rolls and are 30 or 36 inches (762 or 914 mm) wide. They will form metal as heavy as 22 gage. This machine has three rolls. The front two are gear-operated by turning the handle. The back one is the idler roll. It does the actual forming. You can move it up or down to form larger or smaller cylinders. You can also move the lower front roll up and down by the two front adjusting screws to take different thicknesses of metal. To remove the cylinder after it has been formed, you slip the end of the upper, or slip roll, out of place. The lower and back rolls have grooves cut along their right sides.

Fig. 29–1 Parts of the forming rolls, or slip-roll forming machines. (Peck, Stow & Wilcox Company)

These grooves are for forming wire or for forming cylinders when the wired edge is already installed on the workpiece.

Forming a cylinder

1. Lock the upper roll in position. Adjust the lower roll to be parallel to it. Leave just enough clearance between the rolls for the metal to slip in under slight pressure (Fig. 29–2).

2. Adjust the back roll to about the position needed to form the cylinder. Make sure that the back roll is parallel to the other rolls. You can test these settings on scrap sheet.

3. Insert the sheet between the front rolls, and turn the handle. Just as the metal enters, raise it slightly to start the forming. Then lower it to catch the back roll (Fig. 29–3).

4. Continue turning the handle to shape the cylinder (Fig. 29–4). If the cylinder is too big, bring the sheet back to the starting position, and readjust the back roll. After the cylinder is formed, release the upper roll to remove the metal (Fig. 29–5).

Fig. 29–2 Adjust these screws or knobs until the distance between the front rolls is equal to the thickness of the metal.

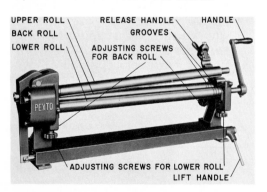

UPPER ROLL
BACK ROLL
LOWER ROLL
RELEASE HANDLE
GROOVES
HANDLE
ADJUSTING SCREWS FOR BACK ROLL
PEXTO
ADJUSTING SCREWS FOR LOWER ROLL
LIFT HANDLE

A   B

Fig. 29-3 Forming a cylinder: (A) Insert the sheet in the front rolls. Turn the handle forward. (B) Just as the metal enters, raise it slightly with your left hand to start the cylinder.

Fig. 29-5 When the cylinder is formed, open the release handle and raise the upper roll to remove the cylinder.

Fig. 29-4 The roll beginning to form the cylinder.

Rolling a cylinder with a fold on both edges

If the sheet has a fold on both edges for making a folded or grooved seam, the process is more difficult (Fig. 29-6). This is because you cannot feed the sheet in from the front.

1. Loosen the upper roll, and insert the metal with one bend just inside the rolls. The back roll must be lowered quite far.

2. Lift the sheet slightly by hand, and turn the handle. When the fold is past the back roll, turn up the back roll to about the position needed to form the cylinder. Then turn the handle forward to do the forming.

3. It is usually a good idea to form the cylinder to a size slightly larger than the finished one. Then, by adjusting the back roll, you can bring the cylinder to finished size by rolling it back and forth.

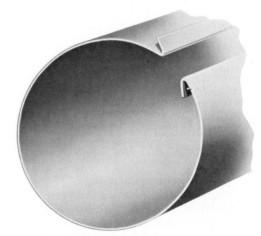

Fig. 29-6 A cylinder with edge folds.

Rolling a cylinder with a wired edge

1. Adjust the front rolls with a slightly wider space at the right side than at the left.

2. Place the sheet between the front rolls, with the wired edge down and in the groove of the correct size (Fig. 29-7). Then proceed as before.

Forming cone shapes

1. Adjust the front rolls as above. Set the rear roll at an angle that is about the same as the taper of the cone, with the left end of the roll nearer the front rolls.

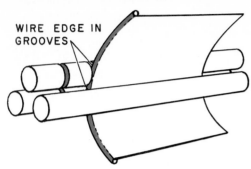

Fig. 29-7 Forming a cylinder with a wired edge.

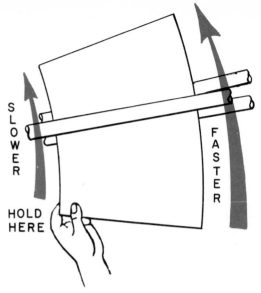

Fig. 29-8 Forming a cone-shaped object. Hold one corner so that one side goes through the rolls faster than the other side.

2. Insert the sheet with the short side to the left and the long side to the right. Hold the short side as you turn the handle. Allow the short side to go through the rolls more slowly than the long side (Fig. 29-8). This forms the cone.

 QUESTIONS

1. How many rolls do the forming rolls have?
2. Which one does the forming?
3. Which roll do you adjust so that the machine can take more than one thickness of metal?
4. After a cylinder is formed, how is it removed from the machine?
5. How do you set the rear roll for forming a cone?

 EXTRA CREDIT

1. Which of the basic machines you study in physics are applied in the forming rolls? Make a sketch of each.
2. Prepare a research report on roll forming in industry.

Unit 30
Making Seams

Seaming is joining sheet-metal parts with mechanical joints. Seams are sometimes soldered to make them watertight. In this unit, you will learn to make some simple seams using the hand tools found in the shop.

Types of seams

A number of different seams are used in sheet-metal work (Fig. 30-1):

1. The *butt seam* has two pieces of metal butted together and soldered.

2. The *lap seam* is made by lapping the edge of one piece of metal over the edge of the other and riveting or soldering them together. The most common kind is the *plain lap*. If the two metal surfaces must align, a

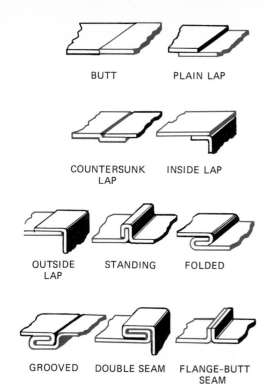

BUTT   PLAIN LAP

COUNTERSUNK   INSIDE LAP
LAP

OUTSIDE   STANDING   FOLDED
LAP

GROOVED   DOUBLE SEAM   FLANGE-BUTT
SEAM

Fig. 30–1 Common seams for sheet-metal joining.

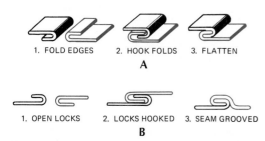

1. FOLD EDGES   2. HOOK FOLDS   3. FLATTEN

A

1. OPEN LOCKS   2. LOCKS HOOKED   3. SEAM GROOVED

B

Fig. 30–2 (A) Steps in making a folded seam. (B) Steps in making a grooved seam.

Hand Groover Sizes		
Number	Width of groove	
	in	mm
6	$\frac{1}{8}$	3
5	$\frac{5}{32}$	4
4	$\frac{7}{32}$	6.5
3	$\frac{9}{32}$	7
2	$\frac{5}{16}$	8
1	$\frac{11}{32}$	9
0	$\frac{3}{8}$	9.5

Fig. 30–3 A hand groover and groover chart.

4. The *double seam* is used to join the bottom to the sides of rectangular or circular containers or to make corner joints on rectangular containers.

Hand groovers

The *hand groover* is used to lock a grooved seam (Fig. 30–3). Hand groovers vary in size from No. 000 to No. 8. The groover should have a groove about 1/16 inch (1.5 mm) wider than the width of the finished seam. For example, hand groover No. 2, which has a 5/16-inch (8-mm) groove, is made to lock a 1/4-inch (6-mm) seam. The common sizes are No. 0, No. 2, and No. 4. See the chart in Fig. 30–3.

Making a folded
or grooved seam

1. Determine the width of the seam, and allow extra material equal to three times the seam width. For example, if it is a 1/8-inch (3-mm) seam, allow 3/8 inch (10 mm). Sometimes, a small additional amount is allowed for the rise in the seam, especially if the metal is heavier than 22 gage. This amount should be about one and one-half times the thickness of the metal. On

countersunk, or *offset, lap* is made. An *inside* or *outside corner lap* may be used on the corners of sheet-metal projects.

3. *Folded* and *grooved seams* have two folded edges hooked together (Fig. 30–2). In a grooved seam, the edges are locked. Note that with a grooved seam, there are three thicknesses of metal above the joined sheets.

Fig. 30–4 For a grooved seam, an allowance of three times the width of the seam must be made. For heavier sheet stock, a small additional allowance is made for the height of the seam.

most projects, add half the allowance to either end of the metal (Fig. 30–4). Sometimes, it is a good idea to notch the corners. This makes a neater seam.

2. Fold the edges by hand or in a bar folder. The metal should be bent as for an open hem. When using a bar folder, adjust the machine to the seam width and fold. If the seam is to be made on one continuous piece, such as a cylinder, *remember to fold the ends in opposite directions* (Fig. 30–5).

3. If the project is to be of some particular shape—cylindrical or rectangular, for example—form it at this point.

4. Place the metal over a solid backing, such as a stake if it is circular, or a flat metal table if it is flat. Hook the folded edges together. To make a folded seam, gently strike

the seam along its length to close it, using a wooden mallet. Avoid nicking or denting.

5. To make a grooved seam, select a hand groover that is 1/16 inch (1.5 mm) wider than the seam. Hold the groover over the seam, with one edge of the groover over one edge of the seam. Strike the groover solidly with a metal hammer to close one end of the seam (Fig. 30–6). Slide the groover along as you strike it, to complete the seam (Fig. 30–7). You can further lock the seam with prick-punch marks about 1/2 inch (13 mm) from either end of the seam.

6. Check the seam after it is locked. Are the joined sheets of metal level? Is the seam well formed, without nicks, and smooth?

Making a double seam

It is very difficult to make a double seam for attaching a bottom to a round, as opposed to a rectangular, container. This is the procedure:

1. Form the sides of the container, allowing an extra amount for the burr or flange around the lower edge, usually about 3/32 inch (2.5 mm).

2. Turn this edge at a 90-degree angle on a burring machine (see Unit 31).

Fig. 30–5 In making a grooved seam on a closed cylinder or a rectangular object, the ends must be bent in opposite directions.

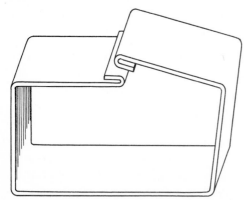

Fig. 30–6 Starting at one end, tip the hand groover at a slight angle and hook it over the edge of the seam. Strike the groover firmly to lock one end.

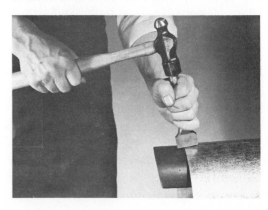

A

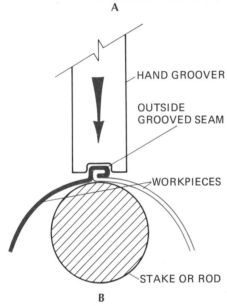

HAND GROOVER

OUTSIDE
GROOVED SEAM

WORKPIECES

STAKE OR ROD

B

Fig. 30–7 (A) Slide the groover along as you strike it, to complete the seam. (B) This is how the locking takes place.

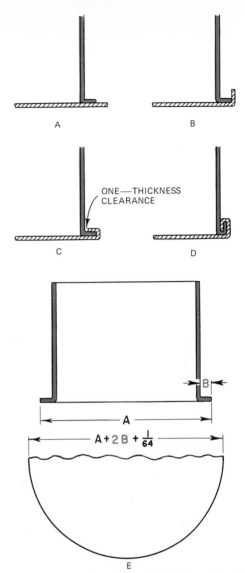

A

B

ONE—THICKNESS
CLEARANCE

C

D

$A + 2B + \frac{1}{64}$

E

Fig. 30–8 Steps in making a double seam on the bottom of a cylindrical container: (A) The container itself with a burred edge or flange. (B) The bottom with a burred edge. (C) The double seam closed. (D) The edge turned. (E) Measuring the cylinder to get the correct disk diameter for the bottom.

3. Now, carefully measure the diameter across the turned edges. Do this at several points to get an average. It is very important that this be as precise as possible.

4. Add to this diameter an amount equal to the width of the two turned edges, plus a small amount for the thickness of the metal, usually 1/64 inch (0.5 mm) (Fig. 30–8).

5. Cut a disk for the bottom to this diameter.

6. Turn the edge of the disk, equal to B in Fig. 30–8, on a burring machine. You may have to practice on a scrap piece.

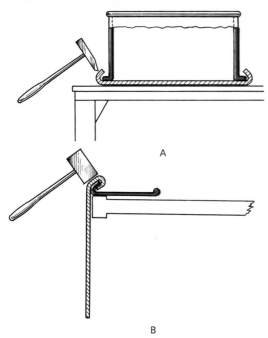

Fig. 30–9 (A) Closing a double seam with a setting-down hammer. (B) Turning a double seam with a mallet. Notice that the container is held over a double-seaming stake.

7. Now, snap the bottom over the burred edge of the cylinder.

8. Hold the bottom of the container flat against a metal surface. Close the seam with a setting-down hammer (Fig. 30–9A).

Turn the container to close the seam gradually.

9. Slip the container over a double-seaming stake. Finish the seam with a mallet (Fig. 30–9B). Strike the edge of the seam with glancing blows as you rotate the container through a quarter turn. Be sure that the inside of the container directly behind the seam is backed by the metal stake.

? QUESTIONS

1. Name the four main kinds of seams.
2. How do a folded and a grooved seam differ?
3. When is a double seam needed?
4. How is the size of the hand groover chosen?
5. How much extra material should be allowed to make a folded or grooved seam?
6. With which tool do you close a folded seam?
7. In double-seaming a cylinder to its disk bottom, what must you do to the edges of each before you can snap them together?

✓ EXTRA CREDIT

Make a display board of the common types of seams. Mount each sample and identify.

Unit 31
Wiring an Edge, Turning a Burr, Beading, and Crimping

Turning in sheet-metal work is forming metal on disk or cylindrical shapes. A *rotary machine* (Fig. 31–1) is used for these opera-

tions. A single *combination rotary machine* will turn, wire, or burr an edge and do beading and crimping (Fig. 31–2). Larger shops have a separate machine for each operation. These operations serve to decorate, stiffen, or prepare a workpiece for wiring or seaming.

Wiring an edge

Wiring an edge stiffens the article and eliminates sharp edges. The wire used is made of mild steel, with a galvanized or copper coating to protect it from rusting. The

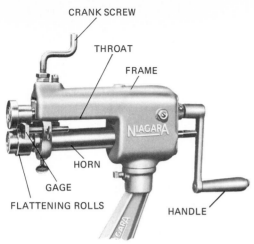

CRANK SCREW
THROAT
FRAME
HORN
GAGE
FLATTENING ROLLS
HANDLE

Fig. 31-1 The rotary machine is used for turning operations in sheet-metal work. (Niagara Machine & Tool Works)

size is measured by the American Wire Gage system. The most common sizes are 10 (about 1/8 inch or 3 mm in diameter), 12, 14, and 18. How an edge is wired depends on whether the wire is put on before or after the article is formed. If the project is a simple cylinder, the wire is put on the flat sheet before rolling. In this case, use the bar folder to turn the edge. You will need only the wiring rolls of the rotary machine to finish the job. If the project is a cone, such as a funnel, the wiring is done after it is shaped. Both turning and wiring rolls are needed. In making a layout for a wired edge, remember to allow two and one-half times the diameter of the wire for the edge.

Turning an edge

1. Install the turning rolls on the rotary machine (Fig. 31-3).

2. Set the gage at a distance equal to two and one-half times the diameter of the wire from the center of the groove.

Fig. 31-2 A rotary machine can perform these operations.

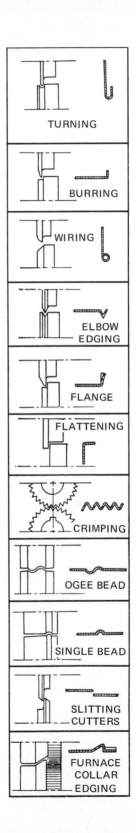

TURNING

BURRING

WIRING

ELBOW EDGING

FLANGE

FLATTENING

CRIMPING

OGEE BEAD

SINGLE BEAD

SLITTING CUTTERS

FURNACE COLLAR EDGING

183

Fig. 31-3 Turning rolls.

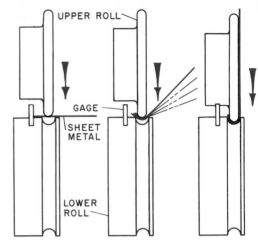

Fig. 31-4 Using the turning rolls to form the edge for a wired edge. Notice how the edge is formed a little at a time.

3. Slip the metal between the rolls and against the gage. Tighten the upper roll until it just grips the metal.

4. Holding the metal against the gage with your left hand, turn the handle with your right hand. Make one complete turn. The metal must track the first time. Never let the roll run off the edge of the metal.

5. Tighten the upper roll a little more—about one-eighth of a turn. At the same time, raise the outside edge of the container a little higher. Make another complete turn.

6. Continue tightening the upper rolls after each turn. Raise the cylinder until the edge is U-shaped to receive the wire (Fig. 31–4).

7. Loosen the upper roll to remove the metal from the machine.

Closing the wired edge by hand

1. Cut a piece of wire to length. If the object is already shaped, form the wire into a ring in the forming rolls of the rotary machine or to a rectangle over a stake.

2. Place the wire in the edge with one end sticking out about 1/2 inch (13 mm). Then, with pliers, squeeze the edge for a distance of about 1/2 inch (13 mm) to fasten the wire in place (Fig. 31–5). Then close the edge with a setting-down hammer (Fig. 31–

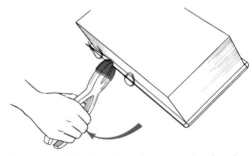

Fig. 31-5 Starting to close a wired edge with a pair of pliers. Squeeze the edge over and around the wire. Cover the jaws of the pliers with masking tape to prevent marring.

Fig. 31-6 To close a wired edge completely by hand, use a setting-down hammer to fold over the metal. Be careful not to dent it.

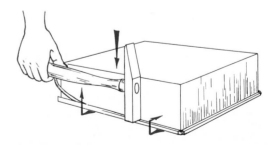

6). This can also be done by bending down the edge with a mallet.

Closing the wired edge by machine

1. Place the wiring rolls on the rotary machine (Fig. 31–7). Adjust the gage. Its distance from the sharp edge of the upper roll should equal the diameter of the wire plus twice the thickness of the metal.

2. Place the project between the rolls with the wired edge up and against the gage. Tighten the rolls at the point where the edge is already turned until they grip the metal.

3. Turn the handle as you feed in the metal to set the wired edge (Fig. 31–8).

4. Loosen the upper rolls, and remove the work.

Turning a burr or flange

The burring rolls of the rotary machine are used mostly to turn a flange, or rim, on a cylinder and to turn a burr on a round bottom in making a double seam to attach it to a cylinder (Fig. 31–9). The second is a tricky operation. It must always be practiced on scrap stock.

This is the procedure for turning a burr on a round bottom (see Unit 30):

1. Place the burring rolls on the rotary machine. Adjust the upper and lower rolls. The distance between the sharp edge of the upper roll and the shoulder of the lower roll should be equal to the thickness of the metal.

2. Set the gage away from the shoulder of the lower roll by a distance slightly less than the width of the burr.

3. Bend a little piece of scrap metal into a U shape to protect your hand from the sharp burr. Place this in the round of your hand between thumb and forefinger.

4. Grasp the circular end piece with your thumb on top and forefinger below on or toward the center of the disk.

5. Holding the edge of the disk firmly against the gage, turn the upper roll down until there is slight pressure on the metal (Fig. 31–10).

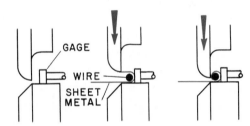

Fig. 31–8 Closing a wired edge, using the wiring rolls.

Fig. 31–7 Wiring rolls.

Fig. 31–9 Burring rolls.

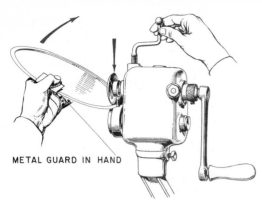

METAL GUARD IN HAND

Fig. 31-10 Using the burring rolls to turn a burred edge on the bottom of a container. Notice that the disk is inserted and that slight pressure is applied to the metal between the rolls.

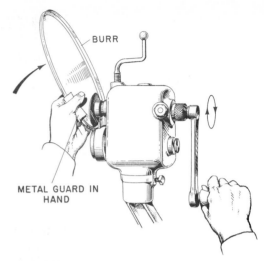

BURR

METAL GUARD IN HAND

Fig. 31-11 The burr has begun to form. The disk is being raised to help form it. The metal guard protects the hand.

6. Turn the handle slowly, carefully tracking the burr. This must be done the first time around. The beginner usually allows the disk to escape the rolls, making tracking difficult.

7. Apply a little more pressure by tightening the upper roll. Then turn the handle a little faster as you slowly raise the disk from a horizontal to an almost vertical position (Fig. 31-11). Continue tightening the upper roll as the burr is formed.

8. Loosen the upper roll to remove the disk.

9. If you have done a good job of turning the disk, the end piece will slip over the flange on the cylinder with a little snap to form the bottom of the container.

10. Turning a flange on a cylinder is a similar operation, except that the edge is turned only 90 degrees.

Beading

Beading is strengthening and decorating containers with either a simple bead or an ogee, or S-shaped, bead. This stiffens the workpiece much as sheet metal is made stronger by corrugation. This operation is quite simple:

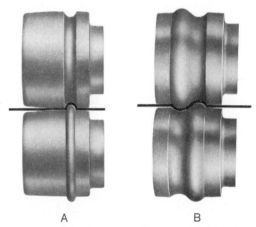

A   B

Fig. 31-12 Using the beading rolls: (A) simple bead, (B) ogee bead.

1. Place the beading rolls on the rotary machine (Fig. 31-12). Set the gage according to where you want the bead.

2. Tighten the upper roll enough to form the metal lightly.

3. Turn the handle, tracking the bead the first time. Continue tightening the upper roll until the bead is completely formed.

Crimping

Crimping is drawing in the edge on the end of a cylindrical object, particularly a heating pipe or stack. It is done so that the object will slip easily into a mating part.

1. Place the crimping rolls on the rotary machine (Fig. 31–13). Adjust the gage to the proper length of crimp.

2. Slip the cylinder between the rolls, with the edge against the gage.

3. Applying moderate pressure with the upper roll, turn the handle to form the first impression.

4. Apply more pressure to deepen the crimp, making sure that the crimping rolls follow the first impression.

Fig. 31–13 Crimping rolls.

3. How much allowance should be made for the edge?
4. When turning a burr on a round bottom, what special equipment do you put on the rotary machine?
5. What is beading?
6. What is crimping? Why is it done?

 QUESTIONS

1. What one machine can wire an edge, turn a burr, and do beading and crimping?
2. What kind of wire is used for wiring an edge?

 EXTRA CREDIT

1. Make a drawing of each sheet-metal operation done on a rotary machine.
2. Prepare a research report on turning machines used in industry.

Unit 32
Fastening with Rivets, Screws, and Adhesives

Metal sheets can be fastened together permanently with rivets (Fig. 32–1). Sometimes, a joint is soldered or glued to make it tight. Adhesives can give a very strong, permanent joint. Sheet-metal screws provide a semipermanent joint.

Fig. 32–1 Learning how to rivet in an apprentice program in an aircraft factory. (McDonnell Douglas Corporation)

187

10 OZ   12 OZ   I LB   2 LB   3 LB

Fig. 32-2 The actual size of sheet-metal rivets.

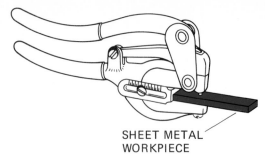

SHEET METAL WORKPIECE

Fig. 32-4 The hand, or hand-lever, punch.

Fig. 32-3 A solid punch. (The Billings & Wilkins Company)

Rivets and riveting tools

Sheet-metal rivets are usually made of mild steel. *Black-iron rivets* have a black iron oxide coating. *Galvanized* rivets have a zinc coating. Both are also known as *tinner's rivets*. They give a strong joint. The size of the rivet is indicated by the weight per 1000. For example, a "1-pound" rivet indicates that 1000 rivets weigh 1 pound (0.45 kg) (Fig. 32-2). All tinner's rivets are flathead. The length of the shank depends on the size. Sizes are shown in Table 32-1. Tinner's rivets are also made of copper.

A *solid punch* is usually used to make the holes for tinner's rivets (Fig. 32-3). These punches are numbered according to size from 6 to 10. Some companies letter the punches from B (3/32 inch or 2.5 mm) to I (3/8 inch or 9.5 mm). Each number fits a certain size of rivet. For example, a No. 8 punch is made for 2-pound (0.9-kg) rivets (see Table 33-1).

Holes can also be made in sheet metal with the *hand, or hand lever, punch* (Fig. 32-4). This punch makes clean, sharp, burr-free holes up to 1/4 inch (6 mm) in diameter in 16-gage (1.6-mm) mild steel. When using this tool, insert the metal between the die and the punch so that the mark for the center of the hole is directly under the punch rod.

Table 32-1
Guide for Selecting Punch, Rivet, and Rivet Set

Gage of metal	Solid punch		Size of rivet (weight per 1000)	Rivet set	
	Letter	Number		Number	Size of hole
30	B	10	10 to 12 oz	8	0.110
28	C	9	14 oz to 1 lb	7	0.128
26	C	9	1 lb	7	0.128
24	D	7 or 8	2 lb	5	0.149
22	D	7 or 8	2 1/2 lb	5	0.149
20	E	6	3 lb	4	0.166

Pull the handle down slowly until the punch is forced through the metal. Release the handle, and remove the workpiece.

A *rivet set* is used to set and head the rivets (Fig. 32–5). It is made in various sizes to match the rivets. Choose the rivet set by number or by matching the rivet shank to the hole of the rivet set.

A *riveting hammer* is the best one to use. It has a flat face on one side and a beveled cross peen on the other. However, a ball peen hammer may also be used.

Riveting

1. Select the correct size of rivets and rivet set and a solid punch or drill.

2. *Lay out the location of the rivets.* If several are to be set along a lap seam, they should be placed *one and one-half to two times their diameter from the edge.* They should be equally spaced along the seam.

3. *Punch or drill the holes.* If the metal is thin, the holes are usually punched. Place the sheets over end-grain hardwood or over a lead block. Hold the solid punch over the place where the hole is to be. Strike the punch solidly with a hammer to form the hole (Fig. 32–6).

4. *Set the rivet.* Place the rivet with the head down on a flat surface or, if cylindrical objects are being riveted together, on the crown of a stake. Slip the metal over it so that the shank comes through the hole. Place the hole in the rivet set over the shank. Then strike the rivet set with a hammer once or twice (Fig. 32–7). This will flatten out the sheet metal around the hole and draw the two sheets together. Do not strike the rivet set too hard. Also, be sure to keep it square with the workpiece because sheet metal dents easily.

Fig. 32–5 A rivet set. (The Billings & Wilkins Company)

Fig. 32–6 Using a solid punch to form holes for riveting. Place the sheet metal over end-grain wood or a lead block.

Fig. 32–7 (A) The hole of the rivet set is placed over the shank of the rivet, and the sheets of metal are drawn together. (B) The cone-shaped hole is used to form the shank or to head the rivet.

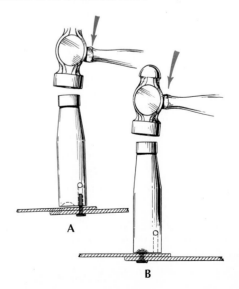

5. *Head the rivet.* Use the flat face of the riveting hammer to strike the shank squarely with several blows. The shank will expand, filling the hole tightly. The top of the shank will flatten a little. Now, place the cone-shaped depression of the rivet set over the shank, and strike the set two or three times to round off the head. You may also use a ball peen hammer to set and head rivets in sheet-metal work (see Unit 23).

6. If you are setting several rivets in a row, it is a good idea to punch and rivet the center hole first. Then punch and rivet the other holes from the center outward.

7. Check your work. Have you dented the sheet metal around the rivet? Is the head well shaped? Do you have the rivets too close to the edge?

Pop rivets are available with either a hollow or a solid core. These blind rivets can be installed quickly and easily. They are inserted and set from the same side of the work with a hand tool (Fig. 32–8). This is particularly useful in assembling hollow sheet-metal objects, such as boxes or ducts.

Expanding rivets are also used for sheet-metal fastening. To use, install the rivet, place it between the jaws of a vise or in a bench-plate hole, and strike the head sharply with a hammer. This will cause the plunger to force the shank of the rivet apart and lock the workpieces together (Fig. 32–9).

Fastening with self-tapping sheet-metal screws

Self-tapping sheet-metal screws are made to cut their own threads in mild-steel sheet and softer aluminum alloys. These screws are a quick, sure means of joining sheet metal. They are used a good deal in making ventilation, air-conditioning, and heating ducts. They are also very useful in home maintenance and repair jobs.

There are two kinds of self-tapping

Fig. 32–8 Inserting a pop rivet.

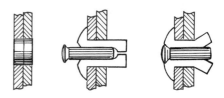

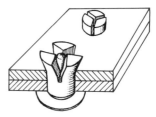
Fig. 32–9 Installing an expanding rivet.

sheet-metal screws. *Type A* is pointed and is made for joining sheet metal no thicker than 18-gage galvanized iron or soft aluminum (Fig. 32–10). *Type B* has a blank point and is used for joining both lighter and heavier sheet stock (Fig. 32–11). Both kinds come in several head shapes with either slotted or Phillips heads. Some common sizes of type A are No. 6 diameter by 3/8-inch (9.5-mm) length, No. 6 diameter by 1/2-inch (12.5-mm) length, and No. 8 diameter by 3/4-inch (19-mm) length.

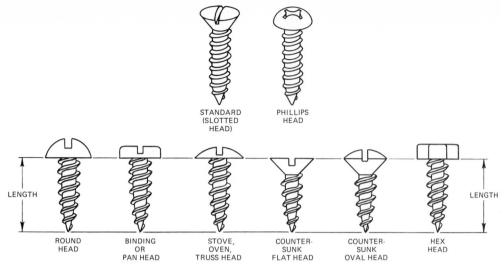

Fig. 32-10 Common head shapes for type A sheet-metal screws.

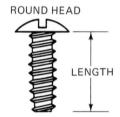

Fig. 32-11 Type B sheet-metal screw.

Installing sheet-metal screws

1. Locate and prick-punch the site of the holes.

2. Choose a drill size that equals the root diameter of the screw. For example, use a 7/64-inch (2.78-mm) drill for a No. 6 screw and a 1/8-inch (3.18-mm) drill for a No. 8 screw. You can also judge the drill size by holding the drill in back of the screw thread. Drill the hole.

3. Line up the hole with a punch. Make sure that the two pieces of metal are held firmly together as the screw is started.

Adhesive bonding

Adhesives are sticky substances such as cements and glues that are used to join surfaces. Adhesive bonds offer a number of advantages over other fastening methods. First, an adhesive bond acts as many tiny fasteners. Thus, the load is distributed uniformly over the entire area of contact. Second, adhesive bonds are inconspicuous. Third, adhesive bonds form a shield between the pieces they join. This reduces the corrosion that can occur when the pieces are of different metals.

Using adhesives

In sheet-metal work, adhesives are used mainly for joining thin sheet or strip parts that are too low in bearing strength for threaded fasteners and too thin to withstand welding heat. In the school shop, you can use adhesives to provide a fast, permanent, watertight joint for small metal parts. You can also use them to fasten metal to other materials such as wood and plastic. Three basic types are in use:

Contact cement is applied to *both* of the sheets to be joined. It is especially useful for adhering one sheet of metal to another or to a piece of wood. The solvent for contact cement is lacquer thinner.

Fig. 32–12 Using epoxy cement to join wood and metal.

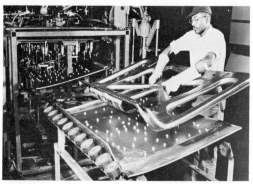

Fig. 32–14 Special hot-melt adhesives are used both in industry and in the school shop. This automobile trunk panel is being joined to the frame with such an adhesive.

Fig. 32–13 A hot-melt glue gun.

Design your project so that you have as wide a joint as possible. Clean the joint surfaces thoroughly. Apply the contact cement to both workpieces, and allow them to dry for about 15 minutes. When the workpieces are dry, carefully place them together. Then put a block of wood over the joint, and rap sharply with a hammer or mallet. *Be very careful: Once you touch the glued surfaces together, they cannot be moved.*

Epoxy cement is a special plastic adhesive that is very tough. It can be used similarly to contact cements except that the joint surface

can be smaller. The solvent for epoxy cement is acetone or a special epoxy cleaner. Use epoxy cement as follows:

1. Clean the workpieces carefully.

2. Squeeze out equal parts of the hardener and resin; mix thoroughly.

3. Apply to *one* workpiece (Fig. 32–12). *Use gloves.* Do not get any adhesive on your hands or face.

4. Press the joint together, remove excess glue, and allow it to dry for about 8 hours.

Hot-melt adhesives are applied with a special gun (Fig. 32–13). They can be used to join metal workpieces quickly and neatly. Hot-melt adhesives come as solid slugs that liquefy when they are heated and **cure,** or resolidify, when they are cooled. To use, insert a slug into the gun, heat it until it is liquid, and press the trigger to run a thin line of glue onto the joint. Press together immediately, clamp, and allow to set. The workpieces can be handled after the glue has hardened. Excess adhesive can be removed with heat. These adhesives can be used to join almost any material. They are widely used in the automobile industry (Fig. 32–14).

QUESTIONS

1. What kind of joint does riveting make?
2. What are sheet-metal rivets usually made of?
3. What coatings are used on tinner's rivets?
4. What shape is the head of a tinner's rivet?
5. What tool is usually used to punch holes for tinner's rivets? To set and head the rivets?
6. Where should you locate rivets along a lap seam?
7. When setting several rivets in a row, which hole should you punch first?
8. Name the two kinds of self-tapping sheet-metal screws.
9. How do you choose the drill size when installing a sheet-metal screw?
10. List some advantages of adhesives over other fasteners.
11. What are the three kinds of adhesives used with sheet metals?

EXTRA CREDIT

Find samples of commercial products showing the various methods of fastening sheet metal together. Show them to the class.

Unit 33
Soft Soldering

Soldering is joining two metal parts with a *solder,* a third metal that has a lower melting point. In **soft soldering,** a tin-lead solder and relatively low temperatures are used. In **hard soldering,** a silver solder and high temperatures produce neater, stronger joints (see Unit 46).

Before you can solder, the following conditions must be met:

1. The metal must be clean.

2. The correct soldering device must be used, and it must be in good condition.

3. The correct solder and flux, or soldering agent, must be chosen.

4. The proper amount of heat must be applied.

If you follow these rules, you will get a good solder joint.

Soldering devices

For most soldering, you will need some type of device to heat the soldering copper. These are the most common kinds:

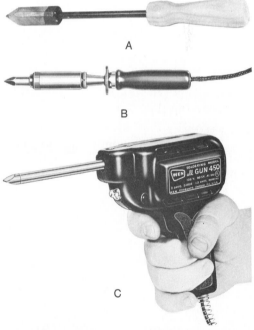

Fig. 33–1 Common heating devices for soldering: (A) a regular soldering copper, (B) an electric soldering copper, (C) an electric soldering gun (Wen Products).

1. *Soldering coppers* are purchased in pairs (Fig. 33–1A). The coppers of a 2-pound (0.9-kg) pair weigh 1 pound (0.45 kg) apiece. This is an average size for regular sheet-

metal work. They are available in smaller or larger sizes, from 3 ounces to 3 pounds (0.1 to 1.4 kg) per pair.

2. An *electric soldering copper* is much more convenient, because it will maintain uniform heat and can be used wherever there is an electric outlet (Fig. 33–1B). Electric coppers are specified by their wattage. They range from 50 to 300 watts. A 150- to 200-watt soldering copper is a good size for most sheet-metal soldering. One as small as 75 watts might be used for electronic work. One as large as 300 watts might be used for rugged work. Another type of electric soldering copper is the *soldering gun* (Fig. 33–1C). This gives instant heat when the trigger is pulled. It is used primarily for electrical work.

Both nonelectric and electric soldering coppers are commonly called *soldering irons*.

3. A *soldering furnace* (Fig. 33–2).

4. A *propane torch* (Fig. 33–3).

5. A *bunsen burner* is sometimes used for sweat soldering (Fig. 33–4).

Fig. 33–3 A propane-gas torch can be used to heat a soldering copper or for direct soldering with heat.

Fig. 33–2 Combination soldering and melting furnace. (Johnson Gas Appliance Company)

Fig. 33–4 A bunsen burner.

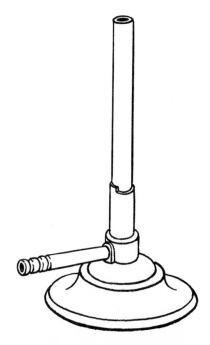

Solders

Most *soft solders* are a mixture of tin and lead. The most common, called *half-and-half,* consists of 50 percent tin and 50 percent lead. It melts at about 420°F (215°C). Solder with more tin, such as 60–40, melts at lower temperatures, about 360 to 370°F (182 to 188°C), and is more free-flowing. Those with more lead require more heat and are not suited for most small projects.

Solder is available in bar, solid wire, and powder forms. More convenient are the acid-core and rosin-core wire types. These have flux in the hollow center of the wire. Soldering paste, containing both solder and flux in paste form, is also available. Solder in preformed shapes is also used for convenience and neatness.

Fluxes

When metal is exposed to the air, a film of oxide, or rust and tarnish, forms on it. The process of oxidation increases greatly when metal is heated. This must be prevented because the oxide tends to keep the metal from reaching soldering temperature and from uniting with the solder. A material called a **flux,** therefore, is used to:

1. Remove the oxide from the metal.
2. Prevent the formation of new oxide.
3. Reduce surface tension so that the molten solder will flow easily by capillary attraction.
4. Assist alloying action of the solder with the workpiece.

There are two types of flux, corrosive and noncorrosive. The first is more effective but must never be used on electrical connections. It must also be removed from any metal after soldering by washing in hot water. The noncorrosive is for all electrical and electronic work. The better commercial kinds can be used on tin plate, copper, brass, and other alloys of copper. There are many

Table 33–1
Soldering Fluxes
for Different Base Metals

Base metal	Flux
aluminum	manufacturer's special flux
brass	cut acid (zinc chloride flux)
copper	rosin (resin)*
galvanized iron	muriatic acid
mild steel	sal ammoniac
nickel silver	cut acid
pewter	rosin
tin	rosin
tin plate	rosin

*Both spellings are used.

kinds of corrosive and noncorrosive fluxes for special purposes (Table 33–1):

A good *corrosive flux* can be prepared in the shop by adding small pieces of zinc to muriatic, or hydrochloric, acid until the zinc no longer dissolves. This solution, called *cut acid* or *zinc chloride flux,* must be mixed half and half with water before using. The zinc must be dissolved in a well-ventilated room. You should do this carefully and wear proper eye protection. *Sal ammoniac* in powder or bar form is a satisfactory corrosive flux. Many types of liquid, powder, or crystal corrosive flux are available under various commercial names.

A very good *noncorrosive flux* is powdered rosin, or resin. Many variations of this in liquid and paste form can be purchased.

Tinning a soldering copper

After a soldering copper has been used for some time, or if it gets overheated, the point becomes covered with oxide. Then the heat cannot flow to the metal. To correct this, the point must be cleaned and covered with solder. The process is called *tinning a soldering copper:*

1. File the point of the soldering copper with a mill file until the clean exposed copper appears (Fig. 33–5).

2. Heat the soldering copper until it turns to yellow or light brown. Then do one of the following:

Fig. 33–5 Filing the point of a soldering copper to remove corrosion and to get a clean, well-shaped point.

Fig. 33–6 One way to tin a soldering copper is to apply an acid-core or rosin-core solder to the point and rub the point on a smooth surface.

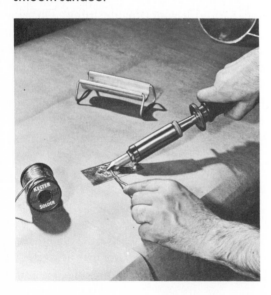

a. Apply acid-core or rosin-core solder to the point (Fig. 33–6).

b. Rub the point on a bar of sal ammoniac, and apply a few drops of solder (Fig. 33–7).

c. Dip the point in liquid flux, and rub with a bar of solder.

3. Wipe the point with a clean cloth to remove the excess molten solder.

Cleanliness

Solder will never stick to a dirty, oily, or oxide-coated surface. Beginners often ignore this simple point. If the metal is dirty, clean it with a liquid cleaner. If it is black annealed sheet, remove the oxide with abrasive cloth, and clean it until the surface is bright. A bright metal, such as copper, can be coated with oxide even though you cannot see it. This oxide can be removed with any fine abrasive.

Fig. 33–7 Another method of tinning a soldering copper is to rub it on a bar of sal ammoniac and apply solder to the point.

SOLDER

SAL AMMONIAC

Fig. 33–8 Applying flux to the seam.

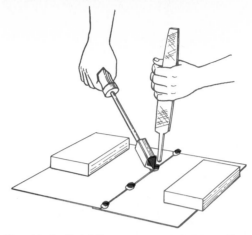

Fig. 33–9 Hold the seam or joint together firmly as you tack it with solder at several points.

Soldering a seam or joint

1. Place the two pieces on a soldering table that has a non-heat-conducting top, such as firebrick.

2. Clean the area of the seam.

3. Make sure that the seam is held together properly. If necessary, place small weights on it.

4. Apply a coat of flux with a swab or brush (Fig. 33–8). Use rosin flux on most metals. A raw-acid flux is needed for galvanized iron. If wire-core solder is used, the area will be fluxed as it is soldered.

5. Heat the soldering copper just until the point can melt solder quickly. *Never allow the soldering copper to become red-hot.*

6. Tack the seam in several places (Fig. 33–9). Put the point of the soldering copper on the seam. Leave it there until the flux sizzles. Then immediately put a small amount of solder directly in front of the point. Never apply the solder directly to the copper, since this merely makes the solder run without joining the two pieces.

7. Start at one end of the seam. Hold the copper with the tapered side flat on the metal until the solder melts (Fig. 33–10).

8. Move the soldering copper along slowly in one direction only, never back and forth (Fig. 33–11). Put more solder in front of the point as needed. If necessary, press the

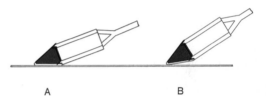

A   B

Fig. 33–10 The correct (A) and incorrect (B) ways of holding a soldering copper on metal.

Fig. 33–11 Move the copper along slowly so that the solder flows into the seam or joint.

197

freshly soldered part of the seam together with a tool such as a file until the solder hardens.

9. Clean the seam with warm running water if acid flux has been used. Baking soda mixed in the water will neutralize the chemical action.

10. Check your work. Is the soldered seam smooth? Are the metals really soldered together? Did you use too much solder?

Soldering a right-angle joint

1. Block up the pieces so that the corner seam is in a horizontal position. Use bricks or charcoal blocks.

2. Apply flux at several points along the joint. Tack the two pieces together.

3. Flow the solder on along the seam.

Soldering an appendage

Handles, feet, clips, and other similar appendages are fastened in place as follows:

1. Apply flux and a little solder at the point where the appendage is to go.

2. Apply a little flux again. Hold the appendage in place. Heat the area until it is sweat-soldered (see below). Hold the appendage with pliers, since it usually becomes too hot to handle before the solder melts (Fig. 33–12).

Sweat soldering

Sweat soldering is soldering two or more pieces one on top of the other. You cannot see any of the solder afterwards. This type of soldering is often used to fasten together several thicknesses of metal to make a heavier part. The handle of a letter opener is a good example.

1. Flux one surface, and apply a thin coat of solder. Flux the opposite surface. Clamp the pieces together with paper clips, small wire clips, or pliers (Fig. 33–13).

2. Hold the pieces over a bunsen burner until the solder oozes out at the edge

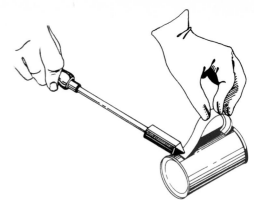

Fig. 33–12 Soldering a handle on a cup. Hold such an appendage with pliers or a glove.

Fig. 33–13 Make several wire clips, as shown, to hold two or more pieces together for sweat soldering.

Fig. 33–14 Hold the pieces to be sweat-soldered over a bunsen burner until the solder begins to ooze out at the edges. A propane torch can also be used.

(Fig. 33–14). For a neat job, use a small amount of solder.

3. Sweat soldering can be used to make a joint. Cover the surfaces to be joined with a

thin coat of solder. Holding the two parts together, apply heat with a soldering copper until they are fastened.

Soldering a box

The sides of a simple box are sometimes soldered to the bottom. Often, the sides are hard-soldered together before the bottom is soft-soldered to the sides (see Unit 46). Solder the bottom as follows:

1. Clean the surface with steel wool. Pay special attention to the area of the bottom to be soldered.

2. Hold the bottom to the sides with black-iron wire, making sure that the joint fits tightly.

3. Add a little flux to the joint.

4. Hold the joint over the flame of the bunsen burner until the flux boils. Move the box back and forth to heat the joint evenly. Reapply a little flux.

5. Touch the joint with wire solder until it flows along the edge. Work quickly to keep oxide from forming.

? QUESTIONS

1. What is soldering?
2. Name five kinds of heating devices commonly used in soldering.
3. What is soft solder made of?
4. How does metal oxidation hinder soldering?
5. Which kind of flux can be used on electrical connections? Which cannot?
6. What must you do when the point on a soldering copper becomes coated with oxide?
7. How can you remove oxide from a bright metal, such as copper?
8. How much should the soldering copper be heated?
9. When soldering a seam with a soldering copper, where do you put the solder?
10. What is sweat soldering?

✓ EXTRA CREDIT

Study the chemistry and physics of soft soldering, and report on (1) applied heat, (2) capillary action, and (3) chemical change of fluxes.

Unit 34
Spot Welding

Spot welding is a pressure-welding process in which the heat is generated by resistance to an electric current. Spot welding is used frequently in sheet-metal fabrication. Two pieces of sheet metal are held together under slight pressure between two copper electrodes. A heavy electric current is then passed through the metal. The resistance of the metal to the current heats those spots on both sheets where the current passes to a plastic, or soft, state. The two pieces are thus welded together (Fig. 34–1). If a spot weld is made correctly, it is stronger than a rivet of the same diameter.

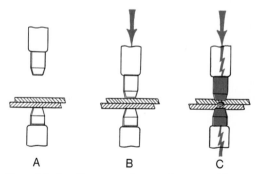

Fig. 34–1 How spot welding is done: (A) Sheets are placed between tips. (B) Pressure is applied to the sheets. (C) Electric current causes sheets to weld by fusion.

Spot-welding machines

Spot-welding machines include portable models that are operated by hand (Fig. 34–

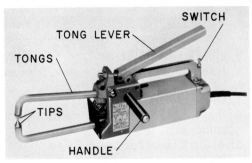

Fig. 34-2 Parts of a hand-operated portable spot welder. (Miller Electric Manufacturing Company)

Fig. 34-4 Spot welding heavy-gage metal parts.

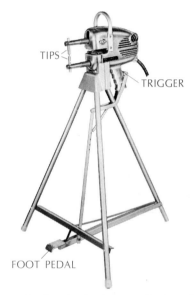

Fig. 34-3 Parts of a foot-operated pedestal spot welder. (Ajax Electric Company)

2) and floor models that are operated by foot (Fig. 34-3). In industry, air-operated or motor-operated machines are used. Spot welders have controls for regulating pressure, heat, and time.

Spot welding

1. Be sure the two pieces of metal are clean. A small spot welder will weld clean pieces of mild steel up to 1/8 inch (3 mm) in combined thickness or two pieces of 20-gage (1-mm) galvanized sheet.

2. Lap the two pieces to be joined about 1/4 to 1/2 inch (6 to 13 mm).

3. Turn on the electric power.

4. Holding the two pieces between the copper electrodes, apply pressure to complete the weld (Fig. 34-4).

Other applications

Spot welding can also be used to join metal bar and rod stock of many sizes. You must check the capacity of your spot welder before doing some of this heavier work.

? QUESTIONS

1. What is spot welding?
2. What generates the heat in spot welding?
3. How does the strength of a spot weld compare with that of a rivet?
4. What other metal pieces can be spot welded besides metal sheets?

✓ EXTRA CREDIT

Study the metal products in your home. See if you can identify parts that were assembled by spot welding.

Unit 35
Industrial Cold-Working Methods

Most of the processes you perform in bench, sheet, and art metal are what industry calls the *cold working* of metals. **Cold working** includes all the processes that change the shape and form of metal, usually in sheets, when it is below softening temperature, commonly at room temperature. The four basic cold-working processes in sheet-metal manufacturing are cutting, bending, press forming or stamping, and spinning.

In industry, cold working is usually preferred to heating because it is less expensive, sizes are more accurate, and there is a better final finish. Also, the grain follows the contour of the shape, resulting in a stronger structure. In the cold-working processes, metal becomes **work-hardened.** Thus, it is sometimes necessary to **anneal,** or soften, the metal at some point during a forming process. The major disadvantage of cold working is that it distorts the grain of the metal in large pieces, sometimes causing it to crack or otherwise rupture.

Cutting

The major methods of metal cutting include shearing and slitting; blanking; piercing; sawing; and flame, abrasive, and chemical cutting. The term **shearing** is generally applied to straight cuts made by two straight blades on sheets and plates. **Slitting** is similar, except that rotating knives are used to do the cutting (Fig. 35–1). In **blanking,** the metal is cut into shapes with a die. A **die** is a tool used to cut or form metal. In blanking, the part cut out is the one that is used (Fig. 35–2). **Piercing** is the same operation as blanking, except that the part that is cut out

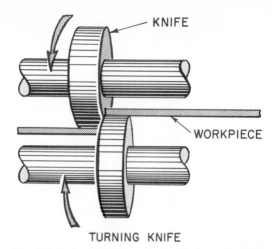

Fig. 35–1 In slitting, note that knives do the cutting. Frequently, a gang, or number, of shears is used to cut sheets into strips by this method.

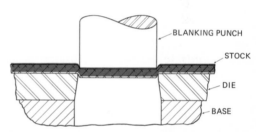

Fig. 35–2 A blanking die used to cut out parts.

becomes scrap. **Punching** is a piercing process used to form a hole or opening in the part. Holes can also be **extruded,** or pushed out. **Perforating** is piercing a series of holes. **Nibbling,** or **notching,** is piercing done along or on the edge of the metal.

Sheet-metal cutting is done by a tool called a **cutting,** or **blanking, die** that is forced together under pressure or by blows from the press (Fig. 35–3). The upper part of the die is called the **punch.** The lower part, the **matrix,** has a recess or cavity. It is usually fastened to the nonmovable part of the machine. The operations performed by cutting dies are called blanking, piercing, trimming,

Fig. 35-3 OSHA standards will require special guards to protect the punch-press operator. (Thomson Industries)

ADJUSTABLE AIR CONTROL
AIR ON UP STROKE ONLY — SHANK
PUNCH HOLDER
PRESSURE PAD PROTECTING PUNCHES
FINISHED PIECE IS   LIFTER PINS OR
BLOWN OUT OF DIE   STRIPPER PINS
                          TO GUIDE STOCK
SHOE
PRESSURE   AIR NOZZLE
PAD   FOUR-STAGE DIE

FOURTH STAGE	THIRD STAGE	SECOND STAGE	FIRST STAGE

CUT OFF OR BLANKING	FINAL FORM	NOTCH AND FORM	PIERCE AND NOTCH	ROLL STOCK

FINISHED PIECE

Fig. 35-4 A four-stage progressive die—from roll stock to finished piece.

or shaving. These dies are often made as sets to do several operations, one after the other (Fig. 35-4).

Bending

Bending is changing the shape of the metal in one direction. Sheet metal is usually bent on a cornice brake, bar folder, or forming rolls. In industry, sheet stock is bent on large mechanical or hydraulic press brakes using sets of dies to form the metal (Fig. 35-5). In Fig. 35-6, for example, a roof deck is being formed on a mechanical press brake. These machines vary in size and design to do a wide variety of bending operations.

Press forming

The most important of the cold-working processes used to mass-produce sheet-metal

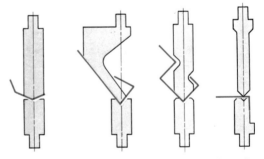

Fig. 35-5 Examples of press-brake dies used to bend metal.

products is **press forming,** or **stamping.** Today, many automobile parts formerly made by such expensive methods as forging,

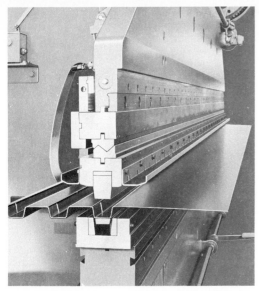

Fig. 35-6 A large mechanical press brake used to manufacture roof decks. (Cincinnati Shaper Company)

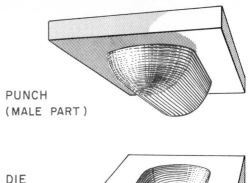

PUNCH
(MALE PART)

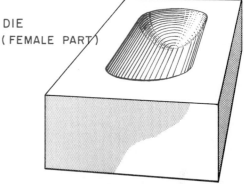

DIE
(FEMALE PART)

Fig. 35-7 The simplest type of forming die.

casting, or machining are now made by stamping. In stamping, dies are used to cut and shape the metal. The dies must be changed for each new type of work. Presses provide the power to operate the dies. The presses are fixed on permanent equipment. They are used for many different operations.

A **forming die** is used to give shape to metal. A simple forming die is shown in Fig. 35-7. This type could be made of wood. A forming die set is shown in Fig. 35-8. Sometimes, the die sets are made to do several operations, one after the other.

Dies are used in either large mechanical or hydraulic presses. In press forming, the actual process of shaping the product is called **drawing**. Drawing forms a flat sheet of metal into a seamless, hollow shape by means of a punch that causes the metal to flow into the die cavity. When a deep, cup-shaped article is made in this manner, the process may be called **deep drawing.** Drawing has the widest application of all sheet-

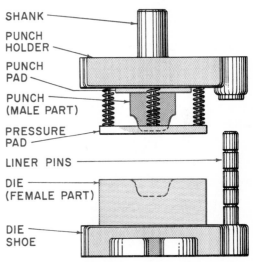

SHANK
PUNCH HOLDER
PUNCH PAD
PUNCH (MALE PART)
PRESSURE PAD
LINER PINS
DIE (FEMALE PART)
DIE SHOE

Fig. 35-8 A complete forming die set.

forming methods. It involves a great variety of techniques. Drawing may be done in a single operation. More often, the drawn part goes through a series of stages to its final form.

Rubber-forming process

Forming metal parts with rubber is commonly called the **Guerin Process.** This method is employed when a limited number of parts of the same kind is needed. A lower die made of steel, hardboard, or aluminum is used to impart the shape. Instead of an upper die, or punch, heavy rubber in a metal frame is used on top (Fig. 35-9). Rubber is, of course, much less expensive than metal dies. When the forming is done, a metal blank is placed over the lower die. The ram is lowered so that the rubber forces the metal around the die.

Press-brake operations are also possible with this technique. Die inserts made of flexible urethane plastic are used in this kind of bending operation. You can see in Fig. 35-10 that only the punch (on top) needs to be changed. The flexible insert can be used for a variety of shapes.

Fig. 35-9 The equipment for rubber forming. The workpiece is placed between the rubber slabs and the dies for forming.

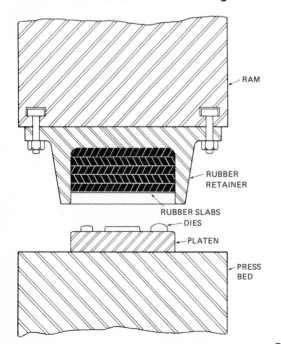

Hydroforming

Hydroforming is another kind of deep drawing. In hydroforming, the dies are reversed. The matrix, or fixed part, of the die is replaced by a flexible diaphragm that can accommodate any shape. The punch that does the shaping of the part is attached to the fixed part of the machine. The blank is placed over the punch, and the forming is done as shown in Fig. 35-11. In this process, the dies are less expensive and can be used for short-run jobs.

Other forming processes

Three other ways of forming thin sheet metal are coining, stamping, and embossing. Stamping and coining compress the metal; embossing stretches it. Often, one of these processes is combined with drawing.

The word *stamping* is used in a general way to refer to all press-forming operations. In a more restricted sense, **stamping** means producing a shallow shape on one side of a blank. This is done with a *stamp*, or male die,

Fig. 35-10 Progressive steps in forming with urethane die pads.

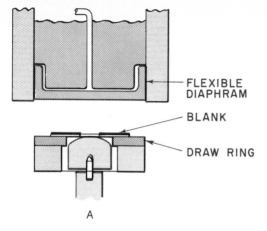

FLEXIBLE DIAPHRAM

BLANK

DRAW RING

A

Fig. 35-11 How hydroforming works: (A) A blank is placed on the blank holder. (B) The forming chamber is lowered and the initial pressure is applied. (C) The punch moves upward into the flexible die member. (D) Pressure is released and the forming chamber raised. The punch is stripped from the finished part.

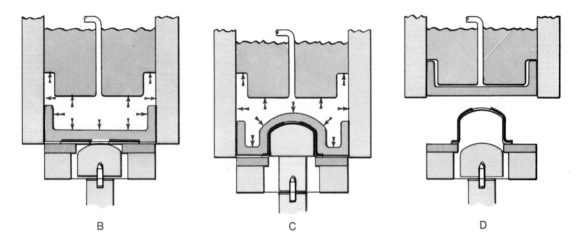

B   C   D

which has a raised pattern cut on it that makes the design.

Coining is forming designs on both sides of a blank at the same time, such as in making coin money. **Embossing** is a shallow drawing process that produces a design similar to metal tooling (see Unit 38).

Spinning

Spinning produces hollow shapes from sheet-metal disks by forcing the metal to take the shape of a rotating hardened mandrel. The workpiece turns with the mandrel. As it does so, it is shaped by pressure tools or rollers that squeeze and stretch it around the

mandrel. Many rocket and missile parts, especially nose cones, are made in this way. Most commercial products are produced by *hydrospinning* or *shear spinning*. In these methods, two or more hardened rollers exert pressure to shape the disks and make them thinner as well (Fig. 35-12).

Cold heading

The process of **cold heading** is chiefly used to make fasteners—bolts, screws, nails, and rivets—from round rod or wire stock (Fig. 35-13). Cold heading is an upsetting operation. The blank of rod or wire is struck on its end by a die. The blow spreads out the end of the blank to produce the head of the fastener. The resulting grain structure makes a very strong part (Fig. 35–14). Most cold heading is done on automatic equipment that cuts the blank from a coil of stock, forms the head and shank of the fastener, and ejects the formed part. Two dies are needed to upset the end of the blank. One holds the blank. The other delivers the forming blow. The blank is inserted from the front of the die. The end of the blank rests against the knockout pin. A suitable amount of the blank protrudes, or sticks out, from the die. The protruding end is then struck with the forming die or punch. The knockout pin moves forward to push the headed part out of the die.

Single-blow heading is illustrated in Fig. 35–15. The end of the blank is formed by a single blow of the punch. The cavity formed when the punch and die meet has the same size and shape as the finished head. Heads with smooth undersides, such as most rivet heads, are usually formed within the punch. Heads with shaped undersides but flat tops, such as most wood screws, are usually formed in the holding die. Parts shaped on both sides of the head, such as carriage bolts, are formed partly in the punch and partly in the dies.

Fig. 35–13 A cold-heading machine. The bolt is shown in its various stages of cold forming.

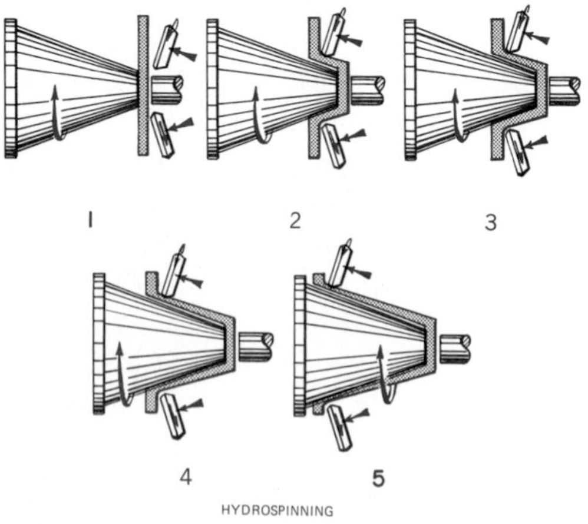

Fig. 35–14 Cold heading uses less material and produces stronger parts than machining.

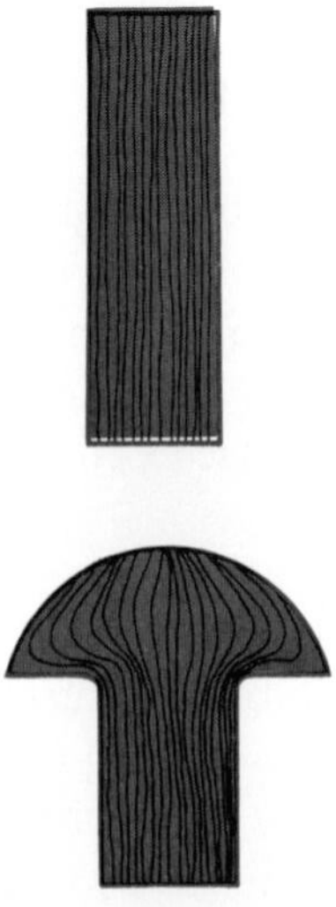

COLD HEADING METHOD

HYDROSPINNING

Fig. 35–12 This missle nose-cone section is being formed by hydrospinning. The operation is very similar to metal spinning, described in Unit 49.

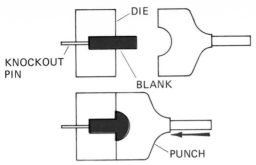

Fig. 35-15 Single-blow cold-heading diagram.

Large or complex heads require more than one forming blow. The two-blow header upsets the blank in two steps. The blank is held in the same die for both blows. However, it is formed by two different punches. The first punch preforms the head into a cone. A cone shape is used because it results in less bending of the blank, especially when large blank extensions are required. The second punch finishes the head. Two-blow heading is illustrated in Fig. 35-16.

Impact extruding

In **impact extruding,** a part is formed by a high-speed blow. The process can be used when the metal is cold or when it is moderately heated to a temperature of 450°F (232°C) or less. In the *reverse* method, a slug of metal of the exact amount needed to form the part is placed in a die cavity. This die cavity controls the bottom and outside walls of the part. The punch shapes the inside. When a high-speed blow is applied to the punch, the metal literally squirts around the punch to form the part (Fig. 35-17). This method is used to make tubes for many types of containers. The *forward* method of impact extruding is less widely used. In the forward method, the dies are of open construction. The slug is often pierced to fit a round projection at the end of the punch. The shape is then extruded by compression. The metal

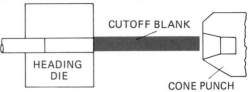

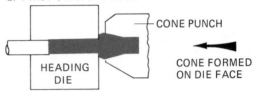

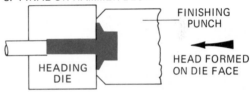

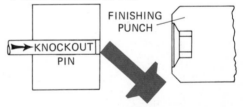

Fig. 35-16 Two-blow cold-heading diagram.

flows in the same direction as the punch stroke—downward (Fig. 35-18).

Other cold-working methods

Cold rolling, like hot rolling, is done by squeezing a workpiece between rotating cylindrical rolls (Fig. 35-19). Cold rolling is normally used only to produce thin, flat products, such as sheet or strip.

207

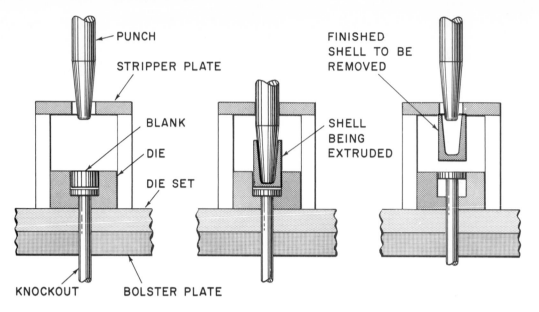

Fig. 35-17 Steps in producing a simple cylindrical part by reverse impact extruding.

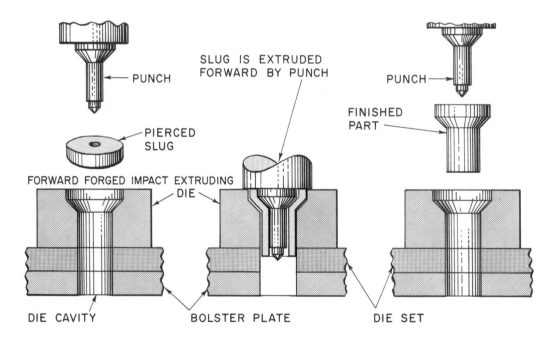

Fig. 35-18 Forward impact extruding.

Cold drawing is used to make many basic products other than sheet and strip. In cold drawing, a rod, tube, or bar is pulled through a hole in a die. The hole is smaller than the starting size of the workpiece. As it is pulled through the die, the workpiece is stretched out and reduced in cross section (Fig. 35-20). One end of the workpiece is usually pointed by grinding or some other method. This is done so that it can be inserted in the die to begin drawing. The equipment grasps the pointed end extending from the die and pulls the remainder of the piece through. A variety of shapes can be cold-drawn by using appropriate dies.

Roll forming is used to form flat sheet or strip stock into straight lengths of various cross sections. Typical shapes are angles, channels, and tube sections. Nearly any shape that can be made by parallel bends in flat stock can be roll-formed. Tubular products are made by bending a strip of metal until its edges meet and then welding the edges together. The material is shaped as it passes through a series of paired, contoured rolls. The roll-forming machine can be compared to a series of small rolling mills arranged in a straight line (Fig. 35-21).

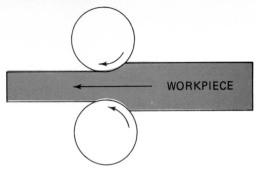

Fig. 35-19 Cold rolling is used to produce thin metal sheets and strips.

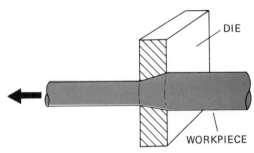

Fig. 35-20 Cold drawing.

 QUESTIONS

1. List some advantages of the cold working of metals. List a disadvantage.
2. Name eight metal-cutting methods.
3. What do you call the upper and lower parts of a die?
4. What device does industry use to bend sheet metal?
5. In press forming, what is the actual process of shaping the product called?
6. What is the advantage of forming metal parts with rubber?
7. In hydroforming, to what part of the machine is the punch attached?
8. How is coining different from embossing?
9. In spinning, what happens as the workpiece turns?
10. What is cold heading chiefly used for?
11. In impact extruding, what kind of force is applied to the punch?
12. How does cold drawing reshape a workpiece?

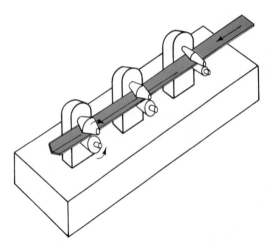

Fig. 35-21 Roll forming is a cold-forming method used to produce angles, channels, and tubes.

 EXTRA CREDIT

1. Select several pieces of metal from the shop, and tell how they were made.
2. Prepare a research report on one of the industrial cold-working processes.

ART METAL AND JEWELRY

Unit 36

Introduction to Art Metal and Jewelry

In *art-metal work,* articles of beautiful design are made from a variety of metals and processes (Fig. 36–1). *Jewelry work* is somewhat similar, except that the articles are smaller, more intricate, and are mostly for personal wear. In *silversmithing,* tableware of sterling silver is made.

Tools and processes

Besides the tool operations used in bench and sheet metal, many special processes are used in art metal (Table 36–1). You will learn about shaping and forming and about surface decorating operations, such as piercing and planishing, fluting, flaring, coloring, and etching. In jewelry and silverware, other surface decorations—such as engraving, enameling, chasing, repoussé, and filigree— are also used.

Engraving is cutting a design on a metal surface with sharp-pointed tools. Engraving on jewelry is usually done by machine, but hand engraving is often done in hobby and craft work. **Repoussé** work is similar to shaping metal foil. The design is made to stand out boldly in relief by placing the metal over a soft substance, such as pitch, and hammering from the front and back with punches. **Filigree** is the art of bending very fine wire into intricate designs. In **enameling,** a permanent, glassy, colored surface is baked on metal, usually copper or silver, in a furnace.

Materials

Nonferrous metals are generally used in art metal and jewelry. Copper, brass, aluminum, bronze, and pewter are the most common sheet materials. These range in thickness from about 36 gage (0.13 mm), for tooling, to 18 gage (1 mm), for raising and piercing. In addition, metal wires, bars, and rods are used. Silver and gold are also used, but they are costly.

Fig. 36–1 Beautifully shaped silverware. (Georg Jensen)

210

Table 36–1
Art-Metal Operations

Cutting Operations	Equipment used
sawing and piercing	hacksaw, band saw, jeweler's saw
shearing	tin snips, scissors, bench shears
abrading	grinder and abrasives
punching	hollow and solid punches
etching	etching liquids and resists

Forming operations	Equipment used
bending	sheet-metal bending tools
spinning	spinning tools and machine
sinking	hammers and forms
raising	hammers and forms
tapping	hammer and tapping tools
chasing	hammer and chasing tools
stamping	hammer and stamping tools
tooling	molding or modeling tools
fluting	hammer and fluting tools
doming	hammer and dapping set
scalloping	scalloping tools
floring	hammer and floring tools

Fastening operations	Equipment used
soldering	soldering supplies
brazing	brazing supplies
riveting	riveting tools
adhering	cement and adhesives

Finishing operations	Equipment used
enameling	enameling supplies and kiln
planishing	planishing hammers and stakes
buffing	buffer and compounds
coloring	coloring chemicals and heating devices
coating	lacquers, paints, and plastic sprays

Art metals can have razor-sharp edges. Be careful to avoid painful cuts and slivers.

Fig. 36–2   Evolution of a fork. From left to right, 12 of over 40 steps in making a fork: the blank, cross-rolled blank, grade-rolled blank, outlined blank, scrap after outlining blank, tined blank, form stamped, finished stamped, flash removed, tine-bar cut off, burrs removed, finished fork. (Reed & Barton)

Processes in manufacturing

Many art-metal operations are similar to those used in industry to shape metal parts. While you will do these things by hand, industry uses large machinery. Figure 36–2 shows the stages in manufacturing a fork.

Opportunities in jewelry and watchmaking

There are about 35,000 people employed as jewelers, jewelry repairers, watchmakers, goldsmiths, and silversmiths. *Jewelers* are skilled workers who make and repair rings, pins, and other ornaments. They use small hand tools and such machines as a jeweler's lathe. They work with gold, silver, platinum, and other precious metals and with precious and semiprecious stones. *Silversmiths* specialize in designing and constructing silverware and tableware.

Many more people enjoy making art metal and jewelry as a hobby. It is a very good leisure-time activity because only a few hand tools and little space are needed and because costs are low relative to the value of the finished article.

1. Name three art-metal forming operations. Three finishing operations.
2. What is engraving? Repoussé? Filigree?
3. What kind of metal is generally used in art-metal work?
4. What are some of the materials jewelers work with?
5. What are the advantages of art-metal work as a hobby?

1. Make a study of the metal crafts of a foreign country. For example, study the history of the English Pewter Guild.
2. Write a report on the mass production of art-metal products.

Unit 37
Metal Tapping, Chasing, and Design Stamping

Designs are pressed into metal surfaces by a number of different methods. In this unit, you will learn about hand processes for producing designs on metal. These processes are tapping, chasing, and stamping.

Metal tapping

Tapping is striking metal repeatedly with a tapping tool to produce a design. By this method, with a little patience and a good design, anyone can make a beautiful object such as a plaque, bookend, letter tray, or tie rack.

Tools and materials

Metal for tapping should be about 30-gage tin plate, sheet copper, brass, or aluminum. If the project is a plaque, you will need other materials for mounting it: a piece of 1/4-inch (6.5 mm) plywood and a number of small 1/8- to 1/4-inch (3- to 6.5-mm) *escutcheon pins,* small roundhead brass nails. The *tapping tool* can be a simple ice pick, a center punch, or several large-size nails ground to different-shaped points. The best tools, how-

ever, are made from drill rod. After the drill-rod points are shaped to different designs, they should be hardened and tempered (see Unit 69).

Metal-tapping procedures

1. Choose a design, and cut a piece of metal to size.
2. Fasten the piece of metal to the plywood with 1/4-inch (6.5-mm) escutcheon pins. Hold them with tweezers or jeweler's pliers.
3. Attach the paper design to the metal with masking tape.
4. Outline the design and border by tapping it with a tapping tool. *Do not strike it so hard that you make a hole in the metal.* Remove the paper design.
5. The background should be stippled in, or covered with uniform dots, with the same tool or with a blunter one (Fig. 37–1). Work outward from the design and inward from the edge. This will keep the metal from stretching too much in one direction.
6. Clean the surface lightly with steel wool or fine abrasive cloth, and apply a coat of clear lacquer.

Chasing

Chasing is tapping with special tools (Fig. 37–2). The design is outlined with *tracing tools. Matting tools* are used to fill in the

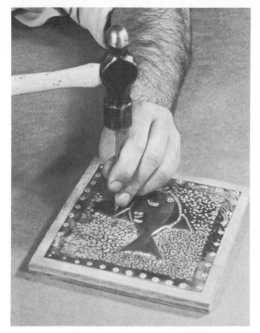

Fig. 37-1 The metal has been fastened to the plywood with escutcheon pins, the design transferred to the metal, and the outline completed. The background is being stippled in to complete the metal-tapping project.

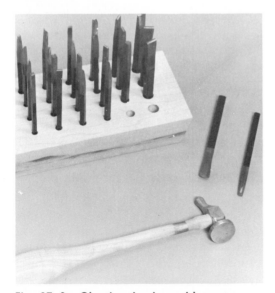

Fig. 37-3 Chasing tools and hammer.

background. A *chasing hammer* is the tapping tool (Figs. 37–3, 37–4). In advanced chasing,

Fig. 37-2 Chasing, the ancient art of decorating silver. (International Silver Company)

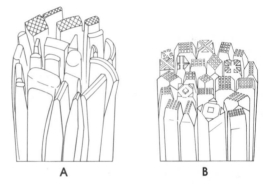

A   B

Fig. 37-4 Chasing tools of various designs: (A) tracing tools, (B) matting tools.

the work is held in a pitch block. For simple chasing, the work can be clamped over a piece of soft wood (Figs. 37–5, 37–6).

Design stamping

Stamping is producing a design on metal by striking it with a punch. Punches for design stamping have intricately shaped points. Many of them are Native American designs. To apply the design, hold the punch over the flat metal, and strike it firmly with a hammer. Never force the design too deeply in the metal or repeat the stamping after it has been done the first time (Fig. 37–7).

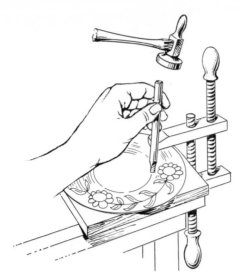

Fig. 37–5   Outlining a chased design.

Fig. 37–7   Note the method of supporting the workpiece being stamped.

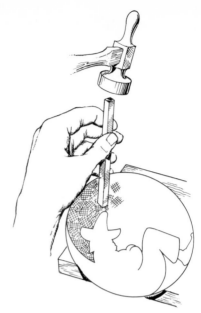

Fig. 37–6   Working down the background of a chased design.

 QUESTIONS

1.   What is metal tapping?
2.   What metals are good for tapping?
3.   What articles make good tapping tools?
4.   How can you keep the metal from stretching while the background is being stippled in?
5.   What special tools are used in chasing?
6.   What tool is used in design stamping?

 EXTRA CREDIT

Develop a design for metal tapping.

Unit 38
Tooling Metal

Metal tooling is creating a bold-relief design on metal foil. A tooled design may appear on wall plaques, lamp bases, overlays for bookends, box covers, calendar covers, picture frames, and many other projects (Fig. 38–1).

Tools and materials

Use No. 32- to No. 36-gage (0.18- to 0.12-mm) brass, copper, or aluminum for tooling. Copper of No. 36 gage (0.12 mm) is best for the beginner. A *combination leather molding tool* that has a broad spatula end and a fine tracing end is often used for tracing the pattern. A *wood molding tool* with two ends— one flat and square and the other round and spatula-shaped—is also needed (Fig. 38–2). For many tracing operations, you can also use such common items as a nut pick, a pointed dowel rod, or an old ballpoint pen. Other materials include old newspapers, steel wool, liver of sulfur, metal lacquer, plaster of paris or patching plaster, and a piece of glass or tempered masonite.

Procedure

A diagram of the tooling process is shown in Fig. 38–3. The exact steps are as follows:

1. Select a simple design, such as a silhouette, a profile, or an etching, as a first project. You must be able to imagine how the design looks in three dimensions.

2. Trace the design on thin paper.

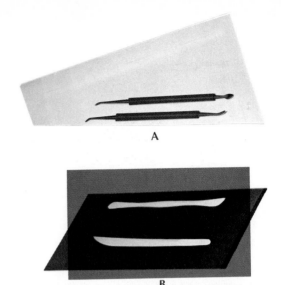

Fig. 38-2 Metal-tooling tools: (A) modelers, (B) smoothing or flattening tools.

3. Cut the metal foil to size with shears or tin snips. Be careful not to kink it. Allow extra metal for mounting.

4. Attach the design to the center of the foil with tape or paper clips.

5. Place the metal and the design over 12 or more sheets of newspaper, a couple of desk blotters, or some other padding.

Fig. 38-1 A wall plaque made by tooling metal.

Fig. 38-3 Tooling procedure: (A) outline, (B) interline, (C) raise, (D) flatten.

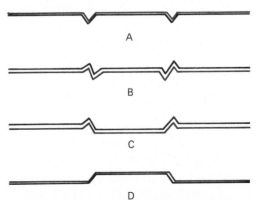

Fig. 38-4 The broad spatula end of the leather molding tool is being used to work out the design from the back. In the foreground, you see the wood molding tool.

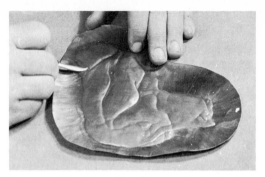

Fig. 38-5 The background is being smoothed to keep it flat.

6. Carefully trace the design with the fine tracing end of a molding tool or with a ballpoint pen. Make sure that the line can be clearly seen. Be careful not to lean on the metal, as this will dent it.

7. Remove the design, and turn the metal face down on the padding.

8. Using the spatula end of the molding tool (Fig. 38-4), work the design out from the outline toward the center. Force the metal down until the design clearly stands out. Use long sweeping strokes, making every one count. As you work down the design, thicken the pad to make it softer.

9. Try to keep the background smooth and flat. During tooling, the background tends to become distorted. To keep it flat, place the metal face up on a hard surface (Fig. 38-5), and flatten the background with the square end of a tool. You can also decorate the background with diagonal or cross-hatched lines.

10. Place the metal face down on the pad again. Continue tooling and flattening until the entire design has been produced.

11. Using your hand as a pad, put in fine detail with a tool with a fine tracing end.

You may have to work on both the front and the back of the metal.

12. Polish the surface with 3/0 steel wool.

13. Color or antique the surface (see Unit 48) and lacquer it (see Unit 51) as desired.

14. Fill the back with some material such as plaster of paris, paraffin wax, molding clay, or Plastic Wood.

15. Mount the design on wood, or frame it.

 QUESTIONS

1. What metals of what thicknesses are best for tooling?
2. Name the tools needed.
3. What tools are used to cut the tooling metal?
4. What materials can be used for padding?
5. What do you use to work the design?
6. What do you use to flatten the background?

 EXTRA CREDIT

Make a display that shows the steps in metal tooling.

In art-metal work, **sawing** involves cutting intricate outline shapes out of metal (Fig. 39–1). Making interior cutout designs is called **piercing.**

Saw frames and blades

The *jeweler's-saw frame* is similar to a hacksaw frame. However, it is lighter and takes smaller blades. These are from 3 to 6 1/2 inches (76 to 165 mm) long (Fig. 39–2). The U-shaped frames commonly come in 2 1/2- and 5-inch (6.4- and 127-mm) depths. Jeweler's blades are sized from No. 6/0, smaller than a thread, to No. 14, over 1/16 inch (1.5 mm) wide. For average light work, use a No. 2/0 or No. 1/0. For slightly heavier work, use a No. 1 or No. 2 (Fig. 39–3). These blades can also be used in a saber saw. If you do not have a jeweler's-saw frame, you can use blades with pinned or bent ends installed in a coping-saw frame.

Fig. 39–1 Complex outline shapes are made by art-metal sawing.

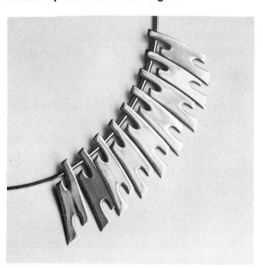

Cutting with a jeweler's saw

1. Adjust the frame so that it is about 1/2 inch (13 mm) longer than the blade. Fasten the blade in one end with the teeth pointing *toward the handle.*

2. Hold the frame against the edge of the bench, pressing the handle with your body, and fasten the handle end. If piercing is to be done, a hole must be drilled in the waste stock and the work slipped over the blade before the second end is fastened.

3. Fasten a bench pin or V-block in a vise or on the end of a table. It should be at

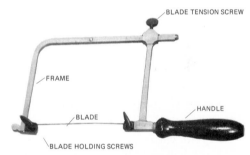

BLADE TENSION SCREW

FRAME

BLADE

HANDLE

BLADE HOLDING SCREWS

Fig. 39–2 The jeweler's saw.

Fig. 39–3 Exact sizes of jeweler's-saw blades.

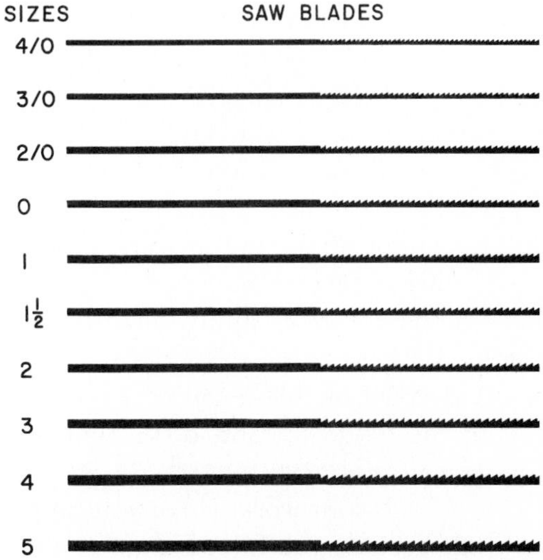

SIZES   SAW BLADES

4/0

3/0

2/0

0

1

1½

2

3

4

5

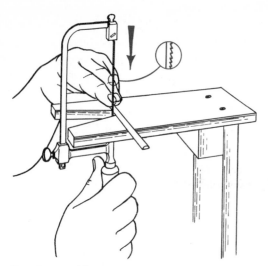

Fig. 39-4 When using a jeweler's saw, be sure to hold the workpiece firmly and to cut carefully. It is easy to break these thin saw blades. Cut on the downstroke.

Fig. 39-5 Art-metal sawing and piercing is smoothed out by working with needle files.

about elbow height when you are seated so that you can sit down and relax as you cut.

4. Hold the metal over the V-block with your left hand. The cutting should be done in the V part of the block. Hold the saw vertically in your right hand.

5. Start sawing in the waste stock with up-and-down movement, using the entire length of the blade. The cutting is done on the downstroke. Try to maintain a uniform, easy motion. Avoid bending the blade, for it can break very easily (Fig. 39-4).

6. Come up to the layout line at a slight angle. Then cut along just outside it. Move the saw a little at a time.

7. Do not apply any forward pressure as you saw, even at a sharp corner. If the blade tends to stick, apply a little soap or wax.

8. To back out of the saw kerf, continue moving the blade up and down while removing it.

9. Check your work. Have you broken the blade because you forced it or tilted the frame? Is the line smooth, needing only a little filing? Have you cut the piece too small?

10. Finish off the cutting by filing smooth with needle files (Fig. 39-5). Be careful not to break these fragile files.

 QUESTIONS

1. What is piercing?
2. How is a jeweler's-saw frame **different** from a hacksaw frame?
3. How do the blades for the jeweler's-saw frames range in size?
4. When the blade is in the frame, **which way should the teeth point?**
5. How much of the blade do you use for sawing?
6. How can you keep the blade from sticking?

 EXTRA CREDIT

Make a tour of a jewelry repair shop or jewelry store. Find out what tools are used by the jeweler to make and repair such things as brooches, pins, earrings, and rings. Report to the class.

218

Unit 40
Annealing and Pickling Art Metals

As metal is shaped, it becomes work-hardened. It must then be **annealed,** or softened, by a heat-treating process. It also becomes covered with dirt and oxide. It must therefore also be **pickled,** or cleaned, in an acid bath. During forming, these two things are done at the same time. After the final shape is obtained, only pickling is needed. This unit is concerned with the annealing and pickling of copper and aluminum. The hardening, tempering, and annealing of steel are discussed in Unit 69.

Pickling solutions

A *pickling solution* is a mixture of acid and water.

 CAUTION

Always pour the acid into the water, never the reverse.

Remember that pickling solutions can be dangerous. Proper steps must be taken to avoid burning your skin, injuring your eyes, or burning holes in your clothing. Mix the solution as follows:

1. Get a glass or earthenware jar large enough to hold the largest project you will be making. The jar must have a cover and must be kept in a well-ventilated place, since acid fumes rust steel tools rapidly.

2. Pour a gallon or multiple of a gallon of water into the jar to fill it half to three-fourths full.

3. Slowly add 10 ounces of sulfuric acid for each gallon of water, stirring the solution with a glass or wooden rod to keep it from overheating.

In metric terms, add 78 mL of sulfuric acid for every liter of water.

Annealing and pickling copper and its alloys

1. Heat the metal to a dull red over a bunsen burner, with a torch, or in a soldering furnace. If you use a soldering furnace, be careful that the hot copper does not touch any old solder. This would pit the metal.

2. Heat slowly and evenly to bring the entire piece up to annealing temperature.

3. Pick up the heated article with copper tweezers or tongs, and *slide* it into the pickling solution. *Never drop it,* making a splash (Fig. 40–1). The rapid cooling will anneal the metal and clean off the dirt and oxide.

4. Remove the article from the solution with the tweezers or tongs. Clean it under warm running water.

Annealing can also be done with water instead of pickling acid, but this does not remove the oxide.

Fig. 40–1 Slide the metal into the acid solution. Never let the acid splash.

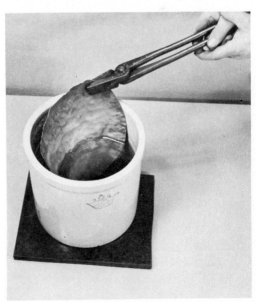

Pickling

When the forming is over and you do not want to soften the project again, place it in the solution without heating. Leave it there 5 to 10 minutes. Take it out with tweezers, wash it under warm running water, and dry it in clean sawdust or with paper towels. *Never touch the project with your fingers after it has been cleaned for the last time in preparation for adding a finish.*

Annealing aluminum

It is difficult to anneal aluminum because it is almost impossible to tell when the metal is hot enough. It is very easy to melt it or burn a hole in it. Rub some ordinary cutting oil or chalk on the surface. Heat slowly until the oil burns or the chalk discolors. Then lay the article aside, and allow it to cool slowly in the air.

 QUESTIONS

1. What must be done to work-hardened and dirty art metals?
2. What is a pickling solution?
3. What must you always remember about mixing acid and water?
4. What color is copper at annealing temperature?
5. In annealing, should the article be heated quickly or slowly?
6. How should an article be placed in the pickling solution? How should it be removed?
7. For pickling only, how long should an article remain in the pickling solution?
8. What can be done to tell when aluminum has reached annealing temperature?

 EXTRA CREDIT

Study the chemistry and physics of annealing and pickling metal. Tell what happens and why.

Unit 41
Sinking and Beating Down Art Metal

Shallow trays, plates, and bowls are formed by **sinking** or **beating down** the metal (Fig. 41–1). This is done in three common ways: sinking rectangular plates in a vise, sinking or beating down in a wooden or metal form, and beating down over a wood or metal block.

Sinking rectangular plates

1. Lay out and cut a piece of metal to a rectangular shape slightly larger than the finished size of the project.

2. Mark a line that shows the area to be sunk.

Fig. 41–1 This aluminum leaf serving tray is a good example of a tray made by beating down in a form. A metal or wooden form of this shape is needed.

3. Cut two pieces of hardwood or angle iron equal in length to the longest side of the metal.

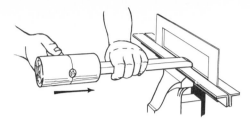

Fig. 41-2   Sinking a rectangular plate.

4. Get a rounded hardwood stick or metal punch and a mallet or hammer.

5. Fasten the metal in a vise between the wood or metal jaws, with the layout line just above the edge of the jaws.

6. Hold the punch just above the vise jaws, and strike it firmly with the hammer (Fig. 41-2). Work along from one side to the other, sinking the metal a little at a time. Rotate the metal a quarter turn and repeat. Anneal as needed.

7. When the forming is complete, the edge will be stretched out of shape. Trim it with snips, and file it. Then decorate the metal. Either the edge or the recessed portion or both can be planished (see Unit 43).

Beating down a tray into a form

1. Select a metal or wooden form with a recessed section of the desired size (Fig. 41-3). For simple, small trays, the top of an electric-outlet box is good. You can make a round, oval, or irregular form by cutting out the center of a 3/4-inch (19-mm) piece of plywood to the right shape and fastening the outside to another piece of plywood. Choose a forming hammer (Fig. 41-4).

2. Cut a piece of metal slightly larger than the size of the tray. Small trays can be made of 24- or 22-gage (0.5- or 0.65-mm) metal. Larger ones require 20- or 18-gage (0.8- or 1-mm) metal. The metal can be rectangular or roughly the outside shape of the finished project.

Fig. 41-3   Forms for beating down. You can make your own by cutting the shape in a piece of plywood and mounting it on another piece of wood.

3. Lay out a line showing the section to be beaten down.

4. Hold the metal over the form or, if you wish, clamp it in place. This can be done by fastening strips of wood around the edge of the metal with C-clamps. The metal can also be nailed to the form at the corners.

Fig. 41-4   Hammers for beating down can be made of wood, plastic, or metal. These are metal.

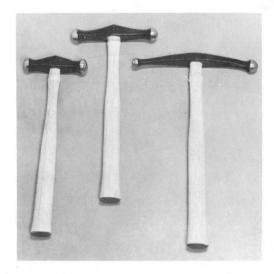

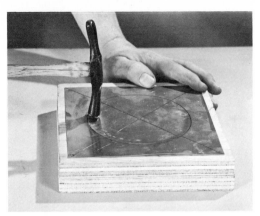

Fig. 41–5 Beating down or sinking a dish in a form. Begin just inside the layout line and strike the metal glancing blows. A metal or wooden hammer can be used. The metal has been fastened to the form with brads, or nails, driven through waste stock in the corners.

These are waste materials that will be cut away later.

5. Use a metal or wood forming hammer or a round-pointed hardwood stick and a wooden mallet. Begin just inside the layout line. Strike the metal with glancing blows to outline the area to be sunk (Fig. 41–5).

6. After you have gone completely around the form once or twice, the metal will require annealing (see Unit 40).

7. Continue forming, working in toward the center in rows until the metal is stretched to the bottom of the form (Fig. 41–6). Then strike the metal with angular blows to form the edge of the recess clearly.

8. If the metal is not clamped, remember to keep the edge flat by striking it with the flat of a wooden mallet (Fig. 41–7).

9. Finish the project by cutting, filing, and decorating the edge as desired.

Beating down over a wood or metal block

1. Select a wood or metal block similar to the one shown in Fig. 41–8 with a cutout portion that will make the kind of recess you want. The advantage of using this kind of block is that a plate of any size can be made. If the block is wooden, fasten two pins in the top of it at a distance from the edge equal to the edge of the tray. Fasten the block in a vise, with the recessed portion extending above the jaws.

Fig. 41–6 Shaping a dish with a wooden hammer.

Fig. 41–7 Flatten the edge of the dish with a mallet several times during the forming operation.

Fig. 41-8 Beating down a dish over a wood or metal block.

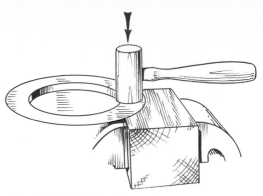

Fig. 41-9 Flatten the edge.

Fig. 41-10 True the bottom of the dish so that it will rest on a table.

2. Cut out a piece of metal to the size and shape of the tray.

3. Hold the metal firmly against the two guide pins. Use a roundnose metal or wooden hammer to strike the metal just beyond the edge of the block.

4. Move the metal a little after each stroke of the hammer, going all the way around the plate. Always keep the edge of the metal flat (Fig. 41-9). Anneal as needed. Success depends on starting the shape correctly the first time around.

5. As the project nears finished shape, strike the metal with sharp glancing blows to form the recessed portion more clearly. Flatten the bottom (Fig. 41-10).

6. Trim the edge, and decorate as you wish (Fig. 41-11).

 QUESTIONS

1. In what three ways can metal be shaped into trays, plates, and bowls?
2. In sinking a rectangular plate, how do you position the metal in the vise?
3. What thickness of metal do you use for beating down a small tray into a form? A large tray?
4. What is the advantage of using a wooden or metal block?

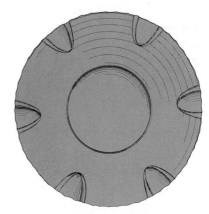

Fig. 41-11 The edge of this tray is decorated by fluting.

 EXTRA CREDIT

Find out how formed metal parts, such as body parts for cars, are manufactured, and make a report to the class.

Unit 42
Raising a Bowl

Bowls, irregularly shaped dishes, and spoons can be raised. **Raising** is forming a shaped piece of flat metal by stretching it with a raising hammer over simple forms (Fig. 42–1). These forms can be used for any size of bowl. *Raising hammers* are made of steel and come in a variety of shapes and sizes (Fig. 42–2).

Raising

1. Find the amount of material needed by bending a piece of wire to the cross-sectional shape of the bowl (Fig. 42–3). By straightening the wire, you can detemine the diameter of the disk.

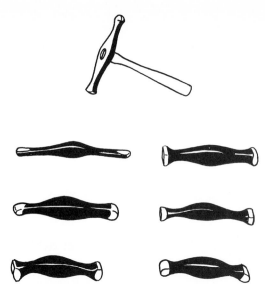

Fig. 42–2   Steel raising hammers.

Fig. 42–1   A form for raising a bowl. You can make your own by gouging out an opening in a piece of hardwood.

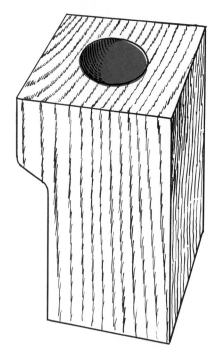

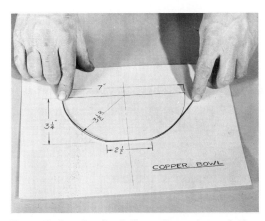

Fig. 42–3   To find the diameter of the metal disk, bend soft-wire solder to the cross-sectional shape of the bowl. You can then measure the length of the wire. Another method is to step off the length with dividers.

2. Select a piece of metal. Use a compass to lay out the required disk shape. Cut the disk out with tin snips.

3. With a pencil compass, draw several circles, one inside the other, on the disk. The center of the disk should be the center of these circles, which should be spaced equal

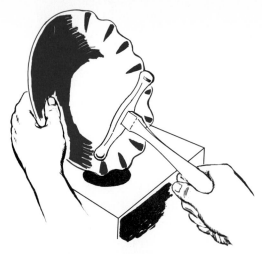

Fig. 42-4   Raising a bowl. Place the metal disk over the form. Hold it at a slight angle to the form. Strike the metal near the edge with a raising hammer. Turn the disk after each blow. Make the blows uniform and overlapping. As the bowl takes shape, lower the angle at which you hold it.

Fig. 42-5   The shapes of the bowl through the various steps of raising.

distances apart. These serve as guidelines for the forming.

4. Fasten the block in a vise with the end grain up. Pound or gouge out a depression in the wood.

5. Place the disk on the block. Then strike it near the edge with the raising hammer. Turn the disk after each blow (Fig. 42-4). Make the blows uniform, and overlap them. Never allow the metal to wrinkle so badly that it folds over, as this would ruin the piece. Continue hammering around the circles until you reach the center of the disk.

6. By this time, the disk will be hard and must be annealed and pickled.

7. When the disk is clean, redraw the circles with the pencil compass.

8. Continue to stretch the metal by hammering it as you turn it (Fig. 42-5). As the forming proceeds, lower the disk over the depression. Do not be discouraged because the bowl looks very crude at this time. An-

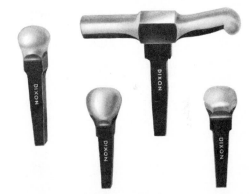

Fig. 42-6   Stakes that can be used to smooth out a bowl. (William Dixon, Inc.)

neal and pickle it often. Continue forming the metal until it is about the shape you want.

9. Select a metal stake that has about the curve of the bowl (Fig. 42-6). Place the bowl upside down over the stake. With a wooden or rawhide mallet, work out the dents and irregularities (Fig. 42-7).

225

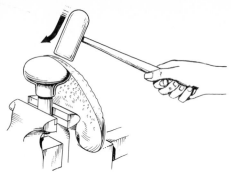

Fig. 42-7 Smooth out the imperfections over a stake. The stake must match the curvature of the bowl. Use a mallet and strike the metal glancing blows.

10. With a surface-height gage, mark the edge true (Fig. 42–8). Trim it with tin snips. File the edges smooth.

11. Anneal and pickle the bowl, and clean and polish it in preparation for planishing.

12. Planish the outside of the bowl with a round-faced hammer (see Unit 43).

13. Decorate the edge, make a base, or add appendages.

Fig. 42-8 Using a surface-height gage to mark a line around a bowl as a guide for trimming the top evenly.

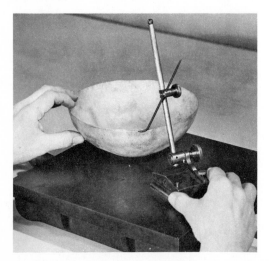

The early forming of the bowl can also be done over a sandbag. Fill a heavy canvas bag about two-thirds full with fine sand. Form a depression in the bag, and proceed as with a wooden form (Fig. 42–9).

The forming can also be done by the crimping method (Fig. 42–10). **Crimping** is hammering a series of depressions in the metal. Divide the disk into several equal parts. Crimp the metal along these lines. Stretch the crimped disk over a stake. Repeat the crimping and stretching until the desired depth is reached.

Raising skill requires many hours of practice.

Fig. 42-9 A bowl can be formed over a sandbag. Strike the metal over a depression in the bag.

Fig. 42-10 Another method of raising a bowl is to crimp the edge over a crimping block. Notice the shape of the hammer being used. The edge is crimped and the bowl smoothed out over a stake. Crimping may have to be done several times during the forming of a bowl.

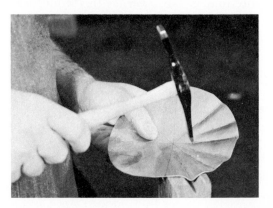

1. What can you use to find the diameter of the piece from which the bowl is to be formed?
2. What is the purpose of drawing circles on the workpiece?
3. What kind of hammer is used for the forming?
4. What tool is used to work out surface irregularities after the forming?

Make a report on the methods of forming used in industry.

Unit 43
Planishing and Decorating

The surface or edge of a tray, plate, bowl, dish, or bottle can be beautified in many ways. A number of these are described in this unit.

Planishing

Planishing is making the surface of metal smooth by hammering it (Fig. 43–1). It is similar to peening (see Unit 18), except that planishing hammers and stakes are used. Planishing removes blemishes, bruises, and irregularities that have developed during the forming. On deep dishes or bowls, the outside surface is planished. On shallow trays or plates, however, the upper surface and sometimes only the edge are planished. To do a good job of planishing, you must have (1) a smooth hammer, (2) a smooth stake, and (3) clean metal.

Planishing a deep bowl or dish

1. Choose a good planishing hammer and a round-faced stake with about the same curvature as the bowl (Figs. 43–2, 43–3). Both should be free of nicks and scratches. Use a buffer and polishing compound to

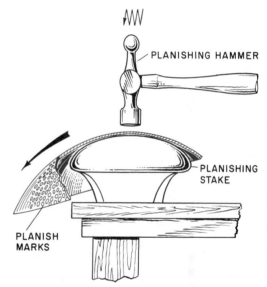

Fig. 43–1 Planishing a bowl. Begin at the center of the project and work outward. Have the blows overlap slightly. Keep the hammer strokes uniform.

remove any that are present. Fasten the stake in a vise.

2. Draw a few circular pencil lines around the outside of the bowl as guides.

3. Hold the bowl over the stake with your fingers underneath and your thumb on top. This will let you hold and guide it securely. Keeping your elbow close to your body, pound with a regular rhythm and uniform wrist movement. Beginners often strike the metal unevenly and too hard. When you

227

Fig. 43-2 Common shapes of planishing hammers. Each hammer produces a different hammer mark.

Fig. 43-3 Planishing stakes. (William Dixon, Inc.)

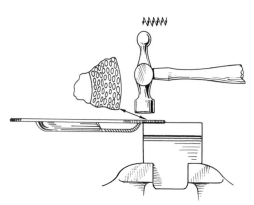

Fig. 43-4 Planishing the edge of a tray.

pound the right way, you hear a clear ring as the hammer strikes the metal. When you do it the wrong way, you hear a dull thud.

4. Begin to planish at the center. Do one area at a time, moving the article a little after each blow. Work from the center outward, following the circles. Have the blows overlap slightly. Rub the surface with fine abrasive cloth to highlight the areas that have been planished.

Planishing trays or dishes

1. Support the surface to be planished over solid metal or a lead block (Fig. 43-4).

2. Planish as described above.

Layout for edge decoration

To lay out the position for decorations that are to be repeated around an edge, do the following:

1. Cut a disk of paper of the same size as the project. Fold the paper into the number of parts in the design.

2. Clip the corners of the folded paper, open it up, and lay it on the metal. Mark the places for the decorations with a pencil or with chalk (Fig. 43-5). If necessary, draw a line from the edge to the center, and locate the exact position of the area to be decorated. This can also be done by trial and error with dividers.

Shaping an edge

After the edge has been shaped and planished, it should be cut to finished size, filed, and smoothed with abrasive cloth. In addition, you may further decorate the edge by filing recesses in it at regular intervals. Strike the edge at right angles with a dull chisel to raise or shape it or to add other decorations.

228

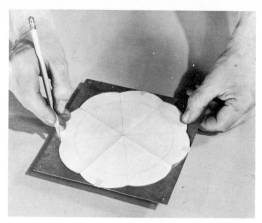

Fig. 43–5 Divide an object into equal parts by folding a piece of paper, clipping the corners, and using it as a pattern.

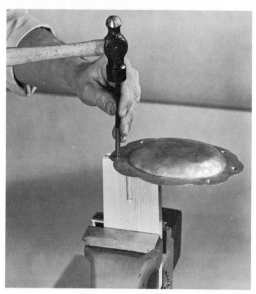

Fig. 43–6 To make a dome, hold the metal over a small conical depression in a wooden form. Strike this spot with a ball peen hammer or a small roundfaced punch.

Doming

A **dome** is a raised, rounded shape that can be placed at equal intervals or in groups around the edge of an object. Domes can also serve as feet on the bottom of a dish or tray. There are three methods for making domes:

1. Cut or gouge a small conical shape in a wood block. Then hold the face of the object over the hole. Strike the back of the metal at the layout position with a ball peen hammer or with a round-faced punch (Fig. 43–6).

2. Cut a piece of pipe that has an inside opening equal to the diameter of the dome. Round the inner edge of the pipe. Choose a ball peen hammer that will fit part way into the pipe. Fasten the pipe in a vise. Hold the item over the pipe, place the ball peen hammer, and strike it with another hammer.

3. *Dapping blocks* and *punches* are used to make domes (Fig. 43–7). They are also used for making half-spheres, which can be soldered together to make a ball (Fig. 43–8).

Fluting

A **flute** is a long, narrow depression in a material. To flute the edge of a flat plate, get a soft piece of wood and a metal rod of the diameter of the flute. Place the rod over the wood. Strike it several times to form the depression. Then place the edge of the plate over the wood, with the metal rod over it.

Fig. 43–7 Punches and a dapping block are used to form small round shapes in metal.

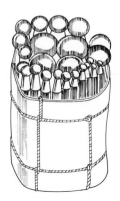

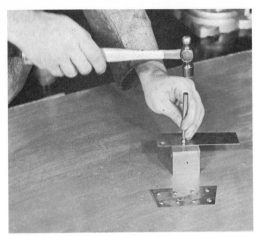

Fig. 43-8 Using a dapping block to form half-spheres.

Fig. 43-9 Fluting the edge of a tray. Note that a groove was made in the wood block.

Strike the rod several times, forming the flute (Fig. 43-9).

On a curved dish, first cut a wooden form that fits the shape of the curve (Fig. 43-10). Gouge out the shape of the flute. Holding the dish over the form, pound in the flutes with a ball peen or forming hammer.

Fig. 43-10 Forms for fluting the edge of a bowl.

Scalloping

Scalloping is forming the edge of metal into a continuous series of arcs. To scallop the edge of a dish, use a wood jig (Fig. 43-11). Slip the metal between the opening in the jig, and bend it. This can also be done with round-jaw pliers that have been heavily taped with masking tape.

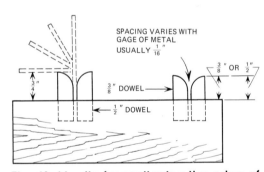

Fig. 43-11 Jig for scalloping the edge of a plate. To scallop the edge, first slip the edge into the jig opening, then bend the metal. Do this evenly all around the edge.

Flaring

Flaring is turning the very edge of metal slightly. On dishes and bowls, flaring should be done over a hardwood block with a slightly rounded corner. Holding the article over the block, strike it with a round-faced wooden or rawhide mallet. To flare the end of tubing, fasten the tube in a simple wood jig, and clamp it in a vise. Get a ball peen hammer that is slightly larger than the diameter of the tubing. Place the ball peen head in the end of the tubing. Strike it with another hammer (Fig. 43-12).

Overlaying

Overlaying is decorating the surface of metal with contrasting material. Cut a piece

230

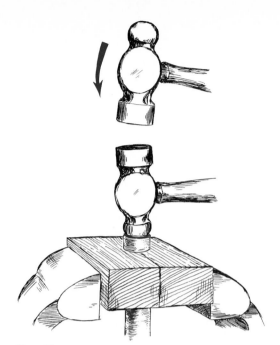

Fig. 43-12 Flaring the edge of a tube.

of decorative wire long enough to go around the edge of the project. Form it into shape. Then sweat-solder it in place.

The surface can also be decorated by cutting out a design in a contrasting metal and sweat-soldering this in place.

 QUESTIONS

1. How is planishing different from peening?
2. How can you tell whether you are handling the planishing hammer in the right way?
3. What can you use to lay out a decoration that is to be repeated around an edge?
4. What is a dome? A flute?
5. What tool do you use to scallop the edge of a dish?
6. What is flaring?
7. How is a decorative wire or other overlay attached to the surface of a project?

 EXTRA CREDIT

1. Make a chart that shows the different kinds of surface decorations and how they can be used. Sketch or make a sample of each kind.
2. Visit a body shop to find out in what ways bumping and planishing resemble the forming operations in art metal. Make a report to the class.

Unit 44
Etching

Etching is a process of surface decoration in which a chemical eats away part of the metal surface. The similar industrial process is called *chemical milling* (see Unit 68).

Materials

Resists are materials used to cover the areas of metals that are not to be etched. For simple etching in which only lines or narrow shapes are cut, *beeswax* makes a good resist. For more complicated patterns, *asphaltum* *varnish* and *acid-resist enamel* applied with a good camel's-hair brush are excellent. For straight-pattern work, the metal can be covered with *masking tape* or *plastic shelving paper*. The area to be eaten by acid can be cut away with a sharp knife (Fig. 44-1).

For etching copper, brass, and pewter, use a solution of one part nitric acid to one part water. Remember the rule about mixing acid and water.

 SAFETY RULE

Pour the acid into the water. Use a glass or earthenware jar to mix and store the acid.

231

Fig. 44-1 **This bookend plate was covered with plastic "sticky" paper before it was immersed in the etching solution.**

To etch aluminum, combine one part muriatic, or hydrochloric, acid and one part water. A nonacid solution can also be used. It comes in powder form and is added to boiling hot water. Use 6 tablespoons of powder to 1 quart of water (75 mL per liter). With this solution, the etching can be done in about 35 minutes.

Etching

1. The surface of the metal must be buffed and perfectly clean. Clean it either with fine abrasives or by pickling it in an acid bath. Then do not touch it. Your finger-prints can ruin the etching because they leave an oily film that acts as a resist.

2. Apply the resist in one of the following ways:

a. Masking-tape method. Cover the article with masking tape, and lay out the design on, or transfer it to, this surface. Cut around the area to be exposed with a sharp knife. Carefully lift off the tape.

b. Asphaltum-varnish or acid-resist–enamel method. Carefully transfer the pattern to the metal by tracing with carbon paper (Fig. 44–2). Paint the varnish or enamel on the areas to be protected from the acid (Fig. 44–3). If the piece is flat or if the entire article must be put into the acid bath, both surfaces must be covered. The edges, in this case, should be given two or three coats. If you are etching a tray or bowl, however, you only have to treat the top surface. This is because you can pour the acid into the object. Be sure to apply enough resist. The area should look black. Allow it to dry for 24 hours.

Fig. 44-3 **Decide what parts of your design are not to be etched. Coat those parts with asphaltum varnish or acid-resist enamel. Apply the resist carefully with a camel's-hair brush.**

Fig. 44-2 **Trace a design from the printed pattern using carbon paper. Hold the pattern and carbon paper in place with masking tape.**

Fig. 44–4 Apply an acid or a nonacid solution by pouring it into the tray. Use a stick with cotton wrapped around to keep the solution moving. This is especially important when only a small amount is poured into a tray.

Fig. 44–5 The completed etched plate.

c. Beeswax method. Melt the beeswax, and coat the surface of your project with a layer about 1/16 inch (1.5 mm) thick. Use an awl or scriber to trace the outline of your design through the beeswax coating. Be sure to press hard enough to reach the metal. Scrape the beeswax off any large areas that are to be etched.

3. Put the article in the acid solution, or pour the acid solution into the article (Fig. 44–4). The time needed for etching depends on the strength of the acid and the depth of etching wanted. Approximate times are 1 hour for copper, 1 1/2 for brass, 1/4 for pewter, and 1/2 for aluminum. Stir the acid during the etching with a narrow wooden stick wrapped in cotton.

4. Take the article from the solution, rinse it in water, and then remove the resist. If asphaltum varnish has been used, clean the article with benzene or paint thinner.

5. Check your work. Is the design clearly outlined? Is the edge ragged? This would be caused by too rapid action or by a poorly applied resist. The result of good and careful work is a fine finished piece (Fig. 44–5).

 QUESTIONS

1. In etching, what happens to a metal surface?
2. What are the materials called that protect the areas not to be etched? List three of these materials.
3. What acid is used to etch copper, brass, and pewter?
4. Name two methods of applying the resist.
5. What does etching time depend on?

 EXTRA CREDIT

Describe the chemical action that takes place in etching. Find your answer in an encyclopedia.

Unit 45
Metal Enameling

Enameling is applying a permanent, glassy finish to the surface of metal. This finish is made of grains of glass, ceramic chemicals, and other colorants. It is fused to the metal by high heat.

Enameling is used in industry to give many metals the good qualities of a glass surface. For example, enameled metal resists acid, heat, erosion, and stains. Kitchen utensils, stoves, refrigerators, bathtubs, and many other objects are covered with enamel. Jewelry, trays, and bowls are typical projects (Fig. 45–1).

Tools and materials

1. *Copper,* 18 gage (1 mm) or thicker, is best because it is easy to shape and will not warp in enameling.

2. An *electric enameling kiln,* or oven, that will heat to about 1500°F (815°C) is needed (Fig. 45–2). A welding torch or gas burner can also be used.

3. A commercial *pickling solution* can be used for copper. One can also be made by

Fig. 45–2   A metal-enameling kiln.

adding one part nitric acid to two parts water.

 SAFETY RULE

Always put the water in a glass or earthenware container, and add the acid to it. Never add water to acid.

4. *Metal enamels* come in many colors and are either transparent (light-admitting) or opaque (light-blocking). Wash enamels before using them (Fig. 45–3). Transparent colors can be mixed together or fired one over the other. If opaque enamels are mixed together, they give a salt-and-pepper effect. They cannot be applied one over the other. Threads and lumps can also be used for interesting effects.

5. An *adhesive* is needed to hold the enamel in place before it is fired. Adhesives include a commercial gum solution, lavender oil, one part powdered gum tragacanth

Fig. 45–1   Enameled plaque. (Thomas C. Thompson Company)

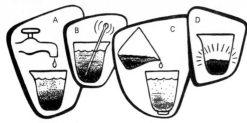

Fig. 45–3 Washing makes enamels more brilliant. Proceed as follows: (A) Flood the enamel with several inches of water. (B) Stir the enamel thoroughly. (C) Pour off the milky water and save it in another jar. (D) Repeat until the poured-off water is clear.

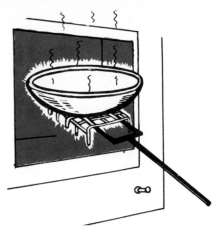

Fig. 45–4 Placing the project in a heated kiln to burn off grease or oil.

Fig. 45–5 Cleaning the metal with metal cleaner or acid solution. Use only copper or wooden tongs to remove the copper pieces.

Fig. 45–6 Scouring the metal with salt and water. Use a cloth, steel wool, or a stiff brush.

mixed in two parts alcohol, or light machine oil.

6. Other materials needed include files, 3/0 steel wool for polishing, salt shakers or 80-mesh sifters, tongs or enameling forks, enameling racks, tweezers, and a small glass tray.

Enameling on copper

1. Make sure the kiln is ready for use. Then turn it on about 1/2 hour before the firing.

2. Cut and form the copper to shape. Smaller pieces should be domed slightly. Enamel shows up much better and is much less likely to crack or chip on a domed surface than on a flat surface.

3. Clean off all impurities on the copper. To remove grease, place the metal in the preheated kiln for a few seconds (Fig. 45–4). Then clean it in the pickling solution (Fig. 45–5). The metal can also be cleaned with a cloth and a paste made of salt and water (Fig. 45–6).

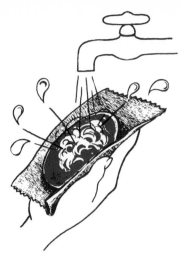

Fig. 45–7 Rinsing the metal thoroughly under running water. Hold the metal with a clean cloth or paper towels to avoid finger marks.

Fig. 45–8 Spraying on an adhesive solution. A solution of salt and vinegar applied to the back will keep the surface from oxidizing.

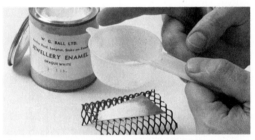

Fig. 45–9 Dusting on the enamel. Dust on a fine, uniform coat of dry enamel. Begin at the edge and work around the piece toward the center. Tap the shaker gently.

4. Rinse the copper under cold water (Fig. 45–7). Then place it on paper towels to dry. Never touch the clean metal with your fingers.

5. Spray or brush on a thin coat of adhesive (Fig. 45–8). No adhesive is needed on a flat piece of copper. Place the workpiece over clean paper on a piece of cardboard or metal that is smaller than the workpiece.

6. Select a base color of enamel. Dust it on as you would apply salt from a shaker (Fig. 45–9). Start at the edge, and work toward the center. Be sure you cover the surface completely. Always pour the excess enamel into a storage jar. If lavender oil is being used as an adhesive, the piece can be fired right away. If a gum solution is being used, spray the piece with the solution again (Fig. 45–10). Let the enamel dry before firing.

7. Check to see if the kiln is at the right temperature, about 1450 to 1500°F (790 to 815°C). If it is, it will show a yellow-orange color. With a wide spatula, lift the piece directly into the kiln. If you use an enameling

Fig. 45–10 If a gum solution has been used, spray the solution over the surface again to hold the enamel particles firmly in place.

rack, lift the piece onto the rack first, and then place the rack in the kiln (Figs. 45–11, 45–12). Enameling can also be done with a torch (Fig. 45–13).

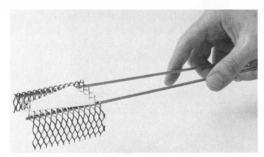

Fig. 45-11 Use a wide-blade spatula to lift the dry enameled piece into the kiln or onto an enameling rack or firing holder.

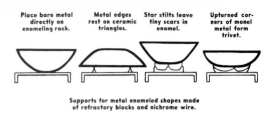

Place bare metal directly on enameling rack.   Metal edges rest on ceramic triangles.   Star stilts leave tiny scars in enamel.   Upturned corners of monel metal form trivet.

Supports for metal enameled shapes made of refractory blocks and nichrome wire.

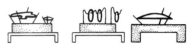

Fig. 45-12 Here are several ways of holding the metal for firing.

8. Now, carefully watch the piece, checking it every 15 seconds. It takes 2 to 3 minutes for the enamel to melt. As soon as this happens, move the piece to the cooler part of the kiln or take it out. The piece will be cool enough to touch after about 10 minutes.

9. Clean the enameled surface with a commercial cleaner, or remove the oxidation with emery, crocus cloth, or steel wool. Then dip it in a pickling solution. If you wish, you can add more color or design by applying the adhesive again and then using a different color enamel. You can also add a design by placing bits of silver, copper, glass, or thread on the surface before applying more enamel. Fire the piece again.

10. File the edge smooth to prevent chipping. Clean the enameled surface with tripoli, rouge, or another buffing compound (see Unit 48). Then apply a coat of clear lacquer.

Attaching jewelry findings

Jewelry findings, such as cuff-link backs, ear screws, or bar pins, can be attached with either a heatless solder or epoxy cement (Fig. 45-14). However, a better job can be done by using soft solder. Soft soldering should be done before the lacquering.

Fig. 45-13 In another method of firing, the part is heated with an air-acetylene flame until the enamel melts and spreads over the surface.

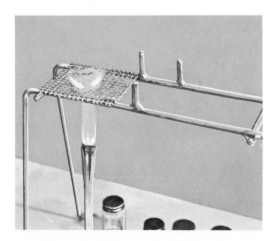

Fig. 45-14 Common findings used in making jewelry.

1. What are the advantages of enameled metal?
2. How much heat does enameling need?
3. Name the two kinds of metal enamels.
4. Why must an adhesive be used in enameling?

5. How is enamel applied?
6. How long does it take for enamel to melt in the kiln?
7. What are jewelry findings?

 EXTRA CREDIT

Make a report on commercial uses for metal enameling.

Unit 46
Soldering Art Metals

Hard soldering is a metal-joining process that utilizes silver solder and high temperatures. It is similar to *brazing* (see Unit 73). Copper, brass, and silver are hard-soldered. Hard soldering produces a neater, more permanent joint than is possible with soft soldering. Special hard solders are used with aluminum. Hard soldering is particularly useful in art-metal work.

Soldering tools and materials

It is important to have a good source of heat for hard soldering. If natural gas is available, a *gas torch* or *blowpipe* with air or with an air compressor is good (Fig. 46–1). A *bunsen burner* with a mouth-type blowpipe is excellent (Fig. 46–2). An *oxy-acetylene welding outfit* is ideal for hard soldering (Fig. 46–3). A *propane gas torch* is excellent for smaller workpieces (Fig. 46–4).

Silver solder can be purchased in three grades: (1) easy, or low-melting, which melts at 1325°F (720°C) and is used only when a single joint is to be made; (2) medium, which melts at 1390°F (755°C), for use on

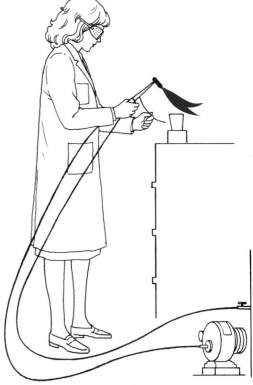

Fig. 46–1   A blowpipe with natural gas and air from a compressor.

the first joint when two joints are to be made; and (3) hard, melting at 1400°F (760°C), which makes the best joint. Some idea of these melting points can be gained

238

Fig. 46-2 Using a bunsen burner for hard soldering.

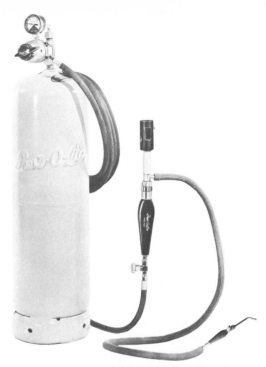

Fig. 46-3 Acetylene tank regulator, hose, handle, and stem for hard soldering.

from the heat colors: 900°F (480°C)—just-visible red; 1200°F (650°C)—dull red; and 1400°F (760°C)—cherry-red. Only the medium grade is needed for most work.

When two or more hard-soldered joints must be made on the same project, solder the first joint, and allow it to cool. Then cover it

Fig. 46-4 Hard soldering using a propane torch for heat. (Bernzomatic Corporation)

with a mixture of polishing rouge and thinner, and let it dry. This will keep the first joint from melting when the second joint is soldered, even though the same solder is used. Once a joint has been soldered, it takes a temperature 15 to 20 Fahrenheit degrees (8 to 11 Celsius degrees) higher to melt it again.

The *flux* can be a paste of borax and water or, better still, a commercial paste flux. A paste solder containing both solder and flux can also be used.

Soldering

1. Clean the joint with a file or abrasive cloth. File a slight V at the joint to hold the solder (Fig. 46-5).

2. Fit the pieces perfectly. Then bind them together with black iron oxide wire to keep them from springing apart when heated. Figure 46-6 shows a ring wired for

239

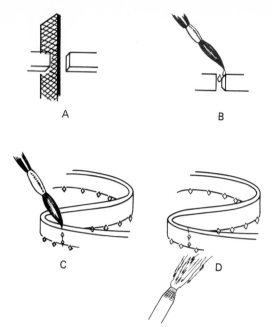

Fig. 46–5 The hard-solder brazing process: (A) filing, (B) applying flux, (C) applying solder snips, (D) applying heat.

6. With the inner point of the flame, heat the joint to the correct temperature. Follow the heat colors as a guide. If possible, heat the joint from the back. Avoid putting the heat directly on the solder. Do the soldering quickly. Do not hold the flame on the article too long. When the solder melts, it will flow or run fast. Remove the heat right away. If pieces of different size or thickness are being joined, apply most of the heat to the thicker piece.

7. Put the article in a pickling solution. Then rinse it with water.

8. Check your work. If the solder rolls into balls and does not join, either the work is not clean or there is not enough heat. The solder is being heated and not the joint. If the joint melts away or the silver burns and smokes, the flame is too hot.

soldering. Place the work over a charcoal block. Put a heat-resistant shield behind the object to reflect the heat. (This shield has traditionally been made of asbestos. However, this substance has been found to be hazardous to health. Therefore, substitutes are being devised.)

3. Flatten the solder if necessary. Cut it into tiny pieces on a sheet of clean paper. Mix a borax-and-water flux to a creamy paste. Paint this on the joint with a small camel's-hair brush. Mix and apply commercial flux the same way (Fig. 46–6).

4. Carefully apply the small bits of solder along the joint with tweezers (Fig. 46–7). Use slightly more than is necessary to fill the joint. The camel's-hair brush is handy for picking up the bits of solder.

5. With the blue part of the flame, preheat the joint until the flux dries out. This will hold the solder in place (Fig. 46–8).

Fig. 46–6 Applying the flux to the joint with a camel's-hair brush. Notice that the ring is wired together so that it will not open when the heat is applied.

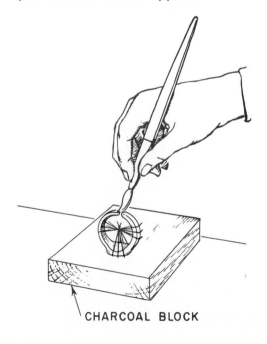

CHARCOAL BLOCK

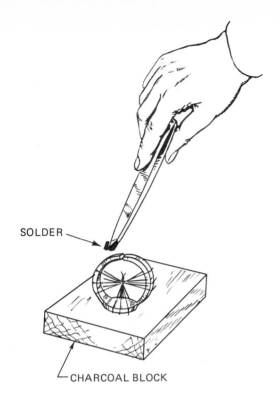

SOLDER

CHARCOAL BLOCK

Fig. 46–7   Applying small bits of solder to the joint with tweezers.

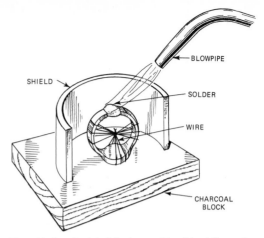

SHIELD

BLOWPIPE

SOLDER

WIRE

CHARCOAL BLOCK

Fig. 46–8   A shield placed behind the object helps concentrate the heat. This makes it easier to solder.

Other fastening methods

For very small workpieces and some jewelry findings, soft solder is sometimes used. A small electric soldering copper is ideal (Fig. 46–9). Epoxy cements also work well.

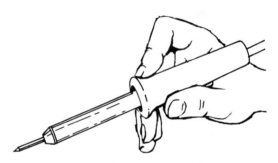

Fig. 46–9   A small electric soldering copper, used to soft-solder small pieces.

 QUESTIONS ▬▬▬▬

1. Which metals usually require hard soldering?
2. How does a hard-soldered joint differ from a soft-soldered one?
3. What are some good sources of heat for hard soldering?
4. What are the three grades of silver solder?
5. How can you keep one hard-soldered joint from melting while you solder another one nearby?

6. Why is it necessary to bind the joint together before soldering?
7. Is the flame applied to the joint or to the solder?
8. How do you know when to remove the heat?
9. What is wrong if the solder rolls into balls and does not run?

✓ **EXTRA CREDIT** ▬▬▬▬

Compare hard soldering and brazing. Describe the differences in materials and procedure.

Leaded stained glass can make a beautiful decoration for windows, lamps, and other items.

Tools and materials

To cut glass, you will need a straight-edge, a circle cutter, glass pliers, a French curve, measuring tape, and an inexpensive glass cutter.

The lead used to join the stained glass is available in 6-foot (1.8-meter) strips and in widths ranging from 1/8 to 2 inches (3 to 51 mm). Normally, lamps take lead 1/4 to 3/8 inch (6.5 to 9.5 mm) wide while panels take lead 3/16 to 1/4 inch (5 to 6.5 mm) wide. The lead is made with single or double channels and with square or curled edges.

Procedure

1. Draw a full-size pattern of your design on heavy wrapping paper. Color it to show what color each piece of glass should be. Remember to leave room for the **heart lines,** the lines between the glass pieces, where the lead will be.

2. Number each section on the pattern. Cut the sections apart.

3. For each section, find a piece of glass of the right color. Be sure the glass is clean. Wash it with detergent, rinse it in warm water, and let it dry. Wear eye protection and gloves when cutting glass. Lay the glass on a heavy piece of plywood. Put the pattern over it.

4. Before cutting the glass, you must **score** it, that is, cut sharp, even grooves in it along the pattern lines. Use a straightedge with a glass cutter for straight lines. Use a circle cutter for outer arcs. Use a French curve and glass cutter for irregular curves. For irregular shapes, make a series of score lines as close to the pattern line as possible.

5. Position the glass on the plywood so that the score line lies along the edge of the wood and the part to be cut away extends out. Tap on the underside of the glass all along the score line. Then, with your hands, press the glass downward quickly to make the break. Do this immediately because glass tends to "heal" itself. Use glass pliers to break off any small pieces left along the lay-out line.

6. Place the cut glass pieces according to the pattern on a piece of plywood. Hold them in place with masking tape.

7. Stretch out enough single-channel lead to go around the edge of the pattern. Stretch out enough double-channel lead to make all the lines between the glass pieces on the inside of the pattern. Straighten the lead strips. When the lead strips are not being

Fig. 47–1 Using horseshoe, or glazier, nails to hold the glass pieces in place before the soldering is done. (Lead Industries Association)

used, keep them in their original packaging to prevent oxidation.

8. Cut the lengths of lead that you need with a sharp cutting tool, such as a saw or shears. Tap the lead carefully with a rubber mallet to avoid crimping or twisting.

9. Place the lengths of lead where they belong among the positioned glass pieces. Put horseshoe, or glazier, nails between the different parts to keep them from moving during assembly (Fig. 47–1).

10. Wherever two lead pieces meet, solder them together using a 40- to 80-watt soldering iron with a chisel tip (Fig. 47–2). Fill the joint with solid-core half-and-half solder. Use rosin flux in most cases. However, if the lead channels are oxidized, use an acid flux. Remove this acid flux after soldering.

Fig. 47–2 Part of the panel is complete. The tools used to cut and join the lead strips are shown in the foreground. (Lead Industries Association)

 QUESTIONS ▮▮▮▮▮▮

1. What kind of metal is used in stained-glass work?
2. What are heart lines?
3. What does it mean to *score* a piece of glass?
4. Where do you use single-channel lead in stained-glass work? Where do you use double-channel lead?
5. How do you attach the lead pieces in a stained-glass project?

 EXTRA CREDIT ▮▮▮▮▮▮

Write a research report on the history of leaded stained glass.

Unit 48
Buffing and Coloring

A number of different methods are used to finish a metal project. Some of the more common ones include *buffing, coloring,* and *coating.* Buffing and coloring are described in this unit. Coating will be discussed in Section 5.

Buffing tools and materials

All small scratches and imperfections must first be removed by polishing (see Unit 21). A bench or hand *power buffer* is good for producing a high shine or luster. A *buffing*

wheel can also be fastened to a lathe or drill press. These wheels are made of cotton, flannel, or felt. They are sewn together at the center, leaving a soft outer edge. To use them, you coat their outer surfaces with an abrasive compound. Use a different wheel for each kind of compound.

The four most commonly used natural abrasive materials are *pumice, tripoli, rouge,* and *whiting.* Pumice or tripoli are for first polishing. Rouge or whiting are for buffing to a highly burnished, or shiny, surface (Table 48–1). There are also many artificial abrasives. These are very fine aluminum oxide abrasive grains and powders mixed with a bonding agent. They are available in stick or cake form.

Table 48-1
Materials for Buffing Metal

Name	Use	Source	Color
pumice	for scrubbing and cleaning; also for cutting down and polishing	powdered lava	white
tripoli	for polishing brass, copper, aluminum, silver, gold, platinum	decomposed limestone	yellowish brown
rouge	to burnish or produce a high color or luster	red iron oxide	red
rottenstone	for polishing precious stones, soft metals	decomposed shale	reddish brown or grayish black
whiting	for final polishing	calcium carbonate (pulverized chalk)	white

Buffing

1. Mount the wheel on the buffing head or other power machine. Hold the stick of compound lightly against the outer surface of the wheel as it turns (Fig. 48–1). Wear goggles and tuck in loose clothing when buffing.

2. Move the project back and forth against the wheel below its center (Fig. 48–2). Put more compound on the wheel as needed. Wipe the project clean.

3. Change to another wheel and a finer compound to finish the buffing.

4. Wash the project in hot water. Dry it

Fig. 48–1 Apply a stick or cake of buffing compound by holding it lightly against the edge of a soft wheel. The buffer should operate at a speed of 1750 revolutions per minute.

Fig. 48–2 Hold the project lightly against the face of the wheel, a little below center.

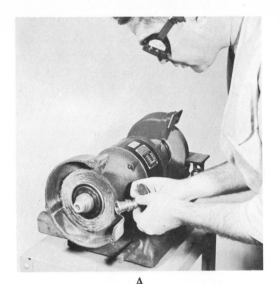

A

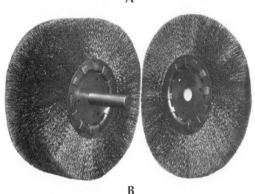

B

Fig. 48-3 (A) For a satin finish, a wire brush can be fitted on the grinder. Always wear safety glasses. Fine bits of wire from the wheel can fly off and injure your eyes. (B) Typical scratch-brush wire wheels.

with a clean cloth or in sawdust. Do not touch it with your hands.

5. To preserve the high luster, coat at once with lacquer, plastic spray, or wax.

Satin finish

A *satin finish* can be applied by lightly holding the project against a turning wire brush (Fig. 48-3). This gives an attractive, softly scratched appearance.

Coloring nonferrous metals

To add interest to the metal surface or to produce a surface that has light and dark tones, you can color it with chemicals. Remember that these are dangerous. Wear an apron, gloves, and eye protection. Always check with your instructor before using chemicals. The chemical most often used on brass, copper, and silver is liver of sulfur, or potassium sulfide.

Apply liver of sulfur as follows:

1. Dissolve a piece of liver of sulfur about the size of a small marble in 1 gallon (4 L) of hot water.

2. Be sure that the article is clean. If necessary, scrub with pumice and water.

3. Dip the article until it turns the color you want. Copper and brass colors vary from brown to black. Silver turns black (Fig. 48-4).

4. If you wish, hand-polish the article to highlight certain areas. In silver work, the crevices are usually left black and the rest highlighted.

To color brass violet, blue, and green, use 2 ounces (60 g) of sodium hyposulfite in 1 pint (0.5 L) of water. Dissolve 1/2 ounce (15 g) of lead acetate in another pint (0.5 L)

Fig. 48-4 Coloring with chemicals. Hold the article with wooden tongs or with pliers whose jaws are covered with masking tape.

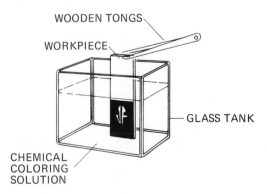

WOODEN TONGS

WORKPIECE

GLASS TANK

CHEMICAL COLORING SOLUTION

of water. Mix the two solutions together. Heat the solution, then dip the work fully into it. Other chemical colors that can be used are shown in Table 48–2.

If you need more or less of these solutions, change the amounts of the ingredients, but keep the proportions the same.

Coloring with heat

Attractive, interesting colors can be given to metals by heating. First, thoroughly clean and buff the article. Then, place it in a heat-treatment oven, heat it with a gas torch, or heat it over a flame (Fig. 48–5). Watch the colors as they appear, and remove the workpiece when the desired colors are present. Quench immediately in water or oil. Rub gently with steel wool to highlight the metal (Fig. 48–6).

Coloring ferrous metals

To color polished iron or steel, apply the solutions according to the instructions below. Unless otherwise indicated, all measurements are by weight.

Fig. 48–5 Coloring art-metal pieces by heat. (Wendell August Forge)

! CAUTION

Use gloves and goggles when working with chemicals. See your instructor before coloring with chemicals.

1. *Blue-black.* Mix 16 parts saltpeter and 2 parts black oxide of manganese. Heat the mixture to 750°F (400°C). Then place the cleaned workpiece into the mixture.

Table 48–2
Formulas for Chemical Finishes for Nonferrous Metals

Brown
4 ounces (120 g) iron nitrate 4 ounces (120 g) sodium hyposulfite 1 quart (1 L) water
Dull matte
1 pint (0.5 L) hydrochloric acid 1 pint (0.5 L) 40% ferric chloride solution
Green antique
3 quarts (3 L) water 1 ounce (30 g) ammonium chloride 2 ounces (60 g) salt
Red
4 ounces (120 g) copper sulfate 2 pounds (1 kg) salt 1 gallon (4 L) water
Pickling and cleaning
1 pint (0.5 L) sulfuric acid 1 pint (0.5 L) nitric acid 4 pints (2 L) water
Satin dip
1 pint (0.5 L) hydrofluoric acid 3 pints (1.5 L) water

Fig. 48–6 Buff and highlight the heat-colored workpieces by rubbing with steel wool. Allow the metal to cool before you buff it. (Wendell August Forge)

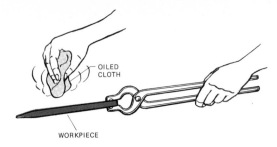

Fig. 48–7 Blackening metal.

Remove the workpiece when you feel it is dark enough. Wipe it dry.

2. *Brown.*

   a. Dip the workpiece in ammonia. Dry it in a warm place.

   b. Dip the workpiece in muriatic, or hydrochloric, acid. Dry it in a warm place.

   c. Dip the workpiece in gallic acid. Withdraw it when the desired color has been reached. Dry it in a warm place.

3. *Bronze.* Heat the workpiece slightly. Paint on a paste of antimony chloride. Let the workpiece stand until the desired shade has been reached. Wipe it dry.

Black oil finish on ferrous metals

Heat the cleaned workpiece and coat it with heavy lubricating oil (Fig. 48–7). Then heat the metal to about 300 to 350°F (150 to 175°C) for 5 to 8 minutes. This will burn off the excess oil and give the metal a black, rust-preventing coating.

 QUESTIONS

1. Name four natural materials used for buffing.
2. How can you give a project a satin finish?
3. What chemical is most often used to color brass, copper, and silver?
4. How can you color metals without using chemicals?
5. List some safety precautions to follow when using chemicals.

 EXTRA CREDIT

Find several other chemical preparations that can be used to color metal. Make a sample of one finish to show to the class.

Unit 49
Metal Spinning

Metal spinning is a machine-shaping process in which a metal disk is revolved on a lathe. As the disk turns, a spinning tool presses it over a form called a **chuck**. Gradually, the disk takes the shape of the chuck. Plates, bowls, and many other objects are made in this way. Some industrial spinning is done by hand in much the same way as in the school shop (Fig. 49–1). Production machines are also used. Spin forming is fre-

Fig. 49-1 A skilled worker spinning a base for a table lamp over a wooden chuck. (Reed & Barton)

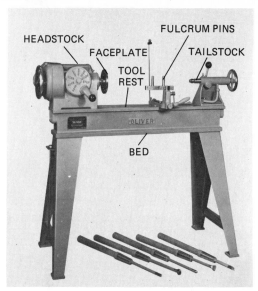

Fig. 49-2 Parts of a spinning lathe.

quently less expensive than other machining.

Equipment, tools, and materials

1. A *spinning lathe* must be solidly built (Fig. 49–2). It must operate at speeds from 300 to 2000 rpm (revolutions per minute). Most spinning is done at 1800 rpm. A *special toolrest* is needed that has a crossbar with holes into which fulcrum pins are fitted. A *live,* or *ball-bearing, tailstock center* is used. The pressure against this center holds the metal against the chuck.

2. *Spinning tools* come in many forms and shapes (Fig. 49–3). They can be bought or can be made from old wood-turning tools. Common ones include:

a. The *all-purpose flat,* or *forming, tool,* used during most of the spinning. One part of the tip is flat for smoothing purposes. The other side is rounded for "spinning to the chuck." The place where the flat and round sections join is also rounded, but with a smaller radius.

b. The *roundnose,* or *pointed, tool,* used for hooking the disk to the chuck at the start of the spinning and for shaping small curves.

Fig. 49–3 Spinning tools: (A) all-purpose flat, or forming, tool; (B) roundnose, or pointed, tool; (C) cutoff, or trimming, tool; (D) beading tool; (E) ball tool.

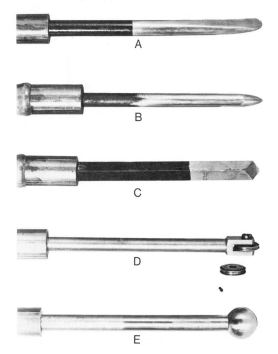

248

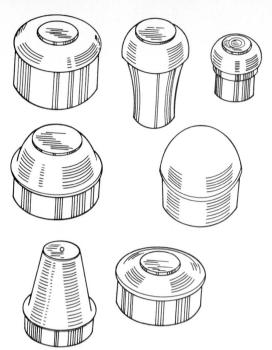

Fig. 49-4   Typical shapes of wooden chucks.

Fig. 49-5   Where the spun shell of the finished article will partially enclose the chuck, a sectional chuck is used. (Aluminum Company of America)

c. The *cutoff,* or *trimming, tool,* used for trimming the extra metal from the edge of the spun object.

d. The *beading tool,* used for turning the edge of a spun project for a beaded lip.

e. The *ball tool,* used for the first steps in spinning hard metals, such as brass and steel. It is used to bring the metal near the chuck but not to finish shaping it over the chuck.

f. The *back stick,* which supports the back of the metal as it is spun. This should be about 1 inch (25 mm) in diameter and about 15 to 24 inches (380 to 610 mm) long. One end should have a flat wedge shape. The back stick can also be used to roll the edge. An old broom handle makes a good back stick.

3. *Chucks* used for spinning can be made of wood, such as oak, maple, or cherry, or of metal. There are two types: the *solid chuck,* used for simple spinning (Fig. 49-4), and the *sectional chuck,* which can be taken apart, for more complicated work (Fig. 49-5). You will use a solid chuck for beginning projects. The chuck can be turned to the desired shape after it has been put on the lathe. A *follow block* fits over the live tailstock center. This is a piece of wood slightly smaller in diameter than the smallest part of the chuck.

4. *Metals* best suited to spinning are copper, aluminum, pewter brass, silver, and certain kinds of steel. Copper, and soft aluminum are most commonly used. When spun, copper and brass must be kept soft by annealing (see Unit 40).

5. The *lubricant* can be yellow laundry soap or a tallow candle.

Spinning a simple bowl

1. Choose a chuck, or turn one in the shape you want. Fasten the chuck to the headstock spindle. Attach the follow block. It should be the same size or a little smaller than the base of the chuck.

2. Cut the disk to size. You can find the diameter by adding the largest diameter of the project to its height. With a little experience, you will be able to do this more accurately. If the edge is to be rolled or turned, allow for a little extra material. The metal should be soft or annealed before you start.

3. Insert the disk between the chuck and the follow block. Turn up the tailstock until the follow block fits snugly against the disk. There are two ways of centering the disk in the chuck:

a. Turn the lathe over by hand, tapping the disk first on one side and then on the other until it runs true.

b. Adjust the lathe to the slowest speed. Turn on the power. Hold a back stick between the edge of the disk and the toolrest. Start with the follow block firmly against the disk. Loosen the tailstock handwheel a little as you press lightly with the back stick against the revolving disk. When it runs true, quickly tighten the tailstock handwheel.

 CAUTION

Centering the disk in the chuck is rather dangerous, so be sure you never stand directly in line with the edge of the disk.

4. Stop the lathe. Adjust the toolrest about 1 1/2 to 2 inches (38 to 51 mm) away from the edge of the disk. Adjust the spindle speed to about 900 to 1200 rpm. Put a fulcrum pin about 1 inch (25 mm) ahead of the disk.

5. Turn on the power. Never stand directly in line with the disk. It could fly out and hit you. Apply only a little tallow candle or yellow laundry soap to both sides of the disk to lubricate it.

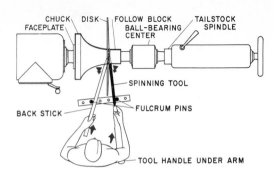

Fig. 49–6 **The metal has been hooked over the chuck. Now the waves and wrinkles are being smoothed out with a spinning tool and back stick. Always keep the metal in a cone shape.**

6. Hook the disk to the base. Choose a flat, or forming, tool. Hold the handle under your right arm, grasping the tool toward the front of the handle with your right hand. Hold the blade of the tool firmly against the fulcrum pin with your left hand. Place the rounded side of the tool against the disk, with the end a little below center. Apply pressure, moving the point of the tool down and to the left while moving the handle up and to the right to seat the metal against the chuck. Once you do this, the metal cannot fly out of the lathe. Work from the center outward. As you do this, the metal sometimes tends to "dish out," causing it to wrinkle. Anneal as needed.

7. Insert a second fulcrum pin ahead of the disk. Hold the point of the back stick against the front of the disk opposite the flat tool that is against the back of the workpiece. Press equally on both tools. Now move them slowly toward the outside to straighten the disk until it is cone-shaped. Always keep the unformed disk to this shape (Fig. 49–6).

8. Stop the machine. Move the toolrest within about 1/2 inch (13 mm) of the outside of the disk. Start the lathe. Trim the edge. Holding the trimming tool firmly on the rest, press in slowly until the tool cuts all

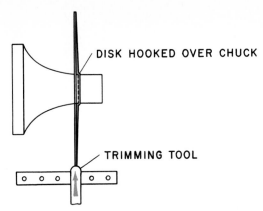

DISK HOOKED OVER CHUCK

TRIMMING TOOL

Fig. 49-7 Trimming the edge of the disk until it runs true.

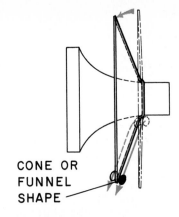

CONE OR FUNNEL SHAPE

Fig. 49-8 Here is the metal disk before and after it has been shaped. The waves and wrinkles are removed and it is kept in a cone or funnel shape.

the way around the outside (Fig. 49-7). File the trimmed edge lightly to remove the burr.

9. Reset the toolholder about 2 to 3 inches (50 to 75 mm) from the disk. Put one fulcrum pin a little ahead of the disk and the other behind it. Hold the flat tool against the toolrest, with the handle under your right arm. Move the handle to the right and up to shape the metal against the chuck. Always keep the point of the tool moving back and forth on the metal in an arc of about 2 inches (50 mm). If you force the metal in one direction only, it thins out and cracks. Also, never let the point of the tool stop and rest on the metal, for this makes ridges. Always be careful to keep the edge from "dishing out" and becoming wrinkled (Fig. 49-8). On shallow dishes, the spinning can be done quickly and can be finished before the metal becomes hard. If a deeper dish is being formed, anneal the metal at this time.

10. Replace the disk, and lubricate both surfaces again. Move the fulcrum pin nearer the headstock. Always place the pin such that you are forming the metal about 1 inch (25 mm) on either side of it. Use the back stick as needed to straighten the metal to a cone shape. Work the metal in the curves and around the corners (Fig. 49-9).

Fig. 49-9 Hold the blade firmly against the fulcrum pin. Here you see one method of holding the tool. (*Popular Mechanics Magazine*)

11. Continue the spinning until about 1/2 inch (13 mm) of the metal is still away from the chuck. Now trim the edge again.

12. Set down the top edge against the chuck with the forming tool.

13. Use a pointed, or roundnose, tool to remove any ridges in the workpiece. Holding it lightly against the metal, move it back and forth (Fig. 49-10).

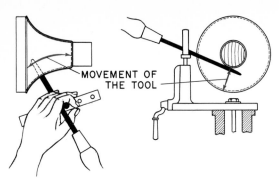

Fig. 49–10 Apply pressure on the metal, and move it back and forth in an arc as shown. Another way of holding the tool is shown here. Notice how the spinning tool moves to follow the arc. Remember that the spinning tool must be guided with the entire body. The pressure of the tool causes the metal to form over the chuck.

14. Polish the outside of the project. Remove the toolrest, and wipe off the lubricant with paper towels or a cloth. Polish the outside with 3/0 steel wool or 300 aluminum oxide cloth. If you want a high luster, buff with fine pumice or rouge. Run the lathe at high speed for polishing and buffing.

15. If the edge is to be double-turned or rolled, spin the metal up to the top of the chuck. Make sure that there is some extra metal left. There should be about 1/4 inch (6 mm) of additional metal sticking out at right angles to the chuck. Trim the edge to this amount. Hold the back stick against the left edge of the metal while holding the flat

tool against the right side. Press with the back stick until the edge starts to turn over. Finish turning or rolling the edge with either a roundnose or a beading tool.

Learning to spin well takes a lot of practice. Always start with a simple project. Keep spinning this until you get it perfect. With time and patience, you will be turning beautiful pieces.

 QUESTIONS

1. What is the advantage of metal spinning over other machining?
2. On what kind of machine is metal spinning done?
3. What metals are best suited for spinning?
4. When preparing to spin a project, how do you find the diameter of the metal disk?
5. What safety precaution should be taken when spinning metal?
6. What shape should the unformed disk always have while spinning?

✔ **EXTRA CREDIT**

1. List some industrial products made by the spinning process.
2. Prepare a bulletin-board display of some very large spun products.

SECTION 5

METAL FINISHING

Unit 50

Introduction to Metal Finishing

Metal finishing is the final process in the manufacture of a metal product. A finish is applied to metals for a variety of reasons and in many different ways. Finishes are used for one or more of the following purposes:

1. To improve the appearance of the product. An example is the attractive chrome plating on appliances, tools, and other products.

2. To prevent corrosion. An example is the finishes that are applied to an automobile body to keep it from rusting.

3. To cover a less-expensive metal with a thin coating of a more-expensive one. An example is table silverware that is made of nickel silver or brass, plated with silver.

4. To improve the wearing quality of surfaces. An example is the superfine grinding done to the moving parts of an engine.

All methods of finishing fall into one of three groups:

1. Adding coating material to the surface, such as in painting and electroplating.

2. Coloring a metal with heat or chemicals, such as in anodizing.

3. Giving some mechanical treatment to the surface, such as by shot peening, sand blasting, or polishing.

Fig. 50–1 Parts of this motor scooter have different finishes. Parts are either chrome-plated or enameled. (Carolina Enterprises)

Look at the metal products you use every day. You see that industry uses many kinds of finishes, often two or more on the same product (Fig. 50–1). Almost every type of finish is applied to one or more parts of an automobile.

What is corrosion?

One of the reasons for applying a finish to metal is to stop corrosion. **Corrosion** is the deterioration, the slow eating or wearing away, of metal. You may have seen a tarnished copper dish. **Tarnish** is the staining and discoloring that takes place when raw metal is exposed to air. It is a kind of corrosion. You have also seen a rusty steel bolt or piece of sheet steel. **Rust** is another kind of corrosion (Fig. 50–2). Water in some form is

253

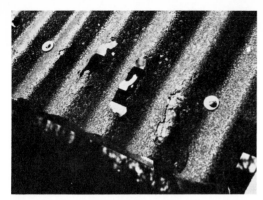

Fig. 50-2 This steel roofing has been eaten away by rust, a kind of corrosion.

necessary for corrosion to take place. The rate of corrosion is affected by use and other conditions. Corrosion results in expensive damage and represents a great technological challenge.

Kinds of corrosion

There are many kinds of corrosion besides tarnish and rust. Corrosion takes place, for example, when unlike metals are joined. It can also be caused by stress and fatigue of metal. Electric currents can cause metals to corrode. Many metals corrode more rapidly when used around acids or salts. Corroding also starts in cracks and crevices or where parts have been assembled. Air pollution can contribute to corrosion. The two most common causes of corrosion are oxidation and galvanic action.

Oxidation is the common deterioration of metals exposed to air, water, or acid (Fig. 50-3). Oxidation results when the oxygen in the air reacts with the surface of the metal. The oxidation process and the resulting corrosion are similar in the common metals. However, the color that results differs. The color will usually be blue-green for copper, black for lead, white or gray for aluminum and zinc, and reddish brown for most kinds of steel.

Most people think only of the rusting of steel as a corrosion problem. Actually, all metals will corrode under certain conditions. For instance, aluminum reacts with air to form an oxide coating. This coating completely covers the metallic aluminum and prevents further oxidation. However, if the oxide is prevented from forming or if it is continually being removed, the aluminum will corrode very quickly. Even stainless steel corrodes when used around many acids. It is important to remember that metals vary in their ability to resist corrosion.

All water is not equally corrosive. Distilled or very pure water is least corrosive. Fresh water is more corrosive. Seawater is most corrosive.

Sulfuric acid is a corrosive material often encountered in industry. It can be present in the air and will corrode metals quickly. Other acids—such as hydrochloric, nitric, and hydrofluoric—will also attack metals. This occurs most rapidly if the metal is dipped into the acid (Fig. 50-4).

Fig. 50-3 This cutaway illustration of an engine shows how rust and scale build up around the cylinder walls. The water in the cooling system causes it to fill up with a corrosive scale.

Fig. 50-4 Staining or eroding metal by placing it in acid. This is what happens in chemical coloring or etching.

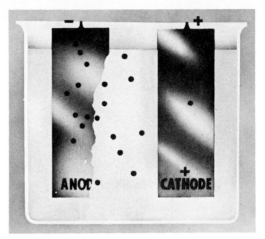

Fig. 50-5 The flow of electricity between the anode and the cathode in metal corrosion. Note how the anode is wearing away.

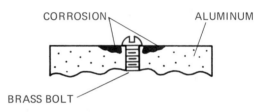

Fig. 50-6 Galvanic action taking place between two different metals causes corrosion.

Galvanic action causes corrosion when two different metals touch one another or are placed in the same vat of water. The metals behave as though they are part of a galvanic cell, or wet battery. The relationship between the rusting of a steel bolt and the action of a battery may not seem obvious. However, the same chemical action is present. It has been proved that corrosion usually involves a small, localized electric current.

In a battery, an electric current is produced by placing two materials, one of which is usually a metal, in a chemical solution. When the circuit is completed, one material, called the **anode,** dissolves. An electric current flows through the solution to the other material, the **cathode** (Fig. 50–5). A piece of metal in contact with moisture behaves like a small battery. The presence of particles, impurities in the air, or contact with some other metal (Fig. 50–6) produces a slight difference of voltage, causing a very small electric current to flow. Galvanic cor-rosion is common whenever two different kinds of metal touch (Fig. 50–7). The corroded metal is always the anode.

Protection from corrosion

Some metals, such as platinum, titanium, and stainless steel, are highly resistant to corrosion. Unfortunately, these are all quite expensive. Therefore, carbon steel, even though it corrodes rapidly when exposed to the elements, is still the most widely used metal in the world. Carbon steels are usually protected by enamel, paint, zinc, or electroplating. Some types of modern structural steel produce a hard, dense coating of rust that prevents further rusting of the steel.

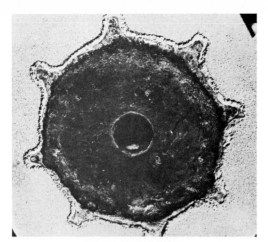

Fig. 50-7 Galvanic corrosion of magnesium where it touches a steel star-shaped core around which the magnesium was cast.

It also eliminates the need for painting or rustproofing structures made of this steel, such as buildings and bridges. Aluminum is usually anodized to help protect the surface.

Zinc, aluminum, tin, and lead can be applied to steel by the hot-dip method. Zinc is the most widely used coating. Steels coated by this method are referred to as *galvanized* or *hot-dip galvanized.* Hot dipping produces a continuous coating that is the thickest available from any conventional process. This thickness gives maximum protection against corrosion. Zinc coatings tend to be somewhat rough, especially as thickness increases. Aluminum coatings are relatively smooth. Both zinc and aluminum coatings quickly develop an oxide that dulls the surface.

Zinc and cadmium coatings are commonly applied to the surface of steel by the electroplating process. A thin, tight, smooth, uniform coating of high purity and good ductility results.

Designing to avoid corrosion

Good design includes selecting the right material. Not only the physical and mechanical properties of a material, but its resistance to corrosion as well, must be taken into consideration. A designer has to know the fundamental principles of corrosion as applied to a particular material.

When the probable cause and type of corrosion has been determined, a variety of methods can be chosen to prevent or minimize corrosion. These include:

1. Painting, coating, or insulating dissimilar metals—the best and least-expensive method for most purposes.

2. Using metal combinations close together in the galvanic series.

3. Avoiding combinations in which the area of one metal is relatively small.

4. Avoiding irregular stresses in design.

5. Using materials made of a metal or an alloy most likely to resist the corrosive environment.

6. Adding suitable chemical inhibitors to a corrosive solution.

7. Keeping dissimilar materials as far apart as possible and avoiding fastening them together by uninsulated threaded connections.

8. Revising the design and insulation to protect against currents.

Stainless steels for corrosion prevention

The **stainless steels** are alloys of iron with chromium, with chromium and nickel, or with chromium, nickel, and manganese. They have one chief characteristic in common—resistance to corrosion. It is the chromium that makes these alloys corrosion resistant.

 QUESTIONS

1. List four reasons for finishing metals.
2. List the three kinds of metal-finishing methods.

3. What is corrosion?
4. What are the two main causes of corrosion in metals?
5. Under what conditions does galvanic corrosion take place?
6. What are zinc-coated steels called?
7. What alloying metal allows stainless steels to resist corrosion?

 EXTRA CREDIT ▐▐▐▐▐▐▐▐▐

1. Write a report on how industry prevents corrosion on bridges and steel buildings.
2. Prepare a display on the types of metal finishing.
3. Prepare a display showing examples of corrosion in various metals.

Unit 51
Opaque and Transparent Finishes

Finishing metal by coating it will preserve it and make it more attractive (Fig. 51–1). In this unit, you will learn of several ways of applying opaque, or light-blocking, and transparent, or light-admitting, coatings.

Wax finishes

The simplest temporary finish for projects used indoors is wax. Warm the metal slightly, and apply a coat of paste wax. Let it dry. Then rub it briskly with a clean cloth. This finish will wear off with time and handling and must be reapplied as needed.

Enamels and lacquers

A colored or transparent finish can be applied with enamels or lacquers. Before applying the finish, make sure the surface is smooth and free of dirt and grease. Lacquer thinner is a good cleaner to use. Clean galvanized steel with vinegar or special cleaners made for this purpose.

Before applying opaque enamels or lacquers to metal, you must use a **primer,** or first coat. It will bind and adhere to the metal, giving a good base. (Transparent finishes need no primer). A red iron oxide

Fig. 51–1 Metal projects are coated to preserve them and make them more attractive. This letter holder has a flat black lacquer finish.

primer is used for most opaque finishes. A zinc chromate primer is good for exterior finishing. Aluminum surfaces that will be exposed to salt water are covered with zinc

257

chromate. However, ordinary lacquers cannot be applied over zinc chromate.

On some metal projects, especially castings, a **filler** may be needed. This is a finish used to fill in the holes in a porous surface before an enamel or lacquer is applied.

Applying enamels and lacquers with a brush

The key to good metal finishing is to have a clean project, a clean finish, and a clean brush. You should work away from drafts and dust.

To apply clear lacquer:

1. Make sure the project is clean and spots are removed (Fig. 51–2).

Fig. 51-2 Clean the project carefully before finishing it.

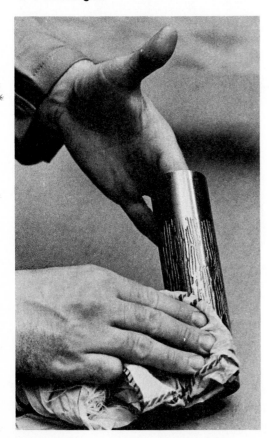

2. Make sure the surface is satisfactorily completed.

3. Now, use clean paper or cloth to handle the project.

4. Warm the metal in an oven if one is convenient. Heating makes the lacquer flow smoothly. Too much heat, however, makes lacquer boil.

5. Use a good brush, and apply lacquer a little at a time (Fig. 51–3).

6. Do not pass over an area a second time.

7. Allow the project to dry in a clean, warm room for an hour or two.

8. Apply a second coat as needed.

9. Clean the brush in lacquer thinner, which is the solvent for lacquer.

To apply enamel:

1. Clean the project carefully.

2. Apply primer or filler as needed. Allow it to dry.

3. Brush on enamel with even strokes (Fig. 51–4).

4. Allow it to dry for several hours. (Follow the instructions on the can.)

5. Apply second and third coats as needed.

6. Clean the brushes in paint thinner or lacquer thinner (Fig. 51–5). Either of these is a good solvent for enamels.

Fig. 51-3 Apply lacquer with light, even strokes.

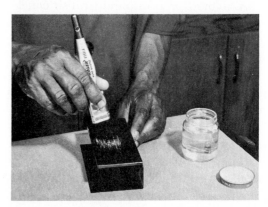

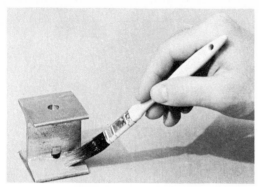

Fig. 51-4 Enamel is applied with a clean brush in light coats.

Wrinkle finish

Many metal goods, such as furniture, heaters, pumps, and novelties, have a wrinkled finish that can easily be duplicated in the shop. This finish has the advantages of covering minor defects and of drying

Fig. 51-5 Clean brushes after each use. Use the right solvent for each finish.

quickly. Choose wrinkle-enamel finish in the color you want.

1. Apply a heavy coat to the surface of the metal with a brush, by spraying, or by dipping.

2. Let this coat dry in the air about 20 minutes. Then place the object in an ordinary baking oven.

3. Heat to 180°F (82°C).

4. Bake the object from 30 to 45 minutes.

5. Turn the oven up to 300°F (150°C) for a short time to harden the finish.

Black antique finish

For a project that has been peened, a very popular finish is antiquing. Apply a coat of black lacquer. Let it dry; then rub the surface with abrasive cloth. This will highlight the metal, leaving black recesses. Apply a coat of clear lacquer. If you use black paint instead of black lacquer, you must use clear varnish as a finishing coat.

Bronze powder finish

Many decorative articles that look like brass, aluminum, or silver are really mild steel covered with a thin coat of powder. This powder can be bought in liquid form or mixed with clear lacquer, then applied like paint. Another effect can be obtained by applying a clear lacquer or varnish and then blowing the powder on while the surface is still wet. Still another method is to apply colored lacquer and then blow on the powder. This gives a two-toned appearance.

Spraying lacquers and enamels

Most industrial finishing is done with spray equipment. Spray finishing can also be done in the school shop. The simplest method is using the spray cans available at paint shops. Follow the procedures for preparing the project (cleaning and so forth) listed above. Then hold the spray can about

259

Fig. 51-6 Spraying is done by holding the can about 12 inches (300 mm) from the project.

Fig. 51-8 Spraying a metal cabinet in a spray booth.

12 inches (300 mm) from the project (Fig. 51-6). Move the can from side to side, and spray a light coat with each pass. Do not spray long in any one area. This will cause runs to appear. After spraying, let the project dry. Apply more coats as needed, or touch up spots you have missed. When you are through, hold the can upside down, and press the button for a few seconds. This will clear all spray from the nozzle cap.

Spray guns are also used in the school shop. This type of spraying takes much practice. Your instructor must show you these procedures. There are different kinds of

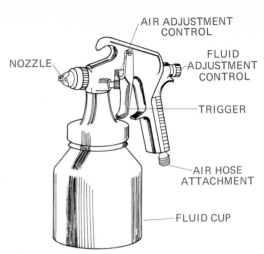

Fig. 51-7 The spray gun, showing the controls and parts.

spray equipment. The most common type of spray gun is shown in Fig. 51-7.

Spraying must be done in a properly ventilated spray booth (Fig. 51-8). Other items needed include an air compressor and air-and-fluid, or paint, hoses. During spraying, the gun should be held perpendicular to the workpiece and 6 to 8 inches (150 to 200 mm) away. Arm motion should be free, similar to the stroke used in spray-can finishing. It is important to clean the equipment properly after use.

 QUESTIONS

1. What is a primer? A filler?
2. Why should metal be warmed before being lacquered?
3. What kind of project looks good with a black antique finish?
4. What can you use to make mild steel look like brass, aluminum, or silver?
5. What happens if you spray lacquer too long in one spot?

 EXTRA CREDIT

Write a report on industrial finishing, describing the methods used to clean the products before finishing.

Unit 52
Electroplating and Black-Oxide Finishing

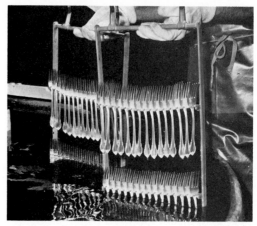

Fig. 52-1 Silver plating is done to give products a durable silver coating. (Reed & Barton)

Electroplating is using electricity and chemical solutions to cover a metal object with a thin coat of some other metal (Fig. 52-1). It is widely used for producing metal-to-metal coatings. The principle of electroplating is simple. An electric cell is created using the object to be plated as the **cathode,** or negative pole. The **anode,** or positive pole, is usually the metal to be deposited. Both are placed in a **plating bath,** which is a solution containing salts of the metal to be deposited. As an electric current is passed through the cell, the metal particles separate from the plating bath and are deposited on the article to be plated. These particles are replaced by metal that either comes from the plating bath or is dissolved from the anode (Fig. 52-2).

Electroplating adds beauty to the product and protects its surface. Also, plating an article can be less expensive than making it

Fig. 52-2 The electroplating process.

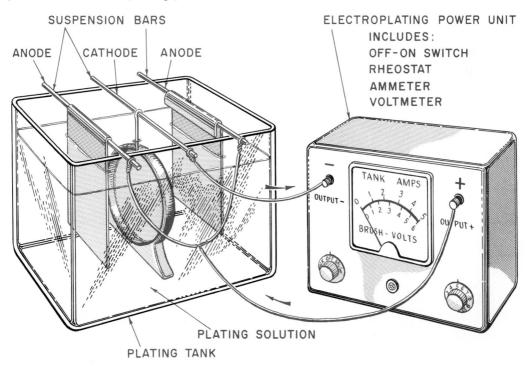

entirely of the metal used for plating. Much silverware is actually made of a fairly inexpensive metal, such as brass or nickel silver, that has been plated.

In commercial electroplating, many different metals can be used in metal-to-metal coating. These include copper, chromium, nickel, gold, silver, and zinc. For decorative plating used for tableware and jewelry, chromium, silver, and gold are common choices. For industrial electroplating, especially of automobile parts, the most common plating is a coat of nickel followed by a coat of chromium. The simplest kind of plating that can be done in the shop is with copper, cadmium, and nickel.

Electroplating equipment and materials

A reliable and easily controlled source of direct current is needed. For small plating setups, a *storage battery* or *dry cell* can be used. However, it is better to use an *electroplating power unit* that permits control of the current and voltage (Fig. 52–3). Other equipment needed includes:

1. *Plastic* or *ceramic electroplating tanks.*

Fig. 52–3 **Typical equipment setup for electroplating in the school shop.**

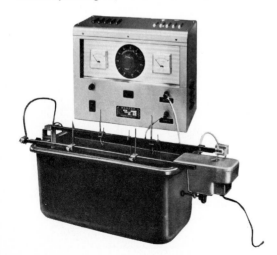

Tanks are needed for each different kind of plating solution. Another tank is needed for cleaning the metal. All tanks should be made of plastic or ceramics.

2. *Small-tank suspension-bar sets.*

3. *Anodes.* These must be the same kind of material as the plating solution. Common ones are cadmium, copper, and nickel.

4. *Plating solutions.* You can mix your own plating solutions, but it is much better to purchase the bath concentrates. These usually contain no dangerous chemicals and are safely packaged in plastic bottles or paper containers. The concentrate is mixed with water. The resulting solution can be stored for reuse either in the plating tanks or in plastic or glass bottles.

Preparing metal for electroplating

Metal to be electroplated must be free of all grease, dirt, oxides, and other foreign matter. *This is essential for good plating.* The first step is to polish and buff the metal to remove all blemishes and to improve the surface luster. Next, dip the article in an acid pickling solution to remove any grease or dirt. A good acid pickle can be made by adding one part muriatic, or hydrochloric, acid to one part water. *Always pour the acid into the water, never the reverse.* Acid should be kept in a glass, rubber, or ceramic jar. After pickling, rinse the metal in cold water. It must be so clean that water on the surface will not bead, or separate into small drops (Fig. 52–4). Never touch the metal with your bare hands after it has been cleaned. Handle it with clean rubber gloves or a piece of clean paper.

Metals for electroplating

Cadmium, one of the soft metals, is used as a rust-resistant coating. When polished, cadmium looks much like silver and is just as hard. To do cadmium plating, first mix the plating solution in a plating tank, and then suspend the cadmium anode from one of the

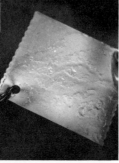

Fig. 52–4 A water test reveals an insufficiently clean metal surface, left, with contamination holding water in bubbles. On a clean surface, right, water flows relatively freely. (Western Electric Company)

suspension bars. Suspend the article to be plated from the other bar, the cathode. The voltage needed is from 1 to 3 volts, depending on the solution. Plating will start immediately. Voltage and current control are important. It is best to start with a low voltage of about 1 to 1 1/2 volts and not more than 2 to 2 1/2 volts.

Copper is used both for coating and as a base metal. It is harder than cadmium but softer than nickel. Nickel plating is also important. Nickel is a hard metal and is used for a rust-resistant coating. It is also used as an undercoating prior to chromium plating, as on automobile parts.

Black-oxide finishing of steels

Black-oxide finishing is a chemical blackening process that uses an oxidizing alkaline bath with a caustic soda base. This solution produces a controlled oxidized surface on steel. The rust metal dissolved from the surface remains in the coating to form a compound similar to the sulfide coloring of copper.

Black-oxide finishes for steels can substitute for plating. The advantages of this process include:

- Attractive glossy or dull black coat, depending upon surface finish.
- Durability and moderate corrosion-resistance in indoor exposure.
- Ease of application with inexpensive equipment.
- One-bath process.
- No dimensional changes.
- Speedy processing.
- Excellent bond for painting and lacquering.

A typical black-oxide solution includes 12 to 15 pounds of sodium hydroxide per gallon of water (1.4 to 1.8 kg per liter). (Concentrations of sodium hydroxide to water vary as water evaporates during the process.) The concentration of sodium nitrate is 5 ounces per gallon (7 g per liter).

To mix the solution, fill the tank one-half full with water. Add the salts slowly, and stir to promote dissolving. Proceed as follows:

 CAUTION

Heat is generated when the salts are added to water, so add only a small amount at a time.

1. Immerse the work in hot (180°F or 82°C) alkali detergent cleaner for 5 minutes.
2. Rinse it in hot or cold water.
3. Immerse the work in a 285 to 290°F (140 to 143°C) bath of the solution until the black coloring is deep and uniform.
4. Rinse the work in clear, cold running water.
5. Dip it in protective oil or wax.

 CAUTION

Aluminum, tin, zinc, and cadmium will dissolve in the black-oxide solution. Introducing these metals will destroy the balance of the solution.

1. What is electroplating?
2. What is a plating bath?
3. Which metals are usually used for electroplating in the shop?
4. What are the ingredients of a typical black-oxide solution?

Write a report on electroplating in the automobile industry.

Unit 53
Industrial Finishing

Industry uses many of the same finishing processes you use in your project work. It also uses others for special purposes. This unit reviews the major industrial metal-finishing methods and materials, some of which you use in making your own projects.

As in the school shop, industry uses paint, enamel, and lacquer to protect products and to improve their appearance. For all metal products used outdoors, a primer coat is applied to retard corrosion. Other industrial finishing methods require special equipment.

Flame spraying

Flame spraying is any finishing process in which a material is melted and sprayed onto a surface to produce a coating. In addition to metals, materials such as glass, ceramics, paper, and cloth can be coated by this process. Metals typically flame-sprayed include carbon and stainless steels, brasses, bronzes, aluminum, and titanium. Sprayed coatings are used to add resistance to wear, corrosion, and heat and to produce parts that have a good strength-to-weight ratio. The three basic kinds of flame spraying are metallizing, thermospray, and plasma flame.

Metallizing is a flame-spraying process that involves the use of metal wire. The wire is drawn through a gun and nozzle by a pair of power-feed rolls. The wire is continually melted in an oxygen–fuel-gas flame and atomized by a compressed-air blast. The air blast carries the metal particles to a cleaned surface either roughed or sprayed with a self-bonding undercoat (Fig. 53–1).

The individual particles mesh to produce a metal coating. Any metal that can be drawn into wire form can be sprayed with a metallizing gun. Wire metallizing is the best choice for all-purpose flame spraying since the coating can be applied fast and at low cost.

A wide variety of metal-coating materials are available. Carbon and stainless steels, brass, bronze, molybdenum, babbitt metal, copper, zinc, aluminum, nickel, monel metal, lead, tin, and cadmium are generally used. Molybdenum is sprayed on the piston rings used in cars in the United States. Metals are sprayed on glass and on cloth and paper to make condenser plates. Copper is sprayed on ceramic resistors and insulators.

Thermospray is the term used to describe the flame-spraying equipment used to apply metals and other materials in powder form. These include alloys of nickel-chromium-boron-silicon, tungsten-carbide mixtures, ceramics such as alumina and zirconia, and some **cermets,** or ceramic-metallic materials.

The powdered materials are held in a hopper that feeds them into a gun. There they are picked up by oxy-acetylene or hydrogen gas mixtures and carried to the gun nozzle. There they are melted instantly and sprayed on a surface by a siphon-jet at the gun nozzle (Fig. 53–2). The design of the gun is simple, ensuring long life and minimum maintenance.

The three basic types of coating materials used in the various thermospray processes are fused-coating alloys, oxidation-resistant metals and alloys, and ceramics. Metallic coatings include nickel-chromium hard-facing alloys, tungsten-carbide blends, stainless steel, copper, and aluminum.

Plasma flame is a technique that involves the use of an electric arc contained within a water-cooled jacket. The process is generally used in high-temperature applications. An inert gas passes through the arc and is "excited" to temperatures up to 30,000°F (16 650°C). A **plasma** of ionized, or charged, gas issues from the torch. It resembles an open oxy-acetylene flame in shape and appearance (Fig. 53–3).

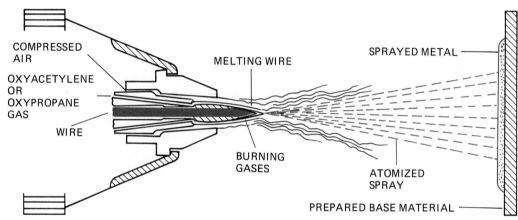

Fig. 53–1   The metallizing process.

Fig. 53–2   The thermospray process.

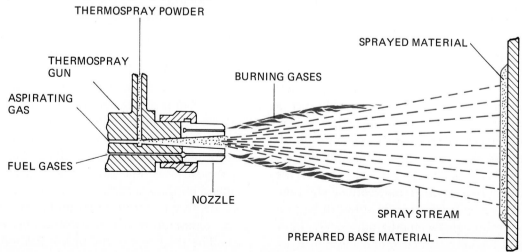

265

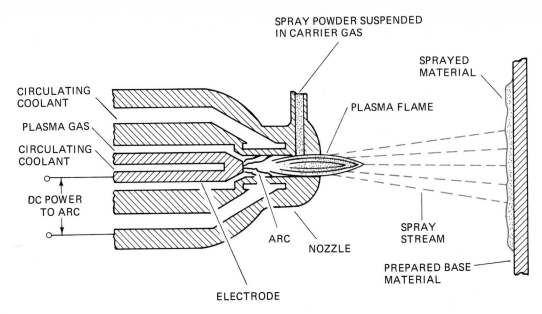

Fig. 53-3 The plasma-flame process.

The properties of plasma-flame coatings are generally superior to conventional flame-sprayed coatings. These include reduced porosity, improved bond and tensile strengths, less oxide content, and high density. The great range of operating temperatures, the variety of spraying materials, and the basic economies of the process give it a wide range of applications. These include the spraying of rocket nozzles, nose cones, and other parts subject to extreme thermal conditions. Parts for large vacuum tubes have also been successfully coated.

Aluminum anodizing

A thin coating of oxide on aluminum helps protect it from corrosion. However, a heavier coating can be produced by a very simple electrochemical process called **aluminum anodizing.** This oxide film, about .01 inch (0.25 mm), is very hard and protects the surface from abrasive and corrosive action. Many varieties of oxide finishes can be produced through the anodizing process. They may be made either clear or colored by dyes.

The color and hardness of the film can vary with the type of aluminum that is anodized.

The usual commercial anodizing process is as follows (Fig. 53–4):

1. The surface is thoroughly cleaned, rinsed, and dried.

2. A finish is applied. The surface of the metal can be given a texture by applying a scratch-brush finish with polishing and buffing wheels or a chemical finish that causes etching.

3. The aluminum is cleaned and again rinsed with water.

4. The actual anodizing is done by a process similar to electroplating. The aluminum object is suspended in an electrolyte, and current is passed through it. This causes a dense aluminum oxide coating to be built up on the surface. This is a conversion coating formed from the metal itself and bonded to the surface. The properties of the film depend on the aluminum alloy used and on the electrolyte composition and concentration, temperature, time, current, and voltage. The thickness of the film is limited by

266

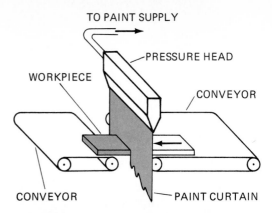

Fig. 53-5   Pressure-curtain coating.

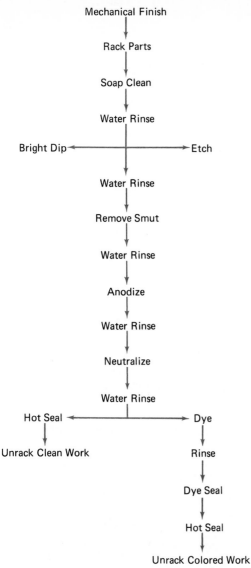

Fig. 53-4   Flowchart for aluminum anodizing.

the fact that it grows from the inside out.

5. The article is neutralized to stop the process. It is then ready for use or for dyeing.

6. A colored coating can be produced on anodized aluminum by introducing *inorganic* pigments within the pores of newly formed oxide coatings. These pigments are especially suitable for exterior use, since they weather well and are reasonably colorfast to sunlight. The pigments give an evenly col-

ored surface and can produce a variety of useful decorative effects. However, the range of colors is limited.

Organic dyestuffs produce more brillant colors than inorganic. They are used to give aluminum coatings a metallic luster. The colors have a clarity and depth that are striking and unusual. Since these dyes are not colorfast to sunlight, they are not suitable for exterior use.

Pressure-curtain coating

Pressure-curtain coating is a method of applying a uniform finish to almost any surface. It can be used to coat any kind of material and many finishes. It is especially valuable in metal finishing. The operation of the pressure-curtain coating system is shown in Fig. 53–5. The coating, under pressure, forms a curtain through which the stock moves. Either the coating or the material may be heated. If the material is heated, the drying time will usually be shorter. Coating material that does not hit the work drains into a collecting bin. It is then pumped through filters back into the pressure head and used again. Thus, very little coating material is wasted. Since the movement of the workpiece through the even curtain is controlled, the finish is smooth and uniform. Applications include furniture, doors, toys, garden tools, and shelving.

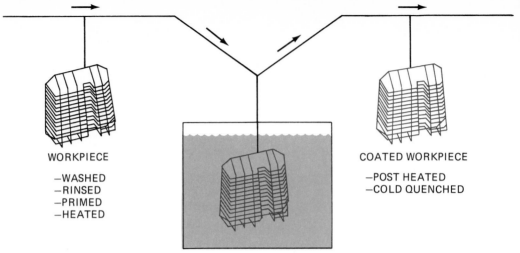

WORKPIECE

—WASHED
—RINSED
—PRIMED
—HEATED

COATED WORKPIECE

—POST HEATED
—COLD QUENCHED

FLUID COATING TANK

Fig. 53-6   Plastic-dip coating.

Plastic coatings

Coating with vinyl plastic is a fast and economical method of depositing heavy layers of decorative, chemical-resistant, and tough material on a workpiece. There are several methods of applying the plastic coat:

1. *Fluid bed.* A heated part is coated by placing it in a bed of powdered plastic resin held in suspension by air.

2. *Electrostatic bed.* A hot or cold object is grounded and held above a fluid bed containing powdered resin that has been charged by a high-voltage source.

3. *Spray.* The preheated article is spray-coated, using a powder spray gun. A collector system is often used to collect extra spray for reuse.

4. *Electrostatic spray.* An electrostatic spray gun is used to spray charged particles of powder onto a hot or cold grounded part. In most instances, powder reclamation equipment is necessary.

5. *Plastic dip.* The workpieces are cleaned and dipped in liquid plastic, then heat-cured (Fig. 53-6).

Since vinyl coating resists wear and the elements, it is used on outdoor hardware, furniture, appliances, sporting goods, and electrical parts. It also has many other applications.

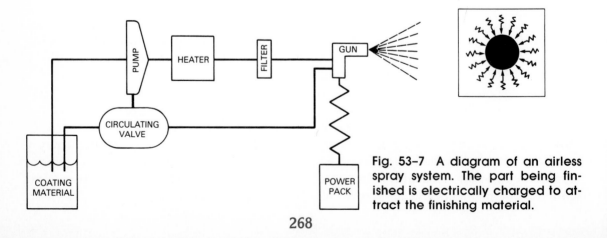

Fig. 53-7 A diagram of an airless spray system. The part being finished is electrically charged to attract the finishing material.

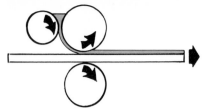

Fig. 53–8 The trend in painting metals is toward continuous processing with pretreatment, coating, and curing integrated into a single operation. Roll coating permits the painting of sheet at high speeds.

Fig. 53–9 These castings have been cleaned by abrasive blasting.

Airless spraying and roll coating

Airless spraying is a method of forcing coating material through a small opening in the spray gun by means of high hydraulic pressure, not air pressure (Fig. 53–7). This eliminates the wasteful "fog" of material created by air pressure with a standard spray gun. Types of airless systems include *cold, warm, hot,* and *electrostatic*. **Roll coating** is a method of applying a coating material such as paint or lacquer to one or both sides of sheets by using rollers to control the flow of the material (Fig. 53–8).

Abrasive blasting

The process of **abrasive blasting,** or **sandblasting,** can be used both for removal and for mechanical finishing. Abrasive blasting removes scale, rust, dirt, and other undesirable coatings. It also produces a soft-peened finish on a metal surface. In this process, work is placed in the chamber and then dry-blasted with a stream of abrasive particles moving at a high speed (Fig. 53–9).

There are several blast-gun systems in general use. One is a hand-held gun that the operator directs at a workpiece. Another is a fixed gun. Mounted in the ceiling of a cabinet, it slides from side to side and can be aimed. The gun flips up and out of the way when not in use.

Abrasive materials used in blasting include silica sand, steel grit, aluminum oxide, nutshell, and glass beads.

Abrasive blasting is used in many cleaning operations. It also can be used to produce surfaces that retain lubricants well and to remove feather burrs and blend tool marks from the surfaces of machine parts.

Other finishing methods

Tin plate is light sheet metal with a thin coating of pure tin applied either by dipping or by electroplating.

Galvanized steel is made in a manner similar to tin plate. A zinc coating is applied to mild-steel sheets.

Terneplate is sheet metal coated with an alloy of tin and lead. It is produced by a continuous process in which cold-rolled steel is immersed in a molten bath of 85 percent lead and 15 percent tin. The lead provides corrosion resistance. However, since lead does not alloy with iron, tin is added to make the alloy adhere. The tin also helps produce a smoother surface. The lead-tin alloy coating solders easily, forms a good bond with paints, and holds lubricants well.

Bluing is a process used to beautify and protect rifle barrels.

Porcelain-enamel finish on metal is obtained by using high temperatures to fuse

Fig. 53–10 Small castings, screw-machine parts, forgings, and stampings may be tumbled as a mass-production method of improving their appearance. Tumbling is also used to deburr and clean small parts.

Fig. 53–11 Using a power scraping tool. (The Dapra Corporation)

grains of glass to the metal (see Unit 45).

Abrasive finishing removes small amounts of material from metal surfaces by grinding, honing, buffing, polishing, or similar treatment. Grinding is done with an abrasive wheel, disk, or belt. It is usually the first step in producing a high polish. Polishing or honing is the second step, producing an even smoother surface. Buffing is done to give metal a very high luster. A satin finish is produced by holding the metal surface against a fine wire brush.

Shot peening, or mechanical hammering, produces a regular pattern of depressions on the metal surface and, at the same time, work-hardens the surface.

Tumbling is placing the workpiece in a rotating barrel to which an abrasive material has been added (Fig. 53–10).

Scraping and spot finishing

Two common methods of finishing the surface of machines that are not otherwise finished are scraping and spot finishing. **Scraping** machine parts by hand is a demanding job requiring top-notch skills and experience. The process is sometimes called **frosting** or **flaking.** A power tool is now commonly used for the process (Fig. 53–11). Another common technique is **spot finishing,** which consists of a pattern of overlapping rings. This operation is done with a dowel.

Deburring

After any machining or cutting operation, the edges of the part usually have a sharp burr that must be removed. This can be done with a wire or abrasive wheel. Several different kinds of machines have been designed to do the deburring automatically, such as on gears and other machine parts (Fig. 53–12).

Marking and decorating metal surfaces

Industry uses a wide variety of methods to mark and decorate metal products. Tools must be identified as to size and use. Materials are often marked to indicate their content. Finished products are marked to identify their contents and/or use. Metal products are decorated for advertising purposes. Some of the most common methods of marking metal include:

1. *Metal stamping.* The simplest and most inexpensive way to mark tools is with a set of steel letters and figures. Guidelines are

Fig. 53–12 Gear-deburring machine. (Acme Manufacturing Company)

Fig. 53–13 A roll-marking machine. (Imperial Stamp & Engraving Company)

marked on the metal product with layout fluid, and then each number or letter is stamped by being struck firmly with a hammer.

2. *Etching* can be used not only for design purposes but also for identification.

3. *Engraving* can be done with an electric engraving tool that has a carbide tip.

4. *Printing* is done on metal primarily with the offset or silk-screen processes. These methods are used mostly to add advertising material or a trademark to the metal surfaces. Metallic materials used for bottles and packages usually have printing on them.

Industrial machines used for metal marking include the roll-marking machine (Fig. 53–13), the stamp-marking typewriter, and the hot-stamping machine.

 QUESTIONS

1. What is flame spraying?
2. What are sprayed coatings used for?
3. Name three techniques of flame spraying.
4. What does anodizing do to an aluminum surface?
5. Which dyes for aluminum are suitable for exterior use?
6. Why does pressure-curtain coating give such a uniform finish?
7. List three ways of applying a vinyl-plastic coating.
8. Why is an airless spray gun better than a standard spray gun?
9. What kind of surface does abrasive blasting produce on metal?
10. What is galvanized steel? Terneplate?
11. What tool is used for spot finishing?
12. Which printing processes are usually used on metal?

 EXTRA CREDIT

1. Prepare a display on industrial finishing methods.
2. Write a research report on an industrial finishing process of your choice.

271

SECTION 6

FORGING

Unit 54

Introduction to Forging

Forging is a method of forming metal by hammer blows or pressure. It is used to shape parts where great strength is needed. Forging improves the quality of the metal, refines the grain structure, and increases strength and toughness (Fig. 54–1). Forging by hand was probably the earliest method of forming iron. The trade is as old as civilization. In hand forging, such as that done by the blacksmith, metal is heated in the forge and shaped over an anvil with various kinds of hammers and tools. In manufacturing, forging is done to shape metal objects that must withstand great stress, such as crankshafts, gears, and axles. It is very much like the work of the old-time blacksmith. However, machine power is used instead of the blacksmith's arm. Moreover, dies, or molds, replace the hammer and anvil.

Forging processes

Forging is a hot-metal forming method related to other processes like extrusion and hot rolling.

Basic equipment in production forge shops includes various kinds of power hammers and presses. To make a crankshaft, for

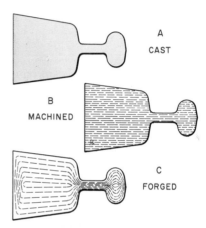

Fig. 54–1   Grain structure of metal produced by different methods of forming: (A) In casting, there is uniform grain structure throughout the part. (B) In machining, the part is weakened at the thin section. (C) In forging, the grain structure is such that added strength is obtained at the thinner sections.

example, a bar of metal is heated to white heat in a furnace. Next to the furnace is the power hammer. The hammer face is shaped something like the outside of the crankshaft. The white-hot metal bar is squeezed between the upper and lower dies. Sharp hammer blows squeeze the hot metal into the dies. Forgings must usually be machined in the machine shop after they are forged (Fig. 54–2).

Fig. 54-2 Stages in forging a crankshaft.

Fig. 54-3 Many forging operations are used in making these attractive ornamental-iron railings.

Occupations in forge work

There are many kinds of workers in the forge shop. The *hammersmith* uses power hammers equipped with unshaped dies to hammer metal into shape. In this kind of operation, the accuracy of the forged part depends on the skill of the hammersmith. The hammersmith must move the heated metal between each stroke of the hammer to give it the right shape. *Hammer operators* use forging machines in which the heated metal is pounded into shape between accurately machined dies called closed dies. This method of forging is used when large numbers of one forging are needed.

Heaters are people who heat the metal to the correct temperature. *Inspectors* check the forgings. *Finishers* grind and chip imperfections and burrs from the finished forgings. *Blacksmiths* forge by hand. They make and repair tools and equipment of various kinds. They must be able to use all types of hand-forging tools. Blacksmiths are employed in many kinds of shops, especially small repair shops.

A closely allied field is that of the *ornamental-iron worker,* who makes and installs wrought-metal decorations for buildings and homes. This worker heats metal and shapes it into artistic designs (Fig. 54-3).

Altogether, there are over 65,000 people employed in forging in the United States, including 15,000 blacksmiths. Most production forging is done near large industrial plants, principally in Ohio, Illinois, Wisconsin, Pennsylvania, Michigan, Indiana, Massachusetts, California, and New York.

Most forgings are made of steel. However, brass, bronze, copper, and aluminum are also shaped in this manner. To be really skillful in a hobby involving ornamental-metal or wrought-metal work, you must be able to do hand forging.

Forge work in the school shop

You will learn to use many different pieces of forge equipment and tools in the school shop. Hammers, tongs, anvils, and anvil tools are commonly used. You must use the forge safely and efficiently. The skills you learn will aid you in making tools such as chisels (Fig. 54-4).

Fig. 54-4 These chisels were hand-forged and finished by grinding and polishing. (Stanley Tools)

❓ QUESTIONS

1. What effects does forging have on metal?

2. What is the difference between the work of the blacksmith and modern production forging?
3. Name two kinds of equipment used in production forging.
4. Why must hammersmiths be so highly skilled?
5. Name some occupations in forging.
6. What are the chief forging metals?

✔ EXTRA CREDIT

Make a list of some of the parts of an automobile that are made by forging. If possible, visit a forge shop.

Unit 55
Hand Forging

Hand forging is useful in making repairs on metal parts around the home, farm, or shop. It is also a good way of making tools and ornamental ironwork.

Equipment

For large ornamental-metal projects, the following forging equipment is needed:

1. The **forge** may be a small gas or oil furnace or a coal forge (Figs. 55-1, 55-2). Blacksmith coal, which is high-quality soft coal, is needed with a coal forge.

2. **Anvils** are made of cast iron, of steel, or with a cast-iron base and a welded steel *face*, or top. The steel anvil is best. The *horn* of the anvil is used for shaping circular metal parts. Various anvil tools fit into the *hardy hole*. The anvil must be solidly mounted for forming the metal (Fig. 55-3).

3. The hot metal is held with **tongs.** There are many shapes, but the most common are those shown in Fig. 55-4.

4. There should be at least two sizes of **blacksmith's hammers.** One of 1 1/2 or 2

Fig. 55-1 Two kinds of gas-forging furnaces. (Johnson Gas Appliance Company)

Fig. 55-2 A coal forge. Notice the hand-operated blower. The forges shown in Fig. 55-1 have motor-operated blowers.

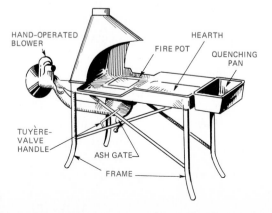

HAND-OPERATED BLOWER

HEARTH

FIRE POT

QUENCHING PAN

TUYÈRE-VALVE HANDLE

ASH GATE

FRAME

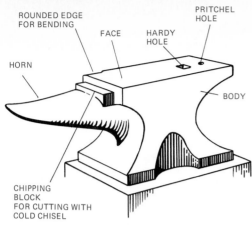

Fig. 55-3   Parts of an anvil.

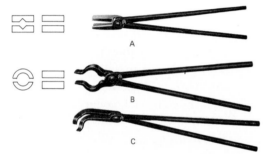

Fig. 55-4   Tongs: (A) flat lip, showing regular and grooved jaws; (B) pickup, showing curved and flat lips; (C) offset.

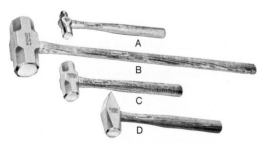

Fig. 55-5   Common hammerheads: (A) ball peen, (B) long-handle sledge, (C) short-handle sledge, (D) cross peen. (Ridge Tool Company)

pounds and another of 3 or 3 1/2 pounds will do all the necessary work (Fig. 55–5).

5. Various **anvil tools** are needed if much forging is to be done (Fig. 55–6). These include top and bottom fullers, top and bot-

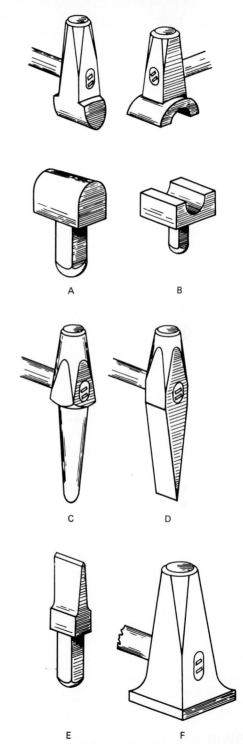

Fig. 55-6   Anvil tools: (A) top and bottom fullers, (B) top and bottom swages, (C) punch, (D) chisel, (E) hardy, (F) flatter.

275

tom swages, punches, chisels, hardies, and flatters.

Building a forge fire

The steps in lighting a *gas* or *oil furnace* follow:

1. Light a piece of paper, and place it in the opening.

2. Turn on a small supply of air. Then turn the fuel valve a little until the furnace lights up.

 CAUTION _____

Never look into the opening as you turn on the fuel.

3. Let the furnace heat up.

4. Turn on more fuel and air until the fire burns with a **neutral flame.** This flame is blue and nonoxidizing.

A *coal fire* is lit in the following way:

1. Clean out the old fire, removing the clinkers and ashes. **Clinkers** are the heavy metallic materials found in the center of an old fire. Save the **coke,** the lightweight material that crumbles easily. This is what remains after gases have been burned out of **green coal,** which is raw coal.

2. Put some wood shavings over the **tuyeres,** or air holes, and light them. Turn on a little air, using either the hand blower or power blower to get the fire started.

3. Add coke to the fire to build it up.

4. Pack dampened green coal around all sides except the front. As the fire burns, add more coal to the outside. If the fire smokes too much at first, poke a hole down the center so that it will burn better. To keep a forge fire neutral, allow it only enough air to burn freely.

Forging

Metal must be brought to the correct temperature before shaping. For example,

Table 55–1
Heat Colors and Comparable Temperatures of Steel

Color	°F	°C
faint red	900	480
dark cherry-red	1175	630
medium cherry-red	1250	680
cherry-red or full red	1375	750
bright red	1550	850
salmon	1650	900
orange	1725	940
lemon-yellow	1825	990
light yellow	1975	1080
white	2200	1200

most mild steel should be heated until it is cherry-red in color (Table 55–1). Tool steel should not be heated to as high a temperature as mild steel. Of course, thinner parts require less heat than heavier and thicker ones. Never allow the metal to become so hot that sparks fly from it.

To heat the metal, always place it in the center in a horizontal position (Fig. 55–7). Never thrust the metal in from the top, with one end at the bottom of the fire. This heats the metal unevenly.

Fig. 55–7 The right way to heat metal in the forge is to point it straight in. Do not stick it down into the fire. This would overheat the end.

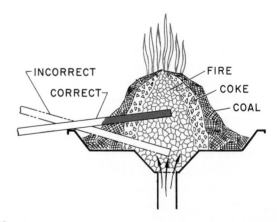

Fig. 55–8 Always wear protective clothing when forging metal.

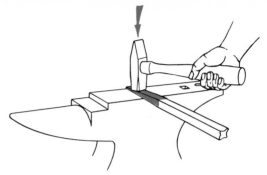

Fig. 55–9 Tapering a cold chisel.

Take the metal out of the fire from time to time to see how it is. It is very easy to burn it. Wear a face protector and special heat-resistant gloves and an apron (Fig. 55–8). Note that these latter items have traditionally been made of asbestos. However, this substance has been found to be hazardous to health. Substitutes for it are now being devised.

Always select the forging hammer best suited to the size of the workpiece. Use a small hammer on thin metal and a larger hammer on heavier stock. Then use your shoulder and wrist for medium blows and your whole shoulder for heavier blows.

The main hand-forging operations are tapering, drawing out, bending, twisting, and upsetting.

Tapering is a shaping process for forming such tools as cold chisels and center punches. It is also done to shape the ends of many wrought-metal projects.

1. Heat the end to be shaped to the right temperature.

2. Grasp the opposite end firmly with tongs. Place the heated section on the face of the anvil. Hold it at an angle equal to about half the amount of taper you want (Fig. 55–9).

3. Strike the heated portion with the flat of the hammer, turning it to keep the tapering even. If the metal is rectangular, make a quarter turn after every few blows. If it is octagonal, turn it to the opposite side. For round stock, turn the workpiece a little after each hammer blow. Make the blows firm and sharp.

4. Always keep the metal at forging temperature. Reheat the metal to a dull red. Then use light hammer blows to smooth out the tapered portion. If a rectangular shape is being tapered, another person can hold a flatter against the tapered portion as you strike the tool to smooth out the taper.

Drawing out is done to make a piece longer and thinner. Figure 55–10 shows a piece of round stock in various stages of being drawn out.

1. Heat the area to forging temperature, to a bright red color.

2. Hammer out the section to a square shape. Use heavy blows that come straight down and are square to the work.

3. Heat the metal again. Form it into an octagon.

4. Round off the section by striking the workpiece firmly while turning it on the

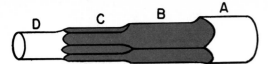

Fig. 55–10 The steps in drawing out a round bar into a smaller diameter: (A) original shape, (B) hammering to square, (C) hammering to octagon shape, (D) hammering again to round.

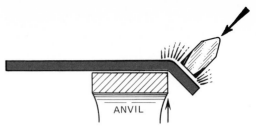

Fig. 55–12 Finishing off the bend. You will need a helper to do this.

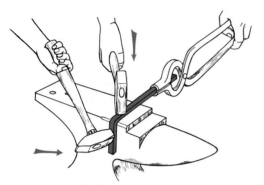

Fig. 55–11 Starting a square bend over the face of the anvil.

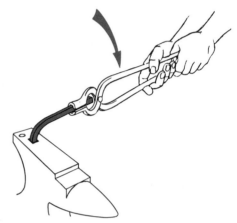

Fig. 55–13 Making a bend by inserting one end of the workpiece in the hardy hole.

anvil face. If you are drawing out square stock, round it off first. If the stock remains square while being drawn out, the metal may crack or distort badly.

Bending is done in various ways:

1. To make a sharp square bend, heat the area at the bend line. Place the workpiece over the anvil face at the point where the corner of the anvil is rounded (Fig. 55–11). Strike the extended portion with glancing blows. Then square off the bend over the corner of the anvil (Fig. 55–12).

2. Another way of bending hot metal is to place it in the hardy hole and pull or bend with tongs (Fig. 55–13).

3. You can also make a right-angle bend by putting the hot metal in a vise, with the bend line at the upper edge of the jaws.

4. Curved shapes are formed over the horn of the anvil (Fig. 55–14). Heat the area. Place the stock over the horn at about the

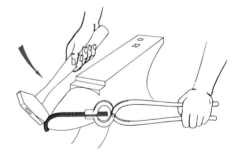

Fig. 55–14 Making a circular bend over the horn of the anvil.

right curvature. Then strike the workpiece with overlapping blows as you move the metal forward to form the curve (Fig. 55–15).

Twisting can best be done by heating the area and then bending the stock in a vise as for cold bending.

Upsetting is the opposite of drawing out. It is increasing the area of the metal by decreasing its length.

1. Heat the section to the proper temperature.

2. If the piece is short, hold it over the end of the anvil, and strike the end to flatten it out (Fig. 55–16). If the metal tends to bend, straighten it out by striking it as it lies flat on the anvil.

3. If the end of a long piece is to be enlarged, heat this area. Fasten the metal in a vise, with the heated end extending above (Fig. 55–17). Strike the end with a hammer to increase the size.

4. Instead of fastening the workpiece in a vise, you can hold it with tongs on the anvil face, with the heated end extended (Fig. 55–18).

Using anvil tools

There are a number of anvil tools that have been designed for special forging operations (see Fig. 55–6). They are held by a second person while the hammering is being done.

Fullers are used to shape round inside corners and angles and to stretch metal. When the forging is worked between the top and bottom fullers, the top fuller is struck with a sledge. The top fuller is often used alone to make depressions on the upper side of a forging lying flat on an anvil. It has a handle like a hammer and is held on the work while a helper strikes it.

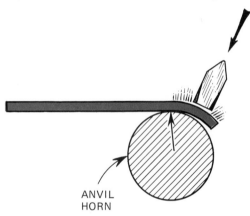

Fig. 55–15 Notice how the hammer is used to strike the metal a little beyond the point at which it touches the anvil horn.

Fig. 55–16 Upsetting both ends of a short piece of stock.

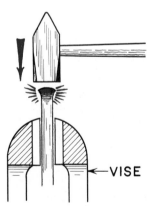

Fig. 55–17 Placing the bar or rod in a vise to do the upsetting.

Fig. 55–18 Holding the bar with tongs to upset one end as it is held flat on an anvil.

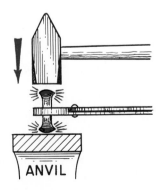

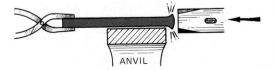

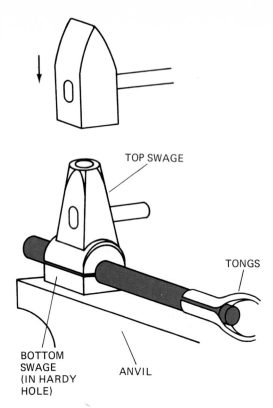

Fig. 55–19 Using the swage to smooth and straighten a forged rod.

thin because a tool used to cut hot metal does not have to be as strong. They are usually ground to an angle of about 30 degrees. They are held over the workpiece and struck with the hammer. Chisels are also used to make grooves or shoulders on the metal. The **hardy** is a hot-and-cold chisel made to fit into the hardy hole of the anvil. It is used mainly as a bottom-cutting tool. Metal is cut by placing it on the hardy and striking it with a hand hammer. The hardy is used for cutting metal bars, wires, and rods. It may be used on both hot and cold steels.

Flatters are like swages, except that they are used with flat workpieces. They are used for smoothing work and for producing a finished appearance by taking out the uneven surface left by the hammer or other tools. Their use requires a helper.

Swages are used for smoothing and finishing. They are made in many sizes, depending on the work for which they are intended. They are used in pairs, each consisting of a bottom swage and a top swage. The bottom swage is inserted in the hardy hole of the anvil. The workpiece is put in the groove of the bottom swage. The top swage, also grooved, is placed over the workpiece and struck to smooth and straighten it (Fig. 55–19).

Punches are placed over a heated workpiece and struck with a hammer. In finishing a hole, the punch is held on the work over the pritchel hole of the anvil. The slug of the stock drops through this hole.

Chisels used in forging are thinner than cold chisels. This lets them penetrate the workpiece more quickly. Their edges are also

? QUESTIONS

1. List the main equipment for forging.
2. What is the safe way to light a gas or oil forge?
3. What are the ingredients for a coal-forge fire?
4. How do you know when mild steel is hot enough for forging?
5. How do you insert a piece of metal into the forging fire?
6. What kinds of safety clothing should be worn in the shop when hand forging?
7. What are the various operations that can be done in hand forging?
8. Name five kinds of special forging tools.

✓ EXTRA CREDIT

1. Study the history of the blacksmith, and explain the importance of the blacksmith in the early development of our country.
2. Write a research report on the industrial production of some hand tools.

As metal is heated, it becomes plastic and, therefore, easy to form. Because of this, industry does much of the mechanical working of metal when it is hot. Many metal products begin in the form of castings, and then are reworked by hot forming, cold working, or machining.

Those methods used to create shapes from heated metals are called **hot forming,** or **hot working** (Fig. 56–1). Hot forming is deforming metal by hammering or pressing it at a temperature higher than its recrystallization point. The **recrystallization point** is the temperature below which a metal's internal structure can no longer be rearranged with ease. Thus, above this point, a metal can be shaped with less force than is needed to shape it when it is cold. Also, because plastic flow *rearranges* the metal at those temperatures instead of *distorting* it, the metal does not work-harden.

Hot forming breaks up the large grains in a casting and gives the material a

Fig. 56–1 Common hot-forming processes.

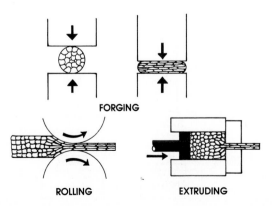

FORGING

ROLLING

EXTRUDING

wrought, or worked, structure. Wrought metal has more uniform properties and is better suited for many uses than cast metal.

Hot forming also stretches out the **inclusions,** the impurities or small particles of nonmetallic elements that are present in all but the purest of metals. These inclusions are stretched out in the directions in which plastic flow occurs during forming. The stretched inclusions are the **flow lines,** or **fiber,** that can be seen on the surface of a cut through a hot-formed part. The flow lines affect the properties of hot-formed parts. A metal has greater load-carrying ability in the direction of its flow lines than it does across the flow lines. For that reason, a hot-formed part is usually designed so that the flow lines run in the direction of greatest load during service (see Fig. 54–1).

There are a number of hot-forming processes used in industry, such as rolling, forging, and extruding. These are described in this unit.

Hot rolling

Hot rolling is an important process in steel, aluminum, and copper mills for forming industrial raw materials. In the hot-rolling process, hot metal ingots go through rolling mills to produce finished products such as sheet, pipe, bar, rod, plate, and others. There are many kinds of rolling mills, but all of them operate on the same principle (Fig. 56–2). The metal ingot is squeezed between two rotating rolls. These rolls are closer together than the thickness of the ingot. The slabs from this first rolling are trimmed, reheated, and rolled again. A final operation is coiling the sheets for easy handling.

Forging

Forging is widely used in industry for hot-forming finished shapes. Rods and bars made by hot rolling are often formed into final shape by forging. Metals that can be

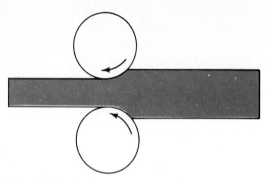

Fig. 56-2 In the rolling mill, the two rotating rolls squeeze the metal between them to form the new shape.

forged commercially include wrought iron, steel, copper, and brass. Aluminum and zinc can be forged at low temperatures.

Industrial forging is forming hot metal by hammering, pressing, or intermittent rolling. The metal is heated to a high temperature. It is then shaped by the pressure applied by one surface, the hammer, as the metal rests on another surface, the anvil. Forged products are remarkably free of concealed or internal defects. Therefore, they have great strength and toughness. For example, automobile parts requiring these qualities, such as the crankshaft connecting rods and wheels, are forged. Hand tools such as wrenches and pliers, hoist hooks, and truck parts are made by forging (Fig. 56-3). When metal has been forged, it has a fibrous structure resembling the grain structure of wood. Like wood, the metal is stronger and tougher in the direction of the grain.

Forging machines

All forging equipment shapes the metal between two dies. One die holds the workpiece. The other delivers the pressure. The dies may be flat surfaces. They may also be cut to correspond to the finished shape of the piece. There are two general kinds of forging equipment: forging hammers and forging presses.

Forging hammers deliver a high-speed impact. This is done by a **ram,** or heavy weight, that is raised and then dropped or driven downward into the workpiece. Forging hammers are usually named by the method used to raise the ram. *Board-drop hammers* have a ram mounted on the ends of vertical hardwood boards (Fig. 56-4). *Air-lift hammers* use air to raise the ram. *Steam hammers* are the largest and most versatile forging hammers. They are constructed like air-lift hammers but operate differently. The ram is raised and driven downward by steam pressure on a piston (Fig. 56-5).

Forging presses are often preferred to forging hammers for many operations. For example, since nickel alloys retain much of their toughness at forging temperatures, the

Fig. 56-3 The wheels and many other parts of this small vehicle are made by forging the metal. (Clark Equipment Company)

Fig. 56-4 A board-drop hammer.

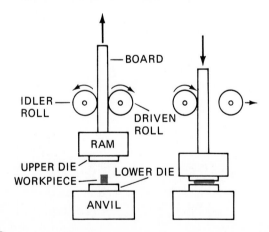

Fig. 56-5 A steam hammer used in industry. (Aluminum Company of America)

slow movement of presses gives the alloys more time to flow into the contours of dies. Also, the squeezing action of presses has a kneading effect on the metal. This causes deeper deformation in the workpiece than is normally achieved with forging hammers. In general, larger forgings can be produced on presses than with hammers. There are two kinds of forging presses: mechanical and hydraulic.

The *mechanical forging press* operates much like a large, slow-moving trip hammer (Fig. 56-6). The ram is mounted vertically. It is moved through a stroke of fixed length and speed by a crankshaft, levers, gears, or other mechanical means. The power source is usually an electric motor. These presses often use automatic transfer systems to move the workpiece from operation to operation.

The *hydraulic forging press* has a large piston attached to the top of the ram, similar to the steam hammer (Fig. 56-7). Hydraulic pressure moves the piston down for the workstroke and up for the return stroke. These presses are sometimes equipped to automatically vary the forging speed and pressure. Hydraulic presses are made in a wide range of sizes.

Fig. 56-6 A mechanical forging press. (E. W. Bliss)

Fig. 56-7 The hydraulic press is used for a wide variety of metalworking operations, including drawing, forging, straightening, cupping, embossing, and coining. Notice that by using hydraulics, or fluid power, a small force applied to the operating lever produces a tremendous force on the ram itself.

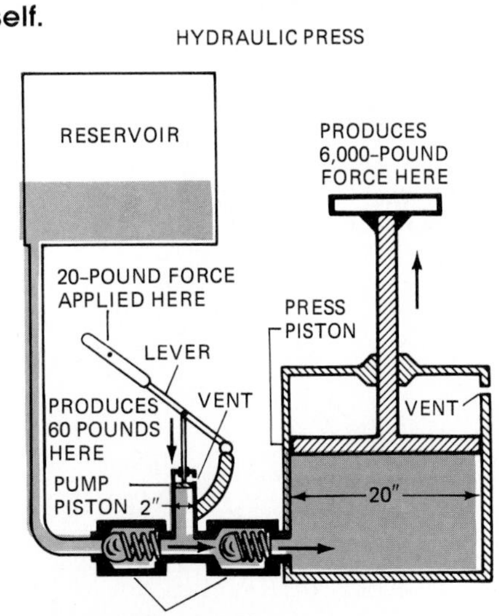

HYDRAULIC PRESS

RESERVOIR

PRODUCES 6,000-POUND FORCE HERE

20-POUND FORCE APPLIED HERE

PRESS PISTON

LEVER

VENT

VENT

PRODUCES 60 POUNDS HERE

PUMP PISTON 2"

20"

BALL CHECK VALVES

283

Forging operations

There are two kinds of forging operations: open-die and impression-die. In **open-die forging,** the workpiece is shaped between dies that do not completely confine the metal. The working surfaces of the dies are either flat or contain only simple shapes. In most open-die forging, the workpiece does not take the shape of the dies. The shape is obtained by manipulation of the workpiece. For example, a round rod can be forged into a square bar by hammering along its length with open, flat dies.

In **impression-die forging,** the workpiece is shaped between dies that completely enclose the metal. The upper and lower dies are cut out so that when they come together, the hollow space between them makes a mold shaped like the forged piece. The workpiece is not manipulated during forging. The entire piece is placed between the dies and hammered or pressed until the metal fills the die cavity (Fig. 56–8).

Before forging can be done, the metal must be heated to working temperature in a large gas or oil furnace. Forging is then done with hammers or presses between the dies. After the forging is complete, the workpiece must be cleaned, heat-treated, straightened, inspected, and often machined.

Other forging methods

Other methods of forging include upset forging, roll forging, swaging, and fullering. In *upset forging,* the shape is obtained by squeeze pressure applied in a horizontal forging machine. In this process, the end of the metal is heated and then placed in two gripper dies that squeeze the metal into shape (Fig. 56–9). *Roll forging* is done in a manner similar to hot rolling. It is done primarily to reduce or taper the ends of bar stock. *Swaging* is a process of reducing or changing a cross-sectional area by revolving the stock under fast blows of the hammer. *Fullering* is used to stretch and thin out a workpiece.

Fig. 56–8   Impression-die forging. Only the bottom half of the die is shown.

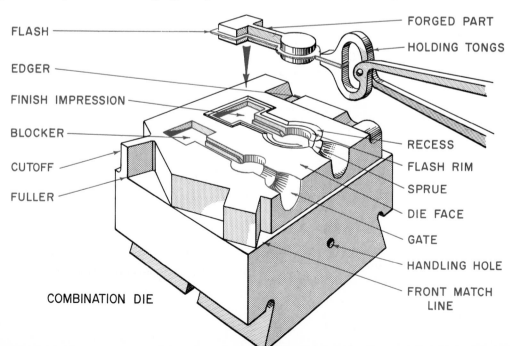

FLASH — FORGED PART

HOLDING TONGS

EDGER

FINISH IMPRESSION

BLOCKER — RECESS

CUTOFF — FLASH RIM

FULLER — SPRUE

DIE FACE

GATE

HANDLING HOLE

FRONT MATCH LINE

COMBINATION DIE

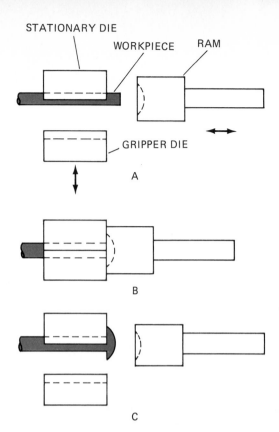

Fig. 56-9 Upset forging: (A) gripping, (B) heading, (C) releasing.

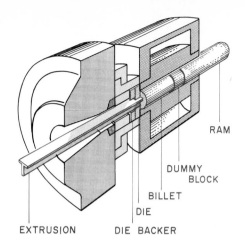

Fig. 56-10 This shows how the die is used in a hydraulic press to produce the extrusion.

Extruding

Extruding is a process in which hot metal is pushed through an opening in a die. The part that is formed has a cross section of the same shape as the die opening. The basic principle of extruding is the same as that of squeezing toothpaste from a tube. The paste is the exact shape of the tube opening. Most extruding is done with the metal heated. However, lead, tin, and aluminum can be extruded cold. The advantage of forming metal by extruding is that long pieces of uniform and complex shapes can be produced.

The first step in extruding metal is to make a die of the shape wanted. This die is placed in a huge hydraulic press (Fig. 56–10). Then a billet is heated. The heated billet is then put in a cylinder behind the die. The hydraulic press applies pressure to the ram, forcing the plastic, or softened, metal through the die opening.

The extruding process is a relatively inexpensive and effective way of producing complex shapes with true and smooth surfaces. Extruded shapes are commonly used in building construction, the automotive industry, and equipment manufacturing.

 QUESTIONS

1. What is hot forming?
2. What is forging used for in industry?
3. What are the two main kinds of forging equipment?
4. What two types of dies are used in forging operations?
5. Name four other forging methods.
6. What is the advantage of forming metal by extrusion processes?

 EXTRA CREDIT

1. Write a research report on industrial forging.
2. Prepare a bulletin-board display of the process of extruding metal.

SECTION 7

CASTING

Unit 57
Introduction to Foundry

Foundry, or **metal casting,** is a very important metalworking process. It is used to produce thousands of different articles, from dental plates to giant hydraulic presses. The art of metal casting is over 5000 years old. It remains one of the world's basic industries. **Foundry** is also the name given to a shop in which metal products are cast. Many metal products used by the average family contain cast parts. Everything from doorknobs, jewelry, and furniture to many parts of bicycles, automobiles, planes, and other vehicles have foundry-made parts (Fig. 57–1). Metal casting is, and has long been, one of the most important recycling industries. This is because much scrap metal is used as a raw material in foundries.

Metal casting involves making a **mold.** A mold has a cavity, or opening, in the shape of the product being cast. Molten metal is poured into the mold. The metal is allowed to cool and harden. It, therefore, takes the shape of the mold cavity.

Foundry processes

Castings are produced by six different processes. They are sand casting; die casting;

Fig. 57–1 The metal frames of these aluminum spurs were cast in the foundry.

permanent-mold casting; shell-mold casting; precision, or investment, casting; and centrifugal casting. They all involve the same general procedures. First, a **pattern** of wood, metal, plastic, or wax is made. In most cases, the original pattern is made of wood. However, in mass-production industries, many castings have to be made from one pattern. In those industries, therefore, the pattern is metal. Sometimes, plastic patterns are used (Fig. 57–2). The pattern must be slightly larger than the finished casting will be. This is because metal shrinks when it cools. However, the pattern has the same shape as the finished casting. The pattern must also be made larger in the areas that may need machining. The vertical sides of the pattern are often tapered slightly so it can more easily be removed from a sand mold.

Fig. 57-2 A glass-fiber pattern. (Fisher Casting Company)

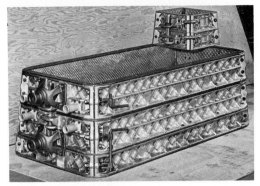

Fig. 57-3 Metal flasks are used in industry. (Hines Flask Company)

The pattern is used to make the mold. In making a sand mold, the pattern is placed in a box called a **flask** (Fig. 57–3). Sand is then packed around the pattern. The flask is

Fig. 57-4 The pattern (top left) and the casting (top right) for the stationary jaw of a vise. The core box in the foreground is used to make the sand core. Sand is packed in the box until it is full and then hardened. Then the core is fitted into the mold. The space taken up by the core appears as an opening in the casting.

made in two or more parts. This is so it can be taken apart and the pattern removed. After the pattern is removed, a **gate** is cut in the mold. This connects the mold to the **sprue hole,** through which the molten metal is poured into the mold. The mold is then closed. Sometimes, the finished casting must have holes or other openings through it. In that case, special sand **cores** are placed in the mold before it is closed (Fig. 57–4). The molten metal is poured into the mold cavity. When it cools, the mold and any cores are broken to remove the casting.

To finish the casting, the unusable parts, such as the sprues and gates, are cut off (Fig. 57–5). The edges of the casting are also smoothed by grinding (Fig. 57–6). The casting is now ready for machining, welding, painting, or other finishing.

Metals used in casting

Most castings are made from ferrous metals, principally gray iron, steel, and malleable iron. About three-fourths of all foundry workers are employed in ferrous foundries. The others work in the nonferrous foundries. There, copper alloys, aluminum, magnesium, lead, and zinc alloys are poured.

287

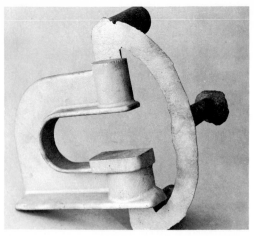

Fig. 57-5 This press body has been cast in aluminum. The waste material, including the sprue, riser, and gate, must be cut off.

Fig. 57-6 Grinding a casting. (Inland Steel Company)

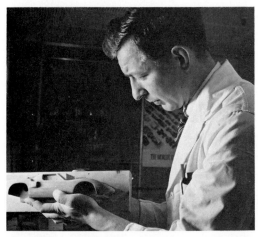

Fig. 57-7 Precision wood patterns are used to make accurate model automobiles.

Fig. 57-8 A coremaker producing sand cores for use in making automobile pistons. (Campbell, Wyant, and Cannon Foundry Company)

Foundry occupations

Foundries employ engineers, scientists, technicians, skilled workers, semiskilled workers, and laborers. The engineer and the metallurgist control the quality of the metal. An engineer also checks the castings and molds and supervises many foundry technicians. The patterns are made by highly skilled woodworkers and metalworkers called *patternmakers* (Fig. 57-7). The molds in the foundry are made by skilled and semi-skilled workers called *coremakers* (Fig. 57-8). The furnace operator is a *melter*. The worker who pours the castings is a *pourer*. The clean castings are finished by workers called *chippers, grinders,* and *finishers.* Altogether, about 450,000 people work in foundries throughout the United States. Of this number, about 80,000 are employed in professional, office, managerial, and sales jobs. There are over 8000 engineers, chemists, metallurgists, and other scientists in the industry.

Types of foundries

There are two basic types of foundries: jobbing and production. The *jobbing foundry*

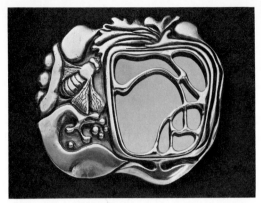

Fig. 57-9 A brooch made by casting. (Sterling Silversmiths Guild of America)

is often very small. There, many different kinds of castings of all sizes and weights are made in limited numbers. Also, one casting is often made to fill a single order. The *production foundry* is usually larger. The work is generally limited to a few patterns from which thousands of castings are made. Most foundry work in the United States is done in the Great Lakes states, on the West Coast, and in Alabama.

Foundry as a hobby

For people who like to make models, pouring small castings can be a lot of fun and a fascinating hobby. Small parts or fittings for model airplanes, trains, and boats can be made in sand, plaster, or metal molds. Those interested in jewelry making can build molds from plaster of paris to make brooches, rings, and other pieces (Fig. 57-9). Many other projects can be made.

 QUESTIONS

1. List some typical cast products.
2. List the six methods of making castings.
3. Name at least five special occupations involved in foundry.
4. What are the two basic kinds of foundries?
5. What kinds of hobbies are related to foundry work?

 EXTRA CREDIT

Find out all you can about one of the major occupations in foundry. Write a report, or give it orally in class.

Unit 58
Making a Metal Casting

There are many interesting projects that can be cast in the school shop by the same methods used in a commercial foundry. Some examples are ashtrays, bookends, paperweights, poker heads and handles, and parts for model engines (Fig. 58-1). The method generally used in the school foundry is **sand casting.** In this unit, you will learn how to make sand castings.

Patternmaking

A pattern is needed to make the sand mold into which the molten metal is poured. Most original or master patterns are made from a good grade of white pine or mahogany (Fig. 58-2). In some cases, the original article can be used for the pattern. A plastic-foam pattern can be used for a single casting. It is not removed from the mold as is a wood or metal pattern. Instead, it is allowed to "burn up" as the hot metal is poured (Fig. 58-3). Cast with a plastic-foam pattern only in a well-ventilated area.

Since molten metal shrinks as it cools, a pattern must be made larger than the actual

Fig. 58-1 Parts for model engines, such as this wheel, can be made by sand casting.

Fig. 58-2 A simple wooden pattern for a house sign.

Fig. 58-3 Plastic-foam patterns are simple to make since the material can be cut easily. (A) A piece of decorative sculpture made with a plastic-foam pattern. (B) A foam pattern for a fireplace poker.

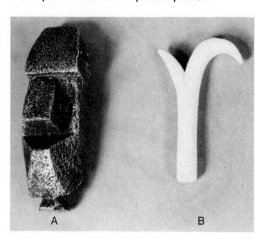

size of the casting. You use a shrink rule to do this. A **shrink rule** is a scale on which the inches are actually longer than regular inches. Shrinkage allowances differ for different materials. Shrinkage does not have to be considered in making small decorative objects.

A pattern must also have **draft.** This means that it must be tapered so that it can be pulled out of the sand mold easily. The **fillets,** the inside sharp corners on patterns, should be made slightly rounded by using wax, Plastic Wood paste, or wood.

Simple patterns are in one piece. *Split patterns,* for round objects or irregular shapes, are made in two or more parts (Fig. 58–4). Sometimes, a pattern is mounted on a **match plate,** with half of the pattern on one side of the plate and half on the other. The match plate will produce a perfectly matching mold. It can be made of wood or metal.

To make a simple pattern like the one in Fig. 58–2, do the following:

1. Cut the background for the pattern from a piece of plywood. Make sure that the edges taper a little to form the draft. If you cut the piece out on a scroll saw, tilt the table 1 to 2 degrees. Then do all the cutting from one side of the blade.

2. Cut out the letters that will form your name in the same way, again allowing for the right draft.

3. Fasten the letters of the background

Fig. 58-4 A split pattern. The completed mold for this pattern is shown in Fig. 58–28.

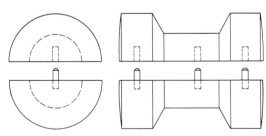

with small brads, glue, or shellac. Use beeswax to form a clean fillet around each letter.

4. Apply at least two coats of very thin shellac. Sand between each coat.

Sand cores

Sand cores are used to provide any needed openings in the casting. Beach or dune sand is mixed with special binders. This mixture is then rammed into preformed boxes shaped like the cores. The cores are turned out onto flat plates or into special supports called **driers.** They are then baked in an oven. They cannot be handled before they are baked. This is because they are very soft and weak and would fall apart. Baking gives a core hardness and strength. Thus, it can withstand the molten metal poured into the mold cavity. After being baked, cores can be handled, pasted together, treated with heat-resistant materials, and stored until needed (Figs. 58–5, 58–6).

There is a quicker process for making cores in school and industry. Mix fine sand with **water glass,** or sodium silicate. Ram this mixture into a core box. Then inject carbon dioxide gas into the mixture. The gas reacts with the water glass. This makes the core hard right away without baking. The core can then be put directly into the mold.

Molding sands

The sand used for making molds is of two basic kinds: synthetic and natural. *Synthetic molding sand* contains certain proportions of many different substances. For example, it may include a clear, washed, pure silica sand mixed with clay, carbon materials, and water. Whatever the kind of sand used, it must be heat-resistant, must stick together, and must retain its shape well. It must also have **permeability.** This characteristic lets the gases from the hot metal poured into the mold escape through the sand. Synthetic sands are used mostly in iron

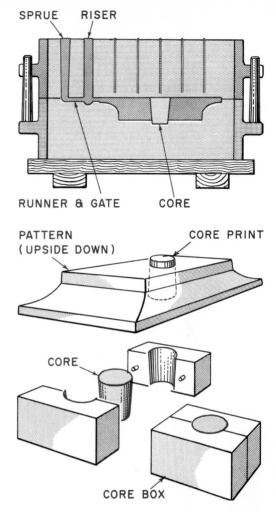

Fig. 58–5 Producing a casting that has an opening in it. A core print on the pattern locates the position of the core that produces the opening in the casting. A core box is used to make the core.

and steel foundries, which require very high temperatures.

Natural molding sand is used just as it is dug out of the ground, with the possible addition of a little water. Natural sands are found principally in the eastern Great Lakes region, in Kentucky, and in Missouri. The natural sands are most widely used for nonferrous metals, which require less heat. New

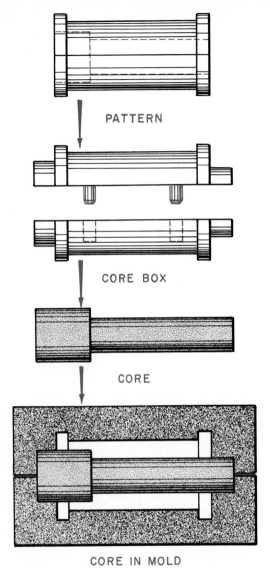

PATTERN

CORE BOX

CORE

CORE IN MOLD

Fig. 58–6 A typical pattern, core box, core, and mold.

moist to your hand. It should break off sharply when you tap it. If you have added too much water, large amounts of sand will stick to your hand.

Parting compound, a dry powder, is dusted between the **cope,** or top, and **drag,** or bottom, sections of the mold. This keeps them from sticking together. You can use a fine beach sand for this purpose, but the commercial parting compounds are better.

Foundry equipment

Some special pieces of equipment are needed for simple foundry work. These include a flat molding board, a flat bottom board, flask weight or clamps, bench rammer, sprue pin, riser pin, draw spike or screw, rapping bar, strike-off bar, riddle, bellows, wet bulb, slick and oval, spoon and gate cutter, trowel, sprinkling can, shovel, and a few other molder's tools (Fig. 58–7). A flask holds the sand mold (Fig. 58–8). It is very important that the molding board be perfectly flat. This lets you get a clean parting between the cope and drag sections of the flask.

A furnace is also needed (Fig. 58–9). For light metals such as aluminum, lead, and zinc alloys, either a large soldering furnace or a special melting furnace can be used (Fig. 58–10). Some metals can also be melted in a forge or with a gas welding torch. However, a melting furnace is best and safest. The metal is melted in a **crucible** (Fig. 58–11). Often, the crucible also becomes the pouring ladle. The crucible is lifted with tongs and placed in a crucible shank for pouring (Fig. 58–12). For protection, the pourer must wear clear goggles, a face shield, and special heat-resistant gauntlet-type gloves, leggings, and apron. Note that these latter items have traditionally been made of asbestos. However, this substance has been found to be hazardous to health. Substitutes for it are now being devised.

sand is light brown, but it becomes dark with use. The sand dries out when used or stored. It must be tempered by moisture. **Tempering** is done by sprinkling water on the sand and mixing it in with a shovel or riddle. The sand is tempered properly when a clump picked up and squeezed retains the sharp impression of your fingers. It should feel

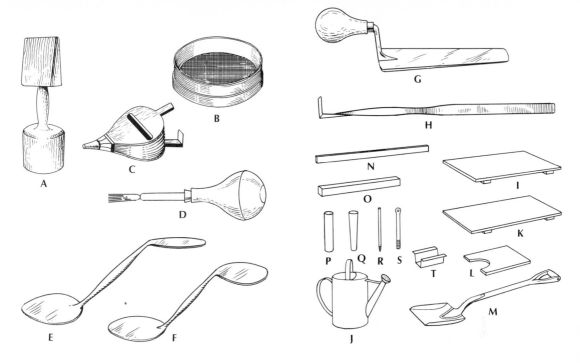

Fig. 58-7   Common items needed in foundry work: (A) bench rammer, (B) riddle, (C) bellows, (D) molder's bulb, (E) spoon and gate cutter, (F) slick and oval, (G) trowel, (H) lifter, (I) molding board, (J) sprinkling can, (K) bottom board, (L) flask weight, (M) shovel, (N) strike-off bar, (O) rapping bar, (P) riser pin, (Q) sprue pin, (R) draw spike, (S) draw screw, (T) gate cutter.

Fig. 58-8   A foundry flask, showing the cope and the drag. (Hines Flask Company)

Fig. 58-9   A soldering furnace and pot used for melting tin and lead.

Fig. 58-10 A small melting furnace.

Fig. 58-11 Kinds of crucibles.

STANDARD SHAPES

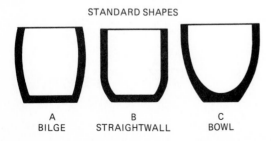

| A | B | C |
| BILGE | STRAIGHTWALL | BOWL |

Table 58-1
Melting Temperature
of Selected Metals

Metal	°F	°C
tin	449	232
babbitt metal	462	239
lead	621	327
zinc	788	420
aluminum	1220	660
bronze	1675	913
brass	1706	930
silver	1761	960
gold	1945	1063
copper	1981	1083
cast iron	2200	1204
carbon steel	2500	1371
nickel	2651	1455
wrought iron	2750	1510

Foundry metals

Practically every metal can be melted and poured into castings. However, many metals have very high melting points (Table 58-1). These must be heated with special equipment. Nonetheless, many of the nonferrous metals can be easily heated with the equipment available in the average shop. Pure lead or **type metal,** an alloy of lead and antimony, is adequate for simple projects. However, lead and lead alloys should never be used for making objects that

Fig. 58-12 (A) Crucible tongs. (B) Crucible shank.

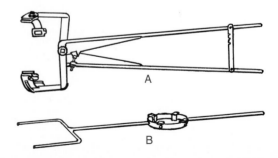

come in contact with food or are likely to be used by small children. This is because lead is poisonous. Aluminum or a die-casting metal alloy are best for the small shop. To help purify the metal and eliminate gas, a **flux** is usually added. This is sometimes done during the melting process. But with aluminum and aluminum alloys, it is generally done just before pouring. Powdered charcoal is used as a flux with lead. Special commercial fluxes are used for aluminum, brass, and other alloys.

Gating system

The **gating system** consists of the openings through which the molten metal runs into the mold (Fig. 58–13). The liquid metal flows with ease through a good gating system. Many problems in producing good castings are caused by poorly designed gating systems. A simple gating system includes the sprue, runner, riser, and gate.

The **sprue** is a vertical opening through which the molten metal enters the gating system. The sprue is formed by a *sprue pin*. This is often a tapered round wood pin. In industry, however, it has been found that a tapered rectangular pin gives better results. The *pouring basin* is a cup-shaped opening at the top of the sprue. The molten metal is poured into this basin, from which it enters the sprue proper. The *sprue base,* or *sprue well,* is a rectangular opening at the base of the sprue. Molten metal fills this base before it enters the runner. The sprue base makes the flow of liquid metal more even by reducing its turbulence.

The **runner** is the horizontal opening through which the molten metal flows to the gates. If the runner is long, it should decrease in size as each gate is passed. This tapering prevents the molten metal from flowing too quickly to the far end of the runner. The *runner extension* is the part of the runner that ex-

Fig. 58–13   A gating system.

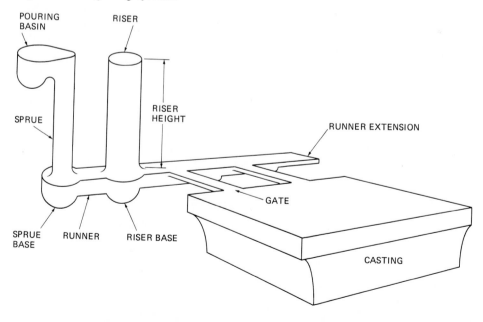

tends beyond the last gate. The first molten metal that is poured into the system contains many impurities. These impurities become trapped in the runner extension. Therefore, they cannot ruin the casting.

The **riser,** which may or may not be needed, provides a reserve of molten metal that helps control the flow of metal to the mold. When aluminum is used for a heavy or thick casting, a riser is not needed. A riser is usually needed for a thin casting with a large area. The volume of the riser must always equal the volume of the mold cavity itself. The riser can be placed directly over the mold cavity or between the mold cavity and the sprue hole. *When casting aluminum, never place the riser on the side of the mold cavity opposite from the sprue.*

A **gate** is a horizontal opening from the runner to the mold cavity. The number of gates needed depends on the size of the mold.

Making a simple mold

These are the steps to follow in making a simple mold:

1. Select or make a pattern of the article or piece to be cast.

2. Place the pattern on the molding board with the draft, or smaller, side up (Fig. 58–14).

3. Make a chalk mark on one side of the cope and drag of the flask. Place the drag face down on the molding board with the pins pointing toward the floor. The flask should be large enough for the pattern, sprue, and riser. The molding board should just cover the flask. It should not be so large that it is hard to handle.

4. Dust the pattern with parting compound.

5. Shovel some molding sand into the **riddle,** or sand sieve. Shake the riddle back and forth over the pattern until the pattern is covered with at least 1 inch (25 mm) of

Fig. 58–14 The pattern is placed on the molding board with the draft up.

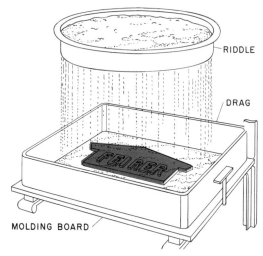

Fig. 58–15 Riddling sand into the drag.

Fig. 58–16 Packing sand by hand.

sand (Fig. 58–15). Then fill the drag about half full with riddle sand. With your fingers, tuck the sand around the pattern and into the corners of the drag (Fig. 58–16). When

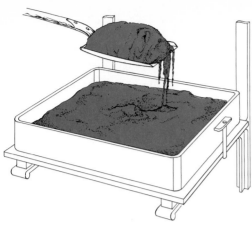

Fig. 58-17 Sand is now shoveled directly into the drag until it is overflowing.

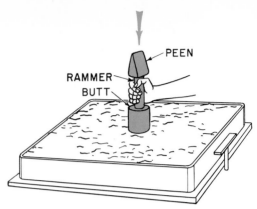

Fig. 58-18 Ram the drag with the butt end of the bench rammer until the sand is firmly packed.

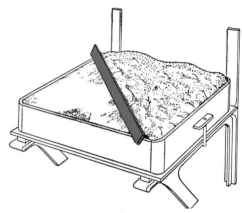

Fig. 58-19 Strike off the drag, using a straight stick or a piece of metal as the strike-off bar. Work the bar back and forth as you pull it across the drag to level off the sand.

Fig. 58-20 Here you see the rammed drag with the bottom board in place. The drag is now ready to be turned over.

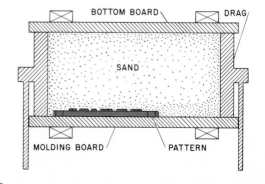

this is done, shovel sand in until it is a little higher than the top of the drag (Fig. 58-17).

6. Using the peen end of the rammer, tuck the sand around the outside edges of the mold first. Then, with the butt end, ram the sand firmly around the pattern (Fig. 58-18). This is very important. In order to get a good casting, you must have a sharp impression of the pattern in the sand. However, if the sand is rammed too hard, it loses its ability to "breathe" and thereby allow hot gases to escape. Ram from the edges, and work toward the pattern.

7. Again, riddle the sand into the drag until it is heaping. Tuck the sand around the edges first and then back and forth over the pattern until the sand is firmly but not too solidly packed.

8. Strike off the excess sand by using a metal or wood bar (Fig. 58-19). This bar should be completely square. Pull the sand off the top of the drag. Then sprinkle a little sand on the surface to form a bed for the bottom board. Place the bottom board on the drag (Fig. 58-20).

9. Holding the molding board and the bottom board tightly together, turn the drag over. Now, lift off the molding board. You

297

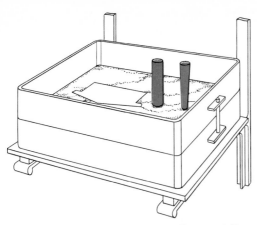

Fig. 58-21 After removing the molding board, dust the surface with parting compound and place the cope in position. Then insert the sprue pin and the riser pin (if one is needed).

will see the bottom of the pattern in the even surface of the sand. This is the **parting line.** Carefully blow off any extra particles of loose sand from the surface with the bellows. Smooth any rough spots with a slick, trowel, or spoon. Then dust the parting line with parting compound. Be careful not to use too much of the compound. An excess would dry out the surface of the sand.

10. Put the cope in place. Make sure that it slips on and off easily.

11. Now, insert the sprue pin. If the casting is quite thick, a riser pin should also be inserted, as shown in Fig. 58-21. The shrinkage that occurs when the metal cools will thus take place in the riser rather than in the casting. Risers are generally larger in diameter than the sprue pins and have no taper. If a split pattern is being used, put the cope part of the pattern in place, and dust in with parting compound.

12. Repeat steps 5 through 8 for the cope section of the flask (Fig. 58-22). Sometimes, the sprue and riser holes are cut with a hollow metal tube *after* the cope has been rammed (Fig. 58-23).

13. To help hot gases escape, it is necessary to vent the mold by punching small holes in the cope or drag section of the mold. These vent holes should go down to within 1/8 inch (3 mm) of the pattern. An old bicycle spoke or a 1/16-inch (1.5-mm) welding rod make good vent rods. You must not damage the pattern. This is the best method for punching the holes: Slowly push the vent rod down until you touch the pattern. Then,

Fig. 58-22 Ram the cope section as you did the drag. Notice that the second half of a split pattern is put on after the drag is turned over. When this is completed, carefully remove the sprue and riser pins.

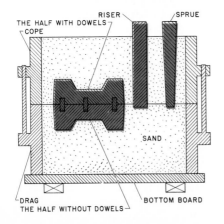

Fig. 58-23 Sprue and riser holes being cut with a hollow metal tube.

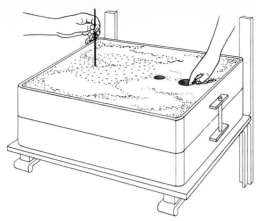

Fig. 58–24 Making a funnel-shaped opening for the sprue hole. The mold is also being vented.

pull it back out about 1/8 inch (3 mm). Take hold of the vent rod at the level of the sand. Now, punch several holes in the sand. Be careful to stop each time your fingers touch the sand.

14. Wiggle the sprue pin around until it becomes loose. Carefully pull it out. Then pack the sand into a funnel shape around the sprue hole. This pouring basin can also be cut with a trowel (Fig. 58–24). Remove the riser pin as you did the sprue pin. It is not necessary to make a funnel here.

15. Lift the cope section of the flask straight up. Set it on its edge out of the way. Make sure the sprue and riser holes are open and clean (Fig. 58–25).

16. With a wet bulb or a camel's-hair brush and a *little* water, carefully moisten the sand around the pattern. Wetting the sand keeps the mold from crumbling when the pattern is removed.

 CAUTION

Water is the worst enemy of molten metal. Do not get the sand too wet.

17. Tap a spike into the wooden pattern. Then lightly rap the spike on all sides until

Fig. 58–25 Remove the cope section, and set it on an edge out of the way.

you can see that the pattern is completely loose in the sand. The spike or a large wood screw can be used to pull the pattern out of the mold. *Now, carefully lift up the pattern* (Fig. 58–26). If you do this right, the pattern should leave a clean-cut imprint in the sand. If the sand crumbles a little, you can repair the mold with a molder's tool. If you are

Fig. 58–26 Lifting the pattern.

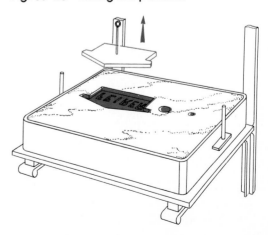

using a metal pattern, screw a threaded rod or bolt into the back of the pattern to remove it from the sand.

18. Bend a small piece of sheet metal into a U shape about 1/2 inch (13 mm) wide. You can use a commercial gate cutter also. Carefully cut a gate, or a small groove, into the drag section of the mold. The size of this gate will depend on the size of the casting. Start with a gate about 1 inch (25 mm) wide and about 1/2 inch (13 mm) deep. Do not try to do this in one stroke. First, cut a small stretch. Then, throw the sand away (Fig. 58–27). When a riser is used, the gate must be cut from the sprue to the riser and then from the riser to the casting cavity. The gate from the sprue to the riser is a little smaller than the gate from the riser to the casting cavity. After cutting these gates, pack down all the loose sand. Then round out the edges where the gates meet the parting line. This is very important. If all the loose sand is not removed from the gates, the molten metal will wash it into the casting cavity. The sand will leave pinholes in the casting.

19. Repair the mold as needed by adding small bits of sand and smoothing them

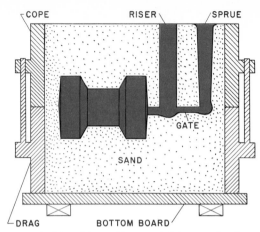

Fig. 58–28　Close the mold by replacing the cope. The mold is ready for pouring. Notice the position of the sprue and riser holes.

down with the right molding tools. Blow off any loose sand with the bellows.

20. Close the mold by replacing the cope section (Fig. 58–28). Carefully guide the cope by putting your fingers along the sides. The pins of the drag should line up with the holes of the cope. Be careful to put the cope back on exactly as you took it off. Do not turn it around. Make sure that the chalk marks are on the same side. Put the mold on the floor, and scatter some loose sand around it. The mold should now be clamped or weighted. If you are not going to pour the casting right away, cover the sprue and riser holes. This will keep dirt from falling into them.

Pouring the casting

 CAUTION

You must wear safety clothing. Put on clear goggles, a face shield, and special heat-resistant, gauntlet-type gloves, leggings, and apron.

Fig. 58–27　Cutting a gate to the sprue and riser holes.

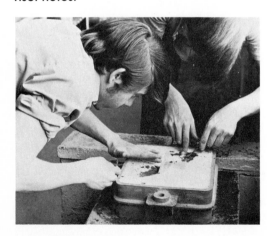

Fig. 58-29 The tip of the lance-type pyrometer is inserted into the molten metal to check the temperature.

1. Select a crucible of the right size. It should be large enough to hold enough molten metal to fill the mold cavity, sprue, and riser. Place the crucible in the furnace. Put in the pieces of metal to be melted. Light the furnace.

2. Heat until all the metal is at pouring temperature. Check often when it is nearing this temperature. Use a lance-type pyrometer for this (Fig. 58–29). Overheating will produce a defective casting. Turn off the furnace, add the flux, and stir. The **slag,** or impurities, will float to the top of the crucible. This should be skimmed off.

3. Take the crucible out of the furnace with crucible tongs (Fig. 58–30). Put it in a crucible shank. Pick up the crucible shank so that your body is parallel to it. Your arm and safety clothing will help shield you from the heat.

Fig. 58-30 Using bent-handle crucible tongs to remove the crucible.

(!) SAFETY RULE

Stand to one side of the mold, never over the top of it.

Pour the metal as rapidly as possible (Fig. 58–31). Once you have started to pour, keep the sprue hole full. Stop pouring as soon as the sprue hole remains full. The metal will start to solidify as soon as it touches the sand. Safe practice is to keep your face and body away from the mold. This is because steam rises from it. Also, metal may spurt up and out of the mold at this time. This is another reason for doing a good job of venting the mold.

Fig. 58-31 Pouring the metal into the mold using the crucible shank.

Fig. 58–32 The cope has been lifted from the cooled mold. Note the cast pieces. (Cerro Corporation)

4. Let the metal cool. The time will vary depending on the thickness and size of the casting. Separate the cope and drag (Fig. 58–32). Shake out, or break up, the mold. Remove the casting. Be careful, because the casting is still hot. You should handle it with tongs.

Finishing the casting

1. A casting is ready to be finished when it is cool enough to be handled with bare hands. Cut off the gates, sprue, and riser with a hacksaw or a metal-cutting bandsaw.

2. You will find that the parting line shows on the casting. This may be filed or ground off and the edges completely smoothed. Castings can be finished in many different ways. Decorative castings can be scratch-brushed, sandblasted, painted, or enameled. In many cases, felt bases are added for such objects as lamps and book-ends. Most commercial castings must be machined on the drill press, lathe, shaper, milling machine, or grinder.

 QUESTIONS

1. What are most patterns for sand casting made of?
2. Define *draft* and *fillet*.
3. What is used to provide an opening in a casting?
4. What are the characteristics of good molding sand?
5. What special clothing must be worn when the casting is poured?
6. What metals can be cast?
7. Name the main parts of a gating system.
8. In sand casting, what is the parting line?
9. What do you call the container in which metals are melted for pouring?
10. In what ways can castings be finished?

 EXTRA CREDIT

1. Make a pattern for a project that will become a part of the school-shop equipment.
2. Make a bulletin-board display of the sand-casting process.

Unit 59
Industrial Casting Methods

Metal casting is one of the oldest industrial techniques. Skilled workers have been making castings for thousands of years. However, until recently the casting process was more an art than a science. Nonetheless, many new casting methods have been developed in industry to meet the ever-increasing demand for metal products (Fig. 59–1). The average five-room home, for example, contains over 2 tons (1800 kg) of metal castings. The average automobile has over 600 pounds (270 kg) of castings. In fact, 90 out of

Fig. 59-1 Huge castings for machine tools.

In school foundries and many small commercial job shops, sand casting is largely a hand process done with very simple tools and equipment. By contrast, the large modern foundry has huge, complex machines that are often controlled by computers. These machines are fed by conveyor systems that eliminate much of the heavy work of the old-style foundry. The modern industrial foundry uses many operations in casting.

First, the melting department provides a continuous flow of molten metal to the molding department. In automotive foundries, the metal is melted in cupolas, or furnaces, fired by coke and high-velocity air. The molten metal runs out through a trough to a holding ladle. There, the molten metal remains until it is needed. Then a transfer ladle is filled with molten iron. This ladle is conveyed to the molding machines by an electrically driven monorail system or a special lift truck.

The sand for cores and molds is stored outside the foundry. Since its level of moisture must be uniform before it can be used, it must usually be dried. This is done in a continuous rotary gas-fired sand drier. The sand is then moved through a series of large machines called mullers. These mix the sand with oil and cereal grain in exact amounts. From there, the sand is taken to the coremaking machines and to the molding department. Many castings have hollow interiors. Special machines are used to make the cores needed to form these hollow sections. Cores are also needed for castings of irregular shape.

At the molding machines, the flask is positioned over the pattern. A controlled amount of sand is dropped on the pattern from an overhead sand hopper (Fig. 59–2). The pattern and flask are jolted, and the sand is leveled and squeezed. Then the pattern is taken out of the mold. If cores are needed, they are put in place at this time

every 100 industries make use of castings either in their products or in the machines that make the products.

Six major casting methods are in general use: sand; die; permanent-mold; shell-mold; precision, or investment; and centrifugal. There are other methods for specialized purposes, such as plaster casting. There are certain advantages and disadvantages in all casting methods. Generally, industry decides on the method to be used mostly on the basis of the quantity, size, and complexity of the parts to be made.

Sand casting

Sand casting is the most important method used in industry. It is low in cost and requires very little complicated equipment. It allows great flexibility in product design. Design changes can be made even after production has begun. Large castings, such as machine bases and transportation equipment, are usually made by sand casting. The major disadvantage of sand casting is that products are less uniform in size. Consequently, products must be made a little larger and later machined down.

Fig. 59-2 A worker using large power equipment to move sand to the molds. (Inland Steel Company)

Fig. 59-3 Positioning a large core in a huge flask. (Inland Steel Company)

(Fig. 59-3). The flask with the mold in it is closed and put on a conveyor. Then the conveyor moves the flask to the pouring station. There, the molten metal is poured into the mold to form the casting (Fig. 59-4). The continuous conveyor takes the mold through a cooling tunnel. This lets the casting cool and harden enough to be removed from the mold at the shake-out area. Then the casting is conveyed to a cleaning room. There, all sprues, gates, and other unnecessary parts and irregularities are removed. Last, the casting is cleaned and inspected. It is then shipped to the machining area. There, all necessary machining is done. A final inspection ensures good quality. Each casting must meet certain standards and must be free of defects. One way to check this is to use an X-ray machine to examine its structure.

Die casting

Die casting is the second most important method of making castings. It is used when a large number of quality parts are needed. In the automobile industry, die casting has been used to make everything from door handles to pistons. Parts as large as engine blocks can be produced by this method. However, there are limits to the size and

Fig. 59-4 Molten metal is poured into the molds. (Reed and Burton)

complexity of the parts that can be made. In addition, only nonferrous metals and alloys are suitable for die casting. Most die castings are made from aluminum or alloys based on zinc. Copper and magnesium are also used.

In die casting, an expensive set of dies must first be machined from alloy steel. These dies are mounted in a huge die-casting machine. This machine has a rugged frame that supports and opens the die halves in perfect alignment. In production, the molten metal is forced into the closed dies under pressure. As the metal goes in, the air is forced out. When the metal has solidified, the dies open and the casting is ejected. For complex castings, a core must be inserted in the dies.

There are two general kinds of die-casting machines: hot-chamber and cold-chamber. The *hot-chamber die-casting machine* is used for metals with low melting points, primarily zinc alloys (Fig. 59–5). The melting pot is built into the machine. The cylinder leading to the die chamber always contains molten metal. The hot-chamber method can produce 300 to 750 castings per hour. The *cold-chamber die-casting machine* is similar except that the cylinder is not in the liquid metal. Instead, the metal is poured into the "cold chamber" through a port from a ladle that holds only enough metal for one casting (Fig. 59–6). The cold-chamber method can be used for casting copper alloys and other metals with a high melting point. The cold-chamber method can produce 60 to 400 castings per hour.

Permanent-mold casting

Permanent-mold casting involves pouring molten metal into a permanent metal mold or die. It is used only to make relatively simple parts (Fig. 59–7). However, the castings made with this process have a better surface finish and grain structure and are more accurate than sand castings. Thus, less machining is needed. The molds consist of two or more parts and must be very accurate. In mass production, they are held in a

Fig. 59–5 The hot-chamber die-casting machine.

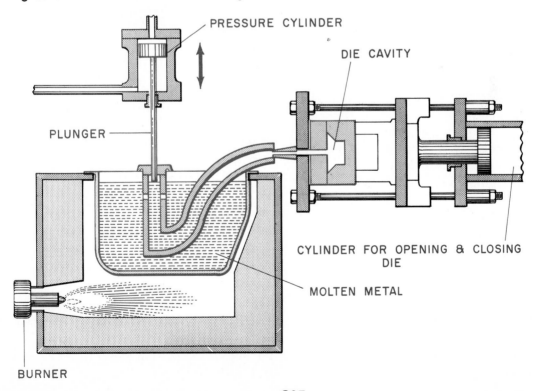

PRESSURE CYLINDER

DIE CAVITY

PLUNGER

CYLINDER FOR OPENING & CLOSING DIE

MOLTEN METAL

BURNER

305

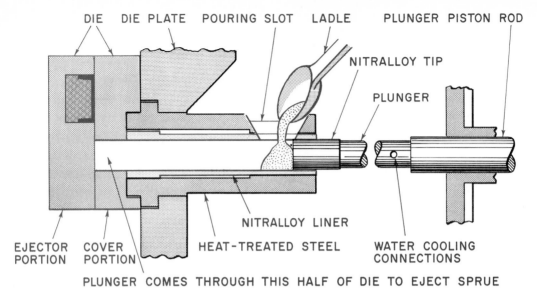

DIE DIE PLATE POURING SLOT LADLE PLUNGER PISTON ROD

NITRALLOY TIP

PLUNGER

EJECTOR PORTION COVER PORTION

NITRALLOY LINER

HEAT-TREATED STEEL

WATER COOLING CONNECTIONS

PLUNGER COMES THROUGH THIS HALF OF DIE TO EJECT SPRUE

Fig. 59-6 The cold-chamber die-casting machine. A measured amount of metal is poured into the machine for each casting.

large machine that rotates through a cycle. These molds are expensive. Thus, this method is used only if a large number of identical castings is needed.

To make the casting, the mold is heated. Then a coating is sprayed into the casting cavity. This provides the insulation needed to prevent direct contact between the metal mold and the molten metal. The mold is filled using the force of gravity. After the metal becomes solid, the mold is opened, and the casting is taken out. If a casting requires an opening, a core is inserted between the two parts of the permanent mold before it is closed for pouring. As in die casting, molds can be reused.

Shell-mold casting

Shell-mold casting uses a mold in the shape of a thin two-part shell. The shell mold is made from dry sand and resin. Never over 5/16 inch (8 mm) thick, it produces an accurate casting with a very smooth surface that needs little cleaning and finishing.

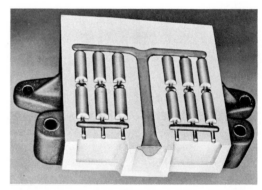

Fig. 59-7 Simple castings made in a permanent mold. Note the sprue hole and the gates through which the molten metal flows to make the 12 castings. (Eaton Manufacturing Company)

A metal pattern must first be produced. Then the pattern is heated. A mixture of sand and resin is applied to its surface to form the thin shell. Any extra sand is removed in a roll-over operation that dumps the sand and resin back into the dump box. The shell is removed in halves from the pattern. It is baked until the resin binder is cured. The resulting mold is very light and thin. The mold halves are then put back together with clamps, adhesive, or some other device (Fig. 59-8). The mold must be supported as the molten metal is poured into it. The mold is broken to remove the casting.

Shell-mold castings are very accurate and have smooth surfaces. Though shell-mold castings are of high quality, the metal patterns and the equipment for making and pouring the molds are expensive. Generally, only small castings weighing less than 25 pounds (11.3 kg) are made by this method.

Investment casting

Investment casting, also called **precision casting** and the **lost-wax process,** is used to make very accurate castings that are too complex for other methods (Fig. 59-9). This technique is used by dentists for making small gold castings for tooth repair. It is also used for jewelry.

The pattern, often very complex, is made by injecting wax into a die. A pattern

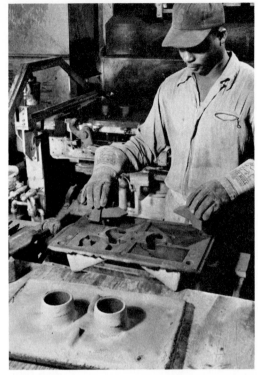

Fig. 59-8 Assembling the shell in preparation for casting.

Fig. 59-9 Steps in the investment-casting method: (A) A pattern is made of wax. (B) The individual patterns are fastened together to form a unit and placed in a flask. (C) Ceramic plaster material is used to cover the pattern. (D) The flask with the patterns in it is turned upside down and then baked to remove the wax. (E) The molds are turned upright and molten metal is poured into the die cavity.

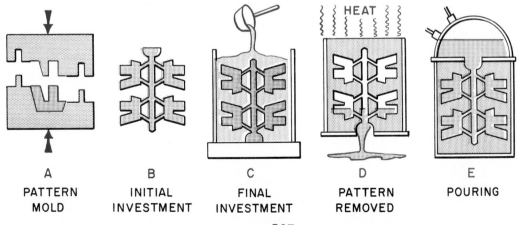

A	B	C	D	E
PATTERN MOLD	INITIAL INVESTMENT	FINAL INVESTMENT	PATTERN REMOVED	POURING

can also be made by hand. The pattern is covered with a fine coating of ceramic investment material, similar to plaster of paris. More investment material is mixed. The mounted pattern is placed in the flask, and the investment is poured in. The filled pattern is then placed on a vibrator to remove all the bubbles. When the investment has set, the flask is placed in a kiln to burn out all the wax. While the flask is still warm, it is locked in a casting machine.

The casting metal is placed in the crucible and heated with a torch until it melts. The lock button on the casting machine is pushed to release the casting arm. This then spins rapidly, forcing the metal from the crucible into the mold cavity. Next, the flask is removed with tongs and soaked in water to soften the investment. The casting is first dipped in a pickling solution and then cleaned with a stiff brush under running water. Defects are touched up with a hand grinder, and sprues, gates, and risers are cut off.

In industrial investment casting, clusters of patterns are joined before investment. The flask is then placed on a vibrating table to pack the material solidly around the pattern. The flask and pattern are turned over and then baked to melt out all the wax. A perfect mold remains for the final casting. The mold is turned over again, and the casting is poured. The casting has the exact shape of the original wax pattern. The mold is broken up to remove the casting. Sprues, gates, and risers are then ground off.

Other casting methods

In **centrifugal casting,** a rotating mold is filled with molten metal. The rotation forces the molten metal to flow into the detailed surfaces of the mold cavity. The spinning continues until all the metal has solidified.

In industry, centrifugal casting is used primarily for making large hollow products, such as pipes.

Plaster-mold casting is very similar to sand casting, except that plaster is used in place of sand. This gives the final casting a smoother finish and greater accuracy. It is possible to produce castings of very intricate design with the plaster-mold method. In plaster-mold casting, wet plaster is poured around the pattern. The plaster hardens with a high degree of detail. The mold is sometimes made in sections. It is baked in an oven for several hours to remove the moisture. All the remaining steps in making a plaster mold—the use of cores, the pouring, and the casting—are the same as for sand casting. The process is used primarily for low-melting-temperature metals, such as aluminum, bronze, and brass.

 QUESTIONS

1. Name six basic industrial casting methods.
2. Which casting method is the most important and is low in cost?
3. What two kinds of machines are used in die casting?
4. In permanent-mold casting and in shell-mold casting, what are the molds made of?
5. What are the other two names for investment casting?
6. What kinds of products are made by centrifugal casting?
7. Plaster-mold casting is similar to what other method?

 EXTRA CREDIT

1. Prepare a research report on one of the industrial casting methods.
2. Collect several castings made by different casting methods. Prepare a display of these, and identify each.

SECTION 8

MACHINING

Unit 60

Basic Machining Methods

Metal machining is one of the most interesting and demanding activities in the school metal shop. Besides making some attractive projects, you will learn many new skills. But just what is machining?

Machining is one of the four major metal-manufacturing methods. The others are hot forming, cold working, and casting (Fig. 60-1). Industry always uses the machining method when a very accurate and smooth surface is needed. However, machining is more expensive than other methods.

In **machining,** metal is turned, shaped, milled, cut, or otherwise reduced or changed by removing chips with machine tools to produce the shape and dimension wanted. A **machine tool** is a power-driven machine used to cut and shape metal. A machine tool can also be defined as a machine that produces other machines. The most commonly

Fig. 60-1 Four basic classes of metal manufacture.

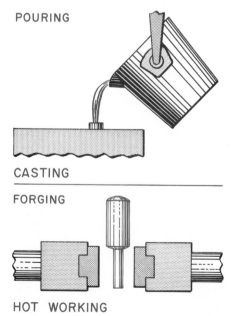

POURING

CASTING

FORGING

HOT WORKING

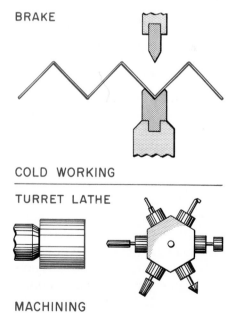

BRAKE

COLD WORKING

TURRET LATHE

MACHINING

309

used machine tools are lathes, milling machines, drilling machines, shapers, and grinders. There are also many special-purposes machines adapted from the basic machine tools.

Basic elements of machining

1. The cutting tool on a machine tool can be of two kinds: *single-point,* as on the engine lathe, shaper, and planer, or *multiple-point,* as on the milling machine, drill, reamer, broach, and grinder. Cutting tools are made from high-speed steel, stellite, carbide, diamond, ceramics, or abrasives (including silicon carbide and aluminum oxide).

2. Materials from which parts are machined are standard bar stock, forgings, or castings. Bar stock may be carbon steel, tool steel, stainless steel, aluminum, a copper-based alloy, or any of the more specialized metals such as magnesium or titanium.

3. Fixtures are used to hold parts for machining. **Jigs** hold the parts and control the cutting tools in machining.

4. Many industrial machines are similar to those found in the school shop, except that they are larger and much more complex.

Basic forms of metal cutting

1. Turning is cutting stock as it revolves on a lathe. A single-point cutting tool is moved against the revolving stock to produce cylindrical shapes, both on the outside and inside (Figs. 60-2, 60-3). Turning can also be done to produce screw threads, to cut tapers, and to do facing, drilling, reaming, counterboring, and chamfering. In the school shop, the *engine lathe,* the most basic of all machine tools, is used to produce cylindrical shapes. However, using it for complex pieces requires a good deal of time to change and adjust the tools and to do the feeding. Turning, drilling, reaming, and tapping

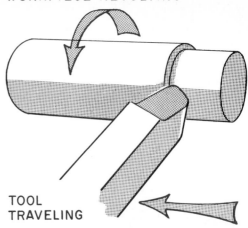

WORKPIECE REVOLVING

TOOL TRAVELING

Fig. 60-2 Simple cylindrical turning is done when the point of a tool moves along as the stock rotates.

must all be done as separate steps. Industry uses special adaptations of the engine lathe for mass production.

The *turret lathe* is a production lathe used to make identical parts. It differs from the engine lathe in that a six-sided turret replaces the tailstock (Fig. 60-4). All six faces of this turret can hold tools of various kinds that can be used on the workpiece, one after another. For example, one face may hold a drill; the next, a reamer; the next, a tap; and so on. As the turret moves backward, it automatically rotates to the next tool. There are

Fig. 60-3 An engine lathe is used to do turning. (DoAll Inc.)

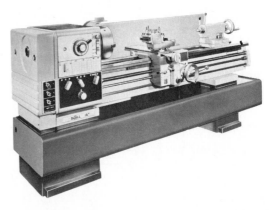

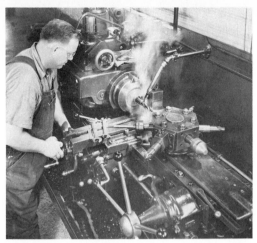

Fig. 60-4 A turret attachment on an engine lathe.

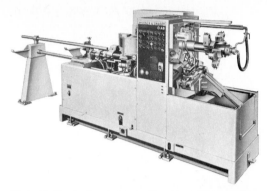

Fig. 60-5 A single-spindle chucking automatic screw machine. (Warner & Swasey Company)

Fig. 60-6 A multiple-spindle automatic screw machine. (Warner & Swasey Company)

also toolholders on the cross slide to hold forming and cutoff tools. Common operations performed in sequence on a turret lathe include drilling, boring, reaming, threading, turning, and cutting off. The order of operations needed determines the arrangement of tools in the turret.

A *screw machine* is a special kind of turret lathe designed for making screws, bolts, washers, and many other small parts in large quantity and with great speed. Since this machine is used only when a large number of identical parts is required, it is usually completely automatic. The screw machine differs from the turret lathe in that the head is designed to hold and feed long bars of stock or tubing instead of castings or forgings. A wide variety of processes can be performed on both the ends and sides of bars. Screw machines are either single-spindle or multiple-spindle automatic (Fig. 60-5). The single-spindle automatic takes only one bar of stock at a time. The multiple-spindle machine has four to eight spindles spaced around a carrier (Fig. 60-6).

Like all mass-production equipment, automatic screw machines operate with maximum efficiency only if they are cor-

rectly tooled up. This means that you must not only select the correct tools, but also choose the right order for doing the operations. In addition, you must correctly relate one tool to the other. For example, before you can cut an internal thread with a tap, you must first produce a hole of the correct size with a drill and a reamer.

A third kind of special-purpose lathe is the *tracer lathe* (Fig. 60-7). On this lathe, a tracer point follows a template. The cross-feed is then operated by hydraulic controls so that it moves in and out in exactly the same pattern. The cutting tool thus duplicates the shape of the template.

Fig. 60-7 A tracer lathe shapes from a template by means of hydraulically controlled cutting tools.

Fig. 60-8 Milling is done as work is fed into or under a revolving cutter.

2. Milling is shaping a workpiece by using a rotating cutting tool that has two or more cutting edges (Fig. 60–8). The *milling machine* is one of the most important machine tools. The work can be accurately controlled so that interchangeable parts can be produced.

There are many kinds of milling machines used in industry. The most basic, like those used in the school shop, are *column-and-knee* milling machines. These are either horizontal or vertical (Figs. 60–9, 60–10). Other industrial milling machines are much larger and more complex. Many special types are available. The *manufacturing,* or *fixed-bed,* milling machine is used for mass production of identical parts. It is made either as a plain, duplex, or special machine. The bed is fixed to the headstock (Fig. 60–11). Another type of fixed-bed milling machine is the *profiling machine,* or *profiler* (Fig. 60–12). It is a vertical milling machine in which the cutter is guided by a tracing arm that follows the outline of the pattern. The profiler is used in shaping curved or irregular surfaces.

3. Drilling is using a rotating cutter to cut cylindrical holes in the workpiece (Fig. 60–13). Drilling machines are used for drilling holes in metal, wood, plastic, and

Fig. 60-9 A small horizontal milling machine. (Bridgeport Machines)

TOOL
REVOLVING

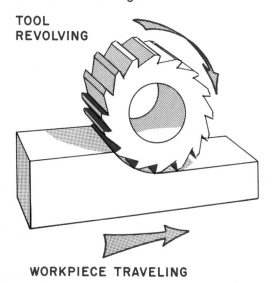

WORKPIECE TRAVELING

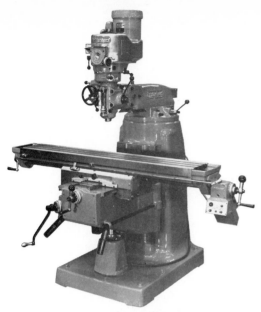

Fig. 60-10 A large vertical milling machine. (Bridgeport Company)

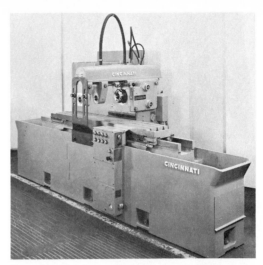

Fig. 60-11 A manufacturing milling machine with a fixed bed. (Cincinnati Milacron Company)

other materials. For simple drilling, a small bench or floor drill press is used (see Unit 14). Industry also uses many other

Fig. 60-12 A multiple-spindle profiler cutting the blades of an impeller for a jet engine. (Cincinnati Milacron Company)

TOOL REVOLVING

TOOL TRAVELING

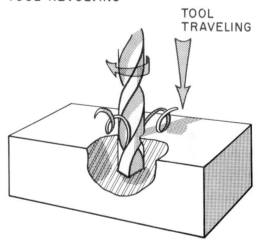

Fig. 60-13 In drilling, a two-lipped rotating cutter is fed into the material. The cutting is done by the two cutting edges. The spiral serves to remove the shavings.

kinds of drilling machines. A *gang drill press* has two or more independently operated drilling heads arranged in a row. The work is moved from one spindle to the next to do different kinds of cutting. On a *radial drill,*

313

Fig. 60-14 A convenient tray holds seven tools for use in this radial drill. (Caterpillar Tractor Company)

the entire drilling head can be moved to different locations for machining holes. The large radial drill has an arm that swings around a column and a precise drilling head that moves along this arm (Fig. 60-14). The

Fig. 60-16 In tapping, threads are produced in holes with a tap.

TOOL REVOLVING

TOOL TRAVELING

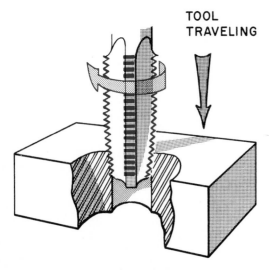

Fig. 60-15 A turret drill. The turret of this machine contains not only drills but also side and end mills, a boring tool, and a tap. (Burgmaster Company)

multiple-spindle drilling machine has at least two and sometimes eight or more spindles that can drill holes at the same time. A *turret drill* uses six or more drilling devices located around a turret. This machine often does drilling, tapping, counterboring, and other operations automatically (Fig. 60-15).

Two other operations that are often done on drilling or special machines are tapping and reaming. **Tapping** is producing threads in holes using a tap as the cutting tool (Figs. 60-16, 60-17). **Reaming** is finishing a hole to exact size with a very smooth interior surface (Fig. 60-18).

4. Boring is enlarging or finishing the cylindrical surfaces of an existing hole. It is done with a *boring machine* (Figs. 60-19, 60-20). The usual method is to use a single-point tool that feeds into the hole while the work rotates. However, sometimes the tool turns while the work is fixed. There are two

314

Fig. 60-17 This production machine cuts threads on the block of an engine as it moves along the assembly line. Six holes are tapped at the same time.

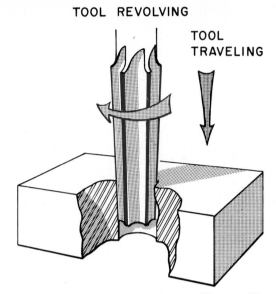

Fig. 60-18 Reaming is done with a multi-edge cutting tool that rotates to enlarge and smooth the surface of a hole.

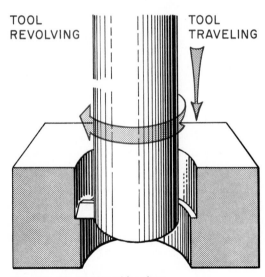

Fig. 60-19 Vertical boring.

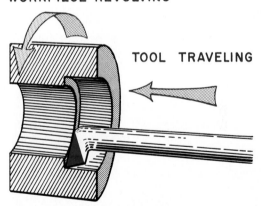

Fig. 60-20 Horizontal boring.

kinds of boring machines: horizontal and vertical (Fig. 60–21). The cutter revolves in a circle of which the axis is either horizontal or vertical. A *jig-boring machine* is really a precision boring machine with a work table that has a slotted surface and a highly precise vertical boring spindle.

5. Surface cutting is shaping metal by making straight-line, back-and-forth cuts across it with machines called shapers, planers, and slotters. These machines can be moved along the workpiece, or the workpiece can be moved back and forth against them. The process is somewhat like planing wood with a hand plane.

The *shaper* uses a cutting tool similar to that on the lathe. The tool is clamped in a tool post. A ram pushes it across the work on

Fig. 60-21 A horizontal boring machine. (Kennametal, Inc.)

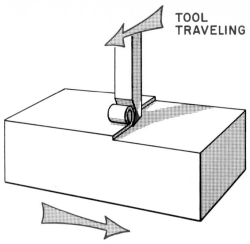

TOOL TRAVELING

INDEXED WORKPIECE FEED

Fig. 60-22 Shaping.

the cutting stroke (Figs. 60–22, 60–23). The ram then raises and withdraws the tool on the return stroke. The work is clamped on an adjustable horizontal table. The table moves a distance of one cut after each stroke. Shapers have no use in mass production, but

Fig. 60-23 A shaper can remove heavy chips. In shaping, the cutting tool cuts on the forward stroke only. (Cincinnati Shaper Company)

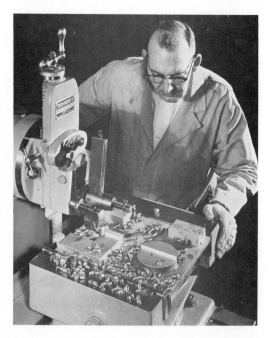

they are sometimes found in small tool-and-die shops. A *slotting machine* is really a vertical shaper designed to machine slots or key seats (Fig. 60–24).

The *planer* is much larger than the shaper. It is used to produce flat surfaces on work that cannot conveniently be cut on a shaper. The work table moves back and forth under a fixed cutting tool. This tool is

Fig. 60-24 In slotting, the tool travels up and down.

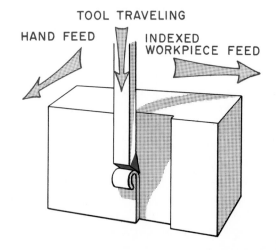

TOOL TRAVELING

HAND FEED   INDEXED WORKPIECE FEED

INDEXED TOOL FEED

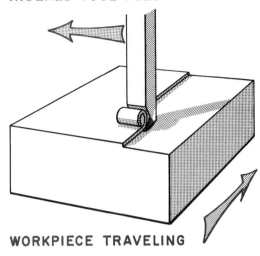

WORKPIECE TRAVELING

Fig. 60-25 Planing.

fed on a crossrail that straddles the table (Fig. 60–25). A planer is sized according to the largest rectangular solid that it can machine. The planer has been largely replaced in mass production by the milling machine.

6. Grinding is removing excess material from a workpiece by using rotating abrasive wheels. There are many different kinds of grinding machines. The *cylindrical grinder* is used on stock that is cylindrical or conical in shape (Fig. 60–26). There are various types of cylindrical grinders. Some hold the

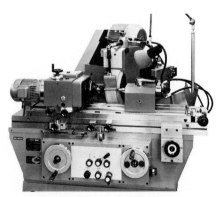

Fig. 60–27 A cylindrical grinder designed for the economical production of parts having different diameters and shoulders. (Alina Corporation)

WHEEL REVOLVING

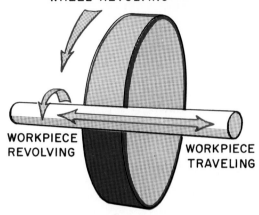

WORKPIECE REVOLVING

WORKPIECE TRAVELING

Fig. 60–26 In cylindrical grinding, the workpiece revolves and moves back and forth against a revolving grinding wheel.

work between centers. On others, called *centerless cylindrical grinders,* the workpiece is neither held nor mounted but is laid on a work rest instead (Fig. 60–27). *Surface grinders* are designed to produce flat, finished surfaces (Figs. 60–28, 60–29). Flat pieces are often finished on *abrasive-belt grinders.*

Fig. 60–28 In surface grinding, the workpiece travels under a revolving abrasive wheel.

TOOL REVOLVING

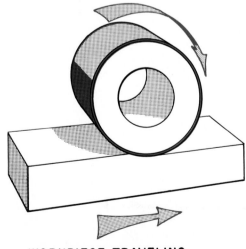

WORKPIECE TRAVELING

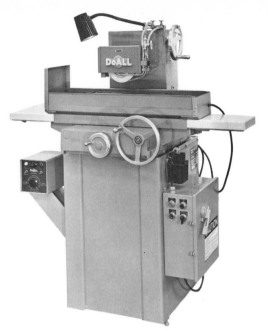

Fig. 60-29　A surface grinder. (DoAll Inc.)

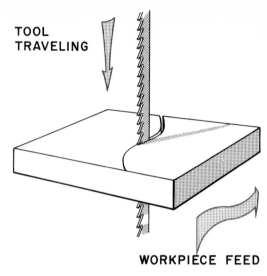

TOOL TRAVELING

WORKPIECE FEED

Fig. 60-30　Sawing is a form of machining.

Fig. 60-31　A vertical band saw in operation. (DoAll Corporation)

Two processes closely related to grinding are lapping and honing. **Lapping** is done with abrasive particles to produce an extremely fine finish. **Honing** produces an even finer finish than lapping.

7. Band machining is cutting stock to size and shape on a specially designed vertical band saw (Figs. 60-30, 60-31). This

machine will produce many shapes both on internal and external surfaces. Rough parts can be made with the vertical band saw more quickly than with other machine tools. This tool is usually used as a first step in machining. If a complicated part must be made, the large masses of material are removed by band machining. Then the part is finished to accurate size by milling or grinding. The same kind of vertical band saw can also be used for **machine filing** (Fig. 60-32).

Other machining processes

There are many other machining processes that are closely related to the ones described above. Often, these can be done on more than one machine. Following are descriptions of four of these processes:

1. Broaching is shaping internal and external parts by pushing or pulling a tapered tool called a *broach* across the surface (Fig. 60-33). The broach has a number of cutting edges somewhat like a file. Each has a slightly larger dimension than the preceding one. A solid broach with teeth on its side is used for finishing holes, enlarging them, or changing their shape from square to some other shape. A hollow broach with teeth on the inside can be used to finish the external shape of work. In industry, specially designed *broaching machines* are used. There are two basic kinds: the push-type and the pull-type. The push-type is essentially a press that has a short, stout broach to cut the material to shape. The pull-type makes use of a hydraulic press to pull the broach through or over the work. Broaching is faster, simpler, and cheaper but less accurate than some other machining processes.

2. Countersinking is cutting a cone-shaped recess on the outer edge of the end of a hole (Fig. 60–34). This process can be done on any drilling machine or lathe and also on certain kinds of milling machines.

3. Counterboring is partially reboring a cylindrical hole to enlarge it for part of its length. The enlarged part forms a shoulder in relation to the smaller part. Counterboring can be done on any drilling machine and lathe and sometimes on the milling machine and grinder.

4. Gear cutting can be done on a *gear-hobbing machine* or on a milling machine. Machining gears is relatively expensive. Therefore, many smaller gears are made of powdered metal on special presses or are cast in plastic.

Occupations in machining

Machining workers are the largest group employed in metalworking. There are over a

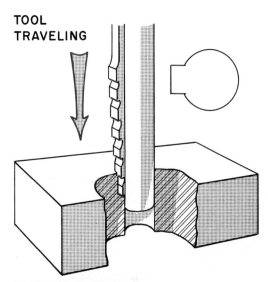

Fig. 60–33 Broaching.

Fig. 60–34 Countersinking.

Fig. 60–32 Machine filing is done with a continuous file that fits on a vertical band saw.

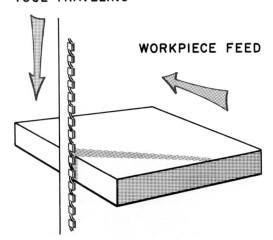

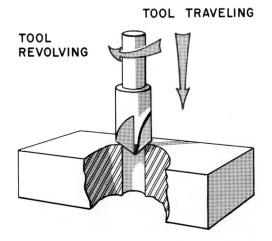

million people working in skilled and semi-skilled machining occupations. Job categories include all-around machinist, machine-tool operator, toolmaker and diemaker, setup worker, and layout worker:

1. The *all-around machinist* can operate several kinds of machine tools, read prints, make precision measurements, and do the skilled work with hand tools needed to fit and assemble parts.

2. A *machine-tool operator* can operate one or two machines but is less skilled in using hand tools and precision measuring tools. Some machine-tool operators merely tend a machine and do very simple, easily learned operations. However, others have more training and can perform more complicated work (Fig. 60–35).

3. *Toolmakers* and *diemakers* are the most highly skilled workers in the metalworking field. *Toolmakers* make and repair jigs and fixtures, as well as gages and other measuring devices. *Diemakers* make and repair the dies or metal forms for shaping metal by stamping and forging. They also make the metal molds used for die casting and molding plastics. Toolmakers and diemakers must be able to use machine tools and precision measuring instruments. More important, they must

know how to use hand tools skillfully. Also, they must know a great deal about machine operations, mathematics, print reading, and other related subjects.

4. *Setup workers* are skilled machinists who install cutting tools and adjust controls of machine tools so that they can be run by less skilled operators. They also teach others how to operate machinery. Setup workers often supervise the work at several machines.

5. *Layout workers* are highly skilled people who mark the layouts or patterns on metal to be machined. They must be able to work carefully from prints, drawings, and other written materials. They also must be able to use precision measuring tools.

Machining offers wonderful job opportunities. Machinists are needed in every kind of manufacturing and for all types of maintenance and repair. Skilled machinists can always find a good job in any state in the nation. There is a machine shop in almost every community. Small ones are called *job shops.* Their work consists largely of general repair or the machining of small numbers of a simple part. In large job shops, called *production shops,* parts are mass-produced.

More experience in general metals will fit you for advanced courses in machine

Fig. 60–35 This machine-tool operator is using precision measuring gages to check the accuracy of the work. (Pratt & Whitney Corporation)

Fig. 60–36 This apprentice is learning the fundamentals of machine shop. (Rockwell International)

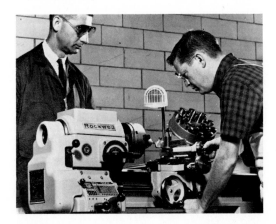

Fig. 60-37 An engineer (right) is discussing a machining project with a technician.

shop. If you become interested in some machining occupation, you will probably serve an apprenticeship. An **apprentice** works for a company or shop in order to learn the trade. An apprentice works with a skilled machinist and also spends a great deal of time receiving related instruction (Fig. 60-36). Skilled machinists can open shops of their own or become supervisors or factory administrators (Fig. 60-37). Additional information on metalworking occupations can be found in Unit 11.

Hobbies such as gunsmithing, model making, and metal spinning generally require machine tools and machine skills. A complete line of small machine tools can be purchased by the hobbyist.

 QUESTIONS

1. Name the four major metal-manufacturing methods.
2. Which is the most accurate?
3. What are machine cutting tools made of?
4. On what kind of machine is turning done?
5. What kind of cutting tool is used in milling?
6. What machines are used for surface cutting?
7. How is a broach like a file?
8. What is countersinking? Counterboring?
9. Name four categories of jobs available in machining.

✓ **EXTRA CREDIT**

1. Make a report on one of the major occupations in machine shop.
2. Write a research report on machining in industry.

Unit 61
Precision
Measurement

Machined products require precision measuring tools to ensure accuracy. Precision measuring tools used in beginning machine shop include *outside* and *inside calipers* and an *outside micrometer* (Fig. 61-1). You will learn to use these in order to do accurate machine-shop work (Fig. 61-2).

Calipers

1. To adjust an outside caliper, hold one leg over the end of the rule. Move the second leg until it exactly fits the correct measurement line (Fig. 61-3).

2. To use an outside caliper, hold it squarely to the work. When you check the

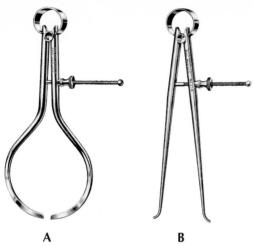

Fig. 61-1 (A) Outside caliper, (B) inside caliper. (The L.S. Starrett Company)

Fig. 61-2 Precision measuring tools are very important in a machine shop. (Lockheed Aircraft)

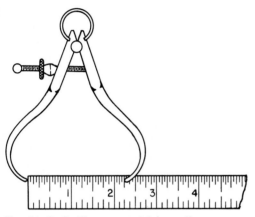

Fig. 61-3 Setting an outside caliper.

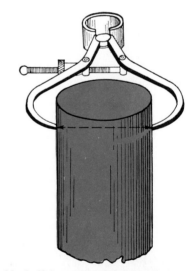

Fig. 61-4 Using an outside caliper.

measurement, the leg should just drag lightly over the work (Fig. 61-4). Hold the caliper lightly so that you can feel when it touches the work.

3. To adjust an inside caliper, place one leg of the caliper and the end of a rule against a machined surface. Adjust the caliper until the other leg exactly fits the measurement line.

4. To use the inside caliper, make sure that the points of the legs touch the work so that the largest diameter is measured (Fig. 61-5). The ends must be at right angles to the work.

5. To transfer a measurement from one caliper to the other, place one leg of the inside caliper against the leg of the outside caliper. Use this as the pivot point. Now, adjust the outside caliper until the other leg just drags across the second leg of the inside caliper (Fig. 61-6).

Reading a customary micrometer

Parts of the outside micrometer are shown in Fig. 61-7. The micrometer works in the following way: There are 40 threads to the inch on the micrometer screw. As it turns, it changes the space between the two measuring faces. The thimble turns with the screw. Each complete turn of the thimble equals 1/40 (0.025) inch. There are 40 lines to the inch on the sleeve. Each time you make a complete turn, you change the reading on the sleeve by one small division. Every four divisions on the sleeve are marked 1, 2, 3, and so on, representing 0.100,

0.200, 0.300 inch, and so on. The tapered end of the thimble is divided into 25 equal parts. One complete turn of the thimble equals 0.025 inch. A turn of the thimble of one twenty-fifth, one small division on the thimble, equals 0.001 inch. The scale on the thimble is marked 0, 5, 10, 15, 20, making it easy to read in thousandths of an inch.

To read a customary micrometer:

1. Look at the number of divisions you can see on the sleeve. In Fig. 61-8, you see one division past the 2, or nine full divisions. This indicates 0.225 inch (0.025 times 9).

2. If the end of the thimble is between two division lines on the sleeve, you must read the scale on the thimble. In Fig. 61-8, you see 21 small divisions past the 0. Therefore, the measurement is 0.021 inch.

3. By adding the reading on the sleeve to the reading on the thimble, you get 0.225 plus 0.021, or 0.246 inch.

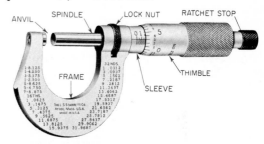

Fig. 61-7 Parts of a customary outside micrometer caliper. (The L.S. Starrett Company)

Fig. 61-8 The micrometer reading is 0.246 inch.

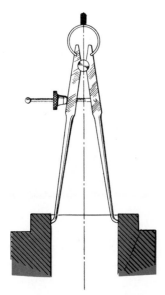

Fig. 61-5 Using an inside caliper.

Fig. 61-6 Transferring measurements.

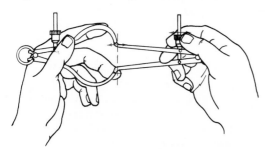

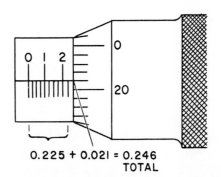

0.225 + 0.021 = 0.246
TOTAL

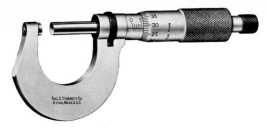

Fig. 61-9 A metric micrometer. (The L.S. Starrett Company)

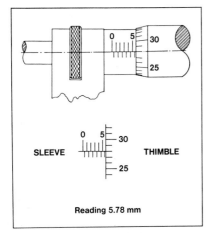

Reading 5.78 mm

Fig. 61-10 Reading a metric micrometer.

Reading a metric micrometer

On a metric micrometer, the pitch of the spindle screw is one-half millimeter (0.5 mm). Thus, one full turn of the thimble moves the spindle toward or away from the anvil by 0.5 millimeter (Fig. 61-9).

The reading line on the sleeve is marked in millimeters (1 mm), with every fifth millimeter being numbered from 0 to 25. Each millimeter is also divided in half (0.5 mm). Each time you give the thimble one full turn, you change the reading on the sleeve by 0.5 millimeter.

The tapered end of the thimble is divided by lines into 50 equal parts, every fifth line being numbered from 0 to 50. Since one turn of the thimble moves the spindle 0.5 millimeter, each thimble division equals

Fig. 61-11 An inside micrometer.

1/50 of 0.5 millimeter, or 0.01 millimeter. Thus, two thimble divisions equal 0.02 millimeter, three equal 0.03 millimeter, and so on.

To read the micrometer, add the number of millimeters and half-millimeters visible on the sleeve to the number of hundredths of a millimeter indicated by the thimble division that coincides with the reading line on the sleeve (Fig. 61-10).

Inside micrometers

A special kind of micrometer is the *inside micrometer* (Fig. 61-11). It is used for precision measurement of the diameters of holes, the widths of slots, and similar areas.

 QUESTIONS

1. Name the two kinds of calipers.
2. On a customary micrometer, what distance does one turn of the thimble equal?
3. On a metric micrometer, how far does one full turn of the thimble move the spindle?
4. What is an inside micrometer used for?

 EXTRA CREDIT

1. Make a comparison between the micrometer and vernier caliper.
2. Explain to the class how the vernier caliper can be used.

Unit 62

The Engine Lathe— Its Parts and Accessories

The **engine lathe** is used to cut or shape metal by revolving the work against a sharp cutting edge. It is the most important machine tool and the one the beginner usually learns to use first. This machine tool is used for a wide range of metal removal and separation operations.

Lathe size

The size of a lathe is determined by the swing and the length of the bed. **Swing** is the largest diameter that can be turned. It is twice the distance from the center to the nearest interference on the bed of the lathe. The *bed length* determines the distance between centers, or the longest piece that can be turned. A common school-shop lathe size is a 9-inch (229-mm) swing with a 3-foot (914-mm) bed.

Parts of the lathe

The lathe has five main parts (Fig. 62–1):

1. The *bed* is the base of the lathe. On top of it are the *ways*, both V and flat. These are rails that support the carriage and the tailstock.

2. The *headstock assembly* is fastened to the left end of the bed. It consists of the *headstock spindle* and the mechanism for driv-

Fig. 62–1 **The major parts of the engine lathe. (Clausing Corporation)**

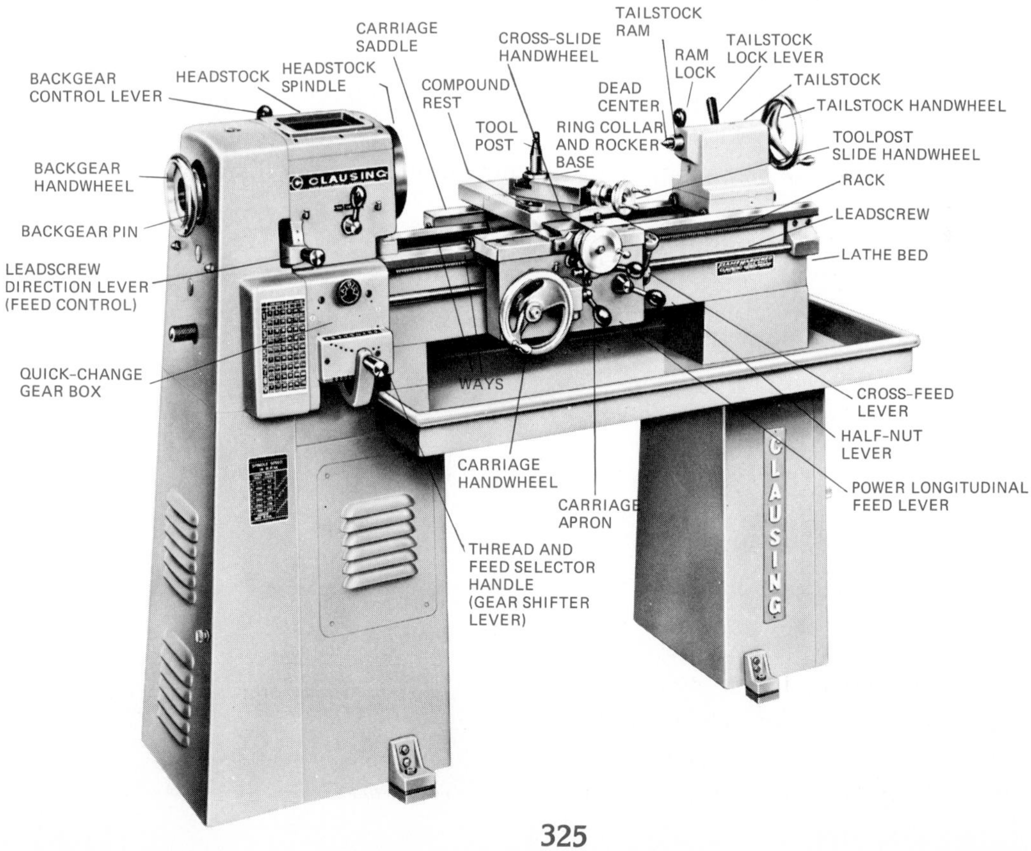

325

ing it. The spindle is hollow, with a tapered hole at the front, or inner, end. A *sleeve* fits into this tapered hole and then into the *live,* or *headstock, center.* A *face plate* or *driving plate* is screwed onto the spindle nose. The spindle controls the speed. The power for turning is provided by an electric motor. On belt-driven lathes, direct-drive power is delivered through belts to a step pulley that turns the spindle. The speed is changed by moving the belts to different positions. To obtain more torque, or turning force, and slower speeds, the *back gear* is used. The *feed-reverse lever* is used to reverse the movement of the lead screw.

3. The *tailstock assembly* is moved along the bed and locked in any position. It has two castings. The lower one rests on the ways. The upper one is fastened to the lower one. The upper casting can be moved toward or away from the operator to offset the tailstock for taper turning. A *hollow spindle* moves in and out of the upper casting when the *tailstock wheel* is turned. This spindle has a taper on the inner end, in which the *dead center* fits.

4. The *carriage* has five parts:

a. The *saddle* is an H-shaped casting that fits over the bed and slides along the ways.

b. The *apron* fastens to the saddle and hangs over the front of the bed. It contains the gears, clutches, and levers for operating the carriage by hand and with power. The *apron handwheel* is turned to move the carriage back and forth. This handwheel is attached to a *pinion* that meshes with a *rack* under the front of the bed.

c. The *cross slide* is mounted to the saddle. A handle is turned to move the cross slide crosswise or toward and away from the operator.

d. The *compound rest* on top of the cross slide can be turned in a circle and locked in any position. It, too, has a slide in which the upper part of the casting can be moved in and out with the compound-rest handle.

e. The *tool post* with the *ring collar* and *rocker base* slides in a T-slot on top of the compound rest.

5. The *feeding and threading mechanisms* consist of a quick-change gearbox, lead screw, and feed rod, as well as the gears and clutches in the apron. The *quick-change gearbox* is directly below the headstock assembly. Power from the left end of the spindle is fed through the gears to this gearbox. The gearbox makes it possible to change the feed and the ratio between the revolutions of the headstock spindle and the movement of the carriage for thread cutting. There are usually two or three levers on the gearbox for controlling the feed and number of threads. An *index chart,* or *plate,* fastened to the gearbox tells you how to move the levers (Fig. 62–2). The *lead screw* and *feed rod* trans-

Fig. 62–2 A quick-change gearbox on a lathe can cut both customary and metric threads. (Clausing Corporation)

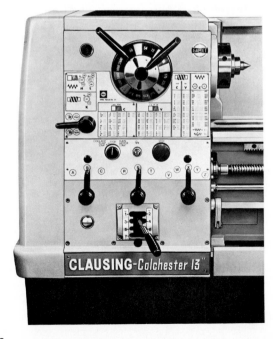

mit the power to the carriage for operating the feed and for thread cutting. To get power for longitudinal, or back-and-forth, feeding, the *feed-change lever* on the carriage is moved to the down (or up) position. Then the *clutch handle,* either a lever or a knob, is turned or moved. To get power for cross feeding, put the feed-change lever in the opposite position. For thread cutting, the feed-change lever is put in the center, or neutral, position to operate the *half,* or *split, nut lever.* This nut closes over the threads of the lead screw to move the carriage.

Fig. 62-3 Some of the levers and knobs that you should be acquainted with in operating the lathe. (South Bend Lathe Works)

Getting to know the lathe

Before machining metal, you should get to know the parts of the lathe and learn how to operate the controls (Figs. 62-3, 62-4):

1. Try the levers and handles with the power off:

    a. Move the carriage back and forth.

    b. Move the cross slide in and out.

    c. Slide the tailstock back and forth, and lock it in position.

    d. Change the position of the belt on the pulley.

    e. Change the feed-reverse lever.

    f. Disengage the bull-gear lock or pin. Pull the back gears in place.

    g. Adjust the feed on the quick-change gearbox.

2. Try adjustments after turning on the power. Operate the carriage with power feed. Also use the automatic cross-feed.

Lathe safety

When using the lathe, you must understand and obey the following safety rules:

1. Do not attempt to operate the lathe *until you have received instruction from your teacher* and have passed a written safety test.

2. Correct dress is important. Remove rings and wristwatches. Roll up your sleeves. Wear an apron. Put on your safety glasses.

Do not wear sweaters or neckties. Tie long hair back or wear a cap.

3. Do not try to lift heavy chucks and attachments alone. Always get help.

4. Make certain your workpiece is set up securely and tightly when using chucks and collets.

5. When holding the workpiece between centers, make sure to use centers of the

Fig. 62-4 If a lathe is to be used for both customary and metric work, then both the cross-feed and the compound rest must be equipped with dials that read in both thousandths of an inch and hundredths of a millimeter. (Sipco Corporation)

right size and with good points. Never use a soft center in the tailstock. Apply oil or white lead to the tailstock center, and adjust it properly. If it is too tight, the point will heat up and burn off.

6. Make sure the tool bits are sharp and ground to the correct shape. Set them at the proper height and angle to the work.

7. Never remove the guards over belts and gears without permission from your teacher. Shut off the power at the switchboard before removing guards.

8. After setting up the lathe, remove all wrenches, oil cans, and other tools from the work area. When the workpiece is held on a face plate, give the face plate one complete turn by hand to make sure the work will not strike any part of the lathe.

9. Stop the lathe before making adjustments.

10. Never measure the workpiece while it is turning.

11. Never use a file without a handle.

12. Never leave a chuck wrench in the chuck. This is dangerous.

13. Keep rags, cotton waste, and brushes away from tools while turning.

14. It is unsafe to have small-diameter work extend more than an inch or two (25 to 50 mm) from a chuck or collet unless it is supported by the tailstock center.

15. Always check in what direction and how fast the carriage or cross-feed will move before you turn on the automatic feeds.

16. Do not run the carriage or compound slide into a turning chuck.

17. If you hear unusual noises from your machine, stop it, and find out what is causing them.

18. Always start and stop you own machine—never let other students do this for you.

19. Do not allow others to fool with or stay around your machine. Accidents happen when your mind is distracted.

ANGLE	DEGREES	ANGLE	DEGREES
END-RELIEF	6	END-CUTTING EDGE	20
SIDE-RELIEF	6	SIDE-CUTTING EDGE	15
BACK-RAKE	8	NOSE	65
SIDE-RAKE	14	NOSE RADIUS	1/8 INCH

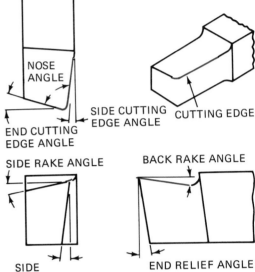

Fig. 62-5 Typical angles of roughing tool for turning mild steel.

Taking care of the lathe

Make sure that you clean and lubricate the lathe whenever you use it. Clean the lathe by brushing off the chips, and then wipe it with a clean cloth. Do *not* blow chips from the lathe with an air hose. This will cause chips to lodge in gears and ways. Oil and grease the lathe, following the lubricating chart that comes with it.

Lathe accessories—cutting tools and toolholders

The *cutting tools*, or *tool bits*, you will use are rectangular pieces of metal made of high-speed steel. They are ground to different shapes for different cutting operations. The *tool angles* shape the point and prevent

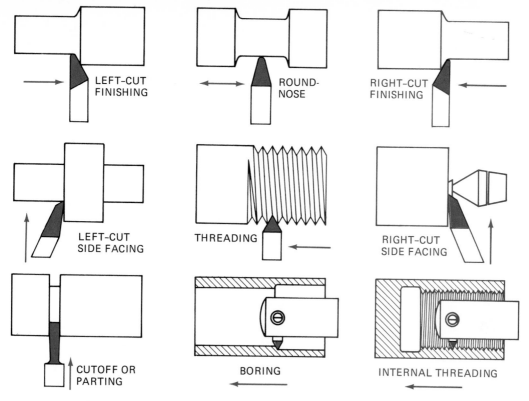

Fig. 62–6 Common cutting tools used on the lathe.

the cutting edge from rubbing on the work after it is machined. The basic angles are *side-relief, end-relief, back rake,* and *side rake* (Fig. 62–5).

The common tool shapes are shown in Fig. 62–6. To grind a roundnose turning tool:

1. Make sure the face of a medium-coarse wheel is trued and dressed.

2. Grind the side-relief angle to about 6 degrees for machining mild steel (Fig. 62–7). Holding the tool bit against the face of the wheel at this angle, move it back and forth a little. Cool it once in a while in water because overheating will soften it. Try to get a single smooth surface. Grind the opposite side in the same way.

3. Grind the *end relief* to an angle of about 6 to 8 degrees for machining mild

Fig. 62–7 Grinding a cutting tool.

steel. Round off the cutting edge to form the nose.

329

Table 62-1
A Simple Table for Choosing the Correct RPM

Material	Average cutting speed		Diameters and rpm			
	sfpm*	smpm**	1/2 in. (13 mm)	1 in. (25 mm)	1-1/2 in. (40 mm)	2 in. (50 mm)
low-carbon steel	100	30	800	400	266	200
tool steel	50	15	400	200	133	100
cast iron	75	23	600	300	200	150
brass	200	60	1600	800	533	400
aluminum	300	90	2400	1200	800	600

*surface feet per minute   **surface meters per minute

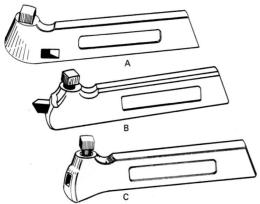

Fig. 62-8 (A) Left-hand, (B) straight, and (C) right-hand toolholders.

4. Grind the side and back rakes at the same time.

Toolholders are *straight, right-hand,* or *left-hand* (Fig. 62-8). Pick the best toolholder for the job.

Speed, feed, and depth of cut

1. Cutting speed is the distance the workpiece moves past the cutting point in 1 minute, as measured around the surface. This is equivalent to the length of chip that would be removed in 1 minute. Table 62-1 shows what the spindle speed must be in order to get the correct cutting speed. Find

out what spindle speeds are available on the lathe you are using. Adjust the belt to get the correct speed.

2. Feed is the distance the tool moves along the bed with each revolution of the lathe. Generally, coarser feeds are used for rough turning and finer feeds for finished turning. These are set by changing the levers on the quick-change gearbox.

3. Depth of cut is the distance from the bottom of the cut to the uncut surface measured at right angles to the machined surface. To reduce the diameter 1/4 inch (6 mm), the depth of cut must be 1/8 inch (3 mm), as adjusted on the micrometer collar of the cross-feed. The beginner usually takes too small a depth of cut with too fine a feed.

 QUESTIONS

1. What is the swing of a lathe?
2. Name the five main parts of the lathe.
3. When the lathe is running, what should you always do before adjusting it?
4. What is cutting speed? What is feed?

 EXTRA CREDIT

1. Make large wood or plastic models of some of the common cutting tools.
2. Prepare a bulletin-board display of the lathe parts.

330

Unit 63
Turning between Centers

Stock must be rough-turned and finish-turned between centers as a first step in making most machine-shop projects (Fig. 63–1). The metal should be about 1/8 inch (3 mm) larger in diameter and about 3/4 inch (19 mm) longer than the completed work if the center holes are to be cut off. It needs to be only about 1/8 inch (3 mm) longer if the center holes are to be left in the finished work. Before turning, the work must be set up accurately between centers.

Setup for turning between centers

Figure 63–1 shows the workpiece held between centers. Notice the following:

1. A *driving plate* is screwed to the spindle of the headstock.

2. A *reducing sleeve* is inserted in the headstock spindle. Then the *live center* fits

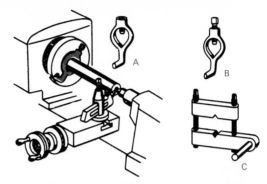

Fig. 63–2 Three common kinds of lathe dogs: (A) safety-screw, (B) bent-tail, (C) parallel-clamp.

into the sleeve. The live center is soft, and the point can be reshaped by turning.

3. A *dead center* is inserted in the tailstock spindle. The dead center is hardened, and the point must be ground to shape.

4. A *lathe dog* is fastened in place to drive the workpiece when it is held between centers. The three most common kinds are the regular bent-tail, the safety-screw, and the parallel-clamp (Fig. 63–2).

Locating and drilling center holes

1. File the burr off the end of the workpiece.

2. Locate the center by scribing arcs with a hermaphrodite caliper or by holding a center head over the end and scribing two lines that cross (Fig. 63–3). A bell center punch (Fig. 63–4) locates and punches the center in one operation.

3. Prick-punch and then center-punch a hole at either end of the workpiece.

4. Select a No. 2 combination center drill and countersink (Fig. 63–5). Drill the center holes on the drill press (Fig. 63–6) or on the lathe by one of the methods shown in Figs. 63–7 and 63–8. Figure 63–9 shows correct and incorrect center holes.

Fig. 63–1 This is how the workpiece should look when turning between centers.

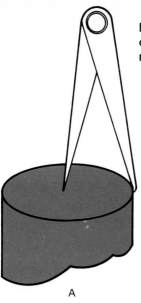

Fig. 63-3 Locating the center on the ends of the workpiece by using (A) a hermaphrodite caliper and (B) a center head.

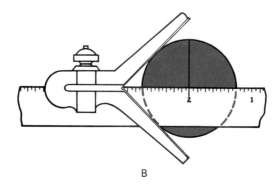

A

B

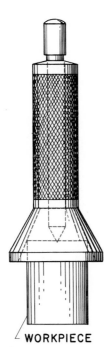

WORKPIECE

Fig. 63-4 Using a bell center punch to locate the center.

Fig. 63-5 A combination center drill and countersink.

Fig. 63-6 Drilling the center holes on the end of the workpiece on a drill press.

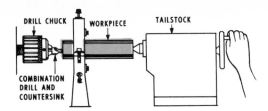

Fig. 63-7 Drilling center holes between centers on the lathe.

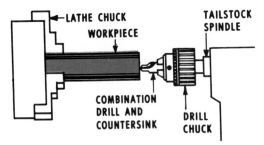

Fig. 63-8 Drilling center holes using a lathe chuck.

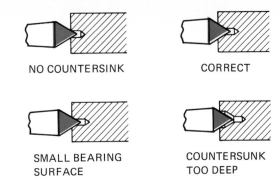

NO COUNTERSINK   CORRECT

SMALL BEARING SURFACE   COUNTERSUNK TOO DEEP

Fig. 63-9 Correct and incorrect holes.

Facing the ends

Facing the workpiece is squaring the ends by making them true and flat (Fig. 63-10). To do facing:

1. Move the tailstock until the dead center just touches the live center (Fig. 63-

11). Be sure the centers are aligned. If they are not, move the top casting of the tailstock toward or away from you.

2. Fasten the lathe dog to one end of the workpiece.

3. Move the tailstock assembly until the opening between centers is a little longer than the workpiece. Lock the tailstock in position.

4. Slip the tail of the lathe dog in the opening in the drive plate. Place the workpiece between centers. Apply a little lubricant to the dead-center hole. Use white lead and oil. Tighten the dead center until the workpiece is held snugly. It should not be so loose that the lathe dog clatters or so tight

Fig. 63-10 Positioning the toolholder for a facing cut.

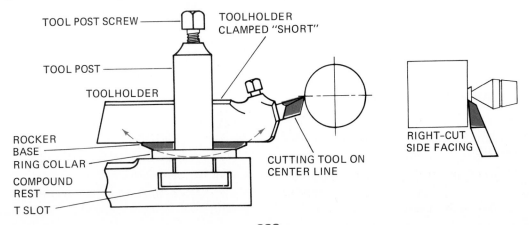

TOOL POST SCREW

TOOLHOLDER CLAMPED "SHORT"

TOOL POST

TOOLHOLDER

ROCKER BASE
RING COLLAR
COMPOUND REST
T SLOT

CUTTING TOOL ON CENTER LINE

RIGHT-CUT SIDE FACING

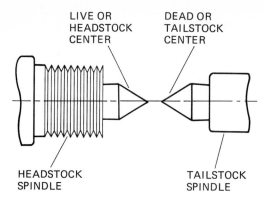

LIVE OR HEADSTOCK CENTER

DEAD OR TAILSTOCK CENTER

HEADSTOCK SPINDLE

TAILSTOCK SPINDLE

Fig. 63–11 Checking the alignment of centers by observing if the point of the dead (tailstock) center touches the point of the live (headstock) center.

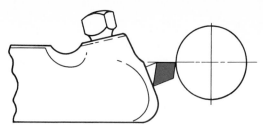

Fig. 63–12 Note that the cutting edge is set on center.

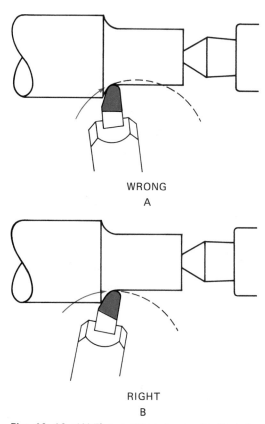

WRONG
A

RIGHT
B

Fig. 63–13 (A) The cutting tool will dig into the workpiece if it moves. (B) The cutting tool will swing out of the way if it moves.

that the dead center becomes scored or burned. Remember that since metal expands when heated, you will have to readjust the dead center after two or three cuts.

5. Place a right-cut side-facing tool in a toolholder with the point well extended.

6. Place the toolholder in the tool post, with the cutting edge at right angles to the centerline. Adjust this by eye.

7. Face the right end of the workpiece, placing your left hand on the carriage handwheel and your right hand on the cross-feed handle.

8. For a rough cut, the tool is fed from the outside toward the center. For a finish cut, the tool is always fed from the center hole toward the outside.

9. Move the carriage to the left until a light cut is taken. Then feed the tool. Reverse the workpiece in the lathe. Then face the other end.

Rough turning

1. Choose a right-cut roughing tool or roundnose tool held in a straight toolholder.

2. Place the toolholder in the tool post, making sure that the toolholder does not extend out too far. The tool post should be at the left end of the T-slot. The face of the tool

must be on center and turned a little away from the headstock (Figs. 63–12, 63–13).

3. Adjust for the correct feed and speed. Check to see how far the carriage can move before the lathe dog hits the compound rest. Check to see that the carriage

Fig. 63-14 **Rough turning.**

will move toward the headstock with power feed.

4. Adjust the outside caliper to 1/32 inch (1 mm) over finished size.

5. Turn on the power. Put your left hand on the carriage handwheel and your right hand on the cross-feed handle. Move the carriage. Turn in the cross-feed until a chip starts to form. Make a trial cut about 1/4 inch (6 mm) wide and deep enough to true up the workpiece.

6. Stop the lathe. Check the diameter with the outside caliper. You may have to make two or three roughing cuts.

7. Turn on the power. Throw in the longitudinal power feed.

8. Check the cutting action. Chips should come off in short pieces. There should be no chattering (Fig. 63-14).

9. When half the cutting has been done, release the longitudinal power feed. Then back out the cross-feed.

(Some machinists prefer not to back out the cross-feed after releasing the longitudinal power feed. Instead, they stop the machine. Then they remove the workpiece, return the carriage to the starting position, reverse the lathe dog, and machine the second end without changing the setting of the cross-feed.)

10. Return the carriage to the starting position. Turn off the power, and check the

diameter. It may be necessary to make one or more additional cuts to turn to rough size.

11. Reverse the workpiece in the lathe. Rough-turn the second half to size.

Finish turning

1. Use a right-cut finishing tool of the same shape as the roughing tool but with a smaller nose radius. The tool should also have a very keen cutting edge.

2. Place the workpiece between centers. Lubricate the dead center. Make a light trial cut about 1/2 inch (13 mm) long. Do not change the cross-feed.

3. Check the machined surface with a micrometer to see how much stock is to be removed. Suppose the machined surface is still 0.006 inch (0.15 mm) oversize.

4. Set the micrometer collar to zero. Move the cutting tool to the right of the workpiece. Turn the cross-feed in 0.003 inch (0.08 mm). Make a trial cut about 1/2 inch (13 mm) long. Then stop the machine, and check the surface again with the micrometer. If necessary, change the micrometer collar to get the correct diameter. Finish-turn the first half of the workpiece.

5. Place a soft copper or aluminum collar around the finished end of the workpiece. Replace the lathe dog (Fig. 63-15). Turn the second half to size. Sometimes, 0.002 to

Fig. 63-15 **Protect the workpiece with a soft collar of sheet copper.**

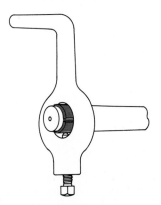

0.003 inch (0.05 to 0.08 mm) of stock is left on the workpiece to allow for filing and polishing.

Turning work to two or more diameters

If the workpiece must be turned to several diameters, do the following:

1. Face one end of the workpiece.

2. Rough-turn the workpiece about 1/32 inch (1 mm) over the largest diameter.

3. Mark the first **shoulder,** or straight part that makes the change in diameter, with a rule and scriber or with a hermaphrodite caliper.

4. Cut a small recess at this layout line.

5. Rough-turn the first diameter about 1/32 inch (1 mm) oversize.

6. Finish-turn the first diameter to the correct size with a right-cut side-facing tool.

7. If there are more than three diameters, turn the second diameter as described above.

8. Reverse the workpiece in the lathe. Face the second end to the needed length.

9. Rough-turn and finish-turn the second end to the correct diameter.

10. Rough-turn and finish-turn the largest diameter.

Filing and polishing

1. Remove the tool post, and adjust the lathe to a high speed. Use a *mill file* or a *long-angle lathe file* to take long, even strokes across the revolving metal. Always keep the file clean. Be careful to keep your arm away from the revolving lathe dog (Fig. 63–16).

2. To get a smooth polish, use a piece of fine abrasive cloth. Apply a little oil to the cloth. Hold it around the revolving work, moving it slowly from one end to the other.

Taper turning

A taper can be turned in several ways:

1. By setting over the tailstock.

Fig. 63–16 Filing on the lathe.

2. By using the compound rest.

3. By using the taper attachment on a lathe. This is the most accurate way.

4. By grinding a form tool.

Turning tapers with tailstock setover

1. Calculate the amount of setover as follows: The setover equals the total length (TL) divided by the length (L) to be tapered times the large diameter (LD) minus the small diameter (SD) over 2.

$$\textbf{Setover} = \frac{TL}{L} \times \frac{LD - SD}{2}$$

In using this formula, remember that the total length is the actual length of the workpiece as it is, not the finished length. This formula is used when the rate of taper is not shown, as in making a center punch or prick punch.

Assume that the rate of taper is known and is expressed in customary measurements, as taper per foot. Then the setover equals the taper per foot in inches times the total length of the workpiece (in inches) divided by 24.

$$\text{Setover} = \frac{\text{taper per foot (in.)} \times TL}{24}$$

Taper in metric measurements is per centimeter, in millimeters. For a metric taper, calculate the setover as follows: Multiply the total length of the workpiece in centimeters times one-half the taper per centimeter in millimeters. The answer will be the setover in millimeters.

$$\text{Setover} = 1/2 \text{ taper per cm (mm)} \times TL$$

Another way to find this setover is to convert the taper per centimeter to a ratio. This is done by multiplying the number of centimeters by 10. For example, a taper of 1 millimeter in 2 centimeters would make a ratio of 1 in 20. At this ratio, a workpiece 20 centimeters long would have a total taper of 1 centimeter, or 10 millimeters. The setover would be half this amount, or 5 millimeters.

2. Loosen the clamp-bolt nut. Adjust the setscrews to move the upper part of the tailstock toward you so that the small end of the taper will be at the tailstock end. There are two ways of measuring the setover:

a. There are two witness, or index, lines machined on the handwheel end of the tailstock. Measure the distance between them with a rule.

b. Measure the amount of setover by holding a rule between the live and dead centers (Fig. 63–17).

3. Place the workpiece between centers as for straight turning. Keep the dead center well lubricated. Choose a thin roundnose tool bit.

4. Start the cutting about 1/2 inch (13 mm) from the right end of the workpiece. If the workpiece is small in diameter, be especially careful that it does not climb over the cutting edge and bend it.

5. Continue making several light cuts until the small end is the correct diameter.

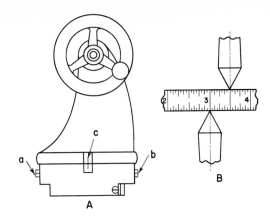

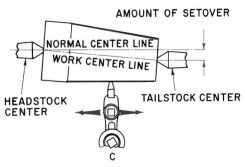

Fig. 63–17 Setting over the tailstock: **(A)** Letters *a* and *b* indicate setscrews, and letter *c* indicates the witness mark. **(B)** Using the rule to check the amount of setover. **(C)** Turning the taper, with the workpiece held between centers.

Measure this with an outside caliper or a micrometer.

Taper turning with the compound rest

For cutting short tapers and angles, adjust the compound rest to the right angle (Fig. 63–18). Do the cutting by feeding the compound rest by hand. The tool will follow the angle set on the compound rest.

Knurling

Knurling is pressing a straight or diamond-shaped pattern on the surface of the workpiece. The handles of some tools are knurled to prevent their slipping from your

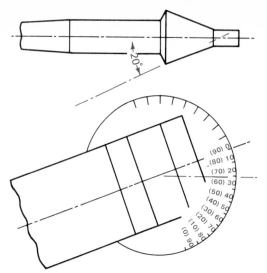

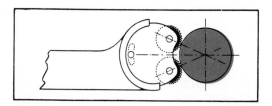

Fig. 63–18 Adjusting the compound rest to cut at an angle of 20 degrees with the centerline or axis. Note that the compound rest has been rotated 70 degrees clockwise.

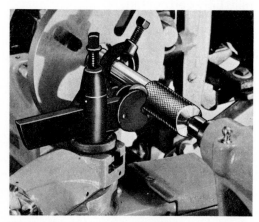

Fig. 63–20 Using the knurling tool. Note the proper position shown in the drawing.

hand. A knurling tool consists of a holder with two hardened steel wheels that form the knurl. To knurl a workpiece, do as follows:

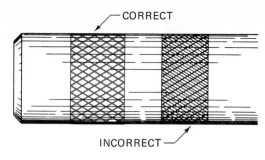

Fig. 63–19 Correct and incorrect impressions for knurling. Both wheels are working in the incorrect knurl, but one is not tracking correctly.

1. Mark the beginning and end of the knurled area.

2. Adjust the lathe to a slow speed.

3. Place the knurling tool in the tool post, with the tool turned a little toward the headstock. The right side of the wheel should touch the workpiece first.

4. Move the carriage to the starting point near the tailstock.

5. Turn in the cross-feed until the wheel presses into the metal about 1/64 inch (0.5 mm). Then apply a little cutting fluid.

6. Turn on the lathe. Immediately use the automatic power feed.

7. Check to see if the tool is working correctly. A diamond-shaped knurling tool should cut a crisscross pattern. If one wheel is not tracking right, release the cross-feed pressure, and move the tool a little to the left. Then start over (Fig. 63–19).

8. If the tool is knurling correctly, increase the pressure, and apply cutting fluid to the surface (Fig. 63–20). Allow the tool to move across the work surface. Clean the wheels often with a wire brush.

9. As the tool reaches the end, turn off the power, but do not release the automatic power feed.

10. Reverse the direction of the carriage. Apply a little more pressure to the wheels, and run the tool back.

1. What part of the lathe holds the live center? The dead center?
2. What does facing do to the end of a workpiece?
3. How should the chips come off during rough turning?
4. In turning work to two or more diameters, which diameter is turned last?

5. What is the setover formula for a taper expressed in customary measurements? For a metric taper?
6. What is knurling?

✔ EXTRA CREDIT ▮▮▮▮▮▮▮▮▮▮

Report to the class on how a taper attachment works.

Unit 64
Machining Workpieces Held in a Chuck

Fig. 64-1 A second method of machining metal on an engine lathe is to fasten it securely in a chuck. Note the use of the safety shield. (Clausing Corporation)

In addition to being held between centers, a workpiece can be held in a **chuck,** or special clamp. The chuck itself is fastened to the spindle nose. Many operations, such as facing, cutting off, drilling, boring, reaming, threading, and turning, can be done in this way (Fig. 64–1).

Kinds of chucks

The *three-jaw universal chuck* is the simplest to use because all three jaws are moved in and out together by turning a single screw with a *chuck key.* It can hold either round or hexagonal workpieces. There are two sets of jaws for each chuck (Fig. 64–2).

The *four-jaw independent chuck* will hold any shape (Fig. 64–3). Each jaw is moved independently.

Installing the chuck

1. Remove the face plate by turning it counterclockwise.
2. Force out the live center and sleeve with an ejector bar.

3. Wipe the threads on the headstock spindle. Apply a few drops of oil.
4. Put a piece of scrap wood or a *cradle* on the ways. Lift the chuck onto it (Fig. 64–4).
5. Clean out the chuck threads.
6. Lift the chuck by placing your hands or fingers in the center between the jaws. Never place your hands under the chuck. Turn it clockwise to start it on the spindle. Lock it in place.

Mounting the workpiece in a chuck

1. On a three-jaw universal chuck, open the jaws until the workpiece slips in. Then tighten with the chuck key. *Always remember to remove the chuck key.*

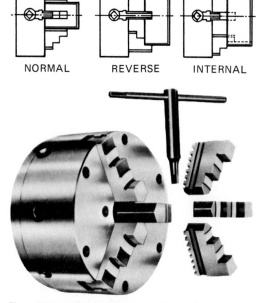

NORMAL   REVERSE   INTERNAL

Fig. 64–2 The ways a workpiece can be held in a three-jaw universal chuck. One set of jaws holds the workpiece either in the normal position or by clamping it internally. The other set holds the workpiece in the reverse position. The chuck key tightens all jaws at the same time.

2. If an independent-jaw chuck is used, open each of the four jaws an equal distance from the center. Use the circular guidelines on the chuck face to do this. Insert the workpiece in the chuck. Then tighten opposite jaws a little at a time until the workpiece is held firmly. Figure 64–5 shows how you can make sure the workpiece is centered.

Facing

1. For rough cuts, choose a left-cut roughing tool. Cut from the outside of the workpiece toward the center. Remember to lock the carriage to the bed with the *carriage-lock screw.* Use the power cross-feed for large-diameter stock (Fig. 64–6).

2. For finishing cuts, use a right-cut facing tool clamped in a left-hand holder. Adjust the holder until the cutting edge is at an angle of about 8 to 10 degrees to the workpiece face. If you set the toolholder at about 80 to 82 degrees, you will be setting the tool at the correct angle (Fig. 64–7). Start at the center, and feed to the outside.

Fig. 64–4 Installing the chuck. (Sheldon Machine Company)

Fig. 64–3 The four-jaw independent chuck. Each jaw is moved independently by use of a chuck key.

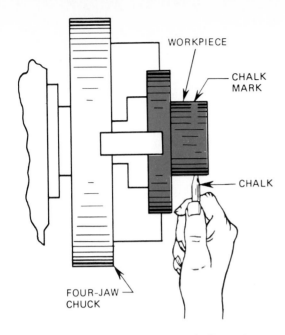

Fig. 64-5 Aligning the workpiece in a four-jaw independent chuck. The chalk will always indicate if the workpiece must be moved slightly in order to center it.

Fig. 64-7 When facing with a cutting tool like that shown, the toolholder should be set at an angle of about 80 degrees to the workpiece.

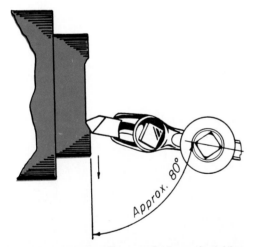

Fig. 64-6 Facing the workpiece held in a chuck. The carriage is locked to the bed by tightening the carriage-lock screw. (Clausing Corporation)

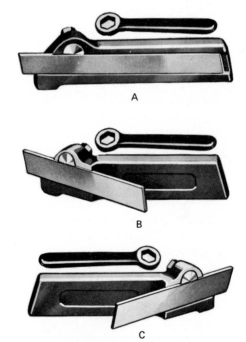

Fig. 64-8 Cutoff tools: (A) straight, (B) right-hand, (C) left-hand.

Cutting off stock

1. Turn the outside of the workpiece as you would if it were held between centers.

2. Use a cutoff tool as shown in Fig. 64-8.

3. Mark the location of the cut. Make sure that the blade is at right angles to the work and on center.

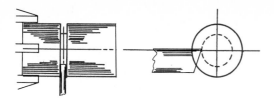

Fig. 64-9 Cutting off with the workpiece held in a chuck.

4. The speed should be about two-thirds that for turning.

5. Feed the cutting tool slowly into the work. Apply plenty of cutting lubricant (Fig. 64-9).

Drilling

1. Remove the dead center, and insert a *drill chuck*. Center-drill the location of the hole.

2. Choose the size of drill needed. If it is large, first drill a pilot hole.

3. Insert the drill in the drill chuck if it has a straight shank. If it has a tapered shank, it can be inserted directly in the tailstock spindle (Fig. 64-10).

4. Adjust for the right speed as in drilling. Feed the drill slowly into the workpiece, applying cutting fluid. Back the drill out several times to clean out the chips. Reduce the feed as the drill breaks through the back of the workpiece.

5. To make a hole of great accuracy, first drill the hole 1/32 inch (0.1 mm) too small. Then bore to 1/64 inch (0.5 mm) undersize. Finally, machine-ream it to exact size. For most work, however, you can drill the hole 1/64 inch (0.5 mm) too small and then hand-ream or machine-ream.

Boring

Boring is done to finish a hole that is not standard size, to trim out a hole in a casting, or to finish a very accurate hole of any size. Use a boring bar with a boring tool ground like a left-cut turning tool (Fig. 64-11).

Fig. 64-10 Drilling with the workpiece held in a chuck. The drill is held in a chuck if it has a straight shank. A taper-shank drill is held in the tailstock spindle.

Reaming

Reaming produces a hole that is accurate and smoothly finished. Hand reaming on the lathe can be done as shown in Fig. 64-12. If a machine reamer with a tapered shank is used, insert it directly into the tailstock spindle. Adjust the lathe for a very slow speed. Turn the tailstock handwheel slowly so that the reamer advances into the workpiece at a slow, steady speed. Never turn the reamer backward.

Fig. 64-11 Using a boring tool to enlarge a hole in metal.

Fig. 64-12 Hand reaming on the lathe. Never use power when hand reaming.

Fig. 64-13 A simple method of cutting internal threads, using a tap.

Fig. 64-15 An arbor press. (Dake Corporation)

Cutting threads

The simplest way to cut internal threads is to use a tap, as shown in Fig. 64–13. External threads can be cut with a die held in a dieholder, as shown in Fig. 64–14.

Turning work on a mandrel

To machine the outside of a workpiece with a hole in it, fasten the workpiece to a mandrel. A **mandrel** is a shaft, rod, or tube that holds the workpiece. Choose a mandrel of the correct size. The size is stamped on the large end. Cover the mandrel with a thin coat of oil. Press it into the workpiece with an *arbor press* (Fig. 64–15). If an arbor press is not available, drive the mandrel into the

Fig. 64-14 Using a button die held in a diestock to cut external threads.

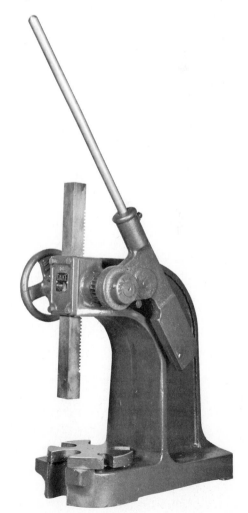

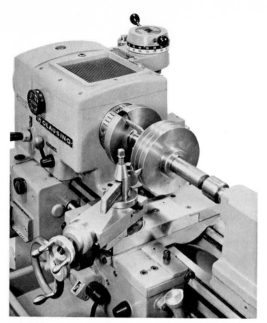

Fig. 64–16 Turning the outside of a work-piece held on a mandrel. (Clausing Corporation)

Fig. 64–17 Turning a workpiece held in a collet chuck. (Clausing Corporation)

workpiece with a soft-faced hammer. Turn the outside of the workpiece as shown in Fig. 64–16.

Other chuck-turning methods

Chuck-held workpieces can also be turned to a desired outside diameter. For long workpieces, use the tailstock center or a steady rest for added support. Shorter pieces can be cut safely without such support. *Collet chucks* are quick-action chucks for easy, accurate installation of workpieces (Fig. 64–17). They come in a number of styles.

 QUESTIONS

1. What operations can be done with the workpiece held in a chuck?
2. How are the jaws moved on a three-jaw universal chuck? On a four-jaw independent chuck?
3. What part of the lathe is the chuck attached to?
4. What kind of drill is held in a drill chuck?
5. At what speed should a lathe operate for reaming?
6. What device should be used to press a workpiece onto a mandrel?

 EXTRA CREDIT

Explain how a collet chuck works and what it is used for.

Unit 65
The Shaper

The **shaper** is a cutting machine that utilizes a tool pushed and withdrawn by a ram and a table for holding the workpiece and moving it after each cut. It is used for shaping horizontal, vertical, angular, and curved surfaces. The size of the shaper is determined by the maximum stroke in inches. This is about the same as the largest cube it will machine. Common sizes are 7 (178 mm), 8 (203 mm), 10 (254 mm), 14 (356 mm), and 16 (406 mm) inches. The

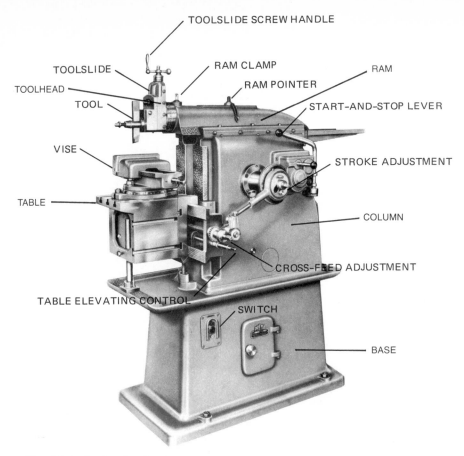

Fig. 65-1 Parts of a shaper.

The following labels appear on the figure: TOOLSLIDE SCREW HANDLE, TOOLSLIDE, RAM CLAMP, RAM, TOOLHEAD, RAM POINTER, TOOL, START-AND-STOP LEVER, VISE, STROKE ADJUSTMENT, TABLE, COLUMN, CROSS-FEED ADJUSTMENT, TABLE ELEVATING CONTROL, SWITCH, BASE.

main parts are shown in Fig. 65–1. Modern industry does not use the shaper much, preferring instead the milling machine (see Unit 66). However, many small shops still have these machines.

Holding devices

1. For most jobs, the workpiece is held in a *swivel vise* fastened to the shaper table. The top of the vise can be rotated so that the jaws are either at right angles or parallel to the ram movement.

2. *Parallels* are used to raise the workpiece above the top of the vise jaws. They are rectangular pieces of hardened steel made in pairs.

3. *Wedges,* or *hold-downs,* are hardened pieces of steel with the back edge beveled to an angle of 2 or 3 degrees and a rounded front edge. They are placed in the vise to hold the workpiece firmly against the parallels (Fig. 65–2).

Cutting tools and toolholders

1. The toolholder can be either a *lathe toolholder* or a *swiveled-head,* or *universal, toolholder* (Fig. 65–3).

2. The shaper cutting tools are the same as those used in the lathe, except for some of the tool angles. Because the shaper feed does not operate during the cut, the *side-relief angle* can be less than for a lathe

345

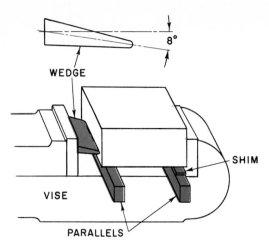

Fig. 65-2 Common accessories used for holding the workpiece include a vise, parallels, and a wedge, or holddown.

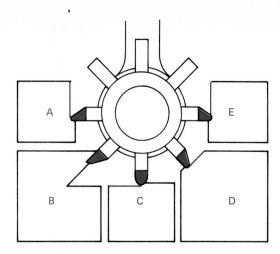

Fig. 65-3 Note how the swivel head can hold the cutting tool for (A) vertical, (B) angular, (C) horizontal, (D) angular, and (E) vertical cuts.

tool. It needs to be only about 3 or 4 degrees. There is no rocker under the toolholder, so the *end-relief angle* cannot be adjusted. It should also be about 3 or 4 degrees. If the cutting tool is held in the lathe toolholder, the end relief on the tool must be ground at about 19 degrees to provide the necessary 3 or 4 degrees. A roundnose tool is used for most simple shaping.

Machining a flat surface

1. Fasten the workpiece in a vise, using parallels and hold-downs. Clamp the workpiece with the long side parallel to the jaws. If necessary, raise the workpiece with parallels. Sometimes, a soft-metal rod is placed between the adjustable jaw and the workpiece. Tighten the vise.

2. Be sure the toolhead is set at zero and the clapper box is centered.

3. Insert the cutting tool in the toolholder. Fasten the holder in the tool post. The toolholder should be turned a little to the right. This is so that the cutting tool will turn away rather than dig in if it slips (Fig. 65-4).

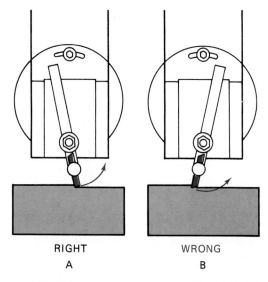

RIGHT
A

WRONG
B

Fig. 65-4 The correct and incorrect way to adjust the toolholder in the tool post. (A) Right: The tool swings away from the workpiece. (B) Wrong: The tool digs into the workpiece.

4. Turn the slide up as far as it will go to avoid too much overhang (Fig. 65-5).

5. If necessary, move the table up or down. To do this, loosen the *crossrail cap*

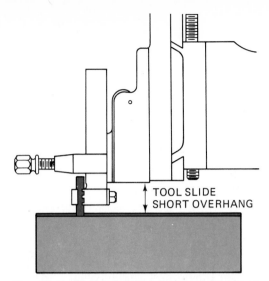

Fig. 65–5 The toolslide is kept up. The tool-holder is also high in the tool post for greater rigidity. Never allow the slide or the toolholder to overhang too much. Raise the table if necessary.

screws directly behind the *column rail bearings.* Also loosen the *table support.* Put the crank wrench on the *vertical screw,* or *table-elevating control.* Move the table up or down. Remember always to tighten the clamping screws and table support. There should be at least 2 inches (51 mm) of clearance between the underside of the ram and the top of the workpiece.

6. Adjust for length of stroke. The stroke should be 3/4 inch (19 mm) longer than the surface being machined. Turn the countershaft or handwheel until the ram is in as far as it will go. Loosen the nut. Put the crank handle on the *stroke selector,* or *adjusting shaft.* A scale on the top of the column and a pointer on the ram show the length of stroke. Turn the crank in either direction until the right length is shown on the scale. Then tighten the nut.

7. Adjust the position of stroke. Move the ram out as far as it will go. Loosen the *ram hand clamp.* Put the crank on the *ram posi-*

tioner. Then turn the crank until the point of the tool clears the front of the workpiece by about 1/4 inch (6 mm). Tighten the ram clamp (Fig. 65–6).

8. Adjust the speed by changing the belt. Most belt-driven shapers have only four to eight possible machine speeds. Speed should be faster for shorter strokes and softer material, and slower for longer strokes and harder material.

9. Adjust for correct feed. The **feed** is the distance the table moves after each cutting stroke. Generally, a finer feed is used with a heavy or roughing cut and a heavier feed with a lighter or finishing cut. To increase the feed, loosen the nut or screw on the *feed-adjustment selector,* or *slotted crank disk.* Slide the end toward the outer edge, then tighten. The feed must be set so that the table advances on the return stroke of the ram.

10. Sit or stand at the front and a little to the right of the shaper. Use the cross-feed crank to move the workpiece to the left and away from you. The cutting will then start at the right edge—the edge nearest you.

Fig. 65–6 See how the cutting tool clears the back of the workpiece by about 1/2 inch (13 mm). This allows the clapper to seat firmly in the box before the next stroke. The tool should also clear the front of the workpiece by about 1/4 inch (6 mm).

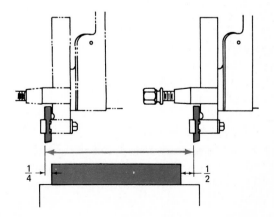

Fig. 65-7 A cutting tool in correct position.

17. Take additional cuts to within 1/64 (0.016) inch (0.4 mm) of the layout line on steel or 0.005 to 0.010 inch (0.13 to 0.25 mm) on cast iron.

18. Increase the speed, use a finer feed, and take a lighter cut to complete the first surface.

Machining a vertical surface

1. Turn the vise with the solid jaw at right angles to the ram stroke.

2. Mark a layout line on the workpiece.

3. Clamp the workpiece so that the end to be machined clears the right side of the vise jaw. Fasten the workpiece in the vise so that the down feed will have to move the shortest distance to complete the cut.

4. Turn the top of the clapper box away from the direction in which the cut is to be made (Fig. 65-8). This is done to make the cutting tool clear the workpiece on the return stroke and to keep it from digging in.

11. Turn on the power. Place your right hand on the *down-feed toolslide handle* and your left hand on the *cross-feed crank*.

12. Turn the cutting tool down very slowly. Move the work toward you until the cutting tool takes a chip about 1/16 to 1/8 inch (1.5 to 3 mm) deep (Fig. 65-7).

13. Turn the cross-feed crank about an eighth to a quarter turn during each return stroke until three or four strokes have been made.

14. Stop the machine to check the surface and cutting action. If the tool is cutting properly, chips will curl away from a steel workpiece and crumble away from a cast-iron workpiece.

15. Turn on the power. Engage the automatic feed.

16. When the first cut is complete, return the workpiece to the starting position. Never cut on both forward and backward motions.

Fig. 65-8 Notice how the clapper box is turned for making the vertical cut.

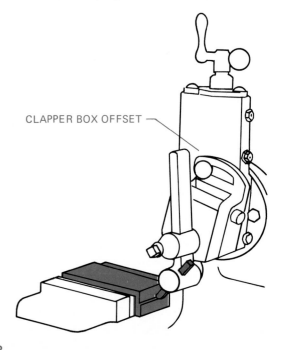

CLAPPER BOX OFFSET

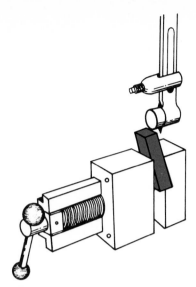

Fig. 65-9 Machine an angle or bevel by clamping the workpiece in the vise, with the layout line parallel to the top of the vise jaws.

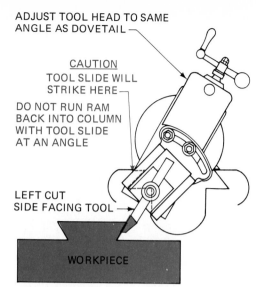

ADJUST TOOL HEAD TO SAME ANGLE AS DOVETAIL

CAUTION
TOOL SLIDE WILL STRIKE HERE

DO NOT RUN RAM BACK INTO COLUMN WITH TOOL SLIDE AT AN ANGLE

LEFT CUT SIDE FACING TOOL

WORKPIECE

Fig. 65-10 Check the action of the ram before making an angle cut.

5. Use the *left-cut side-facing tool.* Mount the cutting tool in the holder and the holder in the tool post.

6. Turn the toolslide up as far as it will go.

7. Move the table to the left until the cutting tool will clear the right end of the workpiece.

8. Turn the slide down to check it. The cutting tool must reach the bottom of the workpiece without too much overhang. Return the tool to the starting position.

9. Turn on the power. Put your left hand on the cross-feed crank and your right hand on the down-feed toolslide handle. Move the workpiece toward you and the cutting tool down until a chip forms.

10. Remove your hand from the cross-feed crank. Then move the cutting tool down about one-fourth to one-half turn at the end of each cutting stroke.

11. Continue machining the vertical surface.

Machining an angle or bevel

1. The simplest way to machine an angle or bevel is to hold the workpiece in a vise, with the layout line parallel to the top of the vise jaws (Fig. 65–9). The angle or bevel is then machined in the same way as a horizontal cut.

2. The second method is to machine it like a vertical cut, except that the head is set at the desired angle. Then move the ram through one whole stroke. Check to see that the slide does not hit the column (Figs. 65–10, 65–11).

Squaring up a block

1. Machine the face, or first, surface (Fig. 65–12A).

2. Place the workpiece in the vise with the face surface against the solid jaw. Put a soft-metal rod of copper or aluminum between the workpiece and adjustable jaw. Check the two surfaces for squareness. Machine the second surface (Fig. 65–12B).

Fig. 65-11 Machining an angle or bevel. Notice how the head has been turned to the correct angle and how the clapper box has been offset.

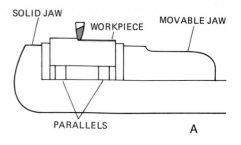

A

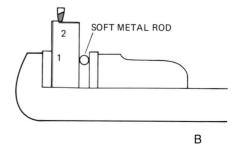

B

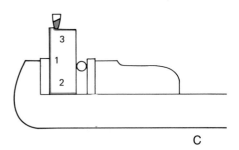

C

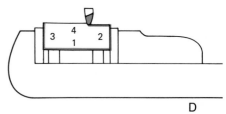

D

Fig. 65-12 (A) Machining the face surface. (B) Machining the second surface. (C) Machining to width. (D) Machining to thickness.

3. Lay out the right width. Place the face surface against the solid jaw, with the second surface down. Machine to the correct width (Fig. 65-12C).

4. Place the face surface on two parallels. Machine to the right thickness (Fig. 65-12D).

5. Machine the ends. If the workpiece is not too long, machine the ends by making horizontal cuts. If it is too long, machine the ends by making vertical cuts.

 **QUESTIONS**

1. On what surfaces is a shaper used?
2. How is the workpiece most often held?
3. In machining a flat surface, how long should the stroke be?

4. What kind of cutting tool is used for machining a vertical surface?

 EXTRA CREDIT

1. What are the differences between a shaper and a planer?
2. Show how a planer works.

Unit 66
The Milling Machine

The **milling machine** uses a rotating tool with two or more cutting edges to shape and smooth metal. Next to the lathe, it is the most useful and versatile machine in the shop. In this unit, only the simplest uses of the milling machine are explained.

Kinds of milling machines and parts

The two milling machines most commonly found in school shops are the *horizontal* (Fig. 66–1) and the *vertical* (Fig. 66–2). Both are called *column-and-knee* machines. This is because the *spindle,* or part that rotates, is fixed in the *column.* The *table,* part of the *knee,* can be adjusted longitudinally (back and forth), transversely (in and out or across), and vertically (up and down) (Fig. 66–3).

On the plain horizontal machine, the spindle is horizontal. On the vertical machine, it is vertical. On smaller vertical machines, the *head* can be turned 180 degrees in a horizontal plane. The head can also be adjusted in a vertical plane to any angle. The

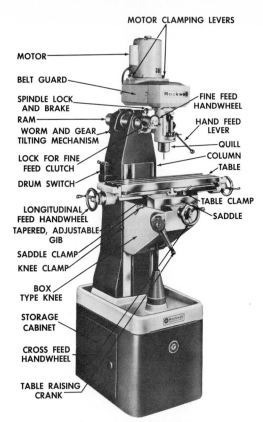

Fig. 66-2 Parts of the vertical milling machine. (Rockwell International Corporation)

Fig. 66-1 Parts of the horizontal milling machine. (Rockwell International Corporation)

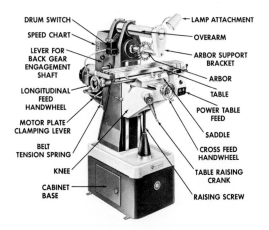

Fig. 66-3 The three movements of the table of a typical milling machine: (A) longitudinal, (B) transverse, (C) vertical. (Clausing Corporation)

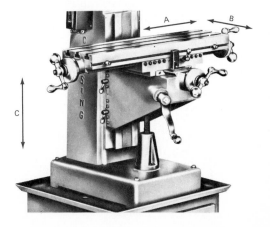

vertical milling machine requires less setup time than the horizontal. It can do a wider variety of operations with the workpiece clamped in the same position in the vise or on the table.

Milling-machine controls

Here are some procedures you should learn:

1. To *change the machine speed,* move the *belt,* as on a drill press. The machine, or spindle, speed is expressed in revolutions per minute (rpm). On most small milling machines, there are eight speeds. The four-step pulleys provide four speeds. By changing the belt position on another set of two-step pulleys, four more speeds are obtained.

Some machines have a *variable speed-control lever.* This permits the quick selection of speeds.

2. To *raise or lower the knee,* loosen the *knee-clamp lever* that holds the knee to the column. Turn the *vertical-feed hand crank* to the left to lower the knee and to the right to raise it. Always clamp the knee in its new position.

3. To *move the table toward the column,* turn the *cross-feed handwheel* to the right. To *move the table away from the column,* turn it to the left. This is called *cross movement.*

4. To *move the table longitudinally* in front of the column, use the *table handwheel* at either end of the table. Turn the wheel to the right to move the table to the right and to the left to move it to the left. Some small machines also have a *table power feed.* On these, the *engaging lever* near the front center of the table is moved to the right to make the table go to the right. *Adjustable stops,* or *trip dogs,* along the front edge of the table control the distance of table travel.

Care of the milling machine

1. Keep the machine clean by brushing the chips away and wiping the table with a cloth.

2. Always wipe the spindle nose before putting in an arbor, adapter, or cutter.

3. Keep the machine oiled according to the chart supplied by the manufacturer.

4. Never leave tools or equipment on the table. Never drop a tool on the table. Remember that this machine is a precision instrument.

5. Handle the cutters and the arbor carefully, using a cloth to protect your hands.

Milling cutters and cutter holders

There are many kinds, sizes, and shapes of *milling cutters.* You will generally use high-speed-steel cutters. A few carbon-steel cutters are also used on small machines (Table 66–1).

On a horizontal milling machine, an *arbor* holds most of the cutters. On a vertical milling machine, the cutters are mounted directly in the spindle or in a *collet.*

Cutting speeds and feeds

Cutting speed is the distance one tooth of the cutter moves as measured on the work in surface feet per minute (sfpm) or in surface meters per minute (smpm). In general, cutting speed is slower for harder materials and faster for softer ones. Cutting speed is not the same as machine speed. The spindle of a milling machine operates at a certain number of revolutions per minute (rpm). If you place a 2-inch (51-mm) cutter on the spindle and it makes one complete revolution, the tooth will travel 2 times 3.1416, or about 6 1/4 inches (160 mm). If a 1/2-inch (13-mm) diameter cutter is used, it will travel only 1/2 times 3.1416, or about 1 1/2 inches (40 mm).

Table 66–2 shows the approximate cutting speeds for carbon-tool-steel and high-speed-steel cutters. To find the spindle speed using customary measurements, use this formula:

Table 66-1 Some Common Milling Cutters and Their Uses

Name	Picture	Use	Type of miller	
			Horizontal	Vertical
plain with helical teeth		for flat horizontal surfaces; to square up a block	X	
side with straight teeth		for light-duty side milling and slotting	X	
half side		for straddle milling	X	
slitting saw with plain teeth		for sawing and cutting narrow grooves	X	
straight-shank end mills with either single or double end		for all end milling, surface milling, and slotting	X	X
taper-shank end mills with two flutes or multiple flutes		for plunge cutting (like drilling), use a two-flute end mill	X	X
shell end mill		for milling larger surfaces; for face and slab milling	X	X

$$\text{rpm} = \frac{4 \times \text{cutting speed in sfpm}}{\text{diameter of cutter in inches}}$$

$$\text{rpm} = \frac{1000 \times \text{cutting speed in smpm}}{3.1416 \times \text{diameter of cutter in mm}}$$

Suppose you wish to machine a piece of mild steel with a high-speed-steel cutter 3 inches in diameter. Then the rpm would be 4 times 80 divided by 3, or about 100 rpm.

To find the spindle speed using metric measurements, use this formula:

Suppose you wish to machine a piece of hard cast iron with a 75-mm high-speed-steel cutter. Then the rpm would be 1000 times 18 divided by 75 times 3.1416, or about 76 rpm.

The machine speed, or rpm, is adjusted by moving the belt, as on a drill press. The

Table 66-2
Cutting Speeds

Materials	Milling cutter materials		
	Carbon-tool steel	High-speed steel	
	sfpm	sfpm	smpm
alloy tool steel	–	28–40	8.5–12.2
tough alloy steel	20–26	40–52	12.2–15.8
medium alloy steel	26–31	52–65	15.8–19.8
cast iron—hard	26–31	52–65	15.8–19.8
SAE 1045 steel	31–38	65–79	19.8–24.1
malleable iron	31–38	65–79	19.8–24.1
SAE 1020 and C1018 (mild) steel	38–46	79–97	24.1–29.6
cast iron—medium	38–46	79–97	24.1–29.6
cast iron—soft	46–60	97–125	29.6–38.1
brass and bronze {medium	60–90	125–180	38.1–54.9
brass and bronze {soft	90–135	180–280	54.9–85.3
aluminum and other light alloys	135–725	280–1500	85.3–57.2

feed, the rate at which the workpiece moves under the cutter, depends on your own judgment. In general, feed is slower for heavy, rough cuts and faster for light, finishing cuts.

When feeding by hand, you tend to move the table too slowly rather than too fast.

Using a horizontal milling machine

1. Check the solid jaw of the vise, as shown in Fig. 66-4. For most work, the vise is set with the jaws *parallel* to the column face. Sometimes, they are at right angles.

2. Fasten the workpiece in the vise. Place it on two parallels so that at least half the thickness is above the top of the jaws.

3. Choose the correct kind and size of cutter. For most work, the tool should be a plain milling cutter. Use one that is a little wider than the workpiece to be machined.

4. Choose an arbor with a hole of the same diameter as that of the cutter. Install the arbor in the spindle, using the *draw-in bar* to hold it firmly in place. Place the cutter between the collars on the spindle so that it is about centered. Make sure the cutter is

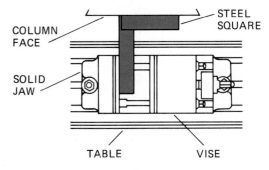

Fig. 66-4 **Checking the alignment of the vise with a steel square.**

held firmly by tightening the arbor nut securely. Also make sure that the *overarm* is clamped tight.

5. Adjust for the right speed and feed. The feed should be *opposite* to the direction of cutter rotation. This is known as *up*, or *conventional*, *milling*. Feeding in the *same* direction as cutter rotation is called *climb milling* (Fig. 66-5). Never try to do climb milling on a small machine.

6. Move the table *transversely* until the workpiece is centered under the cutter.

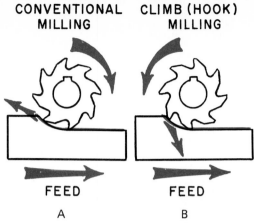

CONVENTIONAL MILLING   CLIMB (HOOK) MILLING

FEED   FEED

A   B

Fig. 66-5 Note the difference between (A) conventional and (B) climb milling.

Fig. 66-6 Setup for side-milling a vertical surface.

7. Turn on the power. Then move the knee until the rotating cutter just touches the workpiece surface. Now, move the workpiece to the left of the cutter. Raise the knee for the correct depth of cut, about 0.015 inch (0.38 mm) for a roughing cut.

8. Feed the workpiece into the turning cutter.

9. After the first cut is complete, stop the machine and check the surface.

 SAFETY RULE

Never feel the finished surface while the cut is being made. Never back the workpiece under the turning cutter.

10. If more cuts are needed, lower the table one full turn. Then move the workpiece to the starting position. Raise the table one full turn plus the amount for the next cut.

11. Side-milling cutters are used to machine vertical surfaces (Fig. 66-6). In *straddle milling*, two half side cutters straddle the workpiece to machine two vertical surfaces.

Using a vertical milling machine

1. Choose an *end mill* that is a little larger in diameter than the width of the cut. However, if the cutter is not wide enough, make two passes across the surface.

2. Mount the milling cutter in the spindle. Most small vertical millers have a collet for holding straight-shank end mills. Insert the cutter. Tighten it by turning the draw-in bar at the top of the spindle or by tightening the setscrews that hold the end mill in place (Fig. 66-7).

3. Make sure the milling head is at right angles to the table, both vertically and horizontally.

4. Secure the workpiece in the vise.

5. Adjust for the right speed and feed.

6. Make sure the spindle is turning in the right direction. A right-hand cutter should turn counterclockwise.

7. Move the workpiece until it is directly under the cutter.

8. Turn the power. Then raise the knee until the cutter just touches the workpiece.

9. Adjust the micrometer collar on the knee crank to zero.

10. Move the table to the right and raise the knee about 0.015 inch (0.38 mm).

11. Move the table until the cutting starts. Then feed it slowly, making a cut across the surface.

12. If much material must be removed, make several cuts.

Fig. 66-7 Installing an end mill in the spindle of the vertical milling machine. The end mill slips into a collet. It is held firmly by tightening the draw-in bar.

Fig. 66-9 Machining the opening for the handle in a hammerhead.

13. Figure 66–8 shows how a bevel or chamfer can be cut with the workpiece in a vise and the head at a 45-degree angle.

Fig. 66-8 Machining a bevel with the head set at 45 degrees.

14. Figure 66–9 shows how to do slotting or to mill a groove or keyway. For a closed-end keyway, use a two-lipped end mill. The vertical milling machine can also be used for accurate drilling, boring, and reaming. To do these operations, the spindle can be moved up and down with a feed handle, just as in the drill press.

 QUESTIONS

1. Name two common kinds of milling machines.
2. On these machines, in what ways can the table be adjusted?
3. How do you change the machine speed?
4. Of what kinds of steel are milling cutters commonly made?
5. What is cutting speed?
6. What is the difference between up milling and climb milling?
7. Name three operations that can be done with a vertical milling machine.

 EXTRA CREDIT

Report on how milling machines are used in industry. Investigate one industry, and show which parts are made in a milling machine.

Unit 67
Precision Grinding

In Units 19, 21, and 48, several kinds of abrading are described. These include grinding, polishing, and buffing. They are all metal-removal processes. In this unit, you will learn how precision grinding is used to finish a metal workpiece to tolerances as close as 0.0002 inch (0.005 mm).

A basic function of machine grinding, or abrasive machining, is to produce cylindrical surfaces, flat surfaces, and internal surfaces or holes. All of these are made with a grinding wheel. The kind of surface to be ground determines the type of grinding operation and the type of grinding machine. For example, if a flat surface is to be ground, the operation is surface grinding and the machine is a surface grinder.

The following paragraphs explain the most basic kinds of grinding operations. These are cylindrical, centerless, internal, and surface grinding.

Cylindrical grinding

Cylindrical grinding is the external grinding of cylinder-shaped parts (Fig. 67–1). These include straight cylinders, multidiameter cylinders, and tapered parts.

In cylindrical grinders, the grinding wheel is mounted on a cross slide with the face perpendicular to the work axis. It is fed to or from the work, either by hand or automatically. It can also be fed parallel to the work. On many machines, the headstock and tailstock are mounted on an auxiliary swiveling table. This table makes it possible for work to be swiveled to grind tapers.

The workpiece is supported between centers. It is rotated and moved back and forth across the face of the grinding wheel. This causes a cylindrical surface to form. The diameter of the cylinder is determined by the distance from the face of the grinding wheel to a line connecting the center points of the workpiece. This distance is, of course, the radius of the cylinder.

Centerless grinding

Centerless grinding is also used for grinding cylinders. The main parts of a centerless grinder are the grinding and regulating wheels and the work rest (Fig. 67–2). The work rest guides the workpiece to the wheel. It also supports the work during grinding.

On the centerless grinder, the cutting pressure of the grinding action forces the workpiece down against the work-rest blade and the regulating wheel. The latter is usually made of a rubber-bonded abrasive. It serves as both a frictional driving and brak-

Fig. 67-1 Cylindrical grinding.

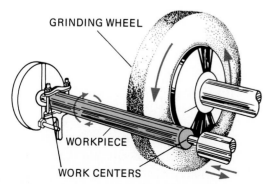

Fig. 67-2 Centerless grinding.

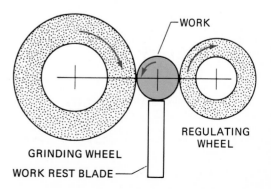

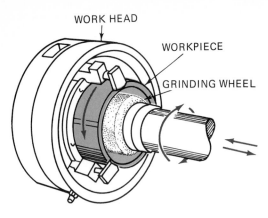

Fig. 67-3 Internal grinding.

ing element, rotating the workpiece at a speed about equal to that of the wheel.

Internal grinding

Internal grinding is done to accurately finish internal surfaces, or holes (Fig. 67–3). It is also done to correct errors from previous operations. These errors might include distortion in heat treating or rough surfaces produced by tools. Straight or tapered holes, through holes or blind holes, and holes having more than one diameter can all be ground on internal grinders. Some machines

Fig. 67-4 Surface grinding.

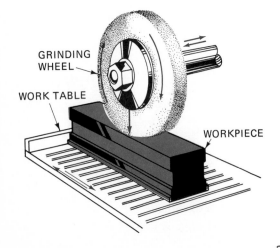

have power feed and traverse feed, though the cycle is manually controlled. Others are fully automatic.

Surface grinding

All grinding is done on surfaces. However, the term *surface grinding* is usually used to describe the process of grinding a flat surface (Fig. 67–4). Machines made for this purpose have horizontal or vertical spindles and rotary or reciprocating tables. There are also various kinds of disk grinders. The surface grinder is the type of grinder usually found in the school machine shop.

The most common kind of surface grinder is probably that having a horizontal spindle and a reciprocating table (Fig. 67–5). The wheel head is mounted so that the wheel can be raised or lowered according to the size of the workpiece. When the wheel head is in place, the wheel can be fed to the work either by hand or automatically.

The table moves back and forth under the wheel. In some simple shop work, hand table feeds can be used. However, in most production work the table travel is controlled automatically. The table travel and speed can be set before the job is begun. Such table speeds are high and may reach 60 surface feet (18.3 surface meters) per minute or more.

Where possible, the workpiece is held on a magnetic chuck built into the table. For mass production, a number of identical pieces may be held on the chuck at one time. After grinding, it is advisable to put the pieces through a demagnetizer. Parts that would be injured by magnetization or that cannot be magnetized must be held by clamps, vises, or fixtures.

Straight-sided wheels that cut with the flat cutting face are usually used in this kind of machine. In grinding shoulders, a recessed wheel can be used. In grinding V's and other shapes, wheels with formed faces are used.

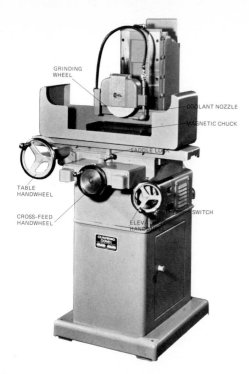

Fig. 67-5 The surface grinder, with parts identified.

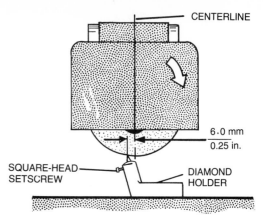

Fig. 67-6 Truing a grinding wheel.

Checking, truing, and dressing the grinding wheel

Before installing the wheel on the spindle, look at it to see if it has any cracks or chips. *Never use a defective wheel.* You should also check for defects by giving the wheel a *ring test.* Insert your index finger in the wheel's center hole. Next, using only this finger, pick up the wheel. Tap the wheel lightly with a wooden hammer or the handle of a screwdriver. You should hear a clear metallic tone.

In mounting the wheel on the spindle, be sure to use blotters. Once the wheel is installed, it must be *dressed,* or sharpened, and *trued,* or shaped, in the following manner:

1. Insert the diamond nib shank as far as it will go into the diamond holding bracket. This will eliminate vibration.

2. Tighten the squarehead setscrew securely.

3. Raise the spindle so that the bottom of the wheel clears the top of the diamond.

4. Set the diamond to the left of the wheel centerlines, as shown in Fig. 67–6. *Never set the diamond to the right of the wheel centerline.* In that position it will grab and dig into the wheel, damaging both itself and the wheel. Also, *never move the table to the right or left when dressing the wheel.*

5. Secure the diamond holder to the table or chuck.

6. Lower the spindle to a point where the wheel's high spot barely touches the diamond.

7. Using the cross-feed handwheel, pass the diamond back and forth across the wheel. Be sure to pass the diamond beyond the wheel face on each pass.

8. For a fine finish, use a slow pass and a down feed of about 0.001 inch (0.03 mm) per pass. For a rough finish, use a rapid pass and a slightly greater down-feed rate.

9. Continue down feeding until the sound of the diamond in contact with the wheel indicates that the diamond is cutting evenly across the full face of the wheel. Use very light cuts and a very slow pass in the finishing stages.

Using the surface grinder

The surface grinder can be used in many machine-shop operations. It can be used to finish the surfaces of cast machine vises, C-clamps, and tools. Following is a description of how the surface grinder is used:

1. Clean all grease and dirt from the workpiece. Dress and true the wheel if necessary.

2. Wipe the magnetic chuck with a clean cloth.

3. Center the workpiece on the chuck. Turn on the switch to hold it in place with magnetism.

4. Adjust the table reverse dogs so that they clear the ends of the workpiece by about 2 inches (50 mm).

5. Turn on the coolant valve, if coolant is to be used. If you are dry grinding, start the dust collector. Set the speed control, and start the table with the three-position switch.

6. Adjust the rate of table feed.

7. Turn on the power.

8. Hand-feed the table in until the workpiece is under the grinding wheel.

9. Turn on the power table feed.

10. Adjust the grinding wheel down until it is near the workpiece. Move the table cross-feed. Continue to feed the wheel down slowly until the grinder just touches the work. This should be the highest spot on the work surface (Fig. 67–7). To make sure, feed the length of the workpiece under the wheel. Feed the grinding wheel down about 0.003 inch (0.08 mm), and start the grinding.

11. Turn the cross-feed out about one-fourth the width of the grinding wheel just as the table changes direction.

12. Grind the entire surface. During grinding, do not let the wheel become soaked with coolant. Measure the height with a surface gage.

13. Dress the wheel. For a high finish, the last grinding should not remove more than 0.001 inch (0.03 mm).

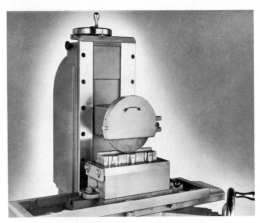

Fig. 67-7   The grinding wheel should just touch the workpiece as grinding begins.

14. After grinding, turn off the coolant, and let the wheel run a few seconds to spin off any coolant it has collected.

15. Check the workpiece carefully to see if all areas are ground. Repeat grinding if necessary.

 QUESTIONS

1. What tolerance can precision grinding achieve on metal workpieces?
2. What are cylindrical grinders used for?
3. In centerless grinding, what guides the workpiece to the wheel?
4. What are internal grinders used for?
5. What kind of chuck is often used in surface grinding?
6. What is a ring test?
7. What must be done to a grinding wheel before it is used?

 EXTRA CREDIT

Write a report on precision grinding in industry.

Unit 68
Advanced Techniques in Metalworking

In addition to the basic ways of forming and cutting metal, many other techniques for doing special jobs have been developed in industry. These methods supplement, rather than replace, the basic procedures described earlier in this book. Some typical examples of these techniques are discussed in this unit.

Powder metallurgy

In **powder metallurgy,** products are made from metal powders, sometimes mixed with nonmetal powders. The first step in powder metallurgy is blending the materials. Then this mixture is pressed into molds of the needed shape and size. The final step is **sintering,** heating the powder in a furnace without melting it (Fig. 68–1). This bonds the powder into a compact material with the right physical properties. Sintering can also occur at room temperature without pressure.

Powder metallurgy is used for many purposes. It is mostly used for making small parts. This is because the process requires very precise dies for doing the forming. Powder metallurgy can be used to make such special products as brake bands. It is often used to combine two metals that do not alloy well together. To make electrical parts for switches, nickel and silver are combined. Nickel has good wearing qualities, and silver is a good conductor. If these two metals were melted together to pour a casting, they would separate like oil and water. However, powder metallurgy makes it possible to combine them. It also makes it possible to combine and press powders so as to make a final product of any needed density. In addition, the powder-metallurgy process is economical. This is because there is no scrap and because machining and finishing are generally not required.

Chemical milling

In **chemical milling** (CHM) metals are shaped by chemically removing part of the metal through deep etching. This industrial process is similar to etching (see Unit 44). In chemical milling, the surface not to be machined is covered with **maskant,** a resistant material. In the next step, either the entire metal part is immersed in an etching solu-

Fig. 68-1 Four basic steps in producing a part by powder metallurgy.

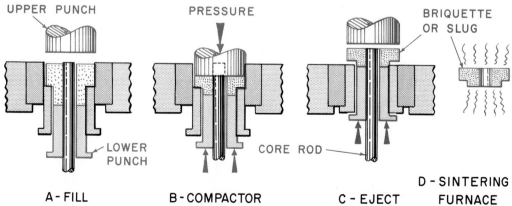

UPPER PUNCH   PRESSURE   BRIQUETTE OR SLUG

LOWER PUNCH   CORE ROD   D - SINTERING FURNACE

A - FILL   B - COMPACTOR   C - EJECT

tion or the acid is sprayed on. This eats away part of the metal not covered with maskant (Fig. 68-2). This method is used mostly to remove metal from irregular surfaces of castings, forgings, and extrusions. When chemical milling is applied to an aluminum casting, the resulting surface will not be smooth because aluminum castings are porous.

Chemical milling is practiced extensively throughout industry, particularly in aerospace manufacturing. The main advantages of chemical milling are that it can be used when the parts have complex shapes; when very hard, tough alloys must be shaped; when thin sections must be cut away; and when metal must be removed across a wide area to a very shallow depth.

Electrical-discharge machining

Electrical-discharge machining (EDM) removes metal by the discharge of a high-current, low-voltage electrical spark between an electrode tool and a workpiece (Fig. 68-3). A power supply provides a series of electrical impulses at a certain rate and voltage. The tool and workpiece are submerged in a circulating dielectric fluid. They are brought close together, and an electrical path forms between them through this fluid. This permits a high-density discharge of current. This discharge removes tiny particles from the surface of the workpiece. These particles are washed away by the fluid. The process continues until a cut or cavity is formed in the workpiece. The cut or cavity has the shape of the tool, but in reverse.

Fig. 68-2 Chemical milling.

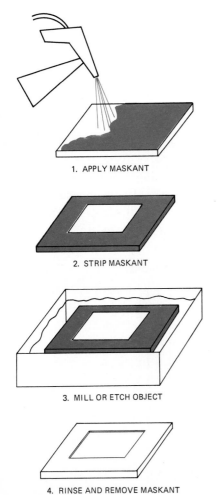

1. APPLY MASKANT

2. STRIP MASKANT

3. MILL OR ETCH OBJECT

4. RINSE AND REMOVE MASKANT

Fig. 68-3 Electrical-discharge machining.

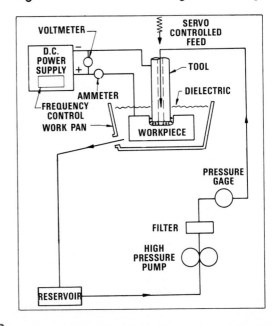

Electrochemical machining

Electrochemical machining (ECM) removes metal by electrolytic action. It is the opposite of electroplating. High-density direct current is passed through an electrolyte solution. This solution fills the gap between the workpiece, or anode, and the shaped tool, or cathode. The electrolyte is, in effect, a part of the tool. The electrochemical reaction removes the metal from the workpiece, ahead of the advancing tool.

Ultrasonic machining

Ultrasonic machining involves cutting materials with a tool and a slurry. A **slurry** is a liquid containing abrasive particles. Ultrasonic machining is a newer method developed for cutting hard materials quickly, economically, and accurately. The machine used has three major units: a frame with an adjustable table, a power and frequency generator, and a pump for circulating the slurry.

In operation, the pump circulates the slurry between the face of the tool and the workpiece. The power unit drives the tool, which moves up and down about 20,000 times per second. Under these conditions, the tool drives the slurry against the workpiece with great force. The abrasive particles do the cavitation, or cutting, by chipping away small pieces of the material (Fig. 68-4). Typical ultrasonic machining operations include drilling, shaving, slicing, and cutting unusual punch and die shapes. Materials such as metal, ceramics, glass, and plastics can be shaped by ultrasonic machining.

Explosive forming

Explosive forming is shaping metal by using dynamite or other explosives (Fig. 68-5). The dynamite bulges, or pushes out, the metal to an exact shape over a die. Equip-

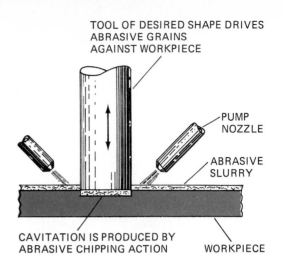

Fig. 68-4 Ultrasonic machining.

ment needed includes a tank of water, a die, a metal blank, and the explosive. The metal blank is placed over the die cavity. The air is then removed from the cavity itself. Next, the device is lowered into the liquid. Finally, the explosive charge is set off. The shock waves from the explosion force the metal into the die, shaping it in a split second. Three or four dies are usually needed to produce a particular shape.

Fig. 68-5 Explosive forming uses the force of an explosion to shape the work.

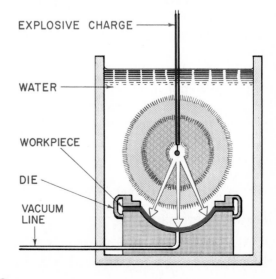

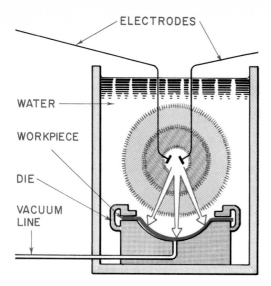

Fig. 68-6   Spark forming.

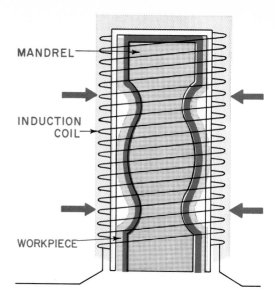

Fig. 68-7   Magnetic forming.

Spark forming

Spark forming is making objects by forcing flat blanks into a die (Fig. 68-6). The required force is provided by the vaporization of a small piece of special wire. An electrical charge is released and transmitted through heavy cables to the wire. When the electrical charge passes through the wire, its resistance is very great. This produces heat that causes the wire to vaporize. When a solid piece of wire is vaporized, its molecules expand rapidly. This rapid expansion has the same effect as the explosion in explosive forming.

The time needed for forming by this method is from 7 to 12 microseconds (millionths of a second). Tolerances are extremely fine. The spark method gives off less vibration than other methods. Thus, there is less disturbance to surrounding activities. Products formed by the spark method include large domes and fuel tanks for rockets.

Magnetic forming

Magnetic forming shapes metal through electromagnetic force. An induction coil is either wrapped around a workpiece or placed within it. Electrical current is sent through the coil, producing a strong magnetic force. This force presses the metal against a shaped mandrel (Fig. 68-7).

Gas forming

In **gas forming,** the combustion of gas is used to drive a ram. The ram moves at high speed and delivers a large amount of energy to the workpiece quickly (Fig. 68-8).

The metal workpiece is first placed in the die. Gas behind the ram is then ignited, driving the ram down on the workpiece with great force. The ram and die form the metal to the exact shape needed.

Gas forming can be used to make products as different as dishes and parts for space vehicles. The metal to be formed can range from a sheet of aluminum to hot metal.

Cold forming

Cold forming produces internal shapes with mandrels and dies without heat. The part to be formed is first drilled and then placed over a mandrel. The outside is then

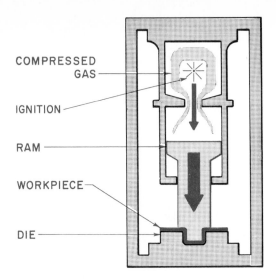

COMPRESSED GAS

IGNITION

RAM

WORKPIECE

DIE

Fig. 68-8   Gas forming.

squeezed by one or more rapidly moving dies. This causes the metal to flow into the correct shape. This method produces complex internal shapes with little or no waste of material (Fig. 68–9).

Orbital forging

Orbital forging is a cold-working method in which metal is pushed out or down into a lower die, depending on the die shape, by a rotating upper die. The upper die is set on a slant. Thus, as it turns, it touches only a small part of the metal at any one time. As a result, forming is gradual and takes far less pressure then a hydraulic press would need to do the same job. Orbital forging also needs no heat or lubrication. With no die-to-metal impact, it is quiet.

The main details on a part, such as the teeth on a gear, are usually formed in the lower die. However, simple contours, such as indented or crowned areas, can be formed on the top surface of a part by the upper die.

Orbital forging is especially useful for making small parts, bevel and face gears, and circular parts.

Photochemical machining

Photochemical machining, or **photoforming,** removes metal by combining photography with chemical etching. This process is related to chemical milling and electrochemical machining. Photochemical machining forms metals into very thin, flat, complex shapes. Large quantities of parts with precise tolerances can be produced.

This technique does not require blanking or piercing tools. It eliminates such defects as tool marks, deformation, and burrs. Machine setup costs are avoided with the photochemical process. Yet the shape or complexity of the end product is in no way restricted.

Most metals and alloys can be photochemically etched. However, special rolling, heat-treating, and annealing techniques produce metal strip and foil particularly well suited to photochemical etching. This metal has qualities such as small grain size and minimum waviness.

The photochemical process has several basic steps, most performed as separate operations. These are precleaning, coating and curing, printing, developing, etching, stripping, and inspection.

Fig. 68–9   A hydraulic press forms cold metal into hard-to-shape parts using extreme hydrostatic pressure. (Western Electric Company)

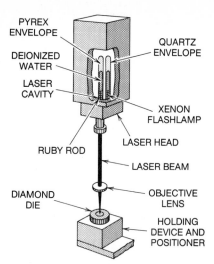

Fig. 68–10 A laser cutting a hole in a diamond die.

Lasers

The laser, one of the major scientific developments, has caused great changes, not only in manufacturing, but also in medicine, communications, and merchandising. The laser was invented by two people named Townes and Schawlow in 1958.

The term *laser* is an abbreviation for *l*ight *a*mplification by *s*timulated *e*mission of *r*adiation. The **laser** produces a very narrow intensive beam of light that can be focused on a spot that is very small in diameter. The way a laser beam operates can be compared with the way a magnifying glass operates when it is used to direct the rays of the sun onto a bonfire to get it started—the intense heat from the small beam of light ignites the wood. The laser produces heat of over 7500°F (4150°C). This concentrated energy will penetrate a variety of materials.

Because the laser ray can be concentrated on such a small spot, it can be used for various manufacturing processes such as cutting, drilling, etching, and welding. All types of materials, including metal, wood, plastic, rubber, and cork, can be cut with the laser beam to very precise designs.

A laser is also used for drilling many different materials, some of which are almost impossible to drill by any other method. For example, the laser can drill (cut) a hole in a diamond die (Fig. 68–10). The laser is also widely used to etch materials. Etching can be done on all kinds of materials. The laser is also very useful in welding difficult materials such as titanium.

Another use of the laser is to measure electronically the sizes of products as they are produced. The laser is used in communications such as the lightwave system that is replacing copper wire to carry telephone messages.

 QUESTIONS

1. What is sintering?
2. Chemical milling is similar to what other process?
3. What shape is the cavity that forms in the workpiece during electrical-discharge machining?
4. Of what is electrochemical machining the opposite?
5. What is a slurry?
6. Name the two forming methods that require an explosive force.
7. What metal-forming method is based on electromagnetic force?
8. What metal-forming method is based on combustion?
9. What metal-forming method is excellent for producing complex internal shapes?
10. What forging method is accomplished without the high noise level usually associated with metal forming?
11. What are the steps in the photochemical-machining process?
12. What do the letters in *laser* stand for?

 EXTRA CREDIT

Write a report, based on recent magazine articles, on the latest developments in laser technology.

SECTION 9

HEAT TREATING AND MATERIALS TESTING

Unit 69
Heat-Treating Metals

After you have machined a center punch, forged out a cold chisel, or made any other small tool, you will find that it is useless until it is heat-treated. **Heat treating** is bringing a metal workpiece to a high temperature to change its properties (Fig. 69–1). The high temperature affects the metal's **grain structure,** a basic physical characteristic. Metal atoms are arranged in characteristic crystal structures. These, in turn, join together to form tiny grains arranged like closely fitting blocks. The effect of heat treating on these grains is usually to either harden or soften the metal. Careful heat treating can give the metal specific properties, such as hardness, toughness, and the like, needed to do a job.

The basic steps in heat treating are:

    1. *Heating* to the right temperature.

    2. *Soaking,* or holding, at this temperature for a certain length of time.

    3. *Cooling* in a way that will give the desired results.

In the school shop, heat treating can be a very simple process that requires few tools. In industry, however, it is a highly scientific operation and takes special equipment.

Fig. 69–1 Heat-treating a part by inserting it in a furnace. Note the safety clothing.

In this section, only the elementary information about heat-treating steel is included. If you want specific information on a particular kind of steel, refer to *The New American Machinist's Handbook*[1] or to *Machinery's Handbook.*[2]

[1]Rupert LeGrand (ed.), McGraw-Hill Book Company, New York, 1955.
[2]Holbrook Horton (ed.), 20th ed., The Industrial Press, New York, 1975.

Heat treatment can also be done on such nonferrous metals as aluminum, copper, and brass (see Unit 40). The process of heat-treating these metals is different, however, and will not be considered here.

The basic heat-treating processes are hardening, tempering, annealing, and case hardening. Each is described in this unit.

Equipment for heat treating

All heat-treating processes use the same basic equipment:

1. A *heat-treating furnace* is best, but a blowtorch, gas-welding torch, forge, or soldering furnace are all good sources of heat (Fig. 69–2).

2. The *quenching bath* can be a pail or other container of fresh water, tempering oil, or brine (salt water).

3. *Forging tongs* are needed to hold the hot metal.

Hardening

Hardening is heating and then cooling steel to give it a fine-grained structure. This process reduces the steel's **ductility,** or ability to be deformed without breaking. It increases its **hardness,** or degree of firmness and strength. It also increases the steel's **tensile strength,** or the amount of stress that it can stand without breaking. Products are hardened to produce sharp-edged cutting tools, to make bearing surfaces wear better, to put the "spring" in a spring, and for many other reasons.

Hardening is done in a furnace fired by oil, gas, or electricity. The metal must first be heated and then rapidly cooled. As steel is heated, a physical and chemical reaction takes place between the iron and carbon in it. The **critical point** or **temperature** is the point at which the steel has the best characteristics. When steel reaches this temperature, which is somewhere between 1400 and 1600°F (760 and 870°C), it is in the ideal

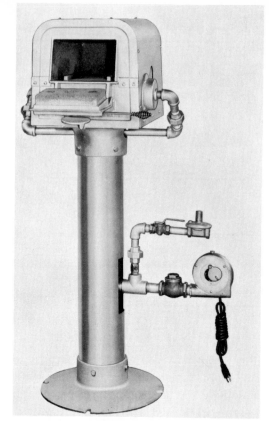

Fig. 69–2   A gas-fired heat-treating furnace that will operate at temperatures of 300 to 2400°F (150 to 1315°C). It can be used for hardening, tempering, and annealing small objects.

condition to make a hard, strong material if cooled quickly.

The critical temperature can be checked by testing with a magnet, by using a pyrometer, or sometimes by observing the color. When a piece of steel is below critical temperature, it is magnetic. When it reaches critical temperature, it is nonmagnetic. The *pyrometer,* an electric thermometer attached to the furnace, accurately registers the temperature in the furnace (Fig. 69–3). Formerly, temperature was determined by observing the color of the hot metal. This is not a very accurate method, however. Even

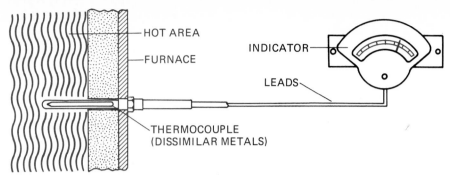

Fig. 69-3 The pyrometer accurately tells the temperature inside the furnace. The thermocouple is inserted in the back of the furnace with leads running to the indicator.

the estimate of an expert can be far off the true temperature.

After the metal reaches the critical temperature, it is **quenched,** or cooled by being plunged into oil, water, or brine. This is done so that the metal will retain the desirable characteristics. If the metal is allowed to cool slowly, it changes back to its original state. When hardened, the metal is very hard and strong and less ductile than it was before.

Exact critical temperatures and quenching procedures are explained in *The New American Machinist's Handbook* and *Machinery's Handbook.*

The procedure for hardening is as follows:

1. Light the furnace, and let it heat up to hardening temperature.

2. Put the metal in the furnace, and heat it to critical temperature. For example, heat high-carbon AISI C1095, a water-hardening carbon steel, to about 1475 to 1500°F (802 to 816°C). (See Unit 7 for an explanation of the AISI system of identifying steels.) For high-carbon steels, allow about *20 to 30 minutes* per inch (25 mm) of thickness for the metal to come up to heat. Allow about *10 to 15 minutes* per inch (25 mm) of thickness for soaking at the hardening temperature.

3. Choose the right cooling solution. Some steels can be cooled in water, while others must be cooled in oil, brine, or air. *Fresh water* is used most often for quenching carbon steels because it is inexpensive and effective. *Brine* is made by adding about 5 to 10 percent common salt to water. Brine helps produce a more uniform hardness. This is because it wets the parts all over more quickly. *Oil* is used for a somewhat slower quenching. It reduces the tendency of steel to warp or crack. Most oils used for quenching are mineral oils. *Air* at room temperature is used to cool steel by merely removing it from the furnace. The steel cools fast enough to harden.

4. Remove the hot metal with tongs, and plunge it into the cooling solution. Agitate the metal by moving it about in a figure eight to cool it quickly and evenly. If the piece is thin, such as a knife blade, plunge the thin edge into the cooling solution as though cutting it. This will keep the project from warping. If one side cools faster than the other, it will surely warp. Never just drop the metal into the quenching bath. If you do this, the heat will create a coating of vapor around the metal that will keep it from cooling quickly.

5. Check for hardness. A correctly hardened piece will be hard and brittle and have high tensile strength. Test this by running a new file across the corner of the work. If it is hard, the file will not cut in or take hold.

Tempering

Tempering, or **drawing,** is reducing hardness and increasing toughness. It removes brittleness from a hardened piece and gives a more fine-grained structure.

Tempering is done by (1) reheating the metal after it has been hardened to a low or moderate temperature and (2) quenching it in air. The tempering heat can be determined by watching the pyrometer or by observing the **temper colors.** As the metal is heated for tempering, it changes color. You can tell by the color about when the correct heat is reached.

Many project parts are completely tempered. Others, such as the cold chisel, are only partly tempered.

The procedures for tempering are as follows:

1. To temper the whole piece, put it in a furnace. Reheat it to the right temperature for producing the degrees of hardness and toughness needed (Table 69-1). Then remove the piece, and cool it quickly. For example, heat water-hardening carbon steel to 425 to 590°F (218 to 310°C), and cool it in water.

2. To temper small cutting tools such as cold chisels, center punches, and prick punches:

a. Harden the whole tool.

b. Clean off the scale near the point or cutting edge with abrasive cloth.

c. Heat a piece of scrap metal until it is red-hot. Place it on a welding or soldering table.

d. Put the tool on the hot metal, with the point extending beyond it.

e. Watch the temper colors. When the right color reaches the point of the tool, quench it in water.

3. Another method of tempering small tools is the following:

a. Fill a metal box with sand.

b. Heat the underside of the box with a gas torch (Fig. 69-4).

c. Clean the hardened tool with abrasive cloth. Place it in the sand, with the point sticking out.

d. Watch the temper colors travel toward the point as the tool absorbs heat.

e. When the right color reaches the point, remove the tool with tongs, and quench it.

4. To temper a knife blade, clean one side of the blade with abrasive cloth. Pack the cutting edge with heat-resistant material. (Note that this has traditionally been done with wet asbestos. However, this substance has been found to be hazardous to health. Substitutes for it are now being devised.) Heat the back of the blade with a bunsen burner or welding torch until the right temper color runs toward the edge. Quench in water.

Table 69-1
Temper Colors of Common Tools

Tools	Color	°F	°C
scriber, scrapers, and hammer faces	pale yellow	430–450	220–230
center punches, drills	full yellow	470	245
cold chisels, drifts	brown	490–510	255–265
screwdrivers	purple	530	275

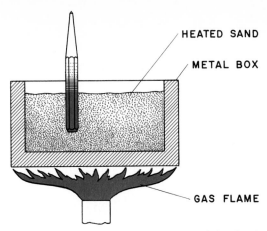

HEATED SAND

METAL BOX

GAS FLAME

Fig. 69-4 Notice that the body of the tool has been inserted in the sand and that heat is being applied to the metal box.

Fig. 69-5 Moving the point of the tool in the quenching solution.

5. To harden and temper small tools at the same time, first heat the tool to critical temperature. Then put only the point of the tool in the quenching solution, and agitate the point (Fig. 69-5). Remove the tool, and quickly clean the point with abrasive cloth. Remember that the handle of the tool will be very hot. Now, watch the temper colors move toward the point. When the right color reaches the point, quench only the point of the tool.

Annealing

Annealing is softening metal to relieve internal strain and to make the metal easier to shape and cut. The metal is heated to the critical temperature and cooled *slowly*. The slower the cooling, the softer the metal becomes. Metals often develop stresses during manufacture. Such stresses can cause steel to warp and castings to warp or crack if not relieved. Metals must often be annealed when they come from the rolling mills or foundry. Annealing gives metals good grain structure and thus makes them easier to machine.

Normalizing is done to put steel in a normal condition again after forging or incorrect heat treating. The steel is heated above the hardening temperature, then cooled in air. This process is very similar to annealing.

You may want to anneal an old file or spring so that you can use the metal to make another project. To do this, heat the article to critical temperature (Table 69-1). Then allow it to cool by one of the following methods:

1. Place it in a pail of sand.

2. Turn off the furnace, and allow the article to cool in it.

3. Clamp the article between two pieces of hot metal, and allow it to cool in air.

Case hardening

Case hardening is hardening the outer surface of ferrous-metal objects. This surface is the **case.** If you add a small amount of carbon to the case of low-carbon steel during heat treating, the case will become hard. However, the core will remain soft and ductile. Case hardening is done to produce parts such as screws for machines, hand tools, and ball and roller bearings. Many methods of case hardening are used in industry. *Cyaniding,* a common one, involves placing steel in molten cyanide. This is very dangerous, however, and cannot be done in school shops. Another case-hardening process, *nitriding,* consists of soaking the part in an oven containing ammonia gas at about 950°F (510°C). The part is then allowed to cool slowly. In *carburizing,* a third industrial method, carbon is added to the steel from the surface inward. The carbon is obtained from one or a combination of the following:

- Wood charcoal.
- Animal charcoal.
- Coke.
- Beans or nuts.
- Charred bone or leather.
- Kasenit (trade name for a nonpoisonous coke compound).

The carbon is added to the steel by the pack, gas, or liquid-salt methods. You will learn to do simple carburizing by the pack method.

The procedure for case hardening using the pack method of carburizing with Kasenit is as follows:

1. Put the project in a metal box or pot, with the Kasenit surrounding the project.

2. Place the receptacle in the furnace, and heat it to about 1650°F (900°C).

3. Leave the box in the furnace 15 to 60 minutes. The mild steel will absorb carbon to a depth of as much as 0.015 inch (0.38 mm).

4. Remove the box with its contents. Take out the project, and quench it. Only the case will harden. The inner core will be relatively soft.

This procedure can be used on hammer heads, piston pins, and other items that must stand a good deal of shock and wear. Case hardening should never be done on products that must be sharpened.

Heat treating in industry

In industry, heat treating is a highly scientific process. It makes available steel with the best properties for each kind of product.

The engineer, technican, and skilled metalworker must know a great deal about the principles of heat treating. The fundamental principles are the same as in the heat treating done in the school laboratory or shop. However, many special procedures and a great deal of specialized equipment are involved. Industry uses large continuous furnaces equipped to provide automatic control for temperature and time. The pieces to be heat-treated move on a conveyor to the furnace. They are held there for the right length of time. They are then plunged into quenching baths. Then the necessary tempering is also done.

Three interesting methods for hardening metal surfaces by heat treating are used in industry. They are induction hardening, flame hardening, and laser hardening.

In **induction hardening,** the metal is put inside a coiled wire in which a current of low voltage and high amperage is flowing (Fig. 69-6). A current is thereby induced in

Fig. 69-6 Closeup of an induction-hardening machine.

Fig. 69-7 A flame-hardening machine. (Cincinnati Milling Machine Company)

Fig. 69-8 A cutaway photograph of an automobile steering knuckle. Note how flame hardening has produced a darker hardened surface where there are threads.

In **laser hardening,** the metal is heated with a laser (see Unit 68). This method is used, for example, on the area around the valve opening in a cylinder block. The block is placed in a revolving table. A laser beam is focused on the valve opening as the table turns. After the hardening temperature is reached, the block is removed from the table and the surface is air-cooled.

the surface of the metal, and it heats quickly. When the hardening temperature is reached, the current is turned off. The heated surface is rapidly quenched with a spray of water. The time required is only 2 seconds. Moreover, the area hardened can be kept very small. Only the surface of the metal is hardened. The core remains both tough and soft. The same equipment can be used for annealing, brazing, soldering, tempering, and other processes.

In **flame hardening,** the metal is heated with an oxy-acetylene flame (Fig. 69-7). Either the torch or the workpiece moves along slowly so that a thin surface layer of metal is heated. Cooling is done with a stream of water or by dropping the workpiece into a quenching tank, which hardens the surface quickly. With this process, only part of the workpiece is hardened. The remainder stays in an annealed condition (Fig. 69-8). This process is particularly useful when only part of a large casting needs to be hardened. For example, on some metal lathes, the ways of the lathe bed are flame hardened.

 QUESTIONS

1. What is heat treating?
2. What are its three basic steps?
3. Name four good sources of heat for heat treating.
4. What liquids can be used to make a quenching bath?
5. What do you call the temperature at which steel has the best characteristics?
6. How can you tell when metal has reached the correct heat for tempering?
7. At what pace is metal cooled during annealing?
8. What is the condition of the core of a steel piece after case hardening?
9. List three industrial methods for hardening metal surfaces by heat treating.

 EXTRA CREDIT

1. Report on the methods used to heat-treat metals used in some familiar products.
2. Find out all you can about how case hardening is done in industry.

Unit 70
Hardness Testing

The term *hardness* suggests the solidity, firmness, and strength of a metal. It refers to strength, wearability, and resistance to erosion. Hard materials are difficult to cut or form into different shapes. Because hardness is not clearly defined, no single measure of hardness can be applied to all materials. Ways of describing hardness include:

- *Wear hardness*—resistance to abrasion, such as by sand blasting.
- *Scratch hardness*—measured in tests used by mineralogists. Heat treaters formerly pressed a new file across the corner of the metal. They could tell about how hard the metal was by the look of the scratch. You can estimate hardness in this way.
- *Machinability*—resistance to cutting or drilling, as determined by special tests.
- *Indentation hardness*—based on the fact that a hard object will dent a soft one. Indentation-hardness tests are the most widely used in testing most metals. They are nondestructive (although they do mar a finished surface), inexpensive, and easy to perform. Four tests most commonly used are the Brinell, the Rockwell, the Vickers, and the Shore. The test selected depends on the specific application and the condition and size of the metal.

Hardness tests are used to compare the hardness of similar metals under similar conditions. In all indentation-hardness tests, a specimen, usually flat, is placed on a rigid platform. An object called an *indenter* or *penetrator* is pressed into the specimen under load. Depending on the kind of test, a hardness reading is made from either the depth or the size of the dent made. The four basic hardness tests are described in this unit.

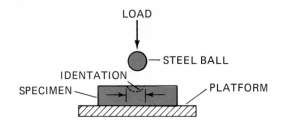

Fig. 70-1 The Brinell hardness test.

Brinell hardness

The *Brinell hardness test* is a method used for testing specimens about 1/4 inch (6 mm) or more in thickness. The testing method is illustrated in Fig. 70-1. The test consists of pressing a hardened steel ball into a metal specimen. It is customary to use a ball with a 10-millimeter (0.39-inch) diameter. The load depends on the material being tested. A load of 3000 kilograms (6614 pounds) is commonly used for medium-hard alloys. A load of 500 kilograms (1102 pounds) is used for soft metals. The diameter of the impression made by the ball is measured with a microscope. It is then converted from a chart to a Brinell hardness number (BHN). The measured hardness is stated as 250 BHN or 100 BHN, for example. The narrower the dent, the higher the number and the harder the metal. This test is best for soft and medium-hard materials (Fig. 70-2).

Fig. 70-2 Measuring the hardness of an aircraft forging with a Brinell tester. (Aluminum Company of America)

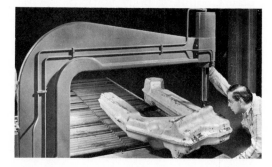

Fig. 70-3 A Rockwell hardness tester with solid-state digital readout. (American Chain and Cable Company)

Rockwell hardness

In the *Rockwell hardness test*, the depth of penetration is used as a measure of hardness. It is fast and easy because the readings are shown directly on a machine (Fig. 70-3). Smaller specimens can be tested better by this method than by the Brinell method. Several kinds of indenters and loads can be used, depending on the specimen. One method is shown in Fig. 70-4.

The Rockwell B and C scales are most commonly used. The B scale uses a 1/16-inch (1.5-mm) steel-ball penetrator and a

Fig. 70-4 The Rockwell hardness test, showing a cone penetrator.

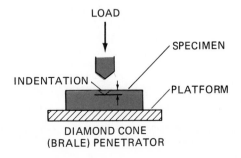

100-kilogram (220-pound) load. The C scale uses a diamond-cone penetrator called a Brale, and a 150-kilogram (331-pound) load. The B scale is for testing materials of medium hardness. Its working range is from 0 to 100 RB. If the ball penetrator is used to test material harder than about 100 RB, it might flatten. Also the ball is not as sensitive as the cone to small differences in hardness.

The Rockwell superficial-hardness tester is a special-purpose machine developed for testing thin sheet metal. It operates on the same principle as the standard Rockwell machine. However, it uses lighter loads and a more sensitive measuring system. Other Rockwell-type machines have been developed for special uses (Fig. 70-5).

Fig. 70-5 A portable hardness tester. (American Chain and Cable Company)

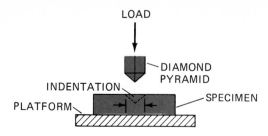

LOAD

DIAMOND PYRAMID

INDENTATION

PLATFORM

SPECIMEN

Fig. 70–6   The Vickers hardness test.

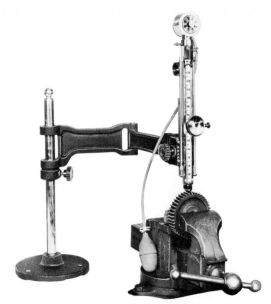

Fig. 70–7   Using the Shore scleroscope to test the hardness of a gear.

Vickers hardness

The *Vickers hardness test* is very precise. It is used mainly as a research tool. As shown in Fig. 70–6, it is similar to the Brinell test. The penetrator is a square-based diamond pyramid. Loads may vary from 1 to 120 kilograms (2.2 to 265 pounds). The square impression made by the penetrator is measured with a microscope. The reading is taken from a reference table that gives the Vickers hardness number, such as 220 VHN or 220 DPH (diamond-pyramid hardness). Vickers test results are slightly higher than those from Brinell tests. Very thin sections of metal may be tested by using small loads.

Shore-scleroscope hardness

The *Shore-scleroscope hardness test* is based on the following principle: If you were to place a mattress on the floor and drop two rubber balls from the same height, one on the mattress and one on the floor, the one dropped on the floor would bounce higher. This is because the floor is the harder of the two surfaces.

In the Shore-scleroscope hardness test, a diamond-pointed hammer is dropped onto the test piece and the rebound, or bounce, is checked on a scale. The higher the rebound, the higher the number on the scale and the harder the metal (Fig. 70–7). The Shore scleroscope is portable and can be used to test pieces too big for other testing machines. Another advantage of the Shore scleroscope

is that it can be used without damaging finished surfaces. The main disadvantage of this machine is its relative inaccuracy. Samples without rigid backing and oddly shaped or hollow workpieces may give incorrect readings.

 QUESTIONS

1. What is the principle behind indentation-hardness tests?
2. In the Brinell test, what does it mean if the steel ball makes a wider dent in one speciman than in another?
3. In the Rockwell test, what is used as the measure of hardness?
4. What is the main use of the Vickers test?
5. In the Shore test, what is used as the measure of hardness?

 EXTRA CREDIT

Write a research report on industrial methods of testing hardness.

Unit 71
Testing Metal Properties

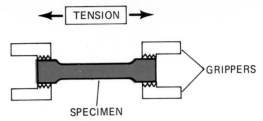

Fig. 71-1 The tensile test.

In metalworking, when force is used to change the shape of a metal, the metal workpiece is said to have been **strained,** or **deformed.** Metals are usually very different after being strained. Strained metal, however, can be restored to an unstrained condition by heating to a high temperature.

Metal can change its shape in three ways when force is applied. First, the metal can change shape while the force is being applied but return to its original shape when the force is removed. This temporary change is called **elastic deformation.** It occurs, for example, when a coil spring is stretched. The spring returns to its original length as soon as the force is removed. Second, a metal can change shape when force is applied and remain in the new shape when the force is removed. This permanent change is called **plastic deformation.** It can occur, for example, when a coil spring is overloaded. Plastic deformation always takes more force than elastic deformation. The third way a metal can change shape is simply by *breaking.* More force is needed for breaking than for either elastic or plastic deformation.

Metal-forming operations change the shape of metal permanently, so they are classified as plastic deformation. The movement of the metal to form a permanent new shape is called **plastic flow.** The forces that cause plastic flow are greater than the forces that cause elastic deformation, but less than the force that causes breaking. The range between elastic deformation and the breaking point is called the **plastic range** of a material. All forming is done in the plastic range. In order to make sure that a metal can be formed, its properties must be tested. You have already learned about hardness in metal and how to test for it. Now you will learn about some other important properties and how to test for them.

Tensile strength

Tensile strength is the maximum *stress,* or force, that a material can withstand before it fractures. Testing for tensile strength is one of the best ways of evaluating metals. The test involves pulling the metal specimen, that is, placing it under tension (Fig. 71-1). The specimen is mounted in a machine that applies a slowly increasing load (Fig. 71-2). This load is measured in customary measurements as pounds of force and in metric measurements as newtons of force. It is recorded throughout the test. Stress is computed from the force and the original cross-sectional area of the specimen. In using customary measurements, stress in pounds per square inch is derived from this formula:

$$\text{Stress (psi)} = \frac{\text{force (pounds)}}{\text{area (square inches)}}$$

In using metric measurements, stress in pascals is derived from this formula:

$$\text{Stress (Pa)} = \frac{\text{force (newtons)}}{\text{area (square meters)}}$$

As the test progresses and the load increases, the specimen stretches until it breaks (Fig. 71-3). This stretching is called

Fig. 71-2 In tensile testing, the sample is mounted in a machine that applies a slowly increasing load. (W. C. Dillon & Company)

Fig. 71-3 This material sample was just broken in a tensile test.

strain. Strain is recorded continuously throughout the test. Strain expressed as a percentage is called **elongation.** Elongation is the percentage of increase in length of the test specimen.

If a metal part is stretched until it becomes permanently deformed, it can be just as useless as if it were broken. The greatest stress a metal can stand without permanent deformation is called the **elastic limit.**

Tensile testing has become fairly well standardized. The size and shape of the specimen depends on the product. Examples are bar, sheet, strip, plate, and tube. Using customary measurements, a round bar specimen with a 0.505-inch diameter has a cross-sectional area of 0.20 square inches. This is a convenient figure for calculating stress from load. For example, if the specimen breaks under a load of 20,000 pounds:

$$\text{Stress} = \frac{20{,}000 \text{ lbs.}}{0.20 \text{ sq. in.}} = 100{,}000 \text{ psi}$$

Using metric measurements, a round bar specimen with a 10-millimeter diameter has a cross-sectional area of 78.5 square millimeters. If the specimen breaks under a load of 89 000 newtons:

$$\text{Stress} = \frac{89\,000 \text{ N}}{0.0785 \text{ m}^2} = 1\,133\,758 \text{ Pa}$$

Specimens for testing sheet, strip, and plate also have standard dimensions. When tubes are tested, the actual tube is used if it is small enough.

The elongation that a metal specimen undergoes during a tensile test is a measure of its ductility. **Ductility** is the ability of a metal to be deformed without breaking. In other words, it is the ability of a metal to be formed by cold-working methods such as bending, deep drawing, spinning, or cold

378

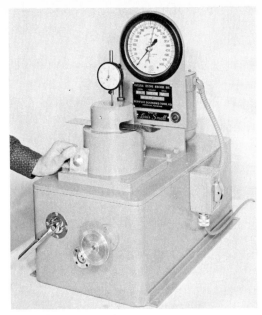

Fig. 71-4 The ductility tester and a test specimen. (Louis Small Company)

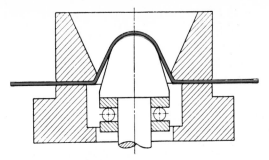

Fig. 71-5 The ductility test.

A compressive test is run on the same machine and in the same general way as a tensile test. However, the force is applied in the opposite direction. In other words, the specimen is pushed together instead of being pulled apart (Fig. 71-6). However, the properties tested are similar. The major exception is that for ductile materials such as steels, a final compressive strength cannot be obtained. This is because the sample keeps compressing until it is flat. Compression tests are usually run on materials such as cast iron or other similar metals.

Compression properties are used in the design of machine parts, structures, and air-

Fig. 71-6 The compression test.

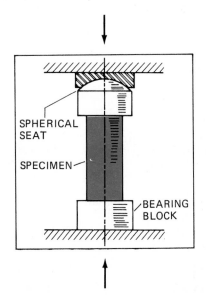

heading. A combination of strength and ductility in a metal is an excellent indication of its suitability for engineering uses (Fig. 71-4). In the *Olsen ductility test,* a piece of sheet metal is deformed by a standard steel punch with a rounded end. The depth of the impression required to fracture the metal is measured in thousandths of an inch (0.001 inch). In the *Erichsen test,* the depth of impression at fracture is measured in thousandths of a millimeter (0.001 mm). The sheet is held between two ring-shaped clamping dies while a dome-shaped punch is forced against it until fracture occurs (Fig. 71-5). The height of the dome is measured by a dial gage.

Compression strength

Compression strength is the maximum compressive force a material can withstand before it fractures. It is measured in pounds per square inch (psi) in the customary system and in pascals (Pa) in the metric system.

craft parts. In many of these applications, selection of the material depends on both strength and stiffness.

Shear strength

Shear strength is the maximum load a material can withstand when that load is applied vertically to the material's surface. It is measured in pounds per square inch (psi) in the customary system and in pascals (Pa) in the metric system. An example of a material under shear stress is a sheet of paper being cut by scissors. The paper is fractured, or cut, because the blades of the scissors apply a stress that is equal to the shear strength of the paper. Bolts and rivets are often exposed to stresses that are similar to the cutting action of scissors. Material used for such parts must have good shear strength.

There are two kinds of shear testing: *double* and *single*. Both types are illustrated by the riveted joints in Fig. 71–7. The double-lap joint (A) is commonly used to connect three pieces of metal. If forces act on this joint in the directions shown by the arrows, the rivet is in double shear. If these forces are

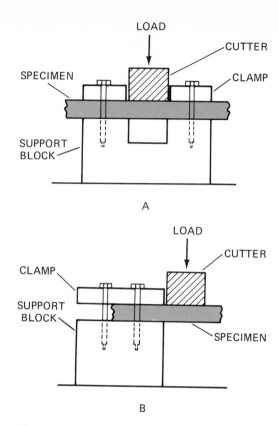

Fig. 71–8 (A) Double-shear and (B) single-shear tests.

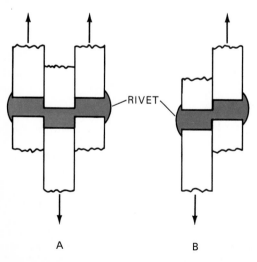

Fig. 71–7   Shear strength is a property required of bolts and rivets.

greater than the double-shear strength of the rivet, it will be cut in two places. The rivet in the single-lap joint (B) is in single shear.

Double-shear strength is measured by mounting a bar specimen in a jig, as shown in Fig. 71–8A. It is placed on the table of a tensile-testing machine. A rectangular cutter on the movable head of the machine contacts the specimen directly over the groove in the block. To reduce bending of the specimen, the clearance between the cutter and groove is small, usually about 0.005 inch (0.13 mm). For accurate results, the edges of both the cutter and the supporting block must be sharp.

To find a specimen's double-shear strength, divide the load required to fracture the specimen by twice the specimen's cross-sectional area. For example, using customary measurements, if a specimen 1/4 inch thick and 1 inch wide breaks under a load of 25,000 pounds, the strength in double shear is as follows:

$$\frac{25,000 \text{ lbs.}}{0.5 \text{ sq. in.}} = 50,000 \text{ psi}$$

In another example, using metric measurements, if a specimen 6 millimeters thick and 25 millimeters wide breaks under a force of 10 000 newtons, the strength in double shear is as follows:

$$\frac{10\ 000 \text{ N}}{0.150 \text{ m}^2} = 66\ 667 \text{ Pa}$$

Testing for single-shear strength is the same as for double-shear strength except that only one end of the specimen is supported (Fig. 71–8B).

Impact strength

Impact strength is the ability of a piece of metal to withstand a hard blow or sudden shock without breaking. This strength is necessary for many applications, such as drilling equipment and automotive and aerospace engines, where shocks occur.

A tensile test is a good measure of metal toughness. However, in this test, the load is increased slowly, not suddenly as in a blow. Thus, it cannot measure impact strength. Special impact tests have been developed to measure the toughness of materials under shock loads. Two of the most common are the *Izod test* and the *Charpy test*. Both are based on the same principle. A pendulum strikes a sharp blow on a specimen, bending or breaking it (Fig. 71–9). Results of the tests are reported as impact strength, measured in foot-pounds (ft-lb) in the customary system and in newton-meters (N·m) in the metric

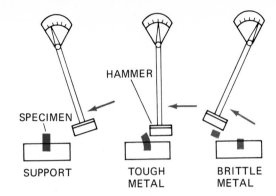

Fig. 71–9 An impact test.

system. This strength is computed from the weight of the pendulum and the difference between the rise of a free-swinging pendulum and the rise of a pendulum that has struck a specimen.

Both Izod and Charpy specimens are notched. The notch is included because a plain flat bar of a ductile material will not generally break with a single blow in these tests. The notches are always carefully machined to standard specifications.

The specimen, method of support, and energy of the pendulum are all quite different for the Izod and Charpy tests. Thus, the test used must always be identified, and results from the two tests cannot be compared. In the Izod test, the specimen is clamped in a vertical position as a cantilever beam. The Charpy specimen is a simple beam supported at the ends (Fig. 71–10).

These tests are most useful for comparing materials of similar strengths and for evaluating the effects of heat treatment, processing variables, or temperature on the same type of material.

Fatigue strength

Fatigue strength is the ability of metal to withstand changing loads without breaking. Such loads occur, for example, in the buffeting of airplane wings and in the pushing and pulling of the connecting rods in piston en-

381

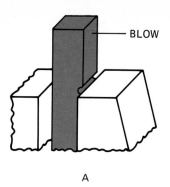

BLOW

A

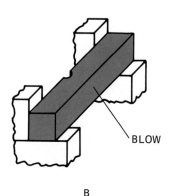

BLOW

B

Fig. 71-10 Support arrangements for (A) the Izod test and (B) the Charpy test.

gines. These push-pull applications of force and on-off applications of pressure are called *cyclic* loads.

During the useful lives of machines that move rapidly and parts that are subjected to severe vibrations, load changes may occur billions of times. Metal fatigue is thought by many to be the most common cause of failure. In fatigue tests, failure is always a brittle fracture. *Fatigue life* is the number of cycles a material can withstand at a specified stress without failure.

There are a variety of fatigue tests, depending on the kind of load applied and the

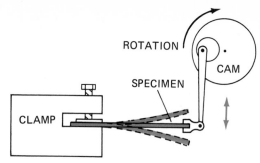

ROTATION

CAM

SPECIMEN

CLAMP

Fig. 71-11 The cantilever fatigue test.

shape of the specimen. One of the most common is the *cantilever test*. This utilizes the Krouse testing machine to test sheet, strip, and thin plate. One end of the specimen is held rigidly while the other is free to move. A rotating cam moves the free end of the specimen up and down until fatigue occurs and the specimen breaks (Fig. 71-11). Stress and number of cycles are recorded automatically.

 QUESTIONS

1. What is the difference between elastic deformation and plastic deformation?
2. In tensile testing, what is applied to the metal specimen?
3. In a compressive test, in what direction is force applied to the metal specimen?
4. What is shear strength?
5. Name the two tests for impact strength.
6. What kind of loads can a metal with fatigue strength withstand?

 EXTRA CREDIT

Write a research report on accidents or disasters caused by metal fatigue or other metal failure.

SECTION 10

FASTENING METHODS

Unit 72

Introduction to Welding and Oxygen Cutting

Welding is fastening metals together using intense heat and sometimes pressure (Fig. 72–1). It is a very economical process and is used in both manufacturing and repair work. When the operation involves heat alone, it is called **fusion welding.** Two kinds of fusion welding are gas welding and arc welding. Using heat and pressure is called

Fig. 72–1 Welding is joining metal parts with heat and sometimes pressure. This illustration shows arc welding. (Hobart Brothers Company)

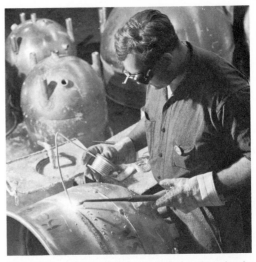

Fig. 72–2 Gas welding is used extensively for making cooking utensils. (Aluminum Company of America)

resistance welding. Closely related to welding is **oxygen cutting,** also called **flame cutting.** In this process, operators use torches to cut metal to shape and size.

Gas welding, one kind of fusion welding, uses a hot flame with a temperature of 6300°F (3480°C) that is produced by burning oxygen and acetylene in a welding torch (Fig. 72–2). The welder heats the metal part by holding the flame near the metal until a molten puddle forms. Then the welder applies a welding rod to build up the weld. Gas welders must know how to choose the right torch tip and welding rod. They must know how to adjust regulators to get the right flame and how to use the torch properly.

Fig. 72-3 Arc-welding a frame for a heavy piece of machinery.

Arc welding, another kind of fusion welding, uses electric power from either an electric generator or a transformer (Fig. 72-3). An *electrode,* which is similar to the welding rod used in gas welding, provides the metal filler for the weld. One cable from the power source is connected to the metal welding table or to the object itself. The other is connected to the holder that holds the electrode. The welder first strikes an arc by touching the metal part to be welded with the electrode. Then the welder withdraws the electrode a short distance from the metal surface, creating an electric arc. The arc produces a heat of about 9000°F (4980°C). This heat melts the metals and also the electrode. The welder moves the electrode along, and feeds it into, the joint. When the electrode is used up, a new one is slipped into the holder, and welding continues. An arc welder must know how to adjust the electric power, how to choose the right electrode, and how to do the welding.

In resistance welding, which uses both heat and pressure, the heat is generated by resistance to the flow of electric current. In manufacturing, resistance welding is done with a machine that brings metal parts together under heat and pressure. The operator merely sets the controls to the correct electric current and pressure for the job and then feeds the work into the machine. Some of the most common kinds of resistance-

welding machines are *spot welders, seam welders,* and *portable spot-welding guns.*

Another pressure-welding process is **forge welding.** Here a blacksmith's hammer is used to apply enough force to the heated metal parts to join them together.

In oxygen cutting, a hot flame is used not to fuse metal, but to cut it. One kind of oxygen cutting is **oxyfuel gas cutting.** In this process, a cutter directs a flame of oxygen and fuel gas on the workpiece until the metal reaches a red heat. Then the cutter increases the amount of oxygen in order to burn or cut the metal (Fig. 72-4). The cutter guides the torch by hand to cut along a marked line. Cutting torches can also be mounted in a machine that follows the layout line.

There are also other kinds of welding. Gas-tungsten arc, submerged-arc, and many others were designed to meet special technological needs. These new developments are described in Unit 75.

Safety

It is important to wear proper equipment when welding. Look at the photographs in this unit. Notice that every welder has eye protection and some safety clothing. Never weld without eye protection. This in-

Fig. 72-4 **This welder is using a torch to remove scale from mechanisms used in continuous casting. (National Steel Corporation)**

Fig. 72–5 Welding technicians work with engineers in experimental work.

cludes special dark glasses. Follow the safety rules given in each unit on welding.

Occupations in welding

There are well over 480,000 welders and oxygen cutters. This number is expected to increase by over 30 percent in the next 10 years. Welders are employed in automobile and aircraft plants, construction industries, metalworking shops, and all kinds of maintenance and repair work. Courses in welding are offered in many public schools. Welding can also be learned on the job. If a weld must meet a certain standard, the welder must first pass a qualifying examination.

There are many different kinds of welding jobs. A *welding operator* operates special welding machines. A *welder* does arc, gas, and special welding. A *welder-fitter* sets up welding work for others to do. Blueprint reading is important in this job. *Welding technicians* work with engineers. They do experimental welding work, run laboratory tests, and build special equipment (Fig. 72–5). *Welding analysts* and *inspectors* examine welded pieces to see if they are correct. If there are flaws, they must find out why. *Welding engineers* and *metallurgists* do experimental and design work on new welding methods and equipment.

 QUESTIONS

1. What is welding?
2. What kind of welding uses heat alone? What kind uses heat and pressure?
3. What are two kinds of fusion welding?
4. What is the name of the process in which a hot flame is used to cut metal?
5. Name some industries that employ welders.

✓ EXTRA CREDIT

1. Make a report on one of the welding processes not discussed in this book.
2. Write a report on occupations in welding.

Unit 73
Gas Welding, Cutting, and Brazing

Gas welding, or **oxy-acetylene welding** (OAW), uses an extremely hot flame produced by burning oxygen and acetylene to melt metal. Brazing is a closely related process. Gas welding is the easiest welding operation to learn (Fig. 73–1). This process is used in almost every school metalworking shop. You will be able to do a fairly good job of welding or brazing low-carbon steels if you master the basic procedure for gas welding.

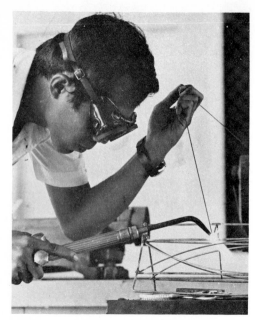

Fig. 73-1 Gas welding is a common joining process learned in the metal shop.

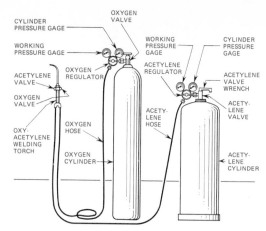

Fig. 73-2 The welding outfit assembled and ready for use.

Equipment

Gas-welding equipment consists of a *cylinder of acetylene,* a *cylinder of oxygen,* two *regulators,* two *lengths of hose with fittings,* and a *welding torch* (Fig. 73-2). The acetylene hose is red. The oxygen hose is green or black. The welding torch is made of copper to give off heat rapidly. The tips come in many sizes. Other items needed are a *welding table* with a top covered with firebrick; a *spark lighter* to light the torch; an *apparatus wrench* to fit the various connections on the regulators, cylinders, and torches; and suitable *goggles* to protect your eyes (Fig. 73-3).

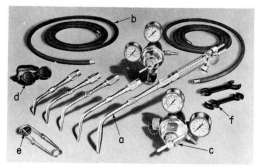

Fig. 73-3 An oxy-acetylene welding outfit: (a) a torch with five tips, (b) a hose, (c) two regulators, (d) goggles, (e) a spark lighter, (f) wrenches. (The Linde Air Products Company)

 SAFETY RULES

1. Never use any oil or grease on or around a welding outfit. Grease and oil can cause a fire when they come in contact with oxygen.
2. Always use a spark lighter to light the torch. Never use matches.
3. Never try to light the torch with both valves open.
4. Always wear goggles when welding.
5. Never let anyone watch while you are welding.
6. Always hang the torches in the right place. Never lay them on the welding table.
7. Always turn off the torch when you have finished a weld.
8. Test for leaks by smearing soapsuds around the fittings and hose connections. Bubbles indicate leaks.

In welding, never guess, experiment, or assume anything. Make sure you know how to weld safely before you start. Always follow the safety rules listed above.

Welding rods and fluxes

Two kinds of welding rods are used in beginning welding:

1. A *mild-steel welding rod* that usually has a copper coating. This coating prevents rusting. In general, use a smaller rod for light welding and a larger rod for heavy welding (Table 73–1). For example, using customary measurements, on 1/16-inch sheet steel you would use 1/16-inch steel welding rod. For 1/8-inch sheet steel, use 3/32-inch rod. If the steel is 1/4 inch thick or more, a rod about 1/8 to 3/16 inch in diameter is used.

2. *Brazing,* or *bronze, rod,* used for brazing. It has a yellow-gold color. Brazing requires a **flux,** a chemical compound that keeps scale, or oxide, from forming. Borax is good, but a commercial brazing flux is better.

Adjusting the welding outfit and lighting the torch

If your welding outfit is not already assembled, follow the assembling instructions supplied with it. To prepare for welding, do the following:

Table 73–1
Recommended Rod Sizes for Oxy-Acetylene Welding

Thickness of metal	Rod diameter in inches
18 gage and lighter	1/16
18 to 16 gage	1/16 to 3/32
16 to 10 gage	1/32 to 1/8
10 gage to 3/16 in.	1/8 to 5/32
1/4 in. and heavier	3/16 to 1/4

1. Choose the correct size of tip for the welding to be done. Generally, a small tip is used for thin metal, a medium tip for medium thickness, and a larger tip for heavy welding. For example, tips with 1/32-inch (1-mm) openings are best for the thinnest metal. The booklet that comes with the welding outfit tells you what size tip to choose. Use the wrench that comes with the welding outfit to remove the new tip. Check the threads on the new tip. Also make sure that the hole at its end is clean and round. Then fasten the tip in place.

2. Put on a pair of goggles, leaving them over your forehead.

3. Make sure that the crossbars on both pressure regulators are screwed out until they are loose.

4. Carefully turn the cylinder valve on the top of the oxygen tank until it is wide open. Always open the valve gradually. With the tank wrench, open the valve on the acetylene about one-half to one and one-half turns—never any more. The cylinder pressure gages on the regulators show the amount of pressure in both tanks. Never stand directly in front of the regulators.

5. Turn in the regulator crossbar on both the oxygen and acetylene until about 5 pounds (34 kPa) of pressure show on the working pressure gages of both. The exact pressure needed can be found in the booklet supplied with the welding outfit.

6. Open the acetylene valve on the torch about 1/4 inch (6 mm). Light the torch with a spark lighter (Fig. 73–4). Adjust the amount of acetylene gas until the flame just jumps away from the tip. This means that there is slightly too much acetylene. Turn the acetylene back a little bit. You have the correct amount when the gas burns with the flame blowing away from the tip. Then turn on the oxygen a little at a time until you get a **neutral flame,** which is the best flame for most welding. This flame has

Fig. 73–4 Using a spark lighter to light a torch. Never light it with a match or another student's lighted torch. Always wear your goggles when gas welding.

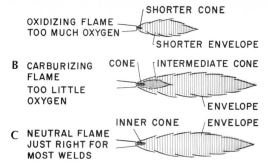

Fig. 73–5 (A) An oxidizing flame. (B) A carburizing, or reducing, flame. (C) A neutral flame.

equal amounts of oxygen and acetylene. It has a full envelope, or outer flame, and a sharp inner cone. If there is too much acetylene, the flame has an intermediate cone between the envelope and inner cone. This is called a *carburizing*, or *reducing*, flame. If there is too much oxygen, the envelope and the inner cone are greatly shortened, and the torch gives off a hissing sound. This is called an *oxidizing* flame (Fig. 73–5).

7. When turning off the torch, always close the acetylene valve first and then the oxygen valve. This prevents a slight backfire, or pop. It also keeps the tip of the torch free of soot. When you have finished welding for the day, first turn off the torch, then close the valves on the acetylene and oxygen cylinders. Next, open the acetylene torch valve to drain the hose. Then, release the crossbar of the acetylene regulator. Last, close the acety-lene torch valve. Follow the same steps in the same order for the oxygen.

Making practice welds

Before you weld a project, you should make some practice welds to learn to operate the equipment.

1. To make an *edge weld without rod:*

a. Use two pieces of 1/16-inch (1.5-mm) or 16-gage (1.6-mm) scrap sheet steel about 1 inch (25 mm) wide and 3 to 4 inches (75 to 100 mm) long.

b. Place the two pieces of scrap steel together on edge or in the form of a little tent (Fig. 73–6). Put goggles over your eyes.

c. Hold the torch in your right

Fig. 73–6 A practice edge weld made without a rod. Note the tent form in which the weld is made.

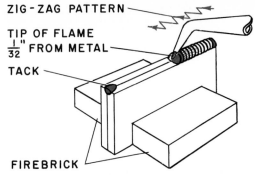

Fig. 73-7 Edge welding without a rod.

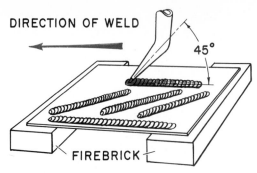

Fig. 73-8 Running a bead without a rod.

hand, with the inner cone about 1/32 inch (1 mm) from the metal. Zigzag it back and forth to tack the pieces of metal together at one end.

d. Then start at the other end, working along the edge with a zigzag torch movement (Fig. 73–7). If you burn through the metal, change to a smaller tip or hold the torch at a slightly lower angle. The greatest amount of heat is applied to the surface when the flame is at right angles to it.

e. Move the flame from one piece of metal to the other, forming a puddle. Then move the torch along from one side to the other as you move it forward. You should practice this a few times until you can join the two pieces together with a weld that has smooth, uniform ripples.

2. To run a *bead without rod:*

a. Choose a piece of metal about 1/8 × 2 × 4 inches (3 × 50 × 100 mm). Place this on the firebrick.

b. Use a tip of about No. 2 size. Adjust for a neutral flame. Remember to place the goggles over your eyes.

c. Hold the tip at an angle of about 45 degrees to the metal, with the tip of the inner cone about 1/32 to 1/16 inch (1 to 1.5 mm) away from the surface.

d. Form a puddle. Then move the torch slowly forward in a weaving or semicircular motion (Fig. 73–8).

e. Make sure that the forward motion and the weaving motion are even to make the bead smooth and regular. If you hold the tip of the torch too long in one place, it will burn a hole through the metal. If you hold the torch too close to the metal, the flame may go out.

f. You can also practice running an edge bead on a piece of scrap metal (Fig. 73–9).

3. To make a *butt weld without rod:*

a. Cut two pieces of scrap steel about 1/16 × 3/4 × 5 inches (1.5 × 20 × 125 mm).

b. Turn a 1/16-inch (1.5-mm) flange on one edge of each piece.

c. Place the pieces with the flange edges together and facing up, about 1/32 inch (1 mm) apart on the welding table.

Fig. 73-9 Running an edge bead without a rod. (U.S. Navy)

d. Hold the torch with the point of the inner flame about 1/8 inch (3 mm) above the flange at one end.

e. Move the torch back and forth in a slight arc until the metal melts and tacks together.

f. Then start at the other end to melt the flange to form a bead. Weave the torch back and forth a little as you work from one end to the other. Keep the molten puddle of metal running to form a smooth, even bead.

4. To run a *bead with added filler:*

a. Choose a piece of scrap stock about 1/8 × 2 × 4 inches (3 × 50 × 100 mm).

b. Select a 3/32-inch mild-steel welding rod.

c. Start forming a puddle, and continue heating the metal in one place without melting a hole. Use a semicircular or weaving motion. If a hole melts through the metal, you have held the flame in one place too long.

d. After the puddle starts to form, add the welding rod to the middle of it (Fig. 73-10). The rod should add about 25 percent more material. Remember to keep the rod in the puddle, not above it, and to direct the flame on the metal, not on the end of the rod. If the tip of the flame is too close to the metal, small blowholes form and the torch may backfire.

e. If you apply the heat mostly to the rod instead of to the metal, the weld will not have good penetration. In this case, the rod merely melts and drops onto the metal, rather than fusing with it.

5. To make a *butt weld with rod:*

a. Cut two pieces of 1/8-inch (3 mm) scrap stock, and place them on the table 1/16-inch (1.5 mm) apart on one end and 1/8 inch (3 mm) apart on the other end.

b. On metal thicker than 1/8 inch (3 mm), one edge must be ground to form

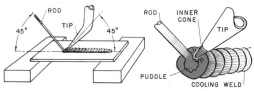

Fig. 73-10 Running a bead with added filler. (The Linde Air Products Company)

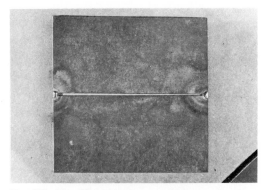

Fig. 73-11 The proper position and spacing for welding sheet metal up to 1/8 inch (3 mm) thick. Tack one side about 1/16 inch (1.5 mm) apart and the other about 1/8 inch (3 mm) apart. Always proceed from the narrower to the wider space. As the weld proceeds, it will draw the pieces together.

a V. Tack the two ends together (Fig. 73-11).

c. Select a piece of 1/8-inch mild-steel welding rod.

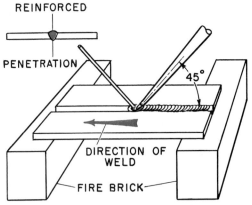

Fig. 73-12 Welding a flat steel plate.

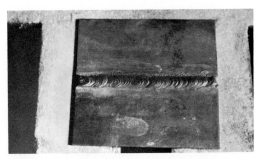

Fig. 73-13 Notice the good bead on this butt weld. (The Linde Air Products Company)

d. Form a puddle on one end. Then begin melting the rod into the puddle to build up the weld about 25 percent.

e. Weave the torch back and forth, moving the rod with just the opposite movement (Fig. 73-12). The bead is formed as shown in Fig. 73-13.

Five basic kinds of welded joints are shown in Fig. 73-14. Practice making them

with and without rods. Most metal projects you make will require only a small weld to join the parts.

Oxyfuel gas cutting

Oxyfuel gas cutting of ferrous materials, especially mild steel, is done with oxygen and the fuel gas acetylene. First, a flame of oxygen and acetylene is used to heat the steel to a bright red color. Then, a stream of oxygen is directed onto the heated area. Where the oxygen touches the heated steel, rapid oxidation causes burning, which cuts the steel apart (Fig. 73-15).

The cutting torch has valves to control the flow of oxygen and acetylene during the heating stage. It has another lever to control the flow of oxygen during the burning stage. Different-sized tips are available for cutting different thicknesses of metal.

Much oxyfuel gas cutting is done with a device that holds the cutting torch and guides it along the work at a steady speed. Large cutting machines have multiple torches that work in unison, cutting several pieces of the same shape at once.

Brazing

Brazing is used to repair metal and to make joints almost as strong as welded joints, without actually melting the metal. It is sometimes also called **bronze welding** or **torch soldering.** The process is somewhat like hard soldering (see Unit 46). Rods and fluxes are available for doing low-temperature welding or brazing on aluminum, copper, and other metals. Following is a description of the brazing process:

1. Know the metal you are brazing. Choose the right brazing rod for the purpose.

2. Cover the work area with *firebricks.* Ordinary bricks contain moisture and can explode under high heat. Protect the surface under the firebricks by covering it with heat-resistant material. (Asbestos paper has

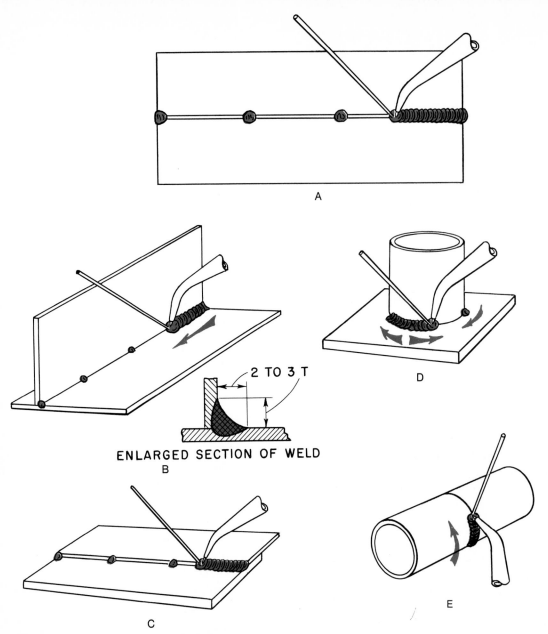

Fig. 73-14 Common kinds of joints or welds: (A) butt weld; (B) tee, or fillet, weld; (C) lap weld; (D) tube-to-plate weld; (E) tube butt weld.

traditionally been used for this purpose. However, asbestos has been found to be hazardous to health. Substitutes for it are now being devised.)

3. Thoroughly clean the metals to be joined. Depending on what must be re-

moved, use a wire brush, sandpaper, and/or *noncombustible* solvent.

4. Before starting work, put on gloves and dark safety glasses. Have handy a fire extinguisher in case of fire and a pail of water to cool tools. Also have on hand tongs

Fig. 73–15 Using a cutting torch that is guided by an electric device that holds the cut straight. (Davis Manufacturing Company)

Fig. 73–16 The correct torch and rod positions for oxy-acetylene brazing.

or longnose pliers for lifting or turning the work.

5. Heat the metals to be joined until they start to get red. Since heavy metal takes longer to get hot, apply heat first to heavier pieces. The torch tip should be about 1/2 inch (13 mm) from the metal surface.

6. If an uncoated brazing rod is being used, dip it in flux.

7. Put the end of the brazing rod in the torch flame (Fig. 73–16). When the joint and rod are hot enough, metal from the rod will flow easily onto the joint. Move the torch flame back and forth over the joint. Repeat these steps as often as necessary. Remember never to melt the rod directly with the torch. Also remember that the metal will weaken if you overheat it. The finished weld should be bright and clean.

8. After the work has lost much of its heat, it can be cooled in a pail of water. However, it is better to let the work cool naturally.

 QUESTIONS

1. Name the basic equipment needed for gas welding.
2. What should you always wear when welding?
3. What size welding-torch tip is used for welding thin metal? For heavy welding?
4. Which is the best flame for most welding?
5. What should you do if you burn through the metal when welding?
6. What happens if you apply heat mostly to the welding rod instead of to the metal?
7. List five basic kinds of welded joints.
8. What are the two stages in oxyfuel gas cutting?
9. What does welding do to the metal that brazing does not?

 EXTRA CREDIT

Make a sample display of the common kinds of welds.

393

Unit 74
Arc Welding

Arc welding, also called **shielded-metal arc welding** (SMAW), is joining metal by means of heat from an electric arc. The pieces to be welded are placed in position. The intense heat of the electric arc applied to the joint melts the metal. At the same time, more metal is added to the joint and mixed with the melted base metal. When all this metal cools, it becomes one solid piece.

Equipment and accessories

There are several basic kinds of *arc welders. Transformer welders* provide alternating current (ac) for welding (Fig. 74–1). The most popular size for school shops and farms has a 180-ampere (A) capacity. Manufacturing plants use transformers with larger out-puts, from 200 to 500 A. A transformer reduces the voltage of ordinary current from the power line and increases its amperage so that high heats can be created. The transformer welder is the cheapest type of welder. It is also easy to maintain. *Motor-generator welders* provide direct current (dc) for welding (Fig. 74–2). Transformers can also provide direct current when equipped with a *rectifier.* Direct-current welders can do certain jobs alternating-current welders cannot do. All welding machines have devices for changing the amount of heat to weld different thicknesses.

Two *cables,* or *leads,* carry the current from the welder to the work and back to the

Fig. 74–2   A motor-generator direct-current arc welder. (The Lincoln Electric Company)

Fig. 74–1   A 225-ampere transformer arc welder. (The Lincoln Electric Company)

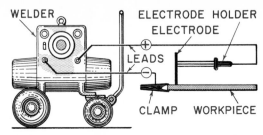

Fig. 74-3 The welding circuit for arc welding.

Fig. 74-4 An electrode holder.

Fig. 74-5 A ground clamp.

Fig. 74-6 Operators must always wear a head-shield helmet for arc welding.

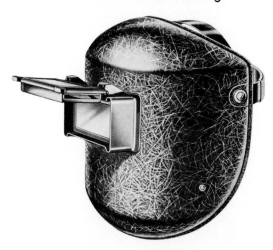

welder (Fig. 74–3). One, the *electrode cable,* is connected to the *electrode holder* (Fig. 74–4). The electrode holder grips the electrode. The other cable, the *ground cable,* is connected to a *ground clamp* (Fig. 74–5). This is attached to the welding table or to the workpiece. An *all-metal welding table* is needed for practice welding and for small jobs that can be placed directly on the table. A *shield* protects the face and eyes from the rays of the electric arc and from heat and molten metal (Fig. 74–6). *Tongs* or *pliers* are used for handling hot metals. A *chipping hammer* is used to remove slag from the weld bead. A *wire scratch-brush* is needed to clean the bead after chipping.

Electrodes

Electrodes are devices used to conduct and emit an electric charge. Those used in arc welding are made of metal wire or rod covered with a hard chemical-flux coating. Their size is determined by the diameter of the core wire. The chemical-flux coating serves several purposes:

1. Part of the flux burns up with the intense heat. This forms a blanket of gas that shields the molten metal from the surrounding air. This keeps the oxygen and nitrogen in the air from forming impurities in the weld.

2. Part of the flux melts, mixes with the weld metal, and floats impurities to the top to form a slag. This slag covers the bead as a crust and protects it from the air (Fig. 74–7).

3. It slows the rate at which the metal hardens in cooling.

4. It affects the way the arc acts during welding.

For dc welding, you must attach the electrode cable to the correct output terminal, or pole. When the electrode cable is connected to the negative terminal of the dc welder, there is *straight,* or *negative, polarity.*

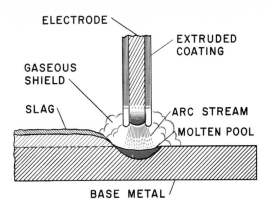

Fig. 74-7 Base metal and the metal from the electrode are fused together by the intense heat of the electric arc. The flux floats impurities to the top to form a slag.

When the electrode cable is connected to the positive terminal, there is *reverse*, or *positive, polarity* (Fig. 74-8).

The American Welding Society has established classifications for standardizing and identifying electrodes. There is also a uniform color code. For example, an electrode that is satisfactory for general welding of mild steel is AWS No. E6013. The *E* means that it is used for the electric arc. The *60* shows the minimum tensile strength (60,000 pounds per square inch, or 413 700 kPa). The *13* indicates that the electrode can be used in all positions for either ac or dc welders. It is also identified by a brown secondary spot. This electrode will produce

Fig. 74-8 Straight polarity and reverse polarity in welding.

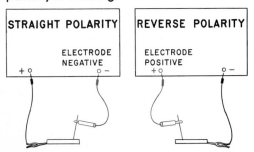

a soft arc and rather light penetration. The penetration is deep enough, however, for most work.

In purchasing electrodes, you must consider the following:

1. Size of electrode needed—diameter of core wire.

2. Kind of welder on which it is to be used—ac or dc.

3. The base metal to be welded—steel, cast iron, nonferrous, and so forth.

 SAFETY RULES

1. Dress correctly. Wear gloves and work clothing that protect your skin from heat, spatter, and arc rays.
2. Wear a shield with the right filter glass. Keep it in the up position when you are not welding.
3. Make sure that the people around you do not watch the arc.
4. Keep away all inflammable materials, such as gas and oily rags.
5. See that the floor around you is clean.
6. Wear safety goggles when you do not have your shield in place, especially for chipping, grinding, and similar operations.
7. Always hold your hand slightly above a piece of metal before touching it to see if it is hot.
8. Make sure that the welding area is well ventilated.

Procedure for practice welding

1. Choose a piece of scrap steel about 3/16 inch (5 mm) thick. Make sure it is clean. Place it on the welding table.

2. Adjust the welder to the right amperage. Set the voltage if a dc welder is used. Use about 100 to 105 A for a 1/8-inch electrode and about 140 to 145 A for a 5/32-inch electrode. Generally, the larger the electrode, the higher the amperage.

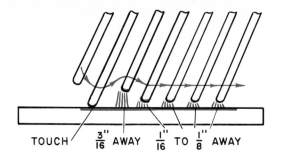

Fig. 74-9 Strike the arc as you would a match.

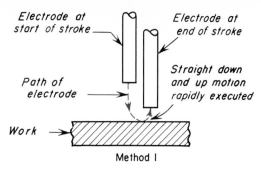

Method I

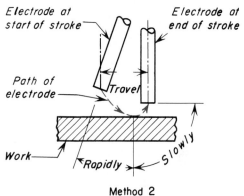

Method 2

Fig. 74-10 Two other ways of striking an arc.

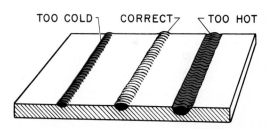

Fig. 74-11 Beads made with an arc that is too cold, with a correct or normal arc, and with an arc that is too hot.

3. Turn on the machine.

4. Drop the shield over your face before you start the arc.

5. To start the arc, grasp the electrode holder firmly. Lower it until the tip is about 1 inch (25 mm) from the base metal. Now, lean the electrode at an angle of about 25 degrees in the direction of travel. Start the arc by scratching the tip of the electrode on the surface of the metal, much as you would strike a large match (Fig. 74-9). There will be a sudden burst of light and spark. Withdraw the electrode a little. The current will jump across the gap, creating the arc. If you hold the electrode on the metal too long, it will fuse with the base metal and stick tight. *If this happens, without raising the shield, break the electrode off quickly by twisting it or releasing it from the holder.* Two other methods of striking the arc are shown in Fig. 74-10.

6. After the arc is started, move it slowly and evenly along the workpiece. Try to maintain an arc length of 1/16 to 1/8 inch (1.5 to 3 mm). You can steady the electrode holder by holding your free hand under the wrist of the hand holding the electrode. You can also steady your elbow against your body or the table as you feed the electrode. Check the arc length by watching the electrode and listening to the sound. When the right setting is used and the correct arc length is maintained, there is a crackling sound like eggs frying.

7. Move the electrode along smoothly and evenly. If you move the electrode too fast, there will be a thin bead and no strength or penetration (Fig. 74-11). If you move it too slowly, there will be too large a bead with a lot of waste metal. Continue to maintain the correct speed until the electrode is melted down to a length of 1/2 inch (13 mm). Then pull it away to break the arc.

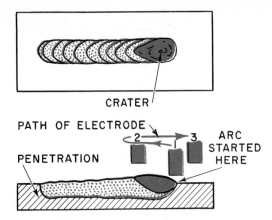

CRATER

PATH OF ELECTRODE

PENETRATION

ARC STARTED HERE

Fig. 74-12 Picking up the weld after inserting a new electrode in the holder. Note that the arc is (1) started slightly ahead of the completed weld, (2) brought back to the crater, and then (3) moved forward.

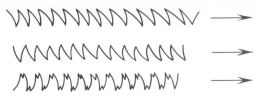

Fig. 74-13 These are some of the weaving motions that can be done in arc welding.

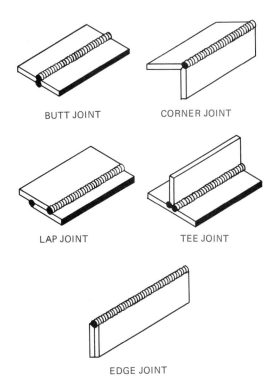

BUTT JOINT   CORNER JOINT

LAP JOINT   TEE JOINT

EDGE JOINT

Fig. 74-14 Five basic kinds of welds used to join metals.

8. To restart the bead, first chip the slag from the crater at the end of the bead and brush off the excess metal. Start the arc a little ahead of the bead, bringing it back to pick up the weld. Then continue forward (Fig. 74–12).

9. Study the bead after you have finished it to make sure you have done it correctly. After you have run a bead, try it again with a weaving motion. This is necessary when you must cover a wider area to weld a joint. The proper motions are shown in Fig. 74–13.

Types of welded joints

Five basic kinds of welds are used to join metals (Fig. 74–14):

1. A butt weld can be made in metal up to 1/8 inch (3 mm) thick without any previous preparation. If the metal is 1/8 to 1/4 inches (3 to 6 mm) thick, bevel one side to form a 60-degree V. For metal from 1/4 to 3/8 inches (6 to 10 mm) thick, grind a V-bevel from one side, leaving a 1/16-inch (1.5-mm) shoulder. Pieces thicker than 3/8 inch (10 mm) should be ground from both sides to form two V's. To make the weld, first tack one end of the two pieces about 1/8 inch (3 mm) apart and the other end 1/16 inch (1.5 mm) apart. A butt weld on thinner material can be made with one pass. On thicker material, it may be necessary to make two or more passes.

2. The **tee,** or **fillet, weld** is used to join two pieces of metal at right angles.

398

Table 74-1
Electrode Size and Welding Current for Various Types of Welds

plate thickness*	1/32	3/64	1/16	3/32	1/8	3/16	1/4	5/16	3/8	1/2 +
For tee and lap welds in flat positions										
electrode size*	—	5/64	3/32	1/8	5/32	5/32	5/32	5/32	5/32	5/32
machine setting**	—	45	65	100	140–150	140–150	140–150	140–150	160–170	170–180
For butt welds in flat positions										
electrode size*	1/16	5/64	3/32	1/8	5/32	5/32	5/32	5/32	5/32	—
machine setting**	30	45	65	100	140–150	140–160	140–160	160	160	—
gap*	none	none	none	1/32	1/32	1/16	1/16	1/8	1/8	—
For corner and edge welds										
electrode size*	1/16	5/64	3/32	3/32	1/8	5/32	5/32	5/32	5/32	—
machine setting**	30	40	65	70	100	140–160	140–160	140–160	160–180	—

* In inches. ** In amperes. The machine settings given are approximate. It may be necessary to set machine higher or lower, depending on welder's skill and welding conditions.

3. The **lap weld** is made in somewhat the same way as a Tee weld. Two pieces of metal are lapped and tacked together. Then the weld is made along the corner.

4. The **corner weld** is used to join two pieces of metal to form a corner.

5. The **edge weld** is used largely on light metal to join two pieces that are flush.

Table 74-1 suggests the right electrode size and welding current for various kinds of welds.

Ventilation for arc welding

Because arc welding produces injurious fumes, it must always be done in well-ventilated areas. In some factories and school shops, arc welding is done in special welding booths containing exhaust ducts, work tables, and welding connections (Fig. 74-15).

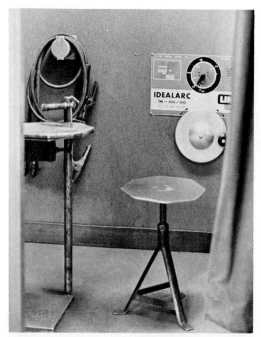

Fig. 74-15 An arc-welding booth in a typical metalworking shop. (The Lincoln Electric Company)

1. What is arc welding?
2. What kind of arc welder is cheapest and easiest to maintain?
3. What are arc-welding electrodes made of?
4. What protective gear should you wear when arc welding?

5. How long should the arc be?
6. Name five kinds of welds.

Make a display board of the common arc-welding electrodes. Show what each kind is used for.

Unit 75
Industrial Welding Processes

You have learned about gas welding and arc welding in the school shop. These processes are also used in industry. However, industry also uses many other special welding processes in manufacturing metal products. These methods are used to weld parts that

Fig. 75–1 The operator activates electrode feed as the trigger is pressed, completing the welding circuit. With the semiautomatic gun, the welder can reach into areas that are inaccessible to the semiautomatic equipment of other processes. (The Lincoln Electric Company)

cannot be welded easily with the gas or arc methods. Industrial processes are often automatic.

One of the problems in welding is the harmful effect air can have on the hot metal. Chemical reaction of the metal with gases in the air can weaken the finished joint. Oxide films, for example, can form on the metal and prevent a good bond. Several methods are used to protect the weld metal from contamination by air until the metal has cooled. The most widely used methods consist of covering the weld metal with a flux or with an **inert gas,** one that will not react with the metal. The method used to apply the flux or inert gas varies with the process. Some of these industrial welding processes are described below.

Self-shielded flux-cored arc welding

Self-shielded flux-cored arc welding (FCAW) uses a continuous "wire" with a core of fluxing and deoxidizing substances as an electrode. This process is an outgrowth of traditional shielded-metal arc welding. In stick welding, it takes time to constantly change the electrode, and the leftover electrode stubs are waste material. In the FCAW process, the electrode wire is coiled and fed in a partly or fully automatic manner to the arc. Semiautomatic FCAW welding is really manual shielded-metal arc welding with very long electrodes (Fig. 75–1).

Gas-metal arc welding

Gas-metal arc welding (GMAW) uses the heat of an electric arc between the workpiece and a consumable electrode. The process is a kind of gas-shielded arc welding. No flux or coating is used on the filler metal. Welding takes place in a "shield" of gas that protects the metal from the air. The process has also been called *MIG*, for *metal inert gas*, *welding*. GMAW is used on alumimum and magnesium and for much production welding.

High speed can be achieved by gas-metal arc welding. The filler metal is a continuous coil of small-diameter wire fed automatically into the joint. Since no flux is used, there is no slag deposit to be removed from the weld bead. The process can be used with automatic welding equipment.

In the GMAW process, power-driven rolls feed the wire through a flexible tube to the welding gun. A hose carries shielding gas, usually argon or a mixture of argon and helium, from a pressurized tank to the gun nozzle. Electrical cables connect the workpiece and filler metal to the power source. During operation, the filler metal slides against an electrical contact inside the feed tube to maintain the circuit. A trigger on the handle of the gun controls both the wire feed and the gas flow. Water is sometimes circulated through the gun to cool it (Fig. 75-2).

Gas-tungsten arc welding

Gas-tungsten arc welding (GTAW) is done with the heat from an electric arc discharged between the workpiece and a nonconsumable electrode made of the metal tungsten. The GTAW process, like the GMAW, is gas-shielded arc welding, using an inert gas and no flux. The difference between the two processes is in the electrodes used. The GTAW process has also been called *TIG*, for *tungsten inert gas*, *welding*.

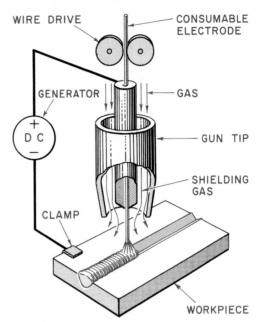

Fig. 75-2 The GMAW process.

Tungsten is used for the electrode because it resists high temperatures and has good electrical characteristics. Welding can be precisely controlled and done in all positions with the GTAW process. Because the electrode does not melt, the arc is extremely steady. GTAW can be done with or without filler metal. The process is used to join thin pieces without filler metal.

The equipment used for GTAW is similar to that used for GMAW. The electrode holder, like the GMAW gun, is connected to a supply of shielding gas. The process is similar to oxy-acetylene welding. An arc supplies the heat and the filler rod is worked by hand (Fig. 75-3).

Submerged-arc welding

Submerged-arc welding (SAW) uses the heat from an electric arc; a shield of loose, grainy flux; and filler metal supplied by an electrode wire to weld heavy workpieces. This process is much like GMAW in that it uses an automatically fed electrode wire

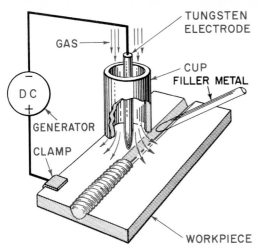

Fig. 75-3 The GTAW process.

of filler metal. The difference is the flux blanket.

In the SAW process, automatic equipment feeds the filler metal into the joint. The power source is connected to the base metal and filler metal. The filler metal slides against an electrical contact inside the tubular electrode holder. The flux is normally stored in a hopper and poured into the joint through a tube mounted in front of the electrode holder (Fig. 75–4).

Plasma-arc welding

Plasma-arc welding uses an inert gas and a transferred, constricted arc. This process replaces GTAW in a number of industrial applications. It offers greater speed at a lower current, better weld quality, greater arc stability, and less sensitivity to process variables. A suitable gas—argon or argon mixed with hydrogen or with helium—is heated and ionized, or charged, into a **plasma.** It flows through the nozzle, protecting the electrode and providing the desired *plasma jet.* However, since the flow rate of the

Fig. 75-4 The SAW process.

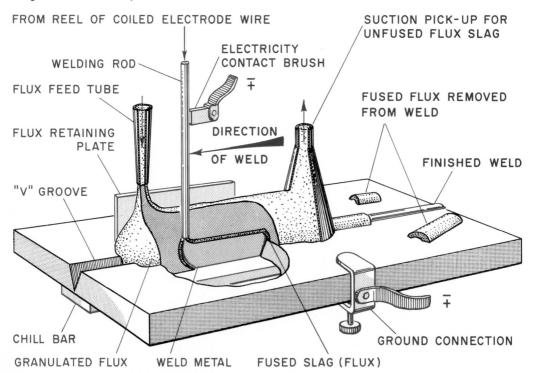

plasma gas is kept relatively low to avoid turbulence and too much displacement of the molten metal, a supplementary shielding gas is required.

In plasma-arc welding, the plasma jet produces a hole, called a **keyhole,** at the leading edge of the weld puddle. The arc passes completely through the workpiece. As the weld progresses, surface tension causes the molten metal to flow in behind the keyhole to form the weld bead.

A plasma-arc welding torch is operated with reverse polarity and a water-cooled copper electrode or with straight connections and a tungsten electrode at currents up to 450 amperes. Power cables at the top of the torch supply power and cooling water to the electrode. Filler metals are used with the plasma arc where more than one weld pass is needed.

Electron-beam welding

In **electron-beam welding** (EBW), the heat needed to melt the joint edges is supplied by an electron gun. This gun can produce temperatures of more than 2,000,000°F (1 100 000°C). The gun focuses a beam of electrons onto the joint line parallel to the existing interface (Fig. 75–5). It can concen- trate a large amount of energy in a spot with a diameter of about 0.01 inch (0.25 mm) or less. Electron-beam welds usually do not require any filler wire. The process is economical for repairing close-tolerance parts.

EBW can be used on materials with thicknesses ranging from about 0.0015 inch to about 2 inches (0.038 mm to 51 mm). It is usually done in a high-vacuum chamber, which minimizes distortion. Lightweight fixtures are needed to hold the parts in place. The flat welding position is commonly used. EBW is either high-voltage (75,000 to 150,000 volts) or low-voltage (15,000 to 30,000 volts).

The weld area must be very clean before welding. This is because the process allows very little time for the escape of any gaseous impurities during the welding. Two passes may be needed with very thin materials to avoid undercutting. The underside of an electron-beam weld sometimes has an undesirable contour that must be removed.

Pulsed-laser welding

In **pulsed-laser welding,** the energy of a laser light beam is focused at the area to be welded (Fig. 75–6). With each pulse, the workpiece is moved to refocus the light one-half spot away. The pulse is normally 1 to 10 milliseconds long. The metal solidifies before the next pulse, so the next area to be welded is not affected by heat from the previous weld. Because very little heat is generated, there is little shrinkage and distortion. Laser welds generally have about one-tenth the distortion of electron-beam welds.

Fig. 75–5   The EBW process.

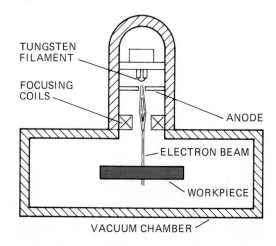

TUNGSTEN FILAMENT

FOCUSING COILS

ANODE

ELECTRON BEAM

WORKPIECE

VACUUM CHAMBER

Fig. 75–6   Pulsed-laser welding.

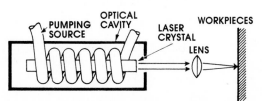

PUMPING SOURCE

OPTICAL CAVITY

LASER CRYSTAL

WORKPIECES

LENS

Since there is no contact with the work, difficult joints can be welded. Also, welds can be made through glass or plastic. The process is effective on small electronic materials, since laser spot welds can be less than 0.001 inch (0.025 mm) in diameter.

Explosive bonding

Explosive bonding uses the force of an explosion to join surfaces. Although some melting occurs, joining does not depend on fusion. The joint has an extremely thin bond area.

The detonation velocity of an explosive must be such as to produce the needed impact velocity between the two metals. The explosives are detonated generally with a standard commercial blasting cap, often along with a line-wave generator for larger charges. When an explosive with a high detonation velocity is being used, the explosive and metal must be separated by a rubber or acrylic buffer.

Explosive bonds are usually wavy or rippled. With metals that form brittle compounds, shrinkage can lead to cracks. Though surface preparation does not have to be as careful as with other processes, surfaces should be smooth to within 0.001 inch (0.025 mm) in the area of the bond.

The widest use of explosive bonding has been to join flat sheet to plate. Tubular transition joints, seam and lap bonds, rib-reinforced structures, and spot bonds also have been made. Explosive spot bonding is particularly useful because the small explosive charges can be packaged and used with a hand-held tool.

Industrial resistance-welding processes

Spot welding, described in Unit 34, and many other kinds of resistance welding are used in industry. Industrial spot welding is used to assemble sheet-metal articles when a

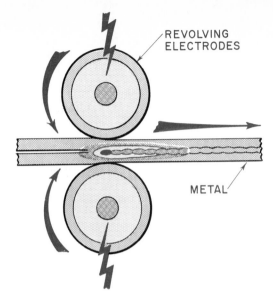

Fig. 75–7 Seam welding.

sealed joint is not needed. A series of welds, similar to riveting, is used along the lap joint. Several spot welds are sometimes made at the same time by multiple pairs of electrodes. The space between the welds depends on the strength needed. This is a speedy, economical production method.

Seam welding is similar to spot welding except that rollers are used instead of electrodes. These allow much more rapid welding (Fig. 75–7). **Flash welding** is used to butt-weld bars, tubes, and sheets. The two workpieces are clamped in dies that carry the electricity. The workpieces themselves act as electrodes. As the dies move together, the workpieces touch, and the welding flash takes place. The molten ends are joined by heat and pressure (Fig. 75–8). **Projection welding** is a method of producing spot welds from projections on the joint surfaces (Fig. 75–9). The parts, held under pressure between electrodes, contact each other only at the projections. The projections melt to form spot welds. In projection welding, two or more spot welds can be made at the same time with one pair of electrodes.

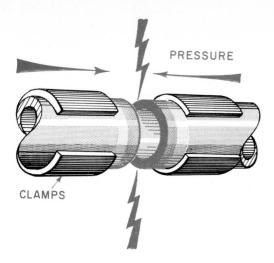

CLAMPS

PRESSURE

Fig. 75–8   Flash welding.

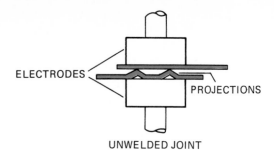

ELECTRODES

PROJECTIONS

UNWELDED JOINT

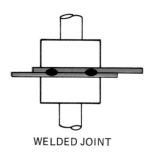

WELDED JOINT

Fig. 75–9   Projection welding.

? QUESTIONS

1. What kind of electrode is used in the FCAW process?
2. How does the electrode used in the GMAW process differ from that used in the GTAW process?
3. What are other names for GMAW and GTAW?
4. How does submerged-arc welding differ from regular arc welding?
5. What is the hole produced in plasma-arc welding called?
6. What temperatures can be produced in electron-beam welding?
7. What is the duration of the light pulse in laser welding?
8. What is the chief use of explosive bonding?
9. Name four kinds of resistance welding used in industry.

✓ EXTRA CREDIT

Write a research report on one of the industrial welding processes.

Unit 76
Industrial Assembly Methods

Assembly, or **fastening,** is the final step in the manufacture of products. A bicycle, for example, is made up of many parts that must be assembled into a final usable ma-

chine. Industry is constantly searching for improved, lower-cost methods of joining parts. Not only the standard fastening methods—such as riveting, soldering, and welding—are used in industry, but also hundreds of very unusual methods. Most metal products can be assembled in more than one way. All assembly methods can be grouped under three basic kinds of fastening: adhesion, cohesion, and pressure. **Adhesion** is assembly

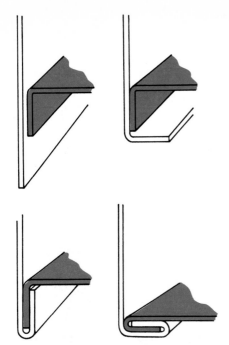

Fig. 76-1 Standing end-lock seam: a typical way of holding two parts of sheet metal together.

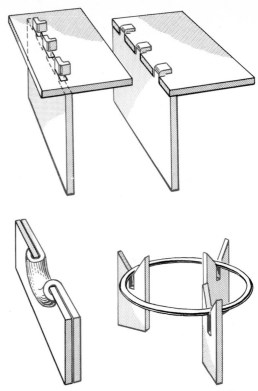

Fig. 76-2 Some methods of attaching parts without mechanical fasteners.

Fig. 76-3 Shapes of retaining rings.

with a material such as an adhesive or solder that holds parts together. **Cohesion** is creating an actual chemical or metallurgical bond between the parts, as in welding. **Pressure** is using a mechanical device such as a screw or rivet to fasten parts together. Some of the more interesting assembly operations are described in this unit.

Interlocking devices

The sheet-metal seam is a typical example of an interlocking device for holding parts together (Fig. 76–1). Industry uses a wide variety of techniques for fastening sheet-metal parts. Twisted tabs or wire, snap-on rings, and crimping methods are but a few ways to assemble such parts without adding any other materials (Fig. 76–2).

The retaining ring is a small washerlike device commonly used in assembly. There are many styles, each with a special use (Fig. 76–3). These rings provide a quick, safe, and secure method of locking pieces together. They are semipermanent in that they can be removed to make repairs.

Fig. 76-4 This automatic soldering machine solders leads to the wire of a telephone printed circuit. The operator is placing the parts to be soldered on the moving assembly line. (Western Electric Company)

Soldering

Soldering is an extremely important fastening method, especially in electronics. Solder seals and secures a joint easily since it melts at a relatively low temperature. Hand, mechanical, and automatic soldering are all done in industry for assembly (Fig. 76-4). Many electronic assemblies require a worker to use a microscope while doing hand soldering.

Brazing

Brazing techniques used in industry are often automatic (Fig. 76-5). This results in faster assembly for precise parts. Preformed brazing-rod material is used to control the amount of braze filler. Automatic furnaces of special design are needed for aluminum assemblies.

Injected-metal assembly

Injected-metal assembly is a quick method that offers many advantages over traditional techniques (Fig. 76-6). The parts

Fig. 76-5 This person operates a machine that does the delicate job of brazing resistors and capacitors on electrical parts. (Western Electric Company)

are aligned, and then molten zinc alloy is injected. The liquid metal flows into the openings and cools quickly to provide a solid fastening. When used for assembly, this alloy is stronger than steel.

Adhesives

Many new adhesives have been developed for use in the aerospace and automo-

Fig. 76-6 Assemblying a gear to a shaft by injecting a molten zinc alloy into the opening. The crosshatched area in the drawings shown above the gear is the zinc alloy bonding material. (Fisher Gauge, Ltd.)

Fig. 76-7 Using a hot-melt adhesive gun. (Nordson)

tive industries. These are especially useful where heat would injure delicate parts. They are also used to prevent the marring of finishes on automobiles. Adhesives are replacing welds in a number of cases.

A simple, quick, and clean method of adhering metals and other materials is with hot-melt adhesives. A hand-held applicator gun delivers a uniform bead of hot-melt adhesive only when the trigger is pulled (Fig. 76–7). The gun is heated electrically and controlled by preset thermostats. The gun grip is insulated. Solid glue cartridges are easily loaded in the gun. The gun mechanism has only a few simple parts. Thus, there is little maintenance. Interchangeable nozzles vary the bead size. Materials joined by this method include metal and metal, plastic and metal, and wood and metal.

 QUESTIONS

1. List the three basic kinds of fastening.
2. What are some ways of assembling parts without adding any fastening materials?
3. What are retaining rings?
4. What sort of assembly is often done under a microscope?
5. What fastening material is used in injected-metal assembly?
6. Why are adhesives used in industry?

 EXTRA CREDIT

Write a research report on one of the industrial assembly methods.

SECTION 11

MANUFACTURING METAL PRODUCTS

Unit 77

Introduction to Metal Manufacturing

From their earliest history, people have made things. Tools, weapons, household utensils, clothing, shelter have all been "manufactured" in one way or another. At first, goods were made by hand with the simplest of tools. Gradually, more complicated machines were used to make products for individual use, for trade, or for sale. Eventually, **mass production** evolved. This is the making of large numbers of identical things relatively quickly and at relatively low cost (Fig. 77-1). Mass production is usually done in a factory with many large, complex machines and a large number of workers.

Modern methods of mass production are based on certain fundamental principles. These are the development of specialized machine tools; the use of transfer machines; the use of jigs, fixtures, and dies; the manufacture of interchangeable parts; and quality control. Following are explanations of these principles:

1. *Development of specialized machine tools.* With specialized machine tools, parts can be made by workers with only limited skills

Fig. 77-1 Tableware is typical of mass-produced products used in daily life. (Dansk Designs)

(Fig. 77-2). Indeed, with **automation,** work is done entirely by machines, reducing—or even eliminating—the need for people. In recent years, automation has been furthered by the use of numerical controls and by the use of transfer machines (see below).

Numerical control (N/C) directs machines by means of information stored on tapes or cards that send signals to the machine at the proper time so that it will do specific operations. In order to use numerically controlled equipment, a skilled worker must first study the working drawings for a product to be manufactured. This person must establish the steps needed for the full machining cycle. These instructions are

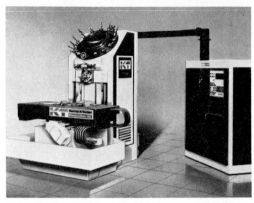

Fig. 77-2 This numerically controlled machining center is typical of a modern machine tool. (Kearney & Trecker Corporation)

Fig. 77-3 Several different kinds of drilling jigs. (Clausing Corporation)

written out in the correct order, just as if a plan of procedure were being made. They are then translated into information that can be put on paper tape, magnetic tape, or punched cards. When these are run through the control machine, the machine does each step in the right order, following the information.

2. *Use of transfer machines.* In most shops, after a part is machined, it is placed in a box and moved to another machine where more work is done on it. In factories with automated production, however, the various machine tools are grouped together along a production line. A **transfer machine** connects the production machine tools. As necessary, the transfer machine positions the part, reverses it, or turns it upside down, all automatically. At the same time, numerical control operates the machine itself. As a result, a group of machine tools connected to a transfer machine can be operated by one or two skilled technicians. There are manufacturing plants today in which these ideas have been carried to the point where a complete product is produced and assembled automatically in one continuous line.

3. *Use of jigs, fixtures, and dies.* A **jig** is a device for holding a piece of work and guid-

Fig. 77-4 A fixture is used to hold this round part for milling. (Boston Digital Corporation)

ing a tool (Fig. 77-3). The jig can be moved with the work. A **fixture,** on the other hand, is fastened to a machine tool and holds one or more pieces in the proper position for machining (Fig. 77-4). However, it does not guide the tool. A **die** is a tool used to cut, shear, press, or otherwise give to the work the correct shape, imprint, or form (Fig. 77-5).

4. *Manufacture of interchangeable parts.* **Interchangeability** means that each part must be made within certain definite dimensions so that it fits *in any one of the final products.* It is impossible to make parts *exactly perfect.* The limits of sizes to which parts can be made must be carefully specified. For some kinds of products, individual parts may vary as much as 1/2 inch (13 mm) in size and still be satisfactory. For other products, such as certain precision parts of a jet engine, the parts must be accurate to within seven millionths of an inch (0.000178 mm).

The basic size of a part is expressed in the specified dimensions. However, it would be impossible and impractical to produce it to this exact size. Therefore, the engineer and drafter establish a tolerance for the part. **Tolerance** is the total range of dimensions allowable over and under the specified dimensions. The **limits,** the largest and smallest dimensions allowed, are usually given after each dimension. They are indicated by a plus-or-minus sign. For example, a part might have to be made to a size of 2 inches (50.8 mm) plus or minus .005 inch (0.13 mm). This means that any part that is 1.995 inches (50.67 mm) to 2.005 inches (50.93 mm) in size would be satisfactory.

Fig. 77–5 A diemaker checking a progressive die. (Western Electric Company)

5. *Quality control.* Industry has developed many kinds of instruments to check tolerances and other standards. **Gages** are inspection tools. These are instruments used to examine parts to see if they meet standards. Some are fixed, such as the plug gage, snap gage, and ring gage. Some are operated by air, electricity, or hydraulics (Fig. 77–6). Determining whether parts meet the specified standards is called **quality control.**

Production resources

Modern industry needs four basic kinds of resources in order to mass-produce products made of metal and other materials (Fig. 77–7). *Natural resources* are the raw ma-

Fig. 77–6 An inspector using an air gage to check the thickness of metal. (Inland Steel Company)

Fig. 77–7 Basic production resources.

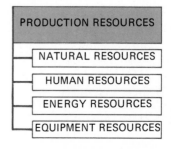

PRODUCTION RESOURCES
NATURAL RESOURCES
HUMAN RESOURCES
ENERGY RESOURCES
EQUIPMENT RESOURCES

411

terials from which people make the goods they need. These include wood, metal, plastic, ceramics, water, earth, air, and chemicals. People must learn to use these natural resources wisely. *Human resources* are the people who design, make, sell, and maintain the products. People use machines in their work, but the machines cannot run alone. Thousands of different skills are needed in production. Each is very important. *Energy resources* provide power for machines and factories. Gas, electricity, coal, oil, gasoline, and atomic energy are all needed to make industry work. *Equipment resources* are the tools, machines, factories, and transport systems used to process raw materials into usable goods. All these resources—natural, human, energy, and equipment—must be carefully organized to produce goods. This system of organization and how it works are the subjects for the remaining units in this section of the book.

Unit 78
Organization of Industry

The factories where products are made are operated by a team of people. The team is made up of managers and skilled workers. The managers are responsible for organizing the resources of industry. They plan the products to be made, purchase raw materials, train workers to do jobs, organize the production line, and sell the goods (Fig. 78–1). The skilled workers are responsible for operating the machines accurately and safely.

Industrial organization

The mass production of goods is a big business. It is necessary for it to be organized

? QUESTIONS

1. Define *mass production.*
2. What are the five basic principles of mass production?
3. What is automation?
4. In what system are machines directed through information stored on tapes or cards?
5. What is the difference between tolerance and limits?
6. What are inspection tools called?
7. What are the four basic production resources?

✔ EXTRA CREDIT

Write a report on how a typical modern product is mass-produced. Examples are bicycles, toys, sports equipment, tools, or machines.

Fig. 78–1 The managers are the organizers and planners of industry. (Caterpillar Company)

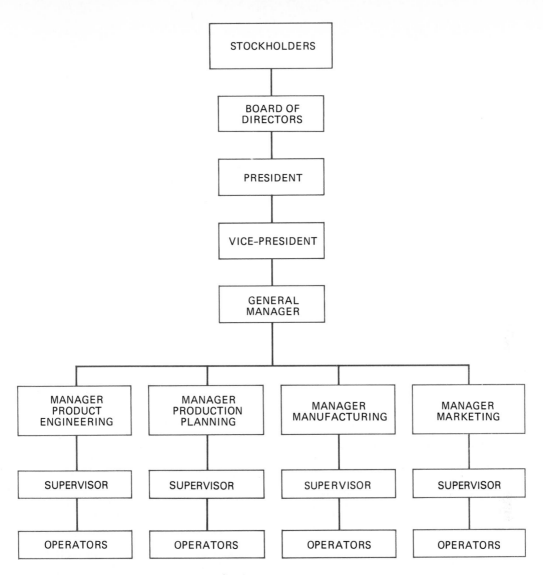

Fig. 78-2 Industrial organization chart.

efficiently. The type of organization used in most large industries is the *corporation*. In a corporation, a number of people pool or invest their money and talents and start a business. The investors are the owners of the business. They are called *stockholders* because they own the stock, or shares, of the company. There are often hundreds or thousands of stockholders in a corporation. The stockholders elect a *board of directors* to run the corporation. The *president* of the corporation is charged with running it efficiently and at a profit. The president is assisted by one or more *vice-presidents*. The *general manager* has direct charge of the factory operations. The general manager supervises several *managers*, each in charge of a special department. A manager is assisted by a *supervisor*, who directs the work of several *operators* or *skilled workers*. The chart in Fig. 78–2 shows the typical organization of a corporation. There are other kinds of business organizations, such as

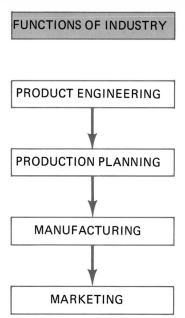

FUNCTIONS OF INDUSTRY

PRODUCT ENGINEERING

PRODUCTION PLANNING

MANUFACTURING

MARKETING

Fig. 78–3   The functions of industry.

proprietorships and partnerships. Jobs with the same duties may have different names in different businesses. The departments or divisions in a production organization are often called the functions of industry.

The functions of industry

These functions of industry are, in fact, the steps a product goes through from the mind of the inventor to the hands of the consumer (Fig. 78–3). These are product engineering, production planning, manufacturing, and marketing.

Unit 79
Product Engineering

All manufactured products are invented, designed, or developed. Part of product engineering is product design, or product research and development.

In the first phase, product engineering, a product is invented, designed, or developed. Special tools, such as jigs, fixtures, and dies, are also designed and made. In production planning, the product is studied to find out what operations are needed to make it. This is much like a plan of procedure. These operations are then fixed into a production schedule. This is part of setting up the production line. Quality control is also a part of this planning. In the next phase, manufacturing, workers turn raw materials into products on the assembly line. Production workers must be trained and supervised. Marketing, the final function of industry, is getting the quality product to the customer and seeing that the customer is satisfied with it.

Each function of industry is described in greater detail in the next several units.

 QUESTIONS

1. What is a corporation?
2. List members of the corporate organization.
3. List the functions of industry.

 EXTRA CREDIT

Prepare a corporate organization chart for a company you might set up in your metalworking class.

Product design

Goods used by consumers must be changed to include the latest technological developments or to meet shifts in public taste. New materials, processes, and products are produced by the product-design part of industry (Fig. 79–1). The design department is a team of people skilled in art, science, and engineering. They combine tech-

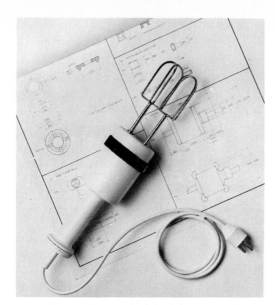

Fig. 79-1 An original design for a hand-held food mixer that was a winner in a design contest. (The Zinc Institute)

nical knowledge of materials, machines, and methods of production with artistic talent. They improve the appearance and functional design of machine-made products. In many instances, they have to consult production supervisors and marketing-research staff for their opinions on the possibility of producing a new product or changing the design of an old product. A team member must be creative, know scientific principles and research methods, be cooperative, and have good business sense.

A first step in the design process is to determine the product to be built. A market survey must be made to discover what people want and need. Of course, the manufacturer already has some ideas and often combines these with the results of the market survey. Research is needed to answer many questions. The design team must design the best product possible using the information obtained from market research and from other reliable sources. After the design has been selected, a model is usually built so that the design can be seen in three dimensions.

At this point, much engineering research goes into product development. Many different people may work on each part of the product. Full-scale models are made. The product is then assembled to see if all parts fit together. Testing is done to see if it will hold up under normal use. Improvements are made where necessary. Management finally approves the design.

Production tooling

After the final design of the product has been selected, the factory must be prepared to produce the parts and assemble them. This involves designing and building machines, dies, jigs, and fixtures and planning new assembly lines. This is called *production tooling,* or *tooling up* (Fig. 79-2). Usually, it is directed by experienced engineers and technicians.

Tooling up consists of four basic activities: (1) deciding what existing machines and tools should be used, (2) ordering needed machines and tools, (3) designing and making all special tools and machines, and (4) supervising the setting up of tools and machines for production. One of the

Fig. 79-2 Developing a layout for a new plant using scale-model machines. (Cincinnati Milacron)

primary aims of the production-tooling department is to reduce the need for skilled labor in machine operations without risking the loss of quality.

QUESTIONS

1. Who is responsible for developing new materials, processes, and products?

2. What is production tooling?
3. List the four basic tasks in tooling up.

EXTRA CREDIT

Prepare a report on the design of a new product, such as a bicycle or a boat.

Unit 80
Production Planning

Once the product has been designed and tooled up, it must be readied for production. This step is called production planning. It involves two main activities: *production control* and *quality control.*

Production control

In a factory, materials and parts move together on assembly lines. These join at different stages of manufacturing until the product is complete. It is the production-control segment of a plant that organizes and plans the manufacturing processes. These include the supply and movement of materials and labor, the use of machines, and assembly and finishing activities.

There may be several weeks or even months of production-control planning before the manufacturing of a product begins. Good planning means that the right material in the right amount is at the right place at the right time. It ensures uninterrupted manufacturing at a minimum cost by avoid-

Fig. 80-1   A sample routing sheet.

PROGRAM		PART NAME					ISSUE DATE		
FOR MODELS		MATERIAL		WT./LBS.		RGH.	FIN.		
				RELEASE					
LINE NO.	OPER. NO.	OPERATION DESCRIPTION		TOOL - MACHINE - EQUIPMENT DESCRIPTION			UNITS REQ'D.	TOOL OR B.T. NUMBER	
1									
2									
3									
4									
5									
6									
7									
8									
9									
10									
11									
12									
13									
14									
15									
16									
17									
18									
19									
20									
21									
22									
23									

ing waste. The production-control department usually works closely with other industrial departments.

The most important tasks of production control are as follows:

1. Writing up *bills of materials,* which specify quantities and kinds needed. These bills are similar to those discussed in Unit 8, except that the quantities are larger.

2. Making *routing sheets,* special forms that list operations in order (Fig. 80–1). These are the same as plans of procedure (see Unit 8).

3. *Scheduling,* which is setting up a timetable for the use of facilities, the flow of materials, and the performance of operations (Fig. 80–2). Schedules are also called progress operations charts (Fig. 80–3).

4. *Dispatching,* which is issuing orders for work on the assembly line.

5. Making a *plant layout,* a plan for

Fig. 80–2 The worker (right) is responsible for operation analysis and scheduling. (Caterpillar Company)

placing machines and work stations on the assembly line (Fig. 80–4). This involves studying bills of materials, routing sheets, schedules, and work orders.

Fig. 80–3   A sample work-schedule chart.

JOB	MON	TUE	WED	THU	FRI

Planned Work: ▬▬▬▬
Actual Work: █████

SYMBOLS USED

A—operator absent
G—green (inexperienced) operator
I—poor instructions
L—slow operator

M—materials holdup
R—machine repair
T—tools lacking
V—holiday

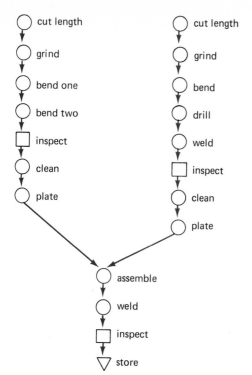

Fig. 80-4 **A sample plant-layout chart for producing a simple school project.**

Left column flow:
cut length → grind → bend one → bend two → inspect → clean → plate

Right column flow:
cut length → grind → bend → drill → weld → inspect → clean → plate

Both flows → assemble → weld → inspect → store

Fig. 80-5 **Inspecting and packaging completed telephones. (Western Electric Company)**

Quality control

Once the assembly line starts rolling, inspection personnel must check often to make certain that defective articles are not being made. The team that establishes standards and periodically inspects the product is called *quality control*. The quality-control team usually uses measuring devices to see if a product is within the standards previously set for it. Interchangeability, the complexity of modern industry, cost considerations, and competition all demand a system for maintaining high quality.

Quality control involves three major groups of activities: prevention, acceptance, and appraisal. *Prevention* includes analyzing records of defects, increasing shop morale, promoting quality coordination, and training personnel to avoid defects. *Acceptance* involves inspecting incoming materials and parts, inspecting and maintaining control gages, inspecting the product, and maintaining testing equipment (Fig. 80-5). *Appraisal* includes checking inspection, investigating customer complaints, checking the marketing quality of the product, and reporting to management. Thus, the appraisal group follows up on and evaluates the previous activities in quality control.

A good quality-control system reduces costs by preventing the waste of materials and labor. It makes mass production, uninterrupted assembly-line operations, and full use of manufacturing facilities possible.

? QUESTIONS

1. What are the two main activities in planning?
2. List the five major tasks in production control.
3. What is the purpose of the quality-control function?
4. What three kinds of activities are involved in quality control?

✓ EXTRA CREDIT

Write a report on Henry L. Gantt, who developed a common progress operations chart. Find out what other charts are used in scheduling.

Unit 81
People and Processes in Manufacturing

Product engineering and production planning prepare for manufacturing. When the product has been designed, tooled, routed, and scheduled, it is ready to be manufactured. Manufacturing is the function of industry that transforms raw materials into useful products through the use of tools, machines, and processes (Figs. 81-1, 81-2). An important element in the manufacturing phase is selecting and training workers. People must work the machines that change materials into finished products.

Personnel management

Personnel management involves hiring, training, supervising, advancing, retiring, and relocating employees. The personnel-management team aims to obtain and maintain an efficient, happy work force.

The first step in personnel management is finding and hiring workers who fit the jobs that are open. If the newly hired people lack the proper experience or education, they must be trained in the best methods for get-

Fig. 81-1 Manufacturing is changing raw materials into useful products. These people are making telephone dialing systems. (Western Electric Company)

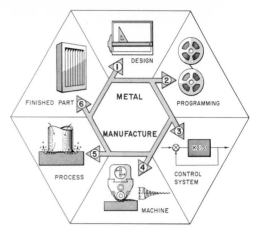

Fig. 81-2 Steps in producing a metal part using modern techniques.

ting the job done. Personnel managers must also be concerned with keeping the employees satisfied while they are working. In order to do this, they must be familiar with both the job and the employee. They must know how the person feels about such things as job, salary, working conditions, career. The personnel department also deals with promotions and demotions and with retirements. It handles relocations—moving people to similar jobs in another place.

Material processing

There is a series of steps that is followed when any product is manufactured. First, raw materials are prepared by being refined and bulked. Second, the prepared raw materials are converted and formed into standard industrial materials. Third, standardized materials are developed into components or into finished products that make up a unit. Fourth, several units or components are put together to form a product. Fifth, the product is made ready for distribution and stored or packaged and prepared for shipment.

The techniques used to transform resources into usable goods are all forms of *material processing*. All these processes can be

419

Fig. 81–3 An automated inspection station. (Inland Steel Company)

classified into four main groups: cutting, forming, fastening, and finishing.

This book describes methods of hand and machine processing. In industry, these are performed on production lines so that they can be done more efficiently. Some of these production lines are automated (Fig. 81–3).

 QUESTIONS

1. What function of industry transforms raw materials into useful products?
2. Name six duties of personnel management.
3. What are the four main ways of processing materials?

✔ **EXTRA CREDIT**

Write an illustrated report on how an assembly line works.

Unit 82
Marketing Metal Products

Marketing is the final function of industry. It involves the distribution of goods to consumers. The marketing department is responsible for moving, storing, packaging, delivering, selling, and accounting for products.

The marketing personnel must know about the customers for the firm's products. For this, they rely on *market research*. Market researchers study consumers' buying habits. They also find out if the customers live in a city, a suburban area, or the country. They learn about the customers' special needs. After collecting and analyzing this data, a company is in a better position to meet the needs of its customers.

Every day, businesspeople make decisions about the selling of their goods and services based on marketing reports. These include such widely differing decisions as forecasting sales; selecting a brand name, package, or design; choosing a new plant location; and determing whether to ship goods by truck, air, or rail.

Major marketing functions include pricing, packaging, advertising, distribution, selling, and service (Fig. 82–1). *Pricing* is determining the amount of money the customers will have to pay for the product. This cost includes the money paid out for materials, labor, and overhead. (Overhead includes the cost of the factory lights, heat, power, and the like). The price must also provide a profit for the business. It is also important to consider the cost of selling and distributing the product. This cost is the amount of money spent to get the product to the right market at the right time. Selling and distribution costs can be as much as two and one-half times the manufacturing cost of the product.

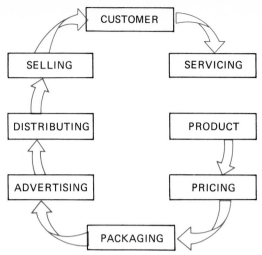

Fig. 82–1 **The different elements in marketing.**

Fig. 82–2 **Good service is now an important part of marketing.**

Packaging is necessary for many, but not all, metal products. Airplanes and automobiles do not have to be packaged. However, such products as tools, lawnmowers, razor blades, and fasteners must be put in bags, cartons, or wrappers. Packages protect products, facilitate shipping and displaying them, and make them more convenient and attractive to customers.

The purpose of *advertising* is to inform consumers about the goods and services on the market. Advertising describes how a product is used and how it works. It tries to convince consumers that one product is better than others available. Advertisements appear in newspapers and magazines, on radio and television, and on billboards and posters.

Distribution involves transporting products from the factory to a store. Goods are moved by rail, air, truck, and ship to markets all over the world. Distribution is closely related to packaging. This is because the products must arrive at their destinations in good condition.

Selling is done in a store, in a showroom,

from door to door, or over the telephone. Salespeople deal directly with the customers. They must know all about the product. They have to be able to discuss it with the people who buy it.

Today, it is not enough to sell products to consumers. The customer also wants to be sold *service* for the product (Fig. 82–2). It is important for the customer to know that the article can be repaired if it breaks. Replacement parts must be readily available. Service industries are growing rapidly because consumers are demanding good service along with good products.

? QUESTIONS

1. What is marketing?
2. Name the main marketing functions.

✓ EXTRA CREDIT

Write a report on market research.

Unit 83
Mass Production
in the School Shop

Fig. 83–1 Mass-producing products in school is a challenging activity. Many students with a variety of skills work together to produce quality goods at a profit. (Republic Steel Corporation)

Fig. 83–2 Work closely with your instructors. They can offer valuable advice. (Junior Achievement, Inc.)

A school activity that is becoming very popular is the mass production of goods by students (Fig. 83–1). Almost any kind of small object can be made—tie racks, school pennants, coat hangers, nameplates, and the

Fig. 83–3 The manager of product engineering should present the product ideas to the class for their consideration. (Republic Steel Corporation)

Fig. 83-4 Pattern for the candle sconce.

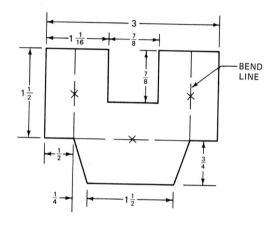

24 GA. ALUMINUM

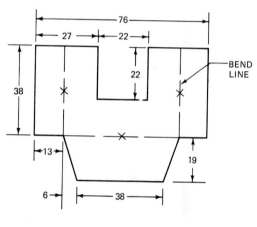

24 GA. ALUMINUM

Fig. 83-5 Customary (top) and metric (bottom) drawings of the brazing fixture.

like. Some of these programs are organized under such titles as Junior Engineers or Junior Achievement. Others are operated only by an individual teacher and class. You can learn about manufacturing by visiting a factory.

Getting started

In starting a mass-production project, the first order of business is to form a corporation and elect or appoint the officers. Study the chart in Fig. 78-2. To do it correctly, you will have to work closely with your teacher. An instructor will sometimes act as president or chairperson of the board of directors. It is the job of this officer to offer advice on the best way of operating your company (Fig. 83-2). Do not appoint the production-line supervisor and operators at this time. They should be chosen later, when you know what product is to be made. They are hired for their special skills.

Product engineering

The manager of product engineering should work with the supervisor and operators. They should be a team that selects three or four suitable product designs. They should make **prototypes,** or samples, of these designs and present them to the class. After class discussion, the final product is selected (Fig. 83-3). For purposes of illustration, assume that you will be making the candle sconce discussed in Unit 8. Study this carefully, and make a prototype of it.

The tooling for this is very simple. You will need only a *pattern* to make the outline and locate the holes and a *fixture* to hold the cup when brazing (Figs. 83-4, 83-5). Make these, and try them out. Be sure they work perfectly.

PROGRAM Colonial Candle Sconce	PART NAME Hanger			ISSUE DATE	
FOR MODELS A-I	MATERIAL 18 ga. black iron sheet	RGH. FIN.			
		WT./LBS. RELEASE			
LINE NO.	OPER. NO.	OPERATION DESCRIPTION	TOOL - MACHINE - EQUIPMENT DESCRIPTION	UNITS REQ'D.	TOOL OR B.T. NUMBER
1	1	cut hanger to size	squaring shear	1	
2	2	apply layout fluid	brush and fluid	1	
3	3	place pattern on hanger - mark outline, bendlines, and holes	scriber, ball-peen hammer, center punch	2	
4	4	cut hanger point to shape	squaring shear	1	
5	5	cut hanger round to shape	tinsnips	2	
6	6	file notches in hanger	round file	4	
7	7	touch up, remove all burrs	belt sander, files	1	
8	8	drill holes	drill press	1	
9	9	remove burrs from holes	file	1	
10	10	make bend #1	sheet metal brake	1	
11	11	make bend #2	sheet metal brake	1	
12					
13					
14					

PROGRAM Colonial Candle Sconce	PART NAME Cup			ISSUE DATE	
FOR MODELS A-I	MATERIAL 3/4" MS Pipe	RGH. FIN.			
		WT./LBS. RELEASE			
LINE NO.	OPER. NO.	OPERATION DESCRIPTION	TOOL - MACHINE - EQUIPMENT DESCRIPTION	UNITS REQ'D.	TOOL OR B.T. NUMBER
1	1	measure 1" pipe lengths	scale, scriber	2	
2	2	cut to size	hacksaw, power	1	
3	3	remove all burrs	grinders and file	1	
4					
5					

Fig. 83-6   Routing sheets for the hanger and the cup.

Production planning

The manager of production planning and the other members of the team should now look at the bill of materials and outline of procedure that are shown in Fig. 8–1. This study should help you understand how product engineering and production planning are related. Then make out a routing sheet for each part—one for the hanger and one for the cup. These are shown in Fig. 83–6. These routing sheets should be tried out by one or two students so that any errors in them can be eliminated.

After the routing sheets are completed, a production-control schedule is made (Fig. 83–7). By studying the materials and routing sheets, you can estimate the time needed to make each part. Time studies can be made to get more accurate figures. Your instructor can be very helpful here. Look at the sample schedule in Fig. 83–8. The days are marked in 5-minute segments. You may choose any interval that is convenient for the length of the class period. You should refer to this chart as production begins. Keep it up to date, so you can tell how you are doing.

A plant-layout chart is then made (Fig. 83–9). Note that every operation is

Fig. 83–7 Preparing production schedules. (Junior Achievement, Inc.)

listed and each inspection and assembly point identified. From this, you can plan the flow of materials through the shop.

Quality-control procedures should be discussed with the instructor. This is a simple project with no moving parts. Therefore, quality control is important but not diffi-

Fig. 83–8   Schedule for candle sconce.

JOB	MON	TUE	WED	THU	FRI
HANGER					
CUP					
ASSEMBLE					
FINISH					

Planned Work: ————
Actual Work: ▬▬▬

SYMBOLS USED
A—operator absent
G—green (inexperienced) operator
I—poor instructions
L—slow operator
M—materials holdup
R—machine repair
T—tools lacking
V—holiday

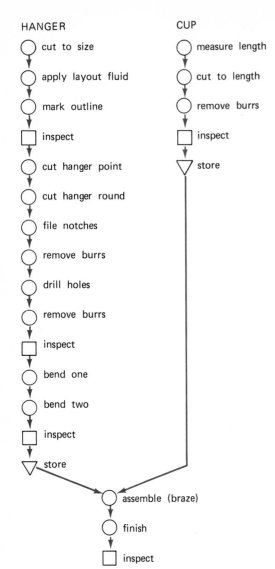

HANGER	CUP
○ cut to size	○ measure length
○ apply layout fluid	○ cut to length
○ mark outline	○ remove burrs
☐ inspect	☐ inspect
○ cut hanger point	▽ store
○ cut hanger round	
○ file notches	
○ remove burrs	
○ drill holes	
○ remove burrs	
☐ inspect	
○ bend one	
○ bend two	
☐ inspect	
▽ store	

○ assemble (braze)

○ finish

☐ inspect

Fig. 83-9 Plant layout for candle sconce.

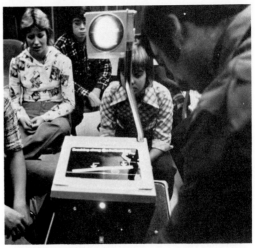

Fig. 83-10 Your instructor can help you in training workers for the production line. (Rohm and Hass Company)

5. Cup crooked.
6. Poor finish or scratches.

Manufacturing

With production planning completed, manufacturing can begin. The first step in the manufacturing phase is selecting operators to work on the production line. You will want many of the class members to take part here. Study the routing sheets, schedules, and layout. Determine how many and what kinds of workers you will need for each job. You may wish to formally interview and hire people. Invite the class members to apply for jobs. Then work with your instructor to train them in the right ways to do the various jobs (Fig. 83–10).

When this training is finished, start the production-line work. Supervisors are very important here. They will have to make sure that safety procedures are followed and that the work is being done correctly and on schedule. Your teacher can be helpful to you.

Marketing

The marketing function is simple if school projects are to be given only to class

cult. You should write out the standards of acceptance you desire. These will help the inspectors be aware of what flaws or errors to watch for. Here is a list of errors that might occur and may need correcting:

1. Poor layout and shaping.
2. Burrs not removed, or sharp edges present.
3. Holes crooked or out of line.
4. Improper bends.

Fig. 83-11 Packaging finished products made in a school manufacturing activity. (Standard Oil Corporation)

Fig. 83-12 The final accounting—did you make a profit? (National Steel Corporation)

members. In this case, the cost of the projects can be computed to determine the price to be charged to each student. However, if they are to be sold to other people, you will also have to solve the problems of packaging, advertising, distribution, and selling.

The price is computed by collecting data on material costs, overhead, and labor costs. Material costs are very easy to collect. Study one of the supply catalogs to get the costs of the materials you used in manufacturing. Overhead costs should include a reasonable estimate of the heat, light, water, and power needed for manufacturing. Include a figure for a fair rental cost of the shop and the equipment and tools used. Finally, add in the costs for labor. Your instructor and school business office can help with this.

Several of the team members can develop packages for the product if these are needed. Remember that the package should protect the product and make shipping and handling easier (Fig. 83-11). You may also wish to prepare advertising posters. Set up a sales booth or sell door to door in your neigh-

borhood. Remember to include marketing costs in your final cost figures. With the final accounting, you can determine if you made a profit (Fig. 83-12). Finally, you should ask how you could have improved the job.

? QUESTIONS

1. What is the first step in doing a school mass-production project?
2. What are the initial samples of a project called?
3. List the typical "paperwork" produced by the production-planning team.
4. What must be done in the manufacturing team before the work actually begins?
5. Pricing is based on what cost figures?

✓ EXTRA CREDIT

Write a research report on how to start a corporation.

SECTION 12

HIGH TECHNOLOGY IN METALWORKING

Unit 84

Computers in the Metalworking Industries[1]

Chances are that by year 1995 there will be more computers than people in the United States. You will want to be comfortable with them, because not a day will go by that you will not be involved with computers in some way. In fact, you are already involved, perhaps more than you realize. When you make a telephone call from a pay phone, the "operator" telling you how much money to deposit actually may be a computerized voice. Your school schedule and reports may be figured by a computer. Many store bills and nearly all bank statements are done by computers. There are also all those computer games you play!

Since computers are everywhere, you are probably getting used to them. As time goes by, you will do more and more with them. This unit introduces you to what it is like to work with computers—work with them when they are being built, being pro-

[1] Some of the material in this unit is supplied through the courtesy of General Electric.

grammed, and being used in different jobs. You will learn how computers are used today and where you may expect to work with them tomorrow. Also you will get an idea of the education and training you will need to work in the computer field.

After reading this unit, you will know and understand computers a bit better and feel more comfortable with them.

Hardware

Computer people have a word for the physical elements of a computer system. They call them **hardware.** The term includes the central processing unit, keyboard, terminals, video displays, printers, and storage units, which are the equipment necessary for the input, processing, and output functions of the system.

Computer hardware is continually changing and also getting smaller and smaller. Systems that once filled an entire room now sit on a desk. The reduced size and increased operating speed of computer hardware make it more versatile and portable. Today you find computers in offices, banks, libraries, factories, warehouses, stores, schools, and homes.

Microcomputers, or personal computers, are small enough to sit on a desk or to carry around. They are general-purpose computers that can do many jobs done on larger machines. These desktop computers may be used just by themselves, or they may be connected by phone or wire to other computers in what is called a computer **network.** In either instance, the personal computer usually consists of five basic units (Fig. 84–1):

1. An *input device,* resembling a typewriter keyboard, which transmits instructions, programs, or information to the computer.

2. A *display device,* similar in appearance to a television set, on which the computer prints out text, graphs, and pictures (printout displayed on such a device is called **soft copy**); a home television set can be connected to the computer to serve as a display device.

3. The **central processing unit (CPU),** which contains the logic and computational chips; this unit is often housed in the same cabinet as the keyboard.

4. The *memory unit,* which controls the disks or cassettes that contain programs and data inserted into the computer.

5. The *printer,* which prints out a typed

copy on paper (this printout is called **hard copy**).

The chip

The **chip** is the all-important electronic building block used in computers. Barely the size of a baby's thumbnail, it is a microelectronic device less than one-eighth as large as a postage stamp. The chip really is complicated electronic circuitry on a silicon base with tiny switches joined by "wires" that are etched on a thin film of metal. The chip can hold millions of electronic "parts."

About 40 years ago, the first digital computer using vacuum tubes weighed over 30 tons. A large air-conditioned room was needed to hold the equipment. By contrast, a single tiny chip can perform 200 times more calculations than this huge first computer with its thousands of vacuum tubes.

In early computers, radios, and television sets, vacuum tubes were used to control and amplify electric signals. Because these "bulb-like" tubes gave off large amounts of heat, they burned out often. In 1947 the **transistor** was invented. This device has replaced the vacuum tube. Over the years, scientists have been able to reduce the size of the transistor by redesigning it. Within 10 years after it was invented, the transistor consisted of a speck of silicon crystal enclosed in a can about the size of a pea. Today the transistors used are smaller than a speck of dust.

A major breakthrough in technology came with the development of the silicon chip. The chip, with its many electronic "switches," is used in such products as computers, watches, calculators, and cash registers and in many items like robots and automobiles (Fig. 84–2).

The function of the semiconductor industry is to make chips. Producing these chips is a very exacting process. First, engineers must design the complex circuitry that

Fig. 84–1 A personal computer, including the keyboard, display device, central processing unit, memory units, and printer. This system also includes a plotter for CAD. (Heath Co.)

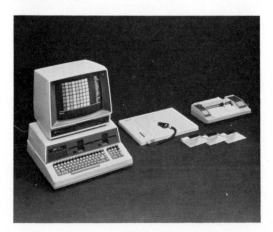

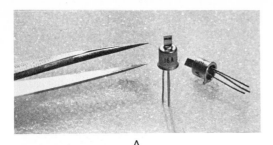

A

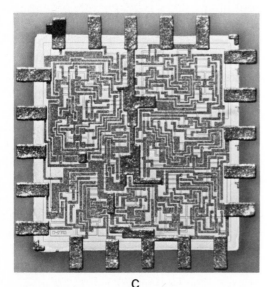

B

C

Fig. 84-2 (A) This tweezer shows how tiny the transistors used in earlier satellite communications were. (B) Individual chips. (C) An enlarged view of the chip showing the integrated circuits. (Western Electric Company)

is to make up the chip. Chips are made for different purposes and with a wide range in the number of electronic switches in the final unit. The electronic circuitry is projected onto the face of a **wafer** (which will later become many chips). The wafers are coated with photoresist, a light-sensitive material that makes it possible for the silicon to accept the design. The circuitry is etched onto the silicon chip. The process is much like that described in Unit 44. The silicon wafer is then covered with a metallic coating which electrically connects the wafer's various switches. Next, each wafer is cut into many chips using a laser beam (see Unit 68). Each chip is then mounted into its own frame and sealed for protection. The frame has tiny lead wires that allow the chip to be connected to other parts of the electronic circuitry in the computer (Fig. 84-3). To get an

Fig. 84-3 Using a high-powered microscope, a technician mounts each chip in a frame and seals it for protection. The frame contains tiny wire leads that allow the chip to be connected to other parts of the electronic circuit. (Western Electric Company)

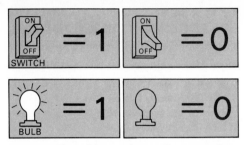

Fig. 84–4 The chip performs the same function as a light switch that turns a light on or off. A light bulb that is lit is equivalent to 1 in the central processing unit. An unlit light bulb is equivalent to 0. (General Electric Corporation)

idea of what a chip would be like to work on, imagine working on a part as tiny as a baby's thumbnail, having to use a microscope to see what is being done.

Remember, the chip with its many switches allows electricity to flow or not to flow, like a light being turned on or off. In a computer, a switch that is "on" represents a 1, and a switch that is "off" represents a 0 (Fig. 84–4). You will learn more about this later when you read about computer math. These electronic switches can be turned on and off at an incredible rate of speed. A large computer, for example, can add more than one million four-digit numbers every second.

Computer math (binary code)

The computer's language is written in **binary** code. It is a simple way of communicating, once you get the hang of it.

If you already understand binary, you know that there are really just two ideas that must be grasped.

The first idea is that the binary system is based on a different number system. Whereas decimal numbers—the kind of numbers we ordinarily use—are built on a base of 10, binary numbers are built on a base of 2. *Base 10* means that when you move

a number one space to the left (and add a zero), the new number is worth 10 times as much as the old number. Another way of saying this is that the number increases by the power of 10. *Base 2* means that every time you move a number to the left, the new number is worth 2 times as much as the original number; the number increases by the power of 2.

Values in the decimal system increase from right to left by the value of the base (10). And values in the binary system increase from right to left by the value of the base (2). By way of illustration:

Decimal: 1000   100   10   1
Binary: 32   16   8   4   2   1

The second idea is that the binary system uses only two numbers: 1 and 0. In other words, you must forget about the numbers 2, 3, 4, 5, 6, 7, 8, and 9. They are never used in the binary system.

How, then, do you count to 2 without using the figure 2? The answer is simple. As we noted, the value of the binary number increases by 2 times as you move it one space to the left. To get 2 in binary, you simply move your 1 space to the left and add zero. Thus, 10 in binary is the same as 2 in decimal.

To visualise this, imagine two racing cars. One has a mileage indicator in the binary system. At the start of a race, mileage indicators on each car read: 00000000. Now watch what happens as they go down the road, as shown in Fig. 84–5.

There is an easy way to convert a binary number to decimal by making a special number line. In a line, going from *right* to *left,* write down the number 1 and then double it to get your next number (2). Keep on doubling each number until you have as many numbers as you need. Note that by doubling each number, you obtain succes-

BINARY		DECIMAL
00000000	start	00000000
00000001	first mile	00000001
00000010	second mile	00000002
00000011	third mile	00000003
00000100	fourth mile	00000004
00000101	fifth mile	00000005
00000110	sixth mile	00000006
00000111	seventh mile	00000007
00001000	eighth mile	00000008
00001001	ninth mile	00000009
00001010	tenth mile	00000010
00001011	eleventh mile	00000011
00001100	twelfth mile	00000012
00001101	thirteenth mile	00000013
00001110	fourteenth mile	00000014
00001111	fifteenth mile	00000015
00010000	sixteenth mile	00000016
⋮	⋮	⋮
01100100	one hundred and one miles	00000101

Fig. 84–5 Here you see the difference between the binary math used in a computer and the decimal math used in both our money system and the metric measuring system. Note that in the binary system the only numbers used for computations are 0 and 1.

sive powers of 2. Your number line should look like this:

$$0 \quad 64 \quad 32 \quad 16 \quad 8 \quad 4 \quad 2 \quad 1$$

Underneath each number match up the binary number. Add the numbers in the decimal number line that correspond to a 1 in the binary number line. For example, take binary number 01100101:

```
0    64   32 16   8 4 2  1
0    1    1  0    0 1 0  1
0 + 64 + 32     +   4 + 1 = 101
```

Each digit—either 1 or 0—in a binary number is called a **bit** (short for *bi*nary dig*it*). This information is important to remember because, as we will see, information moves through a computer a *bit* at a time. While the binary code may seem somewhat awkward to those who are used to the decimal system, it is simplicity itself to the computer. This is because the basic electronic unit (the chip) inside the computer can exist in only two possible states: with the current either on or off.

How a computer operates

To communicate, computers *convert* (change) the numbers, letters, and symbols into the binary code (two digits) of computer math. The digit 1 is like an electric switch or light bulb that is on, and the digit 0 represents the switch or light bulb when it is off. Most personal computers digest information in chains of eight electric pulses called a **byte.** Just imagine these eight pulses as a bank of eight switches or electric light bulbs. When a bulb is on in the series of eight bulbs, it represents a 1, and when the bulb is off, it represents a 0. These eight bulbs can be arranged in 256 different combinations. This is much more capacity than is needed to cover the 52 letters of the alphabet (26 capital and 26 lowercase), 10 numbers, 13 punctuation marks, symbols, musical scales, and other input items that might be needed. To process the input instructions, the "switches" must be turned on or off. The computer "brain" that does the switching is the CPU (often only a single chip for most personal computers). To store excess information, **memory chips** are needed. There are two types of memory chips.

Random access memory (RAM) can be thought of as pages in a notebook where you write in all the information that you would like to use later when performing an operation or figuring out a problem. The information in the RAM chip is there only temporarily and then erased or destroyed just as you might do with the notes in the notebook after you have finished using the information.

The **read-only memory (ROM)** chip is

Fig. 84–6 Using a program on a computer that allows a builder to check various design ideas for floors, walls, ceilings, windows, and doors to determine which items will provide the greatest energy saving. (Owens-Corning Fiberglas Corporation)

like a reference book that contains permanent information that you will refer to again and again when using the computer. The ROM information memory chip is put there by the manufacturer of the computer.

The information in both the RAM and ROM chips is used by the CPU (see Fig. 84–6). The CPU uses the ROM memory chip to find out how to do things, such as show a character on the screen or send output information. The larger the ROM memory unit is, the more functions the computer can perform. Obviously, the more capacity the RAM chip has, the more information you can store on it. For example, a popular personal computer has 128K bytes in the RAM unit and 64K bytes in the ROM unit. The 64K ROM memory chip has permanently stored 524,288 *bits* of information.

Software

Software is the **program,** the detailed instructions that give a computer a complete description of the work it is do to and how it is to do it, step by step.

The people who develop these instruc-

tions are called *programmers,* and you might think of them as translators. They translate the steps for solving a problem into a language a computer can understand.

All kinds of special languages have been developed for communicating with computers. Some might require a simple language for simple problems, while others are very complex for difficult scientific or engineering jobs.

You must understand binary to understand *how* a computer works. However, thanks to the development of *symbolic languages,* you do not have to understand binary to *use* a computer. There is nothing hard about symbolic languages. Most of us hear some kind of symbolic language every day.

Some languages you may run into are Fortran (*for*mula *trans*lation); Cobol (*com*mon *b*usiness *o*riented *l*anguage); Basic (*be*ginner's *a*ll-purpose *s*ymbolic *i*nstruction *c*ode), which was derived from Fortran and Cobol; APL (*a* *p*rogramming *l*anguage), a language for mathematical concepts; and PL/1 (*p*rogramming *l*anguage *1*), which can handle both business and technical problems.

While there are many different computer languages, the four most popular for beginners are Basic, Pascal, Pilot, and Logo.

- *Basic* is used so widely that it is almost the standard microcomputer language. Basic is popular because it is relatively easy to learn and use. A program can be written using only a few instructions. These instructions are easy to interpret since they are in a short-hand form of English.
- *Pascal* was designed primarily for teaching languages. Pascal is used in schools as the language for standardized tests.
- *Pilot* is used by teachers to develop tests and other programs used in teaching.
- *Logo* is used to produce graphics on the screen.

433

COMPUTERS THAT "THINK"

Fig. 84-7 Computers are now being developed that will understand the spoken word so that special languages will not be needed.

In the years ahead, computers will be able to interpret the written and spoken English language as the input language. These computers will eliminate the need for the operator to learn a special language. These advanced computers also will be able to think and reason much like human beings (Fig. 84-7).

The first step in software design is to analyze the problem. This step is called *systems analysis*. A systems analyst, or a group of them, works with the people responsible for the project to figure out just what information is needed, what will be done with it, how quickly it must be processed, and how it is being handled at the moment. The analysis also includes a review of both the availa-

Fig. 84-8 Computer programmers begin with a flowchart. This chart shows the process a computer must go through to print a paycheck. The boxes indicate the work to be done; the diamonds show choices to be made by the computer. Each step of instructions is fed into the machine in a language the computer can understand. **(General Electric Corporation)**

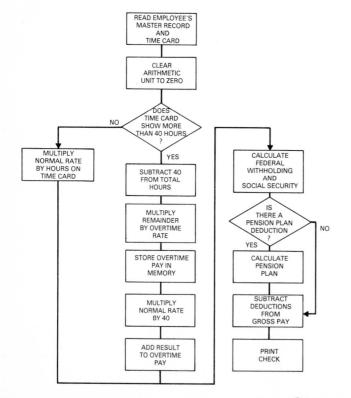

ble computer equipment and possible new equipment to handle the functions.

Next a programmer breaks down the problem into components. One way to do this is to make a flowchart (Fig. 84-8). The flowchart details the logical parts of the problem and the order in which they must be completed.

The programmer then reduces each part to the exact steps the computer must take (Fig. 84–8). Lastly, a computer processor changes each of the steps into a string of 1s and 0s so that the chip knows which switches to turn on and off.

Once the program is written, it is recorded on a **magnetic disk** for personal computers. This disk looks something like a small phonograph record. Some computers use cassettes instead of disks.

Computer careers in metalworking

Computers are used in every phase of metal manufacturing, from the design stage to the finished products. Computers are also a basic part of all office and business practices. Computers are used for accounts receivable, payroll, spare parts requirements, and inventory control, to name only a few uses (Figs. 84–9 to 84–11).

The careers related directly to metal manufacturing include:

Design and manufacturing. This is the rapidly growing field of computer-aided design and manufacturing (CAD/CAM). With CAD, computers translate engineering drawings or mathematical concepts into two- or three-dimensional renderings on a video screen. An object can be looked at from all sides, even from inside in many cases. The engineers involved can analyze a number of designs without the expense of building models (Figs. 84–12 and 84–13). Engineering drawings prepared on a CAD system look the same as those drawn with pencils and drafting instruments.

Fig. 84–9 Using a computer to obtain records about a business. Millions of items can be stored in a computer. (Western Electric Company)

CAD is only the beginning, however. Computers that help design are linked to computers that control manufacturing processes through a technology called *interactive graphics.* The CAM systems for tooling, processing, and testing are designed when the product is designed rather than later. And through CAM, these operations are also controlled electronically.

CAM includes robotics in manufactur-

Fig. 84–10 Computers are useful in every step of business operations. (ASK Computer Systems Inc.)

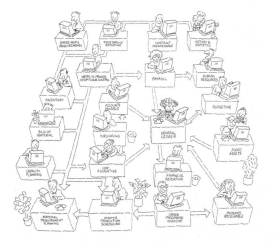

Fig. 84-11 Computers are used in complete office automation. The system includes electronic mailing and filing as well as desktop workstations for clerks, secretaries, professionals, and managers. (Exxon Office Systems Company)

Fig. 84-12 This engineer is doing computer-aided design. The display unit offers a high-quality, three-dimensional display for a new airplane design. (Adage, Inc.)

Fig. 84-13 This engineer is designing a part for an automobile. Notice the clear, true three-dimensional detailed design of the part. (General Motors Corporation)

ing. Robots perform extremely demanding chores such as firing blast furnaces. They also handle monotonous, repetitive jobs, allowing humans to do more complex ones. Robotics is particularly useful in the automobile, appliance, aviation, and heavy-equipment industries.

Engineers. As you might guess, many of the people operating CAD computers are engineers. The type of equipment being designed dictates the type of engineer involved. A bridge would involve a civil engineer; an airplane, an aerospace engineer; a factory layout, a manufacturing engineer; and so on.

There are more than 50 different major specializations within engineering and over 1 million practicing engineers. To all of them, the computer has become a vital tool.

Technicians. Technicians are the engineer's teammates. They need to have expert knowledge of scientific principles, testing, and measuring devices and to know practical ways to apply that knowledge (Fig. 84-14). To meet those requirements, technicians must also have knowledge and experience with computers.

Fig. 84–14 Technicians must be able to test equipment such as this special touch-tone telephone that uses a central processing unit. (Western Electric Company)

Other operators. As computers move into factories, they are also used by people with training in various manufacturing jobs, such as mechanics, electricians, and lathe operators.

Computers in the metalworking laboratory

In a metal technology laboratory, computers can be used for such work as inventory, design of projects, and billing. Educational software (programs) in many areas of metalworking is available, including computerized tests, evaluation, and self-instructional materials.

? QUESTIONS

1. About how many computers will there be in the United States by 1995?
2. Name the five parts of a personal computer system.
3. Describe the chip.
4. What are the two electronic switching units that preceded the chip?
5. Describe briefly how the chip is manufactured.
6. How is the binary code different from decimal numbers?
7. What would the number 14 look like in the binary code?
8. Define the bit and the byte.
9. What is the purpose of the CPU in the computer?
10. Describe the function of the two memory chips.
11. What is the purpose of software?
12. Name three languages used in computer software.
13. Describe the difference between CAD and CAM.

Unit 85
Industrial Robots

The industrial robot is not like the charming robots that traveled the galaxies in *Star Wars*. It is a diving, twisting, thrusting blend of computer and machine tool (Fig. 85–1). Robots are programmable manipulators that can move parts or tools through specific sequences of movements. Just like the other machine tools, robots can repeat the same job for long periods of time with great precision (Figs. 85–2 and 85–3). Some of the jobs robots can do are extremely complex. A robot can be "taught" to do new jobs and use accessories that give it a great range of abilities. Industrial robots can do automatic drilling, milling, boring, cutting, welding, paint spraying, and many other jobs.

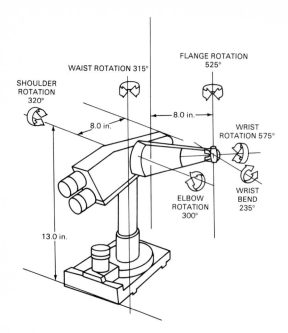

WAIST ROTATION 315°

FLANGE ROTATION 525°

SHOULDER ROTATION 320°

8.0 in.

8.0 in.

WRIST ROTATION 575°

ELBOW ROTATION 300°

WRIST BEND 235°

13.0 in.

Fig. 85-1 This small robot, which is used for medium- to high-speed assembly, has six axes of motion.

The term *robot* comes from the Czech word *robota*, which means "serf" or "forced laborer." The word was first used in a play written over a half century ago. The first commercial robot used in the United States was one developed for the Atomic Energy Commission in 1958 to handle radioactive

Fig. 85-2 A typical heavy-duty industrial robot used in material handling. (Unimation Inc.)

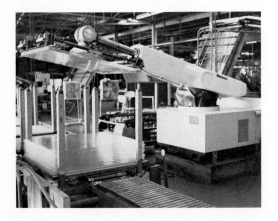

materials. The first robots used on an automobile assembly line were installed in 1962, and since that time, there has been an explosion in robot use in the metalworking industry.

Definition

Robots differ from other automated machinery. A robot is "a programmable device designed to move materials, parts, tools, and specialized devices through a variable of motions for the performance of a variety of tasks." How does a robot differ, for example, from an automated bottle facility? The key word is *reprogrammable*. A robot can perform a variety of tasks once it is programmed to do so, and can be reprogrammed to perform other different tasks (Fig. 85-4). An automated bottling machine, on the other hand, can perform only one task. In the past, it was the practice of companies to build automated assembly lines for producing a single product, such as the subassembly for an automobile engine. Then, when new products were developed, the old assembly line was scrapped because scrapping it was cheaper than converting the line to a new product (Fig. 85-5). Now, with computers and robots, the *flexible manufacturing system* can produce different kinds of products using the same assembly line. (See Unit 86).

Kinds of robots

A typical robot consists of one or more arms (manipulators), hands (end effectors), a controller, a power supply, and possibly an array of sensors to provide feedback information. The robots used in industry are classified according to their industrial use including the following:

● *Pick-and-place robot*—the simplest form of robot. This robot picks up an object and places it in another location. Freedom of

438

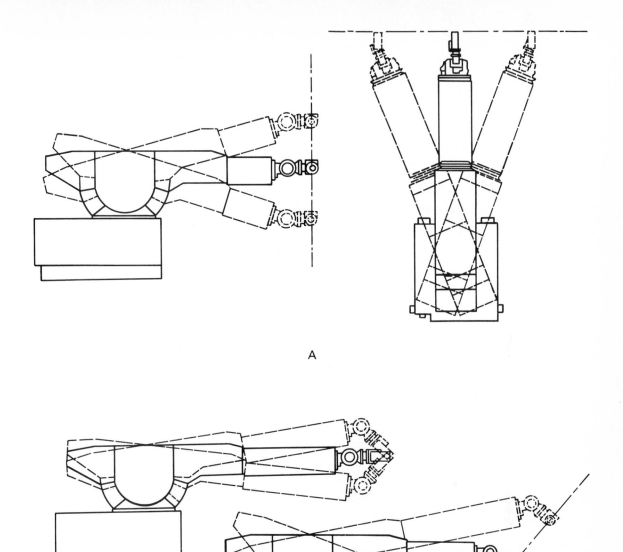

A

B

Fig. 85-3 Robots can move (A) in a continuous path for such operations as weld-ing and spray painting and (B) from point to point for moving products and equip-ment and for assembly.

Fig. 85-4 A large robot used to load, unload, and package parts being produced by other machines.

movement is usually limited to two or three directions (Fig. 85-6).

- *Servo robot*—a robot that uses servomechanisms for the arms and hands to alter direction in midair. There are several kinds of servo robots. Direction is altered by tripping a mechanical switch, and five to seven directions of motion are common, depending on the number of joints in the arm.
- *Programmable robot*—a robot that is driven by a programmable controller that memorizes a sequence of movements and repeats these continuously. This kind of robot is programmed by "walking" the arm and hand through the desired movement.
- *Computerized robot*—a robot run by a computer. This kind of robot is programmed by instructions fed into the controller electronically. "Smart" robots may have the ability to improve upon their work instructions (Fig. 85-7).
- *Sensory robot*—a computerized robot with one or more artificial senses to sense its environment and feed back information to the controller. Senses are usually sight or touch.
- *Assembly robot*—a computerized robot, probably with sensors, that is designed for assembly-line jobs.

Building robots

Robots are produced in many sizes and designs for various kinds of industrial jobs. Robots are made primarily of metal and plastics and contain electronic circuitry, a memory system, a control system, and a power drive to operate the hands and the arms. The control system can be either an electronic control that is manually pro-

Fig. 85-5 A one-product assembly line designed for a specific job. When the product is no longer manufactured, this assembly line will have to be dismantled and a new automatic line built.

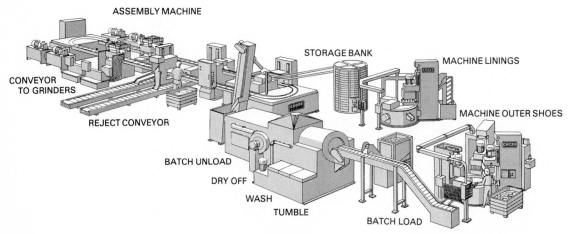

ASSEMBLY MACHINE

STORAGE BANK

MACHINE LININGS

CONVEYOR TO GRINDERS

MACHINE OUTER SHOES

REJECT CONVEYOR

BATCH UNLOAD

DRY OFF

WASH

TUMBLE

BATCH LOAD

Fig. 85–6 A simple pick-and-place robot built by a student majoring in metalwork.

Fig. 85–8 A small robot that is controlled by electronic circuitry. (Feedback, Inc.)

grammed or a computer (microprocessor) control. The power drive can be either hydraulic, electric, or pneumatic. Electric drives to operate the arms and hands are used on smaller robots that handle loads of

Fig. 85–7 A different design for robots that are controlled by a computer. (IBM)

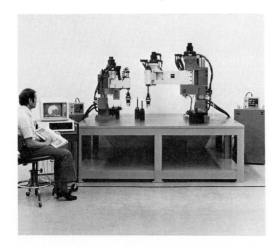

about 22 pounds or less (Fig. 85–8). Larger robots that handle loads of 450 pounds or more use hydraulic drives (Figs. 85–9 and 85–10). A hydraulic system operates by transmitting power and applying it to do work. The parts of a hydraulic system include a pump or compressor, a reservoir to store the oil, relief and control valves, and pipes, tubing, or hoses to carry the fluid. The great advantage of this system is that a small force applied to the control valve produces a

Fig. 85–9 A large hydraulic robot being used to load and unload 20-pound forings into a twin-spindle turning machine, two parts at a time, for inside-diameter machining. (Prab Robot Co.)

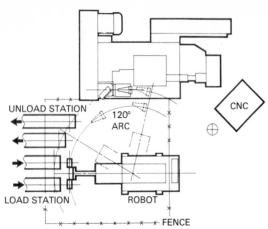

Fig. 85-10 Parts are fed in pairs to a loading station by a conveyor. The hydraulic robot grips both parts, rotating them 90 degrees to bring the part axis from vertical to horizontal. The robot then pivots 120 degrees to insert the parts into the turning machine.

tremendous force on the hands and arms of the robots (see Fig. 56–7). Pneumatic robots use pressurized gas to move the arms and hands.

Fig. 85-11 Robots create a flurry of sparks while welding automobile bodies. (General Motors Corporation)

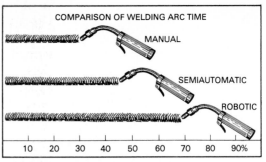

Fig. 85-12 This chart shows how the use of robots can increase efficiency in arc welding. The welder doing the job manually can work only about 30 percent of the time, while the robot performing this same job can operate about 70 percent of the time.

One major use for robots is arc welding. This is a hot, hazardous, and tediously repetitive job. As the result of difficult working conditions, the welder is unable to work with more than about 30 percent efficiency. However, specially designed robots for welding can increase efficiency to an average of 70 percent. By programming the robot to perform the actual labor, a welder can work better and avoid boring, hazardous conditions (Fig. 85–11 to 85–13). One welder can easily position and control several robots.

Another common use for robots is spray painting (Fig. 85–14). Robots produce a more even paint job with less runs and streaks than when the job is done by a worker.

Effect on labor

Robots are having a major impact on all kinds of metal manufacturing. A typical robot working two shifts a day costs about $6 per hour (Fig. 85–15).

Current robots will not replace people in some industrial jobs. Robots cannot react to unforeseen events and changing conditions. Therefore, in many manufacturing plants, robots are combined with people on the as-

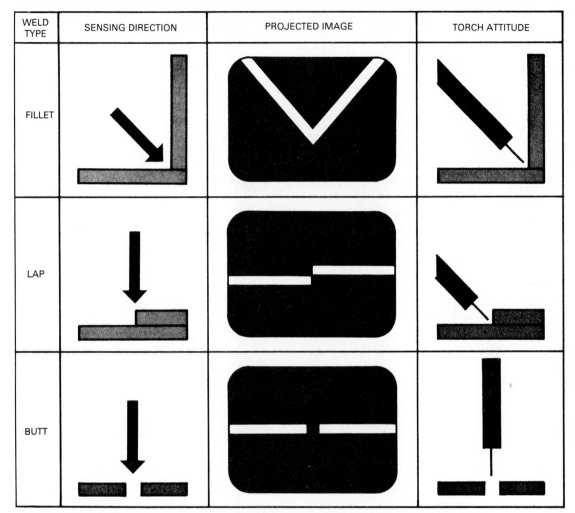

WELD TYPE	SENSING DIRECTION	PROJECTED IMAGE	TORCH ATTITUDE
FILLET			
LAP			
BUTT			

Fig. 85-13 A sensory system used with a robot that is doing arc welding tells the robot to make two passes over the part to be welded. The sensory system has memory storage that controls the robots for many kinds of welds.

sembly line (Fig. 85-16). The robots do the repetitive jobs such as arc and spot welding, grinding, spray painting, stacking, and loading and unloading machines. People do the tasks that require human motor and perceptual skills, eye-hand coordination, planning, judgments, and evaluations.

Robots will replace workers for many of the jobs in manufacturing that have the job title of *operators*. It is estimated that as many as 4 million operators will be replaced by robots over the next 20 years (Fig. 85-17). Some time in the twenty-first century, robots will eliminate almost all routine manufacturing jobs—about 8 million jobs. Robots will also be widely used in undersea and space exploration.

Careers

As robots replace workers for the routine, dangerous, and boring jobs in manufacturing, new job opportunities for people

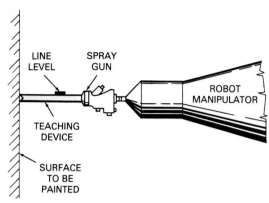

LINE LEVEL

SPRAY GUN

ROBOT MANIPULATOR

TEACHING DEVICE

SURFACE TO BE PAINTED

Fig. 85–14 This teaching device, consisting of a spacer rod or tube with a three-pointed tip and a line level, is used during the pattern (adjustment) process to make sure the robot manipulator (arm) holds the spray gun perpendicular to the surface to be sprayed and at the right distance from it. This would be the responsibility of the *robot technician* in making sure the robot operates properly.

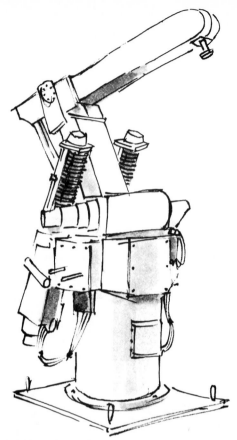

Fig. 85–15 Robots can work 24 hours a day with little loss of time (downtime) for repairs and maintenance.

with advanced technical training will be created. Between 33,000 and 64,000 new jobs in robotics will be created by the end of the 1980s.

Robotics engineers are responsible for designing, testing, and building robots that are productive and safe to operate as well as economical to purchase and maintain. These engineers use computer-aided design and manufacturing (CAD/CAM) systems to perform systems and research methods to manufacture robots economically (Fig. 85–18).

Robotic engineers who work for robot manufacturers are sometimes called *robotics test engineers* or *automation system engineers*. These engineers apply the robotic system to a particular use on a manufacturing assembly line.

Most robotics engineers are employed by private robot manufacturers or robot users. Some engineers work in military and space programs. Others work for colleges

Fig. 85–16 A typical assembly line that combines robots and people to assemble a product.

REASONS FOR USING ROBOTS IN INDUSTRY

- To reduce labor costs
- To improve the quality of the product
- To eliminate dangerous and boring jobs
- To increase the rate of output
- To increase product flexibility
- To reduce waste of materials
- To meet Occupational Safety and Health Act (OSHA) standards for dangerous jobs
- To reduce labor turnover
- To reduce cost of capital equipment

Fig. 85-17 The major reasons manufacturers are using robots in industry.

and universities or vocational and trade schools.

You generally need at least a bachelor's degree in engineering to enter this field. Because robotics technology draws upon the engineering expertise of many different disciplines, engineers who specialize in robotics often have degrees in mechanical, manufacturing, electronics, or industrial engineering.

Robotics courses typically include training in hydraulics and pneumatics, CAD/CAM systems, electronics, microprocessors, integrated systems, and logic.

Robot technicians are needed to install and maintain the machines (Fig. 85-19). The best preparation for becoming a robot technician is a 2-year electronics technician program. Unlike automobile companies, which manufacture generic products (the automobiles have the same basic parts and are serviced in about the same way), each robot manufacturer uses a distinctly different control system. A few of the major manufacturers of robots in the United States include Cincinnati Milacron; Unimation, Inc.; Prab; IBM; DeVilbiss; GM; and GE. Because each company uses a different model of robot, the robot technician must have specialized knowledge to work on a spe-

Fig. 85-18 Robots in production plants today cannot see or feel. They move along a preprogrammed path that never changes, even if the part is out of position. Engineers are working on another generation of robots that will be able to see or feel and react to what they see or feel. Current research is aimed at developing computer vision systems that will allow robots to locate parts that are mixed up. This engineer is placing a part on a conveyor belt. A television camera mounted in the apparatus at the rear views the moving conveyor belt below it and the computer forms a picture of the part. The computer can then match the part with a similar one. The computer tells the robot which one of the parts on the moving belt to pick up. (General Motors Corporation)

cific company's model. For example, a person who can program and repair the electronic circuitry on a Cincinnati Milacron robot would not be able to do the same on a Prab robot. There is very little preventive maintenance on the mechanical parts of a robot. Usually all that is needed is to lubricate the various joints on a regular schedule.

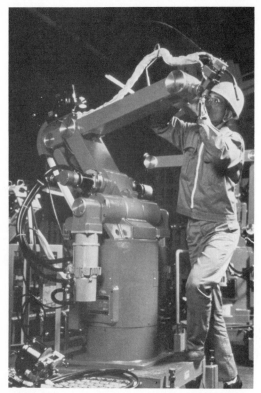

Fig. 85–19 Robot technicians must be able to set up and program the robots for a particular use or purpose. (Analog Devices, Inc.)

? QUESTIONS

1. What is a robot?
2. How does a robot differ from a single-purpose automated machine?
3. Where did the word **robot** come from?
4. Describe a sensory robot.
5. Name the two kinds of power drives used on robots.
6. Which type of power drive must be used if the robot is to pick up heavy loads?
7. What are some of the limitations of the robot?
8. Why will people always be needed in a manufacturing plant?

 EXTRA CREDIT

Read about the future of robots in magazines on technology such as *Technology Today.*

Unit 86
Manufacturing Systems

Manufacturing is concerned with factory production of durable goods using various methods (Fig. 86–1). Manufacturing today is changing so rapidly that it is difficult to keep up with current developments. Only 22 percent of the people in the United States are employed directly in manufacturing. Manufacturing industries are three basic types: custom (customized), batch, and mass production.

Custom production, the first type of industry, means making only one or a very few products of the same design. When you build your own project in a shop or laboratory, you are using this method of manufacturing. Because of developments in CAD/CAM and the flexible manufacturing system (which you will read about later), many more commercial products in the future can be customized (Fig. 86–2).

The second type of industry, *batch* (or *short-run*) manufacturing, is the largest in our economy. In this type, only a limited number of a particular size and kind of product is produced. In batch production, each new model of the product is manufactured with fewer and fewer parts or subassemblies. The

Fig. 86-1 Typical manufactured consumer product—the telephone.

Fig. 86-2 A custom-designed ornament.

try, deals with manufacturing products in high volume. Some of the most common mass production industries include automobile, steel, chemicals, and toys (Fig. 86-4).

All manufacturing is either labor-inten-

Fig. 86-3 Airplanes are typical of *batch*, or *short-run*, manufacturing. Even the same model of plane is customized to meet the desires of different military units.

same parts can be used in a variety of products. One of the best known cameras has only 40 parts, in contrast to over 170 parts in the older models. In batch or limited-line production, the use of both CAD/CAM and the flexible manufacturing system is essential. These techniques make it possible to produce a small number of products at a profit. Information about the parts or products is stored in a computer program, and when necessary, the product can be produced again and again as needed. Today, more and more manufacturing is batch, limited, or midvolume production. For example, 75 percent of all the products used by military services are manufactured in groups of less than 100 units (Fig. 86-3).

Mass production, the third type of indus-

Fig. 86-4 Tableware pieces are typical of small items that are **mass-produced.**

sive or machine-intensive. In *labor-intensive manufacturing*, a large percentage of the cost of the product is in the labor. In machine-intense manufacturing, there is a heavy dependence on expensive machines to produce the part or product with less cost going to labor.

Manufacturing processes include the following:

1. Converting raw materials into industrial materials. For example, using iron ore, coal, and limestone to produce steel or using bauxite ore to produce aluminum.

2. Making industrial materials into standard stock. These standard stock items of plastics, metal, glass, and wood are what you have in the storeroom of your shop or laboratory.

3. Making components or subassemblies. A component is a single item used in a larger product. For example, a transmission of a car is a typical component.

4. Assembling components into finished products. Often, the components will be manufactured in different parts of the country and then brought to a central assembly point.

5. Preparing for distribution. Finished products are stored in warehouses until orders are received from consumers. The finished products are loaded onto trucks, boats, planes, or railroad cars to move them to the consumer.

6. Servicing manufactured goods. Maintenance and repair of manufactured goods after production and during the life span of products are very important.

Traditional automated assembly line

The traditional automated assembly line uses an integral group of machines to perform automatically the necessary operations needed to produce one specific part or product. In addition, through sensing devices fed to an electronic control panel or computer, necessary corrective adjustments are made. However, this kind of assembly line is useful only as long as the same design of part is being manufactured. Once the design is changed, the entire assembly line must be revamped or revised, or a new assembly line has to be built, with a great deal of downtime between model changes.

A typical example of an automobile part produced by the traditional automated system is the cylinder block (Fig. 86–5). The automated system consists of eight major sections (Fig. 86–6). Each section contains a variety of specialized machine tools, transfer equipment, and feedback mechanisms for monitoring the process (Fig. 86–7). The raw cast cylinder block is delivered to the system on skids, the same as for a standard machining process. The operator uses a power hoist to place the engine block in position at the

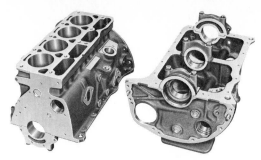

Fig. 86-5 A cylinder block that is to be mass-produced. (The Cross Company)

beginning of the conveyor system. This is the only time the parts are handled manually. All the necessary machining is done as the block moves through a series of specialized machines (Fig. 86-8). After each machining process is completed, the part is moved to its next position by transfer equipment. When necessary, the part is rotated, moved up and down, positioned, and placed in the fixture or jig for the next machining operation (Fig. 86-9). All this is done automatically. Changes in feeds and speed are also accomplished automatically. As the machining is done, the workpiece is continually monitored to make sure it meets established quality standards. The cylinder blocks are even automatically washed before they are given a final inspection. Defective cylinder blocks are automatically ejected. The traditional automated system is still widely used for mass production of parts (Fig. 86-10).

Fig. 86-6 The key to the automated system is a coordinated, integrated system of specialized machine tools, transfer equipment, and feedback mechanisms.

CAD/CAM

CAD/CAM systems are changing the way in which products are designed, drawn, and built. *CAD* is the abbreviation for *computer-aided design*. CAD is a very fast and accurate means of creating and changing drafting designs. CAD is really just an electronic system that is capable of producing a variety of designs with the aid of a computer (Fig. 86-11A). One advantage of CAD is that it eliminates repetition. Once a design is created, it never has to be completely redrawn again. The computer stores all the information so that every design that is created can be kept on file and is always accessible. New designs are made by selecting elements from existing designs and putting them together. Frequently needed design elements, parts, or symbols can be stored in a file in the computer and called up and "plugged" into a drawing as desired (Fig. 86-11B). Another advantage of CAD is that it is very accurate. Line weight is always the same and lettering is standardized since these essentials are part of a computer program. As the designs are redrawn, there is never a variation in quality, as would be true if each new drawing were done by hand. The main change is that the computer has taken over the routine tasks of design. Although drafters still must be skilled in drafting to do the visualizing, they no longer have to worry about such details as line weight and lettering (Fig. 86-12).

CAD is really a kind of "instant" design process because the drafter using the machine can create a new drawing using the elements that are in the storage unit of the computer and see the results immediately (Fig. 86-13). The efficient use of CAD systems depends on the programs (software) that are available. For example, architectural firms will use programs dealing with designing buildings, rooms, floor plans, cabi-

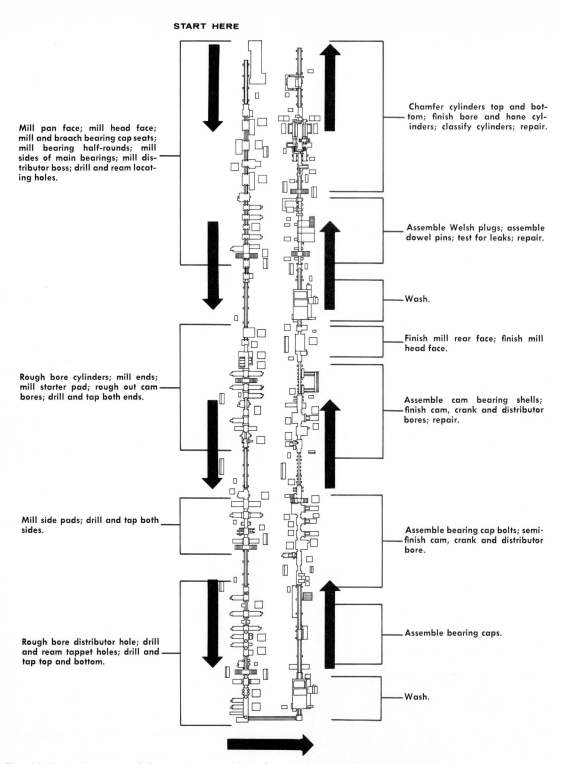

Mill pan face; mill head face; mill and broach bearing cap seats; mill bearing half-rounds; mill sides of main bearings; mill distributor boss; drill and ream locating holes.

Chamfer cylinders top and bottom; finish bore and hone cylinders; classify cylinders; repair.

Assemble Welsh plugs; assemble dowel pins; test for leaks; repair.

Wash.

Finish mill rear face; finish mill head face.

Rough bore cylinders; mill ends; mill starter pad; rough out cam bores; drill and tap both ends.

Assemble cam bearing shells; finish cam, crank and distributor bores; repair.

Mill side pads; drill and tap both sides.

Assemble bearing cap bolts; semifinish cam, crank and distributor bore.

Rough bore distributor hole; drill and ream tappet holes; drill and tap top and bottom.

Assemble bearing caps.

Wash.

Fig. 86-7 A diagram of the automated line for producing the cylinder blocks.

Fig. 86–8 Note the twin milling heads being used to machine the bottom of the cylinder block.

Fig. 86–9 Note how the transfer equipment can move the part, rotate it, and do anything else necessary to keep it moving along to the next machining stations.

nets, and so forth, while manufacturing concerns will use programs for designing metal parts and assemblies. CAD will not eliminate the work of the trained drafter (Fig. 86–14).

While you may not have a chance to use a CAD program in your class, by learning the fundamentals of drafting, you will be in a better position to use CAD in the future as a good drafting and design tool. There are over 1 million drafters in the world, and yet less than 5 percent are using CAD.

*CAM, c*omputer-*a*ided *m*anufacturing, is the other part of the total system. The CAM system takes the design from the CAD system, and by use of computers and numerically controlled machines, produces the product. CAD and CAM are a team that are only two parts of the flexible manufacturing system. This complete system is described next.

Flexible manufacturing systems

A *flexible manufacturing system (FMS)* is an automated line used for the manufacture of a variety of parts at midvolume or batch production. A typical flexible manufacturing system consists of a number of machine tools tied together by work-handling equipment and controlled by a central computer (Fig. 86–15). Robots are used to move and position parts or subassemblies of the work. The flexible manufacturing system includes computer-aided machines, robots, automatic parts carriers, and an automatic quality control center all connected into a single line. The smallest unit in this system is the *manufacturing cell* (Fig. 86–16). A manufacturing cell consists of a system of several machine centers, often not more than five, to do drilling, turning, milling, and other machining operations. Manufacturing cells are directed by a computer or microprocessor.

To develop a flexible manufacturing sys-

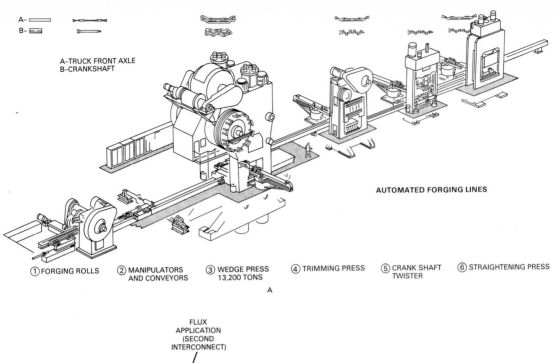

A-TRUCK FRONT AXLE
B-CRANKSHAFT

AUTOMATED FORGING LINES

① FORGING ROLLS   ② MANIPULATORS   ③ WEDGE PRESS   ④ TRIMMING PRESS   ⑤ CRANK SHAFT   ⑥ STRAIGHTENING PRESS
                        AND CONVEYORS   13,200 TONS   TWISTER

A

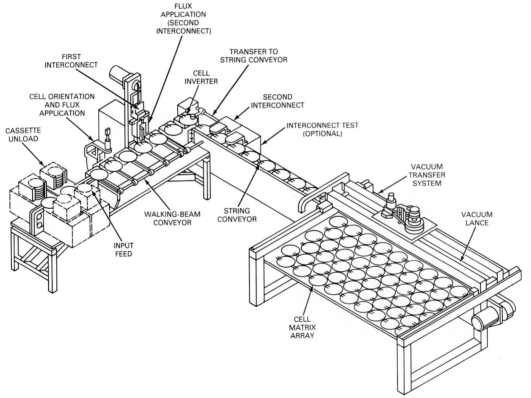

FLUX
APPLICATION
(SECOND
INTERCONNECT)

FIRST
INTERCONNECT

TRANSFER TO
STRING CONVEYOR

CELL
INVERTER

CELL ORIENTATION
AND FLUX
APPLICATION

SECOND
INTERCONNECT

INTERCONNECT TEST
(OPTIONAL)

CASSETTE
UNLOAD

VACUUM
TRANSFER
SYSTEM

VACUUM
LANCE

WALKING-BEAM
CONVEYOR

STRING
CONVEYOR

INPUT
FEED

CELL
MATRIX
ARRAY

B

Fig. 86–10 (A) An automated forging line that can produce front axles, crank-shafts, and other forged parts. **(B)** An automated solar module assembly line. The solar cells are unloaded from cassettes, oriented, and soldered into strings and placed into modules that are used in solar panels for satellites.

452

A

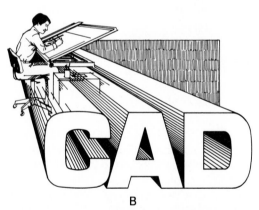

B

Fig. 86-11 (A) A CAD system eliminates the use of a drafting board and instruments. (B) A well-trained drafter who also knows how to use a computer can produce a drawing in a very short time. (Eastman Kodak Company)

and (2) the capability to adjust the line to produce different parts or products using computer software. The flexible manufacturing system must also include a method of transferring the material from one cell to the next. The transfer line may be a variety of devices such as automated parts carriers, continuous transfer lines, or pallet methods of moving material or parts from one place to the next (Fig. 86-18).

The most advanced and complicated flexible manufacturing system is called *computer-integrated manufacturing* (*CIM*). In this system all phases of manufacturing, from the design stage through final inspection, are centrally controlled by a computer. Because CIM is very expensive, only the largest manufacturing companies can afford the system. CIM includes all high-technology advancements, including computers, robots, automated storage and retrieval systems, computerized material handling using driverless transport vehicles, numerically controlled machining centers, and automatic inspection devices.

Fig. 86-12 You must know the fundamentals of drafting before you can learn to do CAD. (Eastman Kodak Company)

tem, first the manufacturing cells must be organized and then the cells assembled into the total flexible manufacturing system (Fig. 86-17). The key to this system is twofold: (1) two-way communication between the cells

A

A

B

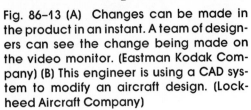

Fig. 86-13 (A) Changes can be made in the product in an instant. A team of designers can see the change being made on the video monitor. (Eastman Kodak Company) (B) This engineer is using a CAD system to modify an aircraft design. (Lockheed Aircraft Company)

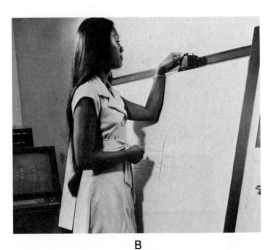

B

Fig. 86-14 (A) A typical CAD unit used in industry. (Cascade Graphic Development) (B) A plotter connected to the CAD unit can produce a full-size engineering drawing in ink on a wide variety of drawing papers and material. (McDonnell Douglas Automation Company)

Fig. 86–15 Numerically controlled machining centers are designed for use when production rates are relatively low and the product mix is relatively high.

Fig. 86–16 Manufacturing cells are the smallest form of flexible manufacturing systems. They are usually fewer than five pieces of machinery capable of performing several machine and inspections functions. (Ex-Cell-O Corporation)

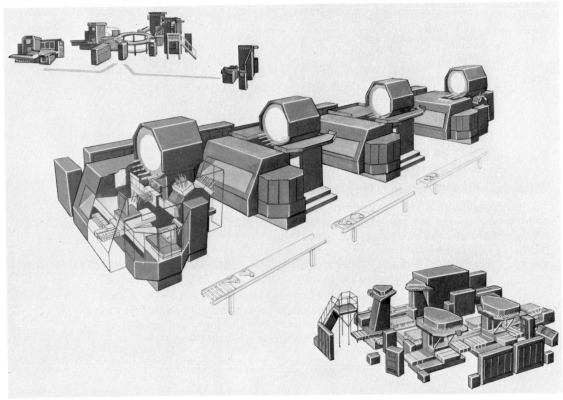

Fig. 86–17 A flexible manufacturing system is an automated production system for the manufacture of families of workpieces at midvolume rates. (Ex-Cell-O Corporation)

Fig. 86–18 Here is a tabletop flexible manufacturing system on which you can learn the typical industrial processes used in this system. This unit includes computers, robots, automated process control, a production line, and optical sensing devices. (ASCI Marketing Group)

Labor-intensive manufacturing

Not all manufacturers use sophisticated equipment to produce their products. Often, manufacturers can maintain a very efficient manufacturing system by using highly skilled individuals. Employees in such companies must have a wide variety of skills, particularly in customizing the products. The individual employee will do most of the operations in assembling the product. Either parts and subassemblies are manufactured by the company, or subassemblies are bought from other manufacturers to use in assembling the final product. One of the most efficient manufacturers of lawn mowers uses this manufacturing system to produce its products (Fig. 86–19).

Fig. 86–19 An all-around skilled machinist can compete successfully when using modern equipment. Because of this fact, skilled machinists, toolmakers, and die-makers are always in demand by industry. (VICA)

 QUESTIONS

1. Name the three types of manufacturing industries.
2. Making a single project in the metal laboratory represents what type of industry?
3. Name the six major steps in the manufacturing process.
4. Define **CAD**.
5. What percent of the drafters in the world use CAD?
6. Define **CAM**.
7. What is a flexible manufacturing system?
8. Can labor-intensive manufacturers compete with manufacturers who use the FMS? Explain.

 EXTRA CREDIT

List the schools in your area which offer 2-year technician's programs in CAD and write a report about the programs.

SECTION 13

PROJECTS

In this section, you will find a number of projects. Making them will help you practice the skills and use the information you are learning in your metalworking course. Some are very simple. They are to be used as beginning activities. Others are more advanced. They can be used only after you have gained skill in certain technical areas.

Remember that these are suggested projects. You should refer to Units 3 and 4 for help in designing projects of your own. After you have done some research and sketching, discuss your design ideas with your teacher. Think of designs that you can use in your room, in your home workshop, or as gifts for your family and friends. The well-designed and well-made project will long be appreciated.

bench metal and wrought metal

Camp Saw. This lightweight yet sturdy camp saw is simple to make. The aluminum tubing is strong but easy to bend. Saw blades for this unit are available at hardware stores at low cost. The length of the saw bow can be changed for other blade sizes.

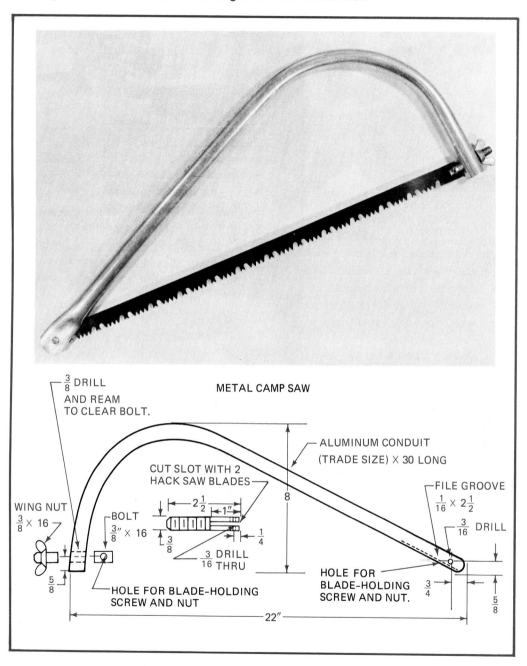

METAL CAMP SAW

Fireplace Set. This attractive fireplace set is made of aluminum. The handles are wrapped with heavy cord or plastic material. The shovel and broom sections can be assembled with rivets or machine screws. A metric-equivalent chart is added if you wish to use metric measuring tools.

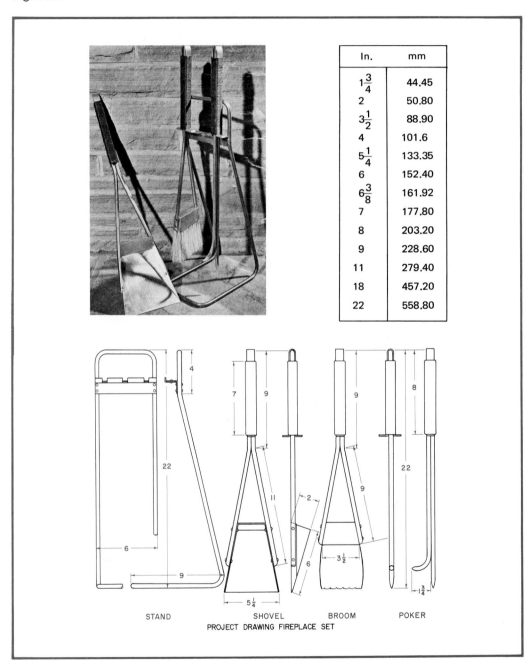

In.	mm
$1\frac{3}{4}$	44.45
2	50.80
$3\frac{1}{2}$	88.90
4	101.6
$5\frac{1}{4}$	133.35
6	152.40
$6\frac{3}{8}$	161.92
7	177.80
8	203.20
9	228.60
11	279.40
18	457.20
22	558.80

STAND   SHOVEL   BROOM   POKER

PROJECT DRAWING FIREPLACE SET

Pickup Tongs. These tongs are a useful tool for the school or home workshop. They are handy for holding hot metal parts and containers. The sizes and shapes of the jaws can be altered to meet special needs.

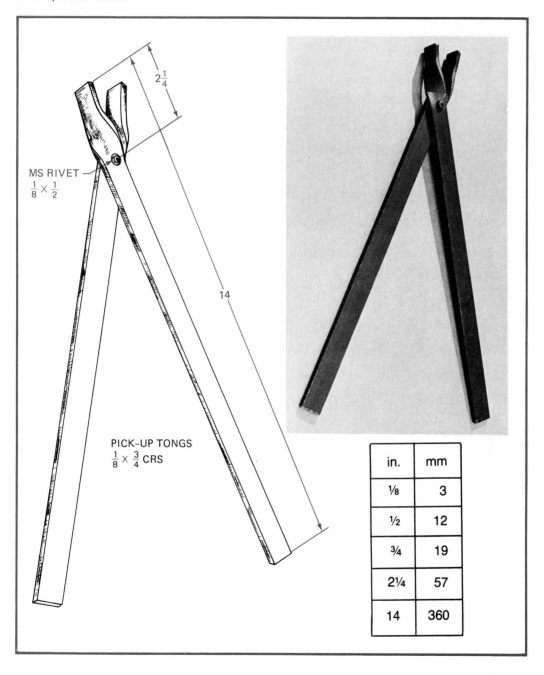

MS RIVET
$\frac{1}{8} \times \frac{1}{2}$

$2\frac{1}{4}$

14

PICK-UP TONGS
$\frac{1}{8} \times \frac{3}{4}$ CRS

in.	mm
⅛	3
½	12
¾	19
2¼	57
14	360

Stack Tables. These tables combine metal and either wood or plastic. The dimensions are given in both inches and millimeters.

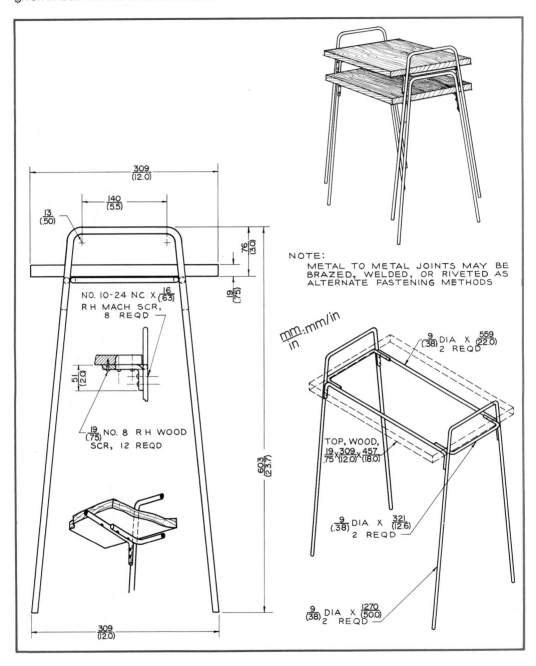

$\frac{309}{(12.0)}$

$\frac{140}{(5.5)}$

$\frac{13}{(.50)}$

$\frac{76}{(3.0)}$

$\frac{19}{(.75)}$

NO. 10-24 NC X $\frac{16}{(.63)}$
R H MACH SCR,
8 REQD

$\frac{51}{(2.0)}$

$\frac{19}{(.75)}$ NO. 8 R H WOOD
SCR, 12 REQD

$\frac{603}{(23.7)}$

$\frac{309}{(12.0)}$

NOTE:
METAL TO METAL JOINTS MAY BE
BRAZED, WELDED, OR RIVETED AS
ALTERNATE FASTENING METHODS

$\frac{mm}{in}$:mm/in

$\frac{9}{(.38)}$ DIA X $\frac{559}{(22.0)}$
2 REQD

TOP, WOOD,
$\frac{19}{.75}$ X $\frac{309}{(12.0)}$ X $\frac{457}{(18.0)}$

$\frac{9}{(.38)}$ DIA X $\frac{321}{(12.6)}$
2 REQD

$\frac{9}{(.38)}$ DIA X $\frac{1270}{(50.0)}$
2 REQD

Caddy Tray. The tray can be used as a desk accessory or as a dressing table. The wire parts can be assembled by brazing. All dimensions are given in millimeters.

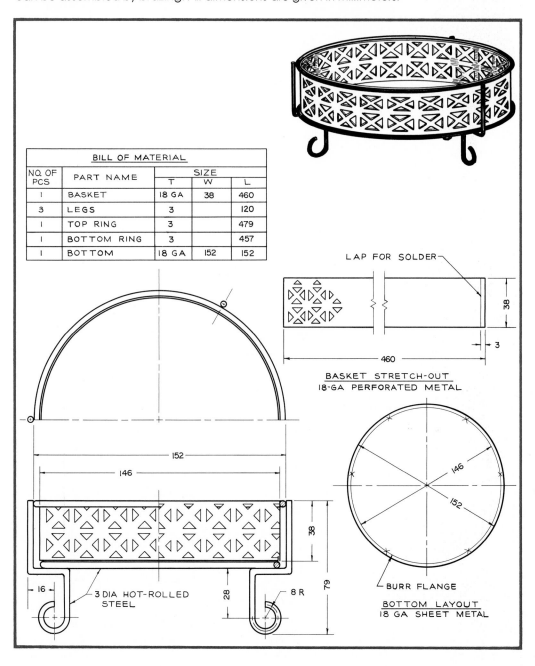

NO. OF PCS	PART NAME	SIZE		
		T	W	L
1	BASKET	18 GA	38	460
3	LEGS	3		120
1	TOP RING	3		479
1	BOTTOM RING	3		457
1	BOTTOM	18 GA	152	152

BILL OF MATERIAL

LAP FOR SOLDER

BASKET STRETCH-OUT
18-GA PERFORATED METAL

3 DIA HOT-ROLLED STEEL

BURR FLANGE

BOTTOM LAYOUT
18 GA SHEET METAL

Fishing Net. This would be an excellent mass production project that your class could sell to people interested in fishing.

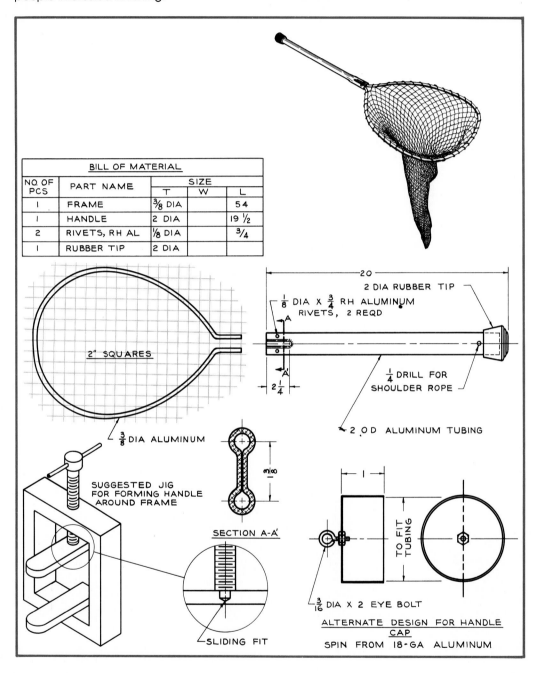

NO. OF PCS	PART NAME	SIZE		
		T	W	L
1	FRAME	$\frac{3}{8}$ DIA		54
1	HANDLE	2 DIA		19 $\frac{1}{2}$
2	RIVETS, RH AL	$\frac{1}{8}$ DIA		$\frac{3}{4}$
1	RUBBER TIP	2 DIA		

BILL OF MATERIAL

2" SQUARES

$\frac{3}{8}$ DIA ALUMINUM

SUGGESTED JIG FOR FORMING HANDLE AROUND FRAME

SECTION A-A'

SLIDING FIT

20

2 DIA RUBBER TIP

$\frac{1}{8}$ DIA X $\frac{3}{4}$ RH ALUMINUM RIVETS, 2 REQD

2 $\frac{1}{4}$

$\frac{1}{4}$ DRILL FOR SHOULDER ROPE

2 O D ALUMINUM TUBING

$\frac{3}{8}$

1

TO FIT TUBING

$\frac{3}{16}$ DIA X 2 EYE BOLT

ALTERNATE DESIGN FOR HANDLE CAP

SPIN FROM 18-GA ALUMINUM

sheet metal

Decorative Planters. Many sizes and shapes of planters can be made of sheet metal. The front of the planter can be richly decorated with scraps from stampings or with perforated or expanded metal.

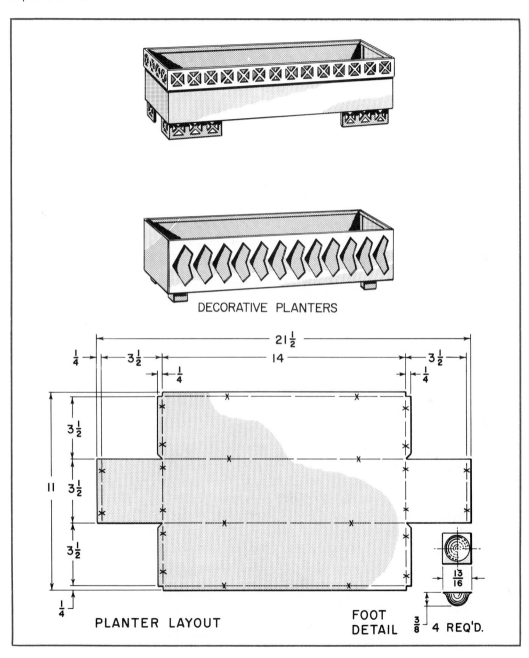

DECORATIVE PLANTERS

PLANTER LAYOUT

FOOT DETAIL $\frac{3}{8}$ 4 REQ'D.

Bird Feeder. These useful feeders can be made in many shapes and sizes. Here is a suggested form. One way to experiment with further ideas is to fold sheets of paper into interesting shapes.

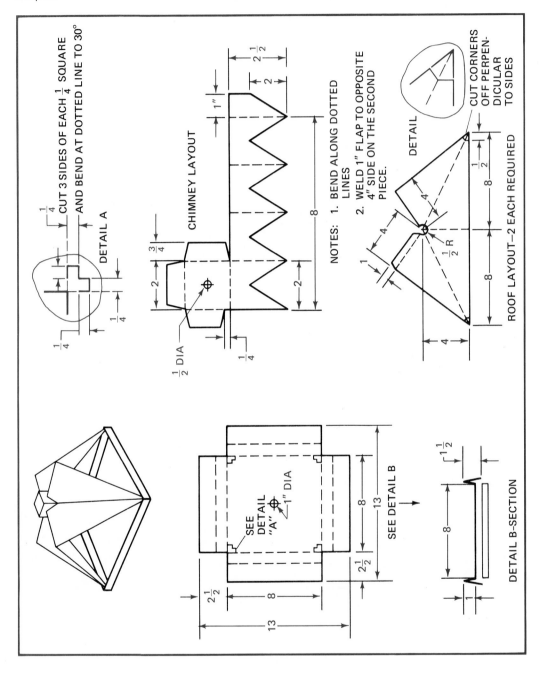

CUT 3 SIDES OF EACH $\frac{1}{4}$ SQUARE AND BEND AT DOTTED LINE TO 30°

DETAIL A

CHIMNEY LAYOUT

$\frac{1}{2}$ DIA

NOTES: 1. BEND ALONG DOTTED LINES
2. WELD 1" FLAP TO OPPOSITE 4" SIDE ON THE SECOND PIECE.

DETAIL

CUT CORNERS OFF PERPENDICULAR TO SIDES

ROOF LAYOUT—2 EACH REQUIRED

SEE DETAIL "A"
1" DIA

SEE DETAIL B

DETAIL B-SECTION

Paper-Pad Holder. This simple metal container is a handy piece for holding sheets of note paper. It can be used on a desk or near the telephone. It can be made in a variety of sizes to match standard paper sizes. Finish it in a color of your choosing.

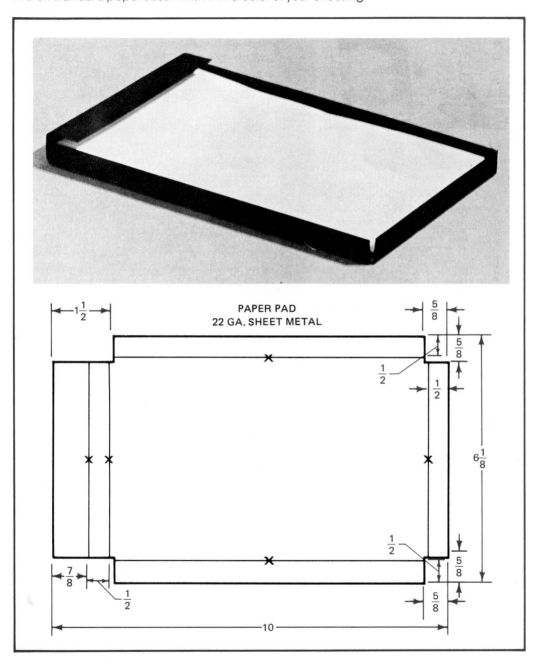

PAPER PAD
22 GA. SHEET METAL

Colonial Hanging Lamp. This beautiful lamp can be made from a few simple materials. Assemble the perforated sheet with pop rivets. Change the bulb by removing the two #8 by 1 1/4 inch flathead wood screws shown at the top of the assembly.

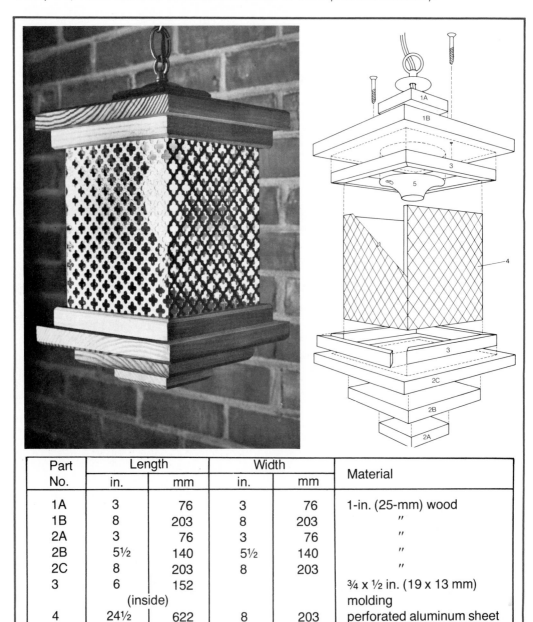

| Part | Length | | Width | | Material |
No.	in.	mm	in.	mm	
1A	3	76	3	76	1-in. (25-mm) wood
1B	8	203	8	203	"
2A	3	76	3	76	"
2B	5½	140	5½	140	"
2C	8	203	8	203	"
3	6 (inside)	152			¾ x ½ in. (19 x 13 mm) molding
4	24½	622	8	203	perforated aluminum sheet
5					standard porcelain fixture

Spice Rack. A handy kitchen accessory to hold all the small cans and jars of spices. Several of these can be mounted on the inside of a kitchen door. All dimensions are in millimeters.

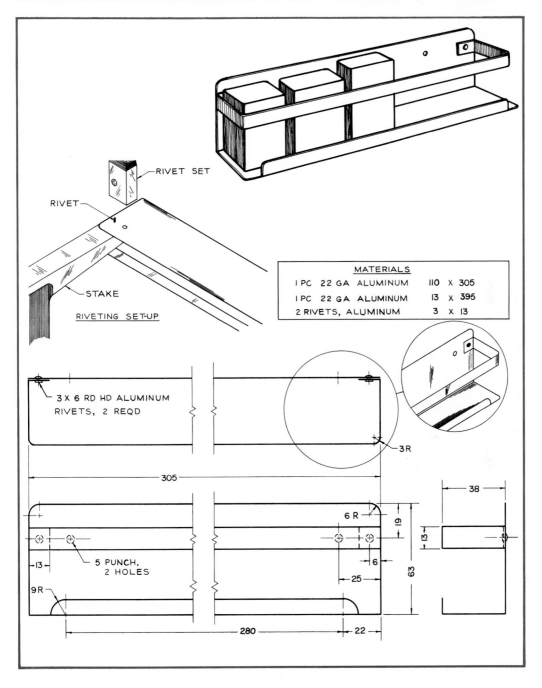

RIVET SET

RIVET

STAKE

RIVETING SET-UP

MATERIALS		
I PC 22 GA ALUMINUM	110	X 305
I PC 22 GA ALUMINUM	13	X 395
2 RIVETS, ALUMINUM	3	X 13

3 X 6 RD HD ALUMINUM
RIVETS, 2 REQD

3R

305

6 R

19

13

5 PUNCH,
2 HOLES

13

6

25

63

9R

280

22

38

Charcoal Hod. This is a very useful item for a patio or around a fireplace. It is great for holding charcoal.

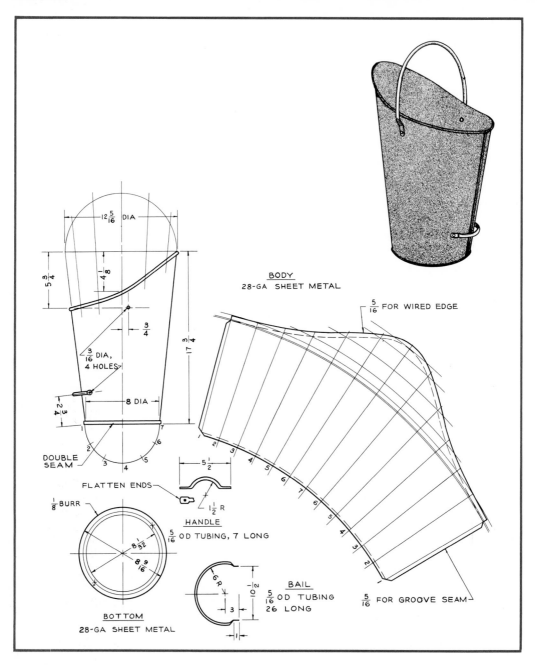

$12\frac{5}{16}$ DIA

$5\frac{3}{4}$

$4\frac{1}{8}$

$\frac{3}{4}$

$\frac{3}{16}$ DIA, 4 HOLES

$17\frac{3}{4}$

$2\frac{3}{4}$

8 DIA

DOUBLE SEAM

BODY
28-GA SHEET METAL

$\frac{5}{16}$ FOR WIRED EDGE

$\frac{5}{16}$ FOR GROOVE SEAM

FLATTEN ENDS

$5\frac{1}{2}$

$1\frac{1}{2}$ R

HANDLE
$\frac{5}{16}$ OD TUBING, 7 LONG

$\frac{1}{8}$ BURR

$8\frac{1}{32}$

$8\frac{9}{16}$

BOTTOM
28-GA SHEET METAL

$\frac{6}{16}$ R

$10\frac{1}{2}$

3

1

BAIL
$\frac{5}{16}$ OD TUBING
26 LONG

470

Mailbox. This useful mailbox will give you practice in laying out, cutting, forming, and assembling sheet metal. The project can be finished with colored enamel.

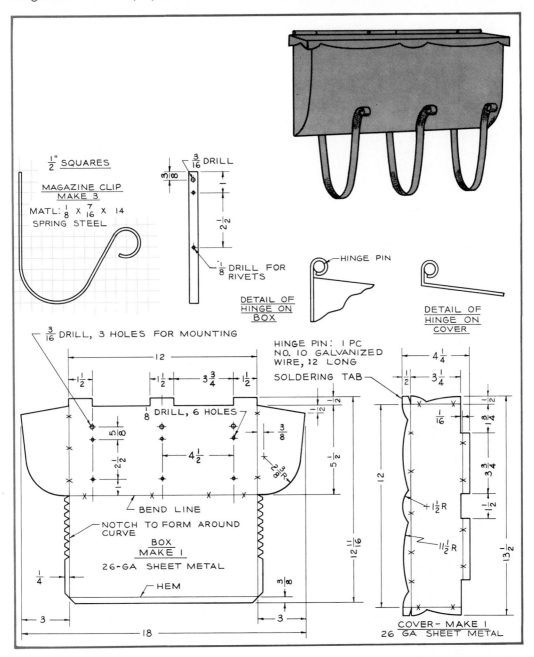

$\frac{1}{2}$" SQUARES

MAGAZINE CLIP
MAKE 3
MATL: $\frac{1}{8}$ X $\frac{7}{16}$ X 14
SPRING STEEL

$\frac{3}{16}$ DRILL

$\frac{1}{8}$ DRILL FOR
RIVETS

$2\frac{1}{2}$

HINGE PIN

DETAIL OF
HINGE ON
BOX

DETAIL OF
HINGE ON
COVER

$\frac{3}{16}$ DRILL, 3 HOLES FOR MOUNTING

HINGE PIN: 1 PC
NO. 10 GALVANIZED
WIRE, 12 LONG

SOLDERING TAB

12

$1\frac{1}{2}$ $1\frac{1}{2}$ $3\frac{3}{4}$ $1\frac{1}{2}$

$4\frac{1}{4}$

$\frac{1}{2}$ $3\frac{1}{4}$

$\frac{1}{8}$ DRILL, 6 HOLES

$\frac{5}{8}$

$\frac{3}{8}$

$\frac{1}{16}$

$\frac{3}{4}$

$4\frac{1}{2}$

$2\frac{1}{2}$

$2\frac{3}{8}$ R

$5\frac{1}{2}$

$3\frac{3}{4}$

$1\frac{1}{2}$

$1\frac{1}{2}$ R

$11\frac{1}{2}$ R

BEND LINE

NOTCH TO FORM AROUND
CURVE

BOX
MAKE 1

26-GA SHEET METAL

$\frac{1}{4}$

HEM

$\frac{3}{8}$

$12\frac{11}{16}$

12

$13\frac{1}{2}$

3

3

18

COVER – MAKE 1
26 GA SHEET METAL

471

Wastepaper Basket. A practical wastepaper container that can be finished by painting.

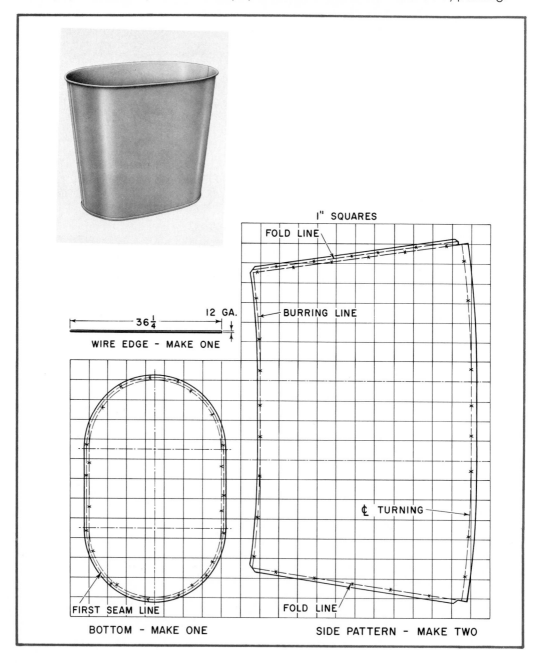

1" SQUARES

FOLD LINE

BURRING LINE

36¼

12 GA.

WIRE EDGE – MAKE ONE

℄ TURNING

FIRST SEAM LINE

FOLD LINE

BOTTOM – MAKE ONE

SIDE PATTERN – MAKE TWO

art metal and jewelry

Mint Dish. Here is a simple yet elegant metal candy dish. The wooden form is shown in the drawing. Other forms can be made for other shapes.

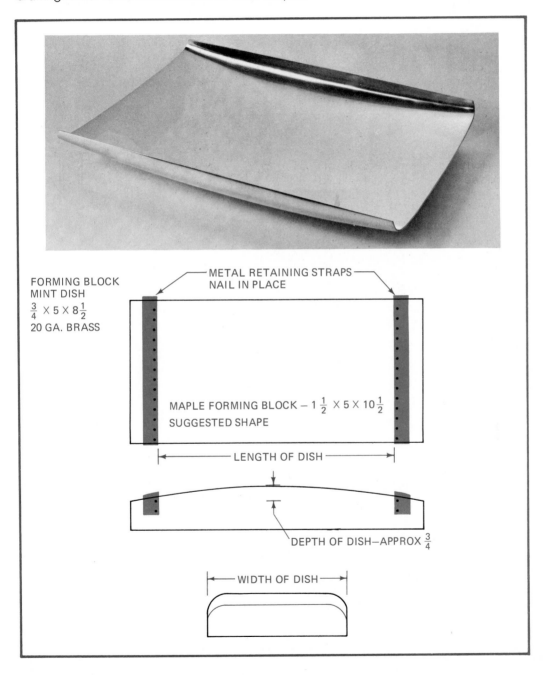

FORMING BLOCK
MINT DISH
$\frac{3}{4} \times 5 \times 8\frac{1}{2}$
20 GA. BRASS

METAL RETAINING STRAPS
NAIL IN PLACE

MAPLE FORMING BLOCK — $1\frac{1}{2} \times 5 \times 10\frac{1}{2}$
SUGGESTED SHAPE

LENGTH OF DISH

DEPTH OF DISH—APPROX $\frac{3}{4}$

WIDTH OF DISH

Metal Box. This decorative copper box has a chased design on the cover. The inside of the box can be covered with flocking. The bottom can be finished by gluing a piece of walnut to it. The box is useful for storing jewelry or other small items.

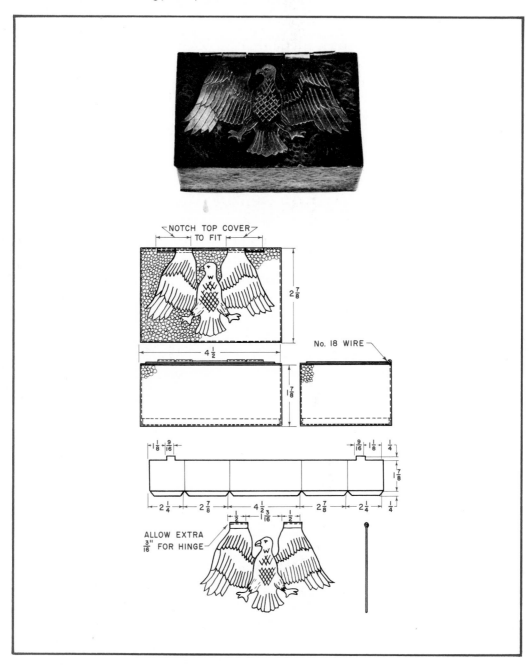

NOTCH TOP COVER TO FIT

$2\frac{7}{8}$

$4\frac{1}{2}$

No. 18 WIRE

$1\frac{7}{8}$

$1\frac{1}{8}$ $\frac{9}{16}$

$\frac{9}{16}$ $1\frac{1}{8}$ $\frac{1}{4}$

$1\frac{7}{8}$

$2\frac{1}{4}$ $2\frac{7}{8}$ $4\frac{1}{2}$ $2\frac{7}{8}$ $2\frac{1}{4}$ $\frac{1}{4}$

$\frac{1}{2}$ $\frac{3}{16}$ $\frac{1}{2}$

ALLOW EXTRA $\frac{3}{16}''$ FOR HINGE

Four Small Projects. Three of these give practice in art metal; the other gives practice in bench metal or beginning machine shop. They include many steps in metalwork.

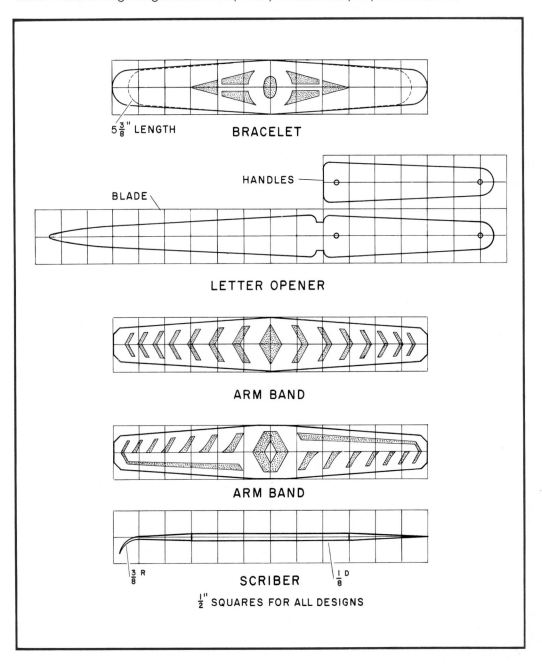

$5\frac{3}{8}''$ LENGTH BRACELET

HANDLES

BLADE

LETTER OPENER

ARM BAND

ARM BAND

$\frac{3}{8}$ R SCRIBER $\frac{1}{8}$ D

$\frac{1}{2}''$ SQUARES FOR ALL DESIGNS

machine shop, foundry, forging, and heat treating

Miniature Tools. This brass tack hammer and plumb bob are two examples of the miniature tools that can be made in machine shop and used for hobby work or as souvenirs. The hammer handle can be knurled to provide a better grip. Any tool can be made to a smaller scale. A metric-equivalent chart is given for convenient reference.

in.	mm
$\frac{1}{32}$	0.79
$\frac{1}{16}$	1.58
$\frac{1}{8}$	3.17
$\frac{5}{32}$	3.96
$\frac{1}{4}$	6.35
$\frac{9}{32}$	7.14
$\frac{3}{8}$	9.52
$\frac{13}{32}$	10.31
$\frac{1}{2}$	12.70
$\frac{17}{32}$	13.49
$\frac{3}{4}$	19.05
$\frac{13}{16}$	20.63
$\frac{7}{8}$	22.22
$1\frac{7}{8}$	117.62

$\frac{3}{8}$ DIA.

$\frac{1}{8}$ DIA. x $\frac{3}{8}$ DEEP

$\frac{1}{32}$ R. x $\frac{1}{32}$ DEEP

45° x $\frac{1}{32}$ CHAMFER

$\frac{1}{16}$ $\frac{9}{32}$ $\frac{13}{32}$ $\frac{17}{32}$ $\frac{13}{16}$

$\frac{1}{8}$ DIA. ROD

45° x $\frac{1}{32}$ CHAMFER

6

PRESS FIT HANDLE INTO HEAD

$\frac{1}{4}$ DIA.

$\frac{3}{8}$ DIA.

$\frac{1}{16}$ R. $\frac{3}{4}$ DIA. $\frac{1}{16}$

$\frac{1}{16}$ R.

$\frac{1}{16}$ R. $\frac{9}{32}$ $\frac{1}{2}$ $\frac{7}{8}$

$\frac{5}{32}$ R.

$\frac{5}{32}$ R. $1\frac{7}{8}$

Bookends. Here are two interesting machine-shop projects. One bookend is made from shallow aluminum channel, backed with contrasting walnut. The decorations are made with a circle cutter or fly cutter. The other piece is made of mild steel. A shaper was used to create the striking cross-textured effect. Both pieces measure 3 by 3 1/2 inches (76 by 89 mm). They are screwed in place. Try your own ideas for decorative bookends.

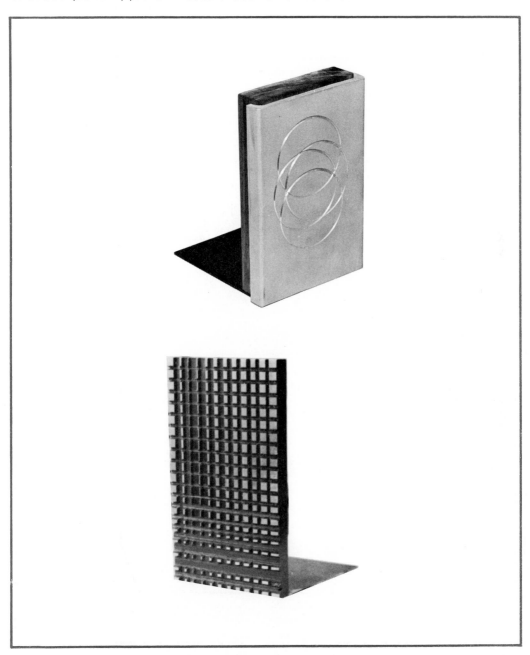

Hobby Knife. A good machine-shop and heat-treating project. The blades must be shaped, heat-treated, and ground.

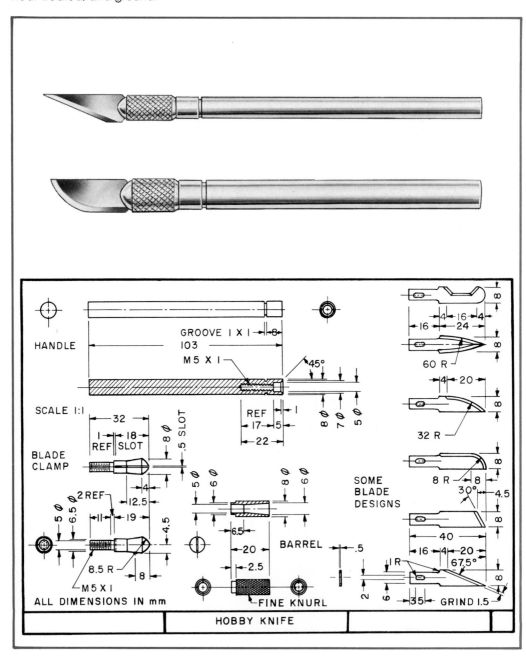

HANDLE

GROOVE I X I — 8

103

M5 X I

45°

SCALE I:I

BLADE CLAMP

32

I — 18
REF SLOT

.5 SLOT

8 Ø

REF

17 — 5

22

8 Ø 7 Ø 5 Ø

2 REF

5 Ø
6.5 Ø

4

12.5

11 19

4.5

8.5 R

8

M5 X I

ALL DIMENSIONS IN mm

5 Ø 6 Ø

6.5

20

2.5

8 Ø 6 Ø

BARREL

FINE KNURL

.5

SOME
BLADE
DESIGNS

8

16 4 16 4
24

60 R

4 20

8

32 R

8 R 8

30°

4.5

40

16 4 20
67.5°

I R

2 6 35 GRIND 1.5

8

HOBBY KNIFE

Paperweight. This project will give you experience in casting (foundry) and machine shop.

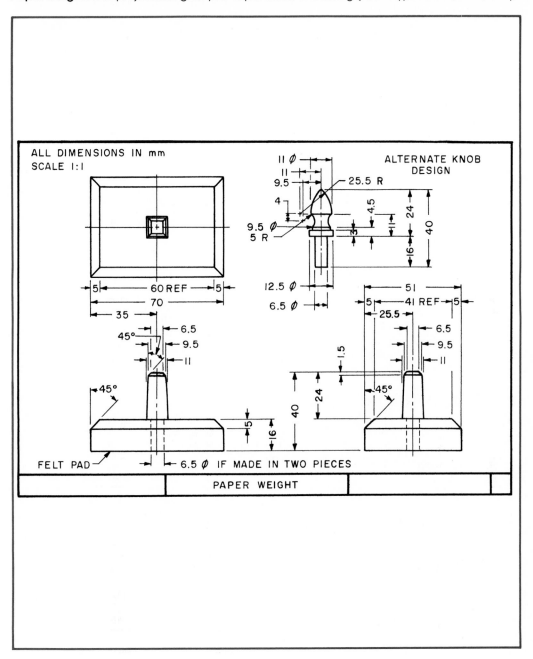

ALL DIMENSIONS IN mm
SCALE 1:1

ALTERNATE KNOB DESIGN

FELT PAD

PAPER WEIGHT

6.5 ⌀ IF MADE IN TWO PIECES

Tack Hammer and C-Clamp. Here are two small machine-shop projects. The heads of the tack hammer can be of cast aluminum.

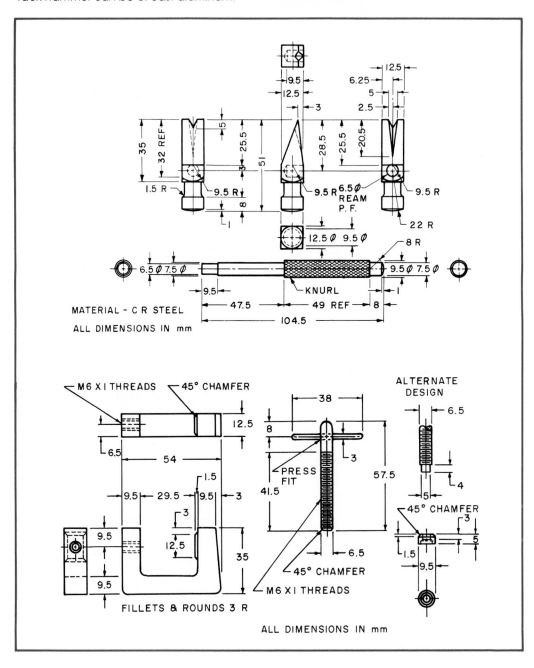

MATERIAL – C R STEEL

ALL DIMENSIONS IN mm

M6 X1 THREADS

45° CHAMFER

PRESS FIT

45° CHAMFER

M6 X1 THREADS

FILLETS & ROUNDS 3 R

ALTERNATE DESIGN

45° CHAMFER

KNURL

ALL DIMENSIONS IN mm

Cold Chisel, Punches, and Screwdriver. These tools will be a good addition to your tool box. They will give you excellent experience in forging and heat treating.

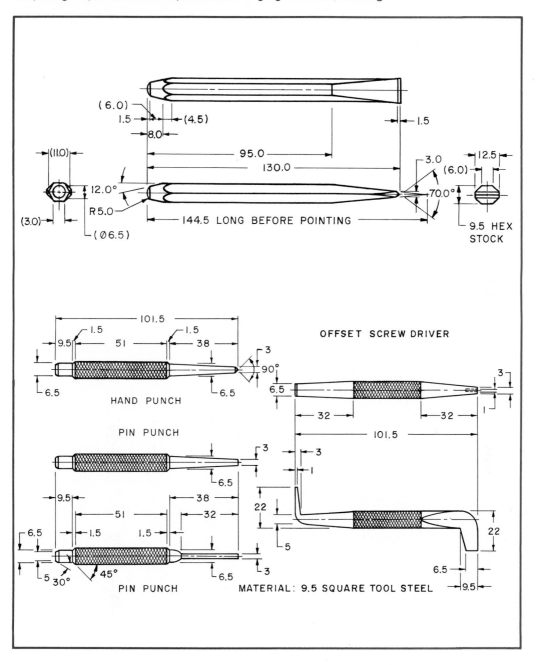

(6.0)
1.5 — (4.5)
8.0
(11.0)
12.0°
R 5.0
(3.0)
(Ø 6.5)
95.0
130.0
144.5 LONG BEFORE POINTING
1.5
3.0
(6.0)
70.0°
12.5
9.5 HEX STOCK

101.5
1.5
9.5 — 51 — 1.5
38
6.5
90°
3
6.5
HAND PUNCH

OFFSET SCREW DRIVER

6.5
32
32
3
1
101.5

PIN PUNCH

3
6.5
3
1
3
22
5

9.5
51
38
32
1.5
1.5
6.5
5 30°
45°
6.5
3
PIN PUNCH

22
6.5
9.5

MATERIAL: 9.5 SQUARE TOOL STEEL

APPENDIX

Metric Conversion Table for Drills

Metric Drills (mm)	Dec. Equiv.	Drills Fractional	Number or Letter
0.1	0.0039		
0.15	0.0050		
0.2	0.0079		
0.25	0.0098		
0.3	0.0118		
....	0.0135		80
0.35	0.0138		
....	0.0145		79
0.39	0.0156	1/64	
0.4	0.0157		
....	0.0160		78
0.45	0.0177		
....	0.0180		77
0.5	0.0197		
....	0.0200		76
....	0.0210		75
0.55	0.0217		
....	0.0225		74
0.6	0.0236		
....	0.0240		73
....	0.0250		72
0.63	0.0256		
....	0.0260		71
....	0.0280		70
0.7	0.0276		
....	0.0292		69
0.75	0.0295		
....	0.0310		68
0.79	0.0312	1/32	
0.8	0.0315		
....	0.0320		67
....	0.0330		66
0.85	0.0335		
....	0.0350		65
0.9	0.0354		
....	0.0360		64
....	0.0370		63
0.95	0.0374		
....	0.0380		62
....	0.0390		61
1.0	0.0394		
....	0.0400		60
....	0.0410		59
1.05	0.0413		
....	0.0420		58
....	0.0430		57
1.1	0.0433		
1.15	0.0452		
....	0.0465		56
1.19	0.0469	3/64	
1.2	0.0472		
1.25	0.0492		
1.3	0.0512		
....	0.0520		55
1.35	0.0531		
....	0.0550		54
1.4	0.0551		
1.45	0.0570		
1.5	0.0591		
....	0.0595		53
1.55	0.0610		
1.59	0.0625	1/16	
1.6	0.0629		
....	0.0635		52
1.65	0.0649		
1.7	0.0669		
....	0.0670		51
1.75	0.0689		
....	0.0700		50
1.8	0.0709		
1.85	0.0728		
....	0.0730		49
1.9	0.0748		
....	0.0760		48
1.95	0.0767		
1.98	0.0781	5/64	
....	0.0785		47
2.0	0.0787		
2.05	0.0807		
....	0.0810		46
....	0.0820		45
2.1	0.0827		
2.15	0.0846		
....	0.0860		44
2.2	0.0866		
2.25	0.0885		
....	0.0890		43
2.3	0.0905		
2.35	0.0925		
....	0.0935		42
2.38	0.0937	3/32	
2.4	0.0945		
....	0.0960		41
2.45	0.0964		
....	0.0980		40
2.5	0.0984		
....	0.0995		39
....	0.1015		38
2.6	0.1024		
....	0.1040		37
2.7	0.1063		
....	0.1065		36
2.75	0.1082		
2.78	0.1094	7/64	
....	0.1100		35
2.8	0.1102		
....	0.1110		34
....	0.1130		33
2.9	0.1141		
....	0.1160		32
3.0	0.1181		
....	0.1200		31
3.1	0.1220		
3.18	0.1250	1/8	
3.2	0.1260		
3.25	0.1279		
....	0.1285		30
3.3	0.1299		
3.4	0.1338		
....	0.1360		29
3.5	0.1378		
....	0.1405		28
3.57	0.1406	9/64	
3.6	0.1417		
....	0.1440		27
3.7	0.1457		
....	0.1470		26
3.75	0.1476		
....	0.1495		25
3.8	0.1496		
....	0.1520		24
3.9	0.1535		
....	0.1540		23
3.97	0.1562	5/32	
....	0.1570		22
4.0	0.1575		
....	0.1590		21
....	0.1610		20
4.1	0.1614		
4.2	0.1654		
....	0.1660		19
4.25	0.1673		
4.3	0.1693		
....	0.1695		18
4.37	0.1719	11/64	
....	0.1730		17
4.4	0.1732		
....	0.1770		16
4.5	0.1771		
....	0.1800		15
4.6	0.1811		
....	0.1820		14
4.7	0.1850		13
4.75	0.1870		
4.76	0.1875	3/16	
4.8	0.1890		12
....	0.1910		11
4.9	0.1929		
....	0.1935		10
....	0.1960		9
5.0	0.1968		
....	0.1990		8
5.1	0.2008		
....	0.2010		7
5.16	0.2031	13/64	
....	0.2040		6
5.2	0.2047		
....	0.2055		5
5.25	0.2067		
5.3	0.2086		
....	0.2090		4
5.4	0.2126		

Metric Conversion Table for Drills

Metric Drills (mm)	Dec. Equiv.	Drills Fractional	Number or Letter
....	0.2130		3
5.5	0.2165		
5.56	0.2187	7/32	
5.6	0.2205		
....	0.2210		2
5,7	0.2244		
5.75	0.2263		
....	0.2280		1
5.8	0.2283		
5.9	0.2323		
....	0.2340		A
5.95	0.2344	15/64	
6.0	0.2362		
....	0.2380		B
6.1	0.2401		
....	0.2420		C
6.2	0.2441		
6.25	0.2460		D
6.3	0.2480		
6.35	0.2500	1/4	E
6.4	0.2520		
6.5	0.2559		
....	0.2570		F
6.6	0.2598		
....	0.2610		G
6.7	0.2638		
6.75	0.2657	17/64	
6.75	0.2657		
....	0.2660		H
6.8	0.2677		
6.9	0.2716		
....	0.2720		I
7.0	0.2756		
....	0.2770		J
7.1	0.2795		
....	0.2811		K
7.14	0.2812	9/32	
7.2	0.2835		
7.25	0.2854		
7.3	0.2874		
....	0.2900		L
7.4	0.2913		
....	0.2950		M

Metric Drills (mm)	Dec. Equiv.	Drills Fractional	Number or Letter
7.5	0.2953		
7.54	0.2968	19/64	
7.6	0.2992		
....	0.3020		N
7.7	0.3031		
7.75	0.3051		
7.8	0.3071		
7.9	0.3110		
7.94	0.3125	5/16	
8.0	0.3150		
....	0.3160		O
8.1	0.3189		
8.2	0.3228		
....	0.3230		P
8.25	0.3248		
8.3	0.3268		
8.33	0.3281	21/64	
8.4	0.3307		
....	0.3320		Q
8.5	0.3346		
8.6	0.3386		
....	0.3390		R
8.7	0.3425		
8.73	0.3437	11/32	
8.75	0.3445		
8.8	0.3465		
....	0.3480		S
8.9	0.3504		
9.0	0.3543		
....	0.3580		T
9.1	0.3583		
9.13	0.3594	23/64	
9.2	0.3622		
9.25	0.3641		
9.3	0.3661		
....	0.3680		U
9.4	0.3701		
9.5	0.3740		
9.53	0.3750	3/8	
....	0.3770		V
9.6	0.3780		
9.7	0.3819		
9.75	0.3838		

Metric Drills (mm)	Dec. Equiv.	Drills Fractional	Number or Letter
9.8	0.3858		
....	0.3860		W
9.9	0.3898		
9.92	0.3906	25/64	
10.0	0.3937		
....	0.3970		X
....	0.4040		Y
10.32	0.4062	13/32	
....	0.4130		Z
10.5	0.4134		
10.72	0.4219	27/64	
11.0	0.4330		
11.11	0.4375	7/16	
11.5	0.4528		
11.51	0.4531	29/64	
11.91	0.4687	15/32	
12.0	0.4724		
12.30	0.4843	31/64	
12.5	0.4921		
12.7	0.5000	1/2	
13.0	0.5118		
13.10	0.5156	33/64	
13.49	0.5312	17/32	
13.5	0.5315		
13.89	0.5469	35/64	
14.0	0.5512		
14.29	0.5625	9/16	
14.5	0.5709		
14.68	0.5781	37/64	
15.0	0.5906		
15.08	0.5937	19/32	
15.48	0.6094	39/64	
15.5	0.6102		
15.88	0.6250	5/8	
16.0	0.6299		
16.27	0.6406	41/64	
16.5	0.6496		
16.67	0.6562	21/32	
17.0	0.6693		
17.06	0.6719	43/64	
17.46	0.6875	11/16	
17.5	0.6890		
17.86	0.7031	45/64	

Metric Drills (mm)	Dec. Equiv.	Drills Fractional	Number or Letter
18.0	0.7087		
18.26	0.7187	23/32	
18.5	0.7283		
18.65	0.7344	47/64	
19.0	0.7480		
19.05	0.7500	3/4	
19.45	0.7656	49/64	
19.5	0.7677		
19.84	0.7812	25/32	
20.0	0.7874		
20.24	0.7969	51/64	
20.5	0.8071		
20.64	0.8125	13/16	
21.0	0.8268		
21.03	0.8281	53/64	
21.43	0.8437	27/32	
21.5	0.8465		
21.83	0.8594	55/64	
22.0	0.8661		
22.23	0.8750	7/8	
22.5	0.8858		
22.62	0.8906	57/64	
23.0	0.9055		
23.02	0.9062	29/32	
23.42	0.9219	59/64	
23.5	0.9252		
23.81	0.9375	15/16	
24.0	0.9449		
24.21	0.9531	61/64	
24.5	0.9646		
24.61	0.9687	31/32	
25.0	0.9843		
25.03	0.9844	63/64	
25.4	1.0000	1	

GLOSSARY

abrade To cut or grind away metal with abrasives.

abrasive A material that will wear away something softer than itself.

abrasive blasting A finishing process in which work is dry-blasted with a stream of abrasive particles moving at a high speed. Also called *sandblasting*.

abrasive finishing Removing small amounts of material from metal surfaces by grinding, honing, buffing, polishing, and similar processes.

access The act of obtaining data stored in the computer.

adhesion The way in which materials such as adhesives or solders fasten parts together.

adhesive A sticky substance, such as cement or glue, that is used to join surfaces.

airless spraying Using high hydraulic pressure, rather than air pressure, to eject coating material from a spray gun.

alloy (n) A mixture of two or more metals. (v) To mix metals to form an alloy.

alloy steel A variety of steel with special properties determined by the mixture and the amount of other elements, particularly metals, added.

aluminum A silvery-white metallic element; lightweight and easy to work.

aluminum anodizing An electrochemical process that produces a hard, corrosion-resistant coating of oxide on aluminum.

angle plate A bracket used to hold workpieces in making a layout.

anneal To heat-treat metal in order to soften it and make it easier to shape and cut.

anode (1) The negative pole of a galvanic cell; the corroded metal in galvanic action. (2) The positive pole of an electrolytic cell.

anvil A heavy block on which metal is shaped.

anvil tool One of a number of special tools used for different forging operations.

apprentice A person who works for a company or shop in order to learn the trade.

arc welding Welding with the heat created by generating an electric arc between the metal workpiece and an electrode. Also called *shielded-metal arc welding* (SMAW).

assembly Fastening together parts to make a complete product.

assembly drawing A working drawing that shows how parts fit together to make a complete product.

automation Using machines that are controlled automatically to do work.

axis A line running lengthwise through the center of a material on which a screw thread is formed.

balance Equality in weight and appearance between the parts of an object.

band machining Cutting metal stock to shape on a specially designed vertical band saw.

base metal The main metal ingredient in a given alloy.

base unit A measuring unit from which other units are derived.

basic oxygen process A way of making steel from pig iron by using oxygen to draw off the carbon.

batch manufacturing (short-run manufacturing) The process of producing a limited number of the same product.

bead (n) A projecting rim, band, or molding. (v) To strengthen and decorate a workpiece by adding a bead.

beating down Forming metal into a shallow hollow shape by hammering it either down into a form or over a block. Also called *sinking*.

bench shears A tool for cutting sheet metal and similar metal pieces.

bench vise A simple vise with two jaws, one fixed and one that moves as a handle is turned. Also called a *machinist's vise*.

bend To change the shape of metal in one direction only.

beryllium A lightweight metal important in the aerospace industry.

binary Having two possible positions: 0 and 1; the 0 corresponds to the *off* position and the 1 to the *on* position of the electronic circuitry.

bit Abbreviation for *binary digit*, one of the two numbers—0 and 1—used to encode (convert) computer data. A bit is expressed by a high or low electric voltage. The bit is the smallest unit of information a computer uses.

black-oxide finishing A chemical blackening process that uses an oxidizing alkaline bath to produce a controlled oxidized surface on steel.

blacksmith's hammer A special hammer used in forging.

blank To cut out a metal part from surrounding waste stock with a die.

blast furnace A large steel shell in which combustion is forced by a current of air under pressure; used especially for refining iron ore.

blind hole A hole cut only part way through a workpiece.

bluing A process used to beautify and protect rifle barrels.

bolt A screw used with a nut.

bolt cutter A special type of shears used to cut metal rods, wire, or bolts.

bore To enlarge or finish the cylindrical surfaces of an existing hole.

brass Any of several copper alloys in which the principal alloying element is usually zinc.

brazing Soldering using a bronze rod for solder and very high temperatures. Also called *bronze welding* or *torch soldering*.

brittleness The tendency of a metal to break easily.

broaching Shaping internal and external metal surfaces by pushing or pulling a tapered tool called a broach across them.

bronze Any of several copper alloys. Common alloying elements used in bronze are tin, aluminum, and nickel.

buff To use abrasives on a metal surface to create a bright, mirrorlike finish or a softer, satin appearance.

burr A thin ridge or area of roughness produced in cutting or shaping metal.

butt weld A weld that fastens parts together end to end without overlapping.

byte A group of eight bits used to encode (convert) a single letter, number, or symbol.

cabinet drawing An oblique drawing in which receding lines are drawn to half size.

carbon A nonmetallic element.

carbon steel A variety of steel classified by the amount of carbon it contains.

case The outer surface of a piece of metal.

case harden To heat-treat ferrous metals so that only the outer surface is hardened.

casting, metal Shaping metal by pouring the metal in molten form into a mold and letting it harden. Also called *foundry*.

cast iron An iron alloy containing 2 to 4 percent carbon.

cathode (1) The positive pole of a galvanic cell; the uncorroded metal in galvanic action. (2) The negative pole of an electrolytic cell.

cathode ray tube (CRT) The video screen that displays data and graphics.

centerline A line that locates the center of arcs and circles or that divides an object into equal parts.

centimeter (cm) One one-hundredth (0.01) of a meter.

central processing unit (CPU) The part of the computer that controls its overall operation. The CPU carries out instructions given to the computer.

centrifugal casting A casting method in which molten metal is forced into a rotating mold.

cermet An alloy of a ceramic and a metal.

charge (*n*) The mixture of substances—such as ore, flux, and coke—placed in a blast furnace or other device in order to produce refined metal. (v) To load a blast furnace or other device with such a mixture.

chase To strike metal with special tools and a special hammer to produce a design.

chemical milling (CHM) Shaping metal by chemically removing part of it through deep etching.

chip A small piece of silicon that is a total semiconductor device. The chip contains microminiaturized electronic circuits.

chisel A wedge-shaped cutting tool used to cut, shear, and chip metal.

chuck (1) In machining, a special clamp for holding a workpiece or tool. (2) In metal spinning, a form that gives its shape to the workpiece.

cinder notch The opening in a blast furnace through which the slag is drawn off.

clinkers Heavy metallic materials found in the center of an old forge fire.

cohesion The way in which a chemical bond or a metallurgical bond such as welding fastens parts together.

coining A stamping process in which designs are formed on both sides of a blank piece of sheet metal at the same time.

coke The material that remains after gases have been burned out of raw coal.

cold drawing Forming a metal rod, tube, or bar by pulling it through a hole in a die.

cold forming Forming internal shapes without

heat by placing metal over a mandrel and then squeezing the metal with one or more dies.

cold heading Forming the head on a bolt, screw, nail, or other fastener by striking the blank for the piece on one end with a die.

cold rolling Forming metal by squeezing it between rotating cylindrical rolls.

cold working The processes that change the shape and form of metal when it is below softening temperature.

components The combination of parts to form a portion of a larger assembly.

compression strength The maximum compressive force that a material can withstand before it breaks.

computer A device that stores information, manipulates data, and solves problems.

computer-aided drafting (CAD) A computer system which enables technical drawings to be produced through a computer on a video screen and then printed as a finished drawing on a plotter.

computer-aided manufacturing (CAM) A system which produces a product using machines controlled primarily by computers.

computer integrated manufacturing (CIM) A manufacturing system in which all phases of production from design to finished product are computer-controlled.

computer language Symbolic notations used to create computer programs such as Fortran, Cobol, Basic, Pilot, and Logo.

cope In casting, the top section of the flask that contains the mold.

copper A warm reddish brown metal, used for much art-metal work.

core A sand shape placed in a mold to provide an opening in a casting.

corner weld A weld that joins two pieces at right angles, forming a corner.

corrosion The slow eating or wearing away of metal.

counterboring Partially reboring a cylindrical hole to enlarge it for part of its length.

countersinking Cutting a cone-shaped recess on the outer edge of the end of a hole.

crest On a screw thread, the top intersection of the thread's two sides.

crimp (1) To draw in the edge on the end of a cylindrical object so that the object can slip easily into a mating part. (2) To hammer a series of depressions in metal to form a bowl.

critical point, or **critical temperature** In heat treating, the temperature at which a given metal has the best characteristics.

crucible In casting, the vessel in which the metal is melted.

cubic decimeter (dm³) An SI metric unit for measuring volume; called a liter when used for liquids.

cubic meter (m³) An SI metric unit for measuring volume; equal to about 30 percent more than a cubic yard.

cure To resolidify, as a holt-melt adhesive does when it cools.

customary system A measuring system used in the United States and formerly used in other English-speaking countries, based on traditional measurement units. Also called the *English* or *Imperial system.*

custom production The process of making one or a few products at one time.

cutting die A die that cuts or shears a workpiece to size or shape. Also called a *blanking die.*

cutting speed The length of the cut made per minute by a machine tool cutting the surface of a workpiece.

data base The collection of information stored in a computer.

data entry device Equipment that will convert data from human-readable form into a code the computer can understand.

data processing Operations performed on data to achieve a particular objective.

debug To locate, remove, and correct mistakes in a program.

decimal system A numerical system which divides units into subdivisions divisible by 10.

decode To convert data from a coded into a human-readable form.

deep drawing Forming a deep, cup-shaped object from sheet metal by forcing the metal into a die cavity with a punch.

deform In metalworking, to apply force to a workpiece to change its shape. Also called to *strain.*

degree Celsius (°C) A unit in the SI metric temperature scale, in which water freezes at 0°C and boils at 100°C.

depth The distance between the crest and the root of a screw thread along a line that is at right angles to the axis of the thread.

depth of cut In machining, the distance from the bottom of the cut to the uncut surface, measured at right angles to the machined surface.

derived unit A unit of measure that is computed from one or more base, supplementary, or other derived units.

detail drawing A working drawing that shows a single part of the product and contains all the information necessary to make the part.

die (1) A tool used to cut, shear, press, or otherwise give work the correct shape, imprint, or form. (2) A tool used to cut external threads.

die casting A casting method in which molten metal is forced into closed dies under pressure.

die cutting Cutting external threads with a die.

diestock A device used to hold dies for cutting external threads.

dimension A measurement.

dimension line In a drawing, a line that shows the dimensions, or distances, between lines. It has an arrowhead at one or both ends and is broken in the center.

disc, or **disk** See *magnetic disk.*

diskette A thin, flexible platter, similar to a 45-rpm record, coated with a magnetic substance and used to store information; a floppy disk.

dividers A two-legged tool used to lay out arcs and to determine the location of holes to be drilled.

dome A raised, rounded shape that can serve as decoration around the edge of an object or as feet for a dish or tray.

draft The taper given to a pattern so that it can be pulled out of a casting mold easily.

drag In casting, the bottom section of the flask that contains the mold.

draw (1) To form sheet metal into a hollow shape by forcing it into a die cavity with a punch. (2) To heat-treat metal to reduce hardness and increase toughness. Also called to *temper.*

dress To sharpen the edge of a grinding wheel by exposing new abrasive grains.

drier In sand casting, a device used to support the sand cores while they are being baked in an oven.

drill (*n*) a device used for drilling. (*v*) To use a rotating cutter to cut cylindrical holes.

drill press A power-driven machine used to do drilling, countersinking, reaming, boring, and tapping.

drill speed The distance a drill would travel per minute if it were rolled on its side.

ductility The ability of a metal to be drawn out thin without breaking.

edge weld A weld that joins the ends of two pieces that lie flush one on top of the other.

elastic deformation A forced change in the shape of metal that lasts only as long as the force is applied.

elasticity The ability of a metal to return to its original shape after bending.

elastic limit The greatest stress a metal can stand without permanent deformation.

electrical-discharge machining (EDM) Removing metal by creating a high-current, low-voltage electrical-spark discharge between an electrode tool and the workpiece.

electric-furnace process A way of making steel from pig iron. It resembles the open-hearth process, but uses electricity to generate heat.

electrochemical machining (ECM) Removing metal from a workpiece by electrolytic action.

electrode A device that conducts and emits an electric charge.

electron-beam welding (EBW) A kind of welding in which the heat is supplied by the beam from an electron gun.

electronic data processing (EDP) The processing of data mainly by electronic digital computers.

electroplate To use electricity and chemical solutions to cover a metal object with a thin coat of some other metal.

elongation The lengthening that a piece of metal can undergo when it is forcibly stretched.

embossing A stamping process that produces a shallow relief design on sheet metal.

emphasis A way of pointing out the focus, or center of interest.

enameling Baking a permanent, glossy finish onto the surface of metal in a furnace.

encode To convert data from a human-readable form into a code the computer can understand.

engine lathe A machine that cuts or shapes metal by revolving the work against a sharp cutting edge.

engrave To cut a design on a metal surface with sharp-pointed tools.

erasable programmable read-only memory (EPROM) A type of memory in which stored information can be erased by ultraviolet light beamed in a window of the chip package.

etching A surface-decorating process in which a chemical eats away part of the metal surface.

expanded metal Metal into which slits are cut and then pulled open, increasing the size of the piece.

explosive bonding Joining metals using the force of an explosion.

explosive forming Shaping metal by using dynamite or other explosives.

extension line In a drawing, a line that is a continuation of a line in the object being drawn. Dimensions are shown between extension lines.

external thread A screw thread cut around the outside surface of a rod or pipe.

extruding (1) In metal cold working, pushing out metal in order, for example, to make a hole. (2) A forming process in which hot metal is pushed through an opening in a die. The resulting part has a cross section of the same shape as the die opening.

facing In lathe work, squaring up the ends of a workpiece by making them true and flat.

fastening Joining together the parts of a product.

fatigue strength The ability of metal to withstand changing loads without breaking.

feed (1) In machining, the distance the cutter advances along the workpiece with each stroke or complete turn, or the distance the workpiece advances with each stroke or complete turn of the cutter. (2) In drilling, the distance the drill advances into the workpiece with each full turn.

ferrous metal A metal that contains a large percentage of iron.

fiber The lines in a hot-formed part made by the inclusions, or impurities, in the metal when they are stretched out during the forming. Also called *flow lines*.

fiber optics A thin ribbon of glass that can be made into cables to carry light pulses over long distances. This process is called *light-wave communication*.

file (1) A hardened steel tool that forms, shapes, and finishes metal by removing small chips. (2) In a computer, a block of information that makes up a group of related data on a disk; like files used in office work.

filigree The art of bending very fine wire into intricate designs.

filler A coat of finish applied to a porous metal surface to fill in the holes before an enamel or lacquer is applied.

fillet An inside sharp corner on a casting pattern.

fixture A device that is fastened to a machine tool and that holds one or more pieces in the proper position for machining.

flaking A machine-finishing process used on machine parts. Also called *scraping* or *frosting*.

flame hardening Hardening metal with the heat from an oxy-acetylene flame; a heat-treating process.

flame spraying Any finishing process in which a material is melted and sprayed onto a surface to produce a coating.

flare To turn the very edge of a metal piece slightly.

flash welding A kind of resistance welding in which the workpieces, which themselves act as electrodes, are clamped in dies that carry the electricity.

flask In sand casting, the box full of sand in which the mold cavity is made.

flat A rectangular steel piece.

flatter A special forging tool used to smooth and finish flat workpieces.

flexible manufacturing system (FMS) An automated manufacturing system which can produce a variety of products on the same assembly line.

floppy disk See *diskette*.

fluid power The transfer of power from one place to another by means of air, oil, or other fluids. When air is used, the system is called *pneumatics*; air-powered tools are frequently used in manufacturing and servicing. When oil is used, the system is called *hydraulics*; hydraulics is used, for example, in braking systems in cars or robots.

flute A long, narrow depression in a material; a groove.

flux A chemical compound used in refining, soldering, casting, and welding to dissolve and remove unwanted substances from the metal.

forge A furnace in which metal is heated and wrought.

forge welding Using the force of a blacksmith's hammer to weld heated metal parts.

forging A hot-metal forming method using hammer blows or pressure.

forging hammer A special hammer used in forging that delivers a high-speed impact.

forging press A machine used in forging to press the hot metal into the desired shape.

forming die A die used to give shape to metal.

foundry (1) Making metal products by casting. (2) A shop in which metal casting is done.

fuller A special forging tool used to shape round inside corners and angles and to stretch metal.

function The action for which an object is specially fitted or used.

fusibility The ability of a metal to become liquid easily and join with other metals.

fusion welding Welding using heat alone.

gage An inspection tool used to determine whether parts meet specified standards.

gage, sheet-metal A metal disk with slots cut around the outside; used to measure the thickness of sheet metal and wire in the customary system.

galvanic action The reaction that causes corrosion to occur when two different metals touch one another or are placed in the same container of water.

galvanized steel Mild sheet steel coated with zinc to keep it from rusting. Also called *galvannealed steel.*

gar-alloy A zinc alloy containing copper and silver to give it strength.

gas forming Forming metal with a ram driven by gas combustion.

gas-metal arc welding (GMAW) A kind of arc welding in which a shield of gas protects the metal from the air.

gas-tungsten arc welding (GTAW) A kind of arc welding done with a nonconsumable electrode made of tungsten.

gas welding Welding using a hot flame made by burning oxygen and acetylene. Also called *oxy-acetylene welding* (OAW).

gate (1) In casting, the horizontal channel through which the molten metal flows into the mold cavity. (2) The controlling element of certain transistors. (3) A logic circuit that has two or more inputs that control one output.

gating system In casting, the system of channels and openings through which the molten metal flows into the mold cavity.

gear cutting Machining gears on special machines called gear-hobbing machines or on milling machines.

general metals The study of all aspects of metalworking.

glazed wheel A grinding wheel on which the abrasive grains have been worn smooth.

golden section A rectangle with a proportion of about 5 to 8.

grain structure The characteristic way in which the grains, or particles, of a metal are arranged together like closely fitting blocks.

green coal Raw coal.

grind To use abrasives, usually affixed to a rotating wheel, to quickly remove relatively large amounts of metal from a workpiece.

grit The grade of abrasiveness of a grinding wheel.

Guerin process A press-forming method for sheet metal in which heavy rubber in a metal frame is used to force the metal over a die.

hacksaw A saw with a fine-toothed blade held under tension in a frame.

hammer (*n*) A tool for striking, driving, and pounding. (*v*) To use such a tool.

hard copy A printout on paper.

harden To heat-treat metal to give it a hard, fine-grained structure.

hardness The degree of firmness or strength of a metal; its ability to resist penetration.

hard-solder To solder using silver solder and relatively high temperatures.

hardware The physical equipment of the computer system.

hardy A hot-and-cold chisel used in forging.

harmony A condition in which the different parts of an object fit and look well together.

heart line In leaded stained glass, a line between the glass pieces, where the lead is placed.

heat treatment Heating a metal workpiece to change its properties.

hem A folded edge used to improve the appearance of a metal object and to strengthen it.

hermaphroditic caliper A tool with one outside-caliper leg and one divider leg, used to locate the center of an irregularly shaped workpiece.

hexagon A six-sided steel piece.

hidden line In a drawing, a line that shows edges and details that cannot be seen.

honing Machining with an abrasive to produce an extremely fine finish.

horizontal band saw A power-driven machine for rough-cutting metal to length.

hot forming Shaping metal by hammering or pressing it at a temperature higher than its recrystallization point. Also called *hot working*.

hot metal In ironmaking, the liquid iron produced by the blast furnace.

hot rolling Shaping hot metal ingots in rolling mills.

hydroforming A kind of press forming in which the punch of the die is attached to the fixed part of the machine and the matrix of the die is replaced by a flexible diaphragm that can accommodate any shape.

impact extruding A stamping process in which a sharp blow from the punch causes a slug of metal to be extruded into the desired shape in the die cavity.

impact strength The ability of a piece of metal to withstand a hard blow or sudden shock without breaking.

impression-die forging A kind of forging in which the workpiece is shaped between dies that completely enclose it.

inclusion An impurity or small particle of non-metallic elements(s).

induction hardening Hardening metal with the heat generated when an electric current is induced on its surface; a heat-treating process.

inert gas A gas that will not react with other substances.

ingot A mass of metal cast into a convenient shape for storage or transportation.

input To transfer data from an input device (such as a terminal) to the computer's memory.

input-output (I/O) The passage of information in or out of the computer.

integrated circuit A semiconductor circuit combining many electronic components in a single substrate, usually silicon.

interchangeability The ability of identical parts to be substituted for each other in the final product.

internal thread A screw thread cut on the inside of a hole.

investment casting A casting method in which a pattern is made of wax and then coated with a ceramic material. The wax is then burned out, leaving a mold cavity into which molten metal is poured. Also called *precision casting* or the *lost-wax process*.

iron A metallic element.

iron notch The opening in a blast furnace through which the refined iron is drawn off.

isometric drawing A pictorial drawing in which the sides of the object are shown 120 degrees apart.

jig A device for holding a workpiece and guiding a tool.

joule (J) The basic SI metric unit for measuring energy or work.

K An abbreviation in the metric system for kilo (1000). A 1K memory chip, however, contains 1024 bits (rather than 1000) because it is a binary device based on powers of 2. A computer that has 16K memory has a capacity of 16 times 1024 bytes of memory.

kerf The width of the cut made by a saw.

keyhole In plasma-arc welding, a hole produced at the leading edge of the weld puddle that aids in forming the weld bead.

kilogram (kg) An SI metric unit for measuring mass; equal to about 2.2 pounds.

kilopascal (kPa) An SI metric unit for measuring pressure.

kilowatt (kW) An SI metric unit for measuring electricity and other forms of power.

knurl To press a straight or diamond-shaped pattern onto the surface of a workpiece.

lapping Machining with abrasive particles to produce an extremely fine finish.

lap weld A weld that joins two pieces that overlap.

laser (1) A machine that produces a very narrow and intensive beam of light that can be focused onto a very small spot. (2) A high intensity beam of light that is emitted over a very narrow frequency range and that can be directed with high precision.

laser hardening A heat-treating process for metal in which the heat is generated by a laser beam.

layout A flat pattern made directly on the metal.

lead A metallic element; one of the heavier metals.

lead The distance a screw will move into a nut in one full turn.

limit In manufacturing a product, the largest allowable dimension over or under a specified dimension.

liter (L) The basic SI metric unit for measuring liquid capacity; slightly larger than a quart.

loaded wheel A grinding wheel that has become clogged with small bits of metal.

logic The fundamental principles and the connection of circuit elements for computation in computers.

machinability The properties of a metal that determine the rate at which material can be removed in machining, the kind of chip produced, the amount of tool wear that occurs, and the kind of surface finish that can be obtained.

machine filing Filing metal stock to shape on a specially designed vertical band saw.

machine tool A power-driven machine used to cut and shape metal; a machine that produces other machines.

machining Giving metal a desired shape and dimension by turning, shaping, milling, cutting, or otherwise removing chips with machine tools.

magnetic disk A flat, circular plate on which data can be recorded.

magnetic forming Shaping metal using the electromagnetic force generated when electricity passes through an induction coil.

magnetic tape A tape on which data can be recorded.

main frame computer A central computer with a huge CPU and memory capacity that serves a number of terminals.

main storage The main memory of the computer. It stores data that are being processed or used currently.

major diameter The largest diameter of a screw thread.

malleability The ability of a metal to be hammered or rolled out without breaking or cracking.

mallet A 9-ounce hammer with a head of lead, brass, rawhide, plastic, rubber, or wood.

mandrel (1) A metal piece that serves as a core around which metal can be cast, molded, bent, or otherwise shaped. (2) A metal piece inserted into a hole in a workpiece to support it during machining.

mask A glass photographic plate that contains the circuit pattern used in the silicon-chip manufacturing process.

maskant In chemical milling, the resistant material placed over the surface not to be machined.

mass production (1) The process of making high volumes of objects. (2) The manufacturing of large numbers of identical objects.

match plate In casting, a device on which a pattern can be mounted, with half of the pattern on one side and half on the other, to make a perfectly matching mold.

matrix The fixed, usually lower, part of a die.

memory Elements in the computer that retain instructions or data used by the central processing unit.

memory chip A semiconductor device that stores information in the form of electric charges.

metal casting See *casting, metal.*

metallizing A flame-spraying process in which metal wire is drawn into a special ''gun,'' melted, atomized, and then sprayed onto a surface to make a coating.

metallurgist A scientist who specializes in metals and their use.

metallurgy The science and technology of metals and their behavior.

meter (m) The basic SI metric unit for measuring length; equal to about 39.27 inches.

meters per second (m/s) An SI metric unit for measuring speed.

metric system A measuring system based on natural units, devised in France in the eighteenth century.

microcomputer A type of computer that is smaller than both the minicomputer and the mainframe computer.

microprocessor An integrated circuit in one chip that provides functions equal to those contained in the central processing unit of a computer. A microprocessor interprets and carries out instructions. It usually can do arithmetic and has some memory. It is a central processing unit on a chip, or a computer system designed around such a device.

millimeter (mm) An SI metric unit for measuring length; equal to one one-thousandth (0.01) of a meter and about one twenty-fifth (0.04) of an inch.

milling Machining metal using a rotating cutting tool with two or more cutting edges.

milling machine A machine that shapes and smoothes metal by means of a rotating cutting tool with two or more cutting edges.

minicomputer A type of computer that is larger than a microcomputer and smaller than a mainframe computer.

minor diameter The smallest diameter of a screw thread.

mold In metal casting, a cavity, or opening, that shapes the product being cast.

molybdenum A metal; used particularly in the aerospace industry.

multiview drawing A drawing that shows two or more views of an object. Also called an *orthographic drawing*.

network A system of interconnected computers which uses terminals for communications.

neutral flame (1) A blue, nonoxidizing flame used in a gas or oil forging furnace. (2) In welding, a flame made with equal amounts of oxygen and acetylene.

newton (N) The basic SI metric unit for measuring force.

nibble To pierce metal along or on its edge. Also called *notching*.

nickel silver An alloy of copper, nickel, and zinc. Also called *German silver*.

nonferrous metal A metal that contains little or no iron.

normalize To heat-treat steel in order to return it to a normal state after forging or after incorrect heat treating.

numerical control (N/C) A system for directing the work of machines by means of tapes or cards that store instructions and then give them to the machines at the proper time.

object line A line in a drawing that represents edges or surfaces that can be seen.

oblique drawing A pictorial drawing in which one side of the object depicted appears close to the viewer and the other sides are slanted.

octagon An eight-sided steel piece.

off-line Not connected to the computer.

on-line Connected to the computer.

open-die forging A kind of forging in which the workpiece is shaped between dies that do not completely confine it.

open-hearth process A steelmaking method in which pig iron is melted with a gas flame in an open hearth shaped like a huge dish.

orbital forging A cold-working method in which metal is pushed out or down into a lower die by a rotating, slanted upper die.

ornamental metalwork Bench-metal work, largely involving simple forming of band iron. Also called *wrought-metal work*.

output Data transferred from the computer memory to a storage or output device.

overlay To decorate the surface of metal with contrasting material.

oxidation The common deterioration that metals undergo when they react with oxygen in the air or water.

oxyfuel gas cutting Cutting metal by heating it with an oxygen-acetylene flame and then burning it with oxygen.

oxygen cutting Cutting metal using a gas flame from a torch. Also called *flame cutting*.

parting compound In casting, a dry powder dusted on the parts of the mold to keep them from sticking together.

parting line In casting, the line on the casting that is made when the two sections of the mold are parted.

pascal (Pa) The basic SI metric unit for measuring pressure.

pattern (1) In sheet-metal work, a flat shape laid out on the metal as a guide for cutting. Also called a *stretchout*. (2) In metal casting, a model in wood, metal, plastic, or wax of the shape being cast.

peen (*n*) A ball-shaped or wedge-shaped end of the head of a hammer that is opposite the face. (*v*) To draw, bend, or flatten metal by striking it with a peen.

perforate To pierce a series of holes in metal, usually to make a design.

peripheral An external or remote device in a computer system. Input-output devices, such as keyboards, printers, magnetic tapes, and magnetic disks, are peripherals.

permanent-mold casting Casting by pouring molten metal into a permanent metal mold or die.

permeability The ability of a substance to permit the passage of liquids or gases through openings or pores.

perspective drawing A pictorial drawing showing an object as it appears to the eye.

pewter A tin alloy containing antimony and copper. Also called *Britannia metal*.

photochemical machining Removing metal using a combination of photography and chemical etching. Also called *photoforming*.

pickle To clean dirt and oxide from metal by immersing it in an acid bath.

pictorial drawing A kind of drawing that looks like a photograph.

pierce To cut out interior waste stock from a metal part with a die.

pig iron Crude iron produced in a blast furnace and then cast into molds.

pilot hole A small hole drilled to make drilling a larger hole easier. Also called a *lead hole*.

pitch On a screw thread, the distance from a point on one screw thread form to the corresponding point on the next form.

pitch diameter For a given screw thread, the diameter of an imaginary cylinder sized so that its surface would pass through the screw-thread forms at the level where the width of the forms equals the width of the spaces between the forms.

planish To make a metal surface smooth by hammering it over a stake or block.

plasma A gaslike collection of charged particles; used, for example, in plasma-flame finishing and in plasma-arc welding.

plasma-arc welding A kind of arc welding that uses a plasma jet of inert gas.

plasma-flame finishing A flame-spraying process in which an inert gas is ionized by passage through an electric arc and then sprayed onto a surface to make a coating.

plaster-mold casting A casting method resembling sand casting, except that plaster is used in place of sand.

plastic deformation A forced and permanent change in the shape of metal.

plastic flow The movement of metal to form a new shape.

plastic range For a given metal, the degrees of force that, when applied to that metal, will change its shape permanently but not break it.

plating bath In electroplating, the solution containing salts of the metal to be deposited, into which are put the object to be plated and the metal to be deposited.

plotter A device used to produce finished drawings from a computer-aided drafting system.

polish To use abrasives to smooth a metal surface and to remove scratches from grinding.

porcelain-enamel finish A finish made by using high temperatures to fuse fine grains of glass to a metal surface.

portable band saw A movable power saw that works like a horizontal band saw.

powder metallurgy The science of making products from metal powders, sometimes mixed with nonmetal powders.

power hacksaw An electrically powered hacksaw.

press forming Creating sheet-metal products using dies to cut and shape the metal and presses to power the dies. Also called *stamping*.

pressure The way in which a mechanical device such as a screw or rivet fastens parts together.

pressure-curtain coating A finishing process in which the coating, under pressure, forms a ''curtain'' through which the stock is moved.

primer A first coat of finish on a metal; it binds and adheres to the metal, giving a good base for later coats.

print A reproduction of a drawing, sometimes called a blueprint.

program A set of instructions, arranged in order, telling the computer to do a certain task or to solve a problem.

projection welding A kind of resistance welding in which projections of welding material on the workpieces are electrically melted to spot-weld the workpieces together.

proportion The way areas or parts of an object are related to each other. For example, a rectangular shape of 5 to 8 is considered good proportions.

prototype In manufacturing, a first sample or model of a new product or design.

pulsed-laser welding Welding with the heat supplied by a pulsating beam of light from a laser.

punch (*n*) (1) A steel rod variously shaped at one end for performing different operations, such as forming, cutting, and embossing. (2) The part of a die that does the forming; usually, the upper, movable part. (*v*) To emboss, cut, or perforate metal with a punch.

quality control Determining whether parts meet specified standards.

quench To cool hot metal by plunging it into water, oil, or brine.

raising Forming a shaped piece of flat metal by stretching it with a raising hammer over simple forms.

ram Any of various guided pieces for exerting pressure or for driving or forcing something by impact, such as the heavy weight used to drive a forging hammer.

random access memory (RAM) In a computer, a memory in which any piece of information can be independently stored or retrieved. Its contents are held only temporarily.

raw materials Materials in their natural form before manufacturing processes change their size, shape, and composition.

read-only memory (ROM) In a computer, a memory chip in which information is permanently stored during the manufacturing process.

ream To finish a hole to exact size with a very smooth interior surface.

reciprocating A kind of portable power saw used especially for sawing metal pipe.

recrystallization point The temperature below which the internal structure of a metal can no longer be rearranged with ease.

recycle In industry, to process used materials so that they can be used again in production.

reducing agent A material that can break down a compound substance, such as iron ore, by combining with one of its components.

remote terminal A terminal that may be miles away and connected to the main computer by telephone or other communication lines.

repoussé Decorated with a design in relief made by placing the metal over a soft substance, such as pitch, and hammering from the front and back.

resist An acid-resistant material used to cover and protect areas on a metal surface that are not to be etched.

resistance welding Welding with heat generated by the resistance of the metal workpiece to the passage of an electric current.

rhythm The effect achieved by repeating a line or shape at regular intervals. Also called *repetition*.

riddle A sieve for sand; used in sand casting.

riser In casting, a vertical channel that provides a reserve of molten metal to help control the flow of metal into the mold cavity.

rivet A device for permanent fastening, composed of a head and a shank.

robot A reprogrammable device designed to move materials, parts, tools, or specialized devices for doing a variety of tasks.

roll coating Applying a coating material, such as paint or lacquer, to one or both sides of sheets using rollers.

rolled steel Steel formed into bars, rods, and other shapes by rolling.

roll forming Cold-forming sheet metal by passing it through a series of paired, contoured rolls.

root On a screw thread, the bottom intersection of the sides of two adjacent screw-thread forms.

round A shaft-shaped steel piece.

rule A ruler, or straightedge.

runner In casting, the channel through which the molten metal flows to the gates that lead to the mold cavity.

rust The reddish, brittle coating formed on iron and other ferrous metals when exposed to moisture; a kind of corrosion.

saber saw A portable power saw used for cutting through thin metal with a clean, even cut. Also called a *portable jigsaw*.

sand casting A method of metal casting in which the molten metal is poured into a sand mold.

saw (*n*) A cutting tool with a toothed blade. (*v*) To cut metal with a saw; especially, in art-metal work, to cut intricate outline shapes with a saw.

scale (1) In a drawing, a device to show the relationship between the sizes as drawn and the true dimensions of the objects. (2) A measuring device; a rule. (3) A coating of oxide on the surface of metal.

scallop To form the edge of a metal piece into a continuous series of arcs.

score To cut sharp, even grooves in glass in order to break it along pattern lines.

screw An externally threaded fastener.

screw plate A set of taps and dies of the most common sizes.

scribe To scratch lines on metal.

scriber The tool used for scribing, consisting of a slender steel rod with a point on one or both ends.

scroll A strip of metal shaped into a constantly expanding circle.

seam (*n*) A joint between pieces of sheet metal. (*v*) To join sheet-metal parts with a seam.

seam welding A kind of resistance welding in which rollers are used instead of electrodes.

self-shielded flux-cored arc welding (FCAW) A kind of arc welding using a continuous "wire" with a core of fluxing and deoxidizing substances as an electrode.

semiconductor An element whose electric conductivity is less than that of a conductor, such as copper, and greater than that of an insulator, such as glass material chemically treated to have electronic characteristics.

set The manner in which saw teeth are bent to one side or the other and the amount of bend.

shaper A machine that uses a tool pushed and pulled by a ram, along with a table that holds the stock and moves it after each cut.

shear To make straight cuts on metal sheets and plates using two straight blades.

shear strength The maximum load that a material can withstand when that load is applied vertically to the material's surface.

sheet-metal gage See *gage, sheet-metal*.

shell-mold casting A casting method that uses a mold in the shape of a thin two-part shell.

shot peening A mechanical hammering process that produces a regular pattern of depressions on a metal surface.

shoulder On a cylindrical part, the straight surface that makes a change in diameter.

shrink rule A rule on which the units are actually longer than regular units; used for figuring shrinkage allowances.

sinking Forming metal into a shallow hollow shape by hammering it either in a vise or down into a form. Also called *beating down*.

sinter To heat a metal powder in a furnace without melting it. This bonds it into a compact material.

slag Impurities in metal that separate out during heating, especially when a flux is added.

slit To cut metal sheets and plates using rotating knives.

slurry In machining, a liquid containing abrasive particles.

soft copy Output that is not in printed form, such as a display on a video screen.

soft-solder To solder using a tin-lead solder and relatively low temperatures.

software A magnetic disk containing the computer program or basic step-by-step instructions to a computer.

solder (*n*) The metal used to make the joint in soldering. (*v*) To join two metal parts with a third metal that has a lower melting point.

spark forming A metal-forming process in which metal is forced into a die by the power created when an electric spark vaporizes a piece of wire.

specification Part of the complete descriptive information needed for manufacturing a product.

spinning A way of forming a sheet-metal disk into a hollow shape by forcing it over a chuck or hardened mandrel while both the workpiece and the chuck or mandrel rotate.

spot finishing Creating a pattern of overlapping rings on a metal surface using a dowel.

spot welding A pressure-welding process in which electricity is passed through very small areas on overlapping parts. Resistance to electricity generates heat, producing the weld.

sprue In casting, the vertical opening through which the molten metal enters the gating system.

square A square-shaped steel piece.

stainless steel Any of several corrosion-resistant alloys of iron with chromium; with chromium and nickel; or with chromium, nickel, and manganese.

stake A device for supporting or giving shape to metal that is being formed.

stamping (1) Forming sheet metal using dies to cut and shape the metal and presses to power the dies; also called *press forming*. In a more restricted sense, producing a shallow shape on one side of a blank with a stamp, or male die. (2) Producing a design on metal by striking it with a punch.

standard unit A unit used in measurement as a standard of comparison.

steel An alloy of iron and carbon.

sterling silver A silver alloy containing copper and other elements to give it hardness.

strain (*n*) The stretching that metal can undergo when force is applied. (*v*) To use force to change the shape of a metal workpiece. Also called to *deform*.

strength The ability of a metal to resist applied force.

style In design, a distinctive or characteristic manner.

submerged-arc welding (SAW) A kind of arc welding performed using filler metal, supplied by an electrode wire, and a shield of loose, grainy flux material.

supplementary unit In the SI metric system, the radian and steradian.

surface cutting Machining metal by making straight-line, back-and-forth cuts across it with machines called shapers, planers, and slotters.

swage A special forging tool used for smoothing and finishing.

swing The largest diameter that can be turned on a given lathe.

taconite A low-grade iron ore.

tap (*n*) A hardened steel tool with a threaded portion, used for cutting internal threads. (*v*) (1) To cut internal threads with a tap. (2) To strike metal repeatedly with a tapping tool to produce a design.

tarnish The staining and discoloring that takes place when raw metal is exposed to air; a kind of corrosion.

technical unit Any of several common derived SI metric units used to measure such variables as speed, force, and pressure.

tee weld A weld that joins two pieces at right angles. Also called a *fillet weld*.

temper (1) To heat-treat metal to reduce hardness and increase toughness. Also called *to draw*. (2) To moisten molding sand.

temper color One of the colors metal turns as it is heated for tempering.

template A pattern made of plywood, sheet metal, or some other material; used as a guide for cutting out many identical parts, especially from sheet metal.

tensile strength The amount of stress a material can stand without breaking.

terminal A device through which data may be entered or received, usually equipped with a keyboard and a display device.

terneplate Sheet metal coated with an alloy of tin and lead.

texture (*n*) The character of a surface. (*v*) To beautify the surface of wrought-metal projects by peening or hammering.

thermospray The flame-spraying equipment used to apply metals and other materials in powdered form as coatings.

thread A helical, or spirallike, groove cut on the inside of a hole or the outside of a rod or pipe.

thread angle The angle formed by the sides of two adjacent screw-thread forms.

tin A metallic element; seldom used except as an alloying metal.

tin plate Light sheet metal of mild steel with a thin coating of pure tin applied either by dipping or by electroplating.

titanium A lightweight metal, used particularly in the aerospace industry.

tolerance In manufacturing a product, the total range of dimensions allowable over and under the specified dimensions.

tongs A grasping device consisting of two pieces joined at one end by a pivot.

tool-and-die steel A variety of steel used when careful heat treating must be done.

tooling Creating a bold-relief design on metal foil by striking it with a molding tool.

toolmaker's clamp A clamp used to hold parts together in making a layout. Also called a *parallel clamp*.

transfer machine In automated production, a machine that connects the production machine tools and positions the part for machining.

transistor A semiconductor device that acts primarily either as an amplifier or as a current switch.

true To straighten and balance a grinding wheel.

tumbling A finishing process in which the work is placed in a rotating barrel to which an abrasive material has been added.

turn (1) In machining, to cut metal stock as it revolves on a lathe. (2) In sheet-metal work, to form metal on disk or cylindrical shapes by using a rotary machine.

tuyere One of the air holes in a gas or oil furnace used for forging.

twist drill A drill with two flutes, or grooves, running around the body.

type metal An alloy of lead and antimony, often used for casting projects.

ultrasonic machining Cutting hard materials with a tool that moves up and down approximately 20,000 times per second and drives the slurry of abrasive grains that do the cutting. The science of ultrasonic phenomena having a frequency above the audibility of the human ear.

vanishing point In a perspective drawing, the point at which various lines meet when they are extended.

V-block A rectangular steel block in which V-shaped grooves have been cut; used to hold round workpieces.

vertical band saw A power-driven machine for cutting stock to size and for cutting out shapes.

video display terminal (VDT) See *cathode ray tube*.

wafer A thin disk of semiconductor material on

which many chips are fabricated at one time. The chips are later separated and packaged individually.

water glass Sodium silicate; used with sand and carbon dioxide for making cores for casting quickly.

watt (W) The basic SI metric unit for measuring electricity and other forms of power.

welding Fastening metals together using intense heat and, sometimes, pressure.

wired edge A sheet-metal edge folded around a piece of wire for added strength.

work hardening The hardening of the grain structure of metal during cold working.

working drawing A drawing used for construction.

wrought Worked, as metal in a forming process.

wrought iron An iron alloy containing almost no carbon; often used for ornamental ironwork.

zinc A metallic element; often used as a protective coating on sheet metal.

INDEX

504